New York, 1955

# THE LITTLE MAGAZINE:
## A HISTORY AND A BIBLIOGRAPHY

# THE
# LITTLE
# MAGAZINE

*A HISTORY
AND A BIBLIOGRAPHY*

BY

Frederick J. Hoffman
Charles Allen
Carolyn F. Ulrich

PRINCETON UNIVERSITY PRESS · 1947
PRINCETON, NEW JERSEY

COPYRIGHT, 1946, BY PRINCETON UNIVERSITY PRESS
LONDON: GEOFFREY CUMBERLEGE, OXFORD UNIVERSITY PRESS

SECOND EDITION 1947

PRINTED IN THE UNITED STATES OF AMERICA
BY PRINCETON UNIVERSITY PRESS AT PRINCETON, NEW JERSEY

# PREFACE

For some years scholarship in twentieth century literature has been recognized as respectable and valuable. Books of criticism, biographies, and literary histories which touch upon one or many of the interesting facts of modern literature have been appearing in appreciable numbers. The work of providing scholars and teachers with adequate equipment for their research also goes on, and it is more than ever needed as they begin to see patterns and divisions in the literary history of the recent past.

Of great value in whatever kind of research or critical investigation we may wish to undertake is a group of magazines which have lived a kind of private life of their own on the margins of culture. These magazines have usually been the sponsors of innovation, the gathering places for the "irreconcilables" of our literary tradition. They have been broadly and amply tolerant of literary experiment; in many cases, they have raised defiantly the red flag of protest and rebellion against tradition and convention. Their careers have been touched upon here and there in the memoirs and biographies which treat of our day. Some few of them are already reasonably well established in our literary histories.

This book is an attempt, first of all, to give to each of these little magazines the attention it merits and the credit it deserves, as an important source of information about twentieth century writing; secondly, to give to the subject as a whole—to all of the magazines—an order and pattern which will help us discover them and learn the special value of each. For, as most of these magazines enjoyed an erratic career, they neither courted the plaudits of conventional critics nor concerned themselves over the efforts of scholars to find them or librarians to collect them. The authors of this book are confident therefore that it will be of considerable value to the many who are curious about the literary history of our century and to the large and ever-growing number of students and critics who want specific information about a number of subjects related to little magazines.

The story of the little magazine is in itself a fascinating and an important part of our history. It is a story of ideas, of experiments in style, and of personalities. It has color, warmth, and humor; it is as wayward and eccentric as are the personalities who are responsible for it. It is a contribution to the social history of our century and a valuable addition to the serious development of its aesthetic awareness. This story is told in the introductory essay of the book. The authors have formulated a definition of the little magazine and have, by way of expanding that definition, made certain generalizations about it. The opening and closing chapters of the essay are a prologue and an epilogue of the story: a definition, an illustration, and in some ways also a defense of the value of the little magazine.

As for the story itself: Chapters II and V are designed as a general survey of each of the two decades (the second and the third) to which they are an introduction. Here the reader will find accounts of some of the little magazines, together with suggestions of their place in the general cultural and literary history of their decade. In Chapters III and IV such magazines as *Poetry*, *Others*, and *The Little Review* are described in some detail, in full appreciation of what is interesting and significant in their careers.

Beginning with Chapter VI, the authors have arranged their discussion of little magazines with a view toward emphasizing certain important tendencies which they illustrate. The later chapters are therefore written with the object of showing the relation of little magazine history to the literary history of the twentieth century in general: the place of little magazines in the history of modern poetic theory and practice; the place of certain magazines in the formulation of modern ideologies and in the story of experimental literature; the relationship of the little magazine to the proletarian development in the thirties; the role of surrealism, vertigralism, and other adaptations of psychoanalysis in modern literary history; and, finally, the contributions of little magazines to modern criticism. In all of these chapters, the attention of the authors is directed toward the history of the magazines themselves—and the careers of their editors and contributors. Some effort is also made, however, when the occasion demands, to review or summarize and to interpret these developments in modern literature.

The bibliography in the second half of the book offers an important service to students of the period. It is arranged chronologically: *within each year* of the chronology the magazines are grouped alphabetically. Thus the reader, if he wishes, may supplement his study of the introductory essay with a survey of the annotated bibliography. In this manner, each division of the book provides a history of its subject.

Some mention ought to be made of the manner in which titles were selected for the bibliography. There are only a few magazines listed which were published before the year 1910, because these earlier magazines form a part of a period in literary history quite separate from that which the authors have accepted as the subject of this book. Those magazines of the earlier period which are included have been accepted because they are representatives of their time or because they point in some way to the history of the little magazine as it is discussed here.

From the hundreds of little magazines published since 1910, the authors have selected a large number for inclusion. The criteria for inclusion are given in part in the definition and discussion of the little magazine offered in Chapters I and XII of the introductory essay. In a sense, however, the selection of titles has also been qualitative. For a magazine must have had, in the authors' estimation, some importance in the history of modern literature or have published some work of merit, before it was eligible for inclusion. This is not to say that all magazines not listed are of no importance; it is simply that those which are included have been subjected both to the tests set down in the authors' definition of the little magazine and to their further qualitative judgment regarding purposes and contents.

The supplementary part of the bibliography contains a separate listing of reviews which do not answer the definition of the little magazine but are of first importance to the student of modern literature and criticism. Such magazines as *The Southern Review*, *The Sewanee Review*, and *The Kenyon Review*, for example, contribute appreciably to the development of criticism in their time. Anyone interested in the little magazines *The Hound and Horn*, *The Dial*, and *The Symposium* will want also to turn to the other group. For that reason, they and others like them are recorded separately. College literary magazines, when they are important "fellow-travelers" of the advance guard, are also given. In short, this section is a record of magazines whose histories are similar to and whose contribution is pertinent to that of the little magazines themselves, but which for one reason or another cannot be included as little magazines.

References of value will be found in a list of books and magazine articles which discuss in some measure the history of the advance guard or of specific little magazines or personalities.

A single, detailed, alphabetical index is provided for both the essay and the bibliography. The index serves to combine for the reader all references to any magazine, person, or tendency which is mentioned in either. Thus he may find quickly any and all pertinent information about a matter of his special interest. The index includes magazine titles, complete cross references (as in the case of a magazine's change of title), editors, and contributors. Also listed are references to "ideas, influences, and movements," when these are mentioned either in the essay or in the bibliography.

The work of compiling materials for the bibliography began with a survey of the meager material already published, which included the short listing by David Moss in *Contact*, Feb.-Oct., 1932, and articles and books written on the subject or about the period. The basic work, however, was done from the files of periodicals found in the holdings of many libraries throughout the country. In view of the extensive search for titles of periodicals on subjects within the range of or related to the little magazines, the task of determining the standards of inclusion often proved arduous and time-consuming. The separate listings of the libraries of Yale, Princeton, Chicago (with the important Harriet Monroe collection), California, Indiana, Buffalo, New York State, and Connecticut Universities were of considerable assistance in the matter of selecting titles and developing the bibliography. Much regional material was located through correspondence with a number of State Universities throughout the country. Frequently valuable information, such as a special issue or a needed record, was supplied from a private collection, and sometimes from a bookshop; occasionally titles were discovered through advertisements appearing in publications of a similar nature. From the records made from all of these sources and the checking with the *Union List of Serials*, it was possible to search the holdings of many large libraries, notably the Library of Congress, the libraries of Columbia, Harvard, and Brown Universities, the American Antiquarian Society, and particularly the extensive files of the New York Public Library, where most of the work was done.

The work was greatly furthered by a grant-in-aid from the American Council of Learned Societies, which made possible the study of material for the bibliography not available in and about New York City. The Graduate School of The Ohio State University also provided funds for the work on two separate occasions.

The authors are grateful to the editors of the following periodicals for permission to utilize material by Mr. Allen which was first published in their pages: *American Prefaces, College English, The Indiana Quarterly for Bookmen, The Sewanee Review, The South Atlantic Quarterly,* and *The University Review.*

A book of this kind, if it is to fulfill adequately the wishes of both its authors and its readers, depends for its success on a great number of persons. It would be impossible to acknowledge here all of the many helpful suggestions, information, and assistance that the compiler of the bibliography has received from many individuals, but appreciation is expressed to H. S. Parsons of the Library of Congress, Donald G. Wing and Grace P. Fuller of Yale University Library, Mrs. Judith S. Bond and Katherine M. Hall of the University of Chicago, Dorothy G. Conklin of Harvard, Charles Adams of Columbia, Lawrence Heyl of Princeton, Mrs. Barbara Cowles of the University of California, and Charles D. Abbott of the University of Buffalo. Among private collectors, James Laughlin IV should also be mentioned. Miss Frances Steloff of the Gotham Book Mart has been of assistance on many occasions. In the preparation of the introductory essay, several persons have offered information and advice: these include John R. Lindsay, Herbert L. Creek, William S. Hastings, Wilbur L. Schramm, and Herbert J. Muller.

A special debt of gratitude is due Miss Eugenia Patterson and Mrs. Eileen C. Graves of the Periodicals Division of the New York Public Library, for their untiring interest and valuable assistance throughout the two years during which the bibliography has been in progress.

May 1945.

F.J.H.
C.A.
C.F.U.

## FOREWORD TO SECOND PRINTING

The changes in the text of the book include some few corrections, where these have seemed necessary; but they consist primarily of additional titles of magazines either started since May, 1945, or discovered by the authors since that date. The index has also been revised, to accommodate new references found in the additions to the bibliography. The index does *not* include references to names in the text of the history, unless these names are associated with at least a sentence of interpretation or comment.

March 1947.

# CONTENTS

## HISTORY OF THE LITTLE MAGAZINE

| | | |
|---|---|---|
| | PREFACE | v |
| I. | INTRODUCTION | 1 |
| II. | THE SECOND DECADE | 18 |
| III. | "POETRY" AND "OTHERS" | 34 |
| IV. | "THE LITTLE REVIEW" | 52 |
| V. | THE THIRD DECADE | 67 |
| VI. | THE "TENDENZ" MAGAZINE | 85 |
| VII. | MODERN POETRY AND THE LITTLE MAGAZINE | 109 |
| VIII. | REGIONALISM AND THE LITTLE MAGAZINE | 128 |
| IX. | POLITICAL DIRECTIONS IN THE LITERATURE OF THE THIRTIES | 148 |
| X. | VARIATIONS ON THE PSYCHOANALYTIC THEME | 170 |
| XI. | THE CRITICAL AND ECLECTIC LITTLE MAGAZINE | 189 |
| XII. | CONCLUSION: REFLECTIONS UPON LITTLE MAGAZINE HISTORY | 218 |

## A BIBLIOGRAPHY OF LITTLE MAGAZINES

| | |
|---|---|
| BIBLIOGRAPHY | 233 |
| LIST OF REFERENCES | 407 |
| INDEX | 413 |

# ILLUSTRATIONS

| | |
|---|---|
| H.D. | Facing page 22 |
| RICHARD ALDINGTON | 22 |
| (Courtesy of the Blackstone Studios) | |
| AMY LOWELL | 22 |
| EZRA POUND | 22 |
| A PAGE OF WYNDHAM LEWIS' "BLAST," JULY 1914 | 23 |
| (Courtesy of John Lane—The Bodley Head) | |
| ERNEST HEMINGWAY'S FIRST PUBLISHED WORK, IN "THE DOUBLE DEALER," MAY 1922 | 28 |
| THREE SKETCHES MADE AT THE "MASSES" TRIAL, 1918 | 29 |
|     ART YOUNG | |
|     FLOYD DELL | |
|     BOARDMAN ROBINSON | |
| MARGARET ANDERSON | 60 |
| ALFRED KREYMBORG | 60 |
| WILLIAM CARLOS WILLIAMS | 60 |
| NORMAN MACLEOD | 60 |
| A TYPICAL CONTENTS PAGE OF "THE LITTLE REVIEW" | 61 |
| FOUR LITTLE MAGAZINE COVERS | 116 |
|     "BROOM" | |
|     "TRANSITION" | |
|     "LAUGHING HORSE" | |
|     "DYNAMO" | |
| THE "FUGITIVE" GROUP, 1930-1931 | 117 |
| JOHN CROWE RANSOM | 117 |

# INTRODUCTION

## CHAPTER I

A CHARACTER in William Saroyan's play, *The Time of Your Life*, suggests that all human problems might be solved if only there were enough magazines to go around.[1] Everyone, he implies, should have the opportunity of seeing himself in print. The results might be most gratifying to politician and policeman alike. Man would no longer quarrel with his fellowman, for his greatest wish would be granted; he would be satisfied, happy, and amiably tolerant of the weaknesses in society. Of course, such a tremendous clearing house for man's literary pretensions has never been provided. Manuscripts still reside in trunks and in desk drawers. But one feature of twentieth century literary history must be noted: hundreds of writers have achieved publication—almost irrespective of their claims to merit or the significance of what they had to say. Since 1912 many of these persons have been published in the scores of literary magazines which have appeared and disappeared to the accompaniment of various forms of pretension, clamor, and editorial oratory.

What is important about this fact is that the best of our little magazines have stood, from 1912 to the present, defiantly in the front ranks of the battle for a mature literature. They have helped fight this battle by being the first to present such writers as Sherwood Anderson, Ernest Hemingway, William Faulkner, Erskine Caldwell, T. S. Eliot—by first publishing, in fact, about 80 per cent[2] of our most important post-1912 critics, novelists, poets, and storytellers. Further, they have introduced

[1] McCarthy, in Act Two. William Saroyan, *Three Plays*, New York, 1940, pp. 88-89.
[2] Charles Allen, "The Advance Guard," *Sewanee Review*, II, 425-29 (July/September 1943).

and sponsored every noteworthy literary movement or school that has made its appearance in America during the past thirty years.

There have been, conservatively estimated, over six hundred little magazines published in English since 1912. Many have been pale, harmless creatures. Fewer than one hundred of them have taken a decisive part in the battle for modern literature, or have sought persistently to discover good artists, or to promote the early work of talented innovators, or to sponsor literary movements. Many of the six hundred have been abortive—some lacking a definable purpose, others editorial discrimination, and still others plain common sense. Some, such as John Malcolm Brinnin's short-lived *Prelude*, irresponsibly followed the will-o'-the-wisp of novelty for novelty's sake.

A little magazine is a magazine designed to print artistic work which for reasons of commercial expediency is not acceptable to the money-minded periodicals or presses. Acceptance or refusal by commercial publishers at times has little to do with the quality of the work. If the little magazine can obtain artistic work from unknown or relatively unknown writers, the little magazine purpose is further accomplished. Little magazines are willing to lose money, to court ridicule, to ignore public taste, willing to do almost anything—steal, beg, or undress in public—rather than sacrifice their right to print good material, especially if it comes from the pen of an unknown Faulkner or Hemingway. Such periodicals are, therefore, noncommercial by intent, for their altruistic ideal usually rules out the hope of financial profit. No doubt little magazine editors would welcome a circulation of a million or two, but they know that their magazines will appeal only to a limited group, generally not more than a thousand persons. And so, financially limited, editors generally caution contributors to banish all thought of remuneration, to be satisfied with payment "in fame, not specie." When there is money for contributors, promises of payment are made triumphantly, always as though such payment is to be made in spite of, rather than because of, the bourgeois system of values.

To the extent that they are not money-minded, such reviews as *The Sewanee Review*, *The Southern Review*, *The Kenyon Review*, *The Yale Review*, and *The Virginia Quarterly Review* may be considered "little." Yet these excellent quarterlies are not little magazines. Intelligent, dignified, critical representatives of an intelligent, dignified, critical minority, they are conscious of a serious responsibility which does not often permit them the freedom to experiment or to seek out unknown writers.[3]

Many editors now contend that "advance guard" is a better name for their magazines than "little." Coming into use during the First World War, "little" did not refer to the size of the magazines, nor to their literary contents, nor to the fact that they usually did not pay for contributions. What the word designated above everything else was a limited group of intelligent readers: to be such a reader one had to understand the aims of the particular schools of literature that the magazines represented, had to be interested in learning about dadaism, vorticism, expressionism, and surrealism. In a sense, therefore, the word "little" is vague and even unfairly derogatory.

The commercial publishers—the large publishing houses and the big "quality" magazines—are the rear guard. In a few instances they are the rear guard because their editors are conservative in taste, slow to recognize good new writing; but more frequently the commercial publishers are the rear guard because their editors will accept a writer only after the advance guard has proved that he is, or can be made, commercially profitable. Whatever the reason for their backwardness, few commercial houses or magazines of the past thirty years can claim the honor of having served the advance guard banner: they have discovered and sponsored only about 20 per cent[4] of our post-1912 writers; they have done nothing to initiate the new literary groups. To their credit, it may be said that they have ultimately accepted any author, no matter how experimental, after he has been talked about for a period of years—sometimes a good many years.

Little magazine history provides us with a bewildering variety of personalities, but they do have certain characteristics in common. Drawing from the widely differing portraits of Ezra Pound, William Carlos Williams, Norman Macleod, Eugene Jolas, Ernest J. Walsh, and other *avant-garde* personalities, we may suggest a composite portrait of the little magazine editor or contributor. Such a man is stimulated by some form of discontent—whether with the constraints of his world or the negligence of publishers, at any rate with something he considers unjust, boring, or ridiculous. He views the world of publishers and popularizers with disdain, sometimes with despair. If he is a

---

[3] We have provided a place for such magazines in the supplementary list in the bibliography; they are important "fellow-travelers" of the little magazines and deserve comment.

[4] See Allen, "The Advance Guard."

contributor and wishes to be published, he may have to abandon certain unorthodox aesthetic or moral beliefs. Often he is rebellious against the doctrines of popular taste and sincerely believes that our attitudes toward literature need to be reformed or at least made more liberal. More than that, he generally insists that publication should not depend upon the whimsy of conventional tastes and choices.

Certainly one of the great values of the little magazine for us, who are anxious to know more about the cultural history of our time, lies in its spirit of conscientious revolt against the guardians of public taste. Freedom from such control frequently leads to confusion. We can have little hope, therefore, for a simple clarification of our age from the little magazine, especially since editors were many and quarrels frequent. There is a tangled and delightful sense of contradiction in the total picture. One gets the impression that many writers, neither having had nor desiring the schooling which a calmer age grants somewhat pompously, were at the business of making up their minds, and liking it very much. The great seriousness with which some of the little magazines pronounced the dawn of a new cultural synthesis is forever being disturbed by the spirit of dada which animated certain others.

In view of the urgent conviction that he has something to say, a would-be editor finds that the resources for beginning a magazine are accessible, though he does not usually see beyond the publication of the first issue of the magazine. Generally he is deeply absorbed in the importance of what he has to say; but his interest in establishing and illustrating his own aesthetic beliefs leads him to neglect such matters as might insure either a wide distribution or a reasonable longevity for his periodical. He is of the advance guard simply because the form and content of his contributions are unusual or violate one or several of the principles upon which material is made acceptable to the commercial magazine.

Thus little magazines usually come into being for the purpose of attacking conventional modes of expression and of bringing into the open new and unorthodox literary theories and practices. One of the most significant contributions of these magazines to twentieth century literature is to give it an abundance of suggestions and styles which popular or academic taste scarcely could tolerate or accept. In summary we may say that little magazines have been founded for two reasons: rebellion against traditional modes of expression and the wish to experiment with novel (and sometimes unintelligible) forms; and a desire to overcome the commercial or material difficulties which are caused by the introduction of any writing whose commercial merits have not been proved.

There are some exceptions, of course; this pattern will not fit every one of the magazines whose individual histories the reader will find in the second half of this book. But it is appropriate to a surprisingly large number.

It has been suggested that the little magazines often pursue a perilous career, steering their courses uncertainly and erratically. Apparently the only certainty about them is the probability of early collapse. Morton Dauwen Zabel, reviewing the current literary magazines in the March 1933 issue of *Poetry*, remarks that "It becomes apparent that the multiplication of these periodicals atones for their individual impermanence; that despite their varying shades of policy and opinion, their functions are ultimately identical and their activities continuous." This is to say that though many die, many more are being born, and that this will continue to be true as long as there are young writers with courage, disregard for the requirements of the "dignified press," a few dollars in their pockets (or an interested friend or two who can pay the bills), and finally an abundance of sheer nerve. What makes the magazines "little" also insures their appearing everywhere and at any time—and disappearing without apparent cause.

It is not surprising that most little magazines are short-lived. The editors and contributors are often disrespectful of the ordinary and legitimate demands of the publishing world—the bare minimum of conformity which typesetters and copyreaders demand of their customers. Frequently editors lose interest in their magazines after the first few issues have appeared. Some editors set more or less definite dates at which the magazine will cease publication. Such, for example, was the reasoning of Director Gorham B. Munson, of *Secession*: "The Director pledges his energies for at least two years to the continuance of *Secession*. Beyond a two year span, observation shows, the vitality of most reviews is lowered and their contribution, accomplished, becomes repetitious and unnecessary. *Secession* will take care to avoid moribundity."[5] Jack Lindsay and P. R. Stephensen prescribed a life of six numbers for their magazine, *The London Aphrodite*, on the ground that "There has never yet been a literary periodical which has not gone dull after the first half-dozen numbers."[6]

[5] Editorial, *Secession*, I, n.p. (Spring 1922).
[6] Editorial, *The London Aphrodite*, v, 400 (April 1929).

Generally, however, the reason for suspending publication is less deliberate. The editor is at present in the hospital and will recover we know not when (*Dyn*); the editor has died, and the magazine cannot be the same without him (*Reedy's Mirror*); the editor has been inducted into the armed services, but the magazine will surely revive after his return (*Vice-Versa, The Little Man*). Most frequent of all reasons are these five: lack or loss of funds; lack or loss of interest; withdrawal of sustaining funds, because of some shift of policy, unpleasant to the backer; government prosecution for some reason or other, usually a matter of censorship; internecine quarrels or misunderstandings.

For the most part, each magazine serves its separate purpose before it dies: that purpose generally is to give finished form and some degree of distribution to the personality and the convictions of its editor or editors. Often these convictions are given editorial form. The editorial statement may be simply an expression of generosity to those who are akin in spirit; it may be (or become) a program or platform; and it may very well be (or become) the expression of some school of political or aesthetic thought which uses the magazine as its voice. A characteristic editorial statement from the little magazines is the following, from the ninth issue of *The New Talent*: "[Writers of *avant-garde* literature are motivated by] the spirit of revolt . . . against artificial boundaries of so-called good taste, against hypocritical 'sweetness and light,' against formalistic strictures of language. . . . [We demonstrate] an awakening . . . of a will to creative truth, a desire for frankness and freedom and honesty in the portraying of the people around us."[7] Such editorial remarks are indicative of the freedom and independence with which *avant-gardists* regarded their positions; they also suggest something of the urgency with which they felt a reform in modern letters was needed. And, in a sense, they underline an aesthetic preoccupation with the need to circumvent any and all restrictions upon experiment in literature. We find these simple ideals developed, practiced, and demonstrated in dozens of little magazines. Their justification is single and simple; their practice varied; their interpretation of literary experiment complex.

[7] E. G. Arnold, Editorial, *The New Talent*, IX, 1-2 (July-August-September, 1935).

## II

One should remember that there were advance guard magazines before 1912. The parent of the American little magazine was *The Dial* (1840-44), edited by Margaret Fuller and Ralph Waldo Emerson. Partly because it always held its standards high, *The Dial* never obtained over 300 subscribers, despite such contributors as Thoreau, Emerson, William Ellery Channing, and Theodore Parker. Most of our nineteenth century periodicals, however, were not very inspiring. Besides *The Dial* only four deserve serious recognition as predecessors of modern little magazines: Henry Clapp's *Saturday Press* (1858-66), and the Chicago *Chap Book*, *Lark*, *M'lle New York*, all of the nineties. The first decade of the twentieth century seemed as barren as any decade of the nineteenth.

The "renaissance" in the little magazines showed its first beginnings around 1910. In 1912 Harriet Monroe succeeded in starting her famous *Poetry: A Magazine of Verse*. Floyd Dell and Max Eastman decided to make *The Masses* a rebel literary magazine, and *The Poetry Journal* was founded in Boston. These and others that followed them in 1913 and 1914 were consciously established to promote a regenerative literature. Little magazine editors knew that there were already writers such as Robinson, Masters, and Sara Teasdale, poets with much to say provided they could find a place to publish consistently. And the editors suspected that there were many unknowns who could be encouraged to write if they were offered a fair chance of publication. How right the editors were we now know from the record of *Poetry*, *Glebe*, *Others*, *The Masses*, *The Little Review*, and the many other little magazines of those opening "renaissance" years. Besides firmly establishing the reputations of Edgar Lee Masters, Amy Lowell, Edwin Arlington Robinson, Sara Teasdale, and others who had received only the slightest attention before 1912, the little magazines, during their first three years, presented such previously almost unknown names as Carl Sandburg, Vachel Lindsay, T. S. Eliot, Wallace Stevens, Marianne Moore, John Reed, John Gould Fletcher, Maxwell Bodenheim, and Robert Frost.

It is impossible in this chapter to do more than mention the influence of individual periodicals in shaping the literary milieu between the two great wars; impossible even to outline the fascinating and often incredible human stories that explain the accomplishments of the advance guard—stories sometimes of tragedy, more often of high comedy, nearly always of courageous sacrifice. In mentioning some of the more important of our post-1912 little magazines, it is convenient to list them as belonging to six major classes—poetry, leftist, regional, experimental, critical, and eclectic. Such a classification is made primarily in the interest of convenience; in many cases the divisions obviously overlap.

Among the more important little magazines devoted exclusively or largely to poetry we might name: *Poetry: A Magazine of Verse* (1912-   ), *The Poetry Journal* (1912-18), *Contemporary Verse* (1916-29), *The Fugitive* (1922-25), *The Measure* (1921-26), *Glebe* (1913-14), *Others* (1915-19), *Palms* (1932-40), *Voices* (1921-   ), and *Smoke* (1931-37). One can safely estimate not only that at least 95 per cent[8] of our post-1912 poets were introduced by such magazines, but that they remained the primary periodical outlets for most of our poets.

January 1911 to April 1917 are the dates of the socialist *Masses*, a magazine which, historically, must be considered a landmark. The first important literary voice of the left-wingers, *The Masses*, especially under the editorship of Max Eastman and Floyd Dell (1912-17), was the American inspiration for the so-called "proletarian" movement of the sociologically minded thirties. The other famous leftwing little magazines are *The Liberator* (1918-24) and *The Partisan Review* (1934-   ). During the thirties there were many ephemeral voices such as *The Anvil, Left, Blast, The Monthly Review, Left-Front, The Little Magazine, The Windsor Quarterly, International Literature,* and *The New Quarterly*.

In 1915 the Midwest finally attempted to free itself from the domination of Eastern publishing influences. This domination usually took one of two forms, demanding either that the midland artist warp his material to conform to a preconceived notion of what represented the Midwest, or that he burlesque his native soil for the amusement of the East. John T. Frederick's *Midland*, printed in Iowa City from 1915 to 1933, was the first coherent voice to insist on the artist's right to present as he honestly saw it the spirit of the vast region between the Alleghenies and the Rockies. The right to interpret truthfully the cultural entity which the writer best knows became the ideal of several other little magazines in the Midwest, Southwest, and Far West. Such quarterlies as *The Frontier* (1920-39), *The Texas Review* (1915-24), *The Southwest Review* (1924-   ), *The Prairie Schooner* (1927-   ), and *The New Mexico Quarterly Review* (1931-   ) derive their inspiration from *The Midland*.

[8] See Allen, "The Advance Guard."

INTRODUCTION 9

The advance guard magazines devoted to experimentalism in one form or another have been more numerous than any other type. They are the magazines that have introduced the literary movements or schools (imagism, dadaism, surrealism, etc.); they are the magazines that have cast a sympathetic eye on the more radical departures from conventional realism; they are the magazines, in short, that are concerned with widening the boundaries of an age dedicated to photographic realism and naturalism. Among scores of these periodicals the most important were the following: *The Little Review* (1914-29), *Broom* (1921-24), *Secession* (1922-24), *The Reviewer* (1921-25), *The Double Dealer* (1921-26), *The Dial* (1920-29), *This Quarter* (1925-32), and *transition* (1927-38). The poetry magazines that have been primarily experimental are: *Poetry, Glebe, Others,* and *The Fugitive*. One might also catalogue as experimental little magazine activities James Laughlin's New Directions Press (1936-   ) and Dorothy Norman's fat semiannual volume, *Twice a Year* (1938-   ).

A fifth group of little magazines specialized in criticism and reviewing, a group represented by *The Dial, The Hound and Horn* (1927-34), and *The Symposium* (1930-33). These reviews were designed as outlets for the intense, brilliant, and mannered critics, of whom T. S. Eliot, John Crowe Ransom, and R. P. Blackmur are fair representatives. Like *The Southern Review* (1935-42) and the present-day *Kenyon Review* (1939-   ), neither of which can be considered a little magazine, *The Hound and Horn* and *The Symposium* inherited much of their temperament from *The Dial* and from T. S. Eliot's British *Criterion* (1922-39), magazines that admired acuteness, urbanity, and sometimes preciousness.

The "eclectics" include some of our most interesting magazines, magazines open to most of the literary currents but generally favoring straight, realistic writing and more or less conventional structural patterns; they are the spiritual heirs of the commercial *Smart Set*, whose years of splendor were between 1912 and 1924. *The Seven Arts* (1916-17) and *Story* (1931-   ) can be included in this group. Many of the eclectic magazines have been and still are associated in some way with university campuses. They are not generally university magazines in the sense of existing simply to glorify the traditions or to inflate the literary accomplishments of the university environment, but they often reflect the tastes and preoccupations of the university community in which they originate. Such, for example, are the Midwestern magazines: *American Prefaces* (University of Iowa, 1935-43), *Accent* (University of Illinois, 1940-   ), *Diogenes* (University of Wisconsin, 1940-41), and *The University Review* (University of Kansas City, 1935-   ). Other magazines, like *The Chimera* (1942-   ) and *Furioso* (1939-   ), were born on a university campus but later moved away from their place of origin.

## III

The individual histories of the magazines that have been mentioned above deserve close attention, and the later chapters will tell many of their stories. At present, for the purpose of illuminating what we have already said, it may be interesting to present an example, a thumbnail sketch, which will contribute to a concrete understanding of the aims and functions, merits and defects, of a typical little magazine. Let us look at the experimental *Double Dealer* for a moment.

The literary revival that began to grow in the East and Midwest in 1911 and 1912 did not take firm root in the South until around 1920. January 1921 saw the first issue of the sprightly New Orleans *Double Dealer*, and a month later *The Reviewer* made its first appearance in Richmond, Virginia.

*The Double Dealer* began by announcing itself "A National Magazine of the South." The editor, Julius Weis Friend, and his associates, Basil Thompson, Albert Goldstein, and John McClure, were out to deceive both the nation and the South "by speaking the truth."[9] It took some time, however, for the editors to determine exactly where to find the truth. At first they told the world (and they did have a worldwide, if scattered, circulation) that they had "no policy whatever but that of printing the very best material [they could] procure, regardless of popular appeal, moral or immoral stigmata, conventional or unconventional technique, new theme or old."[10] They were also worried about the bog into which Southern culture and literature had sunk since the days of the Civil War. In June 1921 *The Double Dealer* remarked: "It is high time, we believe, for some doughty, clear visioned penman to emerge from the sodden marshes of Southern literature. We are sick to death of the treacly sentimentalities with which our wellintentioned lady fictioneers regale us. The old traditions are no more. New peoples, customs prevail. The Confederacy has long since been

[9] Julius Weis Friend, Editorial, *The Double Dealer*, 1, 1 (January 1921).
[10] Friend, "The Magazine in America," *The Double Dealer*, 1, 83 (March 1921).

dissolved. A storied realm of dreams, lassitude, pleasure, chivalry, and the Nigger no longer exists. We have our 'Main Streets' here, as elsewhere."[11]

This call for a regional Southern literature continued spasmodically until early in 1922. But gradually the editors found their true vision, a vision which they had half glimpsed from the beginning; for in that first issue they took the responsibility of appraising the existent magazines, finding that they approved only of *The Dial, The Pagan, The Little Review,* and *The Yale Review.* Since all of these periodicals except *The Yale Review* were interested in experimental writing, the editors of *The Double Dealer* gave some indication of their own purpose and direction by bestowing their blessings upon them.

But even during the first year a considerable quantity of experimental writing was published—and most of it did not come from the South. The work of Sherwood Anderson, Alfred Kreymborg, Babette Deutsch, Maxwell Bodenheim, and Lola Ridge gave the magazine its fire.

After the first year the periodical definitely found its true interest. It became a review that took its place alongside *The Dial* in establishing the early work of the 1920 experimentalists. We find many pages by Hart Crane, Edmund Wilson, Malcolm Cowley, Jean Toomer, John Crowe Ransom, Robert Penn Warren, Donald Davidson, Allen Tate, Ernest Hemingway, and others.

The few articles which have been written about little magazines have failed to give much attention to *The Double Dealer.* Certainly it was a magazine of great merit, one of the foremost leaders of the twenties. Jay B. Hubbell,[12] when discussing Southern magazines in 1934, failed wholly to appreciate the place of *The Double Dealer,* and the Southern commentators have had nothing to say of the three men who discovered some of the best work of their time.

The chief editor and founder, Julius Weis Friend, was born in 1896 in New Orleans, where he has lived most of his life. After serving in France for sixteen months during the First World War, he returned to New Orleans to establish his magazine and to try his hand at writing. When his association with *The Double Dealer* came to an end, he contributed essays and reviews to various magazines and newspapers. Later, during the thirties, he was co-author of three philosophical volumes: *Science and the Spirit of Man, The Unlimited Community,* and

---

[11] Friend, "Southern Letters," *The Double Dealer,* 1, 214 (June 1921).
[12] Jay B. Hubbell, "Southern Magazines," *Culture in the South,* edited by W. T. Couch, Chapel Hill, N.C., 1934.

*What Science Really Means.* His philosophical interpretation of Western history, *The Odyssey of the Idea,* appeared in 1942. This is the man who wished to drive a "pile into the mud of this artistic stagnation which has been our portion since the Civil War."[13]

Friend had the assistance of the poet Basil Thompson, who served in the capacity of associate editor until his death early in 1924. Albert Goldstein was an associate editor for a time. And there was also John McClure, the man who wrote most of the excellent *Double Dealer* book reviews, the same John McClure who later gained some fame as a poet and as book critic on the *New Orleans Times-Picayune.*[14]

The year 1922 was the magazine's great year: it had broken with its regional aspirations and began seriously to sponsor experimental writing. It was the year when the general content of the review reached its highest level of excellence. It was the year when all but one of its important discoveries were printed.

*The Double Dealer's* first introduction of a new writer came in May 1922, with the publication of Ernest Hemingway's "A Divine Gesture." This short, two-page sketch has never been republished and there is no reason why it should be. It is a mildly amusing but slight account of an experience that the Lord God and Gabriel once had in the Garden of Eden. The next issue included the second Hemingway publication, a tough little quatrain, printed at the bottom of a page that also carried a poem written by another man who was soon to become famous.

This new writer was William Faulkner. The poetic "Portrait" of June 1922 tells in six stanzas of two brave young lovers who walk "clear with frank surprise," and "profound in youth," talk of "careful trivialities." The rapid accumulation of such mediocre and sentimental verse as "Portrait" resulted in Faulkner's first volume, *The Marble Faun.*

Jean Toomer and Thornton Wilder appeared for the first time in September 1922. Toomer, in a one-page sketch, writes about a soul called "Nora." Wilder's "Sentences," later to appear in *Cabala,* is a brief piece, probably published because the editor recognized an unusual style.

The October issue contained two poems, "Corymba" and "Dryad," by Donald Davidson, his first appearance outside of *The Fugitive.* The November issue offered verse by John Crowe Ransom, and within the next few months Allen Tate, Robert Penn Warren, and most of the

---

[13] Friend, Editorial, *The Double Dealer,* 1, 126 (April 1921).
[14] Letter, Julius Weis Friend to Charles Allen, July 28, 1941 (unpublished).

other *Fugitive* poets were appearing regularly. Hart Crane, Paul Eldridge, Matthew Josephson, Elizabeth Coatsworth, Malcolm Cowley, Edmund Wilson, and Kenneth Fearing also published some of their early work in *The Double Dealer*, though only Fearing appeared here for the first time (1923). The magazine issued its last number in May 1926. The editors felt that they could "no longer give the requisite time to it."[15]

Thus *The Double Dealer*, though it printed good criticism and book reviews, devoted most of its time to the unearthing of new poetry and fiction. Often it was purposely interested in encouraging a new writer rather than in the quality of his work. Consequently the magazine piled high its record of "discoveries" (whom we need not mention, for they have been long forgotten), and filled many of its pages with second-rate poetry and stories. We can submit in the editors' defense that they clearly recognized a most important function of the little magazine—that of encouraging unknown writers.

*The Double Dealer*, along with *The Fugitive* and *The Reviewer*, stands head and shoulders above the other Southern little magazines. The first discovered two of our best novelists, Hemingway and Faulkner; the second and third brought to fame a round half-dozen of our best present-day poets and critics. All three magazines can stand in the front rank with their more widely chronicled Northern brothers.

Each of the six groups of periodicals that we have mentioned contributed valuably to a regenerative literature. Perhaps those magazines devoted to the experimental philosophies and techniques, magazines such as *The Double Dealer* and *The Little Review*, have most clearly performed the advance guard function. The regionalists or proletarians might, and sometimes did, attain recognition without little magazine help, but the experimentalists rarely could rely on such fortune.

Though the periodicals we have discussed did publish much of the early work of our better writers, they did not actually discover many of them. Most of the reviews printed for the first time a modest two or three. *The Dial*, with its Albert Halper and Louis Zukofsky, is typical.

[15] See *Ibid.*, March 25, 1940. *The Double Dealer* cost on the average of $300 per issue, and "always ran a deficit over and above subscriptions and advertising, which was made up by donations from about forty individuals. Payment for material published started out at the rate of one cent per word for prose and fifty cents a line for verse. This was discontinued after about six issues due to a lack of funds, and for the remainder of the five years no payment was made for material." The average circulation was 1,500.

*Poetry, Story, The Fugitive,* and *The Double Dealer* are the exceptions. *Poetry* has an impressive list that includes the names of many of our best poets. *The Double Dealer* first printed five important persons, and *The Fugitive* first published Donald Davidson, Robert Penn Warren, Laura Riding, and Merrill Moore. None of *Story's* many finds have yet had time to establish a solid reputation.

In what publications, then, did the writers, 80 per cent of whom first appeared in the advance guard reviews, receive their starts? They began their careers in the little, little magazines, in the very short-lived, often wild-eyed, periodicals, the ones such as *Blues* (first published James Farrell and Erskine Caldwell) or *Bruno's Bohemia* (Hart Crane). As we have suggested, there have been hundreds of these ephemera, some of which have been provocative, most of which have been unutterably dreary. Almost every one turns up a considerable number of discoveries. Once in a long while one of the discoveries manages to catch the attention of the more respectable little magazines; and, after a time, he may even attain a reputation that need no longer rely on the moneyless blessings of the advance guard.

## IV

One may speak casually of an Ernest Hemingway's receiving his first half-dozen publications in little magazines and thereby gaining a reputation which the commercial publishers were eager to exploit. But let us be more specific. Hemingway publishes his first story in *The Double Dealer* in 1922. Assume that the editor and a few other people read this story and like it. These people talk enthusiastically of the story and perhaps twice as many read the next Hemingway offering. Soon many admirers are talking—a new name appears in the advance guard. A half-dozen little magazines are printing Hemingway stories and he has several thousand readers. A noncommercial press in Paris publishes his first thin volume, *Three Stories and Ten Poems*. The new writer attracts the attention of the Scribner's office. Finally in 1926 comes *The Sun Also Rises*. A writer has been started on the road to success— by the little magazines and their readers.

Though the best of our writers receive a wide enough acceptance through the little magazines to make them sought after by the conservative periodicals and publishing houses, one cannot help wondering what might have happened if these writers had not been offered a little magazine's encouragement. Many a Hart Crane or Sherwood

INTRODUCTION 15

Anderson might never have been heard from had there been no advance guard; for seeing one's work in print arouses a man's hope, stimulates further effort. This is what Stephen Vincent Benét has in mind when he writes: "The little magazines, of course, are absolutely indispensable. They give the beginning writer his first important step— a chance to see how the thing looks in print. And there's nothing as salutary."[16] This, indeed, is a primary justification.

Despite their promotion of the best of the new writers and literary movements, the advance guard magazines are easy targets for caustic ridicule. The most frequent accusation is that they do not print good writing. Of course there is a good deal of truth in this, and implied in the truth lies much of the strength and weakness of the little magazine. Few persons can take seriously the obvious nonsense that has filled many of the pages of *The Little Review, transition,* or *Broom.* Even the best magazines, *Poetry* and *The Dial,* for instance, have frequently lost their critical balance, been deluded into bestowing praise on an upstart whose only virtue was a facile talent for novelty in phrasing. The readiness with which editors seek for materials of whatever quality is the weakness that plagues the little magazine. Our knowledge of *The Double Dealer* proves, however, that the editor may deliberately accept material which he knows to be second rate, for he sees the marks of a genuine talent behind the stumbling words or unsteady structure of a poem or story. In accepting a manuscript to give encouragement, the editor hopes that the discovery will soon outgrow his awkwardness. More often than not, awkwardness is not outgrown; thus the files of the little reviews lie heavy with frozen material that probably never interested anyone except the author and the hopeful, though probably skeptical, editor. And so, though one must willingly agree that the little magazines contain much that is not of first importance, one must just as willingly grant that there is justification in printing fledgling literary efforts. Nor must one forget that many of the more significant pieces of our time have found their way into the little magazines. The people who suggest that the little magazines do not publish literature might notice the "thanks for permission to reprint" acknowledgments in almost any first volume of reputable stories, poetry, or criticism.

Some persons also believe that the advance guard editors have a tendency to favor the "established" little magazine writers over the

[16] Letter, Stephen Vincent Benét to Charles Allen, September 1939 (unpublished).

meritorious unknown. True enough. Little magazine editors are not free from vanity or oblivious of the desire for prestige. They do favor the "name" writers of their own circle. Yet they do not grant them the same favors that the commercial editor is likely to give his writers. The little magazine does not usually pay for its contributions, is not dependent on advertising, and can ignore names to a far greater extent than the commercial publisher. Several Hemingway stories were refused, perhaps unwisely, by little magazine editors in those first days of Hemingway glory.

Hostile observers also berate the "exhibitionism," "pretension," "snobbishness," and "adolescence" toward which some reviews incline. Exhibitionism there is, nor need one look far to discover pretension and snobbishness. But all of these words connote, in varying degrees, conscious or semiconscious attitudinizing; yet such conscious posturing is rare, not only in literature but in any artistic or mental activity.

But when one comes to the charge that the little magazines are often adolescent, he is forced to grant that the critics have much firm ground under their feet. For if fear and uncertainty are signs of immaturity, as the psychologists contend, then many little magazine contributors and not a few editors are immature. The pioneer, whether he be the wielder of the broad axe, the explorer in the deep jungle of the unconscious mind, the rebel economic theorist, or the innovator of literary surrealism, is often a slightly maladjusted person. Not infrequently it is a feeling of insecurity that has driven him to pioneering, and it is insecurity, combined with an envy for the respectable, that leads the pioneer and rebel unknowingly, and sometimes knowingly, to apologize for his feeling of insecurity with considerable bizarre behavior and intellectual display—display which is designed to emphasize his uniqueness, his superiority. Thus a *Little Review* can convince itself of its ineffable critical discernment by insisting, in all high seriousness, that the dadaists and the machine reveal many of the highest aspirations of man. And *transition* can convince itself of its penetrating insight into the nature of man and the supernatural by talking of divine currents to which man must attune himself. One does not sense pretension nor exhibitionism here, but rather a lack of urbanity, an insecure mind.

Fortunately, one can afford to ignore a good deal of adolescence if courage and daring and genuine accomplishment are also present. All such comment is overshadowed, moreover, by very real contributions. In 1912, in 1920, in 1930, the little magazines were the innovators, and today they are still the innovators. A society needs ever-fresh interpretations and new writers to make these interpretations. Little magazine editors believe that a Hemingway or a Sandburg or a Faulkner may finally lose his power or die and that younger artists must be constantly encouraged. This is why advance guard editors sought out Erskine Caldwell, Albert Halper, and James Farrell in 1929, why they discovered most of the so-called proletarian writers of the thirties, and why in the forties they are still introducing new artists.

# THE SECOND DECADE

CHAPTER II

WHEN Harriet Monroe interviewed Hobart C. Chatfield-Taylor about the prospects for a new poetry magazine, she felt that there was something wrong both with the way poetry was being written and with its reception by the reading public. "The average magazine editor's conception of good verse is verse that will fill out a page. No editor is looking for long poems; he wants something light and convenient. Consequently a Milton might be living in Chicago today and be unable to find an outlet for his verse."[1]

Poetry for the most part was being written as a by-product of the reading of prose. It served many of the functions of prose, but failed in the essential task of the poet—to record the evidence of the senses directly. Ezra Pound was skeptical about the effectiveness of *Poetry* or any other verse magazine in America. It seemed to him that poetry would continue being a scrapbook of sentiment, forever harnessed by rhyme and singsong meter: "Can you teach the American poet that poetry *is* an *art*, an art with a technique, with media—an art that must be in constant flux, a constant change of manner, if it is to live? Can you teach him that it is not a pentametric echo of the sociological dogma printed in last year's magazines?"[2]

One of the values of *Poetry*'s early years was its hospitality to and its vigorous defense of experimentalism in verse. Richard Aldington's "Choricos" was the first publication of the imagists "anywhere," a fact of which Miss Monroe was very proud. Aldington's poems were followed in the January 1913 issue by H.D.'s first American appearance, "Verses, Translations, and Reflections from the Anthology." The

---

[1] Harriet Monroe, *A Poet's Life*, New York, 1938, p. 247.
[2] Letter to Harriet Monroe, *ibid.*, p. 259.

imagist school, which Pound confessed was established to give H.D.'s poems a hearing, was one of the first sources of controversy between the conservatives and the experimentalists. Imagistic poetry strives for precision of statement and a comparative isolation of an image from its affective, sentimental, or sociological context; in Pound's words, the work of the imagists demonstrates their "opposition to the numerous and unassembled writers who busy themselves with dull and interminable effusions, and who seem to think that a man can write a good long poem before he learns to write a good short one or even before he learns to produce a good single line."[3] The verbal economy of the imagists, their striving for poetic purity, is essentially a negative contribution to experiment; it served to revalue the poetic task, and to reinform the poets of the necessities and peculiarities of their craft. The credo of the imagists required a direct treatment of the object or subject of the poem, avoidance of abstractions, romantic or didactic, and a strict and careful attention to metaphoric refinements. What is missing from imagist poems (if it is possible to isolate poems as "imagistic") is the provocative challenge of complex metaphor which so often characterizes later poetry and the intellectual content of that poetry. Imagist poetry is a form of poetic understatement which has the virtue of being limited to the minima of objective reality or subjective appearance. So far as there is any more than superficial or imposed relationship among the arts, the imagistic "color" resembles a fragmentary musical theme. Imagism is admirably suited to the poetic habits of H.D., and may also be said to have tutored the verse of Aldington, but it could not do more than temporarily check the Whitmanism of much American poetry of our second decade. Carl Sandburg's poems occasionally show the effect of the interest in imagism, though he preferred the cadences of Lincoln's speech as he imagined it or the roughly cut catalogic imagery which Whitman's line forced upon his poetic consciousness.[4]

Companion to *Poetry* for a brief time, and in a sense a rival, was *Others* (1915-19), the magazine of Alfred Kreymborg who had earlier helped to edit the interesting little chapbook magazine, *Glebe*. Kreymborg's *Others* was designed to point out that "there were others" writing verse and not being published regularly by Harriet Monroe. The verse of *Others* seems often deliberately clever and shocking, the metaphors strained and the lines arranged like cards in a verbal solitaire.

[3] Ezra Pound, Letter to *Poetry*, I, 126 (January 1913).
[4] See Chapter III, pp. 34-44, for a more complete history of *Poetry*.

Mina Loy's "Love Songs," which appeared in the first issue, were among those which aroused mockery and resentment among the reading public:

> Spawn of fantasies
> Sitting the appraisable
> Pig Cupid      his rosy snout
> Rooting erotic garbage[5]

*Others* is to be remembered for its publication of excellent verse by Wallace Stevens ("Peter Quince at the Clavier"), T. S. Eliot ("Portrait of a Lady"), Marianne Moore ("To a Statecraft Embalmed"), and William Carlos Williams. Its editorial incentive, the inclusion of "others" in the American literary scene, was soon dissipated by the accommodation which these "others" received in *Poetry* and similar magazines. There was little enough quarrel with Harriet Monroe, except on the grounds that her editorial scrutiny had been at times a bit austere and that she sometimes interfered with the poet's given right to "absolute freedom" of expression.

Miss Monroe's Chicago contemporary, *The Little Review*, reflects the utter freedom and irresponsibility which marks much of the history of our literary teens. Ruthven Todd calls the issue of December 1914 "a scrappy repository for anything that happened to appeal to Margaret Anderson, showing neither editorial standards nor a balanced point of view."[6] Todd's close examination of one issue is unfair to the one quality in Margaret Anderson's personality which made *The Little Review* an important magazine—her volatility, which gave her venture the appearance of a rapidly shifting panorama of the literature of its time, or a literary montage with Miss Anderson performing with the scissors. Margaret Anderson was always in control of the magazine; indeed, it would have died at any time she had wished it to. "Life is a glorious performance," she says in her first appearance, and adds, "And close to Life—so close, from our point of view, that it keeps treading on Life's heels—is this eager, panting Art who shows us the wonder of the way as we rush along."[7] The impression given is of breathless racing with life, so that we may imitate it, but may not dare to correct it. Margaret Anderson opposed the intellectualism of her time with an editorial philosophy of "feeling," which reaches its finest development, of course, in the artist. She was interested primarily in the "inner life,"

---

[5] *Others*, I, 6 (July 1915).

[6] "The Little Review," *Twentieth Century Verse*, xv-xvi, 162 (February 1939).

[7] Editorial, *The Little Review*, I, 1 (March 1914).

and claimed that man must be socially free in order to realize his inner being. A little magazine, in her estimation, "should suggest, not conclude ... should stimulate to thinking rather than dictate thought. ... I have none of the qualifications of the editor; that's why I think *The Little Review* is in good hands."[8]

Miss Anderson's magazine had a varied and exciting history. As in the case of *Poetry*, it aroused the interest of Pound, who for some years introduced to it the work of his British friends; and Joyce sent over the manuscript of *Ulysses*, which was to be *The Little Review's* most exciting contribution. The trial of the magazine for its violation of postal regulations against obscenity is told with great animation and some indignation in Miss Anderson's autobiography, *My Thirty Years' War*.[9]

## II

Throughout the early years of America's new freedom, the figure of Ezra Pound looms large. A native of Idaho, for some time a student at the University of Pennsylvania and a teacher at Wabash College in Indiana, Pound ultimately became a confirmed and recalcitrant expatriate. The arrogant and defensive personality which aroused the indignation of anti-Nazis during World War II, in the earlier years endowed him with his most engaging qualities. His was truly the "personality as poet"; so seriously interested was he in the cause of the new poetry that he eagerly grasped every opportunity for placing the work of his friends in the many magazines with which he had influence. His critical remarks are characterized by spasmodic penetration, an arbitrary and cocksure forthrightness, and an obstinate refusal to brook what he considered untimely or petty opposition. His lifelong battle has been with the sentimental abstraction of American and British gentility and oratory. At no time has he compromised with "the people," though he gave Whitman a begrudging compliment in one of the poems published in *Poetry*. In politics this point of view was inevitably to land him, for a variety of reasons, with the Fascists; in literature for a long time it was to act as a candid dissolvent of some of the most stubborn remnants of post-Victorian sweetness and light. Historically Pound must be considered one of the most effective sponsors of experimental literature in our century.

[8] Editorial, *The Little Review*, I, 2 (February 1915).
[9] See Chapter III, pp. 44-51, for a discussion of *Glebe* and *Others*; Chapter IV, pp. 52-66, for a more complete history of *The Little Review*.

John Gould Fletcher first met Ezra Pound in Paris, in 1913; according to Fletcher, Pound was "a pioneer in the last great wave of American expatriates who, like myself, had turned from the West to the East and had come abroad before the European war, bent on submitting their own rude and untaught native impulses to the task of assimilating, and if possible, surpassing the traditional achievements of Europe." This was, in Fletcher's opinion, the true expatriate group, compared with which the exiles of the twenties were ineffectual and truly "lost": "[They] learned nothing much from Europe or America, but largely discovered their own petty and neurotic selves."[10]

Pound and Fletcher planned an "open move" against the localism and feminism of Dora Marsden's *The Freewoman*. From this move came *The New Freewoman*, "An Individualist Review," a curious compound of philosophic editorials, essays on the "new woman," and samplings from modern letters. In January 1914 the magazine changed its title to *The Egoist*, kept its subtitle, and added Richard Aldington as assistant editor. The motto stated in the subtitle is explained in the editorial for December 1913: "If we could get into the habit of describing a man as he feels himself instead of in the terms of the physical image under which he presents himself to sight, we should break through this deadening concept of unity."[11]

In this magazine imagism was to be advanced as the poetic expression of the poetic ego. H.D., Amy Lowell, and William Carlos Williams contributed poems to a collection called "The Newer School." Rebecca West defended these poems as an antidote against the poetry of those who are "unaccustomed to being sacked for talking too much." *The Egoist*, insofar as it reflected Pound's influence, became a review of advanced writing, striking a critical pose and evaluating the prewar tendencies in the political and cultural worlds. In this capacity, it cleared a path for experimentalists and gave them much to think about. The lengthy essays by Dora Marsden on Bergson, Hegel, Nietzsche, and others, though they may be condemned as tedious, pointed to the intellectual preoccupations of an age. A portion of Bergson's *Creative Evolution* was published in the issue of December 15, 1913; and Fletcher, in an essay of April 1917, commenting upon the destructive influence of the war, said, "In order to bear the suffering it has caused we have to effect what Nietzsche would have called a transvaluation of

[10] John Gould Fletcher, *Life Is My Song*, New York, 1937, p. 60.
[11] "Views and Comments," *The New Freewoman*, I, 245 (December 15, 1913).

Richard Aldington

H. D.

Ezra Pound

Amy Lowell

### 6
## BLAST
### years 1837 to 1900

**Curse abysmal inexcusable** middle-class (also Aristocracy and Proletariat).

## BLAST
pasty shadow cast by gigantic **Boehm** (imagined at introduction of **BOURGEOIS VICTORIAN VISTAS**).

**WRING THE NECK OF** all sick inventions born in that progressive white wake.

**BLAST** their weeping whiskers—hirsute **RHETORIC of EUNUCH and STYLIST— SENTIMENTAL HYGIENICS ROUSSEAUISMS** (wild Nature cranks) **FRATERNIZING WITH MONKEYS DIABOLICS**—raptures and roses of the erotic bookshelves culminating in **PURGATORY OF PUTNEY.**

A page of Wyndham Lewis' BLAST, July 1914

values."[12] Publication of original writing was not always discriminating; but Pound's influence secured a first hearing for Joyce's *A Portrait of the Artist as a Young Man*, and later for a part of *Ulysses*.

*The Egoist* affirms the vigorous independence of man as poet, and seeks to encourage him to cast off all intellectual inhibitions, to lose his respect for outworn institutions. We find Wyndham Lewis' *Tarr* published serially, beginning with April 1, 1916. Lewis is the high point of the "aesthetic revolt" against the constraints of *vox populi*; he is the Timon of London. Pound was to say, in defending him, that if the man in the street cannot understand him, "Damn the man in the street, once and for all. . . ."[13] Lewis' *Blast*, which began in June of 1914 and published two issues, was designed as a "death warrant" for the guardians of the past. In place of them it offered "the Vortex," a sort of typographical vacuum sweeper. "Long live the Vortex." "We need the Unconsciousness of Humanity—their stupidity, animalism and dreams." The task of vorticism in *Blast* was "to make the rich of the community shed their education skin, to destroy politeness, standardization and academic, that is civilized, vision. . . ."[14] *Blast* appeared at the beginning of the First World War. It approved of its rival blasts and opposed the Germans on the grounds that they were sentimentally attached to the intellectual society of the French! "Of the two figures—our Genial and Realistic Barbarians on the one side, and the Champions of melodramatic philosophy, on the other, we dispassionately prefer our own side!"[15]

The predecessors of the twenties were conscious of the need for ridding themselves of the "rotten timber" of civilization. Along with the futurism of Marinetti, they offered nothing much more than a destructive cure. Why the violence in their attitude? It seemed a tremendous reaction to the stimulus of irritation. Their apparently indiscriminate iconoclasm has its source in their recognition of themselves as distinct personalities, endowed with an intellect which set them quite apart from the convention-infested world of polite letters on the one hand and the unlettered, unwashed, unthinking masses on the other. Nietzsche seemed a romantic figure to them; his Dionysian scorn for the pale dialectics of Socrates and Plato, his belief that art is above all vigorous and unmeasured—a working agreement between blood and

[12] "The Death of the Machines," *The Egoist*, IV, 45 (April 1917).
[13] "Wyndham Lewis," *The Egoist*, I, 233 (June 15, 1914).
[14] "Manifesto," *Blast*, I, 4 (June 20, 1914).
[15] Editorial, *Blast*, I, 6 (July 1915).

brain—appealed to them. Above all, their rantings were not founded upon any distinct theory of composition; that was to come later. In her explanation of one of the vorticists, Babette Deutsch analyzed the entire group with a fair degree of perception: "It is Pound's too engrossing sense of intelligence crushed by overwhelming mediocrity which wrenches him from the contemplation of beauty to vituperative attack upon vulgar modesty, perverts his worship of perfection to an esoteric artificiality, and stings him to humor that tastes of gall. . . ."[16] In other words, the "blasting" was essentially a destructive, negative, and (perhaps strangely) an intensely personal matter. It did not lay the foundation of any one aesthetic theory or prescribe any mode of action. It was the intellectual turned anti-intellectual by virtue of an intolerable irritation; other than the upsetting of aesthetic plans, it did not disturb the personalities themselves. Perhaps all of this explains why there were no lasting, workable, or consistent plans or theories to replace the institutions and principles which they were partly successful in demolishing. Above all, these men—and especially Pound and Lewis—were individualists, brought together temporarily by the lure of verbal violence, but destined to go their own separate ways in the twenties.

Futurism, however, was well planned. It has been perhaps mistakenly identified as a sort of predecessor to dada. Its entire structure was developed from the fascination which technology and its visible evidences of speed had for its leaders. (It was this preoccupation with speed which caused Wyndham Lewis to dub futurism "automobilism.") Harold Munro, who for a time was attracted by it, printed translations of futurist poems in the September 1913 issue of *Poetry and Drama*: "However deficient in beauty, these poems cannot be said to lack in energy and eloquence," he explains. "We find them constantly invoking all the furies of Nature and of the madman: they are always standing on tiptoe. Their poetry is composed recklessly for immediate and wide circulation and declamation in large assemblies, frequently for purposes of propaganda."[17] The program of futurism is based upon the changed sensibility afforded by the advance of technology: the influence of the telegraph, telephone, and gramophone on the human psyche. The notable results, listed by Marinetti in *Poetry and Drama* were an "acceleration of life," distaste for the traditional and "love of the new and the unforeseen," preference for a life of danger, disappearance of sentimentality ("produced by the greater

[16] "Ezra Pound: Vorticist," *Reedy's Mirror*, XXVI, 861 (December 21, 1917).
[17] "Varia," *Poetry and Drama*, I, 264 (September 1913).

erotic facility and liberty of women"), a union of the psyche with horsepower, and a love for speed as opposed to tedious analysis.

All of these attitudes had been fostered by the quickened perception made possible by technological advances and inventive science. The effect of this point of view upon syntax and style is Marinetti's next problem. Obviously traditional syntax had been based upon a slow and calculated, a logical, use of sensory organs. Degrees of variation in sense perception had always been designated by adjectives, which measured qualities in the external world and in man's response to it. As for punctuation, it was man's way of indicating logical and perceptive pauses—so that a subordinate clause or phrase attached itself to its noun or verb after a definite allowance had been made for its cargo of meaning. The futurist was all for "chucking adjectives and punctuation overboard...." The "Wireless Imagination" demanded absolute freedom of style, "... expressed by disjointed words and without the connecting wires of syntax." Adjectives were mere indicators of the "pace and race of analogies." The infinitive form of the verb, "round and true as a wheel," was indispensable to futurist expression. Thus, the futurist grasp of reality was external and geometric. Its appreciation of syntactic disintegration came essentially from observing the acceleration of sense perceptions. Futurism is therefore distinct from the experiments and theories based upon psychoanalysis which characterize much of the experimental literature of the twenties and thirties.[18]

The First World War has perhaps been overemphasized as a primary cause and determinant of the culture of our day. But it did affect many people in a variety of ways. Aldington left the editorial staff of *The Egoist* to join the forces: Fletcher contemplated enlisting, but was dissuaded. The movement of events was so swift that no one person was able to evaluate them sanely; carnage immediate and intimate deadens the intellect, paralyzes purpose, and acts as a stimulant to anger and fear. For D.H. Lawrence especially, the war was a horrible thing. In some respects he was shaped by it; at least it might be said that much of his *sauve qui peut* philosophy stemmed from his gloomy experiences in the midst of a hostile world. Both foes were essentially at war with him, with his soul, and with what he regarded as precious in man.

Lawrence was above all adversely affected by the economic drives in

[18] F. T. Marinetti, "Wireless Imagination and Words at Liberty," tr. Arundel del Re, *Poetry and Drama*, I, 319-26 (September 1913). For a summary of the history of *Poetry and Drama*, see below, p. 244.

Western culture which in his estimation had made it impossible for man to be true to himself. John Middleton Murry, a companion of these years (the relationship between the two men was to blow hot and cold by turns throughout Lawrence's life), suggested to Lawrence that they "do something about this war." As writers they could scarcely be expected to do anything other than *write* about it—or, rather, write against it. The three issues of *The Signature* were the result.[19] Throughout them appeared a long essay by Lawrence, "The Crown," and one by Murry, "There Was a Little Man." Fiction written by Katherine Mansfield (under the pen name of "Matilda Berry") was the only other contribution. The two essays are a reaction to the war: Lawrence's a more vigorous denunciation of society, Murry's more introspective. For Lawrence the war existed as a monstrous birth, the result of a long-term, illicit misalliance between society and evil. Murry preferred to deny its existence altogether: "Passionately and from the depths of my heart I say 'This monstrous thing does not exist'; there is no real relation between it and me."[20] Murry demanded of society that "it leave [him] alone to work out [his] own justification." Death for him in the accidental or military sense is tragic because it denies the full consummation of the self. Throughout Murry's life as an editor of and contributor to literary reviews, the aesthetic and the moral attitudes warred with each other. This was because he had never made up his mind about the exact complexion of either—and was able to withdraw from one into the security of the other, because indecision allows for much spiritual haven from decision. This was the ground upon which Murry and Lawrence ultimately and profoundly differed; and it is, moreover, the reason why, though Lawrence had followers, Murry's work has for the most part aroused little but adverse criticism.

Why, then, did Murry and Lawrence collaborate in any sense at all? If we are to take Aldous Huxley's portraits of Lawrence and Murry in *Point Counterpoint* literally (and it is obvious that we should be cautious in doing so), they had absolutely no grounds for agreement. Murry was fascinated by Lawrence's vigor. Lawrence had always worn his heart upon his sleeve; Murry kept his securely under lock and key, and frequently left his lodgings without it. This fact should again

[19] It is impossible to give the Lawrence-Murry relationship its full measure of attention in an essay of this sort. The reader is referred to Murry's autobiographies and to his biography of Lawrence, *Son of Woman*, London, 1931, for Murry's interpretation, and to Lawrence's *Letters*, edited by Aldous Huxley, New York, 1932, for Lawrence's views.

[20] "There Was a Little Man," *The Signature*, I, 24 (October 4, 1915).

underline the discrepancy in Murry between editorial promise and ultimate literary achievement. Murry's editorials in *Rhythm* and *The Blue Review* are full of the promise of a vigorous attachment to the purpose of art. Such, for example, is the beautiful intent of the first statement in *Rhythm*: "To treat what is being done today as something vital in the progress of art, which cannot fix its eyes on yesterday and live; to see that the present is pregnant for the future rather than a revolt against the past; in creation to give expression to an art that seeks out the strong things of life; in criticism to seek out the strong things of that art—such is the aim of *Rhythm*."[21]

Murry possessed fine perception of the causes of unrest in his society. More than that, he was to be afflicted with this unrest throughout his life, having early given it the shape of his own ego and kept it within bounds. From that point of view he is able to make such interesting generalizations as this: ". . . the greater part of modern intellectual unrest centers in the middle classes."[22]

### III

Among all of the varying notions one gets of the literary thought and expression of our second decade, one thing stands out: the fact that there were many individuals, each stimulated by some form of aesthetic incentive, all of them held together by a loose unity of aesthetic and moral points of view. The integrity and dignity of the self seemed important above all else. Little magazines, therefore, were often guided and directed by "man alone" rather than by a school of thought or by some doctrinal expression larger than the self. The characteristic little magazine of the teens may be called the "one-man magazine," its editorial policy determining the quality and variety of its inclusions. Need we add that there were many exceptions to this rule?

One approaches the figure of Guido Bruno with no little skepticism and amusement. No other man has ever actually begun and edited so many little magazines, or done so with such wholesale disregard of the proprieties of the publishing world. In rapid though irregular succession appeared *Bruno's Weekly, Bruno's Chapbook, Greenwich Village, Bruno's, Bruno's Bohemia, Bruno's Review of Two Worlds,* and *Bruno's Review of Life, Love, and Letters.* These magazines varied

[21] Editorial, *Rhythm*, 1, 36 (Summer 1911).
[22] *The Blue Review*, 1, 3 (February 1913).

slightly in format, in ambition of enterprise, and in content; but essentially they follow a fairly regular pattern: the exclusiveness of the artist as a person, living in a relatively secure and confined environment, full of small irritations, endowed with an extravagant capacity for indecision about many matters.

The Bohemian, living on "the Happy Island," exercised the prerogative of independence which low rent rates and sympathetic surroundings afforded him. No great literature resulted from such conditions. This is not to say that Greenwich Village was simply the home of congenital idlers who defended Oscar Wilde and complained about the noise of Fifth Avenue busses. There were many other types, some of them quite well aware of what was going on in the world outside, quite ready to allow that world to temper and in some cases to shape their eventual position in the world of letters. In a sense the Village was just a stopping-off place. It afforded young writers the security of a community negligent about decorum; it gave them opportunity for airing their theories in numerous gatherings of loosely organized units, called vaguely "clubs." It was an environment in which much might be begun, if the Village did not become so much a part of one that one simply became stamped as "a part of the Village." Most of all, it was a clearinghouse for ideologies which were in some form or other to affect the thinking of the next two decades. Villagers fought the good fight against middle-class propriety; many of them, however, mistook it for a personal grudge fight, and adapted the weapons of Freud and Marx to close infighting. Others assumed that the struggle against puritanism was larger than themselves, but insisted upon the integrity and sanctity of their own persons, and developed a personal aesthetic and ethic which others might accept if they wished. A third group at some time in the course of their lives were absorbed by one or another of the doctrinal ideologies which have since emerged as the principal source of intellectual conflict. Of course, the Village was also "a business"; but that phase of its life need not detain us.

The editors of and contributors to *The Masses* formed an interesting and curious group in themselves. For them revolt was essentially a personal matter; and, though Marxism and other forms of socialism did form the background for much of their thinking, they looked upon the constraints of bourgeois society for the most part as personal inconveniences or as objects of ridicule and satire. Yet there was an inevitable and a strong socialist leaven which was eventually, when conditions were "right," to convince the editors of *The Liberator* that it had best

# A Divine Gesture
## By ERNEST M. HEMINGWAY

AND then when all was come and gone, the Great Lord God strode out of the house and into the garden, for in the garden he found the deep peace of Rome. Bathtubs stood all around in heavy earnestness. Boot jacks littered the Garden. A thousand broken flower pots were piled into one corner.

"Where is Adam?" asked the Lord God.

No one answered for all the flower pots were tired and none of the bathtubs remembered it was Sunday.

"Where is Eve?" asked the Lord God, pulling at his beard and looking remarkably like Tolstoi.

At once all the boot jacks began to leap and chatter and a flight of blackbirds swooped down into the garden and commenced to strut around, exploring into the flower pots with their beautiful shining bills.

"She is gone out, God," said the largest and weakest bathtub in a heavily earnest manner, "and no man can prophecy the hour of her returning. But I would say that she would return around four o'clock."

The Great Lord God made a divine motion with his hand and the angel Gabriel came swiftly forward from where he had been sitting and let all the water out of the largest and weakest of the bathtubs.

"That would teach him a valuable lesson," remarked the angel Gabriel, and God nodded to him in an absent-minded and approving manner.

"It should," meditated the great Lord God, "and more valuable lessons is what we need in this day and age."

As there seemed nothing more for the angel Gabriel to say and as the water was quite run out of the largest and weakest of the bathtubs, he smiled quietly at God and walked carefully back to his corner, treading cautiously as he went in order not to step on any of the boot jacks which were curling and uncurling in an alarming manner.

"Stop it!" shouted the great Lord God, and at once every boot jack was still. "How often have I told you not to continue that loathsome habit?"

One boot jack nudged another and soon they were all nudging one another and whispering, "We mustn't squirm today. We mustn't squirm to-day. Hy ya ta did eeyay. We mustn't squirm to-day!"

In a little while from whispering the words had changed into a chant and all the boot jacks were squirming more than ever and chanting at the top of their voices, "We mustn't squirm today. We mustn't squirm today. Hy Yah Ta Did Esay! We mustn't squirm today!"

"Stop it!" shouted the Great Lord God in a terrible voice.

Ernest Hemingway's first published work,
in THE DOUBLE DEALER, May 1922

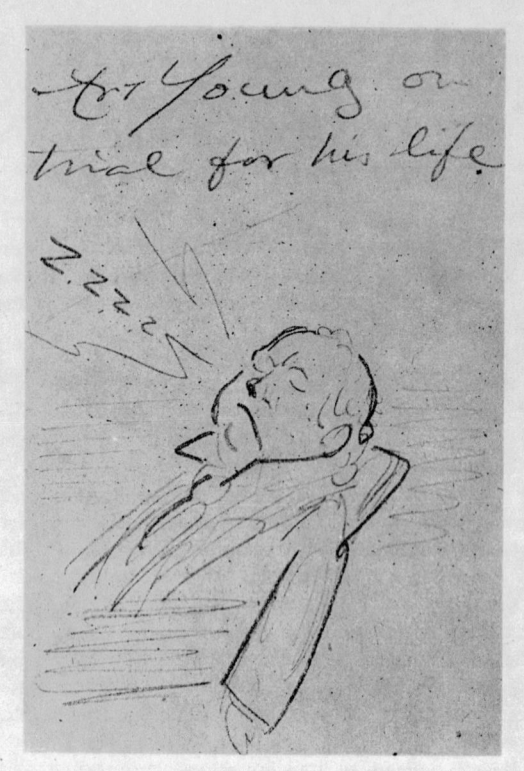

Art Young, by himself

Floyd Dell
by Boardman Robinson

Boardman Robinson
"Who didn't miss an hour of the trial"
by Art Young

Three sketches made at the MASSES trial, 1915

be turned over to the communists. Socialism of this early period—that is, before the revolution in Russia had given Marxism a bargaining power with intellectuals and artists—was a mixture of social realism and poetic romanticism. This accounts for the lyricism of much of *The Masses* verse, for the serious and lengthy discussions on the sexual problem by Floyd Dell. *The Masses* was, after all, a Village magazine. And, somehow, in art conflicts can be resolved in the imagination; or they may be clarified by a visit to a psychoanalyst. Contrast, in the light of what has been said, the editorial statement in the February 1911 issue of *The Masses* with much of leftwing principle of a later date: "Socialism has more to gain from a free, artistic literature reflecting life as it actually is, than from an attempt to stretch points in order to make facts fit the Socialist theory."[23]

The first year of the magazine (1911-12), under the guidance of the noisy and humorless restaurant manager, Piet Vlag, was commonplace enough. Vlag rather pompously announced that his magazine, financed by a wealthy insurance tycoon, was to campaign for the rights of the workingman, rights which evidently were never very clear in Vlag's mind, though he ponderously attacked the high costs of living, war, child labor, and came out in favor of co-operative stores. Vlag also promised that new writers and artists were to be sponsored. Not many were: Art Young was the one noteworthy talent to appear during this first year. By September 1911 *The Masses* was on the rocks; three months passed before the magazine was rescued. During these three months Art Young and a small group of Greenwich Village artists and writers had decided that the magazine must continue. They elected as editor Max Eastman, a former professor of philosophy at Columbia University. Eastman selected Floyd Dell as managing editor and *The Masses* was off on its devil's advocate career of chief baiter of the capitalistic bourgeois.

Unlike most of its latter-day descendants, the Eastman-Dell *Masses* radiated sparkle and humor along with its biting criticism. Its circulation, which according to Eastman rose to an average monthly 14,000, was garnered largely from the socialist and liberal intelligentsia rather than from the working people that the monthly professed to serve.

During 1913 John Reed, Arturo Giovannitti, Lincoln Steffens, and Art Young helped Eastman and Dell carry the battle directly to the capitalistic fortress, and in this year *The Masses* found itself involved in the first of its fiery legal battles. Having accused the Associated Press

[23] Editorial, *The Masses*, I, 3 (February 1911).

of suppressing news because of an antilabor prejudice, the magazine found itself faced with a libel suit; the combatants sparred for two years before the Press, with haughty dignity, announced that it no longer cared to fight. *The Masses* was delighted and forever afterwards poked malicious satire at its defeated opponent. The year 1914 found the periodical busy sponsoring feminism, Negro rights, and pacificism. Some of the most frequently appearing names for this year were John Reed, Mabel Dodge, Robert Carlton Brown, James Oppenheim, and Floyd Dell. During 1915 and 1916 the magazine became more definitely literary. Fiction and poetry began to flow into the editorial offices from such writers as Ernest Poole, Wilbur Daniel Steele, Carl Sandburg, Helen Hoyt, Sherwood Anderson, and Amy Lowell.

After January 1916, *The Masses* was no longer allowed on New York elevated and subway newsstands, for the howling winds of war chauvinism were lashing ever more furiously at the magazine's socialist-pacifist point of view. Finally, in August 1917, the Post Office Department succeeded in barring the periodical from the mails. Undaunted, the editors published issues for September, October, and a final one for November-December. At last the Department of Justice brought a charge against Eastman, Dell, Young, and the business manager, Merrill Rogers, for "conspiracy against the government" and "interfering with enlistment." The trial began in April 1918, dragged on for days, and at last resulted in a jury disagreement. The government prosecution was outraged, insisted on another trial, to be held in September. Again the jury disagreed and *The Masses* considered itself vindicated. Though moral victory was obtained, much of the fight had been taken from the socialist editors and contributors. It was not until March 1918 that the weary forces could again be inspired for battle. In that month appeared the first number of *The Liberator*, edited by Eastman and Young. The pages of *The Liberator* continued the tradition of *The Masses*, but revolt and protest were eventually to be directed to the development of Marxist ideology in its American dress. In 1924 it was given to the communists and merged with *The Labor Herald* and *Soviet Russia Pictorial* to become *The Worker's Monthly*.[24]

The work of Marion Reedy in Saint Louis, though he stood in the vanguard of liberal protest, did not disturb its orthodox contemporaries as much. Reedy was a liberal in politics, not a radical. When the war

---

[24] This story of *The Masses* and *The Liberator* belongs also to a discussion of the leftwing little magazine, and it will be taken up again in a chapter devoted to that subject. See Chapter IX, pp. 148-53.

finally came to the United States, he saw it through a Wilsonian haze, and wrote constantly about the opportunity for liberal reconstruction afforded by our entrance. *Reedy's Mirror* was also liberal in its attitude toward arts and letters. Though Marion Reedy came home from Chicago to scoff at the futurists and cubists, he welcomed the new poetry and praised Harriet Monroe for her efforts in its behalf. The *Mirror* printed the *Spoon River Anthology*, by "Webster Ford," who was revealed as Edgar Lee Masters in the issue of November 20, 1914. Orrick Johns, commenting upon "the *Masses* crowd," indirectly pointed to the virtues of Reedy's magazine by suggesting that "The young men of *The Masses* have none of the social delusions that O. Henry tumbled into so often. They have a sound logic which does them honor, but they rarely show simple feeling. . . . I find *The Masses*, on the whole, vitiated by sentiment, but wrong in feeling. This is partly because that paper has 'a policy'."[25] Liberalism in politics and eclecticism in the arts gave the *Mirror* a reputation for considering all movements amiably. The magazine was therefore a source of information about the arts and a starting point for such men as Masters and Johns. As an intellectual amateur, Reedy delivered himself of opinions on a variety of subjects, from Nietzsche to the psychology of dreams.

Robert Coady's editorship of *The Soil* (1916-17) was marked by no aimless eclecticism. His selection of materials was motivated by a desire to find the most inclusive and the most genuine American art. He was impressed by the native vigor of American activity in many fields; and, like Whitman, he found poetry in all of them. The American art "is not a refined granulation nor a delicate disease—it is not an ism. . . . It has grown out of the soil and through the race and will continue to grow. It will grow and mature and add a new unit to Art."[26] The content of Whitman's poems influenced Coady's magazine, as the form had affected the manner of many American poets. *The Soil* thus is a Whitmanesque catalogue, minus the latter's references to Hegel and other philosophers:

> The rhythm of the ocean cradles the transatlantics,
> And while the heroic express arriving at Havre
> Whistles into the air, where the gasses dance like tops,
> The athletic sailors advance, like bears.
> New York! New York! I should like to inhabit you!

[25] "Wanted—The Real Thing," *Reedy's Mirror*, XXII, 5 (December 12, 1913).
[26] *The Soil*, I, 4 (December 1916).

> I see there science married
> To industry,
> In an audacious modernity,
> And in the palaces,
> Globes,
> Dazzling to the retina
> By their ultra-violet rays;
> The American telephone,
> And the softness
> Of elevators. . . .[27]

Coady recognizes the advantages of taste and aesthetic discipline, but insists that true American art "is as yet outside of our art world"; we cannot find it by running "to this ism and that ist." We need art more than any other nation; but it must be an art which can account for Jack Johnson, Nick Carter, Charlie Chaplin, the East River, and the trip hammer. This preoccupation with the immediate in our environment is accompanied by an appealing respect for aesthetic discipline. Coady's death prevented any synthesis of the materials he had thrown together in his magazine. Other artists, however, have been influenced by Coady's vision and have been fascinated by the diversity of appearances in our American scene.

## IV

In the total picture of our second decade one finds a puzzling complexity and diversity of motive and intention. *Poetry* is begun to give poetry "great audiences"; *Others*, simply to afford a place of publication for young poets, who most assuredly deserved it. Art is regarded variously as a guarantor of individualism, a handmaiden to prerevolutionary socialism, a bludgeon to be used against bourgeois dry rot, and an ivory citadel against the encroachments of civilian boorishness. There is no way of measuring such variety, save perhaps to find in variety itself a form of unity. The fact is that this was a period of doubt, confusion, and conflict. One truth is apparent throughout, however— the artist reserved for himself a certain inviolability of temperament. Thus concessions were made for him, and by him for himself. Further, it may be said that the artist was receiving the first shock of recognition; the world surrounded him with contradictory institutions and prac-

---

[27] Arthur Craven, *The Soil*, I, 36 (December 1916).

tics. The immediate past offered him a variety of ideologies, new to him and not yet assimilated by him. The sciences, metaphysics, psychology, and sociology offered strange and exciting jargons which somehow clashed with the jargon of aesthetics. The huge task of relating all of these disciplines with aesthetics had only begun. Revolt does not become experiment until it affects the language and craft of the artist.

Thus the little magazines of the teens must be considered in the light of their age.[28] It was not an age of indecision; it was an age of predecision. What Joseph Freeman says of his generation demonstrates the transitional nature of the decade: "We were too young to become rigidly set in prewar attitudes, too old to benefit without anguished struggle from a younger generation's conceptual world fashioned by Einstein, Freud and Lenin. Many an idea which was to become common-place a decade later came to us new, startling, incredible."[29]

The war had come before many had made up their minds about its justice or evil, or, for that matter, before they had come to any decision about their world, save that there was much in it that dissatisfied them. In poetry one gets mainly the Whitmanism of the Midwest and the aesthetic precision of the imagists—not, however, a precision encouraged by any larger confidence in poetry as a social expression. "The Wasteland" of T. S. Eliot had been discerned only vaguely. Eliot had already given us a freshman portrait of Prufrock; and suggestive remarks about the wasteland were just beginning to come from the pen of Aldous Huxley, whose point and counterpoint appeared in *The Palatine Review, Coterie*, and other English magazines:

> Weary of its own turning,
> Distressed with its own busy restlessness,
> Yearning to draw the circumferent pain—
> The rim that is dizzy with speed—
> To the motionless center, there to rest, . . .[30]

---

[28] Among the many magazines omitted from the discussion in this chapter, two ought to be mentioned, and the omissions explained; *The Midland*, begun in 1915, in Iowa City, and *The Seven Arts*, issued in 1916-17, from New York City. Since each represents ideally a type of magazine which we are discussing in a separate chapter, we have omitted them from the general survey of the second decade. See Chapter VI, pp. 86-92, for a study of *The Seven Arts*; Chapter VIII, pp. 140-47, for a study of *The Midland*.
[29] Joseph Freeman, *An American Testament*, New York, 1936, p. 112.
[30] "The Wheel," *The Palatine Review*, III, 1 (June-July, 1916).

# POETRY AND OTHERS

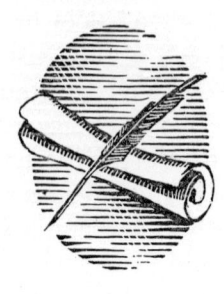

**CHAPTER III**

POETRY: A MAGAZINE OF VERSE celebrated its thirtieth anniversary in October 1942. To hundreds of poets and would-be poets, to many friends in all parts of the world, 232 East Erie Street in Chicago still extends a cordial welcome. But Harriet Monroe is gone.

Friends miss the sight of her small figure out in a back alley, brewing coffee over an open fire for her tea guests. They miss her presence on festive nights when poets read verses, talk late, and eat handsomely. They miss the fear of being rushed across dangerous boulevards by the tugging hand of Harriet, who always crossed with head bent low, refusing to glance either way.

It was in June 1911 that aristocratic Hobart C. Chatfield-Taylor agreed with his friend, Harriet Monroe, that the moment was ripe for the establishment of *Poetry*.[1] A little magazine had been for years a passionate ambition, but Miss Monroe had bided her time until she could see her way clear to financing such a magazine for an extended period.[2] The seeds of a new poetry must blow with some not far distant wind, she knew. And she realized that these seeds must be allowed to settle, sprout, and mature. She knew the danger of early death for this new poetry when it arrived, knew it all too well. There were no magazines in America willing to print much serious new verse.[3]

Let us glance at the so-called quality magazines for the months immediately previous to *Poetry's* appearance. What monthly diet was served by *The Atlantic*, by *Scribner's*, or by *Harper's*, the periodicals which most persons thought of as "good" magazines? They carried

---
[1] Harriet Monroe, "These Five Years," *Poetry*, 34 (October 1917).
[2] Harry Hansen, *Midwest Portraits*, New York, 1923, pp. 257-58.
[3] *Ibid.*

from two to five verse tidbits a month, generally of a highly vapid character, sentimentally designed by such hacksters as Margaret Prescott Montague, Fannie Stearns Davis, Florence Converse, and Margaret Sherwood. Almost completely blind to new talent, *The Atlantic* exhibited during 1912 only one piece of verse by a poet (Amy Lowell) new to the American literary scene. Miss Lowell's fragment must have been a disturbing curiosity to readers who had come to expect quatrains such as "Vision," printed in the August 1912 issue:

> As each slipped from the place
> Where all had walked with me,
> I, on each passing face,
> Saw immortality.[4]

*Harper's* was publishing the same brand of verse. The month *Poetry* made its first appearance, *Harper's* carried a half-dozen lines by Anne Bunner, lines typical of the magazine's poetic tone.

### "O WISE AND STRONG"

> O Wise and strong beyond all need of me!
> Why should I dream, now you have flown so high,
> And I, earth-bound, could never touch the sky—
> Why should I dream you needed me? And yet
> I never, looking in your eyes, forget
> The little lonely child you used to be.[5]

John Hall Wheelock was the only American of ability among the *Harper's* contributors, and the only representative of the younger writers. One might expect a better record from *Scribner's*, and, indeed, we do find Margaret Widdemer once, Arthur Davison Ficke twice, Sara Teasdale twice, and John Hall Wheelock once. Yet this, too, is a remarkably bare poetic cupboard. It is small wonder that Harriet Monroe was fearful for the fate of the new poetry.

But even after Chatfield-Taylor enthusiastically agreed that the time was ripe and suggested a way of attacking the financial problem, Miss Monroe was cautious. She did not immediately rush a magazine to press. That was not her way. Though she was intensely eager for the appearance of *Poetry*, her sanity kept her desire on leash. She was checked by the clear knowledge that such a periodical, if it were to burn

---

[4] Margaret Sherwood, "Vision," *The Atlantic Monthly*, cx, 198 (August 1912).
[5] Anne Bunner, "O Wise and Strong," *Harper's*, cxxv, 674 (October 1912).

with more than an ephemeral flame, must be well prepared for.[6] She wanted a periodical that would print the best the English world had to offer, superior verse not only of 1911 or 1912, but for many years to come. Such a project had to be planned, well thought out. Chatfield-Taylor had suggested the possibility of one hundred Chicagoans, each subscribing fifty dollars for a five-year term.[7] Coming of a pioneer Chicago family, intimate with the educated and moneyed strata of Chicago society, Miss Monroe might easily have mustered sufficient financial resources to give her magazine a trial; she could have done it in a fairly short time; and indeed she did, once she put her mind to this portion of her problem. But there were other details that prevented the appearance of Poetry for over seventeen months. There were vital problems of economy, of selling her idea to poets, of encouraging young unknowns to see the vision of a new art closely integrated with modern life, presenting that life in a simple, direct fashion, stripped of all petrified traditions.[8] There was nothing hastily conceived in Poetry when it finally made its appearance in October 1912.

Poetry was vital from its inception. Its value to America and Britain during the past quarter of a century can scarcely be overestimated, for it courageously stimulated American verse to a height which had been alien atmosphere for many a year. In Poetry's case mere figures are indeed meaningless. To say that it has promoted the reputation of 95 per cent of the post-1912 poets; to mention its distinguished criticism of verse; to talk about the numerous yearly prizes it has given and encouraged other magazines to give, is almost futile. One must browse slowly through its volumes and discover their full flavor for himself.

The first issue of a magazine is likely to be rather unworkmanlike, but Poetry never assumed the necessity of an initial foundering and managed to avoid it. The first 32-page sheaf carried Ezra Pound's high-spirited lines to Whistler, a finely nuanced Mexican sequence by Grace Hazard Conkling, an unpublished poem of William Vaughn Moody, two pieces by Arthur Davison Ficke, and the first published poems of Helen Dudley and Emilia Stuart Lorimer. A presentable first issue, especially when we consider that Harriet Monroe, in order to protect the name of her magazine from a Boston group, had to bring Poetry out a month or two in advance of her original plan.[9] In November,

---

[6] Monroe, "These Five Years," pp. 36-39.
[7] Ibid., p. 35.
[8] Ibid., pp. 36-39.
[9] Hansen, Midwest Portraits, p. 259.

John Reed made his first poetic appearance with "Sangar"; and Richard Aldington and H.D. were introduced to American readers. A month later Rabindranath Tagore translated his own work for the first time into English. In January 1913 came Vachel Lindsay, booming forth his "General William Booth Enters into Heaven." February brought George Sterling. July was to see F. S. Flint and Amy Lowell for the first time in *Poetry*. From October 1913 through March 1914, one finds John Gould Fletcher, Padraic Colum, D. H. Lawrence (January 1914), and Robert Frost (February 1914) in either their first or an early American appearance. Carl Sandburg made his bow with "Chicago," printed in March. With August came Maxwell Bodenheim's first; a month later Rupert Brooke was introduced to this country and Eunice Tietjens made her entrance into *Poetry*; in November of the same year appeared Wallace Stevens. Edgar Lee Masters, having published much of his *Spoon River Anthology* in *Reedy's Mirror*, appeared in *Poetry* for February 1915. Soon thereafter appeared one of T. S. Eliot's first published poems, "The Love Song of J. Alfred Prufrock." In May came Marianne Moore and Floyd Dell. In 1917 we find *Poetry* bringing James Joyce to this country. Edna St. Vincent Millay was printed in August, and Sherwood Anderson in September. Thus runs the parade of names—Malcolm Cowley and Evelyn Scott in November 1919; Grace Stone Coates and Elinor Wylie in April 1921, Elizabeth Roberts and Glenway Wescott, a few months later—and we have glanced only hastily at the first ten years.

The fifteen years that followed 1920 were equally brilliant; we find much of the early work of such artists as, to name only a few, Yvor Winters, H. L. Davis, Hart Crane, Horace Gregory, George Dillon, Archibald MacLeish, Robert Penn Warren, W. H. Auden, Louise Bogan, Ernest Hemingway, Stephen Spender, Allen Tate, Countée Cullen, Hildegarde Flanner, Marion Strobel, Joseph Gordon Macleod, William Empson, Paul Engle, C. A. Millspaugh, Robert Fitzgerald, Marya Zaturenska, Jesse Stuart, Norman Macleod, and R. P. Blackmur. And as one reads these poets, all of them heralded to fame by *Poetry*, many of them first printed by *Poetry*, one is surprised to find that any single magazine could so consistently uncover and recognize the talent of its age. Its alertness to new writers, to new trends, has been little short of phenomenal.

While *Poetry* was doing its work, the quality periodicals were resting in impervious smugness. Perhaps it would be unfair to expect them to brave the dangers of presenting new talent, but we might reasonably assume that they would print talent after it was discovered. It was amazing to watch *The Atlantic* sail serenely through the poetic revival, content until well past 1922 with its writers of 1913—Fannie Stearns Davis, Margaret Prescott Montague, and Margaret Cable Brewster. True, *The Atlantic* did briefly notice Robert Frost in 1915, two years after *Poetry* printed him. A few times it published short Robinson poems; once it noticed Alice Meynell; yet the record through 1930 fails to show a Sandburg poem, or anything by Lindsay, Eliot, Aldington, Pound, H.D., or any of the other newer poets with the exceptions of John Crowe Ransom, S. Foster Damon, and Archibald MacLeish, all published in the late twenties. Nor were *Harper's* and *Scribner's* more alert. They were represented by such names as Charles Hansen Towne, Effie Smith, Hortense Flexner, George Woodberry, and Amelia Josephine Burr, though between 1913 and 1918 the editors saw fit to administer small doses of such established English and American writers as John Masefield, Sara Teasdale, Thomas Hardy, and Bliss Carman. Among the works by younger artists in *Harper's* was a poem by Amy Lowell, one by William Rose Benét, one by Louis Untermeyer. We find Robinson appearing rather frequently in *Scribner's*, however, and three times we discover Arthur Davison Ficke there; John Hall Wheelock was published twice in these five years, Amy Lowell twice, William Rose Benét once. Never do we find a trace, between 1913-18, of the score of other poets who were eventually to assume an important place in American poetry.

Harriet Monroe was born in 1860 of a well known Chicago family, educated at the fashionable Visitation Academy, Georgetown, District of Columbia. Her educational and family environment did much to shear the rougher edges from a somewhat egotistical temperament. There were moments, especially in her later life, when she tended to ride hastily over opposing opinion, when her self-absorption drew her farther and farther from personal relationships. But these blemishes must not blind us to the more dominant aspect of her personality. No one can question her directness and sincerity, her discriminating and sensitive taste. Until her death she maintained a zestful, intelligent interest in the world about her, with a hope for the future which included willingness to innovate.

Living her entire life in Chicago, she may have been stimulated by the youthful buoyancy of the city. During her mature years Chicago's population jumped from half a million to over three millions. Every day brought change. In these years of great hope and struggle, of brimming energy, Chicago was already rapidly becoming the "player with railroads," the "hog butcher for the world," dreaming of an art institute, of great universities, of music; even of becoming the world's literary capital. True, the new city had much rampageous crudeness, but Harriet Monroe's selective mind could estimate these elements of her environment. It was the energy, the ambition, which must have profoundly influenced her and added to the determination that was such a prominent part of her character. Possibly it was the Chicago exuberance of those years which was partly responsible for her frequent journeys to Egypt or to China, for the spirit which brought about her death in 1936. At the age of seventy-six she decided to explore the Peru Inca country and the high altitude brought on heart failure.[10]

This was the woman who founded *Poetry*, who did so much to encourage the revolution in American verse, and who still dominates the little office at 232 East Erie Street. For not the least of her accomplishments was a selection of able associates, persons such as George Dillon, Morton Zabel, and Geraldine Udell, whose literary taste and business ability bid fair to steer the magazine through a second quarter of a century as inspiring as that just past.

There was little of the dilettante in Miss Monroe's personality. Her judgment was thoroughly grounded in a liberal, humanized education.[11] She was distinctly not one to be swept from her feet by literary innovation, nor on the other hand was she one to look at experimenters with suspicious pedantry or condescension. Objectivists, proletarians, and Victorians might hurl their cries of opprobrium at her, and she would weather their attacks, confident of her judgment. Indubitably there were few persons in the America of 1912 better qualified to lead the fight for a new poetry. And it was a fight—nerve-wracking, often bitterly discouraging.

From November 1912, when *Poetry* offered Richard Aldington's "Choricos," incidentally mentioning imagism, until well towards the close of 1920, the magazine fought bitterly for the principles of imagism. Between 1912 and 1915 the new movement was the object of much unfavorable comment, comment which broke into a fury of

---

[10] This portrait of Harriet Monroe is based on statements to Charles Allen by George Dillon, Morton Zabel, Geraldine Udell, Paul Engle, and on Harry Hansen's comments in *Midwest Portraits*, Horace Gregory's "The Unheard of Adventure," *American Scholar*, VI, 195-200 (Spring 1937), and S. Ichiye Hayakawa's "Harriet Monroe as Critic," *Studies in English Literature*, XIV, 1-7 (1934).

[11] Statement to Charles Allen by Geraldine Udell, business manager of *Poetry* and a close friend of Harriet Monroe, September 1937.

invective upon the publication of the first *Imagist Anthology* in 1915. William Ellery Leonard's denunciation, which he managed to organize under four headings, is representative of these fumings:

1. The Imagists can't see straight.
2. The Imagists can't feel straight.
3. The Imagists can't think straight.
4. The Imagists can't talk straight.[12]

Today, looking back on the war years, it is difficult to realize how necessary it was to defend the modest and at least 2,500-year-old statements which the imagists propounded.[13] That literary people shouted in clamorous denunciation against such age-old principles as: "To use the language of common speech, but to employ always the exact *word*, not merely the decorative word, to present an image, to produce poetry that is hard and clear, never blurred or indefinite,"[14] can be accounted for only by the fact that the nation's verse had been for twenty-five years in a state of cant and doldrum.

From the imagist manifestoes and from the early imagist verse of Ezra Pound, Amy Lowell, John Gould Fletcher, Hilda Doolittle, and William Carlos Williams, we are forced to conclude that imagism represented little that was startling. The imagists simply wished to write a poetry sheared of unessential analysis, rumination, and ornament—to base their verse as firmly as possible on clear, precise images. Often their work was slight, mere exercising in descriptions, descriptions too often divorced from human experience. Imagism was, therefore, chiefly valuable as a reassertion of several poetic first principles that had been for some time neglected. The movement was a healthy emphasis, but left us few noteworthy poems.

Out of the imagist movement grew a more profound imagism. Today, we still find the precise image, but the image is put to a use that transcends the function of a simple description. Recent poets have discovered that the use of a series of rapid, often dissociated, images may suggest a final meaning, a meaning which cannot be directly expressed in an image of its own. The surrealist poets are the obvious practitioners of this new imagism, though we need not search far to find it used consciously and with discrimination by others.

In mentioning this defense of imagism, we cannot neglect the simul-

---

[12] Quoted by Glenn Hughes, *Imagism and the Imagists*, Palo Alto, Calif., 1931, p. 56.
[13] *Ibid.*, pp. 3-4.
[14] *Ibid.*, pp. 39-40.

taneous contest which *Poetry*, *The Glebe*, *The Little Review*, and a few less well known magazines, conducted for the *vers libre* exponents. Miss Monroe led the defense, despite the fact that Margaret Anderson of *The Little Review* was more fiery in her advocacy of the poet's right to work outside established forms and traditional metres. *Poetry* was more important than either *The Glebe* or *The Little Review*, however, primarily because Miss Monroe had a greater influence in combating such opinions as that of T. S. Eliot: "*Vers libre* has not even the excuse of a polemic; it is a battle-cry of freedom, and there is no freedom in art,"[15] and the less intelligent harangue of *The Dial's* editor against Miss Monroe's defense of free verse. He damned *Poetry* as a "futile little periodical" for printing Sandburg's "Chicago," and went on to say, still referring to Sandburg, "We have always sympathized with Ruskin for the splenetic words about Whistler that were the occasion of the famous suit for libel, and we think that such an effusion as this [Sandburg's] is nothing less than an impudent affront to the poetry-loving public."[16]

But after such men as Lindsay and Sandburg had crusaded up and down the land, and *vers libre* had become smart, rather than dangerous, and after the *lo's* and *behold's*, the *thee's* and *thou's* had been routed, and after verse had been stripped of "eloquence, grandiloquence, poetic diction—of all the frills and furbelows which had overdraped, over-ornamented its beauty"[17]—after this, there were few persons to deny *Poetry's* accomplishments. Harriet Monroe had conducted a high-spirited, dramatic campaign.

Certainly these first ten years were charged with electricity. Chicago was then a literary center. Those were days when Harry Hansen, Sherwood Anderson, Lindsay, Margaret Anderson, Sandburg, Floyd Dell, Masters, Ben Hecht, and many another gathered at Schlogel's restaurant on Wells Street to discuss *The Little Review*, *Poetry*, new ideas, or technical innovation.[18] Here was a group with a mutually stimulating purpose.

When the fight for free verse and imagism was finally won, most of this literary colony began to drift eastward, first to New York, later and inevitably to Paris[19]; almost everybody left except Harriet Monroe. If it is the role of the little magazine to initiate, to act as the advance

[15] *Ibid.*, p. 73.
[16] Quoted by Monroe, "The Enemies We Have Made," *Poetry*, IV, 63 (May 1914).
[17] Monroe, "Looking Backward," *Poetry*, XXXIII, 34 (October 1928).
[18] Hansen, *Midwest Portraits*, pp. 3-13.
[19] Albert Parry, *Garrets and Pretenders*, New York, 1933, p. 211.

guard for a new movement, then it may be argued that *Poetry* had served its function, that the natural cycle of the magazine had been completed when the Chicago group moved East.

It is not surprising, therefore, to see *Poetry* beginning to share the spotlight with others. Several reputable little magazines, such as *The Fugitive*, began to print good verse, and even the larger quality journals were becoming more friendly towards the new spirit. 232 East Erie Street could no longer monopolize the public imagination, even though the magazine did continue to discover new poets, even though it maintained its leadership in the magazine parade.

Nor was it surprising, since Miss Monroe had a definite preference for simple, direct poetry, that there should come, in time, poets with different views, writers who might be printed with a brave eclecticism, but who could never be taken wholly to heart.[20] The newer poets, when they came in the middle twenties, had to find other organs than *Poetry* for the large part of their work. Harriet Monroe, in many quarters, came gradually to be looked upon not as a rebel, but as a conservative.[21] Objectivists, proletarians, aesthetes, members of every group, began to pout because they could not monopolize the sixty-odd pages of each number. This ill feeling was only partially allayed by Miss Monroe's turning over complete issues to one or another of such groups. The objectivists put forth their poets and critics in February 1931; the Southern writers were allowed an issue under the editorship of Allen Tate in May 1932; proletarians were given a number in 1936. The experimentalists, particularly, publishing a great percentage of their work in such little magazines as *The Little Review* and *transition*, claimed that *Poetry* was not cordial enough towards their writings. Such persons as Ezra Pound and Hart Crane grumbled much, loudly denouncing *Poetry's* skepticism about many of their endeavors.

On the other hand, there were those who raged because the experimentalists were noticed at all. The editor explained why she believed much of their work was valuable, and insisted on the necessity of printing the best of any group—even though it might be tangential to what she considered the main stream.[22] She recalled the motive of the magazine as announced in the second issue:

"The Open Door will be the policy of this magazine—may the great poet we are looking for never find it shut, or half-shut, against his

---

[20] Monroe, "Looking Backward," p. 36.
[21] *Ibid.*, pp. 35-36.
[22] *Ibid.*, p. 36.

ample genius! To this end the editors hope to keep free of entangling alliances with any single class or school. They desire to print the best English verse which is being written today, regardless of where, by whom, or under what theory of art it is written. Nor will the magazine promise to limit its editorial comments to one set of opinions. Without muzzles and braces this is manifestly impossible unless all the critical articles are written by one person."[23]

The years following Harriet Monroe's death in 1936 have given us some very good issues of Poetry. Morton Zabel, George Dillon, and Peter De Vries have cordially left the magazine's door open to new talent. We can mention only a few of the new names that have appeared between 1936 and the present. Karl Shapiro appears to be one of the most promising of this younger group that includes Delmore Schwartz, Dylan Thomas, Richard Eberhart, Ruth Lechlitner, C. A. Millspaugh, Weldon Kees, Paul Goodman, Oscar Williams, Charles Henri Ford, and John Malcolm Brinnin. The publication of the older, more established poets, though not exactly infrequent, is held at a minimum, and those of the older persons who are printed are the ones, such as John Wheelwright, Robert Penn Warren, Louise Bogan, and R. P. Blackmur, who are not as well known as their merit deserves. *Poetry* is still an advance guard fighter.

To discuss the ideals *Poetry* fought for—the contest for the poet's right to proper remuneration,[24] the defense of *The Masses* and other periodicals when they were victimized by war hysteria,[25] the help it extended to many little magazines[26]—would require more space than there is room for here. Besides, the story has been told in Miss Monroe's *A Poet's Life*. Yet mention of what was perhaps its most difficult and long-standing battle must be made—the perpetual problem of every little magazine—the struggle for finances.

*Poetry* spent between nine and ten thousand dollars annually during its opening years, always paying for contributions (about $10 per page), always making a prompt monthly appearance. Later, when it increased its leaves from around thirty to over sixty, its expense account rose to nearly $13,000 yearly.[27] Only a little over a third of this necessary money was contributed by guarantors. The rest had to flow from sub-

[23] *Ibid.*, from November 1912, p. 64.
[24] *Ibid.*
[25] *Ibid.*, IX, 161 (December 1916).
[26] *Poetry* has at various times reviewed the contents of little magazines and given them publicity through articles.
[27] Statement of Morton Zabel to Charles Allen, September 1937.

scriptions, from a modicum of advertising, and from gifts. Miss Monroe had supposed that there were 2,500 libraries able to afford her magazine, had thought there were several thousand cultured Americans who would willingly spend $1.50 a year for an alert poetry magazine. She was seriously disappointed. Try as she would, she could never build up a subscription list of much over 3,000 and usually it was smaller; there was a paid circulation of only 1,400 after the first six years. But through grim determination, the budget always balanced at year's end. There were times toward the close of almost every twelve-month when a cloud of discouragement would descend on the two-room office; it was never definitely certain until the last moment that the magazine could be continued.[28] Especially during the depression of the thirties, doom appeared imminent. An announcement that the magazine would cease publication brought protests, and a few checks from self-sacrificing friends.[29] In 1936 a Carnegie fund donated an emergency grant of $5,000. This money was made to last until 1940. Again, in 1943, *Poetry* was seriously threatened. This financial problem, always a dread specter, must be constantly fought. The struggle entails bitter sacrifices on the part of the staff. Everything possible to make the magazine self-supporting has been tried[30]—everything except a lowering of its standards.

Poets of greatness or near greatness are found every year, but never the great audience that Whitman's line on *Poetry's* cover has always urged. The magazine deserves a great audience, for it carries on today with the same high spirit and intelligence that has made its past record so brilliant.

### III

Among the men active in literary protest, a few may be called the patron saints of the modern little magazine movement. They supported with money, encouragement, and contributions dozens of little magazines, and were associated in some capacity or other with nearly every advance guard movement of the past forty years. Of them, Alfred Kreymborg was the first to enter a little magazine in the battle for a new literature. Two years after the establishment of the first influential little magazine of this century, *The Masses*, and one year after Harriet

---

[28] Monroe, *Poetry*, XL, 31 (April 1932).
[29] Monroe, *Poetry*, XL, 272 (August 1932).
[30] Statement of Geraldine Udell to Charles Allen, September 1937.

Monroe founded *Poetry*, Alfred Kreymborg armed for fight his monthly *Glebe*. The year of *Glebe's* beginning was 1913, the year of its end 1914. But this latter year saw the birth of *Others*, the second of Kreymborg's experimental magazines of poetry. Later, in 1921, with the help of Harold Loeb, Kreymborg launched the elaborately dressed and mildly exciting *Broom*; later still, in 1927, he helped establish, with Paul Rosenfeld, Lewis Mumford, and Van Wyck Brooks, a little magazine activity called *The American Caravan*, an annual volume of new, and supposedly experimental, literature.

Kreymborg was the fifth child of a poor but valiant New York East Side family. He found time for school, books, music, and chess. As a shy young man, working for a music company, he wrote stories, novels, and poetry. But he was unable to sell or give away most of his work. At the time, as we have shown, the quality magazines were not publishing much poetry, and when they did print verse they did not wish to present an unknown or unorthodox writer. Experimental writing or fresh ideas could not be tolerated, Kreymborg believed. Gradually he saw the need of a magazine devoted to the work of such young writers as himself.[31]

In 1908 Kreymborg thought of publishing an *American Quarterly*. He collected manuscripts, subscriptions, and money towards the ideal before he worked himself into a nervous prostration and was forced to give up his project.[32] Not until five years later, when he found himself summering with the painters Samuel Halpert and Man Ray, both of whom lived in a shack near the village of Grantwood, New Jersey, did Kreymborg reopen discussion of the need for a little magazine. Ray worked in a Manhattan print shop where he managed to talk his employer into donating an old press for the prospective magazine. The press obtained, manuscripts and reproductions were hurriedly gathered. Ezra Pound heard of the proposed *Glebe* and immediately forwarded a packet from London which included poems by Pound, James Joyce, Allen Upward, Ford Madox Hueffer (Ford), H.D., Richard Aldington, F. S. Flint, Skipworth Cannell, Amy Lowell, and William Carlos Williams.[33]

One morning the press arrived, stood waiting to be unloaded from a truck. During the unloading the machinery slipped from its moorings, plunged to the ground, and was damaged beyond repair.[34]

Undaunted, Kreymborg left for New York to seek financial aid. He

---

[31] Alfred Kreymborg, *Troubadour*, New York, 1925, pp. 122-31.
[32] *Ibid.*, pp. 129-39.    [33] *Ibid.*, pp. 199-205.    [34] *Ibid.*, p. 205.

thought it possible that support for a projected magazine might be gained in Greenwich Village. Aid was quickly found—from Albert and Charles Boni, then proprietors of the Washington Square Bookshop. The Bonis agreed to finance *Glebe*, and Kreymborg was to be sole editor. One suspects, however, that the first issue, which was filled with the work of a young Californian, George Cronyn, was the doing of the Bonis.[35]

When the Bonis' money had been eagerly accepted, it was understood that Kreymborg was to be unhampered in his editorial inclinations. But the controlling pocketbook gradually usurped power. The Boni brothers favored Europeans; Kreymborg desired the experimental, little known Americans.[36] The editor resigned and *Glebe* foundered. The Bonis retired temporarily from publishing. There had been ten issues of the magazine, extending over a period from July 1913 to 1914.

*Glebe* was one of the first periodicals to sponsor experimental writing, and a great percentage of its contents was imagistic. The magazine was the first to present the imagist, William Carlos Williams. Of course, not *Glebe*, but *Poetry*, was the first to introduce imagism; nor was *Glebe*, with its scant 300 circulation,[37] as influential as the Chicago periodical.

In February 1915 a group of young writers gathered one evening at the Greenwich Village apartment of Allan Norton and his wife. Norton was the editor of the brisk, short-lived little magazine, *Rogue*, and was giving a party for some of his contributors: Donald Evans, Wallace Stevens, Carl Van Vechten, Mina Loy, Kreymborg, and Walter Conrad Arensberg. Kreymborg for the first time met Arensberg.[38] A few days later the two dined in Arensberg's studio on West 67th Street; dinner was followed by a long walk which lasted until three in the morning. There was inspired talk.[39] That two such men as Kreymborg, the romantic experimentalist, and the scholar neoclassicist Arensberg should have so much in common was a little surprising. But the paradox explains itself in their common admiration for Ezra Pound, who in the early 1900's could well provoke any amount of conversation. The two men went to bed exhausted, and four or five hours later awakened to resume their talking. Before the day was finished, a little magazine

---

[35] *Ibid.*, p. 210.   [36] *Ibid.*, p. 211.
[37] Statement, Alfred Kreymborg to Charles Allen, August 1939.
[38] Kreymborg, *Troubadour*, pp. 218-19.   [39] *Ibid.*, p. 220.

had been decided upon—to be dedicated to experimental poetry. Kreymborg was to edit, Arensberg to finance.[40]

To work for new artists, artists who wished to write outside of conventional forms—that was the ideal. Imagism for Kreymborg had become conventional; he was ready to experiment with new structures and free verse rhythms, and he knew that there were other new experimenters, such as Marianne Moore, Wallace Stevens, and Carlos Williams. *Others* would publish their work in the hope that these relatively unknown poets might become more widely accepted. That was the only motive.[41]

Arensberg and Kreymborg had no thought of making money. They believed the magazine might somehow be distributed, but they made no promotion plans. They would simply publish and let the sparks fly where they might; perhaps two or three hundred copies might be disposed of, they thought. For most of the magazine's life 300 was the extent of the circulation, though at times it climbed towards the thousand mark.[42]

The first issue, in July 1915, was well printed on substantial 7-by-10-inch paper, encased in a simple gold coverpiece. It contained ten poems within the sixteen pages, by Wallace Stevens, William Carlos Williams, Ezra Pound, Mina Loy, Orrick Johns, and several less well known persons.

*Others* caused a disturbance from the very beginning. No faint praise was offered; there was either loud acclaim or bitter denunciation, mostly the latter. "The little yellow dog," it was called by those newspaper observers who were disturbed by the verse of Mina Loy and Orrick Johns.[43]

The intimate personal aspect of the magazine is worth a glance. Artists just beginning to be recognized are rarely content to isolate themselves. They must get together, talk it all over, read each other's writings. Kreymborg and his wife, Christine, had retired to Grantwood, New Jersey, after the first issue of the magazine. It was a tedious ride to Grantwood, but every Sunday the *Others* contributors eagerly gathered to talk shop. They would slip in with a sheaf of manuscript in one hand, sometimes a bundle of food in the other. Momentarily the atmosphere would be a little strained.[44] Kreymborg tells us in his autobiography, *Troubadour:* "Like most every other cultural activity of

[40] *Ibid.*, pp. 222-23.   [41] *Ibid.*, p. 222.
[42] Statement, Kreymborg to Allen, August 1939.
[43] Kreymborg, *Troubadour*, p. 235.   [44] *Ibid.*, pp. 238-45.

the new soil, the intercourse of these people was a novel experience. They had to approach it warily and grow up to the art of conversation with a painstaking, self-conscious *tempo* similar to their development as artists. It was not a lack of self-confidence which dictated so shy a contact, but a joyous bewilderment in the discovery that other men and women were working in a field they themselves felt they had chosen in solitude."[45] The mutual stimulation, the chance to meet the fellows of one's craft, was an invaluable incentive to further accomplishment.

These meetings became more frequent in the fall of 1915 when the Kreymborgs moved back into the city. At any hour of the day or night a poet might come up for a chat. The editorial room was the kitchen, and the icebox was its center.[46]

Among the persons who made the Kreymborg apartment a meeting place were Maxwell Bodenheim, William Carlos Williams, Marianne Moore, and Wallace Stevens. All of them published much of their early work in *Others*, and were, along with Kreymborg, Orrick Johns, and Skipworth Cannell, the magazine's most frequent contributors. Of these seven persons Marianne Moore and Wallace Stevens are the most exciting poets. Stevens, endowed with an urbane and quixotic imagination, follows a range from sparkling, witty humor to bland seriousness. He is an impeccable fashioner of melody, color, tone, and pattern, musing whimsically and sometimes wryly, never with passion or torture, about the spectacle of the world, a spectacle which he accepts and bows to with a grave or witty irony of ceremonious elegance.

In those first years before she began writing her acid, almost prosy dissertations, Marianne Moore's work was faster reading than it is today. Yet even as early as 1915 one finds the bizarre image, the juxtaposition of the abstract with the concrete, the wit, irony, and satire, the profusion of rare and esoteric knowledge, and a sharp-cracking cacophony. One must also admire her technical accomplishment; particularly her delicate sense of free verse rhythm, rhythm of such subtle tension that the mind must concentrate carefully to keep afloat and moving with the current.

William Carlos Williams was still pretty much of an imagist in his *Others* days. His driving compulsion was to see the object, to see it with fiery intensity, to see it to the core. To make fierce "contact" with the objective, seeable world became such an ingrained necessity for Wil-

---

[45] *Ibid.*, p. 241.    [46] *Ibid.*, p. 248.

liams that he finally, in 1920, was driven to launch a little magazine to advertise his vision. That magazine he called *Contact*.

Kreymborg naturally appeared several times. Whimsical, given to charming fantasy, striving for the taut, simplified rhythm, he attained many a grave flippancy in his sanguine, well pruned lyrics.

Orrick Johns wrote several of his verses, most of them lighthearted and simple in context and form, but possessing a freshness of wording that gave them a right to be admitted to the experimental *Others*. Maxwell Bodenheim often herded through the pages of the magazine his luxuriant, baroque images. Both Bodenheim and Johns tried their hands at one-act poetic dramas.

These were the artists who made the periodical important. Kenneth Burke was the only person to publish his first work in *Others*,[47] but Bodenheim, Johns, Stevens, Williams, and Moore printed most of their early poems in the magazine. None are great artists in the high meaning of the word, though two of them, Moore and Stevens, are among the finest voices that have sung in America during the past fifty years.

When one considers the poets included in *Others*, and the wide variety of their work, he immediately realizes that the *Others* experimentalism ranged over a wide country. The periodical attempted to push beyond the frontiers of imagism, though some of the poems, especially those of Williams, might well be labeled imagistic. One cannot be certain what exactly the magazine was seeking. Kreymborg might suggest that he was looking for new experimentation with word values and rhythms and structures, as opposed to the narrower concentration on the image. More probably, Kreymborg might say that he was simply looking for new experimental writing.

At the end of the first year, the editor was faced with the problem of financing the magazine himself, no easy task. Arensberg, the classicist, and Kreymborg, the romanticist, could not well agree. During the two preceding years, the editor had worked as a letter writer for a New York financier, four hours a day with an hour off for lunch. A forty-dollar-a-week salary made at this work had previously sufficed, but now, with *Others* needing money, forty dollars was very pitiful indeed, and yet there could be no question of discontinuing the magazine.[48]

[47] Burke reports, in a letter to Frederick J. Hoffman, December 28, 1943, that though he did publish his first writing in *Others*, many of his early pieces went to *Sansculotte*, a little magazine published on the Ohio State University campus, in 1917.

[48] Kreymborg, *Troubadour*, pp. 254-56.

Days of worry—and then the miraculous once again. Alfred Knopf had been watching *Others* with an eager, sympathetic eye. He suddenly proposed that his publishing house bring out a yearly anthology of the magazine's poetry under Kreymborg's editorship. That would help. There were two *Others* anthologies by Knopf, in 1916 and 1917, and one by Nicholas L. Brown in 1918. Almost simultaneously John Marshall, a partner in the Little Bookshop Around the Corner, asked that he be allowed to finance the magazine. Kreymborg readily agreed, and Marshall assumed responsibility for the "material interests" of *Others*.[49] Those early months of 1916 were indeed "prodigious" days.

The editor could relax only for a moment. He went to Chicago, expecting that the magazine's finances would be well taken care of in New York. But soon after arriving in Chicago he received a letter from Marshall stating that he was resigning as patron of the magazine.[50] Once again collapse threatened. Until May 1916 the periodical had made monthly appearances; thereafter it was not so regular. There were only three more issues in 1916, two in 1917, one in 1918, and three in 1919. Doubtless *Others* would have died after 1916 had it not been for the zeal of the magazine's poets who managed to scrape together enough money to bring out some of the numbers.

After a time the contributors were forced to do most of the editing, too, for Kreymborg gradually came to believe that the magazine's usefulness had been outlived. He sponsored it only halfheartedly during the last two years and was willing to allow Williams, Saphier, Bodenheim, Helen Hoyt, Johns, Lola Ridge (who did most of the work), and Kreymborg's second wife, Dorothy, to serve as editors *pro tem.* or in associate capacities.[51] They apparently decided to revive poetic drama, since many of the magazine's pages were filled with one-act plays by Williams, Johns, Djuna Barnes, Bodenheim, and Saphier.

Despite Kreymborg's lack of enthusiasm, and a general scarcity of funds, it was difficult to make an end of *Others*. Kreymborg tells the amusing story in his *Troubadour*, of how "toward the tail-end when Krimmie [Kreymborg] was positive the venture had outlived its usefulness, Lola [Ridge] managed to keep it going a while. Williams, who had soured on the movement to a degree that caused him to pounce on an issue he edited with a grieving, ranting, coroner's inquest he called Belly Music, assured his readers, 'Others is dead,' and promised to bury it with the present issue. The *post-mortem* on the part of Lola, with her happy mania for appearing among moribund things and re-

[49] *Ibid.*, p. 265.   [50] *Ibid.*, p. 279.   [51] *Ibid.*, pp. 330-31.

viving them, puzzled the subscribers. Here was still another number on top of one they had been asked to accept as an obituary. How many times was the thing to die and bob up again?"[52]

But even after the magazine once and for all ceased publication, its spirit continued. The *Others* group had been brought together and it would not disperse. The writers insisted on gathering in Lola Ridge's apartment to read their new work to each other. It was during one of these meetings that Scofield Thayer, who had recently become co-publisher and co-editor of *The Dial*, met many of the people whose work he was soon to begin printing. *The Dial's* poetic tone was really a continuation of the *Others* spirit, even before Marianne Moore became *The Dial* editor in 1925.[53]

*Glebe* and *Others* were two of the first magazines to throw themselves deliberately and with vigor into the fight for experimental poetry. Neither magazine paid for contributions, neither was widely circulated, yet both attracted favorable attention in the right places. To gain a selected but intelligent hearing for their all but unknown contributors was the purpose each magazine set out to accomplish. The significance of *Glebe* and *Others* is no greater or less than the estimate that one places upon the desirability of securing the reputations of such poets as Williams, Moore, and Stevens.

[52] *Ibid.*, p. 330.     [53] *Ibid.*, p. 332.

# THE
# LITTLE REVIEW

CHAPTER IV

The "personal"[1] magazine usually reflects the editor's personality on the cover and on every page. There was Margaret Anderson's very personal *Little Review.*

In explaining the varied career of *The Little Review,* one must keep a close eye on the impulsive temperament of the editor. Margaret Anderson's magazine was started in Chicago with scarcely any plan for financing it,[2] and she published it on sheer will power from March 1914 through May 1929. Stories and novels were accepted which she knew in advance would mean a journey to court, a fine, and not much publicity. She colored her review with much of the enthusiasm of her youth, and it reflects often her sudden shifts in interest. First, it was feminism. Next Emma Goldman came to Chicago and the magazine became a strong sponsor of anarchism. There followed a number of other enthusiasms: imagism, symbolism, dadaism, the machine, and the work of Brancusi, among them. It was an exciting magazine, quixotic, sometimes immature, but always radiating the blue sparks of highly charged feeling.

Many were the stars that danced before Margaret Anderson's impulsive vision. The editor was always drawn to the "marked," the "unusual" experimentalism, the most advanced of all the advanced. Inevitably, there was to come a time when she could glimpse no further horizon.

She was twenty-one when her inspiration came.[3] She had been in Chicago for several months, writing book reviews for *The Dial.* One

---

[1] A term used by Gorham Munson, "How to Run a Little Magazine," *Saturday Review of Literature,* xv, 3, 4, 14 (March 27, 1937).
[2] Margaret Anderson, *My Thirty Years' War,* New York, 1930, p. 36.
[3] *Ibid.,* p. 35.

night she awoke and found life meaningless. Here is the explanation, taken from her autobiography, *My Thirty Years' War*, of how life was given meaning and how *The Little Review* was born:

"So it was for the *Little Review*. I had been curiously depressed all day. In the night I wakened. First precise thought: I know why I'm depressed—nothing inspired is going on. Second: I demand that life be inspired every moment. Third: the only way to guarantee this is to have inspired conversation every moment. Fourth: most people never get so far as conversation; they haven't the stamina, and there is no time. Fifth: if I had a magazine I could spend my time filling it up with the best conversation the world has to offer. Sixth: marvelous idea —salvation. Seventh: decision to do it. Deep sleep."[4]

Whether all of this happened so neatly, or whether the explanation is an instance of the editor's instinct for drama, is of no importance. She suddenly began talking about her marvelous new magazine. She talked so intensely that a young journalist decided to give large monthly portions of his salary for the cause.[5] Immediately she was off to New York for advertising, and she actually collected about $450.[6] In a very short time she was back in Chicago, established in the Fine Arts Building, and announcing her first issue.

Since conversation, inspired conversation, was the *sine qua non* for her, naturally *The Little Review* had to be a critical review, printing fiction and poetry only incidentally. It was a sort of Spingarnish impressionism which was called for in the first issue:

"Its [*The Little Review's*] ambitious aim is to produce criticism of books, music, art, drama, and life that shall be fresh and constructive, and intelligent from the artist's point of view. For the instinct of the artist to distrust criticism is as well founded as the mother's toward the sterile woman. More so, perhaps; for all women have some sort of instinct for motherhood, and all critics haven't an instinct for art. Criticism that is creative—that is our high goal. And criticism is never a merely interpretative function; it *is* creation; it gives birth! It's not necessary to cite the time-worn illustration of Da Vinci and Pater to prove it.'"[7]

Following this announcement came the editor's ambitious article about life and art, referring to Paderewski, Galsworthy, William Vaughn Moody, and Rupert Brooke, studded with many "beauties" and "passions." Floyd Dell expressed a firm belief that love and work

[4] *Ibid.*, p. 35.   [5] *Ibid.*, p. 41.   [6] *Ibid.*, p. 43.
[7] Anderson, "Announcement," *The Little Review*, 1, 2 (March 1914).

are good for women. Margery Currey and Cornelia Anderson (Mrs. Sherwood Anderson) wrote book reviews. Llewellyn Jones, George Burman Foster, George Soule, and Sherwood Anderson contributed articles. Vachel Lindsay told in a poem "How a Little Girl Danced"; Eunice Tietjens contributed a verse about sadness; and Arthur Davison Ficke was represented by five poems. In *My Thirty Years' War* Miss Anderson gives a rather unfair estimate of this first issue when she says: "The first number betrayed nothing but my adolescence. . . . What I needed was not a magazine but a club room where I could have informed disciples twice a week that nature was wonderful, love beautiful, and art inspired."[8]

For the following four or five months she continued her interest in criticism. During the spring and summer there were articles on such subjects as "Futurism" and "The New Paganism," but as the winter of 1914 drew on, she began to neglect criticism. Perhaps good criticism was hard to find. At any rate poets were beginning to appear more and more frequently, especially the imagists who were rapidly capturing Miss Anderson's attention. But let us pause over the titles of the critical articles dealing with art which appeared in these early numbers: "Futurism and Pseudo Futurism," "The Meaning of Bergsonism," "The Germ" (a discussion of the Pre-Raphaelite little magazine), "The New Paganism," and several articles on imagism. *The Little Review's* editor was being caught in an experimental current which stemmed from Baudelaire, down through Huysmans, Mallarmé, and Rimbaud among the French, from the Pre-Raphaelites, Pater, and Wilde among the English, and from Poe and Edgar Saltus among the Americans. It was a current that led to imagism. During 1915 and 1916 Miss Anderson fought on the front line in the battle for imagism.

She was still defending the imagists in November 1916 when her magazine carried sixteen poems by Richard Aldington, but her enthusiasm had been for some months quite apparently on the wane. Impatiently she proclaimed that "The *Little Review* is a magazine that believes in life for Art's sake." As early as August 1916 her impatience had generated into a fever of nervous disgust.

"I have been realizing the ridiculous tragedy of the *Little Review*. It has been published for over two years without coming near its ideal. . . .

"Well—I wanted Art in the *Little Review*. There has been a little of it, just a very little. . . . It is tragic, I tell you. . . .

"Now we shall have Art in this magazine or we shall stop publishing

[8] Anderson, *My Thirty Years' War*, p. 47.

it. I don't care where it comes from—America or the South Sea Islands. I don't care whether it is brought by youth or age. I only want the miracle! ...

"I loathe compromise, and yet I have been compromising in every issue by putting in things that were 'almost good' or 'interesting enough' or 'important.' There will be no more of it. If there is only one really beautiful thing for the September number it shall go in and the other pages will be left blank."[9]

With September came a magazine filled largely with blank leaves. Two pages edified the reader by describing in pen and ink cartoons the light occupations of the editors on their California sojourn: there was the editor beating at her Mason and Hamlin; Jane Heap—recently adopted associate editor, who was to play a considerable role in *Little Review* history—sat astride her broken-down horse; there was a making of fudge and of conversation. Decisive proof that the imagists had lost Miss Anderson's interest. A change was in the offing.

Although *The Little Review* battled strenuously for feminism, anarchism, Ben Hecht, and the imagists, it fought harder to keep alive. The drama is an enlightening and amusing commentary on the fortunes of the unsubsidized little magazine.

In those early Chicago days Schlogel's restaurant, the meeting place of the journalists and literary elite, seethed with Margaret Anderson gossip. "Where is Margaret?" "What's she doing now?" were frequent questions.[10] A person who inspires such fascination, and of whom are written such eulogies as the following, quoted by Harry Hansen in his *Midwest Portraits*, will never lack supporters:

"She was always exquisite, as if emerging from a scented boudoir, not from a mildewed tent or a camp where frying bacon was scenting the atmosphere. She was always vivid, is yet, and beautiful to look upon, and lovely in her mind. There is a sort of high, wind-blown beauty about her; her fluffy hair blows marvelously, her eyes are in Lake Michigan's best blue. And she is valiant, always."[11]

Gushing, but significant for an understanding of how *The Little Review* lived. When Miss Anderson spoke in "gasps, gaps, and gestures," she charmed Harriet Dean into donating energy and money, or Eunice Tietjens into giving a diamond ring.[12] "Unknown people asked me to lunch, urged me to talk about my 'ideals,' and the next

[9] Anderson, "A Real Magazine," *The Little Review*, III, 1-2 (August 1916).
[10] Hansen, *Midwest Portraits*, p. 102.     [11] *Ibid.*, p. 105.
[12] Anderson, *My Thirty Years' War*, p. 68.

day sent a hundred dollars for the ideals."[13] Thus *The Little Review's* credit in the first "ecstatic" year or so. Later money did not flow into the coffers so readily, especially after anarchism was adopted. But always she managed to keep afloat. She lived in apartments without furniture, until one cold April day, when room rent was no longer forthcoming, she piled her oriental rugs on an ancient wagon, moved to the edge of the lake, pitched a tent, and lived there until the following November. During those tenting days the only clothes she possessed were a hat, a crepe georgette blouse, and a blue tailored suit, but everyone thought her well-groomed, for she had found a more expressive way of walking. And besides, the blouse could be washed every night in Lake Michigan.[14]

With the exceptions of the first two or three issues the magazine never garnered much advertising. Businessmen do not advertise in an anarchist magazine. For over a year the editor sought advertising, her indefatigable energy leading her to attempt a witty strategy. In the June-July, 1915, number she ran several pages which might have contained advertisements but did not. Small boxes in the middle of the back pages carried several amusing announcements, two of which deserve quoting:

> Mandel Brothers might have taken this page to feature their library furnishings, desk sets, and accessories—of which they are supposed to have the most interesting assortment in town. I learned that on the authority of someone who referred to Mandel's as "the most original and artistic store in Chicago." If they should advertise those things here I have no doubt the 1,000 Chicago subscribers to the *Little Review* would overflow their store.
>
> Carson, Pirie, Scott and Company ought to advertise something, though I don't know just what. The man I interviewed made such a face when I told him we were "radical" that I haven't had the courage to go back and pester him for the desired full-page. The Carson-Pirie attitude toward change of any sort is well-known—I think they resent even having to keep pace with the change in fashions.[15]

---

[13] *Ibid.*, p. 69.  [14] *Ibid.*, pp. 88-90.
[15] Anderson, *The Little Review*, II, 57, 59 (June-July, 1915).

Of course *The Little Review* expected to collect on some of these gratuitous mentionings, and of course it never did.

The device of giving a party for the Chicago subscribers, admission 50 cents, was tried only once. The attempt to cajole *Little Review* readers into ordering their books by mail through the magazine, which was to receive a percentage of the sale price of the book, was not very successful. The editors had to print their monthly 60 pages from the money that Margaret Anderson enticed from her friends and enemies, from the meager 2,000[16] subscribers who paid at first $2.50 a year and later $1.25, and from the savings of tent economy. Only a heroic need for the magazine kept it from sinking.

## II

And then, in March 1917, began the New York period. *The Little Review* lived for five years, its years of greatness, in two small basement rooms of the old Van Buren house at 31 West 14th Street.

The years following 1916 saw a fiery eruption of experimentalism. The new symbolists were making their first appearances, and Miss Anderson found herself fighting tooth and nail for the right of America to read Joyce, Dorothy Richardson, Eliot, and many another symbolist. Also at this time she began her fight for the privilege of introducing to America such literary movements as cubism, futurism, and expressionism, movements that had hitherto received only the slightest notice in this country.

Symbolism gave the inner self, and particularly the feelings, a more piercing scrutiny than romanticism had ever done. The early symbolist saw more of the complicated and inexplicable in life than the romantic. Such men as Poe, Baudelaire, Huysmans, Rimbaud, Yeats, Mallarmé, and many another used every magic to suggest this complexity of the spirit. The real and the imaginary were confused; fantasy was employed; metaphors were consciously mixed; and often poetry approached music.[17] More recent symbolists have exploited all of these devices and quite a few more. Proust, Joyce, Valéry, Stein, and T. S. Eliot have found life even more intricate than the earlier symbolists, largely because of the speculations of Bergson and Freud—Bergson

---

[16] A conjecture, based on a statement in the June-July, 1915, issue that the magazine had 1,000 Chicago subscribers.

[17] Edmund Wilson, *Axel's Castle*, New York, 1931, pp. 1-25.

with his conjectures as to the influence of memory on our action, and Freud with his ideas concerning the part the subconscious plays in our lives.[18] Quantum physics has also cast its shadow on the thinking of the recent symbolist.

The new romantic cults that came into being between 1900 and 1930 took their cue from symbolism's radical subjectivism and have carried the ideal of exploring the innermost mind of the individual to a near limit.

Futurism was founded by the Italian poet, F. T. Marinetti, whose first manifestoes were published in *Le Figaro* in February of 1909. As we have seen in Chapter II, futurism set itself firmly to the task of abolishing the accepted standards, particularly "history, exoticism, love-stories, syntax, punctuation, conjugations, the stage, concerts, verses, colleges, art-galleries, literary critics and professors." Marinetti, like his dada and surrealist descendants, called for "the revolution of the word," "neologisms, simultaneous and onomatopoeic expression, the substitution of noise for music." *Speed, dynamism, force* were the slogans of futurism. It demanded electric flashings, vitality and intensity, and above everything an expression of the individual ego.[19]

Contemporaneous with futurism came German expressionism and French cubism. Neither cubism nor expressionism sought the frenzied movement characteristic of futurist work, but these three schools were at one in demanding the personal approach to subject matter. Pablo Picasso and his Montmartre group believed the constructive imagination to be constrained by the traditional concept of the need for three-dimensional perspective. The cubists wished to forget perspective, to take their glance at three-dimensional nature, then break it up, and finally rearrange the elements into a world of two-dimensional volumes and planes expressive of a formal and harmonious relationship. There was little cubistic literature, but the movement did strengthen the ideal of self-expression. German expressionism, however, affected all of the arts. "We will transform into plastic form live states of the soul, we will jerk your sensibilities into the most acute response,"[20] runs an expressionist manifesto, and it is suggestive of what such men as Kaiser, Pirandello, and the early Sherwood Anderson were attempting when they selected one aspect of a personality and dramatized it by symbol, distortion, exaggeration, and fantasy. Always the artist's vision of the

---

[18] Regis Michaud, *Vingtième Siècle*, New York, 1933, pp. xviii-xix.
[19] *Ibid.*, p. 408.
[20] Thomas Craven, *Modern Art*, New York, 1934, p. 225.

"psychic state" which he wishes to interpret attempts to be "original."

In April 1917, Ezra Pound became foreign editor of *The Little Review*. Pound knew many of the European experimentalists, and was obviously the person best qualified to find the "beautiful" art which Margaret Anderson sought. Pound wanted an American organ where he, Joyce, T. S. Eliot, and Wyndham Lewis could appear whenever they felt like it—usually about every month. Margaret Anderson thought this "the most stunning plan that any magazine has had the good fortune to announce for a long, long time."[21] The experimentalists having been adopted, the periodical began to appear in green, orange, and red covers, each of which heralded: *The Little Review, a Magazine of the Arts. Making No Compromise with the Public Taste.* Hatred for the "usual," love for the "unusual," became a fetish with *The Little Review*.

The great event of 1918, and probably of *The Little Review*'s history, was the beginning of Joyce's *Ulysses*. For three years the novel ran in installments, four of which were confiscated and burned by the Post Office Department.

"It was like a burning at the stake as far as I was concerned. The care we had taken to preserve Joyce's text intact; the worry over the bills that accumulated when we had no advance funds; the technique I used on printer, bookbinders, paper houses—tears, prayers, hysterics or rages—to make them push ahead without a guarantee of money; the addressing, wrapping, stamping, mailing; the excitement of anticipating the world's response to the literary masterpiece of our generation . . . and then a notice from the Post Office: BURNED."[22]

Government burnings, newspaper charges that the magazine was a purveyor of lascivious literature, nonrecognition of *Ulysses*[23] on the part of intellectuals—all this was but a prelude to the battle over Joyce. The climax came in December 1920 when John Sumner's Society for the Suppression of Vice brought the review before a Special Sessions Court on an obscenity charge. John Quinn, able New York lawyer and patron of the arts (he had donated $1,600 to the periodical), defended the magazine and lost the verdict. The editors were fined $100. Margaret Anderson insisted on going to jail rather than paying the money, but her friends dissuaded her. A woman who hated *Ulysses* paid

[21] Anderson, "Announcement," *The Little Review*, IV, 25 (April 1917).
[22] Anderson, *My Thirty Years' War*, p. 175.
[23] Ibid., p. 175.

the hundred dollars, and the case ended with disappointingly little publicity.[24]

But *Ulysses* was not the only exciting work the magazine printed from 1917 to the end of 1921. Dorothy Richardson's frequent contributions included *Interim*. Sherwood Anderson sent many of his expressionistic stories, later to make up the volume *Winesburg, Ohio*. Ford Madox Ford published his *Men and Women*. Pound was represented by much of his poetry and practically all of the critical papers which later appeared in *Instigations*. There were a good many things by Wyndham Lewis, such as *The Ideal Giant* and *Cantleman's Spring Mate*. Poems, stories, and plays came from William B. Yeats, and there was a single group of twenty-four reproductions from Brancusi's sculpture. Much of the early work of T. S. Eliot, Ben Hecht, Emanuel Carnevali, William Carlos Williams, Djuna Barnes, Aldous Huxley, Arthur Waley, John Rodker, Mary Butts, Jean Cocteau, Louis Aragon, Philippe Soupault, and Francis Picabia found its way to *The Little Review* during these five years. Miss Anderson's pride in her little magazine knew no bounds; well did she know that there was only one answer to her question: "Is *The Little Review* contributing to the mental upkeep of Columbia Gem of the Ocean?"[25]

The magazine performed an invaluable service to America in those years, since it was one of the few outlets in this country for ideas and techniques which were to influence profoundly much of our later writing. Had it not been for the sacrifices and limitless enthusiasm of Margaret Anderson, it is quite likely that the postwar American fiction and poetry would have been slower in its experimental course. "My idea of a magazine which makes any claim to artistic value is that . . . it should suggest, not conclude; that it should stimulate to thinking rather than dictate thought."[26] It was precisely this function that made the periodical an important force in American letters.

How *The Little Review* managed to keep sailing during the late teens is a splendid, if sometimes pathetic, story which we cannot dwell upon. Harriet Monroe, in reviewing *My Thirty Years' War*, remarked: "One kind of courage they had which this reviewer could never attain —the courage to run into debt and print issue after issue without knowing, or indeed caring, where the money would come from to pay for it.

[24] *Ibid.*, pp. 214-21.
[25] "What *The Little Review* Has Done," an advertisement in *The Little Review*, ix, inside back cover (Autumn-Winter, 1923-24).
[26] Anderson, "Our First Year," *The Little Review*, I, 2 (February 1915).

Margaret Anderson

William Carlos Williams

Norman Macleod

Alfred Kreymborg

# THE LITTLE REVIEW

### THE MAGAZINE THAT IS READ BY THOSE WHO WRITE THE OTHERS

MARCH, 1918

| | |
|---|---|
| Ulysses, 1. | *James Joyce* |
| Imaginary Letters, VIII. | *Wyndham Lewis* |
| Matinee | *Jessie Dismorr* |
| The Classics "Escape" | *Ezra Pound* |
| Cantico del Sole | |
| Women and Men, II. | *Ford Madox Hueffer* |
| Bertha | *Arthur Symons* |
| A List of Books | *Ezra Pound* |
| Wyndham Lewis's "Tarr" | |
| Raymonde Collignon | |
| The Reader Critic | |

Copyright, 1918, by Margaret Anderson

MARGARET ANDERSON, Editor
EZRA POUND, Foreign Editor

24 *West Sixteenth Street, New York*

*Foreign office:*
5 *Holland Place Chambers, London W. 8.*

25 cents a copy　　　　　　　$2.50 a year

Entered as second-class matter at P. O., New York, N. Y.
Published monthly by Margaret Anderson

A typical contents page of THE LITTLE REVIEW

And frequently it didn't come, and printers and editors alike were perilously near starvation. It was a gallant adventure—the *Little Review*—and all the audacity and flaming sincerity of youth were in it."[27]

The magazine was swallowing over $10,000 a year. The editors did, indeed, go without food at times. They made their own clothes, did their own cooking and scrubbing, even cut their own hair.[28] As in Chicago, they opened a bookstore in connection with the magazine, this time not on the mail order plan but a regular shop in *The Little Review* office. There was an appeal in 1920 for $5,000 in the hope that one thousand persons would contribute $5 apiece. Once, in desperation, Margaret picked out the tallest skyscraper, took the elevator to the top floor, and began a canvass of the entire building. Several endowments were offered, usually with restraining chains; only those gifts were accepted which left the editor a free hand.[29] In one way and another, "real credit," Miss Anderson's personality, kept the magazine afloat.

The monthly became a quarterly in the autumn of 1921. The handling of mechanical details was becoming a superhuman task. The editors were forcing themselves through the drudgery of reading copy, wrapping, and distributing the periodical twelve times a year. All of this might have been endured.[30] But added to these annoyances was a growing war with the printer, a situation that finally became so unbearable that the editors had to spend days at a time in the print shop goading the printer to his work.[31] No doubt it was physically impossible for a nervous temperament to stand many fights such as the one indicated by the following letter:

> DEAR MISS ANDERSON:
>
> Tomorrow will be a week that I received copy with money in advance as agreed, and was not able to start and will not be able before next week. It is no use Miss Anderson to be so nervous. You want always first-class work and I cannot make. Do you not know that we had war? Workingman is now king. If you would pay me three thousand dollars I will not make good work. This is other times. I wrote you about this many times and will not repeat any more, but wish to say if you pay all in advance and two, three hundred per cent more as now, you must not expect good work or on time. I want no responsibility.[32]

[27] Harriet Monroe, "Personality Rampant," *Poetry*, XXXVII, 98 (November 1930).     [28] Anderson, *My Thirty Years' War*, p. 156.
[29] *Ibid.*, pp. 187-88.     [30] *Ibid.*, p. 157.     [31] *Ibid.*
[32] Anderson, *The Little Review*, VI, 64 (March 1920).

## III

From 1921 on *The Little Review*, taking advantage of a low money exchange rate in France, appeared in a luxurious format, full of bizarre types, printed with inks of many colors. The Autumn-Winter, 1924-1925, issue, with its high quality paper, its elaborate reproductions of Juan Gris's work, its black, yellow, and red headache inks, was a far cry from those issues of the war years when the magazine was printed on a thin, low grade stock, always threatening to disintegrate at the slightest touch.

After the experimental climax in the brilliant works of Dorothy Richardson, Joyce, Yeats, Proust, and others, came a denouement of dadaism. Dada was born at six P.M., February 8, 1916, at the Café Voltaire, Zurich, Switzerland. It was largely the work of Tristan Tzara, a Roumanian. Dada was conscious of a large disgust with western bourgeois culture and war-making. It wanted to destroy the whole cultural structure, beginning with literature and the other arts.[33] The chief attack on letters consisted in writing meaningless sentences, or in composing subjective tales that could be understood only by the author.

Miss Anderson migrated from New York to Paris in 1922, two years after André Breton, Louis Aragon, Philippe Soupault, Paul Eluard, and Tristan Tzara had founded their review, *Littérature*. By the time Margaret Anderson arrived in Paris, *Dadaist Disgust* (the title of a dadaist pamphlet) was on the march, crusading "with all the fists of one's being in destructive action"[34] against a world of silliness, stuffiness, and brigandage. Young men of talent, most of them just out of the trenches, were thumbing their noses at the world, not only through their writings but in individual actions. Fervent young dadaists chased about Paris, interrupting bourgeois plays, burning popular literary heroes in effigy, denouncing religion from churchyards—insulting the hated public in every fashion conceivable. Louis Aragon threatened to wreck the offices of *Les Nouvelles Littéraires* if it continued to mention his name, and carried out his threat when he was next mentioned. He terrified critics by threatening beatings if they dared review his books; no one accepted the dare.[35]

*The Little Review* threw its energy gaily into this fracas, printing

---

[33] Michaud, *Vingtième Siècle*, p. 409.
[34] Malcolm Cowley, *Exile's Return*, p. 159.   [35] *Ibid.*, p. 163.

much of the work of Guillaume Apollinaire, Tristan Tzara, Os-Anders, Louis Gilmore, W. G. Jitro, Louis Grudin, Jean Cocteau, and others, delighted for a time with the dadaist vision of a new world order where the novel, the purposeless, the "marked," the "individual pursuing his individual whims, the artist riding his hobbyhorse, his dada," would rule.

But dadaism finally bogged down when it began to embrace that portion of its manifesto announcing: "Art is a private matter; the artist does it for himself; any work that can be understood is the product of a journalist."[36]

Even before dada had failed, surrealism cropped up, carrying a great deal of dada baggage, but also adding a positive note. Dada's influence on surrealism was fundamental. Dada had cleared the field for the ideal of absolute self-expression. It had suggested art for the individual's sake and had set a precedent for breaking with bourgeois cultural ideology. To some extent dadaism was also responsible for the surrealists' tendency toward a deformalization of language, though the latter group has never been very radical in this respect.[37]

But even with dada, personalized self-expression was confined largely to an exploration of the writer's conscious mind. About 1924 surrealist André Breton (once a dadaist) and his followers assumed the right right to explore their subconscious and unconscious depths. It is true that the symbolists had made gestures in the direction of the subconscious under the influence of Freud and Bergson, but no previous group had explored the mind with the thoroughness of the surrealists. Surréalisme—a term used by Guillaume Apollinaire as early as 1918— shows very little interest in anything above the subconscious.[38]

Breton's group attempts to transcend the reality that our sensory equipment reveals to the conscious mind. It is interested in what the subconscious and unconscious do with the patterns formed by the conscious. The deformations, the grotesques, the magical exoticisms into which the deeper regions transform our ordinary "real" impressions, is the proper subject matter of art, for the unconscious represents a higher reality. Surrealism sets for itself the positive program of systematically exploring the innermost man, an exploration which in its opening years was conducted often through the aids of automatic writing and hypnosis. Spontaneous images are emphasized, and the

[36] *Ibid.*, p. 158.   [37] Michaud, *Vingtième Siècle*, p. 419.
[38] *Ibid.*, pp. 418-20.

real and the imaginary are contrasted by such leaders as André Breton, Philippe Soupault, Louis Aragon, Paul Eluard, Robert Desnos, Joseph Delteil, Benjamin Péret, and Henry Michaux in their efforts to free the imagination, to give it a wider working scope.[39] Commander Breton has formulated the clearest and briefest definition of the literary aspects of the movement that has yet been published. His definition is to be found in Le Manifeste du Surréalisme.

"Surréalisme, n.m. Automatisme psychique pur par lequel on se propose d'exprimer, soit verbalement, soit par écrit, soit de toute autre manière, le fonctionnement réel de la pensée. Dictée de la pensée, en l'absence de tout contrôle exercé par la raison, en dehors de toute préoccupation esthétique du morale. Encycl. Philos. Le surréalisme repose sur la croyance à la réalité supérieure de certaines formes d'associations négligées jusqu'à lui, à la toute-puissance du rêve, au jeu désintéressé de la pensée. Il tend a ruiner définitivement tous les autres mécanismes psychiques et à se substituer à eux dans la résolution des principaux problèmes de la vie."[40]

It is apparent that here is a fusion of the naturalistic empirical spirit with the romantic longing for the "above," the mysterious, the supernatural.[41]

The Little Review entertained surrealism for two years, but gradually the editors became weary. From the winter of 1926 to May 1929 the magazine could find no excuse for publication. The white flag of complete surrender was finally hauled up. It was with a trace of pomposity that the editors delivered the sword in their 1929 capitulation number.

Miss Anderson said in part:

"So I made a magazine exclusively for the very good artists of the time. Nothing more simple for me than to be the art arbiter of the world.

"I still feel the same way—with a rather important exception. As this number will show, even the artist doesn't know what he is talking about. And I can no longer go on publishing a magazine in which no one really knows what he is talking about. It doesn't interest me.

"I certainly couldn't live my life today among people who know nothing of life. It would be as if some one asked me to live seriously

---

[39] Ibid., p. 419.
[40] André Breton, Manifeste du Surréalisme, Paris, 1929, p. 46.
[41] For a supplementary discussion of surrealism, especially as it is developed in several independent surrealist magazines, see Chapter x, pp. 180-84.

all the redundant human drama that undeveloped people like to put you through. Oh no."[42]

The statement "even the artist doesn't know what he's talking about," refers to a questionnaire which had been circulated to the world's most prominent artists, asking such questions as "What do you look forward to?"; "What is your attitude towards art today?"; "Why do you go on living?"

Jane Heap expressed herself volubly in that last issue:

"For years we offered the *Little Review* as a trial-track for racers. We hoped to find artists who could run with the great artists of the past or men who could make new records. But you can't get race horses from mules. I do not believe that the conditions of our life can produce men who can give us masterpieces. Masterpieces are not made from chaos. If there is confusion of life there will be confusion of art. This is in no way a criticism of the men who are working in the arts. They can only express what is here to express.

"We have given space in the *Little Review* to 23 new systems of art (all now dead), representing 19 countries. In all of this we have not brought forward anything approaching a masterpiece except the 'Ulysses' of Mr. Joyce. 'Ulysses' will have to be the masterpiece of this time. But it is too personal, too tortured, too special a document to be a masterpiece in the true sense of the word. It is an intense and elaborate expression of Mr. Joyce's dislike of this time.

"Self-expression is not enough; experiment is not enough; the recording of special moments or cases is not enough. All of the arts have broken faith or lost connection with their origin and function. They have ceased to be concerned with the legitimate and permanent material of art."[43]

And so ended *The Little Review*. The magazine published only two unsolicited writers in its life and was not much given to discoveries. Ben Hecht, with his tale "Life," was the first find. Sherwood Anderson wrote criticism from the beginning and one of his first published stories, "Vibrant Life," appeared in March 1916.[44]

But we can justify *The Little Review*, not on its discovery record, but on its "service" record. It was one of the first to enter the fight for experimental writing, battling for the new movements and for a host of

---

[42] Anderson, Editorial, *The Little Review*, XII, 3 (May 1929).
[43] Jane Heap, "Lost: A Renaissance," *The Little Review*, XII, 5-6 (May 1929).
[44] Sherwood Anderson's first published story, "The Rabbit Pen," was printed in *Harper's*, CXXIX, 207-10 (July 1914).

little known writers who were later designed to become leaders of their generation. Further, the magazine was the first to give us an adequate cross-section view of European and American experimentalism, for it explored, at one time or another in its turbulent life, about every experimental highway and byway. Though much of this experimentalism was freakish, especially after the move to France, the periodical did, despite attitudinizing, erratic editorial whims, and a frequent lack of literary taste, present a great volume of significant work, some of it the most significant of our time. And, as Miss Anderson says, even when the magazine was at a low level it was still suggestive, suggestive especially for the young men of literary inclinations who were first beginning to think of writing between 1915 and 1922. *The Little Review* was a potent charmer; its glamour and strangeness fired the imaginations of many a young Hart Crane and Ernest Hemingway, often suggesting the roads they were to travel. Nor must we forget the spell cast on still other young men, persons who were soon to establish little magazines of their own. *Broom, Secession,* and *This Quarter* were in many respects patterned after the rebel, combative *Little Review.*

There are many reasons for writers, now between forty and fifty years old, to remember gratefully *The Little Review,* and for their insistence that it was the best magazine of their youth.

# THE THIRD DECADE

## CHAPTER V

WRITING for the opening number of *Decision* (January 1941), Stephen Vincent Benét remarks upon the great difference between "A Review of Free Culture" and the magazines of 1921. "There were plenty of new magazines in the America of 1921— but they took freedom for granted, except where John S. Sumner and the Watch and Ward Society were concerned. The fight then was against a particular and rather limited form of censorship; a censorship that tried to keep the writer from handling all sections of life. It seemed an important fight at that time, and I think it was one. . . ."[1]

From the point of view of the forties, the magazines of the twenties might well have appeared unimportant. But that opinion was by no means held by those who edited them and wrote for them. It was an exciting time. The war was over. It had left a great number of "unemployables"—both those of the type of John Dos Passos' Charley Anderson, back from Europe with gunshot nerves, and the other sort, the "aesthetically unemployable." The times were ripe for change; they were years of mockery, open defiance of the Babbitts of Zenith, state of Winnemac, and of Cambridge, Massachusetts, alike. Harriet Monroe's magazine seemed tame, "The nervous guardian of the corn-fed poetic cliché."[2] The heritage of which the twenties took advantage was near by, a matter of a few years past, or of the actual living present. James Joyce had been heard from in the London *Egoist*. Wyndham Lewis was writing, and waiting for an opportunity to launch another magazine. D. H. Lawrence, having survived the war, was carrying on his own

---

[1] "America—1941," *Decision*, I, 9 (January 1941).
[2] Quoted by Samuel Putnam from the *Chicago Daily News*, in "Chicago Letter," *Modern Review*, I, 38 (Autumn 1922).

private quarrel with the world. Greenwich Village had seen *The Masses* go and *The Liberator* arrive, much the same magazine, with the same editors, the cartoons of Art Young, and discourses on marriage by Floyd Dell. In 1917 *The Little Review* had been taken in hand by Ezra Pound (though Margaret Anderson remained the editor), expressing "no respect for mankind save in respect for detached individuals."[3] In 1920 Margaret Anderson was fighting the good fight over the printing of Joyce's *Ulysses* and making italicized faces at Mr. Sumner: the "fundamental principles" for which her magazine lived were

"First, that to a work of art you must bring aesthetic judgment, not moral, personal, nor even technical judgment. . . .

"Second, that only certain kinds of people are capable of art emotion (aesthetic emotion). They are the artist himself and the critic whose capacity for appreciation proves itself by an equal capacity to create."[4]

In November 1920 Pierre Loving, writing in Bobby Edwards' Greenwich Village magazine, *The Quill*, praised André Tridon for his proselytizing in behalf of psychoanalysis: "Like Herbert Spencer, who played a similar part with regard to Darwinism, Tridon is the talented magician whose wand converts the tangled jargon of the various schools into simplicity."[5] In January 1921 *The Double Dealer* appeared in New Orleans, with its slogan, "We shall 'remain only ourselves who can deceive them both by speaking the truth.'" *The Dial*, brought out in 1920 by Scofield Thayer and Dr. Watson, became an active sponsor of modern letters, fulfilling its editorial claim: "If a magazine isn't to be simply a waste of good white paper it ought to print, with some regularity, either such work as would otherwise have to wait years for publication, or such as would not be acceptable elsewhere."[6] And in 1923 *The Playboy* called upon a curious assortment of "sponsors" for its first issue: "D. H. Lawrence, Arthur Schopenhauer, Walt Whitman, Friedrich Nietzsche, Jesus Christ, Robert Hillyer, Elie Faure, William Blake, John Peale Bishop, and Edmund Wilson, Jr., Lord Dunsany, Clive Bell, King Solomon, and Carl Sandburg, Playboys all; let them speak for us!"[7]

In the early years of the decade Harold Stearns, Hart Crane, Malcolm Cowley, and Mortimer Adler were all in the Village, some of

[3] *The Little Review*, IV, 6 (May 1917).
[4] *The Little Review*, VII, 10 (September-December, 1920).
[5] Review of André Tridon's *Psychoanalysis and Behavior*, *The Quill*, VII, 11-12 (November 1920).
[6] Editorial, *The Dial*, LXVIII, 408 (March 1920).
[7] Editorial, *The Playboy*, I, 6 (First Quarter, 1923).

them writing for Joseph Kling's magazine *Pagan*, "A Magazine for Eudaemonists." And *Contact*, which appeared for four issues, carried the appeal of William Carlos Williams for a vigorous and precise native art.

These appearances and statements are merely a sampling of the immense activity which those years witnessed. There is no co-ordination, no directive, among them, but they are intensely alive. The truth is that the artist of the twenties was immensely serious about himself, and a little bewildered. He had ceased long before to be concerned with the Beautiful, the True, and the Good, as abstractions or things in themselves. There was some self-conscious attention in the Village to the artist as artist, but much of that was parading before tourists, deliberately to mislead them into thinking that *The Saturday Evening Post* had been right after all. And one found most of all a consideration of newly discovered ideologies and doctrines—not one, but many, and especially those which could be made to fit the lives and personalities of the artist. For a philosophy or psychology does not "influence" a writer; rather, a writer takes what he finds and molds it to his taste or comprehension.

The Freudian "contagion," which Bobby Edwards maintains was picked up at the Bonis' Washington Square Bookshop, had spread throughout the Village. Freud was disturbed at the American habit of suiting his researches to momentary opportunity, and regarded the Americans with some suspicion for the remainder of his life. Indeed, he had good reason, for psychoanalysis was much abused and misunderstood. "Now the principal motivation of sex," said Bobby Edwards, for example, "is the dreadful ructions of the subconscious mind, which apparently dwells on nothing else. . . . And if you don't let your subconscious do as it wishes you get complexes which do everything from spoiling your digestion to making you a faddist."[8] Doctor Freud, "Satan's little brother," had filled the Village air with discussions of free love, neurosis, and "dream talk," until this "plausible pseudo science" had spread its theories throughout the country, "in spite of the Methodist Church." Floyd Dell was one of a few Villagers whose reception seemed both enthusiastic and intelligent; in fact, Freudianism was for him the companion of Marxism in the fight against bourgeois economic and moral convention. Joseph Freeman also regarded it as a way of liberalizing our attitudes toward sex. He recalls the advice Dell gave him when he visited the Village:

[8] "Bobby's Stuff," *The Quill*, VIII, 25-26 (May 1921).

" 'Have yourself psychoanalyzed. It's the only thing to do. Everybody is being psyched these days. You will unravel your complexes and thus overcome them. You will relive your life, discover its secret pattern, and learn to direct it consciously. Confession has always been good for the soul; now we have a scientific confessional whose catharsis liberates us from the tyranny of our unconscious fears and taboos.' "[9]

Actually psychoanalysis was badly misunderstood in the Village and elsewhere. In its original form it was by no means a ready and easy way of foregoing legal and moral responsibilities. It was not, in the opinion of its founder, a substitute for religion; nor does it prove virgins to be pathetic scoundrels. But one must take into account the complicated nature of the problem of influence. A science, a philosophy, or a psychology will be adapted to a writer's needs, usually in accordance with its availability to his understanding and its adaptability to human applications. Psychoanalysis had a host of explainers—lecturers, popularizers, who simplified its original terms, and by those means made more remote the possibility of our ever understanding their original meaning.

In spite of the inaccurate and almost casual treatment of Freudian theory in the writing of the twenties, the influence of psychoanalysis upon this writing was great and even profound in some cases. Like most theories which enjoyed a popular reception, it suffered misinterpretation and a curiously capricious use of details. In some cases psychoanalysis helped to explain aesthetic motivation: Conrad Aiken, for example, pointed out the role played by the poet's unconscious mind and hinted that the sources of poetry are often hidden and unavailable to critic and reader alike. Frederick Clarke Prescott's book, *The Poetic Mind*, published in 1922, served as a link between the Platonic and the modern ideas of poetic creation, and helped to give Freudianism a critical sanction which impressed both scholars and poets alike. It was he more than anyone else of the early twenties who pointed to the similarity between dreams and poetry: the "evidence indicating a relation between poetry and dreams [is convincing]. In the first place language tends to identify the two, and such identification always indicates a relation."[10] Writers were very much interested in this relationship: if dreams were neglected but rich sources of psychological explanation, they argued, perhaps some of the most difficult problems of language and creation can be solved by a study of them. The many reports of

[9] Freeman, *An American Testament*, p. 244.
[10] *The Poetic Mind*, New York, 1922, p. 22.

the dreams of Harry Crosby and others in *transition* are typical attempts to bring the artist's unconscious to the surface, where it might be examined for clues to the creative process.

And this applies not exclusively to poetry, by any means. The novelist was also intensely interested. Floyd Dell's explanation of the genesis of his novels *Moon Calf* and *The Briary Bush* underlines this interest. "Fiction, like art of any sort," he said in an essay published in *The Modern Quarterly*, "is generated in the unconscious mind, and represents an attempt to work out unsolved psychological conflicts. The conflict within this writer's unconscious mind between the narcistic impulses and the sexual-social impulses is evidently very strong, since nearly all his work has dealt with it."[11]

Though Freud's work had been translated into English as early as 1913, and had been debated at some length in the second decade, the real emergence of Freud as a popular figure, maligned as often as respected, waited for the twenties. The enthusiastic reception of psychoanalysis on each of several levels of comprehension and misapprehension remains one of the marvels of the twenties. He was no longer a source only of psychological curiosity or of medical pique; he became a subject for discussion in both the subway and the drawing room. He was as often condemned as the bête noire of the century as he was unthinkingly accepted as an angel of deliverance. For several reasons, the interest in the controversy over Freud fixed upon two of his books: *The Interpretation of Dreams* and *Three Contributions to a Theory of Sex*. Among his other works, *The Psychopathology of Everyday Life* and *Wit and Its Relation to the Unconscious* caused only a mild disturbance; and his latter-day speculations on myth and the racial unconscious have attracted scarcely more than a few of the writers of our day. Writers of the twenties were drawn to Freud's theories in three ways: 1) they were interested in the dream, its language and its habits; 2) they were attracted by the Freudian explanation of the artist—and, though some of them dismissed the notion of an "aesthetic neurosis" as nonsense, others thought they saw something important in it; 3) and, finally, they welcomed Freud's reinterpretation of sexual and familial themes, believing that some new suggestions for the analysis of character might be borrowed from it. On such individual novelists as James Joyce, D. H. Lawrence, Sherwood Anderson, Waldo Frank, Ludwig

---

[11] "A Literary Self-Analysis," *The Modern Quarterly*, IV, 148 (June-September, 1927).

Lewisohn, and Conrad Aiken, the influence appears to have been great —in some cases avowed, in others perhaps evident though disclaimed.

In one respect, psychoanalysis came very close to the proud, fervent but confused beliefs of the intellectuals: it was, after all, a psychology of the "inner life of the soul"—a psychology which could best explain the reasons for man's valiant but vain struggle to find himself in a world too complex for easy, overt explanations. Eliseo Vivas, discussing D. H. Lawrence's *The Rainbow* in the April 1925 issue of the Philadelphia *Guardian*, put it this way: "They are modern who have thrown overboard the faith of yesterday with all its subtle implications, who have no spiritual rudder or compass, who search in the welter of contemporary tendencies for a guiding light which cannot be found because it has not defined itself and probably never will."[12] Freudian psychology helped to explain their confusion, but did not explain it away. Moreover, it gave them some terms which could be used against the things they disliked. The attack on the Puritan, whose appearance changed curiously from the historical figure by which he had been known, was aided and abetted by such Freudian explanations as that of repression, projection, and sublimation. It is interesting to watch the figure of the American middle class change as it is subjected to various theoretical interpretations. The fat, bloated capitalist of Art Young's cartoons in *The Masses* became a thin, spare, repressed Vermonter in Waldo Frank's portrait of Calvin Coolidge; after he had been thoroughly explained and his sins examined in public by the writers of the twenties, he was to sit for a new portrait in the thirties. In the twenties the trouble with the ruling classes was psychological; in the thirties it was economic. Repression gave way to oppression as the critical war cry.

Nietzsche fared only less badly. He had been early pointed out as the archdevil opponent of conventional society; and, through the agencies of Henry Mencken, Huntington Wright, and George Burman Foster, his criticism of civilization had been equated with the wave of scorn which swept against American conventions and institutions. It was as though he had had America specifically in mind when he wrote *Thus Spake Zarathustra*. Both Freud and Nietzsche were therefore handy ideological weapons against "the great American boor."

The influence of Nietzsche had, of course, an earlier start than that of Freud. It was an important accompaniment to the criticism of society advanced by the men of the nineties. Nietzsche was essentially a spokesman for the artist, who saw in his work justification for the

---

[12] *The Guardian*, I, 267-68 (April 1925).

artist's taking a stand against the errors and stupidities of his civilization. Hence we find Zarathustra quoted in the magazines of the 1890's. In 1896 an essay on Nietzsche by Havelock Ellis appeared in *The Savoy*, a British magazine. Another of these magazines, *The Eagle and the Serpent*, began in 1898, and its title page was decorated with a quotation from Zarathustra.

Perhaps the chief significance of Nietzsche for young intellectuals was that he had (unwittingly, of course) given his blessing to the artist and explained his eccentricities by emphasizing the unusual role of the artist in society. In this respect, the two books, *Thus Spake Zarathustra* and *The Birth of Tragedy*, exercised a major influence, and suited the aesthetes perfectly. The fact that Nietzsche had all but repudiated the artist—or at least was disposed to scorn the poetaster and despise the compromise which artists often made with society—did not seem to interfere with his "use" of Nietzsche as a spokesman. The superb lyricism of passages in *The Birth of Tragedy* thrilled the artist and led him to believe in himself as the superman's right-hand man. Such remarks as the following underlined, in the artist's opinion, his essential difference from the ordinary run of human beings, and glorified his separation from them: "He who approaches these Olympians with another religion in his heart, seeking among them for moral elevation, even for sanctity, for disincarnate spirituality, for charity and benevolence, will soon be forced to turn his back on them, discouraged and disappointed. For there is nothing here that suggests asceticism, spirituality, or duty. We hear nothing but the accents of an exuberant, triumphant life, in which all things, whether good or bad, are deified."[13]

One of Nietzsche's interpreters in our century was James Huneker, music critic, a contributing editor of *M'lle New York*, and a novelist of the twentieth century aesthete. Huneker published a long essay on Nietzsche in 1909, in his book *Egoists: A Book of Supermen*. "Nietzsche is the most dynamically emotional writer of his times," Huneker wrote. "He sums up an epoch. He is the expiring voice of the old nineteenth-century romanticism in philosophy. His message to unborn generations we may easily leave to those unborn, and enjoy the wit, the profound criticisms of life, the bewildering gamut of his ideas; above all, the tragic blotting out of such a vivid intellectual life."[14] The hero of Huneker's *Painted Veils* (written in 1919) is conversant with all of the pundits of his day. His arguments with the priest brother of

[13] *The Birth of Tragedy*, tr. Clifton P. Fadiman, New York, n.d., pp. 179-80.
[14] *Egoists: A Book of Supermen*, New York, 1909, p. 268.

Mona Milton are chiefly defenses of the advance guard ideas of his time. They support, he says, the artist's genuine belief that he is a man "set apart" from the masses. But Milton's attack does not accept such a premise; and he condemns the artist for taking such a stand: " 'Great artists? Yes. But guides to damnation. Moral anarchs, their teaching will lead to the anarchy of physical violence. Mark my words. All Europe will suffer sometime from their doctrines.' "[15]

The great attraction of Nietzche's style, his aphoristic manner of condensing his thoughts and of foregoing obvious order and pattern in his exposition, is at least in part responsible for the misinterpretation from which he has suffered in modern times. But this was not the only reason for his popularity. Nietzsche emphasized the weaknesses of his civilization. His attack upon the life and manners of his contemporaries was thoroughgoing and relentless; his appeal for a revival of pre-Christian pagan morality was enthusiastically received by the artists of the fin de siècle and by their successors in several Bohemian centers of the twenties. Egmont Arens hailed him as a "Playboy" and asked that he be respected and his word heeded. The editorial manifesto of *The London Aphrodite* echoes the phrases of Nietzsche and proclaims the artist's independence on Nietzschean grounds:

"We stand for a point of view which equally outrages the modernist and the reactionary. . . . We declare war against all academicians, whether modernistically disguised or smugly official—against all prophets from the gutters of resentment, whether the noise proceeds from the mere press or exasperated theories of intellectualizing impotence —against all sentimentalists who degrade the emotional theme by trivially pretty modes—against all debauchees of the distracted nerves or ascetics of the intellect who abstract the fluid geometries from their true action.

"We affirm Life, and for definition quote Nietzsche: Spirit is that life which itself cuts into life. We affirm Beauty, and by that term understand a sensual harmony, a homogeneous ecstasy, which, constructing intellectually, yet hates nothing so much as the dry cogs of the objectified and objectifying intellect."[16]

*The Aphrodite* seemed committed, in part at least, to the advertisement of its editors' version of Nietzschean thought; and the Fanfrolico Press offered new translations of Nietzsche to the magazine's subscribers. In one essay, Jack Lindsay called the German philosopher

---
[15] *Painted Veils*, New York, 1920, p. 206.
[16] *The London Aphrodite*, 1, 2 (August 1928).

"The Forerunner," but claimed that those who followed him were far from a living realization of his principles: "They are rather the excreta of inertia upon his energy, the automatic thinning-out of his trumpets." Nietzsche, says Lindsay, saw in what new direction man must face: "Balancing his vision of life as process, flux, will, movement, he introduced (instead of the abstractly incarnated Being of Hegel or the Nirvanic will of Schopenhauer) the symbol of Eternal Recurrence—that is, the liberated essence of man achieving the dynamic judgment. ... He made a fresh moral analysis. ... If we are to remain true to life we must submit incessantly our Apollonian intellect to the Dionysian tumult of experience, ... to escape the static abstraction, we must be for ever dynamically transitional." We stand, concludes Lindsay, "at the gates with Nietzsche, Beethoven and Wagner as the signposts of our future ... themselves our future, if we are to have one."[17]

Nietzsche contributed almost nothing to literary experiment. Though his books have a number of things to say about dreams, about the unconscious, and about several other matters of interest to modern theorists and writers (he had anticipated Freud in a number of ways, as Freud has himself admitted), they are scattered and presented in a fragmentary manner, with no appeal to science and no scholarly pretension about them. He affected the experimental interests scarcely at all, therefore. His chief service was in supporting the artist's notions of his own unusual nature—he has certainly translated eccentricity into saintliness, and writers were grateful to have this sanction for their reckless disregard for "slave morality." Thus he contributed to the development of an attitude. The influence of psychoanalysis was more varied than his; its suggestions were laboriously copied down from clinical experience, and presented in literal translations. While the incentive for accepting Nietzsche was strong but vague, the reasons for listening to Freud and his fellow workers were serious, factual, and in harmony with what most writers knew about the scientific method.

## II

The good fight against tradition was often carried on from remote outposts—Paris, Vienna, Rome, Berlin. The exiles of whom Fletcher spoke so scornfully, the "second generation" of exiles, came—to Paris

[17] "The Modern Consciousness: An Essay towards an Integration," *The London Aphrodite*, I, 4, 5, 23 (August 1928).

chiefly—for a variety of reasons, but principally because living was cheap and one could drink quite openly and quite freely. As Malcolm Cowley expressed it in his poem "Valuta," these men learned soon enough the value of the American dollar on foreign exchanges:

> Following the dollar O following the
> dollar I learned three fashions of eating
> with the knife and ordered beer in four
> languages from a Hungarian waiter while
> following the dollar around the
> 48th degree of north latitude where it
> buys most there is the Fatherland—[18]

Was the movement to Paris entirely escapist or opportunistic? Certainly many young Americans simply stayed there after the war, finding it impossible to return to a dry and dull America. The brave, reckless, "lost generation," pictured in Hemingway's *The Sun Also Rises* and given the status of knighthood by Gertrude Stein, found in Paris a stimulus compounded of dada, Bohemianism, and liquor. But most of all it was the freedom of action and thought which held the Americans in Paris. This attitude is presented satirically by Cowley in *Broom*: "Young Mr. Elkins places an evident value on his facts and yet he collates them around a simple, almost a childish thesis; a single thesis concerning America and Puritanism: Puritanism is bad; America is Puritan; therefore America is bad. . . ."[19]

America was in Paris for more than a holiday. The native land seemed inhospitable to experiment, and the Village seemed a drab place—good enough quarters for freshmen, but not suitable for all-out antipuritanism. The arts are so hedged in by conventional barriers in the "Anglo-Saxon countries" that one cannot see them at all, said the *transatlantic review*: "An ever present strain of puritanism obscures aspects of life that are plain enough to almost all the races."[20] Ernest Hemingway found America hounded by critics, "the eunuchs of literature." Its brightly polished machinery and its paved Main Street had been too little affected by the war. Its morality was comparatively untouched, except for the isolated centers of Bohemianism. In this atmosphere one could not breathe freely enough. One either made money or made Marxist faces at those who did. Why not stay in Europe and "follow the dollar"?

[18] Cowley, "Valuta," *Broom*, III, 250 (November 1922).
[19] "Young Mr. Elkins," *Broom*, IV, 54-55 (December 1922).
[20] "Chroniques: I," *transatlantic review*, I, 196-97 (April 1924).

Exile, then, whether actual or merely spiritual, was a gesture of protest against the automatic censorship which American morality exercised over minds which wished to be free. Much of the writing in the exile magazines sought to justify this move away from America on other than hedonistic grounds. But more material was of and about American things. The expatriation was not necessarily an uprooting. Beyond youthful reasons for moving across the Atlantic, there were no deeply rooted convictions which held the Americans in Europe; and most of them came back again—when the money ran out, or the pleasures were no longer pleasant, or, simply, when the native felt the need of returning to be reoriented to his original points of view. The genuine expatriates—Eliot and Pound especially—had never really thought of returning; Eliot because he was too much in love with things British, Pound because he hated too much the central democratic philosophy of American life and thought it uncongenial to the artist.

Mr. Albert Parry suggests that the principal difference "between the pre-war and the post-war Americans in Paris was the drinking. Before the war, the Americans drank light wines and tried to remain gay gentlemen even when their feet were like pretzels. But after the war, absinthe and cognacs became the fashion; the heavy, dull, leaden drinking was the thing, with liquids indiscriminately mixed. Not the indolent sitting in front of a café, not a philosophic soirée in a studio, but a marathon of reeling from bar to bar over a wide territory—this was the post-war mode."[21] Along with this freedom from the Volstead Act, there was the more riotous freedom of dada; and dadaists were not only members of a "literary movement"; they were master craftsmen in the matter of nihilistic showmanship. The postwar attitude of disrespect showed itself in deliberate displays of riotous and complex flouting of sense and logic.

Just how good (or how bad) this indiscriminate Bohemianism was for the exiles of the twenties it is hard to say. Certain it is that a large number of writers were in Paris at one time or another—and the few who had preceded them (Gertrude Stein, Ezra Pound, for example) had something to do with their coming. Robert McAlmon is inclined to think that exilism (if life in Paris may be called that) did no harm, but that failures in Bohemian centers are given more publicity simply because they are generally in the public eye and can't escape public censure.

[21] Parry, *Garrets and Pretenders*, p. 331.

"It may be that artists who are surest of what they are about, admit fallow periods, or that they do drink, perhaps to boisterous drunkenness, and they don't lack sound-citizen companions. Some realize that Bohemian centers present in concentrated form their share of human types and manifestations. Failures on Main Street seldom get so severely criticized as the same failures loitering about art-centers, because such centers permit extra relaxation, and no producing artist worries about the salvation of other beings whose best mode of living is to remain unproductive. Purposefulness on the part of incompetent people wastes much valuable material. That Montparnasse furnishes a resident and transient background of beings futile to themselves, and destructive in their false contempt of production, does not mean that The Quarter is a disintegrating force for such people as find it a convenient rendezvous for interesting encounters, or for dissipation that appears often excessive and ridiculous."[22]

By 1922 or 1923, McAlmon tells us in his autobiography, *Being Geniuses Together*, there were "quantities" of Americans in Paris. Some of these came escorted by their wives, "who saw to it that they did not over-drink or indulge in companionship with people who could not be of definite service to them."[23] Others, however, spent more leisurely lives, working in an atmosphere of freedom and casualness. But the American magazines and newspapers emphasized the dissoluteness of Paris Bohemian life and pointed out that many Americans were simply wasting away their lives there.

To check up on these accusations, McAlmon and some others toured the Quarter: "We noted down a list of two hundred and fifty names, English and American, and some were the names of persons responsible for the American articles against so-called exiles in Paris.... In that list were the names of none but working writers or painters; one of the writers has since gained the Nobel prize; several others have been Book-of-the-Month Club selections, or bestsellers, or acclaimed great writers." One wonders, says McAlmon, by what strange circumstance of the mind these critics of the exiles could have come to their conclusions, "and what obsession persisted in the writers who returned to America, which caused them to find it necessary to throw off on Paris, a city which gave them material and stimulus, and which helped them to grow up mentally, if they did."[24]

Whatever the reaction of their soberer and more domestic contem-

---

[22] "Truer Than Most Accounts," *The Exile*, II, 42-43 (Autumn 1927).
[23] *Being Geniuses Together*, London, 1938, pp. 104-5.
[24] *Ibid.*, pp. 105-6.

poraries, these young men and women in Paris were able to offer sufficient evidence of their having been at work. Indeed, over most of Europe, in the large cities especially, American and English writers carried on the little magazine tradition. At remarkably reasonable cost, they could issue their own reviews and magazines, and the presence of so many American and English writers insured them against a dearth of talent. These exile magazines differed from their American and British contemporaries in only a few particulars. There was no regional emphasis in them. Having freed themselves from the immediate surroundings of the home country, they were able to sponsor and to tolerate literary experiment freed from any provincial restraints or embarrassments. Yet these magazines were obviously published for "home consumption," and some of them did return to the States; one at least, Pound's *Exile*, was written and edited in Paris, but published in Chicago, as a means of evading the customs officer, against whom its "Ezraordinary" editor railed with his customary vigor.

The list of exile magazines is long, and the motives for publishing them various. Many of them will be discussed in other chapters of this book. *Broom* (1921-24) began in Rome, and moved from there to Berlin, and finally died in New York. *Secession* (1922-24) was first published in Vienna, and traveled from there to Berlin, Reutte, and Brooklyn, New York. All four issues of Pound's *Exile* (1927-28) were edited in Paris. Ford Madox Ford's *transatlantic review* (1924-25) was edited and published in Paris—and lays claim to having been the first to sponsor the writings of Ernest Hemingway (Hemingway had first published in New Orleans' *The Double Dealer*). This magazine of the ubiquitous Ford appeared first and always in sedate format, not unlike that of many more conservative English reviews. But it was not unkind to the *avant garde*; and, though it "featured" Conrad and Ford, it also published the writings of E. E. Cummings, Gertrude Stein, Hemingway, and Pound. Its regular department, "Chroniques," discussed aspects of contemporary life; and, like Waldo Frank (who had "advised" the Paris exiles about their America in a book published in 1919), it commented upon the life of the American middle class, asking this question: "Has life in America been raised to such a high level of physical comfort for all that no sharp inequalities can ever come into being to break down the mechanistic equilibrium that is a moribund pull down to indifference and the death of the spirit?"[25]

[25] Jeanne Foster, "Chroniques III: And from the United States," *transatlantic review*, I, 72 (March 1924).

Arthur Moss, at one time editor of the Greenwich Village magazine, *The Quill*, moved to Paris in 1921, and from there directed the fortunes of the exile magazine *Gargoyle*. It was essentially a survey of Paris intellectual life and published reproductions of modern paintings, comments on the arts, and critical essays on the then reigning inhabitants of the colony. From the editorial sidelines Moss surveyed "these days of drab realism, freudian frightmares, cabellaisian subtleties, and general literary licence."[26]

Other little magazines were also being published in Europe in the twenties and subscribed to by Americans. Ernest Walsh's *This Quarter*, and Harold Salemson's *Tambour*, for example. Then, of course, there was Eugene Jolas' *transition*, begun in 1927 in Paris, but published by old presses in villages near the city. But this most important of all exile magazines deserves and will get separate treatment in another chapter. As for Salemson's *Tambour*, it did not play favorites and objected strenuously to the esoteric exclusiveness of some of its contemporaries. To prove its charitable attitude toward the recent past, it published an issue devoted to the writings of Anatole France (the fifth issue, published in 1930). "We shall assemble all the species, all the tendencies. To our readers will be left the privilege of passing judgment," Salemson said in the issue of June 1930; and, he added, it is stupid to publish a magazine for the exclusive use of the postwar generation, "just as limited, nay, more limited, since those have not yet shown anything, than to publish a review ignoring those under a certain age or of insufficient fame."[27]

The internationalism of the little magazine of the twenties should not surprise us, who know already that the preoccupation of all intellectuals in that decade was with ideas, theories, and experiments, scarcely if at all limited by national boundaries. And we ought not forget that another internationalism was growing in strength. The Red Revolution in Moscow, reported by John Reed for *The Liberator*, had piqued the curiosity of most young men and women of the time. But the real story of the Marxist critic, the proletarian writer, and of the pilgrimage to Moscow, is a story of the thirties. For the most part the men of the twenties enjoyed the congenial atmosphere of Paris (as much of it as their money could buy at the very reasonable exchange rates), and were pursuing ideas and experiments only indifferently related to specific political events and gospels.

[26] "Entr'acte," *Gargoyle*, III, n.p. (October 1922).
[27] Letter to *Tambour*, III, 3-4 (1930?).

## III

The twenties are marked by confusion and cross-purpose, by endless debate and by offended spirit. Above all, they were animated by intense literary activity. Emotions were qualified and induced by one's recent experience in the library or by what Shaw had said in Act Three. Living seemed a momentary pause between one book and the next. What amazes the student who looks back upon that period is its apparent lack of discrimination. Systems of thought ordinarily have a continuity and unity which sets them apart, each from the other. How, then, can one man draw from a dozen and hope to retain any reasonable consistency in his own scheme of things? The truth is that men of the twenties were able to manage it. What Freud had failed to make clear, Schopenhauer explained on Page 263; what Bergson neglected to mention was beautifully given in Chapter Three of Dewey's latest book. What a marvelous assemblage of mutually exclusive elements! The person of Mabel Dodge Luhan sets the absolute limits to which this eclecticism may reach. Each week a different speaker on a different subject. It is all very exciting and instructive. We may at one moment plan a program for re-educating the farmers of Kansas; at another we may send across "sympathetic vibrations" to Lawrence in Italy, making it imperative that he come to America immediately. Next Wednesday we shall visit the new center of euthanasian culture, whose major tenet is that "all is negation" and that a negation of negation furnishes an incentive for action.

The twenties were an age of individualists, who pieced together fragments of books, scraps of conversation, and new recipes, without regard for logical consistency. That is the characteristic of the period. Many men were seriously making up their minds and were confronted by many rather than single solutions to postwar bewilderment. The intellectual pace was too much for a host of minor minds, who gave in eventually to a single solution of their moral and aesthetic dilemmas. Economic event and doctrine acted as the agents of resolution for others. Today scores of the most reckless of individualists have subsided, become domestic, and look upon further novelty with a jaundiced eye. They regard the twenties as an unfortunate period in which "nothing of any consequence happened." They forget that "everything happened" and that they had helped it to happen. They have selected from the many dogmas which they explored then, the one by which they might live, and now stoutly vouchsafe and defend its truth. The turmoil of the twenties was indispensable to the clarification of principles which these men now hold.

It is this merry confusion which makes the little magazines of the twenties stimulating to read. The strong purposiveness or truculent assertiveness of some of the stronger spirits stands out without qualification as representative of the period. The personalities of three men stood out from all others in an age of nervous individualism. Two of them were survivors of the original group of individualists, centered about *The Egoist* of London: Wyndham Lewis and Ezra Pound.

The third, Ernest J. Walsh, who piloted two issues of one of Europe's best American magazines, *This Quarter*, breathed the very air of freedom and accepted that freedom of the artist as the *sine qua non* of the age. It is characteristic of the individualists that they should fall out with each other. Walsh's first issue was dedicated to Ezra Pound, who "comes first to our mind as meriting the gratitude of this generation."[28] The third issue, apparently with the posthumous consent of Walsh, withdraws the tribute. What sort of man was Walsh? The third issue gives abundant evidence of his vigor, his sincerity, and the decidedness of his opinions: "An irreverent man, without standards, without tracks . . . A hard witted man. A fiery-hearted man . . . A NEW MAN with great sounds."[29] In Walsh's posthumously printed essay, "What Is Literature?" he delivers himself of a variety of judgments. Gertrude Stein is a "profound artist but a poor writer"; the influence of *The Dial* upon young writers is "insidious"; the life of *The Dial* and of *The Criterion* "is a tradition without individuality"; *The Little Review* is "too trivial to discuss." Walsh respected no tradition; he tolerated no incentive save that which led man to write without hindrance. In his magazine, editorial taste is always implicit; it does not deliver the knockout blow to literature, but allows contributions to appear unedited. This was a shock to the conservatives, whose prior convictions acted strongly to alter and remodel the contributions they were willing to publish.

Wyndham Lewis, on the other hand, preferred to be called "The Enemy." He would not sponsor any "movement," he said, or hide behind any doctrinal skirts. Here is "merely a person and not a gang!" Since he has thus separated himself from society, he can "resume his opinion" of it. Friendship and tolerance are for him soft and easy; further, they mark every opinion with hedging and compromise. There

---

[28] Editorial, *This Quarter*, I, verso, front cover (Spring 1925).
[29] Editorial, *This Quarter*, III, 9 (Spring 1927).

is no hesitation in *The Enemy*, no "impartiality." In his estimation, the most vicious characteristic of the age is its depersonalization. He will do his best to counteract it. In *The Enemy* many things are condemned —the latter-day primitivism of D. H. Lawrence and Sherwood Anderson; the "dadaism" of Jolas' *transition*; the automatic inanities of Gertrude Stein; the sad confusion of Joyce's "Work in Progress."

Ezra Pound continued from Paris; London had long since exasperated him, and he gave it up as beyond repair. *The Exile* published a few of his cantos, printed the prose of Robert McAlmon and others, and ranted editorially about the two American institutions which seemed most to upset him—the censorship and the national legislative branch. America's "horror" was caused by the inability of Americans to allow the lives of people to remain private: ". . . America is *the* most colossal monkey house and prize exhibit that the astonished world has yet seen."[30] As for revolution, Pound thought it stupid for the artist to advocate it, for the artist is far ahead of any revolution, or counterrevolution.

In 1931 Pound joined Samuel Putnam on the editorial board of *The New Review*. Putnam later repudiated him: "The truth of the matter is," he said in an article published in *Mosaic*, "Pound's mind, such a mind as he has, is capable of expansion only with the greatest difficulty and with exceeding slowness. His is a tight little brain. He dwells in a murky Hinterland of his own into which only now and then a fancied ray of light flickers."[31] Pound became notorious in 1943 and 1944, *persona non grata* for his broadcasts of Fascist propaganda from Italy. He had prepared himself for these by readings in economics; since he cannot brook opposition in any field, his statements in economics are marked by vehemence and dogmatism. They command no respect. Pound is not the "misunderstood" creature, condemned by society to suffer its displeasure. He has been all too easily understood; and our recent understanding of him might serve to dismiss him as charlatan and fool without any effort to evaluate objectively his contribution to modern literature. No one can doubt that this contribution is very important. We ought, therefore, not to let immediate events interfere with our estimate of his ultimate worth.

[30] *The Exile*, I, 92 (Spring 1927).
[31] "Ezra Pound: Cracker-Barrel Revolutionist," *Mosaic*, I, 5 (November-December, 1934). For another latter-day impression of Pound, see William Carlos Williams, "Ezra Pound—Lord Ga-Ga!" *Decision*, II, 16-24 (September 1941).

Our third decade will have to be judged with the tolerance perspective affords the critic. Measurement of its value cannot be made according to the standards it set up for itself. Intellectually it was a unity of disparate elements, a parade of mutually exclusive theories, an anthology of recalcitrance. It had all standards and no standards. It has been the most exclusively "literary" of all decades of the century; that is, its intellectual sponsors derived many of their judgments from books and magazines, and out of them compiled more books and established more magazines. It was a time of experiment, tolerant of contradictions and of indiscriminate effusions. The energies were not channelized, and efforts to synthesize were smashed by strong personal differences or editorial mismanagement.

Harold J. Salemson sums up the experimentalism of the twenties for us in *Tambour's* seventh issue. For the moderns, whatever their persuasion, "art is but a projection of the artist's personality into the world about him, or if we wish, an interpretation of the outside world as related to the artist. In this, modernism has been but a romanticism distinguished by its form."

"Modernists" (that is to say, experimentalists) have been wholly preoccupied with form; this has led to an exhaustion of form, and some new aesthetic direction is necessary. It is necessary to add "matter" to the various "manners" with which the writers of the twenties have experimented. We need, above all, a new point of view, which goes beyond the artist himself: "We demand that the artist look at his day with the point-of-view of his day, as he understands it, and without making us feel his presence in it."[32]

The pressure of events was to furnish a new "matter" for writing in the thirties.

[32] "Essential: 1930 (A Manifesto)," *Tambour*, VII, 5-7 (1930).

# THE
## *TENDENZ* MAGAZINE

CHAPTER VI

At first glance the overwhelming variety and diffusion of enthusiastic but adolescent activity discourages any effort at giving it any order whatsoever. The difficulty of "presentness" in any age is its preoccupation with the immediate environment, physical or intellectual. If there is any difference between the confusion of our second decade and the disorder of the third, it must be sought in efforts which some of the magazines of the latter period made to fashion a synthesis from diverse materials. Beginning with the later years of the war, some men sought for an underlying meaning, of which the diversity of expressions was merely the surface appearance.

The tendenz magazine is, therefore, an important clue to the literature of the twenties. Its aim was first to recognize, second to state, the forward direction of our thought and culture; and, finally, to predict or advocate the ultimate ends and aims of our literary aspiration. Men who piloted such magazines over rough seas were in a sense the "dictators of thought"; and, like most dictators, they were met with criticism civil and uncivil, and led troubled lives. It was a time of assessment of democratic values; and it was the poet's task to state these values clearly, the critic's to draw them together.

The tendenz magazine is a peculiar result of the age. Its product was the critical philosophical essay, companion piece to the creative work found in its pages. Its purpose is primarily to sponsor thinking on a number of issues and to give original thinkers a place of publication. Hence it is editorially more vocal than other types of little magazines, though it may not have a policy any more consistent than, or even as consistent as, its fellows. It is by means of these magazines—the avantgarde magazines of criticism and philosophical discussion—that the major intellectual tendencies of the period may be examined. As we shall see, magazines like *The Seven Arts, Broom, Secession,* and *S 4 N* did support the young, new writers' claim for a hearing; but this was not their only interest. One other distinguishing characteristic these magazines have: their contributors were generally interested in ideas themselves and in the relationship which held between these ideas as they are expressed in philosophy, applied in psychology, and altered and represented in literature. They point to the intellectual future and, on the basis of what they see in contemporary life, suggest one or several tendencies which they feel the world and man must follow. Hence their criticism is often philosophical or sociological, rather than aesthetic. This fact sets them apart from magazines of criticism, whose chief concern is with the analysis of works of art in themselves and with various speculations concerning the nature of the arts.

In times more settled than ours, such magazines might well have echoed tradition or defended and explained it. But there was no general body of "believers" who subscribed unanimously to a self-containing system of thought. There are contradictions and inconsistencies to be found, therefore, in these magazines. As a matter of fact, one magazine, *S 4 N*, attempted to formulate an editorial philosophy from the idea of disagreement and difference—claiming that thought is in general "fluid" and adoption of any one body of thought excludes all others, making intellectual progress difficult and almost impossible.

It is as exciting to follow the winding, errant paths which these magazines took as it is to look at the changes in literary method itself. For the editors of these magazines had their differences of opinion and their quarrels; and the history of ideas in the twentieth century is as varied and bewildering as is the history of the literary art. The first of the magazines we wish to examine is one which belongs to the second decade of the century; but its history is so definitely a part of the career of the *tendenz* magazine that chronology can be safely overruled.

## II

New York's *Seven Arts* flashed across the literary horizon for only a year, from November 1916 to October 1917. In that twelvemonth it powerfully stirred American thought and made a lasting name for itself. James Oppenheim, the editor, and his two associates, Waldo Frank and Van Wyck Brooks, were the leading spirits of a group that saw in the late teens an awakening of national self-consciousness, a restless yearning for a finer vision of destiny than the land had previously known. They saw these evidences of America's coming of age in the new poets who were monthly being promoted by *Poetry*, and they were alert enough to see that there were many young men—as yet all but unknown—eager to express themselves in the drama, the novel, the short story, and criticism.[1] A letter addressed to these unknowns in the summer of 1916 defined *The Seven Arts'* ambitious hope of drawing together and synthesizing their thought:

"It is our faith and the faith of many, that we are living in the first days of a renascent period, a time which means for America the coming of that national self-consciousness which is the beginning of greatness. In all such epochs the arts cease to be private matters; they become not only the expression of the national life but a means to its enhancement.

"Our arts show signs of this change. It is the aim of *The Seven Arts* to become a channel for the flow of these new tendencies: an expression of our American arts which shall be fundamentally an expression of our American life.

"We have no tradition to continue; we have no school of style to build up. What we ask of the writer is simply self-expression without regard to current magazine standards. We should prefer that portion of his work which is done through a joyous necessity of the writer himself.

"*The Seven Arts* will publish stories, short plays, poems, essays and brief editorials. Such arts as cannot be directly set forth in the magazine will receive expression through critical writing, which, it is hoped, will be no less creative than the fiction and poetry. In this field the aim will be to give vistas and meanings rather than a monthly survey or review; to interpret rather than to catalogue. We hope that creative workers themselves will also set forth their vision and their inspiration.

"In short, *The Seven Arts* is not a magazine for artists, but an expression of artists for the community."[2]

The high hope was richly rewarded. The result of this appeal brought forth an amazing number of fine writers, men who shortly were to dominate the milieu. *The Seven Arts* receives the credit for crystallizing in the public consciousness such American names as Sherwood Anderson, John Dos Passos, Eugene O'Neill, Randolph Bourne, John Reed, Van Wyck Brooks, Waldo Frank, and H. L. Mencken, and the Englishmen, D. H. Lawrence and J. D. Beresford. Most of these were

[1] James Oppenheim, Editorial, *The Seven Arts*, I, 52 (November 1916).
[2] *Ibid.*, pp. 52-53.

printed frequently. Other names were made known through critical discussion. Ernest Bloch and Leo Ornstein wrote on their music and Marsden Hartley on his painting. And various articles by the editors commented on little known European writers who have since become prominent.

But before we examine the exciting first number, let us glance at the editors.

James Oppenheim was the oldest of the motivating trio, all of whom —as most little magazine editors have been—were under thirty-five. Born in St. Paul, Minnesota, of financially well established Jewish parents, young Oppenheim soon moved to New York, where he lived the remainder of his life. When he was six years old his father died, and within a short time the family found itself in straitened circumstances. The bitter odds against which he gained a few years of extension work from Columbia University foreshadowed a life of misfortune. To keep alive, the poet was soon forced to write sentimental magazine stories, drudgery for a mythically inclined temperament. His serious need for expression had to find release at infrequent intervals until 1916. And so, when he was offered the opportunity of founding *The Seven Arts* with Waldo Frank, a joyous hope of release sprang up.[3] The magazine, richly subsidized by Mrs. A. K. Rankine, removed the haunting specter of poverty, promised a work which he could enjoy, and offered a yearly salary of around $5,000.[4] He took up his duties with enthusiasm.

Waldo Frank was a cofounder and the associate editor (in reality, managing editor)[5] of the magazine. Well educated, imaginative, and possessor of a good deal of practical newspaper experience accumulated after taking a Master's degree at Yale in 1911, Frank was to a large extent responsible for the form and direction of the magazine.[6] Van Wyck Brooks (who had not yet become an associate editor), Kahlil Gibran, Louis Untermeyer, Robert Frost, Edna Kenton, David Manners, and Robert Edmond Jones heartily seconded Oppenheim and Frank in their attempt to build up a magazine as *An Expression of Artists for the Community*.

In the initial issue, as in those to follow, there was a primary concern with critical material. Romain Rolland wrote on "America and the Arts," Peter Minuit examined the status of our architecture. "Lazy

[3] Dumas Malone, ed., *Dictionary of American Biography*, New York, 1934, XIV, pp. 46-47.
[4] Letter, Waldo Frank to Charles Allen, July 25, 1937 (unpublished).
[5] *Ibid.*, November 30, 1937.
[6] Fred B. Millett, *Contemporary American Authors*, New York, 1940, p. 360.

Verse" was severely censured by Oppenheim. Floyd Dell expressed his thoughts on "Shaw and Religion," Louis Untermeyer on the dance, and Paul Rosenfeld on "The American Composer." Van Wyck Brooks, Waldo Frank, and Allen Upward also wrote articles. Robert Frost, Jean Starr Untermeyer, Kahlil Gibran, and Amy Lowell contributed verse. Stories by Josephine Baker and Berry Bencfield, and Louise Driscoll's one-act play, "The Child of God," finished out the issue of 95 well printed pages—a somewhat smaller issue than the later average of 125 book-size leaves.

The Seven Arts group came together with the purpose of directing the new spirit towards an objective. America must slough off its terrifying preoccupation with material values, react against the emotional sterility, the imaginative barrenness which Edgar Lee Masters' *Spoon River Anthology* so clearly revealed.[7] Such new artists as Sherwood Anderson in this country, and John Davis Beresford and D. H. Lawrence in England, must develop. They must be capable of suggesting to an emotionally starved nation the possibilities of a richer way of life, the need for intuition, and poetic responsiveness. They must give to the nation's outlook a vision which would honor the complete man rather than the person whose single obsession was property and its value.[8]

*The Seven Arts* was knifed by war chauvinism and editorial conflict before it could find many of these artists, but the message was heard and from our vantage point we can see that the magazine influenced American letters and thought profoundly.

During the magazine's year of life there were no fewer than two dozen articles, poems, and editorials written by Oppenheim, Frank, and Brooks—all designed to drive home to the average of 5,000 buyers[9] the need for a new national art and life. Though the American scene was examined from different angles by these three men, their writings revealed a close correspondence of outlook. Brooks persuasively reiterated in his numerous arguments his central theme that "Our ancestral faith in the individual and what he is able to accomplish (or, in modern parlance, to 'put over') as the measure of all things has despoiled us of that instinctive human reverence for those divine reservoirs of collective experience, religion, science, art, philosophy, the self-subordi-

---

[7] Van Wyck Brooks, "Toward a National Culture," *The Seven Arts*, I, 538 (March 1917).
[8] Waldo Frank, "Vicarious Fiction," *The Seven Arts*, I, 302 (January 1917).
[9] Letter, Frank to Allen, July 25, 1937 (unpublished).

nating service to which is almost the measure of the highest happiness."[10] Frank, the cultured and prophetic rebel, found that America needed "above all things, spiritual adventure. It needs to be absorbed in a vital and virile art. It needs to be lifted above the hurry of details, to be loosed from the fixity of results."[11] Not quite as graceful as his two colleagues when it came to exposition, but just as sincere, Oppenheim aspired "as our fathers' fathers did, for something beyond ourselves, which we may love or hate, and to which we may so give ourselves that life acquires an interest, an intensity, a fine rigorous quality that tests us athletically and brings all our submerged powers into play. We aspire to be alive in every part of ourselves." All of these men agreed, too, in their hatred of absolute industrialism. Oppenheim expressed their common feeling when he cried, "Human nature has stronger and angrier hungers than an unrelieved industrialism can meet: and a race that has gone out time and again to suffer and to die for ideas and symbols, for abstract conceptions like 'freedom' and 'democracy,' for visions like that of the Grail and of God, cannot now be content alone with factory-work, or business, or the flat metallic taste of money."[12]

The call for spiritual revolution was linked with an advocacy of social revolution. The editors were definite socialists and among the first supporters of the new Russia, though, as Frank points out, this support was more lyrical than argumentative.

In addition to the heavy salvos of Oppenheim, Brooks, and Frank, there were hard-hitting articles by others who had already acquired some degree of fame. John Dewey wrote "In a Time of National Hesitation"; H. L. Mencken in one of his most brilliant moments exposed the inner thoughts of the supervirtuous who had counted the "lewd" words in Dreiser. Bertrand Russell wondered whether nationalism was moribund. The critic and aesthetician, Willard Huntington Wright (who later became famous as "S. S. Van Dine"), did several articles, and Carl Van Vechten had much to say about music. Dreiser, always ambitious for big things, made a long study of a wide subject: "Art, Life, and America." There was an article on the new artistic stirring in Spain; the author, a young unknown, signed himself "John R. Dos Passos."

With *The Seven Arts'* critical predilections in mind we can thoroughly understand the editors' admiration for the fiction of Lawrence,

---

[10] Brooks, "Toward a National Culture," p. 540.
[11] Frank, "Vicarious Fiction," p. 302.
[12] Oppenheim, Editorial, *The Seven Arts*, I, 504-505 (March 1917).

Anderson, and Beresford. These men may not have been the great artists which the magazine called for; but they were striving in the direction of greatness, probing into man's emotional make-up as well as into his intellect. Frank, in an appraisal of Anderson, held that his significance lay in the fact "that he suggests at last a presentation of life shot through with the searching color of truth, which is a signal for a native culture,"[13] a culture, the author goes ahead to insist, which could never have grown out of a purist intellectualism such as dominated Henry James. For James was too much content with probing man's intellect, representing intellect as the whole man.[14]

Neither Frank nor anyone else in *The Seven Arts* group claimed Lawrence or Anderson or Beresford as first-rate artists. What the editors did assert was that such writers pointed towards a complete understanding of man, an understanding which would take into account the human belly as well as the head—the instincts as well as the conscious reasoning. Frank made no claim for himself, of course, but he was attempting in his short stories much the same thing as Lawrence, Beresford, and Anderson.

Lawrence, Anderson, Frank, and Beresford were not titans, even in their *Seven Arts* period, but among the twenty-nine stories printed in the magazine we find ten of great merit written by these four men. There were "Bread Crumbs" and "Rudd" by Frank; Lawrence's "The Mortal Coil" and "The Thimble"; "Escape," "Little Town," and "Powers of the Air" by Beresford; and four of Anderson's powerful sketches: "Queer," "The Thinker," "Mother," and "The Untold Lie." These were the pieces that were largely responsible for bringing their authors to the American public consciousness.

Of the twenty-nine stories printed in *The Seven Arts* twenty-eight were considered distinctive by Edward J. O'Brien.[15] A *Seven Arts* discovery, Frederick Booth, helped build this imposing record. American letters lost one of its most promising young men when Booth left New York for Florida, was heard from only a few times after 1920, and finally completely vanished from the literary scene.

But before we leave the magazine's short story record let us have a look at its prime novelty, Eugene O'Neill's first short story, "Tomorrow." It is a good tale, despite the rather melodramatic structure. A young Scottish blueblood, Jimmy Anderson, marries an exquisite girl

---

[13] Frank, "Emerging Greatness," p. 73.  [14] *Ibid.*
[15] A calculation based on the ratings given in the 1916 and 1917 volumes of Edward J. O'Brien's *Best Short Stories*.

and goes with her and the British to subdue the Boers. Jimmy, returning one day from the interior, finds his young wife *flagrante delictu* with a staff officer, is heartbroken, deserts his moneyed family, becomes a drunkard, and, after many years of trying to catch again a vision of life's meaning, commits suicide. To be sure, this is a familiar framework, but the deft exploring of the sensitive, complicated Jimmy makes an acceptable story. Mr. O'Neill will not allow reprints of "Tomorrow," and this is too bad, for the tale deserves to be better known.

If *The Seven Arts* could have survived the war hurricane it might have continued indefinitely to urge its ideal of a new America. But the editors, particularly Oppenheim, stood in violent opposition to America's participation in the war. Oppenheim was fiery in his denunciation. He poured out one vitriolic editorial after another in favor of the American pipe dream of isolation from Continental squabbles; he encouraged John Reed and Randolph Bourne to write a series of articles carrying such titles as "This Unpopular War"; he defended *The Masses* against the espionage act; and finally, so hard-hitting was his attack, he brought down on his head the wrath of his magazine's sponsor, Mrs. Rankine. Convinced by her "proper" friends that the editors were pro-German (they were not), she withdrew her subsidy.[16]

"However, we could have gone on," Waldo Frank has said. "Many wealthy men and women, such as Scofield Thayer who later bought *The Dial*, urged us to continue and offered substantial help; but the insistence was that in this case Oppenheim should not be the titular editor, but all three of us together. Oppenheim refused to relinquish absolute authority in form. And on that, the thing foundered. My friends urged me to go on, without Oppenheim; but the draft and a severe illness prevented me from acting at once—and later on I agreed with Brooks that 'the time had come to write books.' My *Our America* [1919] was the first result of that withdrawal from the magazine field."[17]

Thus the magazine died with its task barely begun.

Oppenheim found himself socially ostracized, rapidly becoming a spiritual and physical wreck. Misfortune was again dogging his tracks; finally in 1932 he became seriously ill of tuberculosis.[18] During his black later life he must often have experienced a bleak depression of spirit as he saw the nation return to "normalcy," and advance the motto "two cars in every garage" as the highest ideal of civilization.

[16] Letter, Frank to Allen, November 30, 1937 (unpublished).
[17] *Ibid.*
[18] Malone, *Dictionary of American Biography*, xiv, pp. 46-47.

## III

Vienna, Berlin, Reutte, Brooklyn, New York—all played host to the group review *Secession*. Gorham Munson was editor, or Director, as he preferred to style himself, of the magazine's eight greatly discussed issues. From the spring of 1922 to the spring of 1924, *Secession* boisterously promoted such men as Wallace Stevens, Malcolm Cowley, Hart Crane, Waldo Frank, Slater Brown, Matthew Josephson, and Kenneth Burke—authors on an experimental tangent which appealed to Munson.[19] Though every writer published had appeared a few times previously in *The Dial* and other little magazines, it was *Secession* that drew like-minded American experimentalists under one banner, clarified and focused, and to some extent directed, a trend that had been indicated several years before by *Glebe* and *Others*.

*Secession*, edited by and for the new generation, was typical of many of the 1920 *tendenz* magazines. Like most of the group magazines it was a queer mixture of juvenility, arrogance, and good sense. Like many another, it throws light on the formative years of several writers now famous, and serves to crystallize the temper of a muddle-headed, high-spirited period.

Munson became interested in literary matters in 1916, while still at college. Inspired by *The Seven Arts*, and its introduction of Waldo Frank's and Van Wyck Brooks's work, the young man sought out the literati of Greenwich Village. It was not long before he fell under the influence of *Pagan* and *Little Review* talk and met Hart Crane.

Munson was still in New York in 1919,[20] deep in the intellectual confusion in which many of the young would-be writers found themselves. They were shouted at from all sides. Mencken advised seeing a circus, Hamilton Fish suggested catching a Red, Harding recommended normalcy. Then there was the new literature, more and more introverted and emotional. For the young writer these were the years of floundering indiscrimination, with ideas and attitudes quickly adopted and as quickly dropped. Munson in rapid succession was a socialist, "a supporter of the Soviets," an anarchist.[21] The "yewth" burnt their Racine in July, their Keats in October, their Dreiser and Anderson by Christmas. And when Dreiser and Anderson had been repudiated there was nothing to do but concoct a theory of one's own.

---

[19] Gorham Munson, "The Fledgling Years, 1916-1924," *The Sewanee Review*, XL, 31 (Spring 1932).

[20] *Ibid.*, p. 26.    [21] *Ibid.*, p. 28.

That was exactly what the youngsters did—with the help of the French.[22]

Harold Stearns had recommended the Café du Dôme.[23] There scintillating sparkle might start one on a good train of thought. Stearns sailed, beginning a hegira in which many of the young artists were to take part. Munson was one of the first to go. A few of them ran away with a pretended or real disgust for their native land;[24] most of them were simply seeking excitement and adventure.

The first foreign months brought Director Munson into the company of his old friend, Man Ray. Ray introduced Munson to most of the exiles, and to many of the French literati, particularly the dadaists.[25] And so Munson found himself ready to join in the great American sport of reforming letters, flinging insults, challenging opposing critics to fist fights, and founding little magazines.

It was Matthew Josephson who whetted Munson's latent desire for a review. And it was Malcolm Cowley who wrote the article which fired Munson with the idea of a *tendenz* review. Writing for the "Literary Review" of the *New York Evening Post*, Cowley pointed out that there were certain young writers, as yet but little known, all under twenty-five, who were diverging from the main stream of American letters. Cowley argued that "This Youngest Generation" needed to be brought together in a single magazine. Their influence would thereby spread, their thought clarify. The new rebels, Cowley suggested, were Kenneth Burke, E. E. Cummings, Dos Passos, Foster Damon, and Slater Brown. Munson saw that the idea was a good one, and he enlarged the list to include Cowley, Josephson, Hart Crane, Waldo Frank, William Carlos Williams, Wallace Stevens, Mark Turbyfill, Yvor Winters, and Marianne Moore, with a sprinkling of dadaists. *Secession* was founded not so much to find new writers as to sponsor a group, several of whom had first shown their hands in *Others*.

Munson was twenty-six in 1922. He was just a trifle too solemn to enter wholeheartedly into the boisterous life of the exiled Americans. He may have been a little bewildered by some of his fellow exiles' avocations. It was while "following the dollar," as young Malcolm Cowley merrily had called it,[26] that Munson decided to start a magazine. Where the dollar bought the most, Vienna, was naturally the best

[22] *Ibid.*, p. 46.   [23] *Ibid.*, p. 27.
[24] Parry, *Garrets and Pretenders*, pp. 331-32.
[25] Munson, "Fledgling Years," pp. 28-29.
[26] Cowley, *Exile's Return*, p. 92.

## THE "TENDENZ" MAGAZINE

place to begin. He took a dingy hotel room, and with the very considerable help of Josephson, began editing *Secession*. The first issue cost $20.[27]

But before we plunge into the whirling secessionist scene—before we consider Munson's accusation that Matthew Josephson was a literary fakir, before we judge the charge that Malcolm Cowley was a betraying rapscallion, and before we decide once and for all who won the famous Munson-Josephson fisticuffs match at Woodstock, we had better take a closer look at the literary philosophy held by the group.

In 1928 Munson brought out *Destinations, A Canvass of American Literature Since 1900*. This analysis divides our modern letters into three main streams. There was the "Elder Generation," represented by the neoclassic critics, Irving Babbitt and Paul Elmer More.[28] The "Middle Generation" found its impetus in such spirits as Mencken, Dreiser, Sherwood Anderson, and Carl Sandburg, all, according to Munson, "romantic emotionalists," all reacting against a neoclassical humanism and against the Gene Stratton Porter sentimentalism which dominated the Mauve Decade and the fifteen years following. *Secession* was designed to sponsor the more intellectual "Younger Generation," men of various philosophical outlooks, but bound together by an interest in fine craftsmanship and by their reaction against a blatant emotionalism.[29] This younger crowd, including most of the *Secession* names we have mentioned, might also claim such writers as Ernest Hemingway, Glenway Wescott, and Allen Tate. *Secession*, in seceding from the "Middle Generation," promised a group that was to be the "Maker of a Rainbow."[30]

The first issue made a splendid beginning. The 22 well printed, book-size leaves contained work by Malcolm Cowley, Louis Aragon, Apollinaire, Will Bray (Josephson's pen name), Tristan Tzara, and an article by Munson attacking *The Dial*'s "aimless catholicity." In "A Bow to the Adventurous" the Director set forth rather cockily the magazine's purpose. We quote the last paragraph: "*Secession* exists for those writers who are preoccupied with researches for new forms. It hopes that there is ready for it an American public which has advanced beyond the fiction and poetry of Sinclair Lewis and Sherwood Anderson and the criticism of Paul Rosenfeld and Louis Untermeyer."[31]

[27] Munson, op. cit., p. 31.
[28] Munson, *Destinations: A Canvass of American Literature Since 1900*, New York, 1928, p. 2.
[29] *Ibid.*, p. 3.   [30] *Ibid.*, p. 5.
[31] Munson, "A Bow to the Adventurous," *Secession*, I, 19 (April 1922).

The editor also explained his theory that *Secession* should be discontinued after two years.[32] Two years, five years, the time element varies, but there is no question that most little magazines do have a limited period of usefulness. Editors are prone to lose their rebel spirit or fail to realize when their job is accomplished.

July saw the appearance of the second number, an amusing concoction of high seriousness, comedy, and satirical impertinence, including poems by Cowley, E. E. Cummings, a cover design by Ludwig Kassák, stories by Josephson and Burke, and an article by Slater Brown.

Munson, in this second number, made pertinent observations on magazines: "Interstice between Scylla and Charybdis" classified the little magazines into three types: personal, anthological, and group. The personal magazine, represented by *The Little Review*, "displays the personal weaknesses of its editors: an aggressiveness often resulting from insufficient education, a combative recognition of stupidities it is better to ignore than to waste energy upon, an insufficient respect for the value of literary traditions, general uncertainty as to just where they are sitting or where they are going next, a haphazard taste, a tendency to be imposed upon by a blindalley strangeness. . . .

"The usual occupant of the editorial chair of a personal magazine is a mental gypsy, picturesque, enlivening—undisciplined, indiscriminating."[33]

Then there was the anthology classification. *Broom* was selected as the horrible example: "*Broom* joined the anthology classification. Its doing so was the final disappointment which made *Secession* inevitable. It accepted the principle of the general merchandise store. Have everything in stock, what one customer doesn't want, another will."[34] Of course the group magazine was the thing. "It [*Secession*] will make group-exclusions, found itself on a group-basis, point itself in a group-direction, and derive its stability and correctives from a group."[35]

Came midsummer and Munson decided to go back to America. A co-editor was needed to handle the European affairs. Josephson was naturally selected, for he had helped in the arrangements for starting the review and had supplied well over half the writing for the first two issues. And a third editor was necessary in order that any disagreement might be settled by vote. Kenneth Burke, Josephson's friend, was

---

[32] Munson, "Fledgling Years," p. 33.
[33] Munson, "Interstice between Scylla and Charybdis," *Secession*, II, 31-32 (July 1922).
[34] *Ibid.*, pp. 30-31.   [35] *Ibid.*, p. 32.

selected, his services to begin with the fourth issue.[36] In 1922 and '23 Burke was one of our most promising literary figures. He was publishing in *Secession* and *Broom* the exotic fantasies that were to appear in 1924 in *The White Oxen and Other Stories*; and in several other little magazines, particularly *The Dial*, he was printing the first of his brilliant technical analyses. And so Munson sailed for America, leaving the selection of manuscripts for the August number entirely to Josephson.[37]

The August number carried a Josephson story, "Peep-Peep-Parish," previously refused by Munson. (Josephson says he never heard of Munson's refusal of the story.) This, and the fact that Josephson did not admit in the masthead full responsibility for the number, seems to have disturbed the Director a little, but on the whole the contents were acceptable, including work by Waldo Frank, Burke, Cowley, and Phillipe Soupault—"a lively issue," as Munson called it.[38]

*Secession* was now a success in Munson's estimation. It was a magazine which cost an average of $25 an issue. These issues did not run over 32 pages, never sold many over 150 copies (about 350 copies were distributed gratis)[39] but managed, as their editor intended they should, to stir up controversy. From the first many of the 500 copies found their way into the right hands. Free magazines were sent to literary people in order that the influence on writing might be greater.[40] *Secession* undoubtedly "influenced"—at least to the extent of provoking furious talk. *The Nation, The Dial, The Double Dealer, The Little Review, The Nation and Athenaeum*, the *New York Times*, and T. S. Eliot's newly founded *Criterion* reviewed every number at length. The Director was feeling pretty good, never better than just before the fourth installment appeared.

But he was fighting mad when he saw the fourth issue on a January morning in 1923. Several poems and stories from such persons as Wallace Stevens, Richard Ashton, Hart Crane, Slater Brown, and William Carlos Williams had been forwarded to Josephson in Berlin. According to Munson, Josephson wrote objecting to Ashton's poems, and had been outvoted by Burke and Munson.[41] Josephson in a frisky mood revenged himself by changing one of the Ashton hundred-line masterpieces to a three-line aphorism.[42] This episode of the fourth issue rankled deep in Munson's breast, and was the beginning of open war-

[36] Munson, "Fledgling Years," p. 36.
[37] *Ibid.*, p. 35.   [38] *Ibid.*
[39] Letter, Gorham Munson to Charles Allen, August 26, 1937 (unpublished).
[40] Munson, "Fledgling Years," p. 36.   [41] *Ibid.*, p. 39.
[42] Letter, Matthew Josephson to Charles Allen, April 26, 1938 (unpublished).

fare between the two men. It was about this time that Josephson took a job with *Broom*.[43]

Following the breakup the editors were without a European representative, and *Secession* did not appear again for several months. In the meantime Munson and Burke spread stories to the effect that Josephson was "an intellectual fakir" and discussed Paul Elmer More's dualism as "a unity through a balance of conflicting parts."[44]

Meanwhile *Broom*'s new editor was brewing big poison in Paris and Rome, with the co-operation of the young dadaist, Malcolm Cowley. It was an enormous plot that they boiled and their opportunity came when Burke and Munson finally sent over their material for the fifth number. A young Bostonian, John Brooks Wheelwright, was the *Secession* emissary, having agreed to see the magazine printed while visiting in Italy. Cowley and Josephson caught Wheelwright near Paris and convinced him that the manuscripts sent over by Munson and Burke should be largely discarded in favor of material chosen by Cowley and Josephson. At least this is Munson's story as he told it in the Spring 1932 issue of *The Sewanee Review*. The New Yorkers were mightily amazed when they saw the resulting *Secession*. Not only had stories and articles which New York had never seen been slipped in, but Hart Crane's "To Faustus and Helen" was so badly damaged that it had to be excised.[45]

The charge of intercepting manuscripts and damaging "Faustus and Helen" has been denied by Josephson. He says in a letter to Charles Allen, "I don't remember intercepting manuscripts sent to Europe by Wheelwright. It is quite possible that Cowley and I out-voted Munson, who was 3,000 miles away. Weren't we editors too?"[46] Josephson was no longer an editor, and Cowley never had been, nor was to be. Josephson was something of a dadaist, adhering pretty strongly to the "nothing too serious" article of the dada credo. As Munson has charged, Josephson and Cowley probably prided themselves on their deceptiveness. This is suggested by a statement of Josephson's to Charles Allen: "We were, some of us, young sparks, and not a little malicious to each other. We thought Munson, because of his enthusiasm—but also because of his imposing, waxed, handlebar moustaches—might be of great aid to our cause. As to his poor judgment in literary matters, we thought that could be remedied by management. Naturally Munson,

---

[43] Letter, Josephson to Allen, July 25, 1944 (unpublished).
[44] Munson, "Fledgling Years," pp. 41, 49.    [45] *Ibid.*, pp. 42-43.
[46] Letter, Josephson to Allen, July 25, 1944 (unpublished).

who is a man of spirit and determination, resented such an attitude once it became evident to him."[47] As to the charge that "Faustus and Helen" was mutilated, Josephine has this to say: "Crane sent me his poem for *Broom*, which I liked, set up, and printed, in *Secession* as usual two months ahead of shipping time (by freight). Then he went into tantrums, revised it extensively, wrote a poem of equal length which was to precede it as Part One, and sent me letters weeks after everything was shipped away (printed), asking me to stop press and change everything around. It was a misunderstanding pure and simple; Crane realized this afterward, and we were very good friends later. He came to see me often, and also made a ten mile trip to my house to say good-bye to me before he left on his last journey to Mexico."[48]

The contradictory stories regarding the fifth number are representative of the squabbles that surrounded the publication of the sixth issue. It was a gloomy time for the Director.

Several months before *Secession* died in the spring of 1924, the exiles began streaming back to New York. Along came those two menaces to American letters, Cowley and Josephson, dragging their newly acquired *Broom* behind them. The last months of both periodicals were exciting; fire-spitting was the order of the day.

The growing animosity finally came to a violent and amusing climax in the fall of 1923. Munson, in the late fall, went up to Woodstock, New York, to recover from an illness. While in Woodstock he received a Cowley letter urging attendance at a forthcoming "Younger Generation" meeting. A group of *Secession* and *Broom* contributors would get together and do something about their elders, and they would decide something about *Broom*.[49] Cowley did not know quite what, as he explains in *Exile's Return*:

"We planned, for example, to hire a theatre some afternoon and give a literary entertainment, with violent and profane attacks on the most famous contemporary writers, courts-martial of the more prominent critics, burlesques of Sherwood Anderson, Floyd Dell, Paul Rosenfeld and others—all this interspersed with card tricks, solos on the jew's harp, meaningless dialogues and whatever else would show our contempt for the audience and the sanctity of American letters. We planned to pass out handbills in the theatrical district and make defamatory soap-box orations in Union Square. We planned to continue *Broom* as long as its capital or credit lasted. . . ."[50]

[47] *Ibid.*   [48] *Ibid.*   [49] Cowley, op. cit., pp. 189-90.
[50] *Ibid.*, p. 190.

Munson refused to attend this meeting on the plea of inconvenience; consequently Cowley asked for a written message, to be read at the meeting. Munson sent a letter condemning the group for a lack of purpose and for allowing Josephson and Harold Loeb to associate with it.[51] In his *Sewanee Review* article on his generation and on *Secession*, Munson writes: "I had come to regard Josephson as a literary opportunist, an example of last minutism, a kind of stage player in the arts, to adapt a phrase of Nietzsche. I said these things with emphasis and called him an intellectual fakir. . . . I therefore declined to participate in any group which contained so vulnerable a member."[52]

Cowley insists this letter was written in near blank verse, which he read "with all the intonations of a blue-jawed actor reciting a Hamlet soliloquy." The reading threw *Broom's* party into a half-serious, half-humorous fit. Munson's supporters cried that the rendering was unfair; the other side of the table snorted back that Munson was getting off too easily. Hart Crane and Josephson flew into a violent argument. Glenway Wescott went home. Everybody shouted.[53] Josephson was in such a rage that he vowed a great vengeance. The anticlimax came when Josephson decided to act on his threat. Munson was still at Woodstock, staying with William Murrell Fisher; Josephson was temporarily encamped with Slater Brown and Edward Nagle, a few minutes away from the Fisher cottage. One afternoon Josephson stormed over to the Fishers' and demanded that Munson come out for a fight. Outside the mud was deep and the day was cold, and the Director was loath to fight; yet fight he must, for Josephson was full of accumulated rage. The strange battle began with both men out of training. They were winded so quickly that the proceedings ended as an inconclusive draw, with the adversaries gasping for breath. (Josephson insists that this squabble was more of a "lark" than a serious brawl.)[54]

Clear at last of "the peanut policies in which Cowley and some of his friends were trying to embroil *Secession*,"[55] Munson brought out the last two issues of his magazine but without the help of Burke. Number Seven included "For the Marriage of Faustus and Helen" by Hart Crane, Waldo Frank's "For a Declaration of War," a Burke story, and several poems by Yvor Winters. The eighth issue, coming at the end of

[51] *Ibid.*
[52] Munson, "Fledgling Years," p. 49.
[53] Cowley, op. cit., pp. 191-92.
[54] This interpretation is based on letters from Josephson to Allen, March 9, 1938; from Munson to Allen, January 29, 1939; and "Fledgling Years," pp. 50-52.
[55] Munson, "Fledgling Years," p. 45.

the two-year period *Secession* had marked for itself, was devoted entirely to Winter's discussion of poetic theory.

In a "Post Mortem" Munson summed up what he thought were *Secession's* accomplishments: "The stories of Kenneth Burke in which an important theory of fiction is worked to unprecedented discoveries; several poems by Malcolm Cowley which are assured of preservation in anthologies; the fierce satiric poetry of Cummings; 'Faustus and Helen' by Hart Crane; the verse doctrine of Yvor Winters, a manifesto by Waldo Frank which is the most important statement of aims since Whitman's announcements; these are some of the claims of *Secession* to distinction. The decade promises to be full of action in the literary arts. *Secession* perhaps will be known as the magazine that introduced the Twenties."[56]

Looking back on *Secession* we are inclined to believe that it did not give us the "most important statement of aims since Whitman," and that it did not "introduce the Twenties." We are inclined to believe that it was not an important magazine in any revolutionary sense. Its critical formulations, though crystallizing a tendency, were not the first American statements of secessionism. The review discovered no new writers. But *Secession* was important in the sense that it reinforced and strengthened the rebel fight against the sentimental genteel tradition.

This is partly the reason for considering *Secession* at some length. The other reason for considering it is that with its fights, with its irregular appearances, with its financial struggles, with its subtle admixture of seriousness and juvenility, it helps clarify the giddy aspect of the little magazine story.

## IV

"What of it, if some old hunks of a Sea-captain orders me to get a broom and sweep down the decks? What does that indignity amount to, weighed, I mean, in the scales of the New Testament? Do you think the Archangel Gabriel thinks anything the less of me, because I promptly and respectfully obey that old hunks in that particular instance? Who ain't a slave?"[57]

[56] Munson, "Post-Mortem," a mimeographed sheet included in the bound volume of *Secession*, Spring 1924.

[57] A quotation from Herman Melville's *Moby Dick*. *Broom*, I, back cover (November 1921).

*Broom, Secession, Secession, Broom*—the mention of one suggests the other. Both reviews were products of the half-serious, half-playboy early twenties, and both, for the major span of their short lives, were exiles from their native shore. And, as we have seen, each was the sworn enemy of the other.

But more vital similarity is apparent as we turn the pages of these rival magazines. *Broom* asserted a catholic, eclectic interest in literature; it would publish any good writing, European or American, if the author were little known or unappreciated.[58] *Secession*, on the other hand, professed to be interested in a group, by and large an American group. Actually, however, *Broom's* catholic taste was more talk than action. *Broom* tended to exhibit, especially in its later period, the same literary outlook as *Secession*. Such men as Malcolm Cowley, Hart Crane, and Matthew Josephson were to be found in both periodicals. In the main, *Broom* and *Secession* tell identical stories; taken together they clarify one chapter of little magazine history, and one chapter of our recent literary development.

*Broom* was definitely a magazine of periods. There was the Rome Period, lasting from the magazine's inception in November 1921, until November 1922. Then came a short Berlin sojourn. By March of 1923 *Broom* was preparing to go to New York, ready to heckle America with dada tactics, and to carry on a lively fight with *Secession* and the censors. *Broom* did not win a single skirmish in America, for America would not be heckled, *Secession* would not be cowed, nor the censoring authorities banished from the land. But for the moment let us look to the prenatal days of *Broom* when Harold Loeb and Alfred Kreymborg were talking in Manhattan.

In the late twenties Harold Loeb was regarded as a promising young novelist. In 1920, he was one of the proprietors of the Sunwise Turn Bookshop, located in New York's Yale-Princeton Building.[59] The bookshop sometimes published books and one of the books brought out was a volume of Alfred Kreymborg's plays. So began Loeb's friendship with the erstwhile editor and publisher of *Others*. Naturally, the possibilities of a little magazine were explored. Loeb soon found himself attempting to convert the lukewarm interest of Kreymborg to enthusiasm; Kreymborg, knowing the labor involved in publishing a little magazine, was hesitant. Finally, after Loeb had promised to finance both the magazine and Kreymborg, Kreymborg agreed to share editorial responsibility

[58] "Manifesto I," *Broom*, I, inside back cover (November 1921).
[59] Letter, Harold Loeb to Allen, February 9, 1938 (unpublished).

with Loeb.[60] Loeb sold his partnership in the Sunwise Turn. *Broom* was under way.

The year 1921 was a busy one for the Broomsters. There were manifestoes to write and circulate, publicity campaigns to prepare, writers to interview, manuscripts to collect, and arrangements to be made in Italy, where it was decided to publish the review because of the excellent paper and typographical work that could be obtained there at less than a fourth of the American cost. Loeb early hit upon the title of *Broom*, and this, along with Kreymborg's association with the magazine, titillated the curiosity of the literary world. The periodical was both well known and well thought of before it made its luxurious bow to the world in November 1921.[61]

For it was elaborate, this *Broom*, a "sumptuous" affair, as Kreymborg would have described it, heavy of weight, rich in color, fine in binding and printing; nothing quite like its aristocratic format had ever been seen in America. Fabriano paper was used to carry the printing and reproductions. And "sumptuous" too was the *Broom* editorial office, or rather, palace—a palace rented from a princess of the royal family, and commanding a view of half of Rome. From spacious balconies the editors—by now including Edward Storer and Giuseppe Prezzolini as associates—and their famous artist guests were wont to have afternoon tea and gaze with "chastened" eyes out over the Villa Borghese, the gardens of the Pincio, St. Peter's, and the house in which John Keats had died.[62] A strange setting for a little magazine editorial office.

The first issue of the review was certainly a success in pageantry, a success which was due in no small degree to the Italian associate of the magazine, Giuseppe Prezzolini, who had carefully overseen the periodical's manufacture. There were 96 *Esquire*-size pages, and it was fairly typical, both as to format and content, of all the European numbers. There were elaborate reproductions of the work of such European modernist artists as Stravinsky, André Derain, Juan Gris, Albert Gleizes, Bepi Fabiano, Jacques Lipchitz and William Gropper; there were stories by J. D. Beresford, Donald Corley, and Haniel Long; and there was a great deal of poetry from Amy Lowell, James Oppenheim, Walter de la Mare, Lola Ridge, Edwin Arlington Robinson, Ezra Pound, Maxwell Bodenheim, Robert Frost, and Kreymborg. This issue, like most of the European numbers that followed, cost only $500, in-

[60] Kreymborg, *Troubadour*, pp. 360-61.
[61] *Ibid.*, pp. 361-75.
[62] *Ibid.*, p. 374.

cluding payment to the contributing authors.[63] The review sold for 50 cents a copy, $5.00 a year.

*Broom*, on the cover of that first issue, carried the subheading "An International Magazine of the Arts." Its eclectic intentions were announced in Manifesto I:

"*Broom* is selecting from the continental literature of the present time the writings of exceptional quality most adaptable for translation into English.

"These will appear side by side with the contemporaneous effort in Great Britain and America.

"The painters and sculptors will be represented by the best available reproductions of their work.

"Throughout, the unknown, path-breaking artist will have, when his material merits it, at least an equal chance with the artist of acknowledged reputation.

"In brief, *Broom* is a sort of clearing house where the artists of the present time will be brought into closer contact."[64]

The contents that *Broom* presented during its European stay do not belie the claim made in the subtitle and the above manifesto; *Broom* was, throughout its European experience, pre-eminently international in tone, as have been most of the experimental magazines.

The policy was to be catholic, as is implied in the last paragraph of the manifesto. Both conventional and experimental writers were to be presented—that was the plan. But talk and actual practice are likely to be two different things. The conventional writers were always in the minority after the first issue, as they were in most of the other little magazines that stressed internationalism. Experimentalists dominated the periodical. Such *Broom* contributors as Malcolm Cowley, Matthew Josephson, William Carlos Williams, John Dos Passos, E. E. Cummings, Jean Cocteau, Luigi Pirandello, Gertrude Stein, Kay Boyle, Jean Toomer, and Hart Crane were interested in form and words, in an intellectual approach as against the emotional. They were following the middle generation standard of *Secession*.

Of the contributors Hart Crane deserves special mention, for *Broom* and *Secession*, and other similar experimental periodicals, such as *Bruno's Bohemia* (which first published Crane in 1915), *The Little Review* (which did more than any other magazine to establish his

[63] Letter, Loeb to Allen, February 9, 1938 (unpublished).
[64] "Manifesto I," *Broom*.

reputation), and *The Fugitive, The Double Dealer, Measure, S 4 N, The Pagan,* and *The Modernist* were about the only outlets that Crane could find for his mystically enraptured verse until the publication of the "metaphysical" *White Buildings* in 1926. At the time of *Broom* and *Secession,* Crane had outgrown his attachment to imagism and had begun to master the passionate rhythms, explosive sounds, and hard tensions of thought and tone which were to come to such a magnificent culmination in *The Bridge.*

It is unnecessary to follow *Broom* from issue to issue. There were few dramatic moments while the review remained abroad—excitement came after Matthew Josephson obtained $4,000 to back the review and moved it to New York. Kreymborg resigned as co-editor in February 1922, the break coming over a disagreement as to whether American or European experimentalists were to be stressed, Kreymborg favoring the former.[65] Lola Ridge, an inveterate contributor to little magazines, and an associate with Kreymborg during the last year of *Others,* became an editor of *Broom* for a time. Later, Matthew Josephson began his work with the magazine as associate editor and superintended the magazine's removal to Berlin in November 1922. After four issues in Berlin, Loeb's surplus funds were depleted.[66] *Broom* was threatened with extinction in spite of the fact that it had built a sizable paid circulation of around 4,000.[67] Loeb gave up and went to Paris to write novels. Josephson, to whom *Broom* was given, sailed for America with his newly acquired magazine.

What had *Broom* accomplished while in Europe? Broadly speaking, it introduced unknown or little known European writers and painters to America. *Broom* first presented Pirandello to the English-reading world. When Edward Storer and Loeb received permission to present *Six Characters in Search of an Author,* the review undoubtedly hit its high-water mark. The reproduction of paintings by such men as Picasso was also an important accomplishment. It was influential, too, along with *The Dial* and *Secession,* in helping to establish the reputations of several young experimental Americans.

Josephson and Cowley landed in New York, hoping to set off the fuse of the rambunctious Paris dada spirit, but they soon found themselves too worried about money matters, censors, and Gorham Munson to stir up much noise. As we have seen, the one serious attempt to get

---

[65] Kreymborg, *Troubadour,* pp. 380-81.
[66] Letter, Loeb to Allen, February 9, 1938 (unpublished).
[67] Letter, Josephson to Allen, July 25, 1944 (unpublished).

a dada show under way failed because of the quarrel which followed Cowley's reading of Munson's letter.[68]

The harried *Broom* lasted for only five New York issues. These numbers, greatly reduced in size as compared with the European magazine, came in August, September, October, and November of 1923, and a last one in January 1924, which was never distributed because of the postal censors. Editor Josephson, along with his associates Cowley and Slater Brown, managed to find about $500 a month for the magazine; the printer, who happened to be Josephson's brother-in-law, generously contributed the remainder.[69]

*Broom* did not change its editorial policy under Josephson's management. A good number of European names fraternized with the American experimentalists while the magazine was in New York. No important discoveries were made, although a couple of "fantastics" were first printed. There was the "difficult" Joe Gould, who was first published by *Broom*. Once, after a bitter exchange of letters, he challenged Josephson to a duel.[70] Then there was Charles L. Durboraw, a Chicago paperhanger, who contributed a story called "An Awful Storming Fire, of Her and I on a Journey to the Secret of the Sun, by the Author Who Solved the Mysterious Riddle," printed in the November 1923 issue. This story aroused the ire of "Mr. Smith," the Post Office censor. "Mr. Smith" found "An Awful Storming Fire" after *Broom* had been mailed and he threatened to read the next number before it reached the mail.[71] This he did. He found in the January number a philosophical narrative, "Prince Llan," by Kenneth Burke, which mentioned a "plural breasted woman." That was enough for Mr. Smith. *Broom* was banned from the mail under Section 480 of the Postal Laws. The censoring proved more than the tired nerves and the depleted pocketbooks of the editors could stand.[72] Cowley, who was largely responsible for financing this last number, had worked for over a month borrowing the necessary money to put out the issue. It had been the editors' hope that this number of the magazine would net enough money to allow for further publication, but they now became convinced that the fight was useless.[73]

*Broom* was not an important magazine in the sense that *The Little Review, The Midland, Poetry, transition,* and *The Dial* were important.

[68] Cowley, op. cit., p. 191.
[69] Letter, Josephson to Allen, March 9, 1938 (unpublished).
[70] Ibid.   [71] Cowley, op. cit., pp. 194-95.
[72] Ibid., p. 204.   [73] Ibid.

It was not particularly pioneering. The idea of an international magazine of the arts, introducing at once experimental European and American artists, had first been fostered by Margaret Anderson and later developed by *The Dial*. *Broom* did not, as we have seen, introduce any important writers, though it played its part, along with *The Dial* and *Secession*, in firmly establishing several reputations. *Broom's* importance lies in the fact that it was in the vanguard of an intellectual movement, in the fact that it helped win the fight against the sentimentalities of the genteel tradition.

### V

The stories of *Broom*, *Secession*, and *S 4 N* are in many ways representative of a large majority of the six or seven hundred periodicals that have existed since around 1900. Perhaps these magazines, with their exotic flamboyancy, suggest to most people the typical little magazine. For to most critics, the little magazine spells evanescence, irregular appearance, ill-bred noise-making, ludicrous editorial squabbles, a misty combination of serious endeavor and irresponsible horseplay—in short, an amusing but disturbing spectacle. This is Alfred Kazin's view in his *On Native Grounds*, and it is the estimate of all our other literary historians. That this attitude of disparagement and humorous dismissal is not altogether justified is indubitably proved by the records of *Poetry*, *The Fugitive*, *The Hound and Horn*, *The Dial*, and several other distinguished and well mannered periodicals.

The amazing intellect of Kenneth Burke may well serve as an introduction to *S 4 N*, for he was associated in several ways with the men of *Secession* and *Broom*. Of all critics, Burke was best endowed for the task of handling the rapid transfer of ideas from tradition to experiment. Machinery and the subconscious were in effect cluttering up the intellectual pattern, the one gleaming, the other glowering, in their respective corners. Munson is proud of Burke's achievement in *Secession*, the development of a new "theory of fiction" which is worked to "unprecedented discoveries." Burke's fiction is comparatively unknown. His stories are a cross section of the materials of an artist whose mind grasps instantly both the concrete and the abstract values of any idea. This is the reason for their being tremendous theoretical successes and actual failures; for the narrative form and style fares poorly when it is overweighted by the constant burden of theory. But an assessment of Burke the critic—and he is one of the best modern critics—must begin with a study of the assortment of "demonstrations" which constitute his original contribution to *Secession* and *S 4 N*.

*S 4 N*, like *Secession*, was founded upon the conviction that opposing points of view would by an alchemy of the spirit produce a cultural unity: "That out of a comparison of opposed viewpoints (with attendant attacks and counter-attacks, and with subsequent experimentations and reactive critiques) comes aesthetic progress." This deliberate opposing of points of view resulted in a fascinating variety of essays, stories, and poems, but did not account for the fact that where views differ, personalities might also clash. Such is the sad and final realization of the magazine's editor in the last number; dissatisfaction among members of the editorial board had made a continuation of the magazine unlikely. During its career, many lively critical articles were published, some of them written by former editors of *Secession* and *Broom*; some original writing (such as Cummings' satirical poem, "Beauty Hurts Mr. Vinal") also found its way to its pages. Something in the nature of a summary of *tendenz* writing is to be found in the double number of September 1923-January 1924, which was given over entirely to essays on the work of Waldo Frank. Frank's place among the critics of the twenties was high; and this survey of his work is valuable at least in indicating the high regard with which he was considered.

These magazines—*The Seven Arts, Broom, Secession,* and *S 4 N*—point to a fact both interesting and disturbing. In their various ways they suggested that the need for revaluation of our culture was urgent. But their offerings were so often hindered by personal difficulties and indiscretions that they generally failed to furnish a sure or even an intelligent directive. *The Seven Arts* was perhaps the most consistently well edited and offered the best organization of critical and philosophical thought in our generation. All of these magazines, however, illustrate the search for a new intellectual and cultural incentive and for some form of synthesis of the tendencies of our time.

# MODERN POETRY
## and the Little Magazine

### CHAPTER VII

Perhaps more than anywhere else, experiment in the twenties was reflected in the forms poetry assumed and in the poet's campaign against traditional metrics and forms. Ezra Pound's principal battle in the early years of *Poetry* and *The Little Review* was against the "prosaic" in poetry; and he regarded the traditional respect for rhyme, stanzaic pattern, and metrics as barriers to true poetic understanding. The reasons for the poet's revolt are not hard to find; within certain limits, and with certain qualification, they thought of the science of versification as another of the barriers which tradition had set up against individualist expression and experiment.

Our modern poets in the main looked upon the mass of Romantic verse as damaged both in form and in purpose by the requirement that the poet be insincere—that is, that he frequently substitute a conventional or traditional feeling for things for his more direct or more complex comprehension of them. Much poetry had turned out to be preaching but thinly disguised as versified sentiment. This over-all objection to the influence of traditionalism upon poetic speech was directed especially against those poets whose sentiment was not only traditional but also "literary"—that is, who borrowed their sentiments from books. This is what caused Pound to say to Harriet Monroe: "Every *literaryism*, every book word, fritters away a scrap of the reader's patience, a scrap of his sense of your sincerity. When one really feels and thinks, one stammers with simple speech. It is only in the flurry, the shallow frothy excitement of writing, or the inebriety of a metre, that one falls into the easy, easy—oh, how easy!—speech of books and poems that one has read."[1]

[1] Quoted by Monroe, *A Poet's Life*, p. 267.

Another, related, problem which the modern poet considered in his war on tradition was that of the "structural cliché." In the eyes of many of our poets, structural conservatism was associated with artificiality of sentiment. That is, the balance of rhyme, meter, and stanza with the poet's sentiment seemed to foster an insincerity of thought and emotion. Thus, the experimental attitude was directed against the platitude which the regularity of metrical pattern defended against any "barbarous" interference. Critics of twentieth century literature point often to its preoccupation with form and technique and its neglect of content. In a sense this was true because the modern poet was very sensitive to the limits of traditional and conservative communication. In his eyes traditional poets did not wish to speak for themselves; they simply wished to hand back what they had already received, wrapped in a neat package and tied with old string. Distrust of conservative versification had a beginning in the larger distrust of conservative thought and the compact regularity of trite sentiment. Form and content were inseparable for the rebel; and the language of the conservative impressed him as being the servant of insincerity.

Of course, each period of literary history has its share of experiment in form and technique. But it was natural enough for poets of the twentieth century to look about for some means of breaking the tyranny of sentiment which seemed to them to be the major barrier to genuine poetic expression. It was not so much the artificial limits which any literary form places upon a writer's materials: these limits are in a sense the watermark of the arts. Rather, it seemed that sweet expressions found too comfortable a nest provided for them. The writing of poetry had become too maternal; it lacked vigor. What E. A. Robinson had said in the 1890's seems to be a wish which all young poets possessed. Robinson had pleaded for

> ... a beacon bright
> To rift this changeless glimmer of dead gray,
> To put these little sonnet men to flight
> Who fashion in a shrewd mechanic way
> Songs without souls, that flicker for a day,
> To vanish in irrevocable night.[2]

[2] E. A. Robinson, "Sonnet," *Sonnets*, New York, 1928, p. 21.

## II

In order to oust the platitude from literature, the modern poet suggested several reforms in metrics and a restatement of the values of the metaphor. He sought most of all to avoid the cliché and the commonplace. He believed that the simple logic of declamation and the simple correspondence of the decorative simile were false leads, giving the reader the mistaken impression that tradition was flawless and luminous, like a Watteau canvas.

The controversy over imagism and free verse was only a preliminary scuffle. Imagism was designed to give the poet respect for the purity of an image, to force him to give up many of his stock notions of beauty and sentiment. To hold the image within the limits of essential being; to avoid external or artificial references to the "meaning" of the image; to affirm always that "Poetry should not mean, but be": these are the minima of imagist poetry. And they had been stated and illustrated by the predecessor of imagism, the British intellectual, T. E. Hulme, who died in the First World War, in 1917, and did not therefore live to pass upon the use of his suggestions and principles. Hulme had written only five poems in his life, but they were admirable examples of what the imagists wanted to do. Hulme's interest in some reform of poetic usage was often demonstrated in conversations he had with F. S. Flint and others in London. From these talks, and in Hulme's essays on poetry, the gospel of imagism was formulated. And in the pages of the London *Egoist*, Harriet Monroe's *Poetry*, and other magazines of the second decade (as we have already shown), the principles of imagism were stated and restated, illustrated and advanced.

The results are no longer very impressive. Imagism seems to have been another attempt on the part of practicing poets to defend (and, perhaps, to advertise) what they were doing. But imagism was not without its lasting effect upon poetic practice. Its chief influence was its assertion of the visual quality in experience and its tenacious guardianship of the pure image against the incursion of extraneous, extrapoetic materials—reflections and effusions which destroy the precise outlines of a sensory experience. Allowance is made, of course, for the fact that no sensory experience is without its intellectual accompaniment; a percept without a concept is empty. The full nature of the image is well expressed in Ezra Pound's definition: the image is "that which presents an intellectual and emotional complex in an instant of time."

The advocates of free verse attacked the problem from a similar point of view. The *vers librist* was above all indignant over the suggestion that his verse was formless. He insisted that the form of any expression is implicit in the nature of the poet's attitude toward what he wanted to say—that a pattern resided within, was not superimposed upon, the poetic material. There was neither logic nor aesthetic value in fixed forms. They worked against sincerity of expression by announcing beforehand the form which it was to assume. The conservatives agreed but insisted that traditional form was not as much a handicap as it seemed. Conrad Aiken's remarks in *The Poetry Journal* stated their case: "A poet always uses the maximum subtlety of form which he can completely fuse with what he has to say."[3] More than anything else, however, the advocates of free verse regarded it as a "democratic expression," a kind of verse that "the people will understand," and one which was ideally suited to the "formlessness of modern life." The work of the "Whitmanists" in *Poetry* and *The Midland* seemed substantially to develop this thesis. Vachel Lindsay, Carl Sandburg, Edwin Ford Piper, Edgar Lee Masters, and Arturo Giovannitti all used Whitmanesque free verse as a means of direct communication. It seemed to them a means of avoiding insincerity, of stating the fact or announcing the sentiment without formal delay or abstract equivocation. This is why the *Spoon River Anthology* of "Webster Ford" was so highly regarded by Ezra Pound and the *Egoist* group in England: "The author has escaped from the stilted literary dialect of *The Atlantic Monthly*. He has endeavored to write the spoken language. He has not escaped a few dozen *clichés*, *clichés* of political journalism, *clichés* still hanging over from his 'poetic diction' period."[4]

As for opposition to free verse on the grounds that it was patternless, this of course had to be answered. Professor John Livingston Lowes, for example, could not see that the loose structure and capricious patterns of imagism and free verse were different in any sense from prose description. He argued that many passages in Meredith's novels might easily be arranged in the free verse line and compare favorably, as poetry, with the poetry appearing in the "new journals."[5] But all pattern is the exercise of the imagination upon subject and feeling. As T. S. Eliot said, "It is not our feelings, but the pattern we make of our

[3] "Illusory Freedom in Poetry," *The Poetry Journal*, v, 190 (May 1916).
[4] Pound, "Edgar Lee Masters," *Reedy's Mirror*, xxiv, 11 (May 21, 1915).
[5] "An Unacknowledged Imagist," *Nation*, cii, 217-19 (February 24, 1916).

feelings which is the center of value."[6] Within each line, modern poets argued, the poetic phrase, the very nature and sound of the words, dictated the reading and governed the comprehension of the poetic idea. To impose upon the line an artificial restriction—one not emotionally grasped or imaginatively controlled by the poet—was simply to deny him the right to fashion his line independently and genuinely. As Laura Riding and Robert Graves have put it, "The whole trend of modern poetry is toward treating poetry like a very sensitive substance which succeeds better when allowed to crystallize by itself than when put into prepared moulds."[7]

The writing of imagist and free verse was not without its share of charlatans. Much bad verse was written under the new dispensation. But the controversy acted as an incentive to future experiment. The advantages of the traditional forms, while not neglected—*The Masses* group under Max Eastman, for example, preferred the form of the sonnet—were generally suspect. For more than one reason the moderns approved of the revolt; it called their attention to the possibility of experiment with a variety of forms and meanings; it turned the poet's attention to words and images *per se*; it challenged him to produce originality of thought rather than cleverness of structure; it set up the cliché in the pillory of contemporary scorn.

What is the real difference between the cliché and the metaphor? The easy answer is that the cliché is simply an outworn metaphor, which perhaps has intrinsic value but is now dead as last year's Number One song hit. The differences are more subtle than that. Continuous usage has given the cliché a simple and easy intellectual content; in fact, its meaning is taken for granted and lacks almost all challenge to the poetic imagination. Further, the cliché has become communal, while the metaphor is personal in its use. Modern poets were impressed in the twenties by the importance of aesthetic independence; they wished above all to avoid giving up their birthright by handing it over to tradition. This desire was not motivated solely by a sense of Bohemian exclusiveness. The force of language needed to be secured against any softening of the aesthetic temperament. The poet's sense of difference and his respect for that difference caused him to protect at all costs the use of the metaphor as a source of new and plural mean-

[6] Quoted by Elizabeth Drew, *Directions in Modern Poetry*, New York, 1940, p. 232.
[7] Laura Riding and Robert Graves, *Survey of Modernist Poetry*, London, 1927, p. 47.

ing. Abuses of this conviction caused some critics to condemn the modern movement in poetry; it was made ridiculous, according to one critic, by "tricks of the minor 'new' poet who having learned to look within himself for inspiration thinks that everything he finds on looking within is poetry, as he finds it."[8]

There were contradictions in the position which modern poets assumed—contradictions are plentiful throughout modern literary history. Free verse was used on the one hand for its close approximation to the "common speech"; it was used by the experimenter as a means of achieving a high degree of singularity of speech. Imagism began as the most objective of verse; it was incorporated into the verse of those who regarded the image as the best means of articulating poetic individualism. Note that in the subsequent development of both free verse and imagism, the hardiest of individualists scorned the verse of Masters, Lindsay, and Sandburg. They regarded the French symbolists as their true masters, because these latter seemed to deal with language and metaphor with greater subtlety and with less regard for their values as communicative means.

Eventually the modern conception of the metaphor was to provide an important challenge for the experimentalist poet. Its plurality of meanings gave the performer the reputation of virtuoso, especially since he only rarely indicated the exact meaning which the reader ought to accept. The wide variety of metaphoric usage can be seen in the following illustrations, drawn from the little magazines: Louis Grudin's

> She hung from his arm like a slain snake,
> while he stared through the waves of
> evening for her wake; like an oracle
> over a fowl, he studied her circlings.[9]

Evelyn Scott's

> My joy,
> Sharper than the blades of swords,
> Ran,
> With a white cry,
> Naked through the morning.
> I quenched all the stars
> And went on
> Beyond them.[10]

---

[8] Richard C. DeWolf, *The Minaret*, I, 77 (November 1916).
[9] Louis Grudin, "Solitaire," *Rhythmus*, I, 1 (January 1923).
[10] Evelyn Scott, "Touch," *Rhythmus*, I, 40 (February 1923).

Eugene Jolas'

> At night, when she went to her home in the suburbs,
> She found a rain-dull tedium nodding its bald head
> Against the bleak curtain of her old-maid loneliness.[11]

T. S. Eliot's

>> Let us go then, you and I,
> When the evening is spread out against the sky
> Like a patient etherized upon a table;[12]

and Ezra Pound's

> And we sit here
>> under the wall,
> Arena romana, Diocletians, les gradins:
>> quarante trois rangées en calcaire—
> Baldy Bacon
>> bought all the little copper pennies in Cuba
> Un centavo, dos centavos,
>> told his peons to "bring 'em ini."[13]

Whatever else may be said about this random sampling of modern, little magazine verse, the variety of statements and of poetic usage should impress one immediately. The metaphor is in each an imprecise expression of meaning, and leads the reader away from direct paraphrase. Most of all, the metaphor is freed from its confinement within logical statement and—in many cases, not all—remains a fluid suggestion of a variety of meanings located within the linguistic origins of the words, the allusiveness of the figure, or the "inappropriateness" of the comparison.

Experimentalism in poetry was a challenge to language to rid itself of traditional clichés. In the estimate of the poet, these clichés did not make meaning clear; they made meaning deceptively easy, when what the reader needed was an awareness of complexity. There is no riddle in this. The poet's apprehension of reality was as of a flux of perceptual material, momentarily caught within the boundaries of attention. Fluctuation of sensations caused many strange groupings of ideas, which seemed not actually to exist and yet made a powerful impression

---

[11] Eugene Jolas, "Futility," *Rhythmus*, II, 50 (May-June, 1924).
[12] T. S. Eliot, "The Love Song of J. Alfred Prufrock," *Poetry*, VI, 130 (June 1915).
[13] Pound, "Another Canto," *transatlantic review*, I, 12 (January 1924).

upon the poet. Hence the novelty of much modern poetry is primarily a recognition of the diversity and looseness of incidental associations. The metaphor is likewise an "untrue" statement of fact. The more complex appearances become, the more unusual the metaphor, the more remote from our habitual associations. Modern metaphor is "shocking"; that is, one does not appreciate it by a simple nod of recognition; one does not simply fit it with one's stock notions of "what so-and-so said the other day about the tariff." It violates such conventional recognition, and aims essentially to make the reader discard it altogether, to reform his attention and to reconsider his standards of acceptance. In some cases, the poet may trick him into dropping his platitudes, only to have him find that the metaphor is merely ambiguous and without any reducible meaning of any kind. It is on these terms that one may judge the seriousness of the modern metaphor: its intrinsic value (which is in one sense implicit in the "way of saying") and its value after the reader has acceded to its demands, not before.

### III

It is with the structure of the metaphor and the texture of the line that most poetic theory is concerned. The "Fugitive" group of poets in Nashville, Tennessee, established their own magazine for the purpose of practicing poetry and coming to some theoretical agreement about its function: "The Editors of *The Fugitive* are amateurs of poetry living in Nashville, Tennessee, who for some time have been an intimate group holding very long and frequent meetings devoted both to practice and to criticism. The group mind is evidently neither radical nor reactionary, but quite catholic, and perhaps excessively earnest in literary dogma."[14]

From its beginning in 1922 until its end in 1925, the black-and-gold-covered *Fugitive* puzzled its observers. The first two issues presented a startling array of pseudonyms—such names as "Marpha" and "Henry Feathertop"—thus suggesting to several New York critics that all of the poems were written by John Crowe Ransom. Within the first year, Southern reviewers, troubled about a cryptic editorial, nervously wondered whether the periodical was repudiating the South. Nor was it long before some were crying out against what they thought was

[14] Editorial, *The Fugitive*, I, 34 (June 1922).

Four little magazine covers

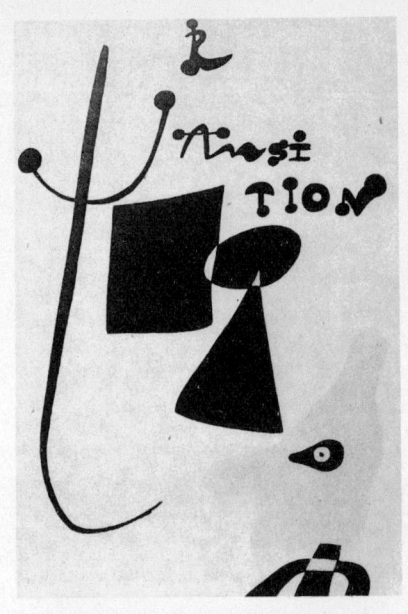

John Crowe Ransom

The FUGITIVE group, 1930-1931. *Reading from top to bottom:* Andrew Lytle, John Crowe Ransom, unidentified, Thomas Warren, Robert Penn Warren, Allen Tate, Mary Davidson, Mrs. Robert Penn Warren, Mrs. Donald Davidson, Caroline Gordon.

"obscurity" or "unintelligibility." Today, some are still befuddled, believing that the magazine was connected with the agrarian movement.

The Fugitive was never filled with the work of one person masquerading under various signatures; it never repudiated the South; it was never unintelligible; it was never a regional or agrarian magazine. What The Fugitive stood for one can easily determine by remembering the early work of its chief contributors: Allen Tate, John Crowe Ransom, Donald Davidson, Merrill Moore, Laura Riding, and Robert Penn Warren.

The magazine was established by a group of seven, all of whom lived in or near Nashville. Some of these seven—Donald Davidson, James Marshall Frank, Sidney Mttron Hirsch, Stanley Johnson, John Crowe Ransom, Alec B. Stevenson—had been meeting for several years to talk of poetry and philosophy, gathering every other Saturday night at the home of Mr. Frank. Allen Tate, who was introduced to the group as a Vanderbilt undergraduate in 1921, has given us a casual and swift glimpse of these meetings in "The Fugitive—1922-25," published in the April 1942 *Princeton University Library Chronicle*. He tells how the young men grouped themselves, somewhat formally, around the chaise longue of the invalided Dr. Hirsch, who, with a grand and authoritarian manner, a manner doubtless accentuated by his pince-nez and "curled Assyrian hair," directed the conversation. "He was a mystic and I think a Rosicrucian, a great deal of whose doctrine skittered elusively among imaginary etymologies,"[15] says Tate. For some time before Tate became a member, the group had been in the habit of writing verse and reading to one another, with Dr. Hirsch sternly ordering the program and calling for criticism of each piece. It was Hirsch who suggested the poetry should be printed as a co-operative undertaking in a magazine, and it was he who suggested the name *The Fugitive*.[16]

That first April 1922 number contained seventeen poems. For the sake of the record we list these works and their authors.

Ego                         by *Roger Prim*
Night Voice             (John Crowe Ransom)
To a Lady Celebrating
   Her Birthday
The Handmaidens

---

[15] Allen Tate, "The Fugitive—1922-1925," *The Princeton University Library Chronicle*, III, 76 (April 1942).
[16] Ibid., pp. 78-79.

| | |
|---|---|
| I Have Not Lived | by *Marpha* (Walter Clyde Curry) |
| A Demon Brother<br>The Dragon Book<br>Following the Tiger | by *Robin Gallivant* (Donald Davidson) |
| Sermons<br>An Intellectual's Funeral<br>The Lighted Veil | by *Jonathan David* (Stanley Johnson) |
| To Intellectual Detachment<br>Sinbad | by *Henry Feathertop* (Allen Tate) |
| The House of Beauty<br>To a Wise Man | by *Drimbonigher* (Alec Brock Stevenson) |

The pen names in several instances were whimsically apt descriptives of the men who assumed them. Roger Prim, who read his verse "in a dry tone of understatement,"[17] possessed a decisive and fierce "primness" that made him something of a leader, though he never pressed his right to command. Robin Gallivant was in 1922 a light-hearted, buoyant romantic who liked to tell of the strange mysteries of far countries, but soon he gave up most of his romanticism. Henry Feathertop was a little proud and vain, as he exaggeratedly admits: "My conceit must have been intolerable."[18] Since the pseudonyms were dropped with the appearance of the third issue, one can guess that they were assumed not so much from a desire to conceal identity as from sheer playfulness.

Walter Clyde Curry, Merrill Moore, William Y. Elliott, and William Frierson were added to the original seven in late 1922 and the early months of 1923. Later still Jesse and Ridley Wills, cousins, and Robert Penn Warren, Laura Riding, Andrew Lytle, and Alfred Starr were elected to the *Fugitive* ranks.[19] "Red" Warren, one of the alert editors of the recently defunct *Southern Review*, and one of our most distinguished poets and critics, was only sixteen when he was admitted into the group. During his first year with the fugitives he roomed with the frolicking Allen Tate and Ridley Wills. Catching from Tate a fine admiration for T. S. Eliot, Warren decorated their room with murals depicting the inspiring sights of *The Waste Land*. "I remember par-

---
[17] *Ibid.*, p. 77.
[18] *Ibid.*, p. 81.
[19] Letter, Donald Davidson to Charles Allen, May 10, 1939 (unpublished).

ticularly the rat creeping softly through the vegetation, and the typist putting a record on the gramophone."[20]

Laura Riding, one of our best contemporary poets, was elected to membership during the last year of the magazine's career. At that time she was the wife of a history professor, Louis Gottschalk, of the University of Louisville. After winning a $100 prize offered by the magazine in 1924, she became a frequent contributor, though her personal connection with the group was somewhat remote.

Merrill Moore, we may well imagine, is the most prolific versifier living. He has written over fifty thousand sonnets since he published his first one in *The Fugitive*, written them in spare moments taken from his successful practice as a psychiatrist in Boston. He always appeared at the Saturday readings with at least ten poems, and once he came with twenty-one.

These were the persons, along with the original seven, who were responsible for the bulk of the material that was published in the magazine's nineteen numbers. Few were the others who gained admission to *The Fugitive's* pages; only infrequently do we find such names as Witter Bynner, David Morton, William A. Percy, Robert Graves, Louis Untermeyer, John Gould Fletcher, and L. A. G. Strong. Of the outsiders perhaps Hart Crane deserves special mention. Tate, early in his career, became a warm admirer of Crane's work, and at Tate's request, *The Fugitive* presented Crane's "Stark Major" in August 1923, and other poems, including the "Lachrymose Christ," in 1924 and 1925.[21]

The magazine was a natural outgrowth of friendship, a unique phenomenon in the history of the recent little magazines. As such there was none of the pretense, the crusading, the yielding to outside pressures, which we find in some other little magazines. It was admirable in its self-sufficiency, in its unconcern for renown. If fame came, and it certainly did, it was not because *The Fugitive* blew its own trumpet. Fame came because the magazine printed some of the best poetry then being written in America. Merrill Moore, the most frequent contributor, flooded the magazine with his experimental and exciting sonnets. Davidson, with such poems as "Advice to Shepherds," "A Dirge," "Echo," and "Hit or Miss," appeared almost as frequently as Moore. Laura Riding explored with a hard, brilliant intensity in most of the later issues. Some of Ransom's best known work, such

[20] Tate, "The Fugitive—1922-1925," p. 82.
[21] Letter, Davidson to Allen, May 10, 1939 (unpublished).

as "The Amphibious Crocodile," "Lady Lost," "Bells for John Whiteside's Daughter," and "Captain Carpenter," first appeared in *The Fugitive*. But there is little point in reciting titles. One might go ahead for pages glibly mentioning the poems of Tate, Warren, Curry, Shipley, Johnson, and Stevenson, but he could never succeed in tapping *The Fugitive's* quality. The verse that appeared here must be read, not simply talked about.

Since *The Fugitive's* aim has often been misunderstood, we quote an editorial, written by Ransom, that fairly and accurately states the magazine's purpose:

"The *Fugitive* exists for obvious purposes and has the simplest working system that we know of among periodicals. It puts in a single record the latest verses of a number of men who have for several years been in the habit of assembling to swap poetical wares and to elaborate the Ars Poetica. These poets acknowledge no trammels upon the independence of their thought, they are not overpoweringly academic, they are in tune with the times in the fact that to a large degree in their poems they are self-convicted experimentalists. They differ so widely and so cordially from each other on matters poetical that all were about equally startled and chagrined when two notable critics, on the evidence of the two previous numbers, construed them as a single person camouflaging under many pseudonyms. The procedure of publication is simply to gather up the poems that rank the highest, by general consent of the group, and take them to the publisher."[22]

Here is the true and best statement. Certainly the entire group refused to acknowledge "trammels upon the independence of their thought" and they were "self-convicted experimentalists."

Why did these men wish to think of themselves as "self-convicted" experimentalists? From what were they revolting? A clue is furnished in the name of the magazine. When Dr. Hirsch suggested the title, he undoubtedly was remembering, as Tate has mentioned, the ancient etymology: "A Fugitive was quite simply a Poet: the Wanderer, or even the Wandering Jew, the Outcast, the man who carries the secret wisdom around the world."[23] If one wishes, however, he can correctly read more into the choice of the name. One can assume that these poets were fleeing from, or attacking, the shackles of sentimental Southern poetry of their day (pillars in the moonlight, pale, mysterious ladies, Uncle Tom, sing-song lassitudes, etc.). In writing their

---
[22] John Crowe Ransom, Editorial, *Fugitive*, I, 66 (October 1922).
[23] Tate, "The Fugitive—1922-1925," p. 82.

verse, as Davidson says, they were fleeing from "poet-laureating, the cheapness and triviality of public taste, even among those supposed to be cultured; the lack of serious devotion to literature, to the arts, to ideas."[24] And they were against "professional Southernism," but by no means against the South, as many observers of the time believed. Rather, as their later agrarian symposium proved, theirs was a respect for the South, or at least a hope for what the South might become.

At the time, however, these poets showed no concern with promoting a scheme for reconstructing Southern life, except insofar as they wished to inject a fresh note into its verse. Thumbing through the magazine, we find little prose, and that little is concerned with aesthetics and astute book reviewing. There is absolutely no evidence that the periodical was agrarian or self-consciously regional. It is not our purpose to tell how several of the group—notably Tate, Davidson, and Warren—later became ardent advocates of literary regionalism, or how they supported the theory that a writer should use the materials of the place, the cultural entity with which he is best acquainted. This is a story in itself and has no relation to the *Fugitive* activity. Nor is it pertinent to consider here that some members later coalesced to sponsor the Southern agrarian movement.

What needs emphasizing, however, as both Davidson and Tate have insisted, was the fortuitous gathering in Nashville of a group of talented Southerners, most of them native to Kentucky and Tennessee.[25] These men not only shared a close sympathy for their historical heritage (a heritage which had a "use for the dramatic and lyrical arts"[26]) but they also shared a brave and intense need to attack the ubiquitous sentimentalities that had taken evil root in their native soil. This was a closely knit group, and the sense of solidarity tended to harden and sharpen the imaginative thinking of the individual minds. It is not too surprising, therefore, that people have noticed similarities in the work of the group.

A few critics are convinced that these similarities derive from the influence of T. S. Eliot and Hart Crane. There may be an element of truth in this observation, especially in reference to Warren and Tate, but that element can be easily overemphasized. There is good

---

[24] Letter, Davidson to Allen, May 10, 1939 (unpublished).
[25] *Ibid.*; see also Tate, "The Fugitive—1922-1925," p. 83.
[26] Tate, "The Fugitive—1922-1925," p. 83.

evidence (the words of the poets[27]) for believing that they worked out for themselves some of the cacophonous and "metaphysical" techniques.

The phrase "metaphysical manner" is dangerous and tricky. Following Cleanth Brooks' brilliant definition in *Modern Poetry and the Tradition* we may define "metaphysical" as the blending of the intellectual with the emotional approach (i.e., irony, satire, ideas, "meaning," juxtaposed with feeling); as the designing of a tight functional structure (the fusion of idea, tone, and imagery into an integral whole); as the striving for "maximum density" (i.e., the inclusion of a wealth of disparate allusion into any given stanza); as the making of the surprising image (i.e., the extended image which carries the thought; the compressed, elliptical image; the pitting of opposites within the image).[28] In varying degrees, all of the group except Moore and Riding exploited this ancient tradition introduced by Donne.

Warren, discussing "Pure and Impure Poetry" in the Spring 1943 issue of *The Kenyon Review*, summarizes and defends ten "undesirable" characteristics which most critics believe should not appear in "pure" poetry (that is, acceptable poetry). Nine of these ten qualities describe the structure and content that Warren, Tate, Ransom, and, to a lesser degree, Davidson, seek in their work.

1. ideas, truths, generalizations, "meaning"
2. precise, complicated, "intellectual" images
3. unbeautiful, disagreeable, or neutral materials
4. situation, narrative, logical transition
5. realistic details, exact descriptions, realism in general
6. shifts in tone or mood
7. irony
8. Metrical variation, dramatic adaptation of rhythm, cacophony, etc.
9. subjective and personal elements.[29]

Perhaps, too, one can see in these four men and in Laura Riding similarities of attitude and theme. All perceive in our rationalistic society a weight of vulgarity and stupidity, and they take a sardonic

---

[27] Letter, Davidson to Allen, July 18, 1941 (unpublished).
[28] Cleanth Brooks, *Modern Poetry and the Tradition*, Chapel Hill, 1939, pp. 39-49.
[29] Robert Penn Warren, "Pure and Impure Poetry," *Kenyon Review*, v, 246-47 (Spring 1943); see also William Van O'Connor, "Tension and Structure of Poetry," *Sewanee Review*, LV, 555-73 (Autumn 1943).

delight in slashing at these vices. All notice symptoms of disunity in themselves, and they struggle fiercely to integrate their natures with the avalanche of complex, unrelated scientific fact that presses against them with a demand for immediate assimilation. Hence the oblique and many-sided approach to their varied material, the abrupt shift in tone, and the use of dense inclusiveness. The world must be examined from as many views as possible.

But one can make too much of the likenesses of theme and attitude, as well as of technique. For the fugitives attacked the vapidities of the world and of Southern literature with individual force and temperamental emphasis. Though Davidson shows many of Ransom's characteristics, especially the irony, satire, and magnificent wording, he is a warmer, less intense, more lyrical spirit. Warren, probing the brain for its tortured, almost demented incertitudes, was more drawn toward native subjects than any other poet of the group and was at the same time more profoundly metaphysical than even Tate. And Merrill Moore, with sly, racy prankishness whipping through his lines, barely manages to skim the periphery of the great tradition. Laura Riding during her early years was not as rigidly denotative or as madly analytical of human nature as she has been of late, but she showed even in 1924 and 1925 a compulsion toward the literal, unimagistic abstraction that makes her more complex and masculine (and therefore more "difficult") than the other fugitives. Indeed, when one considers the variety of approach, he is almost inclined to dismiss any attempt at cataloguing.

A co-operative magazine generally has little chance of surviving for more than a few months. The editorial fights that characterized *Secession* are the usual thing. But the fugitives showed a rare spirit. They were gentlemen who had been friends over a period of years. There was no question of *The Fugitive* becoming a point of bitterness among them, and when it finally ceased publication in December 1925, the reasons were not dissent or lack of money.[30] The editors discovered that they had responsibilities which would no longer permit the labor

[30] Letter, Davidson to Allen, May 10, 1939 (unpublished). The average cost of *The Fugitive* was less than $100 per issue, an expense which was largely taken care of by a small newsstand sale and the one-dollar bills which came from the 300 yearly subscribers. The poetry prizes, offered after the first year, were made possible through the assistance of various patrons, among the most prominent of whom were the Associated Retailers of Nashville, Ward-Belmont College, and Mr. Joel Cheek. For a period of about eighteen months, previous to December 1924, when the magazine was tried as a 32-page bimonthly, Mr. Jacques Black contributed a large share of the necessary money.

and time of publishing a magazine, and one can readily see why. For the periodical had rocketed its poets into the national literary spotlight. Ransom, Tate, Warren, Moore, and Riding had gained a degree of acceptance in the public grace. Davidson published his *Outland Piper* in 1924, and Ransom his famous *Chills and Fever* in the same year. *The Fugitive* had fulfilled its proper function.

Moore, Riding, Warren, and Davidson were the four who received first publication in the magazine, but it was *The Fugitive* that really established the careers of the entire group. The magazine is best viewed as a means by which an entire flank of modern American poets gained recognition; for, though some of the work in the periodical was fledgling and trivial, much of the most estimable verse of Ransom, Warren, Tate, Davidson, Riding, and Moore appeared there. The alert reader feels no inclination to cavil with Mr. Tate's judgment of the *Fugitive* years: "I think I may disregard the claims of propriety and say quite plainly that, so far as I know, there was never so much talent, knowledge, and character accidentally brought together in one American place in our time."[31]

## IV

Modern poetry has above all helped to throw off the cloak of false piety from poetic expression. Since contemporary poets emphasized "the newness of the matter," they found that the old metrical patterns could scarcely accommodate their novelties and were forced to rely upon their own inventiveness and experimental sense. Ransom sees some disadvantage in this condition: "But at least our poet is aware of his own age, barren for any art though it may be, for he can't write like Homer or Milton now; from the data of his experience he infers only a distracting complexity."[32]

The private aesthetic values in such communication, though they may not give the poet great audiences, will at least satisfy him on the score of integrity; any oversimplification of his feeling would inevitably lead to triteness of statement. This consideration of the poet as above all a private person, best equipped to remain honest and original within the seclusion of his own sensibility, is a defense against the demand that the poet take the stump for humanity in general or the proletariat in particular. It is justified by the surprising discovery that

[31] Tate, "The Fugitive—1922-1925," p. 83.
[32] Editorial, *The Fugitive*, III, 36 (April 1924).

the poet's environment is a complex one and that he can best understand and reveal its complexity by accepting no social or sentimental compromise with it. Such a position is indispensable to the full use of the poet's intellectual and emotional resources. He ought not to write within easy distance of Bartlett's *Quotations*, a dictionary of rhyme, and the latest interpretation of Lenin on Marx on Bakunin.

*The Fugitive* is the best argument against its detractors. Since it was published in a university community, its sponsorship of revolt was neither reckless nor unguarded. Since those who wrote for it were poets endowed by nature, the sincerity of its poetics seemed all but proved by the excellence of its contents.

The little magazines are well supplied with other statements of poetic purpose. There were the extreme conservatives of the type of *The Journal of American Poetry*, which looked wistfully back at the glorious prewar days when poets did not substitute eccentricity for charming poetic statement. There were the innumerable statements made by states laureate, who published their own little poetry magazines in the interests of the beautiful and nothing but the beautiful. There were poetry magazines in the late twenties and in the thirties which regarded poetry as just another way of announcing Marxist doctrines. To each of these statements (which overwhelmed the nation's readers by the weight of sheer numbers) were added the temperamental disposition and the political and aesthetic interests of its spokesmen.

It was the integrity of the poet which impressed most critics, though the quixotics of some modern poets distressed the more conservative. Released at least temporarily from conventional metrics, poetry of all the arts seemed best suited to express the age. Poetic activity was marked by a fury and quantity which apparently knew no bounds. This activity was motivated in part by a defiance of the world of convention and business, in which the use of the metaphor was limited to the billboard or the magazine advertisement. Maxwell Anderson, for example, thought it altogether possible "that poetry and art are out of place in the new tradesmen's civilization about to be erected on the ashes. If so we [the editors of *The Measure*] are atavistic. We are born too late, and can't help it."[33] Poetry, in Anderson's opinion, is not the product or expression of a school, but "the output of a keen, egotistical, independent intelligence backed by an extraordinary surcharge of emotion."[34]

[33] Editorial, *The Measure*, I, 24 (March 1921).
[34] Editorial, *The Measure*, II, 17 (April 1921).

Since much of the poetry of our day has been taken up by statement and counterstatement regarding the importance of the aesthetic imperative, poetry may be considered the most advanced of the advanced guard literary arts. The guardians of tradition were considerably reduced in rank; the bulk of the defense of tradition was puerile and useless. Among the ablest of the conservative critics who abhorred "unsightly esotericism" in the arts, Conrad Aiken stands out as quite capable of defending the limits and discipline of traditional form, though his own poetry does not always document his criticism. His opinion, announced as early as 1912 in *The Poetry Journal*, was not unreasonable, though he objected to free verse as an unpardonable excuse for inadequate art. Free experiment, Aiken says, is often a giving-in to "aesthetic fatigue." A strong and competent imagination will not need to resort to forms outside of the traditional ones in order to compensate for its "subjective limitations."[35]

But many of the traditionalists played the theme of "nobility, truth, and goodness" until it must have bored even them. *The Journal of American Poetry*, for example, was established because "the decadent school" had made poetry so unrespectable that it had almost disappeared altogether. The *Journal* would like to disabuse the public of the notion that poetry need be ignoble before it can be published. Thus the definition of poetry as "verse which is exalted in mood and uses poetic diction" is offered as a substitute for modern poetics. London's *Decachord*, though essentially conservative in its point of view, nevertheless offered much intelligent opinion and seemed interested in the "metaphoric purity" of modern poetry. *L'Alouette* expressed itself with some acerbity: "Between the urbane sterilities of our bearded Brahmins and the psychoanalytical clinics of our younger intellectuals, American poetry fares badly indeed."[36]

Inferior criticism was as usual marked by vagueness of idea and a kind of foolish lyricism and archaism:

"The poet who would be read, loved and remembered must listen to the shouts and sighs of humanity at midday, must comfort them under the pyramiding burdens of even. . . ."[37]

"The soul, in its quest for beauty, may find its sustenance in a flower, a sunset, a picture, a strain of music, or a poem. It is a common need—shared by the laborer in the fields, the woman drooping

---

[35] Aiken, "Illusory Freedom in Poetry," p. 187.
[36] Editorial, *L'Alouette*, I, 20 (January 1924).
[37] Editorial, *The Buccaneer*, II, 24 (Winter 1926).

over tasks at home or shop, and the toiler lost in the maze of industrial life."[38]

Such criticism may be considered a part of social rather than literary history. It accounts for a wide variety of mediocre versifying which was published in the name of American poetry. Hundreds of little poetry magazines flourished (and still flourish) in our country on trite appeals to widely shared sentiment, one step removed from birthday telegram No. 8. They were the "backbone" of the nation's literary life. Affecting a love for garrets and for the beautiful, they echoed the commonplaces of our time. Triteness is not necessarily a vice of conventional verse; ultimately the quality of a poem must be measured in terms of the vividness and freshness of its language, its use of the music of the line, the quality of its statement. This is why the struggle for unconventionality in poetic statement is valuable and important; it helped to divide poetry into three types—the mediocre, the competent but unoriginal, and the aesthetically acceptable. The first may be dismissed, for it can readily be recognized in whatever form it appears. The second is marked by an aptitude for imitation and a self-consciousness which is too often covered by generalizations about nature and the Self. The third is the verse which we have been discussing in this chapter. Disputes among important poets—such as the quarrel which Winters and Ransom conduct in their contributions to magazines and in their books—can be explained by the fact that poets are ever mindful of the justice and correctness of their private emotions. However we may ultimately assess the value of modern poetry, the distinction between mediocre and important verse will always be clear.

The qualities and the very texture of modern verse underline the experimental tendencies of our time. Obscurity of meaning is often the responsibility of the reader. Seldom does obscurity exist in and for itself. It is part of the texture of our verse because no strict line of demarcation has been set for the poet's sensibility. And he may be introducing a "new knowledge" simply by pointing out the false simplicity of the old. Likewise, the aesthetic incentive for obscurity has been closely allied with the extremely wide range and the tenuous equilibrium of the poet's sensory experiences. The modern poet may be pardoned the ambiguity of his expression if only it be discovered that our own general range of comprehension has been greatly underestimated in the past.

[38] Editorial, *Westward*, I, 1 (August 1927).

# REGIONALISM
## and the Little Magazine

CHAPTER VIII

Two facts are clear enough. One: there is a large body of American literature that can be called regional. Two: this regional literature has stirred up an immense volume of violent controversy, in print and out of print.

As for the critical controversy, it continues unabated. The defenders and detractors of literary regionalism have piled high a mass of misinformation, wild opinion, deliberate falsification, slanderous bad temper; and the critical confusion that has resulted will not be unscrambled for a long time. We should like to suggest in this chapter that the unscrambling can be accomplished, in large part at least, by a close study of the regional little magazines. In their pages, where regionalism was born and reared, lies the clearest revelation of the major issues involved in regional theory and practice.

The critics who have concerned themselves with regionalism would probably unite on the following description. First of all, most critics, like most laymen, would agree that regionalism is synonymous with ruralism, though these same critics might admit that there is no very good reason for ruling out large urban areas as distinctive regions, or at least as one kind of region. But since tradition has decided that regionalism is ruralism, one may say that regionalism always finds its subject matter in the country or in the small villages, towns, and cities that are closely dependent for their existence on the land. Most critics would agree, too, that any work is regional that consciously attempts to stress the distinguishing geographical, human, and cultural patterns of a regional area such as the Great Plains region or the Southwest desert region. Any artistic work is regional if the artist's *primary* intention is to reveal the natural and social structure of a particular, clearly definable region as it is distinguished from the natural and social structure of any other clearly definable region. Regionalism self-consciously strives to portray the all-inclusive reality of a region; it strives to show the lay of the land, the flow of the rivers, the drift of the clouds and the winds; but above all, it labors to reveal the human beings who work and sweat and die on the land, and to reveal how these human beings have built their social institutions, especially their particular colloquial language. Thus the regionalist's first interest is rarely in human psychology in its typical or "universal" aspects, and to the degree that a regional work approaches the borderline of the universal its regional emphasis becomes less noticeable. How should one classify *My Antonía*, for instance?

Additions to this description can and should be made, though it may be difficult to muster a majority agreement among the critics on either of the additions we wish to propose. The most necessary addition is this: regionalism inevitably, since it seeks the truth about the region, employs the method of objective, factual realism. As a natural consequence of the search for truth, the characters in regional novels are more often than not second-rate people, not often revelatory of man's bravest potentiality. (This depresses a good many critics who believe that a prime function of literature is to ennoble the reader's soul.) The second addition is this: regionalism is marked nearly always by an intense consciousness of nature. Nature, indeed, is sometimes so dominating that the characters are all but lost in the panorama of landscape and far horizons. And frequently nature's molding influence on the individual and on his cultural institutions is made to appear inexorably powerful, marking the fiction with the stern brand of determinism, often pessimistic determinism. Pessimistic naturalism, however, cannot be considered a mark of regionalism, for in more cases than not the tone, situation, and philosophy are optimistic.

The little magazines were the first to promote a regionalism such as has been described; and, since 1915, when John T. Frederick launched his *Midland* in Iowa City, the little magazines have been the movement's staunchest defenders. *The Midland* (1915-33) preferred to speak optimistically of the Midwest land and of its people. Though a good many of the magazine's stories were grim and pessimistic, good cheer, laughter, and love for the land pervaded most of the fiction and poetry. This tone of quiet optimism has also been conspicuous in all of the other regional little magazines, particularly in *The New Mexico Quarterly Review* (1931-    ) and *The Southwest Review* (1924-    ).

*The Prairie Schooner* (1927-    ) and *The Frontier* (1920-39),[1] have favored a more pessimistic interpretation of their regions than have the Southwestern quarterlies. *The Prairie Schooner*, speaking primarily for the Great Plains and the agricultural Midwest, and *The Frontier*, speaking for the mountains and plateaus of the Pacific Northwest, represent sections that are still largely raw and dreary expanses whose people often are forced to live on an elementary and depressing level. Perhaps the refusal to compromise with the bitter, often brutalizing reality of their regions accounts for the suspicion with which some observers have regarded both magazines.

There have also been a good many other little magazines interested in regionalism, though only partially and spasmodically. One thinks immediately of *The Reviewer, American Prefaces, Space,* and the early *Double Dealer*.

The editors of the periodicals mentioned in the two preceding paragraphs have for the most part relied on their actions (the material they printed) rather than on their words (their editorial opinions) in the fight for a new literature. At the rare intervals when they have expressed themselves formally, they have written much as Harold G. Merriam, *The Frontier's* editor, wrote in 1934:

"I should like to have writers understand regionalism not as an ultimate in literature but as a first step, as the coming to close knowledge about the life of the region in which he lives as a first necessity for sound writing, even as knowledge of oneself—'know thyself'—is also a first necessity. The 'universal,' when healthy, alive, pregnant with values, springs inevitably from the specific fact. This conception of the interpretation of life I would oppose to the idea of cosmic-minded people that understanding springs from abstract ideas and images in the mind—in the soul. To such extent regionalism in my judgment, is earth-minded."[2]

An understanding of the motivations that govern regionalist activity is necessary if one is to estimate justly the validity of the regionalist's argument. The regional little magazine gives this necessary understanding. The primary motivation of recent American regionalism is quietly revealed in the first issue of *The Midland*, whose editorial announcement reads in part:

[1] For the purpose of giving a more specific understanding of a representative regional little magazine, we have added to this chapter a somewhat extended discussion of *The Midland*. See pp. 140-47.

[2] Harold G. Merriam, "Expression of Northwest Life," *The New Mexico Quarterly*, IV, 128-29 (May 1934).

"Possibly the region between the mountains would gain in variety at least if it retained more of its makers of literature, music, pictures, and more of its other expressions of civilization. And possibly civilization itself might be with us a somewhat swifter process if expressions of its spirit were more frequent. Scotland is none the worse for Burns and Scott, none the worse that they did not move to London and interpret London themes for London publishers."[3]

Frederick's belief that the "spirit" of "the region" should be more frequently revealed is the first of several such little magazine statements. Thus Jay B. Hubbell, first editor of *The Southwest Review*, announced in his introductory number that he would "especially encourage those who write on Western themes, for it is a magazine of the Southwest."[4] And Harold G. Merriam, writing to Charles Allen in 1938, a year before *The Frontier* ceased publication, stated that the purpose of his magazine was "To reveal the state of civilization in the Pacific Northwest."[5] The conviction of these three men is the conviction of all sincere regionalists and of all sincere regional little magazines. It is a conviction that regionalists take very seriously, for a reason which is broadly hinted at in the last sentence of *The Midland* editorial:

"Scotland is none the worse for Burns and Scott, none the worse that they did not move to London and interpret London themes for London publishers."[6] In other words, the region would be none the worse if its artists would refuse to move to New York to interpret New York themes for New York publishers. This willingness to follow Eastern publishing standards was all-prevalent during the half century following the Civil War, and to a great extent this tendency is still strong, despite the valiant efforts of the regionalists and their little magazines since 1915.

What were these literary standards demanded by the Eastern publishers? They were the moral standards of gentility and refinement. They required a mechanical formula: obvious rising action, wherein virtue and refinement struggled on fairly even terms with crudity and immorality; obvious climax and denouement, wherein virtue and refinement victoriously subdued all evil. The happy ending with good triumphant was a necessity. And there was, of course, a long list of

[3] John T. Frederick, Editorial, *The Midland*, I, 1 (January 1915).
[4] Hubbell, Editorial, *The Southwest Review*, x, 98 (October 1924).
[5] Letter, Merriam to Allen, December 9, 1938 (unpublished).
[6] Frederick, Editorial, op. cit., p. 1.

unmentionable words and actions that had to be scrupulously avoided. Above all, the writer's tone, his attitude, had to be one of sentimental optimism. Such a formula, if it allowed one to write of Winesburgs or Nebraska prairie farms at all (and it rarely did) required that the treatment be highly distorted, burlesqued, or romanticized.

As Henry Seidel Canby has recently made clear in his study of Whitman, the genteel standards expressed, in part at least, the educated public's crusade to mend the nation's manners and morals.[7] For the educated people, including many publishers, had been profoundly shocked with the flood of crudity and brutality that swept the country during and after the hate-releasing Civil War. And so it is a little unfair to cast all the odium of blame for the vapidity of our post-Civil War fiction and poetry on the heads of the publishers. They were the victims, though often sympathetic victims, of the "climate of opinion," of the prevailing temper of the *Zeitgeist*. And needless to insist, so were most of the writers.

But the emphasis on gentility, whatever its origin and despite its motive, was more than a little vicious and dehumanizing. Certainly it was cramping and stifling for the artist, whose first responsibility is to meet life with an unflinching vision. Bound by genteel standards, he was not allowed or could not allow himself to travel far in the direction of realism and honesty. The inevitable revolt against gentility began in the late nineties and the early years of the new century. Stephen Crane, Frank Norris, and Theodore Dreiser were the first rebels. They were soon followed by David Graham Phillips, Edith Wharton, and Willa Cather. Yet these people, all of whom insisted on reporting life realistically, did not receive a wide hearing until about 1915 or 1916 when the realistic frontal attack against refinement and sentimental romance really began in force.

The call that *The Midland* and its successors issued is to be seen as an important flanking movement of this main realistic attack against the deeply entrenched forces of gentility. The Eastern publishers, of course, were the main citadels of the enemy and the obvious focus of the attack. Frederick's motive in asking that the midland artist stay at home and fashion his own literary standards, realistic ones, is the primary motive of all regionalists and of all regional little magazines. Thus Merriam, as late as 1938, could still defend *The Frontier* with the argument that it gave "an outlet to sincere writers whose work is

---

[7] Henry Seidel Canby, *Walt Whitman: An American*, New York, 1943, pp. 278-79.

good but does not appeal to commercial editors."[8] And this is still the argument of the editors of The Southwest Review, The Prairie Schooner, and The New Mexico Quarterly Review.

As we have said, literary regionalism was given its first conscious statement in The Midland and the little magazines that followed it. Yet until the Civil War, American artists and other thinkers had assumed unconsciously much of the regionalist argument. One could, for instance, make a strong case for calling the entire New England group regionalists. And even in the period between the Civil War and the realistic revolt of the late nineties there were the notable exceptions who worked close to the regionalist pattern. One thinks immediately of Mark Twain and William Dean Howells, perhaps even more immediately of such "grim" realists as Ed Howe and Edward Eggleston. Indeed, there is much truth in Pearl Buck's observation that our literature always has been regional, that there is no such fact as a national literature, and that perhaps there will not be such a literature for many years.[9]

Nor must one forget that long before the direct pleas for literary regionalism there was a call, particularly from Frederick Jackson Turner and Josiah Royce,[10] for a cultural regionalism. It was a call which had direct and obvious implications for literary men. There can be little doubt that Frederick was perfectly aware of Royce's Phi Beta Kappa address, delivered in 1902 in the home town of The Midland. Royce said in substance: "Let your province then be your first social idea. Cultivate its young men, and keep them near you. Foster provincial independence. Adorn your surroundings with the beauty of art. Serve faithfully your community that the nation may be served."[11] Obviously there is a marked similarity in purpose to be noted when we compare these thoughts with the words of Frederick which we noticed in the first Midland editorial.

[8] Letter, Merriam to Allen, December 9, 1938 (unpublished).
[9] Pearl Buck, "Introduction to the United States," The Saturday Review of Literature, xx, 12-13 (May 27, 1939).
[10] Turner read his essay, "The Significance of the Frontier in American History," in 1893 and Royce read his paper, "Provincialism," in 1902.
[11] John Paul Abbott, "Regionalism" (unpublished), a summary of "Provincialism," from Race Questions, Provincialism, and Other American Problems, by Josiah Royce.

## II

Merriam's conception of regionalism as it is revealed in the quotation from The New Mexico Quarterly is the conception of all regional magazine editors and of all regionalists. It is a perfectly sound theory. There is no apparent wish to deny the so-called "universal" elements, no apparent wish to promulgate a barren, factual realism. As a theory, it represents the program of most good artists of all times. And so it is not the theory, but the literary practice—the value of the fiction produced—among other things, that leads to dispute.

For in practice regionalism rarely transcends Merriam's "first step," the "coming to close knowledge about the life of the region . . . as a first necessity. . . ."[12] Too often the regionalist fails to probe beyond "the specific fact" to the universals. He is too preoccupied with the region's peculiarity, its eccentric detail, its uniqueness. This is true of even the best—Eudora Welty, Ellen Glasgow, Willa Cather, Robert Penn Warren, Allen Tate, William Faulkner. It is more true of the second best—William March, Paul Engle, Ruth Suckow, Wallace Stegner, Jesse Stuart, Mari Sandoz, August Derleth, James Hearst. It is painfully true of the host of little known regionalists—Loren C. Eiseley, Meridel Le Sueur, John Henry Reese, Spud Johnson, Curtis Martin, Howard McKinley Corning, Ted Olson, Roderick Lull, Upton Terrell, and many others. The writers of these last two groups are often so self-consciously regional that one experiences the unpleasant feeling of being victimized by overseriousness. Regionalism has, in effect, thrown too heavy a stress on the particular, and it would seem that this is a danger inherent in regional theory.

A pedantic and self-conscious preoccupation with the region is a grave fault, but there are other serious shortcomings to be noted. One of these is the brand of realism that the regionalists have adopted. Since their intention is to reveal the region as accurately as possible, the regionalists are naturally committed to some form of realism. Of course the realist need not preoccupy himself too closely with surface detail, with the purely external spectacle of life and nature, as is generously proved by such writers as Proust and Dostoevski. Yet the truth is that our twentieth century American realist has for the most part confined himself within the narrow boundaries of an external factualism.

Our young realistic regionalist, especially as one sees him beginning and developing in our little magazines, tends to stress the outward

[12] Merriam, "Expression in Northwest Life," pp. 128-29.

spectacle more than is usual with the young, developing nonregionalist realist. Insofar as this is true, the regionalist little magazines and the regionalists are less exciting and profitable reading than the best of the nonregionalist little magazines and nonregionalists. Time and time again, particularly in the naturalistic brand of regional fiction, the story is a chronicle of man's bitter physical struggle against an imperturbable, hostile nature. Man may challenge his enemy bravely, may go down to an inevitable tragic defeat gallantly; or, as is usually the case, he may break under the strain, become a hardened, emotionless beast. But however he responds, the focus of interest is directed not on the inner man but on the spectacle of physical, outward action. And this stress on the outward appearance is not limited to naturalistic fiction. It is also characteristic of optimistic pastoralism.

Another serious defect, a defect that can be spotted, however, with almost equal ease in our nonregional realism, is drabness of style. A realistic style need not be leaden and colorless: it can and often should flow with premeditated and vivid rhythm; it can and often should sparkle with the decisive and electric word. By the electric word and the vivid rhythm we mean the kind of tensioned prose that Katherine Anne Porter often writes. We do not refer to the overemotionalized, florid, pseudopoetic style that marks the work of a good many regionalists such as Herbert Krause, whose *Wind Without Rain* is a case in point. For every regionalist with some sense of style, such as Robert Penn Warren or Eudora Welty, there are a dozen writers of weight and drabness. But again one must remember the obvious: this lack of textural richness, this ineptness of phrase and rhythm, is typical of most of our realistic fiction, though the nonregionalist is likely to be a little less pedestrian.

A fourth observation must be made in order to judge our regional literature fairly. Regionalism, being a lineal descendant of nineteenth century local color, often shows evidences of local color faults. A good many regionalist apologists would deny their uncouth heritage, and many others would prefer to have the obvious fact forgotten. But a fact it is, and one need not possess a too perceptive eye to see a good many local color mannerisms in our modern regionalism.

Local color was a varied and many-sided movement, but only two aspects of it are relevant to this discussion—the sentimental romanticism that expressed itself through the pens of such diverse writers as James Lane Allen, Sarah Orne Jewett, Mary Wilkins Freeman, and Grace King; and the humorous exaggerations that showed itself at its frolicking best in the work of such people as Bret Harte, Mark Twain, Petroleum V. Nasby, and George Ade.

The latter group was primarily inspired by the impulse to entertain through laughter. It loved to ridicule frontier uncouthness, especially frontier dialect; it reveled in humorous and satiric exaggeration and distortion of character and situation; it sometimes made humorous, more often careless, use of a broken, episodic structural framework. Much modern regionalism is prone to dialect simply because of its specialness, makes use of the episodic structure for no good reason, deals in exaggeration and distortion simply out of habit. These mannerisms are probably not general, but they are very noticeable in a good deal of our fiction. There is a considerable body of fiction labeled regional being written today that should be labeled "local color" had it been produced in the nineteenth century. We may point to such writers as Jesse Stuart, writers who capitalize on the eccentricities of dialectical language and on the eccentricities of social behavior (e.g., the naïveté of the Kentucky bumpkin).

The little magazines have reacted vigorously against the unhealthy heritage of sentimentalized pastoralism that was indulged in by one school of nineteenth century local color. Only occasionally does one find a story or novel that is suffused with an idealized or romanticized view of reality. But while this tone as a dominant is rarely found, traces of it can sometimes be observed, especially in the form of "poetic" rhapsodizing over the beauties of nature and the virtues of simple country folk. Such traces were noticeable in *The Midland*, and they can be found today in all the regional periodicals. But this mark of local color ancestry is not prevalent enough to be dangerous.

In general, one is safe in asserting that the orientation of our regionalism is radically different from our local color orientation, for though they both put emphasis on place, and though a good many writers have not altogether escaped from some of the local color angles of approach, the basic intentions of the two movements are opposed. One seeks reality, the other a conscious distortion of reality. Since there is this very real difference, both in theory and in action, it is apparent that one can for the most part ignore those commentators who still insist that regionalism and local color are identical.

Finally, many critics have frequently observed another regional error: the tendency to relive a "colorful" past or a nostalgic wish to preserve an outmoded cultural pattern. This is a charge that is persistently and loudly made by all unfriendly critics. And of course there is an element of justice in the accusation, as even the regionalist defenders are forced to admit. Thus Lewis Mumford, one of the warmest champions of cultivating regional differences, at the time he published his brilliant *Technics and Civilization*, in 1934, warned that:

"The besetting weakness of regionalism lies in the fact that it is in part a blind reaction against outward circumstances and disruptions, an attempt to find refuge within an old shell against the turbulent invasions of the outside world, armed with its new engines: in short, an aversion from what is, rather than an impulse toward what may be. For the merely sentimental regionalist, the past was an absolute. His impulse was to fix some definite moment in the past, and to keep on living it over and over again, holding the 'original' regional costumes, which were in fact merely the fashion of a certain century, maintaining the regional forms of architecture, which were merely the most convenient and comely constructions at a certain moment of cultural and technical development; and he sought, more or less, to keep these 'original' customs and habits and interests fixed forever in the same mold: a neurotic retreat. In that sense regionalism, it seems plain, was anti-historical and anti-organic: for it denied both the fact of change and the possibility that anything of value could come out of it."[13]

Though we have noticed evidences of this "neurotic retreat," particularly in some earlier regionalism, we cannot agree that retreat is a besetting weakness. We have not found, in the little magazines or elsewhere, very much of a sentimental backward glance, though backward glancing of a more objective variety there is aplenty. There is little of it in fiction. Such an attitude is more noticeable in poetry, and it is quite evident in regionalist drama. But even in drama the strain is not dominant. Nor do we believe that the charge is true in reference to the exposition, which is the area that Mumford apparently has primarily in mind. Most of the regionalist exposition that has analyzed the past has not been sentimentally nostalgic. It has been for the most part straightforward, objective, historical research—certainly a valuable and necessary activity.

### III

So far we have been mainly concerned with regionalist fiction. There is regionalist poetry, too, and the little magazines have been largely responsible for its development. The most striking fact about the re-

[13] Lewis Mumford, *Technics and Civilization*, New York, 1934, pp. 292-93.

gionalist poetry of the last thirty years is the simplicity of its form and style. The verse is never complex, never "difficult," always works within traditional forms. It has a directness, an openness of word, rhythm, sound, and structure that is unpretentious and a little dull. There is little experiment, unless one wishes at this late date to think of free verse as experiment. The most radical line never ranges beyond the area explored long ago by Whitman, and usually it does not dare trust itself that far. Never can one hope to be stimulated by intricacies and subtleties. But if regionalist verse abounds with clichés, they are not unpleasant clichés, for they have not yet worn too thin. They still possess warmth and dignity, though they are no longer very exciting.

Regionalist poetry, even more than the fiction, is concerned with the outward spectacle. Indeed, much of the verse is pure nature description, a simple chronicling of woodchucks, gophers, frozen creeks, sturdy sycamores, painted deserts, and howling winds. Most of the verse gives man an incidental place, shows him influenced for good or evil by the mighty scenery that surrounds him. Sometimes he is the pitiable and uncomprehending victim of nature's immensity and imperturbability; more often he is entranced before its grandeur and mystery. In either case there is a huge sentimentalism that cannot be blinked.

We refer to the great bulk of poetry that has appeared in the regionalist little magazines; but we might add that these magazines have also published some of the distinguished work. The verse of James Hearst is a case in point. It is typical of a considerable volume of relatively unknown work, poetry which follows a tradition that stresses the importance of man and the values that he may derive from a close association with nature. It is the gentle, quiet, ennobling poetry, the poetry that is honestly convinced that nature offers solace, wisdom, humility, and strength to the man who will live with her. It is a tradition that focuses its eye on man rather than nature as the important consideration.

With the exceptions of *The Midland* and *The Prairie Schooner*, the regional periodicals have published a good many essays and articles, a few on literary regionalism, a good many colored by broader regional interests—economic, political, racial, historical. Indeed, *The Southwest Review* is primarily designed for such articles and essays; and *The New Mexico Quarterly Review* often devotes about half of its pages to such exposition. These two magazines, though unrepresentative in their preference for exposition, are typical in regard to the expository subject matter that they prefer. The nonfiction of these magazines, especially during the past ten years, usually deals with the present-day regional issues, or with plans and suggestions for future regional action. The articles cover a wide range, are likely to examine such diverse subjects as education, political reform, sociology, and economic geography. This serious concern with the present and future of the region is the kind of dynamic, cultural regionalism that Royce called for in 1902, and the kind that Howard W. Odum and Lewis Mumford and all of the best orientated regionalists have demanded. All of the little magazine editors have clearly and persuasively expressed themselves in action concerning the necessity for this dynamic present-day and future-day orientation.

The regional magazines have, however, shown a generous interest in the historical past of the regions. This is especially true of the articles and essays of *The Frontier, The Southwest Review,* and *The New Mexico Quarterly Review,* all of which have conscientiously performed a valuable service in adding to the record of Northwest and Southwest history, folklore, legend, and anecdote.

While speaking of exposition, notice must be given to the book reviewing in these magazines. The reviews are usually of regional titles, though not always. Competent and informative, generally written by academic persons, the critical remarks are sometimes a little heavy and uninspired.

The impression that regionalist little magazines were without reservation dedicated to regionalism is a false one. They have all shown a broad streak of cosmopolitan, eclectic interest. This is especially true of *The Southwest Review,* which inherited a good deal of the dominating cosmopolitanism of the older *Texas Review. The New Mexico Quarterly Review* has also cast its eye beyond regional boundaries, publishing articles on such people and topics as British fascism, Americanism, Trotsky, and D. H. Lawrence. And many of the stories and many of the poems in the magazines are no more regionally colored than the fiction of Hemingway or the poetry of John Malcolm Brinnin. In fact, entire issues sometimes are devoted to nonregional interests. Further, the authors in about 50 per cent of the cases are from outside the region.

All in all, despite obvious shortcomings, the regional periodicals and literary regionalism have much to recommend them. One can agree with Dorothy Canfield Fisher when she praises in a recent essay the regional little magazines:

"They preserve in print, as part of our variegated national riches, writing of excellent quality which for reasons not connected with its quality would not be profitable for national-range magazines to publish. And they supply fine reading for groups of Americans who are especially qualified to savor and enjoy prose and poetry written out of the same kind of life they have known. They break up the large American unit into smaller, diversified parts, which make possible a specialized, intimate communion between authors and readers, out of the question on the large, generalized scale."[14]

But one can also see in these regional magazines a more important function. They serve, first of all, as the primary, advance guard force in the sturdy demand that the writer analyze realistically the life which he best knows. This is a healthy and stimulating emphasis in an America that is often all too eager to keep company with any fashionable literary movement or unprofitable idealism that may happen along. In his insistence that the artist acknowledge his "roots," that he write of the life that he truly understands, the regionalist is simply talking common sense—the common sense upon which all firm artistic structures always have been reared. It is only from such a foundation that an enduring American literature can be constructed.

## IV

*The Midland*'s enviable record could only have grown out of an admirable personality. That personality is John Towner Frederick.

While still an undergraduate at the State University of Iowa, in Iowa City, Frederick launched his *Midland: A Magazine of the Middlewest*. The editor, in 1915, was twenty-three years old, possessed of a discriminating literary judgment, and of a first-rate reason for starting a magazine. The reason stemmed from a recognition that Eastern commercial periodicals were not giving the best of the young Midwest writers an opportunity to be read.[15] *Harper's, The Atlantic Monthly, Scribner's,* and others were at that time more concerned with name writers than with the quality of the fiction they offered their readers. New writers were, every now and again, printed by the money-making periodicals, but they were not likely to be from the midland, for most seaboard editors were determined on one of two things from a trans-

[14] Dorothy Canfield Fisher, "Introduction," *Prairie Schooner Caravan*, Lincoln, Nebraska, 1943, p. 13.

[15] Frederick, Editorial, *The Midland*, XVI, 369 (November-December, 1930).

Allegheny writer. Either he must mold the Middlewest outlook to conform with that of the East, or the Midwest soul must be burlesqued for the amusement of the East. In either case, the writer could not honestly explore the spirit of his native people. Frederick believed his country should write, and *The Midland* was established for those artists who desired to interpret their section realistically.[16] The magazine, edited by one close to the Midwest, began then as an experimental regional magazine.

Frederick had several friends who, between 1910 and 1915, contributed much towards formulating and clarifying the purpose of the magazine as it was announced in that first January issue. Most important of these associates was C. F. Ansley, during Frederick's undergraduate days head of the Iowa English Department. Ansley, more than anyone else, helped direct Frederick's thinking. Then there was Edwin Ford Piper, the regionalist poet, who gave invaluable advice and who was able to secure many of the guarantors who helped support the periodical in its beginning. Three others, undergraduates in 1915, made important contributions: Ival McPeak, R. L. Sergel, and Raymond Durboraw. These five, particularly Ansley and Piper, not only helped in formulating Frederick's thoughts on regionalism, but also offered valuable service in editorial capacities during the magazine's earlier years. And there was one other person whom we must not forget, though she was not officially connected with the review until its last two years when she served as co-editor. That person was the editor's wife. Through the magazine's entire history Esther Frederick helped guide the editorial policy and in other ways made the magazine possible.[17]

How the quiet and unpretentious Frederick slowly built his magazine, maneuvered it into an ever more important position, makes an interesting tale. With what vigor and delight he conducted his magazine for the midland poets and storytellers! "Sacrifice and hardship sustain *The Midland*, but it brings reward in treasure beyond price."[18] There was hardship and sacrifice. Like most little magazines, *The Midland* always trod close to the edge of bankruptcy. Despite the fact that the periodical was given office space by the university, that at various times editorial assistants were supplied by the school, that the Economy Advertising Company in Iowa City always generously provided the

---

[16] Frederick, Editorial, *The Midland*, I, 1 (January 1915).
[17] Statement of John T. Frederick to Charles Allen, September 1937.
[18] Frederick, Editorial, *The Midland*, VI, 2 (Jan.-Feb.-Mar., 1920).

printing at a minimum cost, and that friends contributed varying amounts of money, Mr. Frederick was constantly having to draw from his own income as a teacher to keep his project afloat.[19]

The financial record for 1915 is worth our attention, since it shows the hazards of starting a little magazine. There were twelve issues, each number containing 32 well printed book-size leaves, substantially bound between a tan, simply designed coverpiece. The printing bill ran to $695, postage $72, and other expenses to $57, a total of $826. The income from the subscriptions was $285 (the review sold for $1.25 a year in the beginning, for $3.00 later), and there was $245 from guarantors. Frederick was left to pay a deficit of $263.[20] As Frederick became more certain of his ground, as the magazine increased in importance, it came nearer to self-sufficiency, though it never, before moving to Chicago in 1930, mustered many more than 500 subscribers. On the average Frederick did not have to reach into his own pocket for over one or two hundred dollars per year.[21]

The gradual growth of The Midland was not altogether due to hard work. Tact and personal charm drew to the editor many supporters. Certainly the spirit in which the magazine was conducted accounted for much of its success, as is suggested in the following paragraph, written by Frederick at the opening of his periodical's tenth year:

"It is still to me a joint adventure of readers, contributors, and editor—laborious and difficult but joyous, slightly irresponsible, and devoted most of all to the cause of good fellowship. We are seeking, to be sure, some such things as truth and beauty. But I do not want to be too rigidly convinced that I know what these things are or where to find them. Nor can I tell how long we may journey together. I am content if in this tenth volume we of The Midland, new friends and old, may find something pleasant in our comradeship, and something to be cherished in our freedom."[22]

Here we see the very human quality of the man, the warmth of feeling which drew an ever-increasing number of readers, contributors, and other persons to devote their time and money to The Midland ideal. We can also sense in this quotation the calm dignity which never allowed Frederick to become a missionary crusader. He had a purpose, the challenging of Eastern commercial periodical standards, but never

---

[19] Statement, Frederick to Allen, September 1937.
[20] Frederick, pamphlet enclosed with January 1916 issue of The Midland.
[21] Statement, Frederick to Allen, September 1937.
[22] Frederick, Editorial, The Midland, x, 64 (January 1924).

did his conviction break into ranting tirades. There were, indeed, in *The Midland's* eighteen-year history, not over a dozen pages devoted to criticism of East Coast publishing tactics, and that criticism was free of the ostentatious, reforming tone. Frederick preferred to keep himself in the background, to work quietly and let the results speak for themselves.

*The Midland* record during the first eight years is memorable largely for a great bulk of fine short stories and poetry. Many young writers came with great promise. They came with the honesty that Frederick called for, but they were often undeveloped as storytellers. Hours and days were spent with many of them, criticizing, encouraging, until finally several developed into artists who showed every sign of future accomplishment.[23] This coaching of the young writer is one of the primary justifications of the little magazine. It means that many persons are developed who otherwise might never be heard from. The literary flowering of the last quarter century is, in no small part, the result of little magazine editors' patience in helping the ambitious writer to come into his own. It was Frederick's ill luck that many with whom he spent laborious hours during the first eight years died before they could develop their original promise.[24] Others, like Walter J. Muilenburg, faded after writing a half dozen or a dozen good stories. Perhaps they were not born writers, perhaps they could only thrive under continual stimulation. As far as this generation is concerned, most of the contributors of fiction to *The Midland* in its early years are unknown, though many of these forgotten men certainly produced some fine work, stories which gained for the periodical a growing respect. "The Prairie" and "Heart of Youth," by Walter J. Muilenburg; "The Parting Genius," by Helen Coale Crew; and Harriet Maxon Thayer's "Kindred" are some of the memorable stories from this period. It was during these years, too, that Frank Luther Mott, shortly to become an editor of *The Midland*, began to contribute his first stories, among them the mystically turned "The Man with the Good Face." Then there was Howard Mumford Jones, later to become better known as a critic, who sent his first stories to Frederick.

There was one discovery from the first eight years of which any magazine might have been proud. In 1920 a story "Uprooted," by Ruth Suckow, found its way into University Hall and was published, beginning a cordial relationship between Miss Suckow and Frederick. Several

[23] Statement, Frank Luther Mott to Charles Allen, November 1937.
[24] *Ibid.*

of her early stories were accepted by The Midland and she came to Iowa City in 1922 to become an associate editor.

Practically all of The Midland fiction was realistic. This realism was frequently of the grim, pessimistic variety that has dominated the later regional little magazine. But, in general, The Midland was prone to a quiet optimism, the stories reflecting love for the land, cheerful humor, and faith in man's ability to build a dignified life. This warm and comfortable view of rural culture was usually convincing, though there were times when one suspected traces of sentimental romanticism. However, the mark of sentimentality was rarely obvious enough to destroy the essential truth.

A good deal of the early Midland poetry was regional and it generally revealed the merits and defects of regional verse which we have mentioned earlier. Among the first contributors of verse were Arthur Davison Ficke, Edwin Ford Piper, William Ellery Leonard, Margaret Widdemer, Witter Bynner, Ruth Suckow, and Maxwell Anderson. Only Ruth Suckow, whose first poem was printed in 1918, was discovered by The Midland. Those were the years when Poetry garnered discovery honors.

In 1923 Frederick decided to throw the direction of his magazine from a definitely Midwest basis to a national one. The reasons for this are readily apparent. The magazine had for some time received many manuscripts and most of its subscriptions from other sections, particularly New York and California. But more important, Frederick had come to the conclusion that the Middlewesterner was not the only one tormented by New York's prejudiced demands. Writers from New England, from Mississippi, from any region, faced the same problem as the Dakota artist. The editor believed that the midland was the best location from which to challenge, since it represented a geographic and cultural mean. But until the end in 1933, well over half the stories were by Midwestern writers and about the Midwest region.

By 1925, when Frederick moved back to Iowa City from Pittsburgh where he had been teaching in the University of Pittsburgh for two years, the editorial burdens had become heavier, and because of this he asked Frank Luther Mott to become a co-editor.[25] This was a wise choice, since Mott was well fitted by temperament and training to work harmoniously with Frederick. During the next five years the two men shared responsibility, both editorial and financial. The magazine prospered. In these years The Midland published some of the early work of

[25] Statement, Frederick to Allen, September 1937.

a number of writers who are now becoming famous. MacKinlay Kantor, Paul Engle, Phil Stong, James Hearst, James Farrell, David Cornel De Jong, Albert Halper, Clifford Bragdon, and Marquis Childs were among those who received early recognition from *The Midland*. These were years of hope and aspiration. In addition to the work of the above authors, the magazine printed fine stories by men like Tupper Greenwald, Warren L. Van Dine, Raymond Weeks, Leo L. Ward, and William March. Such stories as March's "The Little Wife" and Weeks's "The Hound-Tuner of Calloway" did much to place the periodical near the top of the little magazine heap. The editors dreamed of the time when their magazine could become a more potent national influence. They were keeping their eyes open for the opportunity for expansion, knowing that it might come.

And by 1930 the time appeared ripe for *The Midland* to take further steps to increase its prestige. Not only Frederick, but such shrewd observers as Edward J. O'Brien, believed that the magazine might do well to seek richer pastures. (O'Brien's early recognition had done much to help the magazine through its first perilous years.) In prefacing his volume of *Best Short Stories* for 1930, O'Brien expressed the opinion that the quality periodicals were dying on their feet. *The Century* had just expired. According to O'Brien, the quality magazines had persisted too long in giving their readers second-best stories whose only recommendations were the canonized names of the authors; the public was ready and eager for a new vitality, from whatever quarter, and would not long be put off.[26] To meet the demand, and for the good of American letters, O'Brien made this suggestion:

"The true remedy for this lagging behind of the better monthlies is probably the establishment of a new national monthly in the Middle West which is nearer the present centre of population. If I may venture a suggestion, I think the time is now ripe for *The Midland* to pool its interests with *The Prairie Schooner*, *The Frontier*, and perhaps one or two other regional periodicals such as *The Southwest Review*, and to issue a full-grown national monthly of belles-lettres in which short stories, poems and essays should be given pride of place. The significance of such a new national periodical would depend very largely upon its interest in discovering new writers rather than in depending upon old ones.

"If *The Midland* chooses to take the lead in this matter, I am convinced, after many years' reflection, that it has the same opportunity to

[26] Edward J. O'Brien, *Best Short Stories of 1930*, New York, 1930, pp. x-xi.

crystallize the best expression of contemporary national life that *The Atlantic Monthly* was able to seize upon its foundation, and that *Harper's Magazine* enjoyed a generation ago. Two generations ago Boston was the geographical centre of American literary life, one generation ago New York could claim pride of place, and I trust that the idea will not seem too unfamiliar if I suggest that the geographical centre today is Iowa City."[27]

Frederick, however, had been considering another plan. Still dominated by his conviction that Eastern publishing influences were unwholesome, still convinced that the Middlewest was the best place to fight back at New York, Frederick decided to move his magazine to Chicago. Perhaps he was more realistic than O'Brien in selecting Chicago rather than Iowa City as the most logical point from which to attack. Chicago, the editor believed, should become the focus "because of its energy, position, printing facilities, and *Poetry*." And so, late in 1930, *The Midland* left Iowa City "with a box of subscription cards and a sheaf of manuscripts—alike slender, sole impedimenta of the editorial office." Though the magazine continued to be printed in Iowa City, its editorial windows now faced "black roofs and the utilitarian facade of a twelve-story garage" on Van Buren Street.[28] Frank Mott remained behind, and Frederick and his wife became co-editors, though Mott continued as an associate and conducted much of the Iowa City business.

Six months after the magazine had been in Chicago it flowered out in a more imposing, two-column format. The periodical was now receiving a great number of good manuscripts. The subscription list grew to 1,200, and about 2,000 copies were printed per issue.[29] During the next six months Benjamin Appel was discovered. To all appearances Frederick's gamble in taking the magazine to Chicago was to bear rich fruit. The magazine was daily assuming a new importance. The integrity of the editor, his unwillingness to be swayed in any fashion by commercial expediency, his fine critical sense, the financial stability which was rapidly being gained, promised much. For a few months *The Midland* prospered as it never had before, and the editor's dream appeared capable of realization. But just at the moment that success seemed assured, an ominous wind began to blow.

Storm clouds had been on the Eastern horizon even at the moment

[27] *Ibid.*
[28] Frederick, Editorial, *The Midland*, xvi, 369 (November-December, 1930).
[29] Statement, Frederick to Allen, September 1937.

Frederick moved to Chicago. Few persons expected these clouds to develop into a serious blow. But the hurricane of financial depression swept westward from the seaboard, striking Chicago with full blast in the winter of 1931. Banks failed, bread lines grew, factories closed, business collapsed. *The Midland* was doomed.

For eighteen months the editor fought a losing battle. Subscriptions fell off; the magazine changed from a monthly to a bimonthly. Meanwhile, Frederick shouldered a debt of a thousand dollars a year,[30] hoping to outride the storm. But by the summer of 1933 the battle was over. We know what the magazine's end must have meant to its editor from the following quotation from the last editorial: "For nearly twenty years I have given to it money and time taken from my work as teacher and farmer, from my reading, from my family life; and though the money and time have been alike sometimes needed and hard to spare, my personal rewards have been great."[31]

Because of its contribution to the development of regionalism, *The Midland* must be ranked alongside *The Dial*, *The Little Review*, and *Poetry*. It was a magazine that discovered and helped many young authors. It published a great volume of excellent fiction. Of the 337 Midland stories that came to Edward O'Brien's notice, 324 were judged of high merit, 105 of them being of such distinction that he gave them his highest rating.[32] Few magazines can boast such a high percentage of excellent stories. But above all, *The Midland* emphasized, perhaps more than any other periodical, what must always be the standard of any little magazine—complete integrity in upholding its standards.

[30] *Ibid.*
[31] Frederick, Editorial, *The Midland*, xix, 56 (June 1933).
[32] O'Brien (a calculation based on the rating of *The Midland* stories from 1915 to 1933, not including the years 1922-23, since the magazine is not rated for those years).

# POLITICAL DIRECTIONS in the Literature of the Thirties

CHAPTER IX

Socialism has long been familiar to the young intellectual. *The Masses, The Liberator,* San Francisco's *Blast,* Emma Goldman's *Mother Earth,* and other magazines have since 1904 "carried the message" in one form or another to the intellectuals and the workers of their time. Margaret Anderson's *The Little Review* sponsored, among other things, a form of "aesthetic anarchism," and there were appearances by Emma Goldman and other left-wingers in its pages. In 1906 Emma Goldman had established the anarchist *Mother Earth,* one of the early sponsors of radical literature in America. Miss Goldman came to the United States in 1886, and she was immediately active in promoting a variety of reform movements. During the second decade of our century, she joined with sympathetic intellectuals, argued for socialism and social reform, was jailed twice, and finally (in 1919), with Alexander Berkman, was deported to Russia. Along with *The Masses* and *The Liberator,* Miss Goldman's magazine influenced liberal thinkers to take a stand somewhat left of center in their attitudes toward the First World War and other contemporary issues. In fact, social and political problems were very much in the minds of men and women of the second and third decades. In 1922, Gorham Munson complained that a little review had difficulty steering a safe course between absence of policy and an overdose of "extraneous" policy. The editors of the latter type of magazine, says Munson, were almost solely interested in "the social, interpretative, philosophical, and psychological significances of literature, rather than in aesthetic meanings."[1]

Socialism and its intellectual sponsors exercised an influence upon

[1] Munson, "Interstice between Scylla and Charybdis," p. 31.

the thought of many writers, an influence which argued for some crystallization of attitude when the proper circumstances might permit. Until the time of the Russian Revolution, however, its influence was formative but not convincing. The first issues of *The Masses*, for example, talked about socialism and advertised Karl Marx cigars for sale, but its editor advocated cooperatives and other variants of mild reform. The real distinction between leftwing magazines before 1930 and those of the thirties seemed to be this: in the early years, the accent was upon criticism of and the need for reform within the capitalist system; after the financial crash, left-wingers gained the confidence of hundreds of writers, and magazines spoke forthrightly of revolution. This latter call was implicit, of course, in some of the earlier magazines, and explicit in a few; but one can scarcely assume that, because *The Liberator* spoke out against the abuses of capitalism in the early twenties and *The New Masses* was founded in 1926, the little magazines were prevailingly leftwing in their political thinking. We ought to regard the period 1904-17 as a "progressive" period, one in which debunking and reform were advanced with varying degrees of belligerency and success; the period 1917-30 as an "aggressive" period, during which issues were being clearly defined and Marxist critics were formulating their principles and exploring the possibilities of full-fledged attack upon capitalist institutions and economics; and, finally, the thirties as an "active" period, during which leftwing ideas were not only adopted by intellectuals but actively promoted as alternatives to capitalist principles. Since the little magazines, along with most other publishing ventures, were to be vitally affected by this last development, it is with it that we should be chiefly concerned. But we might also look briefly upon the earlier career of leftwing ideas and magazines.

*The Masses* emphasized politics, but we can scarcely say that it offered a synthesis of the political and aesthetic points of view. Certainly the articles of John Reed and Mary Heaton Vorse, and the poetry of Arturo Giovannitti argued for a growing strength among the literary leftists. The magazine's editorial advertisements emphasized its desire to "conciliate nobody." It was concerned with feminism, with abuse of the workers in a capitalistic state, with the futility of the war, and with other matters which may also be the concern of Communists but are certainly not the mainstay of Communist doctrine. A poem by Arturo Giovannitti, which appears in the issue of January 1913, expresses imperfectly the sentiment of the magazine, though it scarcely points to anything more positive than sympathy for the downtrodden:

> The dust of a thousand roads, the grease
>   And grime of slums, were on his face;
> The pangs of hunger and disease
> Upon his throat had left their trace;
> The smell of death was in his breath,
>   But in his eye no resting-place.
>
> Along the gutters, shapeless, ragged,
>   With drooping head and bleeding feet,
> Throughout the Christmas night he dragged
>   His care, his woe, and his defeat;
> Till gasping hard with face downward
>   He fell upon the trafficked street.[2]

John Reed reported the strike in Paterson, New Jersey, in the issue of June 1913. Floyd Dell regretted the scarcity of such true revolutionaries as Theodore Dreiser, in the February 1914 number. In April 1914, the magazine carried a discussion of the case of Frank Tannenbaum, who had led a group of derelicts into a New York church and been arrested for his pains. And Louis Untermeyer expressed dismay over the apathy of average America concerning the revolution:

> Yet I felt that this man was going to bring
>     about the revolution—
> Bring it quicker—make it bloodier—
> With his hard, careful apathy, and
>     his placid, shrugging unconcern.[3]

In 1917, when the war issue prevented the full expression of calm or satirical minds, the government suppressed *The Masses*. It reappeared as *The Liberator* in March 1918, with the same editors. *The Liberator* began to talk the language of Marx and Lenin immediately. Yet in the opinion of Joseph Freeman, one of its later editors, ". . . abstract theories outstripped our practical sense of what was revolutionary in art."[4] The conflict between the "aesthetic" and the "actual" revolutionaries was reflected in the career of *The Liberator*. Most of

---
[2] "The Bum," *The Masses*, IV, 15 (January 1913).
[3] "A Customer," *The Masses*, V, 15 (June 1914).
[4] Freeman, *An American Testament*, p. 258.

the historians who have commented on The Liberator are of the opinion that it was but a pale imitation of The Masses. True, the ebullience was absent and one missed, too, the sparkling language that cloaked the artistic and propagandistic Masses' trumpetings for reform.

But the calls for reform were nevertheless to be found. There are all of the old Masses' war cries for feminine equality, racial equality, freedom of speech and of the press, reform of the criminal code, to which were added attacks on the Klan and Prohibition. Yet what is most surprising, almost incredible, was a belligerent demand for revolution as a means of bringing about the socialist state—this not only during the latter months of the war when America was angry and shocked at bloody Russia, but even during the regime of Red-baiting Attorney General Palmer. John Reed explained the Revolution almost every month before his death in October 1920; Maxim Gorky, Nikolai Lenin, Leon Trotsky, and Karl Radek also contributed revolutionary polemic direct from the Kremlin, though much less frequently than Reed. Among the most frequent American contributors were Max Eastman, Floyd Dell, Claude McKay, Michael Gold, Joseph Freeman, Robert Minor, and John Pepper. Certainly The Liberator served the cause of radicalism more than nominally. The magazine finally combined, in November 1924, with the Labor Herald and Soviet Russia Pictorial to become The Worker's Monthly.

In the spring of 1926 The New Masses was founded in New York City, its first editors Egmont Arens, Joseph Freeman, Hugo Gellert, Michael Gold, James Rorty, and John Sloan. Among the fifty-six writers and artists connected in some way with the early issues of The New Masses, Freeman reports, only two were members of the Communist Party, and less than a dozen were fellow travelers. The New Masses had started as an experimental magazine. Published monthly in the beginning, it later became a weekly, at which time it assumed a heavy political emphasis and became increasingly conscious of its responsibility to the Communist Party line. Again the literary interests of its editors locked horns with their political interests. But this conflict was soon to be resolved. In its earlier issues The New Masses is a literary little magazine, modeled halfheartedly upon its older namesake. The editors had decided that it was not to be a Bolshevist journal but a magazine of American experiment. The first issue contained Babette Deutsch's philosophical dialogue between the shades of Lenin and Anatole France, and a number of essays on political subjects. This latter emphasis was soon the predominating one, and in the thirties

*The New Masses* became what it is today: a magazine of leftwing political comment, its attention to literature confined to book reviews and explosive editorials aimed at non-Marxist contemporaries.

The importance of *The Masses* and *The Liberator* for the development of leftist thought ought not to be neglected, though neither magazine possessed the critical seriousness of *The Modern Quarterly* or the downright and almost exclusive devotion to Marx and Russia which animated all but the earlier issues of *The New Masses*. But, in Max Eastman's editorials, in the long, journalistic reports of John Reed from foreign fronts, and in the sketches by Mary Heaton Vorse, we can find positive and persuasive signs of a growing activism. In short, the struggle between comic playboyism and serious reportage went on in the pages of these two magazines almost from the beginning. The men and women of most other magazines looked to Paris—and in the twenties they went there. Those of *The Masses* and *The Liberator* looked to Moscow; and many of them went there through the twenties and thirties to investigate and report on the great socialist experiment. Essentially these two early magazines were both of the Village and of the world outside; the emphasis seemed often to be on Village attitudes and the orientation toward large political issues a Village orientation. It was really after *The Liberator* had given over to *The Labor Herald*, and *The New Masses* had finally decided against going the same route as its predecessors, that the playboy and the serious elements of our early leftist movement were separated: the aesthetic playboy either stayed in the Village with Egmont Arens and others, or went to Paris; some of the more sophisticated and less doctrinaire comments upon local and national society found their way to the pages of *The New Yorker*, which began in 1925 to appeal to the "caviar sophisticates." This division of interests was symptomatic of the growing isolation of interest in serious leftwing criticism, unadorned and uninfluenced by petty preoccupations with capitalist didos, but seriously concerned with the more disastrous cracks in the capitalistic wall.

Perhaps the best explanation of the ambiguous stand of *The Masses* and *The Liberator* was the conviction that there were several solutions to the crisis in capitalism. It was only when the Revolution in Russia had apparently proved the workability of the political tenets of Communism that the conflict between aesthetic and purely socialistic attitudes crystallized into action. *The Liberator* especially performed a yeoman's service in interpreting the Russian Revolution to American intellectuals. The age was after all generous and willing to accommodate one more theory explaining the paradoxes in American society. But it seemed that the intellectuals of the twenties were much more interested in an analysis which was less coldly objective. They regarded Marxism seriously enough, but often looked upon it only as theory. They subscribed to revolution, but they usually insisted that it have the insight of the artist as its *modus vivendi*. Like André Gide, E. E. Cummings journeyed to Russia to see for himself. He was disillusioned, as we know from his reports in *The Hound and Horn*.

*The Modern Quarterly* is one of a few magazines of the twenties in which criticism seemed well founded upon Marxist principle. It attacked the idea of private property without qualification. It was especially vehement in its attack upon the members of "the leisure class," considering T. S. Eliot a spokesman who would "rationalize their defeat into an appearance of victory."[5] Opposed to Jolas and the *transition* call for a "Revolution of the Word," the magazine's editor insisted that language subserves social communication. Any revolution of the word, he said, should have but one purpose: "To make the word a finer because [a] more precise and clarifying form of social communication."[6] As a critical review, *The Modern Quarterly* was bitterly opposed to aesthetic individualism and "eccentricity": "If art is to become other than an amusement for the fatigued merchant, the tired flapper, and the jaded libertine, it must rise from the eccentric to the universal, must transcend the pallid estheticisms of recent years in its endeavor to attain a social beauty commensurate with radical vision and aspiration."[7]

*The Modern Quarterly*, above all, showed most clearly the coincidence of two important preceptors of modern thought—Freud and Marx. To V. F. Calverton, the editor, they were equally important: Freud had located the areas in which modern bourgeois evil had originated; Marx had offered a new society in which "social repression" would be kept at a minimum. Most of the criticism in the magazine shared that conviction; the contemporary writers are discussed often in terms borrowed from psychoanalysis. This union of conflicting (or at least supplementary) theories is characteristic of the intellectual habits of the twenties. As the years moved toward the climax of capital-

---

[5] Ernest Sutherland Bates, "T. S. Eliot: Leisure Class Laureate," *The Modern Monthly*, VII, 17 (February 1933).

[6] V. F. Calverton, "The Revolution-in-the-Wordists," *The Modern Quarterly*, V, 277 (Fall 1929).

[7] V. F. Calverton, "For a New Critical Manifesto," *The Modern Quarterly*, IV, 17 (January-April, 1927).

ism's speculative orgy, before the "crash," Freud received less attention, Marx and Lenin more. Why the partnership at all? The artist who thought most seriously about social problems hesitated to give up his role in society to the organizer, the party man. Freud represented to him a happy and apparently workable union of the aesthetic and moral imperatives; Marxism combined effectively the economic and moral imperatives, but neglected the aesthetic. How could one better save both the world and one's conscience than by bringing Freud and Marx together? The inherent differences did not need to wait long to be discovered. Floyd Dell, who perhaps more than any other writer of the twenties saw Freud and Marx as the cultural sponsors of his time, retired from Marxism almost entirely and consulted psychoanalysis and allied theories of sex for his estimate of society. Joseph Freeman was willing to forget Freud temporarily and join the party, subscribing wholeheartedly to the Marxist solution. His latest novel, *Never Call Retreat* (1943), and his retirement from political controversy suggest a return to psychoanalysis. But most writers were less firmly held by either.

II

This conflict, one of many, was resolved for most writers by that sobering economic crisis known as the depression. In the twenties Waldo Frank had characterized Calvin Coolidge as the last of a long line of repressed Puritan Americans. In 1930, dozens of writers were subjecting Herbert Hoover to a severe Marxian analysis. The change in direction is not entirely accidental. Efforts to achieve an aesthetic synthesis of the diversity of tendencies had failed for two reasons: the aesthetic temperament is often too slow in coming to practicable decisions—witness the failure of D. H. Lawrence's many plans; it was altogether reluctant, until forced by circumstances, to submit to a discipline which seemed alien to its purposes. The circumstances were now apparent; the incentive for isolating the aesthetic temperament from direct social issues had all but disappeared. From the singular and eccentric debate over purity of motive, many writers turned to a direct frontal assault upon the evils of the bourgeois.

Writing about the little magazines in the December 1934 issue of *Space*, John Gould Fletcher remarked the differences between the magazines of 1914-29 and those of the thirties. The former, says Fletcher, were "prevailingly aesthetic; the later crop has been in many cases imbued with proletarian protest, with an atmosphere of Marxism." This "proletarization" he regards as essential to literature: "Somehow, poetry and drama, criticism and history, will have to pass through the same test, will have to emerge again as arts for the people rather than for the select few."[8]

One might easily assume that, with the partial check upon aesthetic immunity, the little magazines would have ceased to encourage experimental writing and have concentrated upon following a strict party line. This, however, was not the case. The *avant garde* retained a fair portion of its independence, and the leftwing writer was given considerable freedom in the form in which he belabored bourgeois capitalism. It seemed only natural, however, that two literary forms should be stressed: free verse and the short story. The former lost much of its experimental quality as it galloped ahead to the rescue of the oppressed. The latter concentrated mainly upon the details of social realism. Proletarian fiction came into its own; and the agrarian realism of *The Midland* enjoyed a revival which necessitated a variety of magazines to accommodate it: *Hinterland*, for example, *The Hub* of Cedar Rapids, Iowa, and *The Midwest*.

What had formerly appeared to the poet to be a delightful immunity from financial worry now aroused resentment. The artist was lost in a capitalist's world; his talents were not wanted, except insofar as they justified the *status quo* or entertained the tired businessman. Said Maxwell Bodenheim, on the status of the artist in a capitalist society: "No proletarian worker on the face of the earth is more shamelessly and deceitfully exploited than is a poet in any capitalistic country."[9] The poet may serve the revolutionary cause, Bodenheim continued, by remaining independent of Communist doctrine and speaking his own mind.

Without qualification, certain magazines swung wholeheartedly to the leftist cause. They mocked the cynicism and despair of literature which either compromised or hesitated on the leftward turn. *Left Front* in Chicago sneered at the "Century of Progress" exhibits being prepared along the lake front. The future, it declared, was not with *that* kind of progress. And Richard Wright sent "A Red Love Note" to his capitalist oppressors:

[8] "The Little Reviews: Yesterday and To-Day," *Space*, 1, 84-85 (December 1934).
[9] "The Revolutionary Poet," *The Little Magazine*, 1, 1 (February-March, 1934).

> My dear lovely bloated one:
> when we send you our final love-notice of foreclosure
> to vacate this civilization which you have inhabited
> long beyond the rightful term of your tenure,
> there won't be any postponements, honey;
> no court delays,
> no five-day notices, darling;
> no continuations, sugar-pie;
> it'll all be over before you know it![10]

In the trilingual magazine *Front*, V. F. Calverton announced the doom of individualism in aesthetics, in no uncertain terms. There is no place in any society for the "precious" confusion of minds. The literary artist must turn to social organization or simply lose his place in the world. In the new society the poet will be looked upon as an "emotional engineer." "The individualistic concept of the artist as a free agent, therefore, is doomed to disappear with the passing of individualist civilization."[11] The dissenting voice of Ezra Pound, who contributed a note to *Front*, made only a slight impression. The progress of *Front* was toward a commitment to leftwing policies. Literature will be considered an art, it implied, only if it aids the workers in their struggle with the *bourgeoisie*.

One of the effects of this movement toward the left was a reconsideration of middle class society in America. Respectability had always been the object of much scornful comment. The artist of the twenties, however, had regarded the revolt against it as a personal matter, as though "respectable" people were doing him a disservice in being unpleasant and disagreeable. The leftist regarded respectability as a wall to be knocked down and removed. For him it was a sign of social apathy, or a veil drawn across the evils in society. Hence the satire in leftwing magazines was directed against aspects of bourgeois life which kept prejudice alive and afforded men a comfortable protection against reality. This is the attitude taken by the leftist poet, H. H. Lewis:

> The orchestra plays,
> And the unragged, unfatigued,
>    parasitical audience,
> Wised to the ways of symphony,
> Gets the point.

[10] *Left Front*, I, 3 (January-February, 1934).
[11] "The Literary Artist in a Mass Civilization," *Front*, I, 19 (December 1930).

How esoteric the fantasia becomes:
How the listeners, not hungry for
    food, lean forward to catch
    the faint, sweet notes . . .

And you damn elite monsters of
    sensitivity,
O blast your perverted souls.[12]

For the most part writers concentrated upon the task of picturing the disgusting lives of the oppressor and the distressing lives of the oppressed. It was the task of literature, it seemed, to describe the hardship of life in a capitalist society—the pity of it, the economic and moral paradoxes which it allowed. All leftwing trends in literature were scanned and appraised by the "official" organ of leftist aesthetics, *International Literature*. Surveys of the work of Sherwood Anderson, Langston Hughes, James Joyce, and other moderns appeared in that magazine from time to time. Joyce, for example, "is one of the greatest representatives of the literature intimately connected with the parasitic decay of Western bourgeois culture."[13] "Work in Progress" is "pure nonsense, the work of a master idling." In this magazine, also, the Marxist interpretation of aesthetics was given careful attention, with the aim of affording leftist writers a direction for their efforts.

The link between experimentalism in literature and radicalism of political point of view is seen in *The Left*, a magazine published by George Redfield and Jay du Von in Davenport, Iowa. Artists who had hitherto believed that experiment is possible only in a *bourgeois* milieu were to be encouraged to try out new forms and techniques, "to express the fresh substance, the faster tempos and rhythms of the new world order. . . ."[14] The magazine supplemented its editorial announcement with such critical essays as V. F. Calverton's "The Need for Revolutionary Criticism," and Harold J. Salemson's "French Letters, Left Face." And in the second issue Donal McKenzie spoke the usual words over the grave of Ezra Pound's literary pretensions: "Pound is an incurable Romantic Liberal," McKenzie said, "toasting his toes at the better Fascisti fires, and trying to rationalize about a system of which he really enjoys the fruits."[15] *The Left* gave space

[12] "In All Hell," *The Rebel Poet*, I, 3 (February 1931).
[13] D. S. Mirsky on James Joyce, *International Literature*, I, 92 (1934).
[14] Editorial, *The Left*, I, 3 (Spring 1931).
[15] "T(h)inker Pound and Other Italian Legends," *The Left*, I, 52 (Autumn 1931).

to the young writers who were underlining in their poems and stories the courage of the worker and the evil of his "owner": Jack Conroy, Norman Macleod, Albert Halper, and S. Funaroff.

## III

Social realism, the form in which leftist literature was frequently written, used the technique of the objective reporter. Selecting a scene, an event, or a person, the author relied upon the facts themselves to tell the story and announce his attitude toward it. The subjects were starvation, strikes, poverty, proletarian heroism. The formula for melodrama, which assumes clear-cut personal representatives of villainy and virtue, was often employed to give reportage an editorial slant, so that the moral might be made more explicit. The writing is marked by self-confidence: the hero, though imprisoned actually or spiritually, is consoled by the thought that his imprisonment is a temporary thing; it will be relieved by death or by some other form of deliverance. This current of comment runs through many of the tales: prejudice, injustice, or oppression are absurd; men act this way only when they are victims of an intolerable economic system; once the system has been smashed, men will be good and above all sensible. The social realist had, therefore, two aims: to impress the reader with prevailing political and economic conditions; to arouse him to indignant action against these conditions. Both leftwing fiction and leftist criticism emphasized these aims. Critics pointed out the literary realism of the recent past, to prove that the description of conditions was not at all falsified. Sherwood Anderson, they said, was not a Communist; yet he too was forced by the relentless urgency of fact to describe life in a capitalist society as drab and inconvenient.

Matters of style were strictly secondary. But the proletarian writer often selected adjectives which best underlined the absurdity and paradox in society. It was also permissible to caricature the enemy enough to remove any respect the reader may have had for his way of life. The selection of scene was often made with the aim of underlining the ironic contrast of undeserving prosperity with undeserved misery. Walter Snow's "Lunch Hour in Wall Street" demonstrates some of these devices: "Old Pietro Vichi, a white walrus moustache drooping below cheeks hollow and slaty as storm-chiseled rock, big, bony hands thrust in shabby overcoat pockets, instinctively ceased his stooping gait, drew a deep breath of the sun-warmed salt-tangy air and threw back his rounded shoulders. His thin blue lips suddenly twisted in pain. . . ."[16] And the concluding lines force the contrast upon the reader's attention, with the aid of large caps and exclamation points: " 'D'ya hear? STARVATION! On the steps of the Sub-Treasury!' "

The futility of attempting in any way to deal with the business mind is emphasized in other *Anvil* stories. The uninformed worker lives in an atmosphere of helplessness which can be relieved only by his learning the Marxist truth, or by committing suicide: "After all, what could you do? After all, it was not anything you could stop." Women on relief have an especially hard time: "The way it is that they think that all the girls and women on relief is bad, that's the way they figures it. Low grade intelligence, they says."[17]

All of this aroused a mixed response. Some critics accused leftwing writers of being single-minded and morbid. There were also matters of style: is one's conviction about social abuses to be a single passport to a literary reputation? Leftwing writers were aware of their limitations, but insisted that, after all, they had a direction, and that ultimately conviction would lead to the fullest exploitation of latent talent. They argued further that no talent would be vitiated by the necessity for nonaesthetic compromise with the quality magazines and with those who controlled them. Social realism was obstinately faithful to the context of actual society, they argued, and it did not hesitate to reflect the misery, the ugliness, the language of the "industrial primitive." The death of the euphemism was immediate and final. After all, wasn't the euphemism a part of middle-class respectability? To replace it with a franker language was evidence of a new kind of "wholesomeness."

The principles of creation applied in fairly equal measure to town and country. The small town is pictured as a dreary, spiritually dead place—with much uninteresting sin committed as a refuge from the dullness of life. Somehow nature, which had in *The Midland* stories inspired the lives of men, now looks impassively upon evil—as it does in this story by Jerre Mangione: "He tried to breathe but leaves got into his mouth. Then he felt his body dropping into space. It turned a somersault, then another. The third time his head hit an iron post.

---

[16] *The Anvil*, I, 5 (May 1933).
[17] John C. Rogers, "Gas," *The Anvil*, I, 15 (September-October, 1934); Meridel LeSueur, "They Follow Us Girls," *The Anvil*, II, 5 (July-August, 1935).

His body lay still. On the hill above, the yellow leaves rustled in the wind."[18]

The development of the short story in the thirties is single in direction, but the requirements of social realism helped to modify the form. Social reportage gave the short story a more limited selection of theme; it reduced the structural requirements of the short story to a minimum and reinstated the implicit moral as a necessary guide to narrative direction. Since the short story is a convenient device for the entertainment of strap-hangers, the overwhelming tendency in popular short fiction had been to offer a well-made unit of action, fitted to the commercial magazine's notion of "what the twelve-year-old is thinking about this season." The formal requirements of such fiction were adjusted to its readability under conditions forbidding more than a fleeting attention to thought content. Its content suited admirably the tastes of a cinema-fed public. The little magazine of the short story had, therefore, an excellent reason for being. Its purposes were two: to convince the reader that a story need not advertise its beginning, its middle, and its end; to present life as it was, at its glamorless worst.

It was inevitable that the story magazines, committed to no social program, should absorb a number of leftwing writers. *Story*, the most successful of the lot, was begun in Vienna in 1931 by Whit Burnett and Martha Foley. In the course of its very active career it printed "short narratives of significance by no matter whom and coming from no matter where." The magazine's principal value is that it served as a proving ground for young writers who were experimenting with the form. The American version of the Chekhovian tale was given a good deal of attention. A simple reflection of the life or mind of a character, given no ethical or psychological clarification, this form marks the development of new experimentation in narrative writing.

When *Story* celebrated its tenth anniversary in 1941, it had published over a thousand stories, about 90 per cent of which were considered distinctive by short story anthologist O'Brien. These stories, always readable, if not quite as fresh and awe-inspiring as Messrs. Burnett and O'Brien and Martha Foley contend, are better than anything else of the sort published in America. They are stories from the pens of such old masters as Saroyan, Hemingway, Faulkner, Kay Boyle, and Caldwell, and from such young talents as Francis Eisenberg, Ludwig Bemelmans, Roderick Lull, and Kresseman Taylor. There have been

---

[18] Jerre Mangione, "His Favorite Color," *Hinterland*, IX, 20 (1938).

a number of discoveries, and a still greater number of writers who have attained prominence through *Story*, though not published there for the first time. In short, *Story* is a convincing refutation of the frequent dogmatic assertions that the little magazine's function was a peculiar flowering of the First World War years, or of the twenties, or of the early depression years.

Stimulated by the success of *Story*, H. E. Bates and Edward J. O'Brien established the English *New Stories* in 1934: "The editors ... do not set forth any definition or classification of the short story as a literary form, to which writers might be expected to conform. ... But they are agreed upon a proper economy of effect and a sensibility to significant detail as essential elements in the best contemporary short stories."[19] Though *Story* and *New Stories* were not established to furnish exempla for Marxist sermons, they were willing to accommodate leftwing writers because these were the literary pace-setters of the moment. The contents of the two magazines during the early thirties are liberally supplied with the names of leftwing storytellers. But this is more an accident of the times than it is a demonstration of any definite editorial policy.

The value of the short story to regionalism in literature has always been great. Midwestern realism had been the special contribution of *The Midland*. In the thirties several magazines were begun which emphasized the short story above all other forms of writing. *The Dubuque Dial*, edited by Karlton Kelm, presented "stories from Iowa." Typical of its contents is Josephine Herbst's "You Can Live Forever," a story of economic conditions in the farm country; the debate in one man's soul over the problem of joining the I.W.W.: " 'They shot him in Salt Lake City,' said Ed. 'But they got fooled. ... Let me tell you. There's more than one way to live.' "[20]

The weight of attention in the *Dubuque Dial*'s stories is devoted to social problems. This is also true of Lee Lukes's *Decade of Short Stories*, which began to appear from Chicago, in 1939: "Its conception has emerged from the girded loins of a memory of ten years of depression, turmoil, years of struggle, followed by a twisted turn to normalcy. The majority of the writers represented here have discovered the true light of their spheres within these years. . . ."[21]

The little magazine had always used stories and prose sketches. But

[19] *New Stories*, 1, 2 (February-March, 1934).
[20] *The Dubuque Dial*, 1, 1-5 (June-December, 1934).
[21] *Decade of Short Stories*, 1, front cover, verso (May 1939).

in the thirties the short story came into its own, to meet a literary need. Writers experimented in a variety of ways with the form, favored by an editorial generosity which is a characteristic of the little magazine in general. This development was not without self-criticism, however. The thirties were an age of "writer's markets," of college literary magazines sponsoring and appraising the undergraduate output. This habit of self-appraisal often had a commercial incentive, but for the most part writers seriously examined the literary value of their work.

Such an appraisal took up a large part of one issue of 1933. Thomas Uzzell praised the radical magazines for their encouragement to young writers, but found that these writers were using them too often as a means of exaggerating the sexual problem in modern society. A literary magazine, said Uzzell, should not be used as a means of satisfying the "curiosity of titillated, unhappy adolescents." Uzzell's second objection was to the radical's apparent assumption that "everything that is merely ugly or merely 'true to life' is worth printing." We should not attempt to imitate the scientist, said Uzzell; rather than seek out the truth, we ought to "sort it out." Joseph Kalar replied to Uzzell, claiming that the emphasis on sex is not the radical magazine's chief stock in trade, for "the 'sexual revolution' is practically accomplished." The radical's important task, said Kalar, is to revalue "existing esthetics and literary ideas through the lenses of a revolutionary ideology." The basis for disagreement in the symposium was essentially the length to which radicalism might go if it wished to retain some degree of literary honesty. This is the burden of Albert Wetjen's objections to *The Anvil*, which, he said, carries the social consciousness theme beyond the limits of art. Radical magazines show no discretion, he complained: "Justified in a revolt, they are inclined to rush into anarchy." The function of the little magazine, in Wetjen's estimation, is in some way to remold the literary tastes of the time; it cannot do so if it subscribes to only one aspect of our life. Fred Miller, however, is glad to see the "arty" little magazine die. It was simply the "tony" expression of the upper middle class; and it has been frightened to death by the depression. And Norman Macleod reiterates the confident purpose of the radical magazine: the little magazine, he says, has a place which cannot be filled by the "bourgeois commercial publications": "Its role is to report the decay of capitalism (in its finest expression), and the growth of the literature of the revolutionary proletariat."[22]

## IV

This 1933 symposium suggests a considerable conflict of opinion over the validity of political radicalism as a sole motivating force in literature. This conflict was more than implicit. Not all writers shifted their point of view overnight; they were not all led to accept a solution suggested to them from a nonliterary source. Artists were generally agreed upon the major abuses in society, but they often remained individualists in the face of strenuous efforts to make them "joiners." Though the radical magazine perhaps represents the strongest characteristic of the time, it was by no means alone in the literary world. Most interesting of all is the little magazine which tried to remain impartial and tolerant of varying ideologies in a time when one ideology made unceasing demands upon the writer's conscience. The career of such a magazine is likely to be perilous, and its pilot at times bewildered about his course. The editorial comment in *Earth's* first issue is typical of such uncertainty: "Just what form the policy of *Earth* will take if we are able to continue its publication, is impossible to decide at this time. That it will contain the clean, constructive expression of young men, though, is certain."[23] Before it had ceased publication, *Earth* was "converted" to radicalism in writing and criticism.

Editors parried the question of quality and purpose, striving (sometimes vainly) to consider manuscripts in terms of quality alone. When *Challenge* was asked why it was so "pale pink," it retorted that the radical contributions "were not literature." The *Windsor Quarterly* began as a little review which "will present through its successive issues a valuable survey of the important trends in modern American literature." Of these trends, the proletarian was the most persuasive; the magazine moved to Mena, Arkansas, in 1934, still open to writers "of all schools," though convinced that the best materials were coming from the leftwing groups. Two essays, considered in the order of their appearance, tell the story of the magazine's leftward progress. In the issue of Summer 1933, George F. Meeter remarked that "To

[22] Symposium on the Status of Radical Writing, 1933, Section II, 122-43 (December 1933-April 1934).
[23] Editorial, *Earth*, I, 1 (April 1930).

measure the worth of an artist or even an individual by the social feeling alone ... is to make but half a judgment."[24] In the Spring 1934 issue E. A. Schachner credited the social revolution with stimulating the only genuine literary activity: "It has remained for the present economic crisis, the deepest and broadest in the history of capitalism, to catapult American writers into the main stream of American life."[25]

A great many writers still believed in the revolution as a private matter, and complained about the sad effects of radicalism upon the development of an aesthetic. The "New Criticism" of Ransom and Tate flourished in *The Kenyon Review* and in some little magazines as well, developing along the lines of a private investigation of sense and metaphor in modern poetry. In California Yvor Winters' *Gyroscope* (1929-30) had argued for a "serious and protracted study of the masters of art and thought, as well as of self and of living human relations."[26] Such magazines as *Fantasy* kept a regular course, allowing only matters of aesthetics and "the larger criticism" to shape their policies. Radicalism in *Fantasy* was confined for the most part to revolution in aesthetic matters—theories and practices in poetry, the poet's role in a nonreligious world, among other things. Perhaps the editor was motivated by an extravagant sense of critical tolerance when he said, apropos of the influence of political matters upon his contemporaries: "Political issues which find increasingly great expression in today's print do not consciously influence our judgment. We should not be above accepting work by Hitler or Stalin or any other dictator if we thought the work worthy—literature has been known before to uphold false or betrayed ideals."[27]

A critical review committed as was *The Symposium* to the accommodation of opposing points of view is especially liable to the difficulties of impartiality in editorial judgment. This magazine of James Burnham and Philip Wheelwright is recognized as one of few important critical reviews in the history of modern criticism. To show the "relations among contemporary ideas," *The Symposium* arranged its articles so that varying lights might be thrown upon the discussion of any problem. Since it had begun in 1930, when radicalism was be-

[24] "Marxian and Universal Art," *The Windsor Quarterly*, I, 120 (Summer 1933).
[25] "Revolutionary Literature in the United States Today," *The Windsor Quarterly*, II, 27 (Spring 1934).
[26] Editorial, *The Gyroscope*, I, n.p. (May 1929).
[27] Editorial, *Fantasy*, VI, 2 (1939).

ginning its drive for domination of literature, its editors found the social problem a constant source of irritation. In April 1933, in "Thirteen Propositions," they stated explicitly their position with regard to Communism. The critical position, they said, does not offer simple alternatives for the solution of any problem, be it social or otherwise. Social revolution, however, appears now to be necessary, since capitalism is an outmoded economic system. But the Communist Party, "the one group that is clear about the aim of the politico-economic program," is not an acceptable agent of such a revolution. Criticism must recognize the social issue, however, "at a time like this."[28] The Symposium had spoken; it was as though these statements had finally cleared the air and taken care of a very vexing problem.

There were no doubts in the minds of those who wrote for The Left Review. In fact, The Left Review had the advantage of bringing together a group of very able writers who had already committed themselves to a leftist analysis of society. "Left Review does not consider literature and the other arts as the domain of a cultivated intelligentsia who condescend occasionally to look down on vulgar politics,"[29] it said. Radicalism in politics is healthful for the arts, The Left Review maintained. Indeed, the social intelligence of a writer who commits himself to a definite program, instead of mumbling vaguely to himself about this sad, sad world, is the genuine source of clear-headed criticism and satisfactory literature. In its pages The Left Review justified its editors' faith. The writing was usually sharp, clear and confident. Critical prose and reportage came from Ralph Bates, Ralph Fox, and others. And the best of the modern leftwing English poets—Spender, Auden, and C. Day Lewis—brought to the social question the unhesitating answer of leftwing sentiment.

## V

Literary expression in the little magazines of the thirties has been affected by the moral and economic emphasis of Marxist influence in several ways. In the first place, critical perception has had to sacrifice certain prerogatives which have been the artist's prized possessions. Openness of mind does not mean vacuity; the aesthetic temperament allowed for a variety of experiences to temper its habits of decision. It

[28] Editorial, The Symposium, IV, 127-34 (April 1933).
[29] Montagu Slater, "The Purpose of a Left Review," The Left Review, I, 361 (June 1935).

was inclined to regard experience as a many-sided source of aesthetic materials. The leftist commitment, while it did not blind the eyes of the writer, nevertheless adjusted their gaze. Perhaps the leftists were justified in calling a halt to dada. But dada is simply the chaos caused by negation; and in most cases it was merely adolescent sport. Leftist literature and aesthetics were bound to put at last a temporary end to the aesthetic view of life as complex; what it gained by eliminating confusion, it lost in forcing the artist into too simple a pattern of opinion and aim.

Secondly, the leftist view of the world directed individual sensibilities to certain aspects of life, and, willy-nilly, closed the eyes of the artist to others. It is not that a revolutionary attitude is harmful to the artist; but his sense of the inequalities in social experience and of the paradoxes in society is not always allowed fullest development if it is shortened by doctrinal necessity. No doubt, many writers were relieved to find so many problems solved for them. But the singular value of the poet, for example, lies in his appreciation of the complexity of the sense world and his expression of the ambiguities which result from linguistic compromise.

Finally, it is perhaps not always good for the artist to accept a ready and easy way through difficulties he seems not willing to solve. For the validity of the artist's position often rests upon a personal acceptance of responsibility. To turn from the first person singular immediately to the first person plural, without any examination of the other members of the declension, may cause the artist to lose much and gain little. In fact, the simple explanation which Marxism offered was often no better than the handy guide to writing and reform which popular psychoanalysts had suggested. There was good reason, therefore, for the hesitation with which many writers plagued themselves before they entered Marxist precincts and the eagerness with which they took advantage of incidents in the Soviet in order to leave those precincts.

The spectacle of the thirties—the dilemma of the artist solved and yet not solved—is nowhere better portrayed for us than in the career of that most interesting of all radical literary magazines, *The Partisan Review*. One of its chief aims was to provide a place for creative writing of leftist character, which was gradually being crowded out of *The New Masses* by the urgent demands of political and economic discussion. It began in New York City as a "John Reed Club" publication—one of many established throughout the country to put the convictions of John Reed into practical action. At its inception *The Partisan Review* is "simply leftist." James T. Farrell published a section from his *Studs Lonigan* trilogy in the first issue; and there were poems from the pen of Joseph Freeman, who at the time was the most sincerely convinced of all leftist writers. Short stories by Ben Field and Tillie Lerner suggested the strong alliance with such other radical magazines as *Left Front*, *Blast*, and *The Anvil*. The magazine's thorough commitment to the precepts of leftist criticism is indicated in the statement made in a review of Jack Conroy's *The Disinherited*: "There is no question why it is so good a book: it grows out of Conroy's own experience as a worker."[30]

The serious critical purpose of *The Partisan Review* is abundantly evident. The development of revolutionary literature "is a progress through a series of contradictions." Criticism must resolve these contradictions. Leftism cannot depend upon any other doctrine than Marxism. Working with *The New Masses*, the editors of *The Partisan Review* "hope to develop a critical atmosphere that will strengthen the most vital forces of our young literary tradition."[31]

In the earlier years the magazine is noted for its inclusion of writers who for the most part had definitely accepted the leftist position. The contents, though of a generally high quality, did not differ essentially from those of many other radical magazines of the time. The writers were confident of tremendous advantages over the lost generation. The survey of the endless city panorama of sensation was given a direct leftist emphasis—the details were so many soldiers mustered in the defense of a cause.

In February of 1936 *The Partisan Review* combined with *The Anvil*. In December of 1937 an editorial announced that the magazine had made the turn and become a mature review: "Any magazine, we believe, that aspires to a place in the vanguard of literature today, will be revolutionary in tendency; but we are also convinced that any such magazine will be unequivocally independent. *Partisan Review* is aware of its responsibility to the revolutionary movement in general, but we disclaim obligation to any of its organized political expressions. . . ."[32] Dwight Macdonald and F. W. Dupee, who had been editors of *The Miscellany*, joined the staff.

[30] *Partisan Review*, I, 56 (February-March, 1934).
[31] William Phelps and Philip Rahv, "Problems and Perspectives in Revolutionary Literature," *The Partisan Review*, I, 10 (June-July, 1934).
[32] Editorial, *The Partisan Review*, IV, 3 (December 1937).

*The Partisan Review* immediately felt the reaction of *The New Masses* to its independent stand. "Such," it said, "is the result of refusing to accept the Party Line in literature." The contents of the magazine changed. Disillusioned, the Party die-hards left, to concentrate their attention upon *The New Masses* and other orthodox journals. Contributions to *The Partisan Review* became (and remain) more definitely literary and critical, less polemic, the political discussions confined to the editorial columns or incorporated into the points of view of certain critics and essayists. The magazine, insofar as it is political in tone, emphasized the "Trotskyist" position—world revolution, opposition to nationalism, and definite disapproval of Stalinist policies.

With the exception of this strong revolutionary attitude in politics, the magazine has steadily increased the number and changed the nature of its literary offerings. *The Partisan Review* has, for example, presented several studies of Henry James, who has been an important mentor and spirit for many *avant-gardists*. André Gide published a section of his comments on the Soviet Union. The experimenters appear often in the later issues. As if in justification of its last move, Herbert Solow presented a statistical survey of the fate of *The New Masses* writers. Apparently, he concluded, few contributors have survived the danger of becoming "enemies" of the Party. In view of the great change in *The Partisan Review's* list of contributors, it is not too much to expect that it will become a literary magazine altogether, abandoning much of its political speculation. This is what is now happening. It is only mildly interested in the political revolution, but still vitally concerned with the evaluation of *avant-gardist* literature. The resignation of Dwight Macdonald from the editorial staff and the acquisition of Delmore Schwartz have certainly helped to change the emphasis. Macdonald has begun publishing his own magazine, *Politics*, in which he hopes to develop his own political and critical inclinations, apart from his former association with *The Partisan Review*.

If we can characterize the literary activities of the thirties at all simply, we might point out their apparent simplicity of direction, for one thing. The problem of man's survival has had a chastening influence. The content of the literature seems to have been predominantly political and sociological. There is less aesthetic eccentricity; writers seem either to have wearied of the confusion of their own contradictions or to have found themselves, at least temporarily. Aside from the large revolutionary haven to which writers retired, there were others to tempt them. It seems also that criticism has "caught up with creation," for good or ill.

Not all of the dadaists made the pilgrimage from Paris to Moscow. The influence of Freud worked strangely and wondrously on an interesting group of writers, whose work has left its mark upon our century. But this development of the thirties deserves extended treatment.

# Variations on the PSYCHOANALYTIC Theme

CHAPTER X

One of the several revolutions advocated in the twentieth century is the "Revolution of the Word." The fault with rational communication, claimed the rebels, lay in its layers of orthodox meaning and in the smugness with which men used it on the level of abstraction. Experimentalists viewed orthodoxy in word usage with much skepticism and suspicion. Language had seemed to die almost earlier than the traditional ideas and institutions which it supported or clarified. This is because language was a product of conscious thought processes and involved the selection of words, phrases, and sentences consonant with the expediency of communication—that is, it has no life of its own, being obliged to submit to any practical device or stratagem the speaker might think of using at the moment. The metaphor was considered by many modern poets as a more suitable index to the complexity of modern life, simply because it offered a variety of suggestions or meanings, which appeared on the surface to be mutually exclusive.

Conscious communication—perhaps best represented by the economy and clarity of an exact, ten-word telegram—is admirably suited to the ordinary affairs of the everyday world. It is also indispensable to verbal understanding; that is, men need to know what their terms mean, to what experience or object they refer, before they can begin to understand one another. But there is another form of understanding, not new in the twentieth century, which defies the slow workings of linguistic change or logical communication. Freud had in several ways pointed to the various devices which men use to evade the social and moral responsibilities of ordinary communication. There were slips of the tongue, at which men laughed; puns, and curious gestures with syntax and spelling, which men used in playful moments; and dream language, which men usually called ridiculous or incredible.

Freud's understanding of the dream is explained with much elaboration and evidence in *The Interpretation of Dreams*, translated into English by A. A. Brill in 1913. According to Freud, the eccentricity of dream language and dream images—composite words, composite persons, distorted sequence of events, and so forth—is caused by the efforts of certain primal drives in the unconscious to elude the censor and gain expression. In other words, the language of dreams is eccentric in the sense that it violates the rules for rational communication. A thoroughly intelligible communication demonstrates the reason fully in command of a linguistic, a logical, or a practical situation.

Those who were impressed by the researches of psychoanalysis thought that it had discovered a key to another kind of life, which might have great possibilities for literature, and especially for poetry. They thought that the language of conscious speech told an old story and an incomplete one. Since many artists in the twenties were dissatisfied with the pattern of conformity they were asked to follow, they found a ready explanation for this unfortunate circumstance. In short, they discovered that they were repressed. Not only did society ask them to submit to a variety of uncomfortable and apparently meaningless codes which seemed to exist solely for the advantage of a social life for which they had little respect; but many of their words seemed to conceal rather than reveal their actual feelings. Their unconscious lives were being withheld from them.

It is easy to see why psychoanalysis attracted a host of amateur immoralists, a flood of opportunists. Much chicanery was excused in the name of Freud; many a seduction was justified—or effected—by a misquotation from his works. To the sincere artist such misappropriation of a psychology was unpleasant. The Marxist's greatest argument against psychoanalysis was that it justified a gay flouting of tradition but offered no serious alternative to the evils of bourgeois society. The novels of the twenties are cluttered with case histories called literature, he said; or these novels offer an interpretation of character which substitutes such terms as "complex," "repression," "censor," and "resistance" in place of genuine insight into human motives.

If this were the sole contribution of psychoanalysis to literature, certainly the new psychology would have to be written off as an unfortunate example of cultural irresponsibility. Indeed, many critics expressed that very opinion. The really serious endeavor, however, which psychoanalysis helped to get under way is the re-examination of language and its relationship to experience and reality. The unconscious life of the soul or mind differed essentially from consciousness; and that difference suggested a means of using language in a new way, consistent with the total life of the poet and not only with his conscious life. Language had therefore to be revised. The word must be considered fluid rather than rigid. Meaning must be so announced that it answered the combined requisites of the external world and the unconscious or inner life of the poet. Words were to regain their original significance, freed of the demands which a cheapened communication had made of them.

## II

Since Eugene Jolas had spent much of his life in Metz, Lorraine—a "bilingual state"—and had in addition acquired English in New York night schools, he was more than commonly interested in problems of language.

Jolas was born of immigrant parents in a small New Jersey town in 1894. His father was a native of Lorraine and his mother a German Rhinelander. When he was two years old his parents returned to Europe and settled in the ancestral home near Metz, then, and for twenty-two years to come, under the German flag and language. There, in the easy tranquillity of prewar Lorraine, Jolas lived more in the "world of prehistoric irrationalism—the *Urwelt der Traume*—than in reality," as he informs us in his as yet unpublished autobiography, *Frontier-Man*. At sixteen young Jolas sailed for America, where he was to remain until 1922, acquiring English in night school and later working on newspapers in Pittsburgh, Chicago, New York, and Savannah. From 1922 until 1925 he was in Paris, Metz, and Strasbourg, publishing his first poetry, working on the Paris edition of the *Chicago Tribune*, talking for weeks on end with young modernist artists, among them Marcell Noll, who gave Jolas a ticket to dada circles. In 1925 Jolas again sailed for America.

This American trip was to influence decidedly the course of the little magazine, *transition*. Jolas was introduced to many of the young insurgent writers who later contributed to his magazine. He met and married the talented linguist and musician, Maria McDonald, who was to be very active in translating and in handling the mechanical details of *transition*. Before long Jolas and Maria deserted what for them was the too nervous atmosphere of New York for the provinces. They went to bilingual Louisiana where Jolas accepted a reportorial job, began translating the young American poets into French, and struck up friendships with Edmund Wilson, Sherwood Anderson, and others of *The Double Dealer* group.

As he translated Robinson Jeffers, Malcolm Cowley, and Vachel Lindsay, the future editor began to contemplate a magazine of his own and considered collaborating with *The Double Dealer* to combat the "bleak realism . . . everywhere triumphant." But on second thought, and because of experiences in interviewing Shriners, he decided that America would never tolerate a review such as he wished. Paris was the only fort from which he could marshal the revolutionary forces of both continents—Paris, where the "subversive impulse would be allowed a wider possibility of action." And so the Jolases sailed for Europe early in the summer of 1926—with plans for a magazine definitely in mind.

In Paris, Jolas began to accumulate the money for his review by resuming newspaper work. After six months on the Paris edition of the *Chicago Tribune*, he was able to make a start. He rented a small hotel room, oiled his typewriter, bought a card table and two ancient chairs, and *transition* was under way. To Anglo-American literature was to be brought the spirit of French modernism; to the Continent, young American rebels were to be introduced. To present a synthesis of German expressionism, of dadaism, and of surrealism; to revolutionize language, to present a new idiom "metaphoric and tropical, an idiom that might express the subtlest nuances of the psyche"—this was the spacious ambition. In the course of a year *transition* would explore the literary currents washing over Europe and America, present them all if they showed "imaginative emancipation" as against descriptive naturalism.

Trouble began with the first issue. Jolas and Elliot Paul made the mistake of publishing their names in the periodical as *gerants*, legally responsible agents. To be legally responsible one must be a citizen of the country, and neither was a French citizen. There were days before the French police, difficult explanations to make, and a confiscation of the magazine, delaying *transition's* appearance for several weeks after the date for which it had been announced.

Finally the review appeared, in April 1927, a compact, bulky magazine of around 150 pages. The paper and printing were fairly good, though the French printer let through a generous number of errors and glued a page of Gertrude Stein's "Elucidation" in the wrong position, a mistake that for a few hours threatened to wreck her health. She was finally pacified when the editor issued a separate pamphlet of the work, much to the amusement of bystanding reviewers. (Miss Stein could use *transition's* pages for any of her material until the publication in 1935 of the *Autobiography of Alice B. Toklas* which carried a great deal of misinformation and misunderstanding concerning the lives and works of several modernists; the 1935 issue of *transition* flung out a *Testimony against Gertrude Stein*, signed by such persons as Henri Matisse and Georges Braque. Jolas washed his hands of Miss Stein with the statement that she had no "understanding of what really was happening about her," and that she might "very well become one day the symbol of the decadence that hovers over contemporary literature."[1]) During its first year *transition* often ran over 200 pages per issue. It paid 30 francs a page for material, hired Elliot Paul as associate editor, and, of course, ran into debt, though it carried a considerable amount of advertising and sold at a subscription price of $5.00. The deficit has always been paid out of the private pocketbooks of the editor and his friends.[2]

*transition* drew many subscribers during its first few months, but the expense account mounted rapidly above the income. To economize, and to escape a growing number of callers at the Paris office, Jolas and his family removed to the edge of a boar-infested forest at Colombay-les-deux-Eglises. The printing of the review was taken from Mayenne to a small industrial town, St. Dizier, some sixty kilometres distant from Jolas' new home. From that time until the temporary suspension in 1930, *transition* was printed in the two-hundred-year-old printing house of André Bruilliard, who conducted his establishment in a leisurely, paternalistic fashion. He donated a small room to the magazine and much of the editing was done from the plant. Commuting between Colombay, Paris, and St. Dizier was done in a dilapidated Ford. The magazine kept its editor traveling, particularly the Joyce section of the review.[3]

Often when a forthcoming issue was announced there would be a general meeting of *transition* friends to help the failing eyes of Joyce

[1] This biographical information is taken from Eugene Jolas' *Frontier Man*, an unpublished autobiography.
[2] Letter, Eugene Jolas to Charles Allen, March 10, 1938 (unpublished).
[3] Jolas, *Frontier Man* (unpublished).

with the revising and rewriting of his galley proofs. Surrounded by innumerable notebooks, the explorer of night would dictate to Padraic Colum, Stuart Gilbert, both of the Jolases, Elliot Paul, Robert Sage, and Lucia and Georgio Joyce. Improvising and correcting would last for days at a time, until the manuscript and the proof sheets were out. Then more proofs, more improvising, until at last the work lay finished. The final proof was sent to Father Christmas, the printing foreman of St. Dizier, who by this time would be near tantrums. At the last minute Joyce would call from Paris to order a minor syntax change.[4]

The eclectic policy of the review during that opening year brought to *transition's* pages some queer bedfellows. Joyce and Stein were printed alongside the new Soviet writers; stories, essays, and poetry were translated from the Spanish, French, and German; the Irish poets, and such Americans as Kay Boyle, Hart Crane, Laura Riding, Malcolm Cowley, Allen Tate, Matthew Josephson, and Horace Gregory were to be found here and there, wedged in between a quantity of surrealism.

The great amount of translation and the proofreading were consuming more time than either of the Jolases had anticipated, and the review was more expensive than expected, although the printing was cheaper than it would have been in America. The advertising and sale of the magazine came far from balancing the cost. *transition* never accumulated many more than a thousand subscribers, though between four and five thousand copies per issue were disposed of. Facing these circumstances, the editor announced the magazine would be a quarterly after April 1928.[5] By this time *transition* had definitely completed its survey period and was ready to strike out on its own with the literary approach which Jolas calls vertigralism.

Certainly one of the major preoccupations of these early years of *transition* was the publication and explication of "Work in Progress." Far from being the "work of a master idling" or a "*divertissement philologique,*" the book which appeared in 1939 was the result of twenty years' work, during which time Joyce contributed little else to modern letters.

"Work in Progress" (its final title is *Finnegans Wake*) is a lengthy experiment in language—both in phonetics and meaning—which has as its basis the philosophy of history written by the Italian, Vico. The

---

[4] *Ibid.*

[5] Jolas, "Transition: An Epilogue," *The American Mercury,* xxiii, 189 (June 1931).

ages of man repeat themselves endlessly, and each man is therefore a prototype of history. How adapt this notion to literature? Carl Jung had described with great clarity the concept of the racial unconscious. He saw in man's unconscious life archaic survivals of the recurrent past which are stored there by a form of unconscious memory. These remnants recur to man only at times when the immediacy of the present or the pressure of conscious life is relaxed.

This was a clue to a literary representation of "all-men." Joyce fixed upon the life of one H. C. Earwicker, a Dublin tavernkeeper, given us as a report of Earwicker's dream experiences after a wearying night in his pub. He is all men—hero, father, incestuous culprit, king, repentant sinner—of all ages, and his three initials H.C.E. ("Here Comes Everybody") are made to fit a variety of historical personages and local persons, distorted by the dream work through the course of the night. Joyce did not use any one influence exclusively. He was a man of great learning and bent all things to his literary purpose. But, to make the language of Earwicker's night life fit the occasion, Joyce employed substantially the devices which Freud had years before outlined and explained in his chapter on "The Dream Mechanism."

Here was the "Revolution of the Word" actually going on—language being revised to explain the totality of life. It was this which chiefly attracted the editor of *transition* to Joyce. *transition* became at its very inception the "laboratory of the word," a champion of its thorough revision to meet the needs of a heightened awareness, a defender against scores of critics who condemned the idea of the "subliminal tongue." In its earlier numbers surrealists published in *transition*, and Jolas has always been moderately interested in surrealist performances. But he was not wholly sympathetic with the surrealist point of view; he especially deplored their apparent triviality and their desire to be eccentric for the sake of eccentricity. In Jolas' opinion, they dwelt too long, and fruitlessly, in the unconscious: "Our conception of literature, however, is not the formalized one of the Surrealists. We believe with them that the artist's imagination should be placed above everything else in importance, but we do not hold with them that writing should be exclusively of the interior. . . ."[6]

The use of psychoanalysis in *transition* should now be apparent. Jolas considered that "science" the discoverer of a new tradition. He regarded its emphasis upon dreams as a significant contribution to aesthetics. But his belief in the value of the dream has its source not

---

[6] "First Aid to the Enemy," *transition*, ix, 175 (December 1927).

in psychology but in the tradition of such German romantics as Novalis and Tieck, such French writers as Stéphane Mallarmé. Jung, who was always interested in the career of *transition*, and contributed to its pages, attracted Jolas more than did Freud, because Jung's contribution to the explanation of the unconscious gave the poet an importance far exceeding that which Freud's theories afforded him. The unconscious is for Jung not simply a dwelling place for primitive instincts but a source as well of the "divine gesture"; it is thus essential for the poet to unite his subconscious or irrational life with his conscious being:

"What really is needed is a new feeling. We need a greater naïveté, a greater simplicity, a greater sense of adventure. The dual realism we think of has the two planes of the subconscious and the instinctive and the physical consciousness.

"The movements of the dream have a value that surpasses all deliberate attempts to emerge into a state of serenity. . . ."[7]

What Jolas most urgently insisted upon was his conviction that a new mythos was needed which would define reality more clearly than ever before. For this reason he demanded that the artist be absolutely free to express himself, without critical or social hindrance. The aesthetic temperament is working its way through to a new, creative language, and the poet cannot be controlled or stopped by the demands of rational communication: "Let the word in prose and poetry find its different planes and its new associations in order to make it impossible that art be again and again the sycophant of reality."[8]

### III

In 1928 Elliot Paul was replaced by Robert Sage as associate editor, and Harry Crosby, Stuart Gilbert, and Matthew Josephson assisted editorially in weaning the review away from surrealist principles. Vertigralism adopted the irrational aspects of surrealism, but did not care to accept the idea of automatic writing or the surrealist Communistic political bias. And *transition* wished to stress language innovation, never a primary concern of surrealism. Thus was born the latest lit-

[7] Jolas, "On the Quest," *transition*, IX, 194 (December 1927). Much information about Jolas' theories of language and literature is either derived from or confirmed in an interview with him by Frederick J. Hoffman, New York City, August 25, 1943.
[8] *Ibid.*, p. 196.

erary method, vertigralism, "the intuitive reaching towards the above," towards the "man who will participate in the collective consciousness of the universe, who will find contact with the . . . world soul."[9]

We notice at once that the surrealistic and transitional interest in irrationalism stems from monotheism. Like its nineteenth century romantic progenitors, transition is strongly pantheistic, seeking to "destroy the dualism between the individual and the universe, idea and reality, spirit and nature, God and world." There are cosmic, supermundane forces in the universe, ideal forces which permeate all nature, including man. But man, by deifying reason and logic, has deadened his response to the supernatural, submerged deep within himself his feeling for the miraculous. "We have within ourselves," claims Jolas, "direct contact with the primitive periods of humanity, as well as with the cosmic forces. Art . . . represents in its most characteristic specimens the wisdom of the ages."[10]

This "wisdom of the ages" reveals itself only now and again—through the dream, hypnosis, automatic writing, and in half-waking states. Hence transition's insistence on the value of the "night mind," upon the revelations of the dream and the borderline experiences of half-sleep. Such is the proper subject of art, for, through the dream, man can again awaken within himself the sense of the wonderful and miraculous which makes life rich and complete.[11]

transition has elaborately connected its theory of the night mind with historical romanticism. It has published hitherto untranslated texts on the dream by Jean Paul, Novalis, Franz von Baader, and Hoelderlin. One of the best expositions of Jolas' interest in the dream is found in the 400-page tenth anniversary issue of his review, No. 27, dated for the spring of 1938. Here Albert Béguin, professor at the University of Bâle, traces the romantic dream interest through Baader, Friedrich Carus, J. J. Wagner, Leibnitz, Herder, Schelling, and others.[12] Jolas and Béguin both oppose rationalism on the same grounds. As Jolas puts it, "The objection I have to rationalism is not its assumption of finality, but its voluntary narrowness. . . . The 'I' has many dimensions."[13] Dream fantasies relate man to the race. Through

---

[9] Jolas, *Frontier Man* (unpublished).
[10] Jolas, "Transition: An Epilogue," p. 190.
[11] Jolas, "Literature and the New Man," transition, xix-xx, 13-19 (June 1930).
[12] Albert Béguin, "The Night-Side of Life," transition, xxvii, 197-218 (Spring 1938).
[13] Jolas, "Transition: An Epilogue," p. 190.

the fantastic, the grotesque, the mystic, the mantic, man begins to understand his true collectivism and common humanity.

It is the editor's conviction that new literary genres are needed to reveal the irrational, and thus the explanation of the review's concern with the myth as a literary form, with the saga, the fairy tale, the legend, and the fable. These are to replace the accepted forms, for they more easily awaken a responsiveness to the fabulous.[14] But these genres are not to be merely an unselected overflow of the irrational. As a reading of the best of *transition* poetry and prose will reveal, the artistic ventures often represent well wrought patterns, exemplify a fine selection of detail, a sensitive feeling for the whole. The work printed in Jolas' collection, *transition stories*, 1930, refutes some of the ill-considered attacks against *transition*.

Jolas refers to the new literary forms with which he wishes to replace the old, and offers examples of them in later issues of the magazine. The "paramyth," for example, he would wish to be accepted as the "successor to the form known heretofore as the short story or *nouvelle*. I conceive it as a kind of epic wonder tale giving an organic synthesis of the individual and universal unconscious, the dream, the daydream, the mystic vision."[15] Paramyths are characterized by verbal innovations; they also employ various languages, the language most suited to the immediate occasion getting preference over others:

"In those days a great disquiet nighthaunted men and women. The monstercities fevercried, the remotest villages sensed the trepidation, ships on the high seas felt electric waves currentcrickling through their bodies...."

"Dans l'atmosphère des frontières quand et la trance of the nighting thoughts wither the harvest of the word-sick is there no train fast enough to hurry up durch die dunkelheit ohne tunnel...."[16]

*transition* is important to a study of experimental literature for a number of reasons. It shows the direction which a serious study of psychoanalysis and allied matters might give an artist who avails himself of the discoveries most pertinent to his craft. The magazine furnishes some evidence of at least one strenuous effort to reconstruct valid aesthetic materials from the life and language of the unconscious. Conscious at first of the dead weight in our language, *transition* devoted much time and energy to a revision of linguistic and syntactic

---

[14] Jolas, *Frontier Man* (unpublished).
[15] Jolas, "Paramyths," *transition*, XXII, 7 (July 1935).
[16] Jolas, "Paramyths from a Dreambook," *transition*, XXIII, 15, 17 (July 1935).

structures; thus it gave *Finnegans Wake* a hearing and defended it against its detractors. Above all, the magazine is experimental and revolutionary, accepting without qualm or hesitation the consequences of experiment upon normal credulity and seeking throughout for a synthesis of diverse materials, more consonant with the nature of complex reality.

## IV

Of many accusations which Eugene Jolas was forced to meet, one seemed persistent. Today many associate surrealism with *transition* and assume that Jolas' latest theories are simply an extension of that doctrine. As we have seen, Jolas agreed with surrealism in some matters and disagreed with it on certain fundamental issues. For one thing, the surrealists seemed to begin and end in Freud. They considered the eccentricities of the unconscious literary ends in themselves. In a sense they too revolted against the vapidities of ordinary language usage; but they remained within the clinic of the psychoanalyst. Surrealism lacked purposive direction; that is, it succeeded in transferring the content of the unconscious to paper and canvas with little or no intercession or reorganization by the artist. This is at least the confirmed opinion of Jolas and other critics. Freud had not been interested in the unconscious for its own sake. His clinical investigations were undertaken for the purpose of therapy. The surrealists, however, attempted to equate the unconscious with reality. They are the true irrationalists of the century.[17]

They have had ample opportunity to speak for themselves. In the twenties *The Little Review* published a number of them, as we have already seen. Edward Titus' *This Quarter* devoted the entire issue of September 1932 to them. More recently James Laughlin gave over a section of the 1940 *New Directions* annual to the manifestoes and writing of surrealists past and present. Several of the most lively current little magazines are devoted to the surrealist cause. In many respects surrealism is a continuation of dada—in its repudiation, especially, of all things conventional and logical. As the dadaists had attempted to show their contempt for convention by constantly distracting their audiences by noisy *non sequiturs*, so surrealist poetry and prose defy comprehension by irrational sequences of metaphors and by typographical excesses.

[17] See Parker Tyler, "Beyond Surrealism," *Caravel*, IV, 2-6 (1935); Jolas, "Surrealism: Ave atque Vale," *Fantasy*, VII, 23-30 (1941).

Surrealists have carried on their fight against the "exterior world" without abatement. The demands of such a world, they say, stifle the poetic imagination. The base of operation for this battle is the unconscious. This realization of the unconscious as the source of all criticism of the external world is Freud's contribution to their doctrine. Poetry is a complex of many startling figures, given only the order which they possess in the unconscious. Hence we have a variety of grotesqueries: the clam plays the accordion on a blue-paper night, and if elephants wear neckties, how can grandmother bake a cake?

In such recent magazines as *Arson*, surrealists have become self-critical, though they adhere with fair consistency to their original manifestoes. Nicholas Calas, for example, suggests that the debt to Freud is incalculable; yet he believes that most of his fellows were overly enthusiastic about the symbolism of the unconscious: "Left to themselves, these images always recurred with increasing monotony, and the more the reader knew of psychoanalytical methods the clearer became the family relationships of the images, with the continual repetition of sex-complexes. What in 1925 was bold and original gave ten years later the effect of intolerable repetition. . . ."[18] This is a recognition of the limitations not of the unconscious but of the psychoanalytic method of free association. The images of the unconscious are freer and less repetitious than the documents of the clinic represent them. Thus, the roles of the poet and of the psychoanalyst are made explicit. The latter watches over the patient's flow of words and images, gives them a control and supervision that is essentially scientific and not aesthetic. The poet, therefore, is the only true believer in the imagery of the unconscious. He is a hero who explores with great courage an inner world, and goes there unequipped with a psychoanalytic camera or gun.

Jolas objected as well to the political beliefs of the surrealists. They are Marxist materialists in their assumption of a world free of any and all supernatural controls. They are "Communists" also, but only in the destructive or negative sense of that term—that is, they agree in looking upon all institutions as rigid, inflexible, and stupid. They had better be called aesthetic anarchists, since true validity for them resides only in the individual unconscious. They are opposed most of all to any external form of regimentation—and rational communication is dead beyond recall, in their estimation (though they use it in their neatly worded manifestoes). Can they offer a program for mod-

[18] Nicholas Calas, "The Light of Words," *Arson*, I, 16 (March 1942).

ern society? In their opinion, the time is especially right for the fulfillment of a surrealist program. André Breton, for example, declares that surrealism offers a lively means of bringing "the boldest solutions to problems posited by current events": "Surrealism will never find a more favourable period for its program, which is to render to man the concrete empire of his functions: the plunge in the diving-bell of automatism, the conquest of the irrational, the patient comings and goings in the labyrinth of the calculus of probabilities, are still far from having been brought to an end. The present circumstances remove all utopian aspects and give them a *vital* interest of the same importance as laboratory researches. . . ."[19]

The magazine View, established by Charles Henri Ford in 1940, suggests in its subtitle that truth is best seen "Through the Eyes of the Poets." It is especially important in a skeptical world, it says, that the matter of truth be left to the artist. The integrity of the artist will allow him to make no compromises with reality. There is little distinction, they maintain, between the painter and the poet, in this regard. Surrealist painting and poetry are treated in View as similar expressions, since the unconscious views truth fully as often in pictorial as in verbal images. What may appear grotesque is only a deeper and therefore more complex truth. Thus, the use of metaphor by surrealist poets—as indeed, the pictorial metaphors of painters—is an imaginative rendering of the unconscious, as in the following example by Robert Horan:

> In the bed of cities they climb the stair
> of hooded flowers; trust in the first
> grapes of disease.
>
> Deranged within the houses of their blood,
> they watch whatever bush of silver
> shocks the water. (Their fists of net.)[20]

Meaning is not to be attached to such work by any prior critical device. It must be accepted as naïve, irrational, and without precise location in time and space. A poem must not mean, but live "the way children, dreams and myths live." It is perhaps unfair to both to associate the surrealist view of metaphor with that of the "new criticism" of Ransom and others. The fact is that the one sees metaphor

[19] Arson, I, 5 (March 1942).
[20] Robert Horan, "Deceptions of Brass," View, I, n.p. (June 1941).

from a purely irrational point of view. The result is poetry that is meaningless in any traditional or rational sense. The other explores the endless possibilities which the metaphor has for meaning and relates each of them to a structure calling for complex rational appraisal. Thus experimentalism has provided at least two widely separate versions of the metaphor. In the case of Ransom, Empson, and Wheelwright, the metaphor has plural meanings, but they enrich rather than confound the understanding. The surrealists, on the other hand, while opposing the neat circumspectness which is afforded by abstract oversimplification, prefer that their work be accepted as valid only within the unconscious. Which is, of course, to say that it is not possible to evaluate it from any point of view save that of the poet himself.

The issue of *View* for October 1942 may suggest further developments in surrealist practice. It is called the "Vertigo" number. Its chief concern is to show the aesthetic possibilities of arrested or confused sensation. The progressive stages of vertigo represent a rapid release from the grasp of the mind: "Whoever is prey to it renounces any measurement, refuses to maintain against the undivided forces of exterior menace the independence, energy and initiative of a will master of itself. Instead of a being working on objects and striving to compose them in his own image, vertigo means that he yields to their weight and follows them where they lead. . . ."[21]

Surrealism is the most enthusiastic and boisterously alive of all irrational aesthetics. There is little or no clue as to future direction, since the very doctrine implies a kind of anarchic solipsism in each of its followers. If the vigor of such magazines as *View, Arson,* and *VVV* are any index at all, surrealism is destined to remain with us for quite some time. Contradictions reside in large numbers within its generous limits; but contradictions are after all seen only by those who appraise a thing from a rational point of view, and surrealism is deliberately and by definition illogical. It rests its case upon the belief that the imagination of the artist must be kept free from meddling by any self-avowed rationalist critic.

The championship of the imagination is not left exclusively to the surrealist, of course. The magazine *Dyn,* edited by Wolfgang Paalen, appeared for the first time in April-May, 1942. In his appraisal of recent aesthetics, Paalen gives credit to the efforts to "give a new collective basis to artistic creation through the liberation of the uncon-

[21] Roger Caillois, "Vertigo," *View,* II, 7 (October 1942).

scious."[22] Surrealism has been correct in dispelling the notion of mere representation in painting and poetry, *Dyn* says. But it is peculiarly limited by its insistence upon the unique importance of the unconscious in all creation. Such a preoccupation may well eventually curb the imagination. *Dyn* regards absolute freedom of the imagination as the most important aesthetic prerogative, and will brook no interference with its proper function: "Absolute refusal to subject one's conscience to no matter what sort of obligatory service of conscience; obligatory conscientious refusal to obey any slogan that distinguishes between means and ends: here is what this morality instructs us to undertake for our immediate activity."[23]

## V

This statement suggests a continued battle against social regimentation of the spirit. If one but glances at the struggle against rigidity in modern society, he will notice that the most persistent champions of freedom have all in one way or another accepted the life or characteristics of the unconscious as a point of departure. Their brilliant criticisms of effete society have not often been matched by constructive counterproposals. But they have been united in censuring society for censoring individuals. In this connection, those men to whom fell the task of preaching the Laurentian gospel have been extremely active. D. H. Lawrence wrote two books on Freud: *Psychoanalysis and the Unconscious* and *Fantasia of the Unconscious*. While he granted Freud's great importance in drawing the attention of modern thinkers to the psychology of the unconscious, he listed him with the "meddling scientists." Science, says Lawrence, is the monstrous and efficient device by which orthodoxy keeps the life of the spirit within bounds.

Life for Lawrence was a series of emotional tensions. Emotional crises whip the blood into strenuous activity. Intellection, associated with any natural act, deprives it of its vitality. Thus his attack upon modern morality, modern science, modern squeamishness of all sorts —in the art gallery, the chapel, the school. The loudest and most persistent pleas for an understanding of Lawrence's way of life appear in *The Phoenix*, begun in Woodstock, New York, in 1938, by

[22] Wolfgang Paalen, "The New Image," *Dyn*, I, 8 (April-May, 1942).
[23] Paalen and others, "Suggestions for an Objective Morality," *Dyn*, I, 19 (April-May, 1942).

J. P. Cooney. Cooney's opposition to the mechanics of modern living follows strictly the views which the master presented in the novel *Women in Love*. The man who plows the field, maintains Cooney, is performing a ritual in which his body is renewed. But "a man seated upon some unliving, atheistic, monstrous machine and directing it with controls and levers as it efficiently and coldly rapes the fields— that, to me, is frightful."[24] Likewise, all social theories based upon the regulated automatism and monotonous repetition of a machine's movements are doomed to failure. It is the purpose of *The Phoenix* to gather together the men and women who share this view, perhaps eventually to establish the community of spirits which Lawrence had always wished to begin.

Members of this group included Henry Miller, Michael Fraenkel, and Derek Savage; Lawrence presided posthumously over their meetings and shared well in the magazine's representation. Miller, the European editor, submitted a chapter from his unpublished book, *The World of Lawrence*, and praised him as "the most alive, the most vitalizing of recent writers." For Lawrence, says Miller, the body has an almost mystic significance. In contrast with him, Proust and Joyce are representative of the decay of our times. Their brilliance was wasted on an endless recounting of modern disintegration and passive acceptance of death. Theirs is a picture of the "world-as-disease." And Miller opposes the figures of Baron Charlus and Leopold Bloom with that of the gamekeeper Mellors of *Lady Chatterley's Lover*.

Throughout the successive issues of *The Phoenix*, this contrast is maintained. Modern fiction and poetry are sick in spirit and preoccupied with slow decay and death. As Derek Savage put it, "This fatigue and boredom we have noticed in the poetry of writers of the latterday industrial revolution is symptomatic of the distress of individuals in a mechanistic environment. Life under metropolitan conditions suffers an internal impoverishment which is the result of divorce from the fullness of natural things."[25]

Lawrence's chief contribution to those who liked his way of life is his emphasis upon primitivism as a means of successful revolt against decadence in society. *The Phoenix*, perhaps naturally, took a stand against World War II, regarding a clash of mechanized military forces as abhorrent. War was the logical result of an exaggerated mechanism

[24] "An Open Letter," *The Phoenix*, I, 23 (March-April-May, 1938).
[25] Derek Savage, "Creativeness and Social Change," *The Phoenix*, II, 103 (Spring 1939).

in society—coldly calculating impersonal destruction of human beings. In this magazine there is a direct opposition of "the life of the blood" to the "life of the brain." There is almost nothing said directly about psychoanalysis or about the life of the unconscious. But the major emphasis is upon irrational life closely allied with positive instinctual drives and freedom from any kind of social or intellectual rigidity.

The Phoenix's European editor is one of the interesting enigmas of our century. His writing is brilliant and facile, his subject matter a parade of the grotesque and the scatalogical. Miller has contributed much to avant-garde publications: transition, Horizon, and The Phoenix, among others. New Directions has published some of his work in its various annuals, and the New Directions Press has presented some of his books. In 1937 Miller and several of his friends took over a magazine called The Booster, apparently at the time an aid to American tourists in Paris, supervised by the American Country Club. With the issue of September 1937, The Booster presented a remarkably changed appearance to its startled readers. Surrounded by conventional advertisements of tourist agencies and businesses, there were the unconventional writings of Miller, Alfred Perles, Lawrence Durrell, William Saroyan, and others. The changed policy was announced in the editorial of the September issue. In fact, The Booster was to have "no fixed policy," except to be "eclectic, flexible, alive," a "contraceptive against the self-destructive spirit of the age." Shortly after the appearance of this issue, the respectable men who had previously owned the magazine published a statement "denying responsibility" for its contents. The advertisements disappeared and the name was changed to The Delta.

The burden of Miller's writings in The Booster and its successor is his advocacy of creative life among biological and metaphysical byways. He suggests that we are wrong in protecting ourselves from death—that we should face death and terror with full recognition of its challenge and its beauty. Much of modern society is suffering a "living death," from its fear of facing the fundamental drives of nature. Miller's attitude resembles a kind of incestuous pantheism, borrowing as it does from the secret places of human functioning and exaggerating their importance. He seems to have expanded upon Lawrence's primitivism and to have made an aesthetics of psychiatry. The earth is an "enormous womb," a place where everything is brought to life. Life itself was glorious for Lawrence, and he did not hesitate to regard all healthy demonstrations of it with enthusiasm. Miller, however, is much more interested in the processes by which life appears and moves toward organic death. The birth trauma is in a sense a basis for Miller's point of view. The world is really "nothing but a great womb, the place where everything is brought to life."[26]

This philosophy of life as darkness and desire for death—the organic striving always to become inorganic—is derived in large from psycho-medical researches into the unconscious. The fundamental reaches of the human personality are the dark areas in which are bred the neurotics of our day. In his analysis of the painting of Hans Reichel, Miller gives expression to his own beliefs:

"This cosmological eye is sunk deep within his body. Everything he looks at and seizes must be brought below the threshold of consciousness, brought deep into the entrails where there reigns an absolute night where also the tender little mouths with which he absorbs his vision eat away until only the quintessence remains. Here in the warm bowels, the metamorphosis takes place. In the absolute night, in the black pain hidden away in the backbone, the substance of things is dissolved until only the essence shines forth. . . ."[27]

Psychoanalysis has thus played an important though secondary role in the literature of the thirties. A great number of writers have discovered the unconscious and seen in it many things. In a number of cases they have been content to concentrate their attention upon it. Failure to recognize that man is after all a conscious being does not encourage a sensible view of his entire life. The most important contribution which both the science and the literature of psychoanalysis have made to modern thought is the recognition that man's life is not all surface brightness and social mannerism. The full pressure of this realization may cause an overemphasis upon the dark areas of life, an inverted view which is held by chains fully as strong as the chains of economic servitude, and much harder to break. Obviously the most interesting results have been achieved in the experiments with words and metaphors. These have caused a realignment of our aesthetic valuations of linguistics and may well serve eventually to give the syntactic distortions of the dream the serious consideration they merit. But communication is still the basis for social operation; and present conditions in world planning and social strategy will not tolerate pure aesthetic anarchy.

[26] Henry Miller, "The Enormous Womb," *The Booster*, IV, 21 (December 1937-January 1938).
[27] Miller, "The Cosmological Eye," *transition*, XXVII, 323 (April-May, 1938).

In short, the psychoanalytic clinic has been a most suggestive and provocative source of literary experiment. Despite several attempts to make Freud and Marx companion revolutionists, their influence has been in all but a few cases diverse; the appeals have been to different kinds of aesthetic temperament. Marx has challenged for the most part the social conscience of the artist—has made him self-conscious and a little embarrassed about his claims to uniqueness in a world demanding selfless co-operation. Freud has suggested a means of insuring the individualism of the artist.

More than anything else, the artist has been frightened by the imminent loss of his aesthetic prerogatives. The old issue of art versus propaganda has recurred many times in the last few years. The writers who grew up in the twenties are a bit surprised and not a little displeased by the appeals of Van Wyck Brooks for a "primary literature"; they see in them a revival of the "trimmed lamp" days, when the artist bowed down reverently before the sanctity of sweetness and light. They prefer to have their attitudes punctuated by irreverence and revolt. Principally, they regard any kind of conformity with suspicion, even that accorded to the "new society" which Marxist doctrine promises. Thus the interest in psychoanalysis gave a few writers of the thirties some distraction from Marxist preoccupations.

# THE
# CRITICAL AND ECLECTIC
## Little Magazine

CHAPTER XI

It is natural enough that *avant-garde* literature should have its own sponsors and apologists. Criticism in the little magazines is a very lively part of their history. In many cases, it is a defense of the literature published in this month's issue, or an anticipation of what will probably be published in next month's issue. It is generally an appraisal of work in the making or just recently completed. More than that, *avant-garde* criticism is an explanation by the artists themselves of what they are doing, or contemplating. We can expect as little unity or pattern in this kind of criticism as we have found in experimental writing. The appearance, in *transition*, of essays in "exagmination" of Joyce's "Work in Progress" before that work had been completed is certainly an excellent example of the way *avant-garde* criticism works. While much of conservative criticism looks to the past (the recent or classical past) for guidance, and strives for a unity in its critical system, criticism in the little magazines is more inclined to look upon the immediate present, or to search the future for critical perceptions. These are the general differences; and, in a sense, they remove advance guard criticism from the danger of its being incorporated into any academic history of criticism.

Much of the literary criticism of the little magazines is to be found in their editorial columns; indeed, the idea of an editorial accompaniment to literature in the making is an interesting innovation in the history of criticism. We may be quite sure that a study of *avant-gardist* criticism will have to take seriously into account the variety of editorial statements, manifestoes, and proclamations which form so interesting a part of little magazine history. We have not so much to determine the accuracy of critical appraisal of past literature as we have to judge the relationship between critical pronouncement and literary product. The editorial may speak positively of a new literary development, but that development is not always evident in the pages of the magazine. On the other hand, the editorial often acts in the role of critical guide to a group of reader-sightseers, who wish to know what is happening in strange new lands and are grateful for any Baedeker supplement their editors may supply.

It is possible to suggest several types of criticism in the little magazines: there are the editorial "barkers" who announce the wonders to be found inside the tent and assure you that they are worth your patience and interest. There are editor-critics who have founded their magazines for the purpose of telling their readers that the world is going this way or that, and that a new literature must be found to celebrate tendencies or to hasten the advent of a new dispensation. A third type of critical attitude we may call the eclectic—an attitude which exhibits a smiling generosity to many types of literary novelty but remains discreetly noncommittal about their eventual worth. Finally, there is the magazine which is made in the editor's own image (and often at his own expense), designed to accommodate his own writings and the writings of those select and fortunate few who may agree with him sufficiently to supply appendix and footnote to the text.

Above all, criticism in the little magazines has been a vigorous defense of what was happening in *avant-garde* writing. We have our own critical guides on the way, and have abandoned the thought of waiting for time to offer a lovely perspective or for scholar-critics to furnish a historical summary or a scientific classification. Further, advance guard criticism has been vitally interested in the formal aspects of literature. Though there are many efforts to apply historical and biographical instruments of interpretation to literature, the predominating note has been indicated by formal analysis and explication. This is probably due to the presence of many men who have acted in the dual role of artist-critic. The idea that an artist is best equipped to explain his own work may not always lead to satisfactory results; but it has certainly succeeded in giving the world more statements and announcements of purpose than has ever been the case in previous literary history.

One other interesting service is performed by criticism in the little magazines: here we discover the writers of our time actually growing; critical statements by them are very important as sections of their intellectual autobiographies. Next to the formal innovations which *avant-gardists* have forced upon our attention, the most interesting fact about these magazines is their glimpses and insights into the intellectual career and the psychological constitution of their contributors. The important members of the *avant-garde* have been very generous in this matter. If Emerson and Thoreau had had a way of publishing their daily observations, the remarks in their journals, they would have enjoyed a privilege similar to that possessed by modern writers. There are two fashions in which these daily speculations have found their way to publication: a magazine like *The Adelphi* or *The Criterion* has published regularly these observations, and the files of those magazines furnish a running account of the points of view of their principal intellectual sponsors; on the other hand, little magazines, anxious for the fame and backing of an *avant-gardist* who has already had his apprenticeship, are often glad to print anything which he is gracious enough to send them. The remarks of Ezra Pound on all aspects of civilization, the arts, and the soul are scattered in a hundred little magazines; William Carlos Williams, Norman Macleod, Henry Miller, and other advance guard celebrities also make numerous appearances in a variety of little magazines.

Before we examine a few of the little magazines devoted specifically or largely to critical matters, we might look briefly at some representative editorial statements. These do not so much give an orderly outline of *avant-garde* criticism as they furnish an insight into editorial temperament. The first of them is by Harriet Monroe and demonstrates her editorial acumen, her steady but studied willingness to give new writing its day and to clear the way of conservative impediments to its reception. "The world which laughs at the experimenter in verse," says Miss Monroe in the second issue of *Poetry*, "walks negligently through our streets, and goes seriously, even reverently, to the annual exhibitions in our cities, examining hundreds of pictures and statues without expecting even the prize-winners to be masterpieces."[1]

Quite without great critical significance, but representative of the editorial ambitions of many minor little magazines is this announcement in the first issue of *The Minaret*: "We are not Cubists, Futurists, or Imagists. We do not pretend to stand for the past or future, but for the present. We have a single aim, and that is to produce a magazine that we hope will appeal to those who are fond of good literature. In a word, we are Americans interested in the literature of our own country, but we believe that by publishing in this magazine, in the

[1] "The Open Door," *Poetry*, 1, 63 (November 1912).

future, translations of the modern French and German poets, we are enriching our own literature."[2] More aggressive, and certainly more in keeping with little magazine editorial manners, is this announcement by William Carlos Williams in the first issue of the earlier *Contact*: The magazine, says Williams, is "issued in the conviction that art which attains is indigenous of experience and relations, and that the artist works to express perceptions rather than to attain standards of achievement: however much information and past art may have served to clarify his perceptions and sophisticate his comprehensions, there will be no standard by which his work shall be adjudged. . . . We are here because of our faith in the existence of native artists who are capable of having, comprehending and recording extraordinary experience."[3]

One editorial attitude which is frequently demonstrated in the little magazines is an invitation to "the best new writing," regardless of its popularity or its standing in conventional literary circles. This policy is announced in dozens of little magazines. In a sense it argues no policy at all, but it encourages the publication of unknowns who might otherwise not see the light of print. Such is the avowed attitude of *The Double Dealer*, which, say its editors, "is entering upon its career with no policy whatever but that of printing the very best material it can procure, regardless of popular appeal, moral or immoral stigmata, conventional or unconventional technique, new theme or old."[4] Sometimes this attitude is merely amiably generous; at other times it is a shrewd recognition of the need for respecting an artist's individuality and for not interfering with his work—certainly an attitude important to the history of little magazines. Ernest J. Walsh's *This Quarter* believed substantially in this "hands off" policy; and the poetry magazine *The Measure* practiced it in an interesting way by changing its editors each quarter. As if to underline this policy, Maxwell Anderson, *The Measure*'s first editor, speaks of the poet's individuality: "Good work is not the product of a school, not a mere blend, but the output of a keen, egotistical, independent intelligence backed by an extraordinary surcharge of emotion. . . . Without a distinct, fighting individuality the poet is indeed lost."[5] Again we find the policy of noninterference with contributors announced in Vincent Starrett's *The Wave*, which, says Starrett, does not believe in imposing rules upon writers. "Excellence

---

[2] Editorial, *The Minaret*, I, cover (November 1915).
[3] Editorial, *Contact*, I, 1 (December 1920).
[4] Editorial, *The Double Dealer*, I, 83 (March 1921).
[5] Editorial, *The Measure*, II, 17, 19 (April 1921).

of form and adequacy of treatment, therefore, are the only tests, and even these tentative 'rules' are not inelastic. In short, we shall print what pleases us, hoping that it will please you."[6] Policy for many of these magazines resides in the literature printed in their pages; it is "a living, dynamic thing," says Edwin Seaver in 1924. "It is the spirit of the magazine, not a label. It is constantly changing, constantly renewing itself."[7]

Implicit in all of these comments is the desire to avoid the sins of the commercial magazines, to make available the pages of little magazines to their writers with as little interference as possible. It is not mere generous passivity which governs these editorial statements; these magazines do not want to publish *anything*, regardless of worth, but they certainly refuse to stand in the way of work which is interesting and valuable but contrary to conservative demands. One of the ideas governing editorial sentiment in the little magazines is the assumption that the general reading public is not always anxious to receive new and strange writing; the public wants "hardware, tinsel, and cheese—classified goods," says *The Pilgrim's Almanach*. "If your way of expressing yourself fails to fall in line with the classified requirements of the business—out you go!"[8]

But these quotations suggest only one kind of critical attitude—one central to the service a little magazine performs in literary history, it is true; but not exclusive or unique. The ardent, positive editorial usage to which such vigorous exponents of their ideas as Wyndham Lewis and Ezra Pound put their magazines affords an insight into another type. Lewis' several magazines—*Blast, The Enemy, Tyro*—existed mainly for the purpose of allowing their editor to expound and expand his own points of view. So also were the "one-man" magazines of Michael Monahan and Guido Bruno, in the second decade of the century. In other words, little magazines may well announce, not so much a policy as a personality; and the critical importance of this type of magazine can be measured in terms of the qualities and defects of that personality. When Lewis speaks of *The Enemy* as sponsoring "merely a person; a solitary outlaw," he is accepting the critical responsibility as well as enjoying the prerogatives of single sponsorship. Similarly, Pound's editorial statements in *The Exile* are to be judged in terms of person and not of school. The privilege and the responsibility are both his.

[6] Editorial, *The Wave*, I, 42 (January 1922).
[7] "Why 1924?" 1924, I, 33 (July 1924).
[8] Editorial, *The Pilgrim's Almanach*, I, 3 (1925?).

But criticism in the little magazines is not to be found exclusively in their editorials. The critical articles which supplement original writing are usually comments upon them, announcements of new critical principles by which the new writing might be judged, or a searching into such fragments of past literature which might be said, by accident or by cultural coincidence, to have afforded a haphazard precedent for contemporary experiment. In the little magazines avowedly interested in criticism itself, two characteristics may be noted: an interest in formal aesthetic questions and in careful, close aesthetic analysis; and a concern over cultural synthesis, usually based upon principles derived from a study of the arts. These two tendencies are often observed together in one magazine. The habit of minute analysis of literature would seem at first glance to argue a retreat from larger and more important issues, with which literature should be linked, in the opinion of many critics. But these critics seem to overlook the fact that intensive analysis of literature may not be an "escapist" device at all. Certainly the critical interest in formal analysis, exclusive of biographic or moral influences, has a purpose quite other than that of escaping responsibility or making literature an idle preoccupation for cultural aristocrats. There are two motives for this kind of analysis: to free literature from its minor position as being mere decoration for large, loose moral and social generalizations; and to consider literary language, poetic language in particular, from the point of view of its being a new way of organizing experience—in short, another kind of knowledge. Literary criticism of this sort comes close to being an appendix to epistemology; but its preoccupation with problems of knowing ought not to surprise us, for we have always recognized in poetry a certain daring exercise of the imagination, which distinguishes itself from the reason by its habits and its product as well. The "poetic way of saying," as I. A. Richards has abundantly proved, demands an appreciation of paradox and ambiguity, characteristics of language which are generally avoided by logicians and moralists alike.

Certain criticism, therefore, has confined itself to the examination of literature as a way of knowing, a form of intellectual and imaginative organization of experience, whose results are richly different from those of other modes. This critical manner does not argue an aristocracy of taste or an exclusiveness of manner, but a fresh view of literature—or, rather, a view so very obvious that it has been overlooked in the scramble for more "vital" and more dubious justifications for literature. Much of the critical discussion associated with this development has gone on in magazines only incidentally related to little magazine history: such "fellow travelers" of *avant-gardism* as *The Kenyon Review, The Southern Review,* and *The Sewanee Review.* The interest has been taken up by the academic mind, as Alfred Kazin has charged. But it is the academic mind with a difference. Most of the university men who discuss "the new criticism" have been or are poets who are interested in their art from a theoretical point of view as well; their connection with universities is not to be condemned but applauded.

The general development of *avant-garde* criticism can be described in some such way as this: first of all, the editorial sponsors of *avant-garde* literature are jealous of the distinction which a writer possesses and anxious that he retain his independence of popular taste and of any rigid controls over his expression. The little magazines act, therefore, as a means of encouragement, and their policy is generously and bravely eclectic. Exceptions to this generalization occur in the "one-man" magazines, in magazines partially or totally committed to political or social doctrines, and in magazines whose aim is cultural synthesis rather than aesthetic freedom. Such was the state of *avant-gardism* in the twenties. In the thirties there are three types of critical attitude; ordinarily each of them is immediately obvious, both in the editorial pages and in the contributions themselves. The first of these represents a partial or total submission to Marxist political doctrine. We have already examined the effect of this point of view upon its followers. The second is marked by a preoccupation with literary form and by an attempt to establish a modern aesthetic—chiefly in the nature of poetic theory to accompany poetic practice. The third and last of these critical developments is an outgrowth of the critical eclecticism of the twenties, but it is also an expansion of it: it is marked by a broad (and not always a discriminating) tolerance of *avant-garde* materials, wherever they may be found, an attempt to evaluate these materials *pari passu,* and an interest in such European developments in literature as seem generally to be in sympathy with *avant-gardist* aims. The character of this eclecticism is different from that of the twenties in at least this respect: it is less interested in novelty for its own sake, less enthusiastic about unknowns, more selective and more anxious to find the "classics" of *avant-gardism* (the paradox in this last phrase is unavoidable; the critical eclectics of the thirties were interested in "monuments" of contemporary literature) and to publish them. In the remaining pages of this chapter, we shall look at several critical and eclectic magazines at close range, as a means of elaborating upon what we have said.

## II

The *Dial* is an ancient and honorable name in American magazine annals. A group headed by Ralph Waldo Emerson and Margaret Fuller established the first *Dial* in Cambridge, Massachusetts, in 1840. It was a critical magazine that never drew over three hundred subscribers. In the best little magazine style, it fought for a spiritual rather than a commercial ideal, preferring to die in 1844 rather than sacrifice its transcendental philosophy. *Dial* No. 1 was the father of the American little magazine.

In the year 1880 a Chicago publisher, Francis F. Browne, revived the name *Dial*, and until 1916 there was published in Chicago a sedate, critical fortnightly review which insisted that it was the legitimate son of Emerson's *Dial*; it reviewed books promptly and often competently, but it lacked the imagination and fire of the transcendental periodical. Not until Martyn Johnson became president and owner of the magazine in 1916 was there a change from an academic and imitative monthly to a serious critical review. After a period during which C. J. Masseck was editor, Johnson hit upon George Bernard Donlin for the job. Donlin assembled a progressive staff and a list of contributing editors that included Conrad Aiken, Randolph Bourne, Padraic Colum, Van Wyck Brooks, and John Macy. The magazine was moved from Chicago to New York where, late in 1918, it was again revamped under the editorial leadership of Donlin, Harold Stearns, Scofield Thayer, Clarence Britten, John Dewey, Thorstein Veblen, and Helen Marot. Under them *The Dial* became an organ of liberal opinion, in direct competition with *The Nation* and *The New Republic*. With a contributors' list that included Harold J. Laski, Charles Beard, Robert Morss Lovett, and Gilbert Seldes, it was soon being distributed to over ten thousand persons. But by 1919 the periodical was in trouble; quarrels among members of the staff and financial difficulties bedeviled Johnson, who, after exhausting himself by dining out with people from whom he vainly tried to solicit money in exchange for *Dial* stock, was glad to sell out to Scofield Thayer and Dr. J. S. Watson, Jr.

The Martyn Johnson *Dial* had sponsored the sort of criticism that was advanced by *The Seven Arts* group. It was a liberal criticism, a criticism that diligently explored the American literary heritage, ancient and contemporary, for its ideas, attitudes, and philosophies. It was not criticism of literature from an aesthetic or technical approach at all, but simply an estimate of American thought as revealed in literature.

The purpose was to examine the national literary accumulation, to estimate it from a liberal point of view, to suggest what should be retained and what should be discarded. In short, the purpose was to discover the foundation on which to construct the American future. This critical approach, represented by the early writings of such men as Waldo Frank, Van Wyck Brooks, and Randolph Bourne, was both valuable and necessary, and its aim of liberalizing and humanizing the American outlook was largely accomplished. But the approach did not add much to our comprehension of art as such, of the qualities that distinguish art from abstract expositional discourse. This criticism made little attempt to explain either the nature of the artistic structure or the value of such a structure to the human mind as a satisfying and meaningful experience. The methods and aims of this insurgent group of Americanizers, though they were to be frequently announced throughout the twenties and early thirties in Mencken's *American Mercury*, by 1920 had already become unpopular with certain younger critics. These younger men were to find the new *Dial* of Watson and Thayer much more congenial to their concept of the proper function of a literary critic than the older *Dial* had been.

The critics who gravitated to the new *Dial* did not care to think of literature as primarily valuable for its expression of ideas or philosophies, though they were willing to admit that such might be one of its associate functions. They believed that art is satisfying and meaningful primarily as form, as a concrete and vivid organization of experience. They conceived it to be their main responsibility, therefore, to discover and clarify the texture and structure of a work—to indicate its artistic form. This method of close textual reading had long been popular in France, where it was first stated and to an extent practiced by both Taine and Sainte-Beuve. Remy de Gourmont had elaborated the method of detailed explication, and it was he more than anyone else who inspired both Ezra Pound and T. S. Eliot, the first American practitioners of the French approach.

Both Pound and Eliot printed much of their early criticism in *The Dial*. They, along with Kenneth Burke, Yvor Winters, and several other only slightly less brilliant men, introduced a new criticism to America—a criticism of learning and insight, and a criticism that kept a close eye on the organization of the work under discussion. Today, looking back upon the nine years of *Dial* activity, one might say that America learned from *The Dial* critics more about the artistic process and more about the value of art as experience than it had learned during our entire previous history.

Though *The Dial's* criticism stressed the analysis of technique and structure, it did not travel as far toward a detailed and extended structural examination as did the work of the later "new critics" of literature. Nor were *The Dial* writers as sternly objective as the structuralists of the next decade. For frequently *The Dial* group insisted on asserting their personal responses to the artistic work, and in some cases, as with Marianne Moore and Charles K. Trueblood, the personal response became heavily subjective and impressionistic—became more a revelation of personal taste and sensitiveness than an objective analysis of form. To the extent that *The Dial* critics gave reign to their subjective responses they were impressionists; to the extent that their impressionism was circumscribed by comments on form and technique they were objectivists. Perhaps the typical *Dial* critic is best seen as a member of a transitional group that stands halfway between the Huneker type of intelligent impressionist and the objective analyst who later developed and practiced his method in the pages of *The Hound and Horn* and *The Southern Review*.

One other point about *The Dial's* criticism remains to be noted, and it is a point that should be stressed in reference to *The Hound and Horn*, *The Symposium*, and many of the critical little magazines of the thirties and forties. That is, their intense concern with all forms of experimentalism, and their willingness to explore beyond our national boundaries in search of it. *The Dial* and most of our critical reviews that followed it exhibited a generous and discriminating international and cosmopolitan outlook, a fact that sets them in radical opposition to the main body of nineteenth and early twentieth century American criticism.

### III

According to Dr. Watson, *The Dial* might have steered quite a different course, had it not been for Randolph Bourne's death. "When Thayer first laid plans for the magazine it was his intention, in which I concurred, to divide the magazine into two sections, literary and political. As his political editor he selected Randolph Bourne, for whom he felt great admiration. Bourne agreed to take full charge of this department. However Bourne's death in the second winter of the influenza epidemic put an end to the scheme. Certainly there were other authorities in this field, but none was quite what Thayer wanted. When we finally obtained control of the *Dial* some months later we agreed to limit ourselves to literary, artistic, and philosophical matter."[9] Thus it happened that one of the most distinguished critical reviews of our time made its initial appearance in January 1920, published from New York.

Scofield Thayer and Dr. Watson were wealthy and had a keen interest in and understanding of what was happening in American and European letters. They were both determined to print a magazine for writers and art rather than for circulation and advertising, both of which they might easily have obtained. For the circulation leaped from the 8,000 of the Johnson *Dial* to around 18,000 during the first four years of the Watson-Thayer regime. But as the circulation grew larger, the yearly deficit increased, reaching $50,000 during two of these years. Advertising might have been solicited, but it was apparent, as Dr. Watson points out, that that would have interfered with the magazine's proper function. Though advertisements were accepted, they were not regarded as a sustaining source of income. And so the circulation was allowed to fall to its natural level, varying between two and four thousand during the last five years.[10]

Few persons know much about Dr. Watson. He is a shy, retiring man, who, through his generosity, has had a considerable part in the encouragement of modern literature. He was more than president of the magazine. Scofield Thayer officially edited *The Dial* until early in 1925, and Marianne Moore thereafter; but Watson actually was a coeditor from beginning to end, though Miss Moore took much of the responsibility after April 1925. Born in 1894, Watson graduated from Harvard in 1916, after which he obtained an M.D. He became an editorial reader for the Browne *Dial* in 1910. In 1918 he joined with Thayer to support James Joyce and *The Little Review* in their exciting fight with the censor over the right to print *Ulysses*. He appeared anonymously or under the pseudonym of "W. C. Blum" in *The Dial*, writing astute book reviews, translating *A Season in Hell*, or discussing Rimbaud "with a quietness amounting to scandal."[11] Until 1924 Watson and Thayer, along with their professional managing editors and

[9] Letter, J. S. Watson to Charles Allen, May 25, 1943 (unpublished).

[10] *The Dial* was a periodical of distinguished, if not elaborate, appearance, usually of about 100 well printed and well designed pages, decorously clad in a tan coverpiece, and selling for $5.00 a year.

[11] Marianne Moore, "The Dial: Part II," *Life and Letters Today*, xxviii, 6 (January 1941).

able secretaries, Eleanor Minne and Sophia Wittenberg (who later married Lewis Mumford), conducted much of the magazine's business: reading manuscripts, conferring with contributors, overseeing the burdensome mechanical details connected with the make-up and printing. In 1925 Watson moved to Rochester, New York, where he has since lived, working at medicine and experimenting with motion pictures, at least three of which, *The Fall of the House of Usher, Lot in Sodom,* and *Highlights and Shadows,* have elicited much favorable comment.[12]

Even less of Thayer is known than of Watson. During the past ten years Thayer has become a half-legendary memory around New York; everyone who knew him has a private version of his personality and it is next to impossible to estimate the truth from the contradictory reports. He was born apparently in 1890 and graduated from Harvard in 1912 (dates not verified). As we have seen, he helped to reorganize the Johnson *Dial* into a magazine of liberal opinion, and he shared with Dr. Watson much of the responsibility during the first four years of the later review. He contributed book reviews, a few critical articles, and some estimable verse (which in 1925 was about to be published in book form but unfortunately never appeared) to his periodical[13]; and he provided the exciting German color reproductions of the magazine's frontispieces, which "in themselves justify Hugo von Hofmannsthal's feeling that *The Dial* was 'just the contrary of blasé and routinier.' "[14] Thayer suffered a nervous and physical breakdown in 1925 and has never completely recovered.[15]

Marianne Moore has honored Watson and Thayer with a gracious tribute in her charming reminiscences of *The Dial* that appeared recently in *Life and Letters Today*.[16] She says: "Above all, for an aesthetically inflexible morality against 'the nearly good enough'; for non-exploiting helpfulness to art and the artist, for living their own doctrine that 'the love of letters knows no frontiers,' Scofield Thayer and Dr. Watson stand foremost...."[17]

Marianne Moore was the real editor from April 1925 until the end, according to Dr. Watson. According to Miss Moore, Dr. Watson was

---

[12] This information has been provided in letters from J. S. Watson (May 25, 1943) and Marianne Moore (August 16, 1939) to Charles Allen (unpublished).
[13] Letter, Watson to Allen, May 25, 1943 (unpublished).
[14] Moore, "The Dial: Part II," p. 6.
[15] Letter, Watson to Allen, May 25, 1943 (unpublished).
[16] Part I in the December 1940 issue, pp. 175-83; Part II in the January 1941 issue, pp. 3-9.
[17] *Ibid.*, Part II, p. 8.

the real editor, though he was in Rochester most of the time. The reader can decide for himself whom he wishes to call editor. Several persons who were associated with the magazine share our opinion that Miss Moore was the actual editor, though Watson certainly helped in passing judgment on the manuscripts. After graduating from Bryn Mawr, Miss Moore taught in the Carlisle Indian School and later was an assistant in the New York Public Library. Alfred Kreymborg was her first American discoverer and sponsored her verse in his *Glebe* and *Others*. By the early twenties she had firmly established herself as a leader of the younger generation of experimental poets. She received *The Dial* Award in 1924, and a few months later was persuaded to join the magazine. She agreed with the "understanding that she was to be in the office only in the mornings."[18]

These three, Watson, Thayer, and Miss Moore, were the main pilots of *The Dial*. They were assisted editorially, in the following order, by Stewart Mitchell, Gilbert Seldes, Alyse Gregory (who married Llewelyn Powys), Kenneth Burke (who in 1927 followed Paul Rosenfeld as *Dial* music critic), and Ellen Thayer (Scofield's cousin), all of whom worked at one time or another in the capacity of managing or assistant editor. Seldes and Burke were on several occasions in sole charge of the magazine.

Miss Moore has told us a little about the atmosphere in which these people worked. "There was for us of the staff a constant atmosphere of excited triumph—interiorly, whatever the impression outside; and from Editor or Publisher a natural firework of little parenthetic wit too good to print—implying that efflatus is not chary of surplus."[19] These pleasant exchanges took place in the Greenwich Village *Dial* home, which Miss Moore describes for us: "I think of the compacted pleasantness of those days at 152 West 13th Street, and the three story brick building with carpeted stairs, fireplace and white mantelpiece rooms, business office in the first storey front parlour, and of the plain gold-leaf block letters, *The Dial*, on the windows to the right of the brown stone steps leading to the front door."[20] Outside on the street the flower-crier and the fish peddler sang their wares. Of the fish man Kenneth Burke remarked: "I think if he stopped to sell a fish my heart would skip a beat."[21]

*The Dial* announced itself as a magazine interested in the best of

[18] Letter, Marianne Moore to Charles Allen, July 2, 1941 (unpublished).
[19] Moore, "*The Dial*: Part I," p. 178.   [20] *Ibid.*, pp. 175-76.
[21] *Ibid.*, p. 176.

European and American art, experimental and conventional. That was the pronouncement, and it has been unreservedly accepted by several commentators. *The Dial*, like *Broom*, was experimentalist, despite work from the pens of Thomas Mann, Maxim Gorki, Gerhardt Hauptmann, Bertrand Russell and George Saintsbury (who would send his criticism only to *The Dial* among American magazines), none of whom were particularly conventional, for that matter. That the review had its definite inclination, that it did not really believe in the diffuse eclecticism it preached is not difficult to prove.

For there were *The Dial* Awards, given once a year from 1921 to 1929, to the American writers whom Watson and Thayer believed to be making significant contributions to our literature. These awards, not to be thought of as prizes such as the yearly competitive *Poetry* prizes, were given "to afford the recipient an opportunity to do what he wishes and out of that to enrich and develop his work."[22] Of course the awards were given to those writers who most nearly expressed the philosophy and aesthetics of the editors. We can look at the complete list and see what kind of experimentation pleased *The Dial*: for 1921 Sherwood Anderson, for 1922 T. S. Eliot, for 1923 Van Wyck Brooks, for 1924 Marianne Moore, for 1925 E. E. Cummings, for 1926 William Carlos Williams, for 1927 Ezra Pound, and for 1928 Kenneth Burke. There is a remarkable consistency of selection indicated here. These persons were all experimentalists, and most of them either were *Others* contributors or might easily have been. If this is not proof enough of the magazine's literary predilections, one can convince himself further by leafing through the volumes and noticing the great amount of space given to experimentalists other than the ones just mentioned, space given to writers such as Malcolm Cowley, Glenway Wescott, Conrad Aiken, Hart Crane, Yvor Winters, Jean Toomer, Paul Valéry, and Waldo Frank, to name only a few.

Of course the experimentalists did not completely dominate the periodical. One need only remember the appearances of such men as George Moore, Ivan Bunin, Anatole France, Logan Pearsall Smith, Gerhardt Hauptmann, and George Santayana—all of whom followed more conservative literary traditions than the main body of contributors. It was the printing of these more established men that aroused the ire of the editors of other experimental little magazines. *The Hound and Horn* editors in 1927 saw a betrayal of the cause and accused *The Dial* of being old and tired. Undoubtedly the tone of the magazine did

[22] Moore, "The Dial: Part II," p. 8.

become more conservative with age, but until the end it was safely in the advance guard ranks.

We have mentioned in passing a few of the writers from whom the periodical secured its material. Let us glance a little more closely at the actual contents. The magazine knew what it wished to do from the very beginning; it knew the writing it wanted and actively sought its writers, paying at the rate of 2 cents a word for prose, $20 a page for verse. Though the contributors were not always the same, a surprisingly large number who published in the first year published in the years that followed.

*The Dial* was primarily a critical review, and the proportion of criticism to poetry and fiction rarely varied, with over three-quarters of every issue devoted to critical essays, book reviews, art, music, and theater commentary. The remaining quarter was given to stories, poems, and art reproduction. An analysis of any one year, therefore, will afford a fairly accurate insight into the history of the magazine.

We may select 1920 for a sampling, beginning with criticism and reviewing. In 1920, as in later years, the editors were determined to print intelligent, critical analyses of living or recent writers and artists; and so we find such essays as Charles K. Trueblood's on Edith Wharton; Arthur Symons' study of Thomas Hardy; E. E. Cummings on Gaston Lachaise; and Van Wyck Brooks on Mark Twain's humor and satire. Besides the essays on specific writers and artists, there were critical explorations of such broad literary and aesthetic subjects as "The Structure of Chinese Poetry," by John Gould Fletcher; "Introducing Modern Art," by Henry McBride; "Modern Poetry," by Maxwell Bodenheim. Books, hundreds of them, were reviewed, always competently, often brilliantly, by such writers as Robert Morss Lovett, Henry McBride, Conrad Aiken, Babette Deutsch, Charles K. Trueblood, E. E. Cummings, Louis Untermeyer, Gilbert Seldes, Deems Taylor, Lincoln MacVeagh (who established the Dial Press, which had no direct connection with the periodical), and Paul Rosenfeld.

During the first year about forty poems were printed, the usual average for the following years. They were written by people who were frequently published later: Evelyn Scott, Conrad Aiken, Maxwell Bodenheim, Alfred Kreymborg, Marianne Moore, E. E. Cummings, Ezra Pound, Hart Crane, Witter Bynner, Elizabeth J. Coatsworth, Djuna Barnes, and Carl Sandburg.

The stories, as always, were few. There were "Crumbled Blossoms," by Arthur Schnitzler; "The Door of the Trap" and "The Triumph of the Egg," by Sherwood Anderson; "The Boss" and "Desire," by James Stephens; "Mrs. Maecenas," by Kenneth Burke; and "The Political Horse," by Manuel Komroff.

As many reproductions of line drawings, paintings, water colors, and sculptures were offered as there were poems. We find the work of Charles Demuth, E. E. Cummings, Charles Burchfield, Gaston Lachaise, Boardman Robinson, and many others reproduced for 1920.

Miss Moore has observed that *The Dial* was "never embarrassed by an over-abundance of able fiction."[23] Sherwood Anderson, D. H. Lawrence, Kenneth Burke, Jean Toomer, A. E. Coppard, Konrad Bercovici, Manuel Komroff, Katherine Mansfield, Albert Halper, Louis Zukofsky, and Llewelyn Powys were the fictionalists who appeared most frequently. D. H. Lawrence found that *The Dial* was the only English or American periodical consistently enthusiastic about his work, and many of his stories and poems appeared between 1921 and 1929. Noteworthy in 1924 was Thomas Mann's *Death in Venice*. Edward J. O'Brien judged 100 per cent of the 125 stories printed in the magazine to be distinctive.

Some of the better known *Dial* poets who did not appear in our 1920 list are: T. S. Eliot ("The Wasteland," November 1922), William Carlos Williams, E. Allen Ashwin, Malcolm Cowley, W. B. Yeats, Marianne Moore, Glenway Wescott, Yvor Winters, Richard Aldington, Joseph Auslander, George Dillon, Orrick Johns, and Louis Zukofsky.

Many reproductions of modern painting, drawing, and sculpture were presented, especially the work of Gaston Lachaise, Burchfield, John Marin, Rockwell Kent, Picasso, David Edstrom, Giorgio de Chirico, Henri Rousseau, Archipenko, Georg Kolbe, Matisse, Brancusi, André Derain, Carl Hofer, Maillol, Epstein, Městrovič, Adolph Dehn, Marie Laurencin, Paul Manship, E. E. Cummings, and Modigliani. Not only were reproductions printed, mostly in black and white, a few in color, but the review carried a discriminating monthly art commentary, written by Henry McBride. In addition, there were many articles on the fine arts by Thomas Craven, Paul Rosenfeld, and other critics. *The Dial* certainly served modern art well, with more knowledge and taste than any other little magazine of its day.

The fighting, alert book review section was also the best of its time; it was led by such people as Gilbert Seldes, Malcolm Cowley, Marianne Moore, Lisle Bell, Paul Rosenfeld, Kenneth Burke, Henry McBride,

[23] Moore, "The Dial: Part I," p. 178.

George Saintsbury, T. S. Eliot, Robert Morss Lovett, Philip Littell, John Cowper Powys, Llewelyn Powys, Dr. Watson, and Scofield Thayer. Some of the reviews by these people were unsigned, particularly many of those by Bell, Moore, Thayer, and Watson. More than once the sharp honesty of the criticism vexed a publisher or author, as is indicated by the following sentences from a letter of reply that Kenneth Burke wrote to an irate advertising manager who had complained of a tardy and unfavorable notice. "Why not give *The Dial* credit. As you have said, under our silence the book went through five editions. Now that we have spoken there may never be a sixth. . . . We are, you might say, reviewing a reprint—a courtesy not all gazettes will afford you. . . ."[24]

There is no possibility of giving an adequate description of the number of excellent critical essays. A few names and titles must suffice. There were Thomas Mann, with his famous essay on "Tolstoy"; T. S. Eliot on "Marianne Moore," and "Ulysses, Order and Myth"; Paul Rosenfeld on "Randolph Bourne"; John Cournos on "Chekhov and Gorky"; Van Wyck Brooks on "Henry James"; Logan Pearsall Smith on "Sainte-Beuve"; George Saintsbury on "Abelard and Heloise"; and Kenneth Burke—many times—with magic pieces such as "Realism and Idealism," "Engineering with Words," "Psychology and Form," "The Correspondence of Flaubert," and an essay on Gertrude Stein. A listing of even the most outstanding articles would cover several pages.

The last issue of the review carried a short, cryptic sentence announcing that the magazine could not get along without contributors. This was not the reason for the end, however. By 1929 Watson was absent from New York for months at a time. Editorial consultations were difficult, and "what had begun as a spontaneously delightful plotting in the interest of art and artists, was becoming mere faithfulness to responsibility."[25]

*The Dial* was one of the most important of the American experimental reviews. It represented more material than any other magazine, and to a greater number of readers; therefore, its leavening influence was far greater than that of its nearest competitor. The periodical, because of its financial stability and the self-effacing character of its editors, traveled serenely through its nine years, unattended by the flashy excitement that accompanied such magazines as *Secession*, *Broom*, and *The Little Review*. The Dial's story is one of accomplish-

[24] Moore, "*The Dial*: Part II," p. 3.
[25] Letter, Moore to Allen, July 2, 1941 (unpublished).

ment and value, and we must not forget that the review helped secure the reputations of many experimentalists by giving them early and frequent publication. Among these were Sherwood Anderson, Albert Halper, Jean Toomer, Glenway Wescott, Kenneth Burke, Evelyn Scott, E. E. Cummings, George Dillon, S. Foster Damon, Louis Zukofsky, Yvor Winters, Witter Bynner, and Elizabeth J. Coatsworth. Louis Zukofsky and Albert Halper were the only discoveries, an unimpressive record that is accounted for by the magazine's policy of discouraging unsolicited manuscripts.

To further a cosmopolitan literary outlook, to fight the spiritual inertia and insularity that characterized most of America, and above all to establish a new method of literary criticism—this was the goal and the achievement of one of the best advance guard critical magazines that ever existed in America.

## IV

*The Hound and Horn* rode an exciting hunt between 1927 and 1934 in search of a new criticism. The magazine was born September 1927, in Cambridge, Massachusetts, as a "Harvard Miscellany," financed by a wealthy young undergraduate, Lincoln Kirstein. Associated with Kirstein as editors were R. P. Blackmur, Bernard Bandler II, Varian Fry, and A. Hyatt Mayor. In 1929 the subtitle was dropped, with the apologetic explanation that it "misrepresented" what the review was trying to do. The fact that Harvard men had contributed most of the material was "largely accidental."[26]

Accidental or inevitable, during the first two years *The Hound and Horn* showed a strong Harvard influence. It presented photographs and reproductions of alma mater's undistinguished decorative sculpture; it declared that it was serving as a "point of contact between Harvard and the contemporary outside world"[27]; it announced an intention of publishing critical dissertations on Harvard's literary great: T. S. Eliot, Irving Babbitt, George Santayana, Henry James, E. E. Cummings, Conrad Aiken, and Henry Adams. Several of these were published and are excellent. Yet even in this early period, despite the surrounding college atmosphere, it carried itself with an urbane air, patterning its conduct after *The Dial* and Eliot's *Criterion*. The reviews of books, magazines, and the arts were excellent. Critical articles of acuteness found a

[26] "Comment," *The Hound and Horn*, III, 5 (October-December, 1929).
[27] "Announcement," *The Hound and Horn*, I, 6 (September 1927).

major place, and the young Harvard undergraduate editors managed to strengthen an important critical direction by seeing the advantages of a criticism devoted to close structural and textural examination.

The October-December, 1929, number saw the subtitle "Harvard Miscellany" discontinued. That same month, in outlining their editorial position, the editors agreed that they did not believe in "special dogmas," such as humanism, surrealism, classicism, America, etc.[28] They further proclaimed that "a sound philosophy will not produce a great work of art and a great work of art is no guarantee that the ideas of the artist are sound. Consequently our standard for judging the arts is technical. We demand only that the given work should be well done. ... We may feel that certain false ideas mar a work of art and partly defeat the artist's aim. But a picture, a poem, and a story have their intrinsic value quite apart from their association with theory."[29] This quotation is significant for an understanding of the review, indicating as it does an admiration for the artistic form itself, which is always the primary concern of the artist—the ethical and philosophical implications, in the nature of the imaginative process, generally being of secondary and often fortuitous consideration. The editors went ahead to announce their intention of seeking criticism designed to "seize the central point of any subject, and [to] discuss that with all the learning, logic and insight it can command."[30] The thought is not clear in this statement, but it seems to call for that close analysis of structure and texture which the director of the "New Criticism," John Crowe Ransom, has so insistently advocated, and which *The Hound and Horn* so insistently practiced. That criticism, of course, is well illustrated by Yvor Winters and R. P. Blackmur, two of *The Hound and Horn*'s assisting editors and frequent contributors. Both of these men, with the other "new critic" editor, Allen Tate, were influential in setting the magazine's tone and in obtaining manuscript. This "new criticism," so brilliantly practiced in recent years by Cleanth Brooks, John Crowe Ransom, Robert Penn Warren, Allen Tate, T. S. Eliot, Yvor Winters, and especially R. P. Blackmur, was probably not formulated in the mind of Kirstein as precisely as in the minds of his three associates, Tate, Winters, and Blackmur, but Kirstein was warmly sympathetic with the method of close, objective analysis. *The Hound and Horn* was the first American periodical to sponsor intensively and knowingly a critical method that has been so genuinely rewarding.

[28] "Comment," *The Hound and Horn*, III, 5 (October-December 1929).
[29] *Ibid.*     [30] *Ibid.*, p. 6.

Blackmur, one of the most important modern structural critics, published some of his first work in the review.

"There has been no clique or group of writers definitely connected as a body with the magazine.... There has been little coherent editorial policy as such"[31]; these are words taken from the review's final issue, words fortunately belied as far as criticism is concerned. And, like *Broom* and *The Dial*, the magazine also had its fiction and poetic bias, a bias revealed by the choice of authors and material. As one glances through the list of the more important and frequent contributors of poetry and fiction, he notices that most of them would ordinarily be considered experimentalists.

By the fall of 1930 *The Hound and Horn* had moved both its editorial and executive offices to New York. Lincoln Kirstein, who during the first three years had been the leading activator of the review, now became chief editor, executive, and financial angel. In 1931 he became sole owner and editor, assisted by Allen Tate and Yvor Winters as regional editors. Kirstein was born in Rochester, New York, in 1907, and is the author of a novel *Flesh Is Heir*, a verse volume *Low Ceiling*, and several works on theatrical dancing.

Though *The Hound and Horn* did not discover any noteworthy writers, it assisted generously in establishing the reputations of several authors who have since become well known. Josephine Johnson, Erskine Caldwell, Richard P. Blackmur, Merle Hoyleman, Alvah Bessie, Katherine Anne Porter, Francis Fergusson, David Cornel De Jong, Raymond E. F. Larsson, John Brooks Wheelwright, Dudley Fitts, and A. Hyatt Mayor were all befriended by the magazine at a time when they were struggling for recognition. Some of Katherine Anne Porter's masterly stories that were collected in the 1930 *Flowering Judas* appeared in such advance guard periodicals as *transition* and *The Hound and Horn*. Kay Boyle had published in the little magazines since the time of *Broom*. Encouragement was given to several others, but they have as yet failed to establish themselves.

Usually less than a quarter of the issue was devoted to poetry and fiction. Criticism and reviewing were the main interests. *The Hound and Horn's* Art, Book, and Music Chronicles were equaled only by those in T. S. Eliot's *Criterion*. Books were reviewed by A. Hyatt Mayor, Allen Tate, Dudley Fitts, R. P. Blackmur, Yvor Winters, Lincoln Kirstein, John B. Wheelwright, Francis Fergusson, and Marianne

---

[31] "Comment," *The Hound and Horn*, VII, n.p. (July-September, 1934).

Moore. Distinguished critical essays from Blackmur, Winters, Louis Zukofsky, S. Foster Damon, Paul Valéry, Henry Bamford Parkes, Bernard Bandler II, Tate, Francis Fergusson, Donald Davidson, Edmund Wilson, Newton Arvin, Marianne Moore, and Edna Kenton made the quarterly a worthy competitor and successor of *The Dial*. The "Homage to Henry James" number (Spring 1934), to which many of the magazine's writers contributed, is indicative of the high critical tone.

*The Symposium* ought to be mentioned at this point, for it was a periodical whose name is rightly associated with that of *The Hound and Horn*. Though it never found enough money to pay its contributors or to afford the rich paper and fine printing that always marked *The Hound and Horn*, *The Symposium* was nevertheless worthy of its wealthier brother. It published such people as William Phillips, Herbert Read, C. R. Morse (an art critic of high intelligence), Henry Bamford Parkes, Louis Zukofsky, Philip Blair Rice, Cudworth Flint, John Dewey, Kenneth Burke, Justin O'Brien, Robert Cantwell, William Troy, and Austin Warren, all of whom contributed critical essays— essays that generally dealt soundly with established masters of the past rather than with the contemporary artists who interested *The Hound and Horn*. During its last year *The Symposium* became more actively interested in the modern scene, even going so far as to make room for poetry and fiction, most of which was not very distinctive. On the whole it was a more conservative, less stimulating periodical than *The Hound and Horn*.

Both *The Hound and Horn* and *The Symposium* took much of their temperament from *The Criterion* and *The Dial*, and both of the former, like their two descendants, *The Southern Review* (1935-42) and *The Kenyon Review* (1939-    ), were designed as outlets for the intense, brilliant, and sometimes mannered critics, of whom Yvor Winters and R. P. Blackmur are fair representatives. After its first two years *The Hound and Horn* was not nearly so concerned as *The Dial* had been in general discussion of aesthetics or literary philosophy, as naturally it could not be, since structural analysis is chiefly interested in a particular object.

*The Hound and Horn* was a beautifully printed review. It measured about ten by six inches and averaged around 150 pages per quarterly issue. Contributions were paid for at the rate of from $3.50 to $5.00 per page for prose, and from $5.00 to $7.00 for poetry. The average circulation, from 2,500 to 3,000 copies, was not high enough to support the magazine financially, even though the editors went unpaid.[32] *The Hound and Horn* was forced to cease publication at the end of its seventh volume in the fall of 1934.

Aside from their intrinsic value as capable though sometimes uneven reviews, *The Hound and Horn* and *The Symposium* helped in suggesting the courses of the maturer *Southern Review* and *Kenyon Review*. The former of these, under the guidance of Cleanth Brooks and Robert Penn Warren, was one of the finest critical periodicals this country has ever known; and John Crowe Ransom's *Kenyon Review* has continued in the vanguard of American criticism. *The Southern Review* was defeated after eight volumes by the woolly intellectual apathy that had made an end of *The Hound and Horn*; and one always fears that the same lassitude will drive *The Kenyon Review* to surrender. One can hope, however, that it will somehow survive, and that, with the help of a rejuvenated *Sewanee Review* (which has found money to run since the ancient year of 1892 and is now edited by Allen Tate), our "new criticism" will be further encouraged to its full development. Intelligent magazines are needed to free us from the exaggerated and often pointless moralistic bondage that has fettered our literary discussion. If the five or six thousand people who should legitimately maintain publications devoted primarily to literature rather than ethics and ideas could bring themselves to concerted action, we might reasonably obtain the exciting reality of an American criticism eclipsing in understanding any insight that has ever appeared in our language. Already we have Cleanth Brooks, R. P. Blackmur, and Yvor Winters, all of extraordinary critical perception.

## V

At this writing the large annual volume, *New Directions*, published since 1936 by James Laughlin from his press in Norfolk, Connecticut, is one of the best of the experimental publications upholding the flag that *The Little Review* and *The Dial* carried so bravely. There have been nine volumes, each presenting between three and seven hundred pages, each filled with more material than most little magazines show in twelve issues. *New Directions* is more frankly in search of experimental writing, both American and European, than is any other

[32] Letter, Doris R. Levine (Business Manager of *The Hound and Horn*) to Charles Allen, April 25, 1939 (unpublished).

present-day advance guard venture. Unfortunately less than 50 per cent of the anthology deserves serious consideration as literature.

James Laughlin, a member of the Pittsburgh steel family, gained an early recognition. When he was eighteen he began publishing short stories and poetry in several of the little magazines. He was twenty-two, still a student at Harvard, when he founded the New Directions Press in Cambridge, Massachusetts. Since that time, the firm has acquired offices in Norfolk, Connecticut, and in New York City, and its publishing activities have been greatly expanded. Laughlin's principal editorial assistants are Hubert Creekmore and (quite recently) Robert Lowry.[33]

Besides the annual volumes, there is the New Directions Press, which has been publishing the fictional, poetic, and critical volumes of such well known experimenters as William Carlos Williams, Ezra Pound, and of such young, relatively unknown experimentalists as Delmore Schwartz and Kenneth Patchen. This well financed, experimental press has published over one hundred and forty printed volumes; already it has done more to disseminate and encourage international experimental writing than any former or present-day publisher. If the press can continue for another ten years, or even five, it will undoubtedly be known as one of the most significant literary landmarks of twentieth century America. But the ever-increasing flow of remarkable volumes does not tell the whole story. Laughlin has three other plans in operation.

The first: the notion of "Poets of the Year." This is a series of 32-page monthly pamphlets, each devoted to the best verse of an important poet. It has now been discontinued.

The second: "The New Classics Series." The neglected works of recent or living modern authors are reprinted.

The third: "The Makers of Modern Literature Series" offers critical studies of authors, experimental or traditional, who have had a continuing influence upon modern literature.

Let us consider Laughlin's motivations for his various projects. What we have to say applies both to the anthologies and to the more important projects of the Press. All of his activities, as he cheerfully admits, are essentially little magazine activities, and he is willing to accept the occasional financial risks.[34] Laughlin has not been reticent about expressing himself in *New Directions* editorials and articles.

---
[33] Statement, James Laughlin to Hoffman, 1947.
[34] Statement, Laughlin to Allen, 1939.

Several times during recent years he has reiterated his purpose—"New Directions has published well over a hundred books," one statement runs. "Some have been much better than others, but all were the work of writers who deeply believed that writing must remain an art and that it must not be degraded to the level of mass production business."[35]

Laughlin's interest in experimentalism is thus frankly an eclectic interest. It is an interest, like *The Dial's* and *The Hound and Horn's*, that ignores national boundaries, and it is an interest that often makes forays into the nineteenth century. One of the strongest motivations of the New Directions front is the desire to make more widely known the significant experimentalisms of the western world of the past one hundred years. Experimental writing makes up about one-fourth of New Directions publications. Advertising of the experimental great has been carried on by printing the original work of the masters, by encouraging critical estimates of them, and by editorial exhortation urging the world to read them. Often, as in the case of Franz Kafka, all three forms of publicity are used persistently and loudly.

When Laughlin speaks of "the healthy evolution of literature," he also has in mind the "healthy evolution" of society, for he believes that the new society, a society that will solve the problem of distribution after the fashion of Major Douglas, must be firmly built on language. Thus we are not surprised to find the editor wholeheartedly applauding the work of such semanticists as Richards and Ogden. Laughlin insists that economics, sociology, and psychology are not as competent as they may appear in solving our problems because these sciences are chained to words which no longer have unequivocal meaning. Vague words befog our thinking processes. If we cannot think, we cannot find our way out of the endless forest.[36] And so the function of the literary experimentalist—for example, E. E. Cummings —is to juxtapose words and phrases, to "shock the mind into fresh analyses." He must help mold a new language; he must help solve our social problems. Experiment with language and we improve the public's interest in clear and intelligent thinking.[37]

This experimenting with language is closely akin to experimenting with the imagination. In our blind adherence to reason and scientific investigation, we have neglected to search the inner recesses of our beings. We must explore deeper than a mere observation of surface

---
[35] Advertisement in The New York *Times Book Review*, Oct. 6, 1946, p. 50.
[36] Laughlin, "Preface," *New Directions in Prose and Poetry*, 1936, n.p.
[37] Ibid.

detail will allow us. One other way of enriching the reader's consciousness of language and literature is that of increasing his awareness of foreign literatures. This New Directions has helped to do: one-third of its publication in recent years has consisted of translation (bilingual) of important foreign language texts.

These are the reasons for New Directions, both the Press and the anthology. But they are both committed to more than a mere accommodation of experiment; in fact, as Laughlin's recent statements make clear, they are interested in "non-commercial literature," whether experimental or traditional in form or matter.

From a study of the *New Directions* annual volumes several observations are possible. First, one notices, as he did with the older *American Caravan* and as he does with the present-day *Twice a Year*, a marked variety in the nature of their offerings, and some differences in quality. Laughlin quite legitimately defends the publication of many of his less distinguished pieces on the ground either that they are suggestive or that he is offering encouragement to promising talents. Above all, he argues for integrity in writing, which, he feels strongly, may be weakened by a writer's submission to various commercial and "journalistic" pressures in American publishing. He is anxious to protect that integrity, at the occasional risk of publishing the work of writers who have not yet achieved maturity, whether in style or mastery of subject.

The volume has gradually put a greater emphasis upon the more radical experimentalisms—and this may be applauded. In the beginning there was much prose that approached in appearance, if not in implication, the domain of objective realism. More and more the editor has sought out fantasy, showing a special friendliness to the imagination which employs dream materials and mechanisms.

Also, one can readily see that the annual has, especially during its first two years, given considerable space to the older, better known experimentalists. Lately less well known names are being printed, and this is all to the good, for the yearly volume ought to be primarily for young and relatively unknown writers. The Press can take care of the more established artists. Several of the newer writers—David Kerner, Kenneth Patchen, Paul Goodman, Weldon Kees, Eudora Welty, Richard Eberhart, Montague O'Reilly, and Delmore Schwartz—have already made great strides. If these and others continue to grow, *New Directions* will have a sizable group whom it can claim the honor of having helped to establish.

As *New Directions* has grown older and more secure, its editor has become increasingly aware of his responsibilities and opportunities. The 1940 volume carried an editorial announcement in which Laughlin squarely faced his record. He believed that he had not been severe enough in demanding that a writer show a sense of literary form. He had published too many writings which could be defended only on the assumption that linguistic and imaginative experiments are justifiable in themselves.[38] He announced that he would demand form, and by form he did not mean "a return to literary corsets, bustles, and buns": he was not calling for plots or "similar horrors." "What I ask is that the parts of a piece of writing be in some way joined together—and the joining need not be logical either—and that, if possible, that joining contribute something, of itself, to the complete meaning of the whole."[39]

So much for *New Directions*, the yearly volume. By the end of 1946 the New Directions Press had published around 140 volumes, most of them distinguished, many of them selling for $2.50 or less. Laughlin's good friends, Pound and Williams, appear most frequently. The writing of the latter is still alertly alive and increasingly significant, though much of Pound's work, while interesting and suggestive, appears fragmentary, confused, and, most vexing of all, tinged with a refractory and perverse exhibitionism.

"The New Classics Series" (reprints of moderns who are out of print or difficult to obtain) is one of the most important contributions of the New Directions Press. Significant also is "The Makers of Modern Literature Series." Among the many books in this rapidly growing series are sound and interesting studies of James Joyce, by Harry Levin; Virginia Woolf, by David Daiches; Nikolay Gogol, by Vladimir Nabokov; Garcia Lorca, by Edwin Honig; E. M. Forster, by Lionel Trilling; and E. A. Robinson, by Yvor Winters. Two other projects, begun in 1946, supplement these ventures and will gain in importance in the next few years: "The Modern Readers Series" (new editions of great books that have gone out of print) and the "Selected Writings Series" (one-volume editions, containing representative selections from the work of modern writers).

January 1941 saw the inauguration of "The Poet of the Month Series" (later known as "Poets of the Year"), with twelve attractively designed pamphlets issued annually, pamphlets which include some of the best work of many modern poets, as well as selections from the

[38] Laughlin, "Preface," *New Directions in Prose and Poetry*, 1940, pp. xiii-xv.
[39] *Ibid.*, p. xiv.

poetry of the past. The series was discontinued in 1945 because of inflationary printing costs. During its three and one-half years, forty-two numbers were published, each one individually designed and printed by a fine press.

Since the Press serves much the same purpose as do the anthologies, we may regard New Directions as an important and alert sponsor of what can best be called "non-commercial" writing. Both Laughlin and James T. Farrell (the latter's long essay on the future of American writing appeared in *New Directions* number nine) agree that much needs to be done to resist an increase in commercial temptations for young writers. The publication of "non-commercial" writing by New Directions—and this writing may be traditional as well as experimental in form—serves to encourage the normal development of writers, and thus to fortify them against the desire for easy fame and money. "We have instances," said Laughlin in *New Directions* nine, "of men like James Joyce who carried on through years of difficulty and never compromised in any way. But how many Joyces may there have been who had not the strength for such an ordeal?"[40]

## VI

Thus *The Dial*, *The Hound and Horn*, *The Symposium*, and the New Directions ventures demonstrate advance guard criticism and editorial selection at their best and most interesting. The first three are expressions of critical taste and practice, carrying as they do much of the burden of critical defense and explication of modern literature. The value of Laughlin's various enterprises lies in his intelligent and enthusiastic eclecticism. In a sense, eclecticism argues a policy—a searching for examples in all times and places, of the work which most interests the writers of our own times. It is a kind of cultural exchange, based on an interest in finding a precedent for immediate tastes and a justification for present practices. As a result, literatures of several nations and cultures are brought together, collated, and reshaped.

One of the consequences of international depression in the thirties was to arouse the interest of peoples in one another, and in their several cultures. Thus *The Partisan Review* has published some of the stories of Franz Kafka, several estimates of his work by Max Brod and others, a long critical essay on Thomas Mann, Eugene Jolas on James Joyce, and Professor Vigneron on Marcel Proust. In fact, if the writers

[40] Laughlin, "Editor's Note," *New Directions*, 1946, p. xvii.

of the late thirties have shown some advance toward a synthesis of literary values, it is suggested in the wider distributions which "foreign" authors have enjoyed, with the help of such cosmopolitans as James Laughlin, Edwin Muir, and Samuel Putnam. Laughlin's New Directions Press has published Kafka, Lautréamont, Rimbaud, Baudelaire, and others. Muir's magazine, *The European Quarterly*, was published in London in 1934, "to attempt to establish a sympathetic contact between the intellectual life of this country and that of the Continent."[41] Studies were published of Russian revolutionary literature, of English poetry, of German and French poets; and translations into English were offered of the work of Garcia Lorca, Sergei Essenin, and Søren Kierkegaard. In a sense the attitude toward literature has matured. In the time of Samuel Roth's *Review of Two Worlds*, the impression of foreign literatures seemed deliberately casual, the object of translation "to increase the gaiety of nations." *The European Quarterly* and *Europa* are a collection of serious studies and earnest endeavors to reach an international understanding through an appreciation of diverse cultures.

*Europa*, whose European editor was Samuel Putnam, was produced from New York in the years 1933 and 1934. Its aim was essentially to inform the peoples of America and England of the status of the arts in Continental Europe. Clive Bell reported on French painting, David Ewen on "Music under the Swastika," William Koslenko on Dostoevski; the Russian theater was given ample attention. And Mussolini reported on Fascism in his country. This generosity toward all elements in European cultural life was not likely to act as an aesthetic dissolvent of political differences. It lacked the motivation of a singleness of purpose, such as was enjoyed by Moscow's *International Literature*. The "panoramic view" cannot prove to be anything more than interesting; its inclusiveness has obvious disadvantages.

Another "news letter of the arts," *The Literary World*, supplements *The European Quarterly* as a center of information about international literature. Again it is Joyce, Kafka, and Mann who receive much attention, as well as André Gide and Louis-Ferdinand Celine. The recent interest in Kafka is here acknowledged and abetted by the entire issue of July 1934. Franz Kafka, a Czech writer who died in 1924, left a number of manuscripts which his literary executor, Max Brod, saved from destruction, in a pardonable disobedience of Kafka's wish. The three novels—*The Castle*, *The Trial*, and *Amerika*—have been more than adequately supplemented by a number of shorter pieces which

[41] Editorial, *The European Quarterly*, 1, 2 (May 1934).

have appeared from time to time in the little magazines. In general it may be said that Kafka's posthumous and presumably unwished-for reputation has been the responsibility of the little magazines, which have been more than willing to accept the word of Max Brod and Edwin Muir regarding his importance. *The Partisan Review, The Literary World, transition, Twice a Year,* and the New Directions annuals and Press have done most to bring this important writer out of seclusion. (Among the commercial publishers, Alfred Knopf has been alert to Kafka's importance as well, and has published two of his novels.)

"Kafka has fully expressed the modern mentality in its German mood," said Denis Saurat in *The Literary World*. It is this earnest desire to assess the aesthetic contribution of European literature that marks an important though minor theme in the thirties. In a sense, it served to supplement and to qualify the enthusiasm for a world revolution. It suggested, not a counterrevolution, but a study of the complexity of the international scene. More than that, it demonstrated that the culture of the twentieth century was coming of age. The appraisal and encouragement of European literatures played a large role in the years immediately preceding the second war of our generation, and it remained strong during the war itself. The complexion of the little magazine may well change in the forties under its influence.

The import of criticism in the little magazines is great for the continuance of *avant-gardism*. Literary criticism may be either a servant or a master of literary creation. The giants of the critical world who announce in stentorian tones what may and may not be written in a given decade are not always the best companions or guides. The healthful and meritorious service of *avant-gardist* criticism resides in its defense of new modes, its search for critical justifications of the modern temper, and its cosmopolitan indifference to arbitrary political and geographic limits to creative work. Most important of all, of course, is the presence in critical magazines of authors discussing their own craft and debating the merits and limits of the aesthetic mode. The presence in large number of purely critical and eclectic magazines argues the willingness of the artist to survey his world and to set some sort of estimate upon the bulk and weight of creative activity in the immediate past. For the most part, these critical magazines are characterized by a generous accommodation of a variety of theories and by a desire on the part of the artist to know more about himself.

# CONCLUSION:

## Reflections upon Little Magazine History

**CHAPTER XII**

The financial instability of little magazines, while it provides an entertaining history of editorial oddities, does not give the avant-garde much assurance of a more than day-to-day existence. As long as social and cultural conditions warrant or demand experiment, little magazines compensate for their impermanence by the great number of new arrivals. Avant-garde ideas are thus like seeds thrown carelessly about on cultural soil. There was no question of survival in the twenties and thirties; they were a time calling for ceaseless literary endeavor, and providing the means in a variety of interesting ways. But the first five years of this decade were difficult ones for little magazine activities. Wars are a great drain upon personal and national energies. Writers have had little time for their trade. Many of them were occupied with nonliterary tasks, by necessity or by choice. The public was often indifferent to their predicament.

The poet's trumpeting for a political and military cause may very well improve the quality of radio and cinema fare. But in so submitting to the demands of an issue too large and too immediate to be solved personally, he has necessarily and obviously to abandon any personal views which may run counter to it or confuse its singleness of direction. The war demands neither contemplation nor equivocation; the poet must forego both in the interests of action. The effects upon him, though perhaps only temporary, are nevertheless felt. This problem is brilliantly analyzed for us by Andrews Wanning in a recent issue of *Furioso*. To write stirring and yet good poetry in a time of war, he says, "would need skill in the use of words, some dramatic imagination, and a certain indifference to the immortality of one's work."[1] The

[1] "Ruminations Over the Dilemma of Poets in Wartime," *Furioso*, II, 47 (1943).

technique of direct persuasion is, however, not entirely consistent with the poet's more complex view of his world. The emotional quality of such persuasion is direct, unequivocal, and available in dozens of journalistic accounts of events. But the egocentricity of the poet must be abandoned. This egoism, of which much has already been said in this essay, is not of necessity antisocial, but it does judge public events from an aesthetically private vantage point. The poet demands that the privacy of his judgment be respected. The pressure of events may well force him into a kind of poetic journalism, employing the obvious idiom of cultural commonplace, the kind of political comment to which the reader turns to be assured of what he already believes in.

Another disadvantage of such times as these is the tacit acceptance of a circumscribed language for poetry. Patriotism has a simple language all its own. Heroism demands abstractions and slogans, by which a human act is viewed as typical rather than individual. Any subtlety of interpretation is a definite barrier to understanding on this level. For this reason, the poet is limited in his choice of materials and in his attitude toward them. A single act of courage must be regarded as typical of the courage of a nation; the treachery of the enemy is also seen as an all-encompassing evil. This necessity strikes a hard blow at the integrity of the poet; for he is frequently called upon to make poetry out of public emotions of which he has had little or no personal knowledge. Occasionally a poet of some conviction and talent may so treat an incident for its inherent aesthetic value, allowing the reader to look at its beauty or tragedy without interference. This is the case in Dylan Thomas' poem, "Among Those Killed in the Dawn Raid Was a Man Aged One Hundred":

> When the morning was waking over the war
> He put on his clothes and stepped out and he died,
> The locks yawned loose and a blast blew them wide,
> He dropped where he loved on the burst pavement stone
> And the funeral grains of the slaughtered floor.
> Tell his street on its back he stopped a sun
> And the craters of his eyes grew spring shoots and fire
> When all the keys shot from the locks, and rang.[2]

The ideal of the artist is by no means completely abandoned, even in a time of absorption in international military affairs. Indeed, some writers are more than ever convinced that "Now" is the time for a re-

[2] *New Poems*, Norfolk, Connecticut, 1943, n.p.

newed affirmation of aesthetic aims and purposes. The danger, they declare, is imminent; the real enemy is the host of men and the pressure of circumstance which will serve to mislead the artist. The little magazine, therefore, needs to be rededicated to a very serious purpose:

"So it is necessary for the real artists and intellectuals and scientists to be continuously alert to the attempts to divert and confuse them, and it is necessary for them to define and understand more and more clearly their own and their contemporaries and their predecessors work, and to know the nature of their society and of past societies, and to ensure that work which they are doing will be presented and find its audience and produce the full effect of its validity and not be suppressed by the thousand and one means the controlling group has of effecting suppression."[3]

The affirmation of the poet may seem strange in these times, but it has the entire valid history of twentieth century experiment supporting it. In the opinion of William Carlos Williams, whose entire life has been linked with this history, the poem remains the primary means for focusing the world. This value should not be "seduced by political urgencies." The poem is a definition of reality; that definition must not be allowed to become a trite political commonplace. The political complexion of any society, says Williams, is only the "surface show." Beneath it life is a complex of warring motives, which only the poet can understand. Successful campaigns to secure a unity of purpose may be tolerated and indeed are necessary in times of emergency, but they must not be mistaken as the true reality.[4]

Thus there are some little magazines striving to hold to the sanctity of the aesthetic imperative. The right to disagree, because one's conscience does not allow agreement, is hard to maintain in a time when right and wrong seem so simply divided and so dependent upon the fluctuations of military power. But such a magazine as *Retort* has held to it, in the face of increasing pressure against all but the single major disagreement with Fascism and the totalitarian state. The magazine was begun in 1942, "as an organ of expression for the independent left, those radicals who have lost faith in the traditional dogmas and ready-made formulas of the revolutionary movement, but who have not succumbed to despair or made their peace with the status quo."[5]

[3] "The Program," *Now* (New York), 1, 5 (August 1941).
[4] "Midas: A Proposal for a Magazine," *Now* (New York), 1, 18-24 (August 1941).
[5] "Retorting," *Retort*, 1, 56 (Spring 1943).

The all-out drive against Nazism has recently occupied the attention of many little magazines. Some of them began with a deliberate intention of avoiding commitment on social and political issues but have since the outbreak of war unhesitatingly joined the anti-Nazi front. *Wales*, for example, a magazine of great merit, has announced its intention of opposing Nazism of all sorts, including the "local variety": "Our fight will be against any establishment of Fascist principles in this country. When we have finished the war there are forces which will gladly set up such a system in this country. That is what we shall have to fight if we are to live."[6] Similarly, *The New Alliance* of Edinburgh committed itself to a struggle against the enemy in 1940.

England's *Horizon* began in 1940 with the intention of biding its time. In the opinion of its editor, Cyril Connolly, political activity has too often acted to prevent the creation of good work. It is the privilege of the artist to wait for social issues to "clear of themselves." "Our standards are aesthetic," he told his subscribers, "and our politics are in abeyance. This will not always be the case, because as events take shape the policy of artists and intellectuals will become clearer, the policy which leads them to economic security, to the atmosphere in which they can create, and to the audience by whom they will be appreciated. At the moment civilization is on the operating table and we sit in the waiting room."[7]

The effect of such an announced policy upon the appearance of the magazine was immediate. The emphasis of the first issues is upon the direct impression of the poet and upon the critic's large evaluation of culture. The value of the magazine is that it encouraged writers to write "on the subjects about which their feelings are deepest," and thus avoided the superficial glare of the political headline. Inevitably, perhaps, the magazine shifted its position, as the war became more immediate, shocking the artist into joining in one way or another. Here the dilemma of the artist in a time of war was brilliantly illustrated. In his own mind he was perhaps desperately opposed to authoritarian control; yet this opposition is after all only one side of his desire for independence. And, in the opinion of such men as Stephen Spender, the war has asked for a response which is beyond the poet's competence. To Spender's apparent return to the doctrine of poetic immediacy, enunciated by him in such places as the Penguin *New Writing* and in his recent book, *Life and the Poet*, more determined and convinced

---

[6] Editorial, *Wales*, x, 254 (October 1939).
[7] Editorial, *Horizon*, I, 5 (January 1940).

critics objected strenuously. The British *Now*, reviewing Spender's most recent remarks, declared that his doctrine of aesthetic freedom was essentially a false one and harmful to his own work: "The contradictions implicit in his own attitude, most notably his refusal to admit art as something fashioned by its time, have led Mr. Spender to the slack writing and over-simplification contained specially in the first and last chapters, and at intervals all through his book."[8]

The titles of two American magazines, *Decision* and *Direction*, might well give a clue to their respective reasons for being. *Decision* was established by Klaus Mann in January 1941. He was supported by an impressive board of editorial advisers, which included his distinguished father. The magazine announced itself as "A Review of Free Culture," committed to the establishment and clarification of "a new *humanism*" which would counter the depersonalizing effects of Nazi tyranny. In *Decision* the aesthetic and moral incentives were to be firmly united in a cause; yet Mann did not wish its contribution to fall prey to the accusation of chauvinism. "We shall try," he said in *Decision*'s first issue, "to approach the great problems of modern life, not with the perfunctory curiosity of reporters nor with the routine pathos of politicians, but with the consuming fervor a good philosopher experiences in examining the intricacies of some vitally significant moot question, a good soldier when fighting for the cause he believes in."[9]

In its twelve numbers one finds a variety of direct or indirect comments upon the necessity for a free culture, given the unity of fervent partisanship for a cause. In most respects, *Decision* demonstrates better than any other magazine of its time the strength of political conviction in the artist and the power which a political decision can be given if it is backed by aesthetic agreement. One of the magazine's weaknesses, however, is the direct result of this sincerity. Out of respect for the courage of Nazi-held countries, *Decision* presented "anthologies" of the work of various writers from each of them. The nationalist motive for selection is an artificial one at best. There is also much confusion over the question of one's attitude toward the nation in which so many of the contributors had found a temporary refuge. How far can one go in praising American literature without overstepping the bounds of gratitude? It was a pardonable weakness to find many Europeans grateful to America and a little self-conscious about it all. *Decision* might ultimately be praised for its excellent and compara-

---

[8] Julian Symons, "A Poet in Society," *Now* (London), 1, 70 (1943).
[9] "Issues at Stake," *Decision*, 1, 7 (January 1941).

tively calm estimate of the culture of its time; the symposiums on political matters and social action, though very necessary to the magazine, will not serve to insure its place in our literary history. The contributions of Thomas Mann, therefore, are likely to prove the most significant documents published in its pages.

The *Direction* of Darien, Connecticut, while it was financially able, utilized some of the devices of the popular photographic magazine, in an effort to impress the importance of the arts upon its readers' consciousness. The magazine expresses confidence in the artist's role in society. The world can do much worse than accept the artist's interpretation of society, it argues, for he lives in the consciousness of "order from chaos"; forces of revolution "move through him." Hence *Direction* presented writers who were aware of their world and might also "take some part in the building of the future." *Direction* may be regarded as a popularized cultural guidebook to the present and future. The third number presented a collection of writing done by workers in the Federal Writers' Project, and discussed the economic value to the artist of national subsidies, especially in view of the financial uncertainty of little magazine efforts. Such problems as federal aid to writers are particularly difficult, however, because they encounter the fundamental issue of aesthetic liberty versus political commitment.

The difficulty of managing the little magazine's financial career seems especially to have taken the center of attention in the last few years. The race against indebtedness has been lost in spite of a variety of expedients: reduction of a magazine's size, irregularity of appearance, appeals sporadic and desperate for aid in a financial crisis, and too often suspension temporary or permanent. Keeping the little magazine alive will continue to preoccupy those who are convinced of its value. James Laughlin's New Directions efforts have solved the problem in Laughlin's own generous way. Universities have become a more important sponsor of little magazines. Federal subsidy is a third possibility. Without some definite assurance of continuation, which will allow the artist freedom of expression, the little magazine might well be in danger of disappearing.

What will be the future direction of the *avant-garde*? There is the question of the policies it will assume, and the related problem of its effect upon the society of letters. Is experiment a temporary, provisional thing? Are we entering upon a long period of aesthetic silence, during which our attention will be concentrated upon international politics and economics? Marxism has given much of our literature a directly political reference, and the impact of the war is not likely to remove such an emphasis. Not that literature is likely to become a succession of political reports. But the attention of many who at one time welcomed individualism is now turned toward international military and political affairs. The European cultural reviews that we have already mentioned underline that fact; and a recent addition to their number, *Review: 43*, has the same motivating purpose.

The little magazines will certainly continue in the forties, perhaps more and more drawn within the intellectual boundaries of the university campus. Many of the *avant-garde* are now teaching: Norman Macleod at Briarcliff Junior College; Yvor Winters at Stanford University; Robert Penn Warren at the University of Minnesota. R. P. Blackmur is with the Institute for Advanced Study, in Princeton. John Crowe Ransom has never left the academic world. It is possible, therefore, that those who have entered academic communities will bring with them the aesthetic prerequisites of their *avant-garde* activities and will encourage a host of new writers by granting them similar freedoms. If that is the case, the little magazine will continue in somewhat altered form. Its financial problem, while not altogether solved, may not harass the editors quite as much. But its editorial complexion is likely to change at intervals of several years, and there will be fluctuations of quality and direction. Of course, there have been university reviews of past years which have been *avant-gardist* in their sympathies. It is not altogether impossible, however, that some universities will not want to be represented by what they mistake for radical thinking, and magazines will under those conditions appear and disappear, shifting place of residence as they have in the past. Many of the *avant-garde* distrust the university atmosphere, or rather have never regained the confidence they lost by virtue of their original experience with it.

About the desirability of preserving the continuity of little magazine history there can be no doubt. As long as there exists within any nation a condition which puzzles the artist with its contradictoriness, or its confusion, or its injustice, there will be an environment favorable to further experiment. Even though we might assume that all readers have accustomed themselves to all experimental forms (few subscribe to that hope), the native contrariness of the artist will always force him to protest against the *status quo* in literary taste, to debunk the prevailing notions as faddist, and to announce his view of the world of sense and society as indispensable to the salvation of culture's good repute.

Finally, it is possible that the *avant-garde* will become conservative, even reactionary, in its theory and practice. It is not altogether ridiculous to imagine a revolt, sponsored by little magazines, against what are now viewed as revolutionary literary forms and styles. A cry for "Intelligibility!" may arise from the rank and file of unknown writers, who may forthwith establish mimeographed sheets quoting from the poems of John Greenleaf Whittier and other "primary" writers. This, however, is the least likely of all probabilities.

## II

The printed page reveals only a part of the freshness and originality of the writer as person. Our century is blessed and cursed with a most amazing number of documents telling the story of its aesthetic adolescence. While much has been done, by Frederick Lewis Allen, Mark Sullivan, and others, with the political and social eccentricities of the twenties and thirties, the little magazines offer an abundance of material for rounding out the picture of those years. The men and women of the time—what were they like? In what way were the irregular issues of their magazines put together? On what basis and with what preparation? That is a fascinating story in itself, and it can illuminate the total picture with an infinity of detail. We have already noted the influence of personalities in the making of little magazine history. By way of conclusion, we might add a few details to the story.

Little magazine history is filled with incident; the struggle against censorship, for example, was of the utmost importance to editors, for freedom from censorship was one of the terms which had to be accepted before modern literature would have a hearing. Guido Bruno's magazines took up the issue constantly. Bruno was indignant, on one occasion, to find that John S. Sumner had suppressed a book by Alfred Kreymborg. Sumner, reasoned Bruno, by suppressing the book was preventing the only effective way of eliminating vice, for it is only by candid discussion of human weakness that man will learn to distinguish good from evil.[10] We have noticed the battle which *The Little Review* fought over the printing of Joyce's *Ulysses*. *The Laughing Horse* also committed an indiscretion: one of its first numbers printed

[10] "Is It Indecent to Expose Vice?" *Bruno's*, I, 21 (January 20, 1917).

a letter of Lawrence's and it was obliged to move its offices from California to New Mexico. Accordingly, the magazine was much exercised over the question of censorship and aesthetic liberties; the entire issue of February 1930 is devoted to that question. Among the notable arguments which the magazine advanced during its career was that offered by Arthur Davison Ficke. Literature, said Mr. Ficke, cannot be made "safe for democracy": "Until life changes its character into a thing of stainless morality, literature must reflect life with all its lights and shadows. You cannot make literature aseptic until you have made life aseptic, and no large-minded man would wish to do so."[11]

This was a battle against popular moralities, in which all of the *avant-garde* joined eagerly. They were agreed upon this one thing at least—that censorship must not interfere with what they had to say, that they would rather go to court for having said it than settle out of court at a price their conscience refused to pay.

Malcolm Cowley, looking back upon the days of dada, "superrealism," and Village antics, tells us that there was a strain of irony in the age, irony deliberately made evident by the "tongue-in-cheek" attitude which most aesthetes adopted toward their announced integrity of purpose:

"There were occasions, I believe, when Greenwich Village writers were editorially encouraged to write stories making fun of the Village, and some of them were glad to follow the suggestion. Of course, they complained, when slightly tipsy, that they were killing themselves— but how else could they maintain their standard of living? What they meant was that they could not live like *Vanity Fair* readers without writing for the *Saturday Evening Post*."[12]

The truth is that those days were marked by eccentricity of behavior, some of it deliberate, some casual, and much of it a natural enough exercise of what a variety of persons considered the artist's prerogative. Revolt was on the surface somewhat bewildering to outsiders looking in upon its strange manifestations. And it was quite natural for such magazines as *The American Mercury* to regard the carnivalism of revolt as simply the reverse side of the bourgeois coin. The *Mercury* was not dear to the hearts of the *avant-gardists*. In the first issue of that magazine, Ernest Boyd wrote an article called "Aesthete, Model 1924." Mr. Boyd denounced the aesthetes of the twenties for regarding themselves slightly, and behaving themselves ludi-

---

[11] "The Problem of Censorship," *Laughing Horse*, v, n.p. (1923).
[12] Cowley, *Exile's Return*, p. 68.

crously. In fact, he said, they were simply repeating the history of the nineties. The essay seems to have affected the writers in question rather unpleasantly. Their counterblow was *Aesthete, 1925*, a single-issue magazine which appeared in February 1925. Mr. Allen Tate, one of the intractables included in Boyd's attack, explains that "Except for the story by Slater Brown, the entire magazine was written over a Saturday night in January, 1925, and through most of the following day at the old Broadway Central Hotel, in New York."

Present at the meeting of indignant "aesthetes" were Tate, Brown, Kenneth Burke, Malcolm Cowley, John Wheelwright, Hart Crane, Matthew Josephson, "and one or two others whom I can't remember after seventeen years."[13] William Carlos Williams sent in his contribution by mail. *Aesthete, 1925* was born of indignation, and its contents give full witty measure of the collective grudge borne Mencken and Company. "Every article contained in this issue of *Aesthete, 1925* is guaranteed to be in strictly bad taste," reads the editorial announcement. John Wheelwright contributed a parody "chat," "Little Moments with Great Critics." Hart Crane's "Chanson" ridicules the editorial pompousness of "Mr. M.":

"I"
said Mr. M. as we crossed the street together
"am compelled to reject this
poem..."

At that moment a terrific detonation interrupted his
dictum
and Mr. M. soared into space astride
the lid of a
man-hole

The last I saw of him he was miles high
trying to climb off
in suchwise did Mr. M. ride into Heaven.
Hallelujah!

On the inside of the back cover was an advertisement for the "Mencken Promotion Society," written by Kenneth Burke. "We want smirks instead of piety," it reads. "We want to think it is intellectual to drink beer."

[13] Allen Tate, a letter included with the Princeton University Library copy of *Aesthete, 1925*.

Such is a single incident in the history of the little magazine and of those who wrote for it. They were alternately gay and serious; and if it is not always possible to distinguish the gaiety from the seriousness, we may be comforted by the reflection that both are, in the twenties at least, eccentric as measured by the standards of any settled age. "Talented, hard-working and intelligent people have always had their excesses and their ridiculous moments," says Robert McAlmon in another connection. "Vide, the Greek philosophers, the Elizabethans, our law-makers, etc. Their unexpurgated lives are worth study."[14]

Take but a few of the *Aesthete, 1925* group. What is the summary of their accomplishment? In what way and to what ends do their lives influence our judgment of the value of our literary history? Cowley and Josephson were dadaists in Paris, and they plagued the serious-minded Gorham Munson with their editorial whims and antics. Cowley is now a literary editor of *The New Republic*. Josephson has written creditable and popular biographies of Zola and Rousseau, and has contributed to the literature of debunking with his books on American wealth and power. Kenneth Burke bids fair to become one of America's most important critics. His most recent book, *The Philosophy of Literary Form*, is a masterful study of the philosophical ingredients of poetic imagination. Tate, the "Henry Feathertop" of *The Fugitive*'s first issue, has alternated between teaching at Princeton University and writing poetry and criticism, and has recently taken over the editorship of *The Sewanee Review*. John Wheelwright and Hart Crane have died, but they left an important poetic legacy.

The point is not that the "aesthetes" of 1925 have settled down, sobered up, or died off, but that their experiences have provided us with more than a pleasant reading of memoirs. It is regrettable, say some critics, that so many little magazines "died to make verse free." The objection of these critics to the period is that total freedom has wasted poetic energies: that the artist, afforded a free run of verse and gin mill alike, has not been disciplined; that some writers might have written the poetry they were capable of writing, had they not dissipated their energies in an age which gave them neither conventions to respect nor models to follow. It is impossible to answer such a criticism without referring again to the peculiar nature and the undoubted advantage of an experimental environment. What makes the work of those times an apparent confusion of contradictory tastes is, after all,

[14] "Truer Than Most Accounts," *The Exile*, II, 43 (Autumn 1927).

the very milieu. Only a small part of the total product of any age, as Harriet Monroe said in an early issue of *Poetry*, can be regarded as truly great, of lasting value. The apparent confusion of a time such as the twenties may well militate against excellence and may offer no precise aesthetic discipline by which creation can assume a recognizable shape and form.

These are the difficulties of an age. The little magazines were in a sense partner to the confusion which puzzles the historian and the critic alike. Designed to encourage the unknown writer, to afford opportunity for him to appear in spite of his times, their editorial generosity tolerated new verse and new prose in quantity; there must therefore have been a tremendous bulk of doggerel and "trash." In fact, though no statistical survey has been made or need be made, much more than half of the total production deserves no more than a first hearing. Nevertheless, writers were never before received and encouraged to continue as they have been in the little magazines of our century. It is impossible to say that the writers whom we accord some respect today would have been better off without the influence of the little magazine, or that they might have realized their powers more fully had they been subjected to an influence more disciplinary and founded upon a more consistent, traditional, and discreet aesthetic.

The importance of all these first efforts, however, lies in their availability for a just estimate of our times. Of their intrinsic value it is perhaps best not to say too much. But it is possible to argue that freedom of experiment does not damage the spirit of an age, and that in a majority of cases the capable artist will not be flattered beyond hope of recovery by having a bad poem or story see the light of print. This is because, more than in any other literary period, the writers of our time tempered their enthusiasm with self-criticism. Since more materials were published, poets were more critical about the eventual merit of their work. Above all, the little magazine acts as a mirror of its age, reflecting all that goes on within it. Scarcely a discussion in the Village, or a reading, or a riot, which did not find its way in some form or another to publication.

All of this may give us an opportunity for critical appraisal which we have never had before. If the little magazines did not sponsor the unilinear development of a single dogma, they did encourage the safe accommodation of many. If they are guilty of granting the printer's impartial accolade to much that is of no value, they saved a great many writers the agony of uncertainty about the merit of their work. If they do not afford an easy method of evaluating our times, they at any rate reward conscientious search with an agreeable abundance. The little magazine is, after all, not more nor less than the persons who produced it, the critics who abhorred it, the writers who welcomed it. Impulsiveness in aesthetic matters may not be the best motive for producing works of lasting value, but its accumulative result is an extremely honest, naïve, and audacious representation of a many-sided and tumultuous period.

# A BIBLIOGRAPHY
# OF LITTLE MAGAZINES

# A NOTE ON THE BIBLIOGRAPHY

Each of the items in the bibliography offers abundant and important information about its magazine. All data is taken from Volume 1, No. 1, of the publication, whenever possible. When No. 1 proved unavailable, the earliest issue at hand was consulted, and in some cases specific information has been supplied from the Union List of Serials. The order in which the details are provided is given below, with exceptions and explanations.

1. The Full Title and Subtitle. A few exceptions occur when a magazine is better known by a subsequent title, as in the case of *The Mirror*, which ran for the first five years as the *Sunday Mirror*.
2. The Publishing Body: society, club, or university.
3. The Original Date and the Closing Date. The plus sign indicates that the magazine is still current; the question mark (?), that some part of the data is not definitely known.
4. Frequency. The term *Irregular* is used to show changes of frequency or discrepancies of consecutive numbering. Occasionally a magazine is entered only for that period during which it answers the requirements which the authors have established for a Little Magazine: e.g., *The Dial*, 1920-29.
5. The Place of Publication. If the history of the magazine is noticeably affected by change of place of publication, such changes are given: e.g., *The Little Review*, *Broom*, and *Secession*.
6. Irregularities: change of title; merger; suspension, when exact dates of unpublished issues are not certain the period of suspension between known dates of issues is so indicated, e.g. "suspended between Dec. 1906 and Nov. 1908."
7. Supplements.
8. Editors. When appearing successively, their dates of office are given. When changes of editorship are frequent, or the magazine continues through many volumes, only a few outstanding names are noted, followed by the words "and others." Many associate, contributing, and foreign editors are mentioned, if they are persons of some importance to the period.
9. Book Reviews and Illustrations.
10. Indexes. The term *Index* indicates that each volume contains an index; cumulative indexes are given with volumes and dates; irregular indexes are noted as found in the files studied.

11. Symbols. Indicate the libraries where magazines were studied. Where symbols are omitted, material was obtained from private collectors.

### KEY TO SYMBOLS

b—University of Buffalo
br—Brown University
c—Columbia University
ctu—University of Connecticut
cu—University of California
h—Harvard University
icu—University of Chicago
lc—Library of Congress
mos—St. Louis Public Library

mwa—American Antiquarian Society Library
nn—New York Public Library
ou—Ohio State University
p—Princeton University
pp—Free Public Library of Philadelphia
uo—University of Oregon
y—Yale University

Notice of special features, special issues, and other useful information is given in the annotation. To this Mr. Hoffman has added information pertinent to a magazine's history: mention of important contributors; a brief discussion of the policy and scope of the magazine (often illustrated by quotation from important editorials); and frequently some suggestion of the magazine's place in little magazine history. It may generally be said that the length of an annotation is some indication of the magazine's value and importance. Often the annotation provides comparisons of the magazine with others of its type, or with those belonging to the same period.

May 1945                                                                                           C. F. U.

# BIBLIOGRAPHY

## 1891

THE MIRROR. Mar. 1, 1891-Sept. 2, 1920. Weekly. St. Louis, Mo. bk. rev. (Mar. 1, 1891-1895? as: *Sunday Mirror;* May 30, 1913-Sept. 2, 1920, *Reedy's Mirror.*) (Superseded by *All's Well, or The Mirror Repolished,* Dec. 1920.)             MOS NN
Editors: M. A. Fanning (Mar. 1, 1891-1892); William Marion Reedy (1893-July 29, 1920); Charles J. Finger (Aug. 5-Sept. 2, 1920).

The *Encyclopedia of the History of St. Louis,* by William Hyde and Howard L. Conrad, states that "*The Mirror* was founded March 1, 1891, by M. A. Fanning—who was its first editor—and James M. Calvin. It underwent several changes of ownership until it fell into the hands of William Marion Reedy"; and the *Dictionary of American Biography:* "The owner of this journal [*Sunday Mirror*], James Campbell, in 1893 put him [Reedy] into the editorial chair and in 1896 made him a present of *The Mirror.*"

William Marion Reedy performed a service for Midwestern America when he assumed editorship of the old *Mirror.* From 1913 to 1920 the magazine, known as *Reedy's Mirror,* played an important part in American letters. Primarily concerned with local and national politics, Reedy nevertheless had a lively interest in the arts, and reported on them for his readers. Many noteworthy St. Louis authors began their careers in *The Mirror:* Zoe Akins, Sara Teasdale, Fannie Hurst, and Orrick Johns. Among other contributors were Edgar Lee Masters, Babette Deutsch, Carl Sandburg, Vachel Lindsay, Charles J. Finger, Maxwell Bodenheim, William Rose Benét, Vincent Starrett, Witter Bynner, James Huneker, and Edna St. Vincent Millay.

*The Spoon River Anthology,* first printed in *The Mirror,* began to appear on May 29, 1914, and continued almost without interruption until January 15, 1915; most of the poems were signed by Masters' pseudonym: "Webster Ford." In 1920 Edna St. Vincent Millay's *Aria da Capo* and her sonnet sequence made their first appearance also in its pages. *Reedy's Mirror* is the best guide to "advanced" Midwestern opinion of the second decade.

## 1894

THE CHAP-BOOK; being a miscellany of curious and interesting songs, ballads, tales, histories, etc. May 15, 1894-July 1, 1898. Semimonthly. Chicago. bk.rev., illus., index (in each vol.: v. 1-8, May 15, 1894-May 1, 1898). (Absorbed by *The Dial,* 1898.)    NN
Editor: Herbert Stuart Stone.

"Herbert Stuart Stone, [was] assisted for the first two months by Bliss Carman, and from Sept. 1, 1894, by Harrison Garfield Rhodes." (From *A History of Stone & Kimball* . . . by Sidney Kramer.)

The Chicago *Chap-Book* is an important source book for the literature of its day. It is one of few literary magazines of the nineties which can be called the predecessors of the little magazines of the twentieth century. In the course of its career, *The Chap-Book* published such writing as Henry James's novel *What Maisie Knew,* serialized; prose by W. B. Yeats and verses by Stephen Crane. Other contributions include poetry by William Vaughn Moody, Bliss Carman, Madison Cawein, Julian Hawthorne, John Davidson, G. E. Woodberry, and Clinton Scollard; and fiction by Hamlin Garland, Arthur Morrison, Thomas Hardy, and Neith Boyce.

## 1895

M'LLE NEW YORK. Aug. 1895-Apr. 1896; n.s. Nov. 1898-1899. Fortnightly. New York. illus.     Y
Editor: Vance Thompson.

Under the editorial leadership of Vance Thompson, who is joined later by James Gibbons Huneker, as associate editor, and with the assistance of Thomas Fleming and T. Powers, artists, *M'lle New York* presents its subscribers with a gay, satirical, comical review of contemporary affairs. The influence of Huneker is pervasive, and is abundantly manifested in publication of his critical essays on music and American prejudices, and his prose sketches, which embody many of the qualities of his larger works: a mild cynicism and a sense of the mockery of "sacred institutions," combined with an insight into the aesthetic values in the arts. The art of cartooning is exhibited by the work of T. Powers, which appears almost regularly. But it is in its deliberate acceptance of its editorial position that *M'lle New York* makes an enduring mark as a little magazine: "*M'lle New York* is not concerned with the public. Her only ambition is to disintegrate some small portion of the public into its original component parts—the aristocracies of birth, wit, learning and art and the joyously vulgar mob." The intellectual interests of the time—the music of Wagner, the poetry of the French Symbolists, the aesthetic statements of the 19th century bête noir, Nietzsche—are all present, explicitly used or implicitly accepted.

## 1899

BELTAINE; an occasional publication. (Irish Literary Theatre.) May 1899-Apr. 1900. Irregular. London.     NN
Editor: W. B. Yeats.

One of several magazines of the Irish Literary Theatre, W. B. Yeats's occasionally issued periodical is interested primarily in calling to the attention of its British neighbors and advertising the current works of Irish playwrights. To that end, the magazine publishes a series of essays on the theater in Dublin, explanations of and comments upon the current plays, and excerpts from these plays. Some of these essays are reprinted from such other magazines as *The Dome*. Among those contributing critical essays are W. B. Yeats, Lionel Johnson, and George Moore.

## 1901

SAMHAIN; edited for the Irish Literary Theatre . . . Oct. 1901-Nov. 1908. Irregular. Dublin.     NN
(Suspended between Dec. 1906 and Nov. 1908.)
Editor: W. B. Yeats.

The issue of November 1908 states: "There has been no *Samhain* for a couple of years, principally because an occasional publication, called *The Arrow*, took its place for a time."

Another of W. B. Yeats's magazines of comment upon Irish dramatic and cultural affairs, *Samhain* is spoken of by Yeats as follows: "Many years ago I brought out an occasional publication called, according to the season, 'Beltaine' or 'Samhain'; it contained my defence of the Abbey Theatre, its actors and its plays. Though I wrote most of it, Synge's 'Riders to the Sea,' some of Lady Gregory's little comedies, as well as my 'Cathleen ni Hoolihan' appeared first in its pages." (*On the Boiler*.) Yeats's *Cathleen ni Hoolihan* appeared in the issue of October 1902. J. M. Synge's *Riders to the Sea* was published in the issue of September 1903. There are several plays in the Gaelic, and some translations from the Gaelic by Lady Gregory.

## 1903

THE GREEN SHEAF. 1903-1904. 13 issues a year. London. illus.　c
Supplements.
Editor: Pamela Colman Smith.

A little magazine, handsomely printed and illustrated, the contents of which are a selection of verses and brief prose sketches by British writers. Among these should be mentioned poetry by A. E., Christopher St. John, John Masefield, and Yone Noguchi; and prose fiction by A. E. and John Masefield. W. B. Yeats contributes a prose essay, "Dream of the World's End," to the second number (1903). There are several translations from the Gaelic by Lady Gregory. A supplement to No. 7 prints A. E.'s drama, *Deirdre*.

◆

THE PAPYRUS; a magazine of individuality. July 1903-May 1912. Monthly. Mount Vernon, N.Y.　NN
(Suspended, Sept. 1906-June 1907.)
(Superseded by *Phoenix*, June 1914.)
Editor: Michael Monahan.

Like its successor, *The Phoenix*, Michael Monahan's *The Papyrus* is a "one-man" magazine which consists chiefly of editorial matter, supported and illustrated by quotations from his favorite authors. "I am putting forth this magazine," Monahan says in his first issue, "because all my life has led up to it and for years it has been the dearest wish of my heart." In the course of the magazine's career, Monahan delivers himself of many opinions, on diverse subjects, and discusses literature and writers at some length. There are contributions from such early twentieth century poets as Richard Hovey, Richard Le Gallienne, and George Sterling. European contributors include Wm. Ernest Henley, Maxim Gorky, Arnold Bennett, and Arthur Symons.

## 1904

DANA; an Irish magazine of independent thought. May 1904-Apr. 1905. Monthly. Dublin. bk. rev., index.　NN
Editor: John Eglinton?

The Irish literary magazine *Dana* is important for its place in the history of several prominent Irish literary figures. As an expression of the literary life of Dublin in the early part of the twentieth century, *Dana* expresses itself as anxious to avoid the "stigma" of provincialism or nationalism: "Since the days of the worthy Thomas Davis . . ." reads one editorial, "Irish literary enterprise has concerned itself mainly with the aim of securing the nationality of Irish literature by the choice of Irish subjects, the revival of the Irish language, and so forth. . . . They [Davis and his colleagues] carefully skirted and stepped aside from the fundamental questions of life and thought which lay in their way, and they set the fashion—which has lasted to this day and is the cause of a certain hollowness in the pretentions of Irish literature—of trying to promote an artificial and sentimental unity in Irish life by carefully ignoring all those matters as to which Irishmen as thinking and unthinking beings hold diverse opinions." The first number of *Dana* publishes for the first time George Moore's "Moods and Memories," a part of his *Memoirs of My Dead Life*. Other contributions to this and subsequent issues of the magazine include poetry by Padraic Colum, Oliver St. John Gogarty, Seumas O'Sullivan, and A.E., and essays by John Eglinton, Padraic Colum, R. B. Cunningham-Graham, Stephen Gwynn, A.E., and Jane Barlow.

## 1906

THE ARROW. (The Abbey Theatre.) Oct. 20, 1906-Aug. 25, 1909; Summer 1939. Irregular. Dublin. illus. NN Editor: W. B. Yeats.

A magazine of comment on the theater, chiefly by W. B. Yeats, and on Yeats's own literary career, *The Arrow* also contains play lists of the Abbey Theatre, Dublin.

The Summer 1939 issue is a commemoration number, celebrating the career of W. B. Yeats with contributions by John Masefield, F. R. Higgins, Gordon Bottomley, Edmond Dulac, William Rothenstein, W. J. Turner, Oliver St. John Gogarty, Lennox Robinson, and others. There are illustrations by Jack B. Yeats, Charles Shannon, Sean O'Sullivan, Max Beerbohm, and Edmond Dulac.

✧

THE SHANACHIE; an Irish miscellany illustrated. [Summer 1906]-Winter 1907. Quarterly. Dublin. illus. NN *Editor not established.*

One of Dublin's several literary and art magazines, using the varied talents of its literary community of the early part of our century. The magazine pays some attention to Irish theatrical matters, but it is also interested in other aspects of Irish culture and in the "attractiveness of its scenery and folk," as the series of essays by J. M. Synge attests. The interest in speculation on matters of aesthetics is demonstrated by essays by J. B. Yeats, John Eglinton, and W. B. Yeats. Contributions include poems by Padraic Colum and stories by J. M. Synge and Lord Dunsany.

## 1908

THE MASK; a quarterly illustrated journal of the art of the theatre. 1908-1929. Florence, Italy. bk.rev., illus., index. (Suspended, May 1915-Mar. 25, 1918, 1919-1922.) NN Editor: Edward Gordon Craig.

The erratic but exciting career of *The Mask* is in itself a commentary upon the history of the progressive theater, demonstrating as it does the struggle of the artist against the pallid and sentimental "realism" of box-office dramatics. The magazine is at least in part a vehicle for the expression of Gordon Craig's ideas; they appear frequently and impressively. The earlier issues are much concerned over the question of realism in drama: Craig announces in the October 1908 issue that "the theatre, with its realism, will end in the music hall, for realism cannot go upwards, but always tends downwards." *The Mask* is interested not only in the future of the theater, but also in suggestions which the past has provided in technique, stagecraft, and source materials. There are many articles on the history of the stage, including excellent treatments of "the architecture of Shakespeare's plays," the Commedia Dell' Arte, and the Morris dance. All such essays are illustrated admirably by reproductions of original drawings and engravings of theater history and art taken from both the past and the present. *The Mask* throughout its volumes is a unique piece of printing and editing. The magazine had some difficulty weathering the storm of World War I; its appearances are erratic during those years, and its format changes with the varying fortunes of its sponsors. From 1919 to 1922 the magazine is forced to suspend altogether. Throughout its career, *The Mask* remains steadfast in its championship of an "art theatre" and in its opposition to a crass realism and a commercially governed or controlled stage. The courage and competence of its contributors make it an indispensable source for the student of modern drama and stagecraft.

MOODS; a magazine of individual contributions. Nov. 1908-May 1918. Monthly. New York. bk. rev., illus., index (in v. 4 and 5, June 1911-May 1912). NN
(Suspended, Feb.-Nov. 1910.) (Dec. 1910-May 1918 as: *The International.*) Editors: B. Russell Herts (Nov. 1908-Oct. 1912; with Jay H. Donohue, Edward Goodman, and Garibaldi M. Lapolla, Nov.-Dec. 1908); George Sylvester Viereck (Apr. 1912-Apr. 1918), and others.

Richard Le Gallienne and Blanche Shoemaker Wagstaff appear in the various capacities of editor, associate editor, and contributing editor. From June/July 1909-Dec. 1910, Lee Simonson and Rhys Carpenter appear as foreign representatives.

*Moods* participates in a variety of the controversies of our second decade and is especially interested in feminism, featuring a number of articles on that subject. But it is also important for its publication at an early date of the work of writers who subsequently acquired either distinction or reputation in modern letters. Among the contributions of this sort are poems by Louis Untermeyer, Ludwig Lewisohn, James Oppenheim, and Joyce Kilmer.

## 1910

NINETEEN-TEN MAGAZINE. 1910. Irregular. New York. illus. (Nos. 1-2 are dated January and February, 1910; nos. 3-5 omit months.) C
Editor: Charles Buckels Falls.

A little magazine which presents the sketches of Boardman Robinson and C. B. Falls, the light verse of Franklin P. Adams and Arthur Guiterman, and two short stories by Theodore Dreiser, among other contributions.

THE OPEN WINDOW. Oct. 1910-Sept. 1911. Monthly. London. illus., index. *Editor not established.* C

*The Open Window* is an illustrated monthly magazine, whose purpose is "the expression of that free vision of things which is more definitely associated with the word art." The contents of the magazine are "of a quality imaginative rather than controversial." Each issue is supplied with black and white drawings. Among the contributions are poems by James Stephens, C. E. Wheeler, D. L. Sulman, Walter de la Mare, John Drinkwater, and others; prose fiction by Edward Thomas, Hugh de Selincourt, E. M. Forster, R. Ellis Roberts; prose essays by Alfred E. Zimmern, C. J. Holmes, Lord Dunsany; and dramatic sketches by Gilbert Cannan and Yone Noguchi.

✧

THE VILLAGE MAGAZINE. 1910, 1920, 1925. Springfield, Ill. illus. NN
Editor: Vachel Lindsay.

*The Village Magazine* is Vachel Lindsay's own production: he is artist, poet, and commentator in one. In Lindsay's own words, it is a "one number magazine—the number to be steadily improved after due meditation." The first issue appears in 1910, and there are two later "imprints" of it, in 1920 and in 1925. In each of the latter cases, new materials are added, though these additions do not constitute a new issue of the magazine. The purpose is clearly to present Lindsay's own version and interpretation of a magazine, which he defines (using *The Standard Dictionary* as source) as "A house, a room or a receptacle in which anything is stored, specifically a strong building for strong gunpowder and other military stores." *The Village Magazine*, in its original issue and in the two "imprints," contains editorial matter—informal, semiphilosophical, homey essays—many of Lindsay's poems, and his own drawings in black and white.

## 1911

THE MASSES. 1911-1917. Monthly. New York. bk.rev., illus. NN (Suspended, Sept.-Nov. 1912.) (Superseded by *The Liberator*, Mar. 1918.)
Editors: Thomas Seltzer (Jan.-Apr. 1911); Horatio Winslow (May-Dec. 1911); Piet Vlag (Jan.-Aug. 1912); Max Eastman (Dec. 1912-Dec. 1917).

Among contributing editors are: Floyd Dell, John Reed, Louis Untermeyer, Mary Heaton Vorse, Arthur Bullard, William English Walling; art editors: Art Young, George Bellows, Boardman Robinson, and H. J. Glintenkamp.

The early issues combine an interest in socialism and co-operatives with some attention to the arts. Beginning with the January 1913 issue, *The Masses* becomes the mouthpiece for the young radical and intellectual of New York City. Its policy, through most of the years of its existence, is guided in the main by Max Eastman and Floyd Dell. The interest in the arts is as active as participation in radical politics. Throughout World War I, it adopts a position of belligerent pacifism, directing much of its energy to demonstrating the uselessness of war. This policy leads to its suppression in 1917, by the United States government. The early work of Louis Untermeyer, Carl Sandburg, Harry Kemp, Randolph Bourne, William Rose Benét, John Reed, Walter Lippmann, and others appears in its issues. Arturo Giovannitti, young radical Italian poet, contributes frequently. *The Masses* presents a good cross-section of the radical thinking of our second decade.

RHYTHM; art, music, literature. Summer 1911-Mar. 1913. Quarterly. London. bk.rev., illus. NN (Superseded by *The Blue Review*.) Supplements.
Editors: John Middleton Murry with Katherine Mansfield and Michael T. H. Sadler (Summer 1911-June 1912).

*Rhythm* seeks for some kind of aesthetic key to the future: ". . . an art that strikes deeper, that touches a profounder reality, that passes outside the bounds of a narrow aestheticism . . ." John Middleton Murry's insistence upon the intimate relationship of art with society is but the beginning of his search for values through a study of the humanities. The magazine publishes the criticism of Murry, some of his poetry, short stories by Katherine Mansfield, poems by Harold Monro, W. H. Davies, Rupert Brooke, and others. D. H. Lawrence makes one of his first appearances, with an article on the Georgians. The magazine is very much interested in the Russians; Katherine Mansfield's short stories show the influence of Chekhov.

❖

VISION; a quarterly journal of aesthetic appreciation of life. Spring 1911-Spring 1912. New York. illus. NN
Editor: Walter Storey.

*Vision's* chief emphasis is upon an aesthetic evaluation of life. To this end, it publishes essays on literary criticism and history and inspirational essays, poems, and sketches. Most of the issue for Spring 1912 is taken up by a long essay by Vachel Lindsay, called "The New Localism: An Illustrated Essay for Village Statesmen."

❖

THE WESTMINSTER MAGAZINE. Dec. 1911-Winter 1944; n.s. Spring 1945 +. Quarterly. Oglethorpe University, Ga. bk.rev., index (v. 23, Spring 1934-Winter 1935). NN

(Absorbed *Bozart* and *Contemporary Verse,* Spring 1935.) (1935-Autumn 1938 as: *Bozart-Westminster.*)
Editors: Robert England (Winter 1932-Winter 1935); James Routh and Thornwell Jacobs (Winter 1932-Winter 1944); T. C. Wilson and Ezra Pound (Spring/Summer 1935); Edward J. O'Brien and Virginia Stait (Spring/Summer 1935-Winter 1944); Thornwell Jacobs (Spring 1945+).
*Issues previous to Winter 1932 not consulted.*

The poetry in *The Westminster Magazine* varies considerably in form and quality. As a Southern magazine it attempts to avoid sectionalism in its contents, preferring to draw from a much wider range of contributors. The most important issue is that of Spring-Summer, 1935, which is called an anthology of Modern English and American Poetry, collected by T. C. Wilson, John Drummond, and Ezra Pound. Among the British poets published are W. H. Auden, Richard Eberhart, Hugh MacDiarmid, and Ruthven Todd. The American contributors include Kenneth Fearing, Kenneth Patchen, Philip Rahv, Muriel Rukeyser, James Laughlin IV, Frederic Prokosch, Louis Zukofsky, E. E. Cummings, John Wheelwright, William Carlos Williams, Marianne Moore, and others. Most of the poems in this issue had already been published in other magazines.

## 1912

THE ANTIDOTE. Dec. 21, 1912-June 12, 1915. Irregular. London.   ICU
Editor: T. W. H. Crosland.

*The Antidote,* edited by T. W. H. Crosland, with the backing of Lord Alfred Bruce Douglas, is a kind of counter-revolt against the "resurgence of the younger writers." "We may say," says an editorial in the first issue, "that the younger writer of 1912 has arrived at the conclusion that he is 'it,' and that there never has been, and there never will be, anything like him." Contributions include poems by Lord Douglas, Siegfried Sassoon, and T. W. H. Crosland.

✧

POETRY; a magazine of verse. Oct. 1912 +. Monthly. Chicago. bk.rev., index. cum. index: v. 1-60 (Oct. 1912-Sept. 1942).   NN
Editors: Harriet Monroe (1912-1935); Morton Dauwen Zabel (1936-Oct. 1937); George Dillon (Nov. 1937-Aug. 1942); Peter De Vries (Sept. 1942+); Jessica Nelson North (Sept. 1942-Mar. 1943); Marion Strobel (Apr. 1943+).
During the early years of the magazine Ezra Pound was the foreign correspondent and Alice Corbin Henderson, Eunice Tietjens, and Helen Hoyt were assistant editors.

The first issue of *Poetry* marks the turning point in American poetry of the twentieth century. What we refer to as "modern poetry" had been given some slight attention in the Chicago *Chap-Book.* But for the most part young writers were neglected, discouraged from experiment by the editorial policies of the commercial press. Harriet Monroe's editorship was at first prompted by a desire to give all poets a hearing. Through the influence of Ezra Pound, who in 1912 became her foreign correspondent, she turned her attention to the new poets and to the championship of new verse forms. Her courage helped to save the magazine from occasional financial depression; her intelligent judgment, and that of her first assistant editor, Alice Corbin Henderson, gave it a consistently high rate of creditable performance. The most exciting years of *Poetry* were the first ones, 1912-1917, when the debate over free verse and imagism seemed vital. The list of poets who published in *Poetry* includes almost everyone who has since become important in American and British letters. T. S. Eliot published some early work in *Poetry*. One of Robert Frost's first American appearances was here; Vachel Lindsay's first appearance as a contributor to periodicals occurs here. Among those whose earlier poems appeared in *Poetry* are Wallace Stevens, Richard Aldington, H.D., William Carlos Williams, D. H. Lawrence, and Ezra Pound. In later years *Poetry* has published verse of high quality, but has relinquished its domination of modern poetics to several admirable English and American poetry magazines.

◆

THE POETRY JOURNAL. Dec. 1912-Mar. 1918. Monthly. Boston. bk.rev. (Suspended between July 1913 and Feb. 1914.) NN
Editors: William Stanley Braithwaite (Dec. 1912-July 1913); Richard M. Hunt (Feb. 1914-May 1915); Edward J. O'Brien (June 1915-Feb. 1916); Edmund R. Brown and Blanche Shoemaker Wagstaff (June 1915-Mar. 1918).

After having "lost the race" with *Poetry* in the matter of first appearance, *The Poetry Journal* settled down to become a more conservative voice for American poetry. In its editorials and in an essay by Conrad Aiken, the magazine announced some slight alarm over developments in modern poetry. Its contributions include poetry by Conrad Aiken, Louis Untermeyer, William Rose Benét, John Gould Fletcher, Alfred Kreymborg, Amy Lowell, Witter Bynner, Richard Aldington, William Carlos Williams, Louis V. Ledoux, Arthur Davison Ficke, and others.

◆

THE POETRY REVIEW. (The Poetry Society.) 1912+. Monthly. London. bk. rev., index. NN
(Supersedes *Poetical Gazette*.)
Supplement: *Poetry of To-day*, 1919+.
Editors: Harold Monro (Jan.-Dec. 1912); Stephen Phillips (Jan. 1913-Nov./Dec. 1915); Galloway Kyle (Jan. 1916+).

Under the editorship of Harold Monro, *The Poetry Review* tries to bring poetry to a wider group of readers, and is anxious also to improve the content and form of poetry itself. "Poetry should be once more seriously and reverently discussed in its relation to life, and the same tests and criteria applied to it as to other arts." Beginning with Vol. 2, *The Poetry Review* comes almost entirely under the control of the British Poetry Society, and Stephen Phillips replaces Harold Monro as editor. For a study of Monro's role as sponsor of modern letters, one should follow Vol. 1 of *The Poetry Review* with an examination of Monro's later magazine *Poetry and Drama*. In his brief career as editor of *The Poetry Review*, Harold Monro publishes the writings of Ezra Pound, F. S. Flint, Rupert Brooke, and others.

◆

ROOT AND BRANCH; a seasonal of the arts. 1912-1919. Quarterly. Bognor, Sussex, Eng. illus. NN
Editor: James Guthrie.

A British quarterly, *Root and Branch* publishes poetry and prose of the second decade of British writers, and many drawings. Included among the contributions are the poetry of Gordon Bottomley, W. H. Davies, Daniel Phaër, Katharine Tynan, Eleanor Farjeon, and others, critical essays by John Freeman and others, informal prose essays by Edward Thomas.

◆

THE TRIPOD; a magazine of art, literature and music. Apr. 1912-? Monthly. Cambridge, Eng. bk. rev. P
*Editor not established.*

*The Tripod* shows an interest in old and new letters and arts. Among its critical essays is one on the music of Richard Strauss and one on modern painting. A prose sketch by Lord Dunsany and an article by Marinetti appear in its pages.

❖

THE WILD HAWK; a periodical of beauty and freedom. 1912-Jan. 1935? Monthly. Woodstock, N.Y. illus. (Nov. 1916-Jan. 1935? as: *The Plowshare*.) (Suspended, Dec. 1920-Jan. 1934.) C P
Editors: Hervey White (with Allan Updegraff, Carl Eric Lindin, and others, Nov. 1916-Jan. 1935?).

*The Wild Hawk* is a literary periodical of one-man exhibits, containing short stories, one-act sketches or dialogue with some verses. It also contains both prose and poems by Allan Updegraff and translations by Carl Eric Lindin of *Socialization of Art* by George Pauli and *The Flying Dutchman* by August Strindberg. It is artistically designed and published by the Maverick Press of which Mr. White is the proprietor. *The Plowshare*, "evolving" from *The Wild Hawk*, includes poems by Pres Hubbard, short stories by Alberta Williams, Kenneth White, and Pres Hubbard, and critical essays by Kenneth Burke and Gorham B. Munson.

## 1913

THE BLUE REVIEW; literature, drama, art, music. May-July 1913. Monthly. London. bk.rev., illus. C
(Supersedes *Rhythm*.)
Editor: John Middleton Murry.

*The Blue Review* is established "on co-operative principles," a number of writers pledging themselves to contribute without payment for nine months, "at the end of which time, a profit-sharing scheme comes into operation." John Middleton Murry and Katherine Mansfield, associate editor, again unite with D. H. Lawrence to further the cause of the arts. The magazine makes a noble effort to cover all events of interest to the "advanced" student of the arts. D. H. Lawrence discusses Thomas Mann. The magazine is an important document in the history of the Lawrence-Murry-Mansfield relationship.

❖

THE GLEBE. Sept. 1913-Nov. 1914? Irregular. Ridgefield, N.J.
Editor: Alfred Kreymborg. NN

The product of Alfred Kreymborg's editorial interests and of the financial strength of Albert and Charles Boni, the ten issues of *The Glebe* were pioneers in the sponsorship of experimental writing. From Ezra Pound, Kreymborg received a package of imagist Mss, which he put into one of *The Glebe's* best issues. Included in this imagist number are the poems of Ezra Pound, James Joyce, Richard Aldington, and William Carlos Williams. *The Glebe* has the distinction of having presented the first of Williams' published works. Other issues of *The Glebe* published translations from the Russian of Leonid Andreyev and the German of Frank Wedekind.

❖

THE LANTERN. Feb.-Oct. 1913? Irregular. Chicago. illus. NN
(Mar. 22-May 20, 1913, as: *Saturday Night Lantern*.)
Editors: Curtis J. Kirch and Milton Fuessle.

*The Lantern* is an expression of Chicago's varied aesthetic interests. Guido Bruno appears here, with some of the articles which are to be published again and again in his own magazines. In general, it is a magazine of literary appreciation rather than a place for original or "new" writing.

THE NEW FREEWOMAN; an individualist review. June 15-Dec. 15, 1913. Semimonthly. London. bk.rev.  NN
(Superseded by The Egoist, 1914.)
Editor: Dora Marsden.

Thirteen issues of The New Freewoman reflect a variety of tendencies in English letters. Though dedicated to the cause of feminism and sponsored by such women as Harriet Shaw Weaver, Joyce's "fairy godmother," and Dora Marsden, it opens its pages to the ubiquitous Ezra Pound, who uses them to call attention to the new poetry and aesthetics. During its brief career, it accommodates itself to the poetry of Ezra Pound, Richard Aldington, William Carlos Williams, and others. With the issue of December 15, 1913, Richard Aldington becomes assistant editor.

❖

POETRY AND DRAMA. Mar. 1913-Dec. 1914. Quarterly. London. bk.rev., index.  NN
(Superseded by Chapbook, July 1919.)
Editor: Harold Monro.

In the first issue of Poetry and Drama Harold Monro explains that his earlier venture, Poetry Review, had been so effectively handcuffed by the British Poetry Society that he was forced to break away from it altogether, to set up his own magazine. This, then, is Monro's first independent editorial expression. Monro's interest in modern letters, as distinct from the "faded gentility" which he sensed in the post-Victorians, is revealed by the list of contributors to Poetry and Drama. American poetry is reviewed, and some of it is published. The editor is properly impressed by Ezra Pound, and prints some of his poetry. Monro is also temporarily excited by futurism; the issue of September 1913 is perhaps the best early treatment of the subject in English. Contributions also include the poetry of Robert Frost, Rupert Brooke, John Gould Fletcher, D. H. Lawrence, Richard Aldington, and Amy Lowell.

## 1914

BLAST; review of the great English vortex. June 20, 1914-July 1915. (Only two issues.) London. illus.  NN
Editor: Wyndham Lewis.

The title reveals much about this early effort of Wyndham Lewis. The manifesto, signed by Wyndham Lewis, Ezra Pound, Richard Aldington, and others, expresses violent discontent with the *status quo* and with all (other) efforts to alter it. Blast is typography's closest approximation to dynamite. The contents are chiefly editorial, though the magazine does publish stories by Rebecca West and Ford Madox Hueffer, and poetry by T. S. Eliot and Ezra Pound. Lewis' and Pound's disagreement with Victorianism is called vorticism, which seems in essence to mean loud and vigorous dissatisfaction with all things sick and dying and with all patent remedies for the world's ills.

❖

THE EGOIST; an individualist review. 1914-1919. Bimonthly. London. illus. (Supersedes The New Freewoman.)
Editors: Dora Marsden (Jan.-June 1914); Harriet Shaw Weaver (July 1914-1919).  NN
Dora Marsden relinquishes her editorship in June 1914, but remains as contributing editor. Richard Aldington, H.D. (Hilda Doolittle), and T. S. Eliot appear as assistant editors.

With substantially the same directorship as The New Freewoman, The Egoist has contributions by Ezra Pound, Richard Aldington, H.D., John Gould Fletcher, Harold Monro, Amy Lowell, Marianne Moore, Helen Hoyt, William Carlos Williams, Ford Madox

Hueffer, John Rodker, and others. Pound, Aldington, and H.D. vigorously sponsor the imagist movement. The influence of Dora Marsden gives the magazine a philosophical tone, and there are many evaluations of modern thought from her pen and by such other writers as Huntley Carter and Harriet Weaver. Joyce's *A Portrait of the Artist as a Young Man* makes its first appearance here, beginning February 2, 1914, and continuing until September 1, 1915; a series of extracts from *Ulysses* is printed in *The Egoist* beginning with January/February 1919 and following for the next few months.

❖

THE LITTLE REVIEW; literature, drama, music, art. Mar. 1914-May 1929. Irregular. Chicago; New York; Paris. bk.rev., illus.  NN
Editors: Margaret C. Anderson (with Jane Heap, 1922-1929).

Frequent editorial announcements by Margaret Anderson proclaim *The Little Review* as a "magazine that believes in Life for Art's sake, in the individual rather than an Incomplete people ... a magazine written for intelligent people who can feel; whose philosophy is Applied Anarchism, whose policy is a Will to Splendor of Life...." Miss Anderson's personality gave her review a freedom of choice and a range of material at times resembling chaos, at others responsible for important contributions to modern letters. *The Little Review* may roughly be said to have gone through three phases of development:

1914-April 1917: The early, "formative" years, in which Miss Anderson's tastes and enthusiasms brought together diverse contributions and sponsored a variety of ideas and "movements": Nietzsche, Bergson, anarchism, feminism, and psychoanalysis were recognized and discussed. Contributors included Sherwood Anderson, Vachel Lindsay, Eunice Tietjens, Maxwell Bodenheim, A. D. Ficke.

April 1917-1921: The "Ezra Pound period," during which the magazine became an important document for modern letters (Ezra Pound took over the foreign editorship). James Joyce's *Ulysses* ran from 1918-1921, finally causing its sponsors a trial and costing them $100. Pound's sponsorship brought poems by W. B. Yeats, Hart Crane, Richard Aldington, T. S. Eliot, John Rodker; prose by Wyndham Lewis, Eliot, and Pound, among others.

Autumn 1921-May 1929: *The Little Review* became a quarterly in Autumn of 1921 and moved to Paris in 1922, where it appeared irregularly, and attached itself to cubism, dadaism, and other developments then current in the Paris of the American expatriate. Jean Cocteau, Guillaume Apollinaire, Tristan Tzara, and Kenneth Burke appear in its pages. The issue of May 1929, its last, contains a series of statements by writers who had contributed in the past, and final apologia by Margaret Anderson and Jane Heap.

❖

NEW NUMBERS. 1914. (Only four issues.) Ryton, Gloucester, Eng.  NN
*Editor not established.*

The object of *New Numbers* is simply to publish the new verse and verse dramas of the four contributors: Lascelles Abercrombie, Rupert Brooke, John Drinkwater, and Wilfrid Wilson Gibson.

❖

THE PHOENIX; a magazine of individuality. June 1914-Dec. 1916. Monthly. South Norwalk, Conn. index (in each vol.: v. 1-3, June 1914-Nov. 1915). (Supersedes *Papyrus*.) (Absorbed by International [N.Y.])  NN
Editor: Michael Monahan.

Michael Monahan's *Phoenix* is an excellent example of the "one-man" magazine, a continuous editorial on a great variety of subjects, supplemented by quotations from the great and the "near-great" and by a few original contributions. As such, *Phoenix* is interesting historically, but reflects the limitations of its editor. Among those who occasionally accompany the editor are Richard Le Gallienne, Frank Harris, and Richard Aldington.

## 1915

BRUNO CHAP BOOKS. 1915-May 1916? Monthly. New York.   NN
Supplements: Special series.
Editor: Guido Bruno.

One of many publishing ventures by Guido Bruno in his garret in Washington Square. Some of the material had previously been published in the Chicago *Lantern*. Alfred Kreymborg's early poetry, called "Mushrooms," is published here and in other Bruno magazines. A special issue, 1915, presents Richard Aldington and "The Imagists."

✧

BRUNO'S WEEKLY. July 1915-Sept. 1916. New York. illus.   NN
(Absorbed *Greenwich Village*, Dec. 1915?) (Superseded by *Bruno's*, 1917.)
Editor: Guido Bruno.

Bruno's magazines are valuable for a study of Greenwich Village, though they are the despair of the bibliographer; Bruno publishes and republishes his materials. Much of this magazine is devoted to a discussion of the bohemian, and of bohemianism in general; local issues are often touched upon. The range of editorial interest is great. Contributions come from Alfred Kreymborg, Marianne Moore, Vincent Starrett, Ford Madox Hueffer, and others. Discussions of European literature and culture are frequent; especial attention is paid to Oscar Wilde.

GREENWICH VILLAGE. Jan. 20-Nov. 1915. Semimonthly. New York. illus. (Absorbed by *Bruno's Weekly*, Dec. 1915?)   NN
Editor: Guido Bruno.

The editor discusses at some length 1) himself; 2) his interests; and 3) his community. Many of the same contributors appear here as appear in Bruno's other magazines: Alfred Kreymborg, Richard Aldington, Hippolyte Havel, and others. Editorial conscience does not interfere with two striking characteristics of Bruno's publications: duplication of materials and borrowing from other periodicals. The magazine is valuable for its impressions of the Village.

✧

THE GYPSY. May 1915-May 1916. (Only two issues.) London. illus.   NN
*Editor not established.*

*The Gypsy* appears, during war years, with an elaborate format and many art reproductions; the magazine's appearance under adverse conditions is explained on the grounds of the indispensable value of the Artist in society: "Expressed in many forms Art has this plain moral: we must have it, we cannot do without it." There are poems by Richard Le Gallienne, Arthur Symons, Walter de la Mare, and others; and stories by Arthur Machen, J. D. Beresford, and Katharine Tynan.

✧

INWHICH; being a book in which I say just what I think. June 1915-Nov. 1916. Monthly. Detroit, Mich. illus. Editor: Norman Geddes.   NN

A magazine of comment by Norman Geddes on various subjects, its aim to bring "The newest and best ideas in art to those who understand and are striving to realize its connection with life." Geddes discusses such subjects as "the new theater," art and "the people," and ethics and the law. Poems are contributed by Harold Hersey and others.

❖

THE LANTERN. Mar. 1915-Mar. 1918. Monthly. San Francisco. index (except v. 3, Apr. 1917-Mar. 1918). NN
Editors: Theodore F. Bonnet, and Edward F. O'Day.

The San Francisco *Lantern* demonstrates the fortunate results of excellent though eclectic editorial tastes. It is one of the few American magazines of the teens which emphasizes and publishes a representative selection of British writings. Bonnet's numerous critical articles call attention to Charles Baudelaire, in whom he is especially interested, and Heinrich Heine. Among the foreign contributors to this magazine are D. H. Lawrence, A. E. Housman, Hilaire Belloc, Siegfried Sassoon, Laurence Housman, and W. H. Davies.

❖

THE MIDLAND. Jan. 1915-Mar./June 1933. Monthly. Iowa City, Iowa. bk. rev., index. NN
(Absorbed by *The Frontier*, Nov. 1933.)
Editor: John T. Frederick (with Frank Luther Mott, Jan. 1925-Mar./June 1933).

Begun by John T. Frederick in Iowa City, *The Midland* is for most of its career a regional magazine, and that fact has much to do with the type of fiction and poetry it publishes. Frederick describes his magazine as a "modest attempt to encourage the making of literature in the Middle West." The fiction is primarily Midwestern in locale, and "realistic" in type. The importance of the magazine lies in its encouraging Midwestern writers "to stay at home and write." It serves to clarify the position of Midwestern writers and to point to that region as deserving of literary treatment. It therefore possesses all of the attributes and defects of a magazine thus circumscribed. A number of writers, some of them native to the region, contribute their earlier writings: poetry by William Ellery Leonard, Howard Mumford Jones, Edwin Ford Piper, Paul Engle, Lizette Woodworth Reese, Maxwell Anderson, Vincent Starrett, Mark Van Doren, and others; stories by August Derleth and others.

❖

THE MINARET. Nov. 1915-Oct. 1926. Monthly. Washington, D.C. bk.rev. (Suspended, July 1917-Apr. 1923.)
Editor: Herbert Bruncken. NN

"We have a single aim, and that is to produce a magazine that we hope will appeal to those who are fond of good literature." As a literary magazine, *The Minaret* begins with the object of capturing some of the reputation of Harriet Monroe's *Poetry*. But its list of contributors is scarcely as impressive. Among those who submit their early poems are Horace Gregory and Kenneth Fearing. Other contributions include poems by Robert H. Schauffler, Gamaliel Bradford, Oscar Williams, Margaret Widdemer, and Marya Zaturenska.

❖

OTHERS; a magazine of the new verse. July 1915-July 1919. Monthly. Grantwood, N.J. NN
Editors: Alfred Kreymborg (July 1915 - Sept. 1916; Feb. - Apr. / May 1919); (June 1917, *editor not established*); William Saphier (Dec. 1917-Feb. 1918).

Among associate editors are: William Carlos Williams, Helen Hoyt, Maxwell Bodenheim, Lola Ridge, and Orrick Johns.

*Others* begins as a place for those whose poetry has not appeared, or has appeared only infrequently, in *Poetry*. Because of this almost accidental "policy," it publishes verse which is more boldly experimental, more "imagistic than the imagists." But the circumstance of publication scarcely establishes an editorial precedent. The intelligence of the editors, though questioned at the time by conservatives, succeeds in affording a place for diverse poetical styles. In some respects, therefore, *Others* is a landmark in the development of modern poetry, a fact which needs no more evidence than the list of contributors: Marianne Moore, Conrad Aiken, Mina Loy, Ezra Pound, H.D., Wallace Stevens, T. S. Eliot, Amy Lowell, John Gould Fletcher, Richard Aldington, and others.

⋄

POESY; a magazine for the lover of the muses. 1915 - Nov. 1917? Irregular. Bishop Auckland, Eng.　　　　　NN
Supplements.
Editor: Edward F. Herdman.
*Issues previous to Nov. 1915 not consulted.*

This magazine "has been promoted to afford a medium through which those possessing poetical talents can have their efforts published in a more permanent and attractive form than is necessary in Newspapers and Periodicals." This purpose is supported by the awarding of poetry prizes and the publication of much verse by unknowns.

⋄

ROGUE. Mar. 15-Sept. 15, 1915. Semimonthly. New York. illus.　　NN
Editor: Allan Norton.

A none too serious magazine, *Rogue* during its brief Greenwich Village career, which is coincident with World War I, presents the writings of an important group, many of whom transfer their literary affection to *Others*. *Rogue* is important for its poetry by Wallace Stevens, Mina Loy, Alfred Kreymborg, and Witter Bynner. Gertrude Stein makes a brief appearance.

SIGNATURE. Oct. 4-Nov. 1, 1915. Fortnightly. London.　　　　　　　C
Editors: D. H. Lawrence, Katherine Mansfield, John Middleton Murry.

Because John Middleton Murry and D. H. Lawrence wish "to do something" about World War I, *Signature* appears for three issues. Both Lawrence and Murry contribute essays which run in all three issues: Lawrence's "The Crown" and Murry's "There Was a Little Man." A study of them reveals the great contrast of the two temperaments; they are important documents for the Lawrence-Murry controversy. "Autumns" and "The Little Governess," by Matilda Berry (pseudonym of Katherine Mansfield), also appear in No. 1 and No. 2-3 respectively.

## 1916

THE AJAX; a monthly magazine for lovers of literature. 1916-1921? Alton, Ill.　　　　　　　　　　　　NN
Editor: C. Victor Stahl.
*Issues previous to 1917 not consulted.*

*The Ajax* is blessed with a very active editorial interest in the discussion and controversy over "the new verse"; though almost all of the poetry in its pages is "traditional," the magazine grants editorially at least the theoretical virtue of the contemporary experiment with verse techniques. Contributions to *The Ajax* include poetry by Paul Y. Anderson, C. Victor Stahl, Byron Emery, Helen Hoyt, and Carleton Beals. The magazine takes the conservative position in the controversy over free verse.

⋄

THE CHIMAERA. May-July 1916? Bimonthly. Port Washington, N.Y. bk. rev., illus.　　　　　　　　　Y
Editor: William Rose Benét.

William Rose Benét's little magazine exhibits materials written by literary artists who since the second decade of our century have achieved positions of some importance in modern American letters. Among these may be noted poems by Louis Untermeyer, Jean Starr Untermeyer, Amy Lowell, Leonard Bacon, Stephen Vincent Benét, Alter Brody, Marianne Moore, Laura Benét, Helen Hoyt, and William Rose Benét; a short story by Waldo Frank; and prose sketches by Paul Rosenfeld.

❖

CONTEMPORARY VERSE. 1916-1929. Monthly. Philadelphia. index (in each vol.: v. 5-20, 1918-1925; v. 23-25, Dec. 1927-1929). NN (Absorbed by *Bozart*, Jan. 1930.) Editors: Howard S. Graham, Jr. and Devereaux C. Josephs (1916); Samuel McCoy (1916-1917); James E. Richardson (Jan.-Oct. 1917); Charles Wharton Stork (1917-1925); Henry Morton Robinson (Jan.-May/July 1926); Lucia Trent and Ralph Cheyney (Dec. 1926-Dec. 1929); Benjamin Musser (Dec. 1926-Dec. 1929).

*Contemporary Verse* begins in some measure as an upholder of traditional verse forms; the editors insist that "there is no point in the use of *vers libre*, unless it is illuminated by a great idea, as in the case of Whitman." Free verse, however, does appear. Among the limited number of fairly important contributors are Joseph Auslander, Winifred Welles, Mark Van Doren, Leonora Speyer, and Parker Tyler.

❖

FORM; a quarterly journal containing poetry, sketches, articles of literary and critical interests combined with prints, woodcuts, lithographs . . . Apr. 1916-Jan. 1922. London. bk.rev., illus. NN (Suspended between Apr. 1917 and Oct. 1921.)
Editors: Austin O. Spare (with Francis Marsden, Apr. 1916-Apr. 1917, and W. H. Davies, Oct. 1921-Jan. 1922).

A British magazine of the arts, *Form* publishes "examples of the best contemporary work in Literature, Fine Art, Music and Criticism; without discrimination in favour of any school or group." Its contributions include poetry by Walter de la Mare, W. J. Turner, Edith Sitwell, Harold Monro, Siegfried Sassoon, Robert Graves, Wilfrid Gibson, Osbert Sitwell, W. B. Yeats, Laurence Housman, W. H. Davies, and Aldous Huxley; prose sketches and essays by Logan Pearsall Smith, W. H. Davies, Arthur Waley, Richard Aldington, Robert Graves, and others. As for the examples of the arts presented in this magazine, they are found in "one or other of the varied forms of expression appropriate to printing—lithographs, pen drawings, calligraphy, decoration, and the like." Accompanying these illustrations are a number of essays dealing with the form and substance of the arts.

❖

THE PAGAN; a magazine for eudaemonists. May 1916-Jan. 1922? Monthly. New York. bk. rev., illus. NN (Mar., July-Aug. 1920, not published.) Editor: Joseph Kling.

Joseph Kling's Greenwich Village magazine is important for two reasons: 1) it illustrates admirably the fortunes and manners of the truly *avant-garde* publication; 2) in its pages appear the early writings of many important modern poets: Malcolm Cowley, Hart Crane, Eugene Jolas, and Virgil Geddes are a few. Kling deliberately tries for a magazine which might represent the aesthetic statement of Greenwich Village life. Some of the editorial defiance of convention appears self-conscious. But the atmosphere is congenial to the young intellectual and poet: many join the group at least for a time. The student of Hart Crane will need to examine the magazine. Other contributors include Gorham Munson, Royall Snow, Fiswood Tarleton, Mortimer Adler, Oscar Williams, Virgil Geddes, and Theodore Dreiser. Hart Crane appears in the issues of 1918 as one of the associate editors.

✧

THE PALATINE REVIEW. Jan./Feb. 1916-Mar. 1917. 4 issues a year. Oxford, Eng.   c
Editor: T. W. Earp?

One of the important English little reviews, *The Palatine Review* appears during the dark days of World War I. Editorially the magazine expresses concern over the fact that ". . . writings of the day evidence a confusion of warring private impulses, a mutual exclusiveness. . . ." The *Palatine Review* is especially noted for its inclusion of many contributions by Aldous Huxley —poetry, fiction, and criticism. T. W. Earp provides one of the earlier critical estimates of the French poet, Charles Peguy, who has recently been republished and revalued. Clive Bell contributes a story, and Philip Heseltine an essay on the music of his time.

✧

THE POETRY REVIEW OF AMERICA. May 1916-Feb. 1917. Monthly. Cambridge, Mass.   NN
Editor: William Stanley Braithwaite.

William Stanley Braithwaite's second poetry magazine, strongly backed by Amy Lowell, succeeds in publishing a number of important poets; John Gould Fletcher, Alfred Kreymborg, Richard Aldington, Conrad Aiken, Eunice Tietjens, Witter Bynner, and others. Amy Lowell submits an example of her polyphonic prose. The editorial incentive is generally "The desire to serve the art of poetry and to consolidate public interest in its growth and popularity—to quicken and enlarge the poetic pulse of the country. . . ."

THE QUARTERLY NOTEBOOK. June 1916-Apr. 1917. Kansas City, Mo. illus.   NN
Editor: Alfred Fowler.

The object of *The Quarterly Notebook* is to bring to the front of the stage the artists of the time—to combine that effort with studies of the traditionally great. Ezra Pound contributes a translation of a Japanese play, with an introductory note.

✧

THE SEVEN ARTS. Nov. 1916-Oct. 1917. Monthly. New York. bk. rev. (Absorbed by *The Dial*, 1917?)   NN
Supplement, Apr. 1917.
Editor: James Oppenheim.

Waldo Frank and Van Wyck Brooks are associate editors, and Louis Untermeyer, Robert Frost, David Mannes, and Robert Edmond Jones appear among those on the advisory board.

*The Seven Arts* is important primarily for its great contribution to American criticism. Its principal reason for publishing is its conviction that the arts are in a sense crucial to a civilization and its "faith . . . that we are living in the first days of a renascent period, a time which means for America the beginning of that national self-consciousness which is the beginning of greatness." The list of contributors is long; and many of them contribute a body of criticism which remains important for the history of American thought. Since these writers—Randolph Bourne, Van Wyck Brooks, Waldo Frank, James Oppenheim—were not always in agreement, the war proved a fatal stumbling block. But few magazines can equal, through their entire lives, the vitality or significance of this short-lived magazine. In addition to criticism, the magazine carries poetry by Robert Frost, Carl Sandburg, Amy Lowell, Stephen Vincent Benét, and others; fiction by Sherwood Anderson, S. N. Behrman, Eugene O'Neill, and D. H. Lawrence.

THE SOIL; a magazine of art. Dec. 1916-July 1917. Monthly. New York. illus.  NN
Editors: R. J. Coady and Enrique Cross.

Robert Coady seeks for an American art in the immediate and familiar: "There is an American Art. Young, robust, energetic, naïve, immature, daring and big spirited." In the "arts" which enjoyed the widest possible interest Coady tries to find a native aesthetic for America: photography, engineering, prize fighting, the dime novel. His magazine is therefore an interesting document which reveals one man's search for a popular aesthetic. Included in the contents are the prose of "Nick Carter" and poems by Wallace Stevens and Maxwell Bodenheim.

✧

THE STRATFORD JOURNAL; a forum of contemporary international thought. Autumn 1916-Jan. 1925. Frequency varies. Boston. bk. rev., index (in each vol.: v. 1-5, Autumn 1916-Oct./Dec. 1919).  NN
(Suspended, July 1920-Mar. 1924.)
(June 1924-Jan. 1925 as: *The Stratford Monthly*.)
Editors: William S. Braithwaite (Autumn 1916-Sept./Dec. 1917); Henry T. Schnittkind (Autumn 1916-Jan. 1925); and Isaac Goldberg (Jan. 1918-Jan. 1925).

The ambitious plans of *The Stratford Journal* include translations from foreign literatures, criticism, and "the best foreign and American poetry." The emphasis is mostly upon writings of Europeans, especially the Russians.

## 1917

ART AND LETTERS. July 1917-1920. Quarterly. London. illus.  C Y
Editors: Frank Rutter (with Charles Ginner and H. Gilman, July-Oct. 1917, and Osbert Sitwell, Summer 1919-Spring 1920).

*Art and Letters* provides space for many of the writers of the late teens. Herbert Read's poetry and his careful criticism of contemporary letters are an important part of its contents. T. S. Eliot contributes poems and critical essays. There are stories by Katherine Mansfield and Dorothy Richardson; poems by Richard Aldington, the Sitwells, Aldous Huxley, and Siegfried Sassoon.

✧

THE BLIND MAN. Apr. 10, 1917-? Irregular. New York.  CtU
Editor: Henri Pierre Roché?

A magazine of "The Independents," *The Blind Man* sponsors or calls for a revolution in attitudes toward the arts. "New York, so far ahead in so many ways," says Henri Pierre Roché in the first issue, "yet so indifferent to art in the making, is going to learn to think for itself and no longer accept, mechanically, the art reputations made abroad." The magazine's chief purpose is to advance the cause of independent and radical artists who have pursued their work in some disregard for the conventions; to this purpose is added a defense of private and special exhibitions to afford these artists a showing. Mina Loy contributes a brief note to the first issue on the artist and the public and on the problem of "educating" the latter in terms of its aesthetic interests.

✧

BRUNO'S. Jan.-Apr. 1917. Weekly. New York. illus.  NN
(Supersedes *Bruno's Weekly*.)
Editor: Guido Bruno.

*Bruno's* varies only in format and very slightly in content from other Bruno magazines. The editor is preoccupied with such matters as the absurdity of American censorship. To this question Alfred Stieglitz adds his comment.

❖

THE LYRIC. May 1917-July/Aug. 1919?
Monthly. New York.                    NN
(Suspended, Mar.-Dec. 1918.)
Editors: S. Roth (with F. Tannenbaum, 1917).

Beginning as a magazine for Columbia University people, *The Lyric* soon expands its scope to include contributions from a number of important writers outside campus limits: Amy Lowell, John Gould Fletcher, D. H. Lawrence, William Rose Benét, Babette Deutsch, E. A. Robinson, and others. The purpose of *The Lyric* is simple—to afford a place for poets to publish. There is no wearisome or pretentious editorial doctrine to interfere with or in any way to qualify that purpose.

❖

THE MADRIGAL; a magazine of love lyrics. July 1917-Jan. 1918. Monthly. New York. illus.            NN
Editor: Gustav Davidson.

*The Madrigal* is slight, but true to its subtitle, since it confines itself to publishing love lyrics, most of them as highly decorated as the magazine's format. Contributors include Edwin Markham, Gustav Davidson, William Rose Benét, and Odell Shepard.

❖

THE QUILL; a magazine of Greenwich Village. June 30, 1917-May 1929. Monthly. New York. bk. rev., illus. (July-Dec. 1926, May 1927-May 1929 as: *The Greenwich Village Quill*; Feb. 1927 as: *Overtures*.)      NN
Editors: Harold Hersey (June 30, 1917); Arthur H. Moss and others (July 1917-July 1918, Jan. 1920-May 1921); Millia Davenport Moss (Aug. 1918-Dec. 1919); Robert Edwards (June 1921-June 1926); Henry Harrison (July 1926-May 1929).

Among the contributing editors are: Pierre Loving, Mary Carolyn Davies, Benjamin De Casseres, Harry Kemp, Willy Pogany, Hendrick Van Loon, Hans Stengel, Max Bodenheim, Helene Mullins, Lucia Trent, Clement Wood, Ralph Cheyney, Benjamin Musser.

During the editorship of Bobby Edwards the magazine becomes an excellent guidebook to cultural activity in Greenwich Village. Edwards' aim is primarily to present the artists of the Village, and to defend it against its detractors and defamers. Discussions of free love, the conventions, psychoanalysis, and socialism give *The Quill* its value; they represent Villagers as serious and gay by turns, rather self-conscious, and anxious to live up to the best of their several reputations. Edwards is aided by contributions in prose by Floyd Dell, Maxwell Bodenheim, Arthur Moss, Benjamin De Casseres, and others. Later issues contain much information about the history of Greenwich Village.

❖

RONGWRONG. [1917]-? Frequency not given. [New York.] illus.
*Editor not established.*

A magazine of some dadaist inclinations, *Rongwrong* contains offerings in the French by Francis Picabia, Carl Van Vechten, and others; in English by Carl Van Vechten. The prose of Van Vechten is written along the lines of early experimental writing and suggests dadaism in its use of disassociation and illogical sequence of ideas and images: "Her poor severed head clung by a shred to her bleeding body, still cringing with the reproach of the rod, but she strode on regardless."

❖

THE SANSCULOTTE. Jan.-Apr. 1917. Monthly. Columbus, Ohio. illus.
Editor: James Light.

Inspired and controlled by undergraduates of Ohio State University, *The Sansculotte* is interesting primarily for the light it throws upon the literary careers of two of America's most important literary critics, Malcolm Cowley and Kenneth Burke. Burke and Cowley contribute an appreciable share of the magazine's contents. There is some promise of future greatness in these early verses and sketches, though the contributors reveal considerable immaturity. Perhaps the most interesting fact about their writings is the breadth of intellectual interests which they demonstrate. The editorial statement on the first issue is marked by a kind of vague enthusiasm for the integrity and isolation of the aesthetic position: ". . . The underlying reality in life is given meaning and force by art . . . art and literature are the interpreters, the coordinators of what meaning there is in men and their surroundings. . . . Our care is for literature for its own sake, as far as possible." The second issue carries some verses by Ludwig Lewisohn, who was on the faculty of Ohio State University at the time. They are marked by a certain prewar idealism, which Lewisohn is careful to explain in a note: "These verses were written before the war. Their idealism seems facile enough now." *The Sansculotte* reveals its principal contributors as extremely young artists whose minds are not yet made up, and whose aesthetics have not yet been formulated.

✧

SLATE; a magazine for teachers who are not dead; and for their friends. Jan.-May 1917. Monthly. New York. bk. rev. illus.   NN
Editor: Jess Perlman.

*Slate*, as its subtitle suggests, is a magazine whose purpose is to stir up interest in reforms in education: "*Slate* desires to fill its pages especially with the literary and artistic productions of those who are teachers; and with the unfettered opinions of both teachers and their friends on all subjects that are pertinent to the problems of education and of life." Its five issues publish spirited editorials; and cartoons somewhat in the style of *The Masses*, with special emphasis upon abuses in the world of education. Together with these, there are poems by Louis Untermeyer, Kenneth Burke, Haniel Long, Malcolm Cowley, Witter Bynner, Pierre Loving, Royall Snow, and Helen Hoyt; and essays by Floyd Dell and Scott Nearing.

✧

THE SONNET. Feb. 1917-Mar./Apr. 1921. Bimonthly. New York.   NN
Editor: Mahlon Leonard Fisher.

Within its self-imposed limits, *The Sonnet* acquits itself admirably. "The sole aim of *The Sonnet* is to publish poetry so well thought of by its makers that they were willing to place it within strict confines." In June 1937 "The First Printing of a Wylie Sonnet" was published as a supplement to this magazine.

## 1918

BRUNO'S BOHEMIA; magazine of life, love and letters. Mar.-Apr. 1918. Monthly. New York. bk. rev., illus.
Editor: Guido Bruno.   NN P

*Bruno's Bohemia* differs only slightly in appearance and content, and not at all in editorial policy or general attitude, from Bruno's other magazines. The first issue, that of March 1918, includes a poem by Harold H. Crane, "Carmen De Boheme," one of Hart Crane's earliest published poems.

✧

THE COUNTRY BARD. 1918+. Quarterly. Madison, N.J. index (v. 1-4, 1918-Autumn 1930).   NN

(June 1945+ as: *The American Bard.*) Editors: Clarence A. Sharp (1918-Spring/Summer 1935); Margarette Ball Dickson (Fall 1935/Winter 1936+).

*The Country Bard* begins as a means of publishing the verse of its editor, who decides, with the issue of Autumn 1919, to make his magazine the meeting place of "a brotherhood of country bards," and opens its pages to fellow pastoral poets. The magazine features verse on subjects rural and rustic. Mr. Sharp speaks, in frequent editorials, against "this esoteric stuff," a label he applies to experimental verse of his time, and advocates a return to the simplicity of "the older poetry." Among the contributions, those by Jay G. Sigmund may be singled out as deserving of mention.

❖

THE LIBERATOR. Mar. 1918-Oct. 1924. Monthly. New York. bk. rev., illus. (Supersedes *The Masses*. United with *Labor Herald* and *Soviet Russia Pictorial* to form *Worker's Monthly*, Nov. 1924.) NN
Editors: Max Eastman (Mar. 1918-Apr. 1923); Chrystal Eastman (Nov. 1918-Feb. 1921); Floyd Dell (Mar. 1921-Apr. 1923); Robert Minor (Mar. 1921-1924), and others.

Arturo Giovannitti, John Reed (foreign correspondent from Russia), Boardman Robinson, Louis Untermeyer, Art Young, Eugene V. Debs, Michael Gold, Mary Heaton Vorse, Howard Brubaker, William Gropper, Claude McKay, Charles W. Wood, Joseph Freeman, Upton Sinclair, and Scott Nearing are among others who appear in various editorial capacities.

Like *The Masses*, of which it is a continuation, *The Liberator* underlines both the aesthetic and the social interests of its contributors and editors. The career of these two magazines runs parallel with and in large measure reflects the gradual channelizing of the artist's social and political interests, until such time as the Marxist interpretation of art threatens to eliminate all other evaluations of the period. This duality of interest inevitably causes a conflict, both within the artist's own mind and in editorial offices; this conflict is admirably interpreted by Joseph Freeman in *An American Testament*. *The Liberator* does, however, show a more specific interest in the actual problems of American Communism than did *The Masses*; its lines and policies are sharpened, and both are brought close to the aims and practices of American leftism of the early twenties. The magazine also accepts the responsibility of interpreting the Russian Revolution to America, and reports on the anarchist trials and other events in America of interest to workers.

In addition to the regular editorials by Max Eastman, mainly on political matters, and the frequent essays by Floyd Dell on the "sexual crisis in America," *The Liberator* carries much verbal and pictorial satire on capitalism and its institutions; the cartoons of Art Young are featured, as they were in *The Masses*. They are supplemented by drawings by Robert Minor and Boardman Robinson, among others. Contributions include the poetry of Eastman, Dell, Genevieve Taggard, Joseph Freeman, Arturo Giovannitti, Sandburg, Bynner, Babette Deutsch, and others; prose by Elmer Rice, Stuart Chase, John Reed, S. N. Behrman, and others.

❖

THE MARIONNETTE. Apr. 1, 1918-Aug. 1919? Monthly. Florence, Italy. bk. rev., illus., index. NN
(Cover title: *The Marionnette To-Night . . . at 12-30.*)
Editor: Gordon Craig.

*The Marionnette* is a little magazine of the puppet theater. "A performance for fools. A Democratic performance. A Diplomatic performance. . ." Gordon Craig writes on the history of marionettes. Like its older and larger brother, *The Mask*, this magazine confines itself to the interest in and capacities of a single craft. Articles link puppetry with history, aesthetics, and literature. The magazine also contains the texts of many old and rare marionette dramas.

❖

YOUTH; poetry of today. Oct. 1918-Aug. 1919. Bimonthly. Cambridge, Mass.    NN
Editors: Royall Snow and Jack Merten (with Donald B. Clark, Oct. 1918-Feb. 1919).

Among the associate editors are: Grace Hazard Conkling, John Erskine, Stephen Vincent Benét, Maxwell Anderson, Katherine Lee Bates, Genevieve Taggard.

Edited by a group of Harvard undergraduates, but in no other way associated with the university, *Youth* publishes some important contributions by John Gould Fletcher, Malcolm Cowley, Maxwell Anderson, Conrad Aiken, E. A. Robinson, and Amy Lowell. The magazine is called *Youth*, says Royall Snow, because "Youth has eternally been a symbol of vitality and growth."

---

## 1919

AENGUS; an all poetry journal. Midsummer 1919-? Frequency not given. Dublin.    ICU
Editor: D. L. Kelleher.

Aengus "arose from a club of 8 writers. Each one in turn produces a number of the paper. He is free to change format, price, title, etc., so long as he keeps prose out and stands the financial risk of his issue." Contributions include poetry by Richard Rowley, Anna G. Keown, H. Stuart, F. R. Higgins, E. R. Dodds, C. O'Leary, H. O. White and D. L. Kelleher.

❖

BRUNO'S REVIEW OF LIFE, LOVE AND LETTERS. Apr. 1919-? Monthly. New York. bk. rev.    NN
Editor: Guido Bruno.
*Issues other than April 1919 (v. 19, no. 1, consecutive series) not consulted.*

One of several Bruno magazines which participate editorially in the events of our second decade, and link that decade with its past by references to the writings and ideas of the decades preceding it. The contributors include Lord Dunsany, Thomas Burke, Vincent Blasco Ibanez, and Frank Harris.

❖

COTERIE. May 1919-Winter 1920/21. Quarterly. Oxford, Eng. illus.    NN
(Superseded by *New Coterie*, Nov. 1925.)
Editors: Chaman Lall (May 1919-Autumn 1920); Russell Green (Winter 1920/21).

Beginning with the Dec. 1919 issue, Conrad Aiken becomes one of the American editors, and T. S. Eliot, T. W. Earp, Richard Aldington, Aldous Huxley, and Wyndham Lewis are listed as members of the editorial committee.

With liberal support by American editors and poets, Chaman Lall makes of *Coterie* an outstanding magazine of art and letters. Though it reflects a conscious effort to be distinctive, the magazine demonstrates the wisdom and taste of its editors. English and American contributions include poems by Aldous Huxley, Conrad Aiken, T. S. Eliot, John Gould Fletcher, and Herbert Read.

❖

THE DAMN; a magazine of humor, satire and irony. Sept. 1919-? Frequency not given. New York.
Editor: Em Jo.

The Damn "believes that a society based on Billy Sundays, Ole Hansons, New York Timeses, Wilsons, Prohibitions and Luskers cannot and ought not to be taken too seriously: It must be laughed at." There are humorous sketches by Gorham Munson, Paul Eldridge, others; poems by Ralph Cheyney.

❖

THE FREE SPIRIT. Feb. 1919-Winter 1921. Monthly. New York. bk. rev., illus.    P
(Suspended, 1920.)
Editor: Rose Florence Freeman (with Joseph Ishill, May 1919-Winter 1921).

A little magazine, varied in its contents, which include free verse poems by Rose Florence Freeman, Peter Altenberg, Alfred Kreymborg, and others, and essays in appreciation of Oscar Wilde and Edwin Arlington Robinson.

❖

GOOD MORNING; the weekly burst of humor, satire and fun . . . May 8, 1919-Oct. 1921. New York. illus.   LC NN
(Superseded by *Art Young Quarterly*, 1922.)
Editors: Art Young (with Ellis O. Jones, May 8-July 10, 1919).

Art Young's humorous weekly amply demonstrates his jovially satirical opposition to the postwar *status quo*. Both in cartoon and essay, the writers for *Good Morning* ridicule the sober efforts of international diplomats and puncture the inflated ego of the returning soldiery. Much of the material is political in its nature, but *Good Morning* is valuable as another example of social satire, contemporaneous with *The Liberator*. Among the artists who draw for the magazine are Boardman Robinson, Hendrick Van Loon, Peggy Bacon, and William Gropper.

❖

MODERNIST; a monthly magazine of modern arts and letters. Nov. 1919-? New York. bk. rev., illus.   NN
Editor: James Waldo Fawcett.
*Issues later than Nov. 1919 not consulted.*

The editor of the *Modernist* pledges that the magazine "will strive to be an expression of our own time and our own work. The interpretation of the ideals and events in which we ourselves have part, the service of humanity to the limit of our ability, is the burden of our task." In the first issue we find poetry by Hart Crane, Ralph Cheyney, and Hazel Hall; critical essays by James Waldo Fawcett, Gorham Munson, and Theodore Dreiser.

❖

THE MONTHLY CHAPBOOK. July 1919-1925. London. illus., index (no. 1-12, July 1919-June 1920; no. 13-24, July 1920-June 1921).   NN
(Supersedes *Poetry and Drama*.) (Suspended, July 1921-Jan. 1922. 1924 and 1925 complete in one number each.) (Jan. 1920-1925 as: *The Chapbook*.)
Editor: Harold Monro.

Like all of Harold Monro's efforts, *The Monthly Chapbook* makes important and interesting contributions to modern poetry and aesthetics. Published during most of its career as a genuine "chapbook," it affords single writers or representative groups ample space for full expression; the later issues are magazine issues, with greater variety in contributions. *The Monthly Chapbook* prints essays on poetry and poetics by T. S. Eliot, F. S. Flint, Richard Aldington, and others; a symposium on poetry and the modern world takes up all of No. 27 (July 1922). Almost all important poets of our times are represented in *The Monthly Chapbook's* table of contents: Richard Aldington, John Gould Fletcher, Maxwell Anderson, Robert Frost, E. E. Cummings, Conrad Aiken, Wallace Stevens, Marianne Moore, and others.

# BIBLIOGRAPHY

THE OWL. May 1919-Nov. 1923. Irregular. London. illus.   NN
(Nov. 1923 cover title: *The Winter Owl.*)
Editor: Robert Graves.

The Owl "has no politics, leads to no new movement and is not even the organ of any particular generation. . . . But we find in common a love of honest work well done, and a distaste for short cuts to popular success." Such an editorial policy, though it would seem to leave out of consideration much that is of interest in modern letters, actually affords an opportunity for publication to a variety of interesting and important writers. Among the contributions are poems by John Masefield, Siegfried Sassoon, Vachel Lindsay, John Crowe Ransom, and Robert Graves.

❖

THE OXFORD OUTLOOK. May 1919-May 1932. Irregular. Oxford, Eng. bk. rev. illus.   NN
(Superseded by *New Oxford Outlook,* May 1933.)
Editors: N. A. Beechman, Beverley Nichols, and others.

A semiuniversity organ, *The Oxford Outlook* nevertheless demonstrates considerable freedom from academic restraints. Its university association is reflected chiefly in essays on language, on the poets, and on political matters. Its interest in contemporary letters is manifested by the publication of poems by Richard Goodman, Cleanth Brooks, Stephen Spender, Edith Sitwell, Robert Graves, and others; critical prose by C. M. Bowra, John Middleton Murry, Stephen Spender, and others.

❖

PLAYBOY; a portfolio of art and satire. Jan. 1919-July 1924. Irregular. New York. illus.   NN
(Suspended, June 1921-Feb. 1923.)
Editor: Egmont Arens.

Egmont Arens attempts a magazine of elaborate format, with many art reproductions and some fragments of literature. The editorial policy results in scattered and varied contributions, some of them of importance for modern letters. Among these are portions of Sherwood Anderson's *A New Testament,* and critical essays by D. H. Lawrence and Egmont Arens. James Joyce's essay, "The Day of the Rabblement," is reprinted in the first issue of 1923.

❖

S 4 N (S 4 N Society.) Nov. 1919-July 1925. Monthly. Northampton, Mass.   NN Y
(Combined with *Modern Review* to form *Modern S 4 N Review,* Aug. 1926.)
Editor: Norman Fitts.

Gorham B. Munson, E. E. Cummings, Thornton Wilder, Jean Toomer, and Stephen Vincent Benét appear among those on the editorial board.

*S 4 N* tells its own story in numerous editorials. It is born of the idea that controversy is in an important way a "constituent of the arts." The result of such policy is brilliant critical tension, which leads finally to the dissolution of the "S 4 N Society." Norman Fitts's clearest statement of policy is "That out of a comparison of opposed viewpoints (with attendant attacks and counter-attacks, and with subsequent experimentations and reactive critiques) comes aesthetic progress." The magazine is an opportunity for the critical minds of Kenneth Burke, Gorham Munson, Norman Fitts, Waldo Frank, John Peale Bishop, and others; poetry is contributed by Hart Crane, E. E. Cummings, Harold Vinal, Allen Tate, John Peale Bishop, and others; fiction by Kenneth Burke, Thornton Wilder, Ramon Guthrie, among others. A complete issue, that for September 1923/January

1924, edited by Gorham Munson, is devoted to criticism of the work of Waldo Frank. A letter from Mrs. Ramon Guthrie explains the origin of the name, S 4 N: "If I remember well, no title for the magazine had yet been decided upon when the first issue was ready to be sent out. On the cover of the magazine the editor and printer had written 'Space for Name' which became S 4 N and remained as the final name of the magazine."

❖

VOICES. 1919-1921. Irregular. London. bk. rev., illus.     H NN
Editor: Thomas Moult.

Thomas Moult's London Voices resembles its American namesake in its general concern over the preservation of poetic and aesthetic values. The contents of the London magazine consist mainly of the poetry of British writers. Several efforts are made to discuss the relationship of poetry with society and with the other arts; among the critics represented are John Middleton Murry, D. H. Lawrence, and Alan Porter. Poems are contributed by Lascelles Abercrombie, W. H. Davies, John Middleton Murry, Richard Aldington, John Gould Fletcher, A. E. Coppard, D. H. Lawrence, and others.

## 1920

ALL'S WELL, OR THE MIRROR REPOLISHED. Dec. 1920-Nov./Dec. 1935. Monthly. Fayetteville, Ark. bk. rev. (Supersedes *Reedy's Mirror*.)   NN Supplement, [1923?].
Editor: Charles J. Finger.

*Reedy's Mirror*, repolished and transferred to Arkansas, and later to Philadelphia, Pa., becomes an organ for the editorial opinion and selection of Charles J. Finger. During its post-Reedy career, it is a vigorous expression of uncensored opinion, though the literary contributions are not equal in importance to those of its predecessor: among them are included poems by Glenn Ward Dresbach, Howard Mumford Jones, Vincent Starrett, George Sterling, Harold Vinal, C. E. S. Wood, and John Hall Wheelock; and critical essays by Gorham Munson and C. E. S. Wood.

❖

THE APPLE (of beauty and discord). 1920-1922. Quarterly. London. illus.
Editor: Herbert Furst.     NN

Another elaborate English magazine of art and letters, "'The Apple' has only one policy: to entertain its readers with living literature and art collected from many gardens and culled occasionally from the ever living, ever fruitful orchards of the past...." Its aim is above all aesthetic, to the exclusion of all but a few "extraneous" political matters. There are a great number of articles on "the arts," and many reproductions. Included among the contributions are critical articles by Ezra Pound, T. Sturge Moore, and Montgomery Belgion; poetry by Robert Graves, Louis Golding, A. E. Coppard, Osbert Sitwell, John Rodker, and others.

❖

BRUNO'S REVIEW OF TWO WORLDS; a magazine of life, love and letters. Nov. 1920-Nov. 1922. Monthly. New York. illus.     NN
Editor: Guido Bruno.

This magazine has all of the editorial peculiarities of Bruno's other magazines. In it Bruno gives full play to his wide acquaintance with the world of letters and art, discussing issues of the day and including reports from contemporary Vienna and Prague. Freud and Joyce receive interesting notices.

❖

CONTACT. Dec. 1920-June 1923; [n.s.] 1932. Irregular. New York. illus.

Editors: William Carlos Williams and Robert McAlmon.   B NN

*Contact* was brought out in 1920 by William Carlos Williams, whose co-worker was Robert McAlmon. Williams had had poetry published in *Others* and *Poetry*, but he wanted to establish his own magazine, because, as he states in his first editorial, he had "faith in the existence of native artists who are capable of having, comprehending, and recording extraordinary experience." In its first five issues *Contact* publishes critical essays by Kenneth Burke, William Carlos Williams, Robert McAlmon, and Marianne Moore; poems by Mina Loy, Williams, McAlmon, Marsden Hartley, Wallace Stevens, Kenneth Burke, John Rodker, Glenway Wescott, and Kay Boyle.

The "new series" of *Contact*, begun in February 1932, with William Carlos Williams at the editorial helm, presents a more impressive appearance than its predecessor. The three issues of this series (a fourth was prepared, but never published) are of definite value to the history of American avant-gardism. Williams' justification for the magazine is that most published writing is either that which "can be sold at a profit," or "scholarly writing which only the erudite enjoy"; independence of the pressures behind both kinds of writing is vital, Williams maintains, if true values in literature are to be preserved. The contents of the later series include the poetry of E. E. Cummings, Louis Zukofsky, Parker Tyler, William Carlos Williams, Nancy Cunard, Carl Rakosi, Yvor Winters, and Fred Maxham; the fiction of Nathaniel West, Eugene Joffe, Erskine Caldwell, Robert McAlmon, William Carlos Williams, Nathan Asch, and others. Two of S. J. Perelman's burlesque commentaries upon modern life appear. Of interest to the student of little magazine history is one of the first bibliographies of that subject, compiled by David Moss.

❖

THE DIAL. (v. 68-86, 1920-1929.) Monthly. New York. bk. rev., illus., index.   NN
Editors: Scofield Thayer (with Marianne Moore, July 1925-July 1929).

During the early part of 1920 Gilbert Seldes was associate editor.

From 1920 to 1929, under the successive editorship of Scofield Thayer and Marianne Moore, *The Dial* consistently prints important contributions in modern fiction, poetry, and criticism, including translations from the German, French, and Russian, and philosophical essays by George Santayana and Bertrand Russell. Though it has little of the ordinary financial difficulty of the little magazine, *The Dial* is truly avant-garde in its editorial attitude toward the world of letters and of magazine publishing: "If a magazine isn't to be simply a waste of good white paper, it ought to print, with some regularity, either such work as would otherwise have to wait years for publication, or such as would not be acceptable elsewhere." Kenneth Burke enlivens its pages with some of his best critical essays, and his translations from Thomas Mann and Oswald Spengler; Sherwood Anderson's short stories have a hearing. English writers are abundantly represented; D. H. Lawrence's poetry and short stories appear frequently. The long list of poets who publish in *The Dial* includes Marianne Moore, T. S. Eliot (whose "Wasteland" had its first American publication here), William Carlos Williams, Conrad Aiken, Ezra Pound, W. B. Yeats, H. D., E. E. Cummings, Hart Crane, Malcolm Cowley, Carl Sandburg, and many others.

❖

THE FRONTIER; a literary magazine. (University of Montana.) May 1920-

Summer 1939. 3 issues a year. Missoula, Mont. bk. rev., illus., index (in each vol.: v. 8-19, Nov. 1927-Summer 1939).   NN
(May 1920 as: *The Montanan;* Nov. 1933-Summer 1939 as: *The Frontier and Midland.*) (Absorbed *Muse and Mirror,* Apr. 1932; *The Midland,* Nov. 1933.)
Board of editors with H. G. Merriam.

*The Frontier* is a "pioneer endeavor to gather indigenous northwest material. It offers itself to readers and writers as a non-commercial channel for expression." The contributions, poetry and prose, are of a truly regional character: Indian lore in narrative form; poems dealing with hills, canyons, and other Western phenomena; articles on Western history and folk lore. In its early years *The Frontier* is a college literary magazine, from 1920 to 1928. Beginning in 1928, its contents show a larger attention to important writing outside the campus limits, though it remains a regional magazine. Among the contributions are poems by Lew Sarett, Howard McKinley Corning, Norman Macleod, Katherine Tankersley Young, Raymond Kresensky, and others; stories and sketches by James Stevens, Grace Stone Coates, and many others; and many studies of the Northwest as a region and of its literature.

❖

NEW NUMBERS. Oct. 1920-? Frequency not given. Saint Paul, Minn. illus. Editor: Hall Alexander.   Y
*Issues other than Oct. 1920 not consulted.*

Saint Paul's little magazine publishes, among other things, poems by Helen Hoyt, Floyd Dell, E. Merrill Root, Oliver Jenkins, and Bernard Raymund.

❖

THE OCCIDENT. (The English Club, The University of California.) (v. 74-85, Jan. 1920-Feb. 1925.) Monthly. Berkeley, Calif. bk. rev., illus.   Y
Editors: Clarence David Greenhood (1920-?); H. R. Luck (1922-1923); Ellsworth Stewart (1923-1924); Vernon Patterson (1924-1925).
*Incomplete file. Issues earlier than Jan. 1920 and later than Feb. 1925 not consulted.*

The English Club of the University of California publishes a magazine which contains many contributions from Western writers and a variety of special essays on the culture of the Far West. The issues of March 1924 and February 1925 are special poetry issues. Among the contributions are poems by Idella Purnell, Witter Bynner, Hildegarde Flanner, and Paul Tanaquil.

❖

PARABALOU. 1920-1921. Irregular. Farmington, Conn.   NN
*Editor not established.*

"A pamphlet of poems by seven of the younger American poets." Two of the seven, Archibald MacLeish and Stephen Vincent Benét, are of some importance in modern American letters. A study of their poetry will have to include their earlier poems in *Parabalou.*

❖

RAAB'S REVIEW. May 1920-? Monthly. Milwaukee, Wis.   ICU
Editor: Helen Raab.

Modeled upon the format and contents of some of Guido Bruno's many little magazines, Helen Raab's magazine contains, among other things, poetry by Alfred Kreymborg, fiction by Lord Dunsany, and some critical remarks by the editor and by others. The cover design for the first issue is done by Djuna Barnes.

❖

RAINBOW; drama, literature, music, art. Oct.-Dec. 1920. Monthly. New York. illus.   P

Editors: Boris de Tanko and Horace Brodsky.

"To-day, not only does the artist receive scant appreciation from the public, but he is in no way considered an important and useful member of society. This is just what we want to try and remedy. We want everyone to understand that art is the most important factor in life...." *Rainbow* publishes poetry and articles on poetry, painting, and the drama.

---

### 1921

L'ALOUETTE; a magazine of verse. Jan.-Mar. 1921; Jan. 1924-1938? Irregular. Malden, Mass. bk. rev. NN
Editor: Charles A. A. Parker.

Editorially *L'Alouette* seeks a position somewhere between "the urban sterilities of our bearded Brahmins and the psychoanalytical clinics of our younger American intellectuals." There are a few contributions from Mackinlay Kantor, Josephine Johnson, and Howard McKinley Corning.

✧

THE AMERICAN INTERCOLLEGIATE MAGAZINE. Dec. 1921 - Dec. 1922. Monthly. Trenton, N.J. NN
Editor: Francis Ward Newsom.

A literary magazine "for college men and college women which purposes to present to the public work representative of the college students of America." Its aim is to select from college poetry and prose the best of its current product, and to make it available to an audience wider than that possible for any single college literary magazine. Among the contributions are poems by T. S. Matthews, Ralph E. Greene, Albert L. Hydeman, and David Newton; prose fiction by Harriet B. Ralston, Jane M. Cassidy, and David Newton; and criticism by T. S. Matthews and Schuyler B. Jackson.

BROOM; an international magazine of the arts. Nov. 1921-Jan. 1924. Monthly. Rome; Berlin; New York. bk. rev., illus. NN
Editors: Harold A. Loeb (with Alfred Kreymborg, Nov. 1921-Feb. 1922; Slater Brown, Matthew Josephson, and Malcolm Cowley, Jan. 1924).

During the early period of the magazine's publication, Slater Brown, Matthew Josephson, and Malcolm Cowley, among others, appear as associate editors and Lola Ridge is mentioned as the American editor.

*Broom* is actually "two magazines under one name." Its conservative period, under Loeb and Kreymborg, stamps it as an excellent little magazine, with admirable format and ambitious but conservative editorial direction. Selections are made with the aim of being nonprovincial, but the contents are rarely distinguished. Under the influence of Matthew Josephson and Malcolm Cowley it becomes an exciting but erratic and short-lived magazine. Josephson takes full advantage of his editorial prerogative; his essays are stimulating and provocative. As a whole, *Broom* may be considered a magazine more valuable for its criticism than for the examples of original writing printed in its pages. But both its history and its reflections upon contemporary thought and writing are important to a study of modern thought; this is especially true of its articles on the "exile" in American letters. Prose criticism is contributed by Matthew Josephson (under both his own name and a pseudonym, Will Bray), Malcolm Cowley, Conrad Aiken, Alfred Kreymborg, Harold A. Loeb, Gorham Munson, Jean Toomer, and others; among the short stories printed are those by Sherwood Anderson, James Stephens, Manuel Komroff, and J. D. Beresford; poetry is contributed by Lola Ridge, Lew Sarett, William Carlos Williams, E. E. Cummings, Ramon Guthrie, and others.

THE DOUBLE-DEALER. Jan. 1921-May 1926. Monthly. New Orleans. bk. rev., illus., index (except v. 8, Nov. 1925-May 1926). NN
Editors: Julius Weis Friend, Basil Thompson (Jan. 1921-Feb. 1923), and John McClure (Mar./Apr. 1923-May 1926).

For the period ending June 1922, Vincent Starrett appears as Chicago correspondent, John V. A. Weaver as New York correspondent, and Arthur Symons and Alfred Kreymborg as foreign correspondents.

Both in its aims and in its achievement, The Double-Dealer illustrates well the merits and defects of the little magazine. It shifts in editorial policy from regional to national emphasis. It publishes some of the earliest poems of the brilliant young Southern poets, Allen Tate, John Crowe Ransom, Donald Davidson, Robert Penn Warren; and it has the privilege of printing Ernest Hemingway's first published "work"—a very brief and ineffective short prose sketch, "A Divine Gesture." But it can best be credited with remaining true to its editorial policy, that of "printing the very best material it can procure, regardless of popular appeal, moral or immoral stigmata, conventional or unconventional technique, new theme or old." The editors are not always able to get the "very best"; there are many dreary stretches of mediocre material. But the final weight of important contributions is entirely in the magazine's favor: poetry by Louis Untermeyer, Hart Crane, Oscar Williams, Babette Deutsch, William Faulkner, Richard Aldington, Mary Austin, John Gould Fletcher, H. D., and others; prose by Sherwood Anderson, A. E. Coppard, William Faulkner, Carl Van Vechten. Thornton Wilder and Jean Toomer appear for the first time in the September 1922 issue.

GARGOYLE. Aug. 1921-Oct. 1922? Monthly. Paris. illus. BI Y
Editor: Arthur Moss.

In the early twenties Arthur Moss left Greenwich Village for Paris, where he edited Gargoyle, a little magazine of modern letters and of comment upon European art and life. Gargoyle's running commentary upon the achievements of Paris' motley group is adequately illustrated by reproductions of paintings by such men as Isaac Grunewald and Georges Bracque. The advance guard is the subject of much discussion in its pages. Contributions include poetry by Hart Crane, H. D., Malcolm Cowley, and Robert Coates; fiction by Malcolm Cowley and Robert Coates; and critical comment by Florence Gilliam and Arthur Moss.

❖

THE LYRIC. Apr. 1921+. Frequency varies. Norfolk, Va. bk. rev., illus., cum. index: v. 13-15 (1933-1936); v. 16-18 (1937-1939). NN
Editors: John R. Moreland (Apr. 1921-Oct. 1923); Virginia Taylor McCormick (Nov. 1923-Aug. 1929); Leigh Hanes (Sept. 1929 +).

Except for a few appearances by important poets, The Lyric has to be satisfied with the work of poets of minor stature. Some of the more gifted contributors include Robert Hillyer, Lizette Reese, C. Day Lewis, Witter Bynner, John Gould Fletcher, and Merrill Moore. Among the more talented minor poets are Paul Engle, Winifred Welles, Leonora Speyer, and Helene Mullins.

❖

THE LYRIC WEST. Apr. 1921-Dec. 1927. Monthly. Los Angeles, Calif. bk. rev., index (v. 4-6, Oct. 1924-Sept. 1927). NN
Editors: Grace Atherton Dennen (Apr. 1921-Mar. 1925); Roy Towner Thompson (Oct. 1924-Aug./Sept. 1925); Al-

lison and Ethelean Tyson Gaw (Oct. 1925-Nov. 1927); Neeta Marquis and Nina Maud Richardson (Dec. 1927).

*The Lyric West*, intended originally as the "Poetry" of the Far West, succeeds occasionally in publishing verse of some importance. Its editorials speak at length of the "educative" value of verse. The content is weighted down by "feminine verse"—delicate in sentiment, "correct" in form, competent, but often bordering on the cliché in metaphor. There are some fortunate appearances by Rolfe Humphries, Lew Sarett, Genevieve Taggard, Ted Olson, Babette Deutsch, and Vachel Lindsay.

❖

THE MEASURE; a journal of poetry. Mar. 1921-June 1926. Monthly. New York. bk. rev., index (except no. 61-64, Mar.-June 1926). NN
Editorial board: Maxwell Anderson, Padraic Colum, Agnes Kendrick Gray, Carolyn Hall, Frank E. Hill, David Morton, Louise Townsend Nicholl, George O'Neil, Genevieve Taggard, Joseph Auslander, Elinor Wylie, Louise Bogan, and others.

*The Measure*, one of a few important American poetry magazines, is interesting for its policy of electing an editor-in-chief and an assistant editor each quarter, from a larger editorial board. The result is a diversified editorial policy, and the contributions do not discredit the scheme. The selection of verses is almost uniformly of importance to American literary history. The range of contributors includes Robert Frost, Conrad Aiken, Wallace Stevens, Genevieve Taggard, Maxwell Anderson (who is the first editor-in-chief), Louise Bogan, Hart Crane, Elinor Wylie, Hervey Allen, and Donald Davidson.

❖

THE NEW PEN; devoted to the publishing of new writers' work and criticism of it. Nov. 1921-Apr./May 1922. Monthly. New York. NN
Supplement.
Editor: J. Moses.

One of several little magazines which publish criticism of their own work, a device aimed at helping contributors to improve their style and selection of subject matter. "By publishing a new writer's work in one issue and criticism of it in the following, the system of class instruction is employed and must result beneficially for those who are earnest and eager to learn." Among the contributions which this policy is successful in getting are poems by Jay G. Sigmund and Helene Mullins.

❖

THE REVIEWER. Feb. 15, 1921-Oct. 1925. Semimonthly. Richmond, Va. bk. rev., index (v. 5, 1925). NN
(Absorbed by *Southwest Review*, Apr. 1926.)
Editors: Emily Clark and Hunter Stagg (Feb. 15, 1921-Oct. 1924), (with Margaret Freeman, Feb. 15, 1921-Jan. 1923, Mary D. Street, Feb. 15, 1921-July 1923?, and James Branch Cabell [Oct.-Dec.1921]); Paul Green (1925).

Emily Clark's magazine, in its brief career, publishes much writing of first importance and much of less than first-rate quality. Its original purpose is to give free rein to Southern writers. James Branch Cabell edits three issues, and in other ways expresses a mild, patronizing interest. Some of the earliest poetry of Lynn Riggs appears in its pages—as does criticism by Edwin Muir, and fiction by Joseph Hergesheimer and Julia Peterkin. Contributions are extremely varied, having only the interest in promoting Southern letters as a guiding policy. In its last year, under Paul Green, the magazine acquires some unity of approach, and the regional interest is given consistent and unified attention.

THE SATURNIAN; a journal of art and literature. June/July [1921]-Mar. 1922? Irregular. Cleveland, Ohio    NN
Editor: Samuel Loveman.

In this magazine, the editor presents his own poetry and translations by him of the poetry of Heinrich Heine, Charles Baudelaire, and Paul Verlaine. In an essay on "Modern Poetry," issue of March 1922, he inveighs strongly against contemporary experiments, as a result of which, he says, "The few who steadfastly remain aloof, find themselves as steadfastly ostracized or outmoded."

✧

TEMPO; a magazine of poetry. June 1921-Winter 1923? Irregular. Danvers, Mass. bk. rev.    BI Y
(Absorbed by *Larus*, Feb. 1927.)
Editor: Oliver Jenkins.

A little magazine of poetry, *Tempo* publishes, among others, contributions by Haniel Long, Joseph Kling, Henry Bellamann, and Waldo Frank.

✧

THE TYRO; a review of the arts of painting, sculpture and design. 1921-1922. (Only two issues.) London. illus.    LC
Editor: Wyndham Lewis.

Another of several magazines under the editorial guidance of Wyndham Lewis, *The Tyro* announces as its object, "To be a rallying spot for those painters, or persons interested in painting, in this country, for whom 'painting' signifies not a lucrative or sentimental calling, but a constant and perpetually renewed effort. . . ." So that it might not neglect the literary arts, T. S. Eliot contributes "Notes on Current Letters," and there are poems by Robert McAlmon. Among those writing critical essays are Wyndham Lewis, John Rodker, and Herbert Read.

VOICES; a journal of verse. Autumn 1921+. Bimonthly. Boston. bk. rev.
Editor: Harold Vinal.    NN

*Voices* is patterned after, and resembles in many respects, Harriet Monroe's *Poetry*. The ideal of the magazine, in the words of Harold Vinal, its editor, "has been to give space to the new poets who need a hearing." Both in its poetry and in many of its critical statements, *Voices* gives a strong impression of its interest in and insistence upon the "subjective source and quality" of poetry. There is much alarmed ado over the "surrender" of some modern poetry to the harsh realities of "the modern distemper." *Voices* wishes to preserve poetry or to rescue it from the danger of modern attacks upon its sensibilities: "A poem is always to a greater or less degree a subjective matter, and complete objectivity in poetry is as unattainable as it is in philosophy or mathematics which strive to be the most objective of the sciences." Besides this critical-historical interest, *Voices* is important for the editorial discrimination of Mr. Vinal, which lifts it far above the level of many of its contemporaries and gives its list of contributions distinction and merit. The quality of the performance is not consistently good; the Muse blows hot and cold. Yet in its twenty or so years, *Voices* has given us the work of many important poets: Allen Tate, Mark Van Doren, Robert Penn Warren, Kenneth Fearing, Donald Davidson, Kenneth Patchen, Genevieve Taggard, and Hildegarde Flanner, among them.

✧

YOUTH; a magazine of the arts. 1921-Jan. 1922? Monthly. Chicago. bk. rev., illus.    ICU Y
Editors: Sam Putnam and H. C. Auer, Jr.
*Issues other than Oct. 1921 and Jan. 1922 not consulted.*

A magazine of critical comment and creative writing, *Youth* publishes poetry by Oscar Williams, Pierre Loving, Eunice Tietjens, Samuel Putnam, Oliver Jenkins, Henry Bellamann, and others; short stories by Edith Chapman, Basil Thompson, and Albert Goldstein; and critical essays by Ben Hecht, Clara Whiteside, and Emanuel Carnevali. In November 1921 appeared a parody of *Youth*, called *Puberty*, whose contributing editors were listed as "Julius Caesar" and "Q. Caius Lucretius." The contributions to *Youth* were parodied in name, title, and contents. Typical contributions to the parody issue are the story, "Erotic Doorknob—A Censored Chapter," by Achilles Hector, and the poem, "The Hour of Hate," by Miss Tummyfull.

---

## 1922

THE ADELPHI MAGAZINE. June 1922. (Only one issue.) London. illus.   NN
Editor: Henry Danielson.

The single issue of this magazine, beautifully printed, contains short stories by Deverell Dagnal, Bernard Muddiman, Jack Darmuzey, Alexander Griffiths, E. Powys Mathers, and Addington Osgoode; a poem by Walter Adolphe Roberts, and one unsigned poem.

✧

ART YOUNG QUARTERLY. First Quarter, 1922. (Only one issue.) New York. illus.   LC
(Caption title: *The Soldier; Art Young's first quarterly.*)
Editor: Art Young.

The *Art Young Quarterly* is primarily a review which draws for its materials upon Young's earlier magazine, *Good Morning*, but it contains as well some of his own work not published elsewhere.

CAPRICE; a poetry art magazine. Oct. 1922-May 1923. Irregular. Los Angeles, Calif. bk. rev.   Y
Editor: David N. Grakowsky.

A little poetry magazine which publishes, among others, poems by Louis Grudin, Harold Vinal, Jay G. Sigmund, Oscar Williams, Lew Sarett, and Sam Putnam, and several explanatory essays on modern poetry.

✧

CLAY; a quarterly literary exhibit. (Clay Guild.) Spring 1922-Summer 1923? Brooklyn, N.Y.   P Y

"The contributing authors of *Clay* aim at just publishing their work periodically, submitting themselves to the public without any intermediary." Contributions include poetry by Alter Brody and Henry Goodman, and prose fiction by Henry Goodman.

✧

THE FUGITIVE. Apr. 1922-Dec. 1925. Bimonthly. Nashville, Tenn.   NN
Board of editors: Walter Clyde Curry, Donald Davidson, Merrill Moore, John Crowe Ransom, James M. Frank, Sidney Mttron Hirsch, Stanley Johnson, Alec Brock Stevenson, Allen Tate, and others. Added December 1922, Jesse Ely Wills, Ridley Wills; February 1924, Robert Penn Warren; March 1925, Laura Riding. *In absentia* William Y. Elliot, William Frierson.

*The Fugitive* began at Vanderbilt University in April 1922, an attempt to commit to print the poetry and discussion of a small group of young students and teachers. These men—Allen Tate, Donald Davidson, John Crowe Ransom, Merrill Moore (Robert Penn Warren was added later)—have already established themselves as spokesmen for modern poetics and as poets of no mean merit. The magazine bears the distinctive mark of their undoubted genius in creation and their competence in criticism. Though most of them are in a nominal sense "academic men," the magazine from the start disavows any university ties, other than admitting that creation, and even experiment, is not particularly disturbed by the academic environment. The contributors to the first issue gave themselves pseudonyms, which were abandoned in the third. These poets "acknowledge no trammels upon the independence of thought, they are not overpoweringly academic, they are in tune with the times in the fact that to a large degree in their poems they are self-convicted experimentalists." Other poets who contributed from time to time include Hart Crane, Louis Untermeyer, John Gould Fletcher, Robert Graves, Witter Bynner, Harold Vinal, George Dillon, L. A. G. Strong, and David Morton.

❖

THE GOLDEN HIND; a quarterly magazine of art and literature. Oct. 1922-July 1924. London. bk. rev., illus. Editors: Clifford Bax and Austin O. Spare. NN

Like *Form* and other English magazines of art and letters, *The Golden Hind* is elaborate in format, rich in art reproductions of woodcuts, lithographs, pendrawings and prints, and carries a substantial number of important contributions: poems by F. S. Flint, W. H. Davies, and Laurence Housman; short stories by Aldous Huxley, Ethel Mayne, and Joseph Hergesheimer; and critical essays by Alec Waugh and Ford Madox Hueffer.

❖

LAUGHING HORSE; a magazine of satire from the Pacific slope. (University of California.) [Apr. 1922]-Dec. 1939. Irregular. Berkeley, Calif.; Guadalajara, Mexico; Santa Fé and Taos, New Mexico. bk. rev., illus. CU NN Supplements, nos. 1-2. Editors: Roy E. Chanslor and James T. Van Rensselaer, Jr. ([Apr. 1922]-Sept.? 1923); Willard Johnson ([Apr. 1922]-Dec. 1939).

In the first three issues the editors wrote under pseudonyms, Roy E. Chanslor as "L 13," James T. Van Rensselaer, Jr., as "Noel Jason," and Willard (Spud) Johnson, as "Bill Murphy" and "Jane Cavendish."

Two items in the early issues caused the editors some trouble, and especially Chanslor, who was jailed, tried, and acquitted, "on the charge of printing obscene matter." The items, both of them sent in by Spud Johnson from New Mexico, were a D. H. Lawrence letter and some excerpts from Upton Sinclair's *Goose Step*. With the eighth issue, *Laughing Horse* moved into the Southwest and became the special problem child of Spud Johnson. The history of this lively periodical (given briefly in a letter from Johnson to Mrs. Barbara Cowles of the University of California) is an interesting chapter in the story of the little magazine; its contents are an addition to the literature of the Southwest.

Since *Laughing Horse* exists primarily for the purpose of presenting the Southwest in letters, D. H. Lawrence's visits to Taos are given considerable attention. Lawrence's contributions to the magazine are what make it important for modern literature, and it is indispensable to a student of Lawrence. The issue of April 1926 is a special Lawrence number. In addition, there are contributions in poetry by Mabel Dodge Luhan and Arthur Davison Ficke, and critical essays by Ficke, D. H. Lawrence, Mary Austin, and others. An issue on censorship contains statements from Upton Sinclair, Lincoln Steffens, A. A. Knopf, John Dewey, Sherwood Anderson, and others.

*Laughing Horse* has published twenty-one numbers; Johnson promises that "Laughing Horse No. 22 will probably be published in Taos—after the war."

MANUSCRIPTS. Feb. 1922-Mar. 1923. Irregular. New York.   NN
Edited and published by contributors.

An original publishing effort, sponsored and financed by its contributors, *Manuscripts* may be expected to vary considerably in content and outlook. Among the contributions are poems by William Carlos Williams and criticism by Waldo Frank, Herbert Seligmann, Kenneth Burke, and others. Considerable attention is paid to photography as an art and to Alfred Stieglitz as an artist.

❖

THE MILWAUKEE ARTS MONTHLY. Sept. 1922-Mar./Apr. 1923. Milwaukee, Wis. bk. rev., illus.   NN
(Jan./Feb.-Mar./Apr. 1923 as: *Prairie*.)
Editor: Samuel Pessin.

The aim of *The Milwaukee Arts Monthly* is originally to prove the healthy state of American literature and to give evidence thereof. It is one of the more important documents of Midwestern letters, though the range of its contributions is not limited to the Midwest: poetry by Carl Sandburg, Virgil Geddes, Yvor Winters, John Fletcher, Louis Untermeyer, and others; prose by Conrad Aiken, Jean Toomer, Grant Code, and others.

❖

MODERN REVIEW. Autumn 1922-July 1924. Quarterly. Winchester, Mass. bk. rev.   NN
(Combined with *S 4 N* to form *Modern S 4 N Review*, Aug. 1926.)
Editor: Fiswoode Tarleton.

The brief but admirable career of Fiswoode Tarleton's *Modern Review* is a credit to the *avant garde* in America. The editors present interesting and sometimes important writers, and offer penetrating criticism of aesthetic matters. Contributions include poetry by Virgil Geddes, Allen Tate, Yvor Winters, and Maxwell Bodenheim; prose by Jean Toomer, Fiswoode Tarleton, Samuel Putnam, and Virgil Geddes. Putnam and Geddes also appear as contributing editors. The similarity in intellectual tastes and interests with those of the *S 4 N* group leads ultimately to a joining of their forces.

❖

THE NOMAD. Spring 1922-Summer 1924. Quarterly. Birmingham, Ala.
Editor: Albert A. Rosenthal.   LC NN

Rosenthal, previously with Joseph Kling and *The Pagan*, begins his own magazine in Alabama, publishing some of the writers who had appeared in Kling's magazine. "It has set no policy, but welcomes all forms of verse in its pages, especially the work of younger poets." Contributing poets include Ralph Cheyney, Harold Vinal, Helene Mullins, John R. Moreland, Joseph Kling, Jay G. Sigmund, Jean Toomer, Clement Wood, Samuel Putnam, and Carl Carmer.

❖

THE POETS' SCROLL; published in the interest of the younger poets. 1922-Apr. 1934. Monthly. Platter, Okla. index.   NN Y
Editors: Estil Alexander Townsend (1922-Nov. 1932); Wilbur T. Townsend (Dec. 1932-Apr. 1934).

A little poetry magazine which publishes a great variety of poems, among which are some few by Margaret Ball Dickson, Anton Romatka, and Jesse Stuart.

❖

SECESSION. Spring 1922-Apr. 1924. Irregular. Vienna; Berlin; Reutte, Austria; Florence, Italy; New York. bk. rev.   NN
Editor: Gorham B. Munson (with Matthew Josephson, Aug. 1922-Jan. 1923, and Kenneth Burke, Jan.-Sept. 1923).

Secession is interesting primarily for the personalities who made up its staff. Like those of *S 4 N* they disagree brilliantly, and underline the confusion that was criticism and creation in the twenties. Munson's own explanation: "Secession was, so to speak, a trial balloon cut loose for a short time and manned by a green crew." The great earnestness of its "director" is not always matched in his co-editors; but, in spite of the editorial turmoil (which, in fact, is part of its very interesting picture), the magazine affords an opportunity for brilliant (though sometimes only half-serious) criticism and creditable creation. The poetry and prose of Malcolm Cowley are important; much of Kenneth Burke's fiction is found here; Hart Crane's poetry appears. Other contributions include the poetry of Wallace Stevens, Marianne Moore, and William Carlos Williams. Yvor Winters' essay in poetics takes up all of the last number. Secession should be studied with *S 4 N*, as companion critical documents, indispensable to an understanding of the twenties.

❖

THE WAVE; a journal of art and letters. Jan. 1922-Oct. 1924. Irregular. Chicago; Copenhagen. illus. NN
Editor: Vincent Starrett (with Thomas Kennedy, Oct. 1924).

Vincent Starrett's Chicago little magazine fulfills adequately the requirements of independent literary creation: ". . . we shall print what pleases us, hoping that it will please you." The magazine prints very little of an experimental nature. Among the contributions are poems by Haniel Long, Maxwell Bodenheim, Oscar Williams, Allen Tate, and Witter Bynner; short stories by Arthur Machen and Vincent Starrett; and criticism by Carl Van Vechten and Llewellyn Jones.

## 1923

CASEMENTS; to the glimpses of youth, the time of most vivid feeling of truth and beauty. (Brown University.) Jan. 1923-June 1924? Bimonthly. Providence, R.I. NN Y
Editors: G. L. Cassidy, Leighton Rollins, H. D. Haskins, and others.

Brown University's literary magazine presents material of uncertain quality, much of it immature, some of it showing promise and achievement. Among the contributions which lend credit to the magazine are poems by Padraic Colum, George Woodberry, Harold Vinal, Joseph Auslander, Gamaliel Bradford, and Katherine Lee Bates.

❖

THE CHICAGO LITERARY TIMES. Mar. 1, 1923-June 1, 1924. Semimonthly. Chicago. bk. rev. LC NN
(Feb. 15-Apr. 1, 1924 as: *Ben Hecht's Chicago Literary Times.*)
Editor: Ben Hecht.

*The Chicago Literary Times*, edited and for the most part written by Ben Hecht and Maxwell Bodenheim (associate editor), is famous for its broad ironies and its parodies of the literary life of Chicago and New York. It is primarily a literary "stunt," immensely amusing, and has to be accepted as such. It is arranged in newspaper format, its shrieking headlines announcing "events" improbable and ludicrous. Ben Hecht's *1001 Afternoons in Chicago* appears in each issue, as does Bodenheim's "authorized" but incredible autobiography. Ring Lardner and Samuel Putnam also contribute. The magazine is a thoroughly enjoyable bit of "history" of Chicago's Bohemianism and how it grew.

❖

FOLIO. 1923-? (One issue only.) New York. illus. NN

Published by a group of contemporary artists and writers, each of whom is responsible for one page.

The motivating purpose of *folio* is to give each contributing artist freedom to select and to be responsible for his own work, without the hampering restrictions of editorial control. "There is no 'angel,' no editor, no cliques, no policy. Only the post-office is censor." In *folio* "the artists have entire freedom. They own it, sponsor it, and pay for it, themselves." Among the contributions are poems by Horace M. Kallen, Alfred Kreymborg, Countée P. Cullen, Donald Davidson, Horace Gregory, and Edwin Seaver.

❖

FOUR. Oct. 1923-Jan. 1925. Quarterly. Los Angeles, Calif. illus.    NN

"It is a portfolio of experiment in which four individuals attempt to present as a group, their latest work. . . . Four will reflect a drastic workshop wherein the group discuss the elements of life, particularly their interpretations through the medium of poetry." The four are H. Thompson Rich, W. H. Lench, David N. Grokowsky, and Yossef Gaer.

❖

FUTURIST ARISTOCRACY. Apr. 1923-? Frequency not given. New York. illus. Editor: N. L. Castelli.    ICU

*Futurist Aristocracy* is established for the purpose of explaining and illustrating the principles of futurism. A manifesto contributed by F. T. Marinetti suggests that "the essential elements of our poetry shall be courage, daring, and rebellion," and that literature, which has "hitherto glorified thoughtful immobility, ecstasy, and sleep," will, under the futurist dispensation, "extol aggressive movement, feverish insomnia, the double quick step, the somersault, the box on the ear, the fisticuff." These and other statements are given illustrative support by means of drawings by Charles Sheeler, Horace Brodzky, Rubczac, and John Marin, in the first issue.

❖

GERMINAL. July 1923-1924. Monthly. London. bk. rev., illus.    NN
*Editor not established.*

The magazine of the "Germinal Circle," whose purpose is "to assist in the artistic expression of current thought in order to bring art into contact with daily life and to use it as a means of expressing modern ideas and aspirations." Included are a number of translations from Russian writers: a short story by Maxim Gorky, and poems by Alexander Blok.

❖

THE GUILD PIONEER; prospecting on the frontier of arts and letters. (The Pioneer Writers Guild of America.) Jan.?-Sept. 1923. Monthly. New York. bk. rev., illus.    NN
Editors: David P. Berenberg, Ione M. Sweet, Lucy S. Clelland, and others.
*Issues previous to May 1923 not consulted.*

The Pioneer Writers Guild is an organization of "young writers who were meeting the usual coolness on the part of the existing papers, not because they represented any startling innovation in form or content, but because they were not nationally known." The literature presented by the magazine is in many cases immature; some of it shows promise. Contributions include poetry by Clement Wood and fiction by Norman Fitts.

❖

THE HUE AND CRY. June 30, 1923-1929? [n.s.] June 9, 1945+. Weekly. Woodstock, N.Y. illus.    LC NN
Editors: Frank Schoonmaker and William Harlan Hale (June 30, 1923-1929?); Ellen Robinson (June 9, 1945+).

*Issues between 1926 and 1929 not consulted.*

The object of *The Hue and Cry* is to express "the significant side" of Woodstock, N.Y. This magazine reflects the varied activities of the Woodstock community; it includes gossip about the arts, art reproductions, and some creative work: poems by Richard Le Gallienne, Glenway Wescott, and James Rorty, for example.

❖

THE LARIAT; a monthly roundup of western discussion and criticism . . . Jan. 1923-June 1929. Portland, Ore. bk. rev., index.   NN
Editors: E. Hofer (Jan. 1923-Dec. 1927); Frank J. Bellemin (Jan. 1928-June 1929).

The magazine is interesting for its belligerent defense of "pure and wholesome literature." The editor claims that the writers of the West have never been either prudish or smutty. There is much criticism of the "degenerate school" of modern letters—a school which includes writers of sex novels and the imagist poets.

❖

MANIKIN. 1923. (Only three issues.) Bonn, Germany; New York.   B
Editor: Monroe Wheeler.

The three issues of Monroe Wheeler's *Manikin* publish, among others, the poems of William Carlos Williams and Marianne Moore, and a collection of Janet Lewis' poems, called "The Indians in the Woods." Each issue is devoted to the work of a single author.

❖

THE MEDIATOR. Mar. 29, 1923-? Semi-monthly. Chicago.   ICU
Editor: Steen Hinrichsen.

The Mediator is established by the artist, Steen Hinrichsen, who is also associated with the magazine, *The Wave*. The editorial of the first issue suggests that *The Mediator* is an answer to a specific need felt by Mr. Hinrichsen: "It seems difficult, if not completely impossible, to expect active interest from artists and writers in a publication edited by a member of the one group. To remedy this and to preserve the unrestricted freedom of the editor of *The Wave* in his efforts to present only such finished products as his individual taste and judgment may choose, *The Mediator* has been conceived." The first issue publishes critical essays by Anthony Angarola, Ivan Sokoloff, Christian Whartoe, and John Drury.

❖

THE MODERN QUARTERLY. Mar. 1923-Fall 1940. Baltimore. bk. rev., index (v. 5, Winter 1928/29-Winter 1930/31).   NN
(Suspended, 1930-1931.) (Feb. 1933-June 1938 as: *The Modern Monthly*.) (Fall 1940, "V. F. Calverton Memorial Issue.")
Editors: V. F. Calverton (Mar. 1923-Summer 1940); Richel North (Mar.-Dec. 1923); Morton Levin (Mar. 1923-Fall 1924); Savington Crampton (Mar.-Dec. 1923); Samuel D. Schmalhausen (May/Aug. 1928-Autumn 1932); Max Eastman (Mar. 1934-Apr. 1935, Fall 1940); Edmund Wilson (Mar. 1934-Apr. 1935).

Others who appear in various editorial capacities include Ernest Sutherland Bates, Carleton Beals, Bruno Fischer, Nina Melville, S. L. Solon, Diego Rivera, Thomas Benton, Jerome Davis.

*The Modern Quarterly* is an organ of leftwing criticism of America. Under the very active and intelligent editorship of V. F. Calverton, it surveys and analyzes most of the important writers of its time. Its chief critical weapons are Marxism and psychoanalysis. The issue of Fall 1929 is of interest for its debate with Jolas and the *transition* group over the "Revolution of the Word." Critical articles are contributed by a large number of writers, including Waldo Frank, Floyd Dell, Michael Fraenkel, Rolfe Humphries, Herbert Read, and Sherwood Anderson.

❖

PALMS; a magazine of poetry. Spring 1923-Mar./Apr. 1940. Quarterly. Guadalajara, Mexico. bk. rev., illus.    NN
(Suspended, June 1930-Oct. 1936.)
Editors: Idella Purnell (Spring 1923-May 1930); Elmer Nicholas (Nov. 1936?-Mar./Apr. 1940), and others.

Among the associate editors appear Witter Bynner, Haniel Long, David Greenhood, Eda Lou Walton, and Joseph Auslander; among contributing editors are Hildegarde Flanner and Vachel Lindsay.

This distinctive little poetry magazine is published under the intelligent direction of Idella Purnell, friend and student of Witter Bynner. Among the contributions are poems by Bynner, Helen Hoyt, Harold Vinal, Willard Johnson, Lynn Riggs, Oliver Jenkins, Mabel Luhan, Ruth Lechlitner, Carl Rakosi, Marjorie Allen Seiffert, Countée Cullen, Donald Davidson, Hildegarde Flanner, John Crowe Ransom, Merrill Moore, and Genevieve Taggard.

❖

PEGASUS; a magazine of verse. 1923-1924. Bimonthly. San Diego, Calif. bk. rev.    LC Y
Editor: W. H. Lench.

A little magazine of verse which publishes, among others, the poetry of Henri Faust, Howard McKinley Corning, Helene Mullins, and Ben Field.

❖

RHYTHMUS; a magazine of the new poetry. Jan. 1923-May/June 1924. Monthly. New York. illus.    NN
(Suspended, Aug. 1923-Apr. 1924.)
(Superseded by *Parnassus*.)
Editors: Oscar Williams (with Gustav Davidson, Jan.-Feb. 1923, and Gene Derwood, June/July 1923-May/June 1924).

*Rhythmus* features the writing of important modern poets, accommodating them with an attractive format. Its appearance is, in fact, a bit "precious"; editorial sympathies, though never dogmatically announced, seem to be with whatever experimental writing is available. Contributions include poems by Amy Lowell, John Gould Fletcher, Edna St. Vincent Millay, Conrad Aiken, Louis Zukofsky, and Waldo Frank. The issue of May/June, 1924, is entirely given over to the verse of Eugene Jolas, free verse reminiscences of his days as a news reporter.

❖

VISION; a literary quarterly. May 1923-Feb. 1924. Sydney, Australia. illus.
Editors: Frank C. Johnson, Jack Lindsay, and Kenneth Slessor.    NN

An Australian literary magazine, *Vision* announces as its object "primarily to provide an outlet for good poetry, or for any prose that liberates the imagination by gaiety or fantasy." Its editors suggest that the postwar spirit, "that disintegrating condition of mind that is obsessed by physical decay," needs in some way to be abandoned and that consciousness ought soon to take "an upward turn." In the hope of turning the modern reader away from its brooding over postwar futility, *Vision* publishes poems by Hugh McCrae, Kenneth Slessor, Jack Lindsay, Robert Fitzgerald, and others, along with short stories, and some few critical essays on modern letters.

❖

THE WANDERER. June 1923-Nov. 1924. Monthly. San Francisco.    NN
Editors: Ethel Turner and Will Aberle.

The *Wanderer* is opposed to those who would seek the superficial "sweetness and light" in literature, and is moderately interested in the search for "new modes" in poetry. Its contributions include poems by George Sterling, Rolfe Humphries, Ted Olson, and Margaret Widdemer.

## 1924

THE BUCCANEER; a journal of poetry. Sept. 1924-Dec. 1926. Monthly. Dallas, Tex. bk. rev.     NN
(Suspended, Aug.-Dec. 1925.)
Editors: William Russell Clark (Sept. 1924-July 1925); Dawson Powell (1926).

The *Buccaneer* is a little poetry magazine, whose pages accommodate a great variety of poets, a few of them of considerable importance in modern American letters. Among the contributions worthy of special mention are poems by John Gould Fletcher, Joseph Auslander, Maxwell Bodenheim, Langston Hughes, and Margaret Widdemer.

✧

THE CIRCLE; a journal of verse. (The American Poetry Circle.) Jan. 1924-Nov./Dec. 1938. Bimonthly. Baltimore.     NN
Editors: Leacy Naylor Green-Leach (Jan. 1924-Apr./May 1937); Marcia Lewis Leach (June 1937-Nov./Dec. 1938).

The *Circle* is for the most part the expression of a single personality, that of its editor. There are occasional poems by Harold Vinal, Ralph Cheyney, and Ernest Hartsock. Clement Wood appears during 1925 and 1926 as a contributing editor.

✧

THE DECACHORD; a magazine for students and lovers of poetry. Mar./Apr. 1924+. Bimonthly. London. bk. rev. (Suspended, Aug. 1926-Jan. 1927, Mar.-June 1931.)     NN
Editors: Charles John Arnell (Mar./Apr. 1924-Jan./Feb. 1931) Philippa Hole (July/Aug. 1931+).

The *Decachord* ". . . owes its existence to the generous and (pecuniarily) unrewarded loyalty of its splendid contributors in this (uncommercial) fellowship in Art." Together with the verse published in its pages (much of it of excellent quality), critical articles on modern poetry are featured. For a period of years Edwin Faulkner appears as consulting editor and his essays on poetry are valuable contributions. Poets published in *The Decachord* include C. Day Lewis, Humbert Wolfe, Siegfried Sassoon, Robert Graves, Wilfred Childe, and Hugh MacDiarmid.

✧

THE DILL PICKLER. (Dill Pickle Club.) [1924-1925]. Irregular. Chicago. illus. Editor: Jack Jones.     NN

The official spokesman for the Dill Pickle Club of Chicago (Jack Jones, proprietor), which "is chartered in the state of Illinois as a Non-Profit organization for the Promotion of The Arts, Crafts, Literature and Sciences." The *Dill Pickler* is a mixture of the *Chicago Literary Times* type of burlesque journalism and the local-pride type of Bohemianism exhibited also by Bobby Edwards' *Quill*. It is an interesting document for the history of American Bohemianism. Volume I, No. 3, is a poetry number, and includes a sketch by Samuel Putnam on the reasons for the failure of much good poetry to receive a hearing, and a brief note on poetry by Llewellyn Jones.

✧

THE FORGE; a journal of verse. June 1924-Fall 1929. Quarterly. Chicago. bk. rev., illus., index (v. 3, Autumn 1927-Autumn 1928).     NN PP
Editors: Sterling North, Stanley S. Newman, Dexter Masters and others.
*Issues previous to Spring 1926 not consulted.*

Among others George H. Dillon appears as associate editor.

The *Forge* was founded in 1924, by the Poetry Club of the University of Chicago. Some of its contributors have subsequently become well known in modern letters; two of them, Jessica Nelson North and George H. Dillon, have been associated with *Poetry Magazine*. Among the promising young writers who contribute poetry to *The Forge* are Willard Maas, Ruth Lechlitner, Paul Engle, and Raymond Kresensky.

❖

THE GALLEON. Jan. 1924-Summer 1925. Quarterly. Kansas City, Mo. illus., index (v. 1, Jan.-Oct. 1924). (Oct. 1924-Summer 1925 as: *The Golden Galleon*.) (Supersedes *Miscellanea*.)
Editor: Alfred Fowler.     NN

A little magazine of creative and critical writing, *The Galleon* publishes, among others, the poems of Mahlon Leonard Fisher, George Sterling, Margaret Widdemer, William Rose Benét, and George Edward Woodberry; critical essays by Vincent Starrett, Margaret Widdemer, and Holbrook Jackson.

❖

GENTLY, BROTHER; a magazine of ideas. Mar.-Apr. 1924. Monthly. San Francisco. bk. rev.     LC
Editors: Lloyd S. Thompson and Chester W. Bonier.

The San Francisco little magazine, *gently, brother*, succeeds in gathering a few of the leftwing contributors to the New York magazine, *The Liberator*, but it does not announce a specific political policy: "The magazine will be without what is commonly thought of as a 'policy,'" it says in its first issue. "We believe in a few things—liberty, intelligence, beauty, doubt—and these will constitute the motif of the magazine. We do not always agree with each other, and on this we rely to keep *gently, brother*, from becoming stagnant. Upon one thing, however, the editors are in accord, resolved: that they will never praise a cause solely because they foresee its success, nor condemn one because it appears hopeless." Among the contributions are poems by Genevieve Taggard, George Sterling, Lloyd S. Thompson, James Rorty, Michael Gold, and others; prose by Michael Gold, Carter Brooke Jones, Maurice Browne, James T. Van Rensselaer, Jr., and others.

❖

THE GUARDIAN; a monthly journal of life, art and letters . . . Nov. 1924-Oct. 1925. Philadelphia. bk. rev., illus.     NN
Board of editors: Abraham N. Gerbovoy, Madelin Leof, Abe Grosner, and Herman Silverman.

*The Guardian* is one of a number of American little reviews. Critical and creative matter share equally in its table of contents. It is, above all, very much alive to and aware of modern letters, and contributes much to a discussion and evaluation of them. Waldo Frank, Kenneth Burke, Bernard DeVoto, and Gorham Munson print work of some importance to criticism. In the field of original writing, *The Guardian* presents poems by John Crowe Ransom, Allen Tate, John Gould Fletcher, Maxwell Bodenheim, and Genevieve Taggard; and prose fiction by Robert McAlmon.

❖

INTERLUDES; a magazine of verse. (Writers' Guild of Maryland.) Jan./Mar. 1924-1932/33. Quarterly. Baltimore. bk. rev., illus.     NN
Editor: William James Price.

Another of a group of little poetry magazines, sponsored by a writer's guild in the hope of discovering talent and furnishing it with an opportunity for publication, *Interludes* has the sponsorship of the verse Writers' Guild of Maryland. Among the poems published are those by William James Price, Howard McKinley Corning, Raymond Kresensky, Benjamin Appel, Ralph Cheyney, and Norman Macleod. Beginning with the issue of Spring 1930, *Interludes* becomes a "Magazine of Poetry and Prose" and publishes some fiction.

❖

MUSE AND MIRROR; a poetry magazine of the Northwest. (Seattle Poetry Club.) June 1924-Autumn/Winter 1931/32. 3 issues a year. Seattle, Wash.　　　　　　　　　　　NN Y
(Absorbed by *Frontier*, Apr. 1932.)
Editors: Whitley Gray (June-Aug. 1924); Helen M. Samsel (Sept. 1924-Sept. 1926?); Helen Maring (Oct. 1926-Autumn/Winter 1931/32).

A small poetry magazine which publishes some of the poems of Ernest Hartsock, Audrey Wurdemann, Howard McKinley Corning, David Cornel DeJong, and Jesse Stuart.

❖

1 9 2 4; a magazine of the arts. July-Dec. 1924. Monthly. Woodstock, N.Y. bk. rev., illus.　　　　　　　　　　NN
Editor: Edwin Seaver.

Under the capable editorship of Edwin Seaver, *1924* is an important review of modern letters. In it Munson and Pound quarrel over the intelligibility of "The Wasteland." Seaver's conviction is that a magazine should have no dogmatic policy: "For policy, if it be worth anything at all, is a living, dynamic thing. It is the spirit of the magazine, not a label. It is constantly changing, constantly renewing itself." In addition to a number of valuable critical articles, *1924* publishes the poetry of Hart Crane, Yvor Winters, Edwin Seaver, E. E. Cummings, and William Carlos Williams.

NINETY-EIGHT-SIX. 1924?-1926? Fortnightly. Colorado Springs, Colo.　Y
Editors: B. S. C. and L. L. C.
*Issues other than Jan. 7 and July 10, 1926, not consulted.*

A little magazine of poetry and informal gossip about the arts, *Ninety-Eight-Six* publishes, among others, poems by Ralph Cheyney, Louis Ginsberg, and Henry Harrison.

❖

ORPHEUS; a private journal of poetry. Dec. 1924-? Frequency not given. Pittsburgh, Pa.　　　　　　　　　　ICU
*Editor not established.*

A little magazine of poetry, *Orpheus* publishes, among others, poems by Stanley Burnshaw, Haniel Long, Robert Clairmont, Paul Sandoz, and Thomas Boggs.

❖

PARNASSUS; a magazine of poetry. 1924+. Frequency not given. New York.　　　　　　　　　　　　　　　B
(Supersedes *Rhythmus*.)
Editor: J. Nolan Vincent.

A little poetry magazine, *Parnassus* publishes, among others, the verse of Katherine Lee Bates, Clement Wood, Henry Bellamann, Helen Hoyt, Arthur H. Nethercot, Samuel Putnam, Eugene Jolas, and Harold Vinal.

❖

PHANTASMUS. May-July/Aug. 1924. Monthly. Pittsburgh, Pa.　　　　NN
Editor: J. G. Edmonds.

*Phantasmus* is a review of critical and creative writing. Sherwood Anderson's *A Story Teller's Story* runs in several issues. Ernest Boyd and Herbert S. Gorman publish important statements about American literature. There is poetry by Alfred Kreymborg, Witter Bynner, Genevieve Taggard, and others.

THE SPINNER; an Australasian magazine of verse. Oct. 1924-1927. Monthly. Melbourne, Australia. illus., index. Editor: R. A. Broinowski.   NN

The Spinner, published in the interests of advancing the cause of Australian poetry, prints, among others, the poems of Myra Morris, Adrian Lawlor, R. A. Broinowski, Molly Howden, Dorothea Mackellar, and E. M. England.

❖

TO-MORROW; the new Irish monthly. Aug.-Sept. 1924. Dublin. illus.   C
Editor not established.

To-Morrow is an important Irish little magazine. The editors "proclaim that we can forgive the sinner but abhor the atheist and that we count among atheists bad writers and Bishops of all denominations." Among the contributions are poems by W. B. Yeats and stories by Liam O'Flaherty and Lennox Robinson.

❖

THE TRANSATLANTIC REVIEW. (Text in English and French.) Jan. 1924-Jan. 1925. Monthly. Paris. bk. rev., illus., index.   NN
Editor: Ford Madox Ford.

Ford Madox Ford's "exile" review reflects the editor's interest in Conrad and in modern criticism. Ford's Paris-American friends join him in producing a review of considerable value; among them are Ernest Hemingway (whose criticism is more in evidence than his creative writing), Robert McAlmon, E. E. Cummings, and Ezra Pound. Gertrude Stein publishes a part of her "The Making of Americans." A selection from Joyce's "Work in Progress" appears in the issue of April 1924. There is much discussion of the America which the "exiles" have left behind—as though they are trying to justify their absence from native shores. For this and for other reasons, the magazine is an important literary document for the student of the twenties. Contributions include poetry by E. E. Cummings, Ezra Pound, William Carlos Williams; fiction by Robert McAlmon, John Dos Passos, Ernest Hemingway, Dorothy Richardson; and criticism by William Carlos Williams, Ford Madox Ford, and others.

## 1925

AESTHETE. Feb. 1925. (Only one issue.) New York. bk. rev., illus.   P
Editor: Walter S. Hankel.

Allen Tate explains that Aesthete, 1925 was an answer to an article by Ernest Boyd in The American Mercury, which had attacked the younger generation "on the ground that they were repeating the attitudes and the posturings of the aesthetes of the '90's. . . . Except for a story by Slater Brown, the entire issue was written over a Saturday night in January, 1925 and through most of the following day. . . ." (Typed statement included in Princeton University copy of Aesthete, 1925.) The single issue of Aesthete, 1925 is therefore a satirical reply by the "younger generation"—which includes, in this case, John Wheelwright, Slater Brown, Hart Crane, Allen Tate, Matthew Josephson, Kenneth Burke (who writes the advertising script for the back cover), and William Carlos Williams.

❖

THE BOHEMIAN. Jan.-Apr. 1925? Monthly. Toledo, Ohio.   NN
Editor: Ronald Walker Barr.

A small magazine of verses, which includes some few poems by Ernest Hartsock, Eda Lou Walton, and Paul Tanaquil, among others.

❖

THE BOHEMIAN; a journal of art and satire. Winter. [c 1925]-? Quarterly. Chicago.   ICU
Editors: Olin Joslin and H. A. Joslin.

A magazine of creative, critical, and satirical writing, *The Bohemian* contains, among other things, poems by Ottie Gill, Don Harper, and Anne Mary Seccombe, and fiction and prose sketches by Joseph Kalar, H. A. Joslin, and Earl Walters.

❖

CONTEMPORARY POETRY; a monthly publication devoted to the younger poets of the English language. Mar. 1925-1927. Dublin. bk. rev.   NN
(Spring 1926-1927 as: *Contemporary Poetry and Song*.)
Editor: G. Edmund Lobo.

The first editorial announces that *Contemporary Poetry* ". . . is being published primarily in the interests of the poets who are as yet unknown to a reading public." The magazine's tastes are, on the whole, conservative; another editorial assures us that "the paradox of *free* verse is outside the scope of the purely poetical magazine."

❖

THE DUMBOOK. Apr. 1925-Dec. 1926. Monthly. Mill Valley, Calif. bk. rev., illus.   LC Y
(Nov. 1925-Dec. 1926 as: *The San Francisco Review*.)
Editors: G. I. Marten (Apr.-Nov. 1925); David Warren Ryder (Apr. 1925-Dec. 1926); Marie de L. Welch (Dec. 1925-Dec. 1926).

A magazine of interest to students of the literature of the Pacific Coast, *The Dumbook* also discusses problems social and political of the California area. Its contents include poetry by Ingeborg Torrup, Robert Schlick, and John Laurvik, a translation by Arthur Ryder from the Hindu Panchatantra, fiction by William Woodbridge, and essays by Carey McWilliams and James Stevens.

❖

FANTASIA. Jan. 1925-? Monthly. South Pasadena, Calif. bk. rev., illus.   NN
Editors: G. Bishop Pulsifer and George Hill Hodel.

A little magazine of poetry, whose purpose as the editors see it is "To offset the cacophonous drabness of daily life, to introduce the stranger harmonies, the rarer harmonies. . . ." *Fantasia* publishes, among others, poems by Sadakichi Hartmann, Beulah May, and W. A. Beardsley.

❖

THE GAMMADION. 1925?-Autumn 1926? Quarterly. Birmingham, Ala. bk. rev.   Y
Editor: Jack Nelson.
*Issues other than Autumn 1926 not consulted.*

The *Gammadion* contains a varied assortment of writings, among which a poem by Carl Carmer and a short story by Jay G. Sigmund may be singled out as deserving of mention.

❖

GOLDEN QUILL; a quarterly magazine of verse. Summer 1925-Spring 1926? Muscatine, Iowa. bk. rev.   NN
Editor: Carroll D. Coleman.

A small magazine of verse which includes a few of the poems of Jay G. Sigmund, Ernest Hartsock, Henry Harrison, and Raymond Kresensky.

❖

THE GYPSY; Cincinnati all poetry magazine. 1925-1937. Quarterly. Cincinnati, Ohio.   LC Y
Editorial board: H. A. Joslen, George Elliston, Halley Groesbeck, T. C. O'Donnell, and others.

A little magazine of verse, which publishes, among others, the poetry of Willard Johnson, Clement Wood, Joseph Kalar, Frances Frost, Michael Fraenkel, Norman Macleod, Raymond Kresensky, Padraic Colum, Alfred Kreymborg, Conrad Aiken, Lucia Trent, John Dillon, and Glenn Ward Dresbach. Two issues of *The Gypsy* (the first is misspelled *Gipsy*), edited by H. A. Joslen, were published in Norwood, Ohio. Though these issues bear no date, they are presumably "experimental issues," probably published before the magazine moved to Cincinnati. For this reason they are included with the Cincinnati magazine, and their contents are considered as belonging with those of that magazine.

❖

THE HARP; a magazine of verse. May 1925-Feb. 1932. Bimonthly. Larned, Kan. bk. rev. NN
Editors: Israel Newman (May 1925-Aug. 1926); May Williams Ward (Sept./Oct. 1926-Jan./Feb. 1931); Eunice Wallace (Mar./Apr. 1931-Jan./Feb. 1932).

A small magazine of verses which has published some of the poems of Howard McKinley Corning, George H. Dillon, Hervey Allen, Clement Wood, George Sterling, Ludwig Lewisohn, Benjamin Musser, Genevieve Taggard, Harold Vinal, Alfred Kreymborg, Eunice Tietjens, Paul Engle, Mary Austin, and others.

❖

INTERNATIONAL ARTS. July-Aug. 1925. Monthly. New York. bk. rev., illus.
Editor: Joseph Kling. Y

In *International Arts* Joseph Kling presents a variety of contributors, who write poems, short stories, and sketches, and critical essays and reviews. Among the contributions are poems by Stanley Burnshaw, Kenneth Fearing, Oliver Jenkins, Helene Mullins, and Michael Fraenkel; short stories and sketches by Paul Eldridge and John Loftus; a review by Fraenkel of "The Reality Element in the Drama"; and several drawings and sketches.

❖

THE MESA; a quarterly magazine of poetry. (Colorado Springs Poetry Society.) Jan.-July/Sept. 1925. Colorado Springs, Colo. NN
Editor: Albert Hartman Daehler.

A little magazine of poetry, *The Mesa* "is committed to no particular school or fashion in poetry; its only program is a sincere devotion to beauty, whether it be found in the traditional forms of English verse or in any of the many interesting patterns evolved by recent experiment." Among the contributions are poems by Margaret Tod Ritter, Ted Olson, Russell W. Davenport, and Harry Noyes Pratt.

❖

THE NEW COTERIE. Nov. 1925-Summer/Autumn 1927. Quarterly. London. illus. NN
(*Supersedes Coterie.*)
*Editor not established.*

*The New Coterie* aims for a certain distinction in format and content. "It will ... welcome contributions from all writers who satisfy the sole criterion of merit, whether they have already received general recognition or not." As one of many English magazines of arts and letters, *The New Coterie* publishes the contributions of many important modern writers: stories by Liam O'Flaherty, D. H. Lawrence, H. E. Bates, Karel Čapek, and Louis Golding; the poems of Robert McAlmon, John Gould Fletcher, and Aldous Huxley.

❖

OPEN VISTAS; a bi-monthly of life and letters. Jan.-Dec. 1925. Stelton, N.J. bk. rev., illus. P
Editors: Hippolyte Havel and Joseph Ishill.

*Open Vistas* carries much editorial comment; the format and selection of material resemble slightly those of Monohan's *Phoenix*. Hippolyte Havel's own statements about art and the social life are of primary interest, in view of his own career as a Greenwich Villager and a rebel. There are poems by Rose Florence Freeman, Israel Newman, and others. The magazine also contains excerpts from writers of the past.

THE ORACLE; a magazine for the lovers of literature and literary workers. (The Writers' Guild.) Mar. 1925-Sept. 1928. Quarterly. New York. bk. rev. (Absorbed by *Bozart and Contemporary Verse*, Mar./Apr. 1930.)  NN
Editor: William Albert Broder.

The principal aim of *The Oracle* is to encourage young writers, both through criticism of their work and through publication of the work of better known artists, examples of "the finished product." In an article on Sherwood Anderson, Maxwell Bodenheim lays all the faults of that writer at the door of his "meeting with Sigmund Freud." Among the more important contributions are poems by Oliver Jenkins, Raymond Kresensky, Michael Fraenkel, Kathleen Tankersley Young, and Ralph Cheyney.

❖

THE OUTLANDER. June?-Aug. 10, 1925? Irregular. Ann Arbor, Mich.  Y
Editors: Mary Elizabeth Cooley, Sue Grundy Bonner, and Dorothy Tyler.
*Issues other than July 27-Aug. 10, 1925, not consulted.*

The *Outlander* is "privately printed" by Mary Elizabeth Cooley, Dorothy Tyler, and Sue Grundy Bonner. Poems and stories are contributed by the three editors.

❖

PAN, POETRY AND YOUTH. June 1925-Apr. 1926. Monthly. Notre Dame, Ind. bk. rev.  NN
Editors: Charles Phillips and H. McGuire (with Dennis O'Neill, Mar.-Apr. 1926).

Among those of the advisory board are: Edwin Markham, Conrad Aiken, Witter Bynner, Carl Sandburg, Don Marquis, Vachel Lindsay, John G. Neihardt, Ina Coolbrith, Maxwell Bodenheim, and George Sterling.

"*Pan* wants to prove that there are young people today who can write poems as beautiful as dusk-tinted clouds, and prose as forceful and clean-cut as obelisks." The contributions are for the most part slight, though there are poems from the pens of Benjamin Musser, Willard Johnson, Louis Ginsberg, and Glenn Ward Dresbach. A special Vachel Lindsay number, April 1926, features that poet's "The Babbitt Jambouree."

❖

THE PILGRIMS ALMANACH. [1925-1926.] Irregular. New York. illus.  NN
Editors: Ivan Narodny (with Robert W. Chandler, No. 2, [1925]).

The magazine of a select group of artists and writers, *The Pilgrims Almanach* announces early and often the revolt of the young intellectual against the despiritualizing effect of the machine and of business life. "Our minds are shadows of our machines and markets. Our stage, art and altar are petty professional specialities pursued by men and women like every other industrial work." By means of reproductions and poetry, drama, and allegorized fiction, the members of this group translate their rebellion into art. The group includes Ivan Narodny, Benjamin De Casseres, and "Jenghis Khan, Jr."

❖

THE TANAGER. (Grinnell College.) Dec. 1925+. Quarterly. Grinnell, Iowa.
Editors: Frank Dewey (Dec. 1925-June 1926); Wayne Gard (Dec. 1925-Mar. 1930); Roma Kauffman (Dec. 1925-June 1926); Margaret Lemley (Dec. 1925-May 1927); Eleanor Lowden (Dec. 1925-Mar. 1927, May 1930-July 1933), and others.  NN
Upon relinquishing the editorship, Eleanor Lowden continues her association with *The Tanager* until June 1942.

Grinnell College's quarterly sponsors writing not only from campus sources but also by writers of some note from beyond campus boundaries. Though there are some few essays on matters beyond the province of the arts, the bulk of the material includes critical and original writing. Among the contributions are poems by Lew Sarett, Raymond Kresensky, Carl Sandburg, Jay G. Sigmund, Paul Engle, Howard Nutt, Alan Swallow, and George F. Meeter; short stories by Jay G. Sigmund, Roderick Lull, August Derleth, Raymond Kresensky, Hubert Creekmore, Karlton Kelm, Hallie Flanagan, William March, Eudora Welty, and others. The great bulk of the original writing is by Midwestern writers.

❖

THIS QUARTER. Spring 1925-Oct./Dec. 1932. Paris; Milan; Monte Carlo. bk. rev., illus., index (v. 4, Sept. 1931-June 1932). NN
(Suspended, Summer 1927-June 1929.) Editors: Ernest Walsh (1925-1926); Ethel Moorhead (1925-1927); Edward W. Titus (1929-1932).

Ernest J. Walsh and Ethel Moorhead manage three brilliant issues of *This Quarter*: Spring 1925 (Paris); Autumn-Winter, 1925-1926 (Milan); and Spring 1927 (Monte Carlo). The third issue is published after Walsh's death; it is a memorial to him, publishes much of his criticism, and defends him against his detractors. Basically the editorial policy of these issues is founded upon encouragement to rather than interference with new writers: "The artist will be edited in these pages in terms of himself . . . we are against literary politics and literary politicians. . . ." The first issue is dedicated to Ezra Pound, and contains a series of tributes to him; the third issue retracts the dedication, and visits the editorial fury of Miss Moorhead upon his head. Included among the contributions to the first three issues is the poetry of Yvor Winters, Isidore Schneider, Ernest Walsh, H. D. (fragment of a verseplay), Ezra Pound, Eugene Jolas, and Kenneth Fearing; fiction by Ernest Hemingway, Kay Boyle, Robert McAlmon, "Bryher" (McAlmon's wife), James Joyce (an extract from "Work in Progress"), and Morley Callaghan. *This Quarter* is resumed in Paris in the Summer of 1929, under the editorial direction of Edward Titus. Its new appearance is honorable but less exciting. Titus presents many translations from the German and French, and is concerned with "prize award" poems. The issue of September 1932 presents one of the best treatments of surrealism to be found. Included among the contributions to Titus' magazine is the poetry of Robert P. Warren, William Carlos Williams, Aldous Huxley, E. E. Cummings, Yvor Winters, Selden Rodman, J. Bronowski, Louis MacNeice, and Paul Eluard; criticism by Paul Valéry, Richard Aldington, Stefan Zweig, Ludwig Lewisohn, and Joseph Wood Krutch; fiction by Ernest Hemingway, Erskine Caldwell, Sherwood Anderson, James T. Farrell, and Karlton Kelm.

❖

TWO WORLDS; a literary quarterly devoted to the increase of the gaiety of nations. Sept. 1925-June 1927. New York. index (v. 1, Sept. 1925-June 1926). NN
Editor: Samuel Roth.
Arthur Symons, Ezra Pound, Ford Madox Hueffer, and Paul Morand appear as contributing editors.

Samuel Roth's magazine, dedicated "to the increase of the gaiety of nations," publishes, among other things, selections from James Joyce's "unfinished work" (*Finnegans Wake*), probably without Joyce's authorization. The magazine is interested in, among other matters, the Oscar Wilde question, and publishes much discussion of it. Translations from the French (by Arthur Symons) and the Russian are frequent. Contributions also include poetry by Louis Zukofsky, Carl Rakosi, Yvor Winters, and D. H. Lawrence.

VERSE; the quarterly review of verse. Winter 1925-Winter 1926. Philadelphia. bk. rev.   NN
Editor: Tod.

The contributing editors are: Katherine Lee Bates, Maxwell Bodenheim, William Stanley Braithwaite, Glenn Ward Dresbach, Robert Frost, John G. Neihardt, Jessie B. Rittenhouse, Lew Sarett, Witter Bynner, and Margaret Widdemer and others.

Among the contributions to the little magazine of poetry, Verse, are the poems of Glenn Ward Dresbach, Margaret Widdemer, and Harold Vinal.

## 1926

THE AMERICAN PARADE; a quarterly magazine—without policy. 1926. (Only four issues.) New York. bk. rev., illus.   NN
Editor: W. Adolphe Roberts.

The editor of *The American Parade* prefers not to announce any aesthetic or social theory; he is interested, however, in American life, and welcomes any capable literary expression of it. Walter Haviland's studies of the "seven American arts" recall Robert Coady's more vigorous championship of American life, in *The Soil*. The magazine is bitter about the expatriates in Paris. The editorial position tends to emphasize the platitude in aesthetics: Art is "the expression of an ecstasy. It is the spirit's overflow of emotion. . . ." Among the contributions we note poetry by Helene Mullins, George Sterling, Richard Le Gallienne; stories by Louise Townsend Nicholl, Louis Adamic, Orrick Johns, Gamaliel Bradford, Jacques Le Clercq.

❖

THE DRIFT-WIND; a tramp magazine issued for the love of literature. Apr. 1926+. Monthly. North Montpelier, Vt. index. cum index: v. 1-16 (Apr. 1926-June 1942).   NN
(June 1927+ as: *Drift-Wind from the North Hills*; other slight variations.)
Editors: Walter John Coates (Apr. 1926-July/Aug. 1941); Nettie Allen Coates (Sept. 1941+).

*Drift-Wind* begins as an amateur poetry magazine. Its exclusive purpose is to popularize Vermont poets, traditional and new. During its long career it enlarges its scope of interest to include other than Vermont poets and improves its contents. Though it is not one of the nation's important poetry magazines, it is a tribute to the patience and persistence of its editor. Contributions of some note include the poetry of Norman Macleod, Harold Vinal, Frances Frost, Ralph Cheyney, and August Derleth.

❖

FIRE!! devoted to younger Negro artists. Nov. 1926-? Quarterly. New York. illus.   Y
Editor: Wallace Thurman ("in association with Langston Hughes and Zora Neale Hurston").

This little magazine of Negro writings publishes, among other things, poems by Countée Cullen, Langston Hughes, and Helene Johnson, and short stories by Wallace Thurman and Gwendolyn Bennett.

❖

THE LANTERN. (American Literary League.) Nov. 1926+. Irregular. New York. bk. rev.   NN
Editors: C. B. McAllister, Margarette Ball Dickson, and Joseph Dean (Nov. 1926-Jan./Feb. 1929); Anne Arrington Tyson (Mar./Apr. 1929-Winter 1930), and others.

Upon relinquishing her editorship, Margarette Ball Dickson remains as contributing editor until Oct./Nov. 1931.

A magazine of poetry, announced as the "official organ of the American Literary League," The Lantern publishes some of the poems of Benjamin Musser, Stanton Coblentz, and Oscar Williams.

❖

MODERN S 4 N REVIEW. Aug. 1926-? Monthly. Boston. bk. rev. (Formed by the union of S 4 N and Modern Review.)     MWA
Editor: Norman Fitts.

The editors of Modern Review and S 4 N combine forces with interesting results. Much the same critical controversy goes on in the new magazine as was characteristic of S 4 N. The contributors to Modern S 4 N Review are much the same as those who made the other two magazines interesting additions to little magazine history. Controversial swordplay over the merits of Gorham Munson's Secession takes up a sizable portion of the issue for August 1926. Contributions include poems by Malcolm Cowley, E. E. Cummings, and Thaddeus Piper. Fiswoode Tarleton appears as associate editor.

❖

NEW MASSES. May 1926+. Monthly. New York. bk. rev., illus.     NN
Editors: Egmont Arens and Hugo Gellert (May 1926-Apr. 1928); Michael Gold (May 1926-Sept. 1933?); Joseph Freeman (May-Oct. 1926, June 1927-Apr. 1928); James Rorty and John Sloan (May-Oct. 1926); William Gropper (Feb. 1927-Apr. 1928), and others.

Among the contributing editors are Sherwood Anderson, Carleton Beals, Van Wyck Brooks, Howard Brubaker, Stuart Chase, Floyd Dell, Max Eastman, Waldo Frank, Arturo Giovannitti, H. J. Glintenkamp, Lewis Mumford, Eugene O'Neill, Lola Ridge, Carl Sandburg, Genevieve Taggard, Art Young, Norman Macleod, and many others.

Though the New Masses was soon enough to turn to a serious consideration of political and economic issues, its earlier issues (1926-1932) deserve inclusion here because they continue the spirit of the old Masses and The Liberator. No. 1 presents a mock "Dialogue in Limbo" between Anatole France and Lenin, written by Babette Deutsch, and cartoons by William Gropper. Other contributions include Robinson Jeffers' poem, "Apology for Bad Dreams," and poems by Mark Van Doren, Witter Bynner, and George Sterling. The contents of the early issues are a mixture of radical political comment and satire (both in cartoons and in editorial essays) and the writing of poems and stories only incidentally related to the leftwing movement. There are poems by MacKnight Black, Lola Ridge, Eugene Jolas, Carl Rakosi, Kenneth Fearing, Horace Gregory, and others; and stories by David Gordon, D. H. Lawrence, Whit Burnett, and others. Cartoon drawings by Boardman Robinson and Art Young remind the reader of The Masses and Liberator days. Critical essays by Joseph Freeman appear frequently in these early volumes; also printed are essays on one and another aspect of leftwing criticism by Genevieve Taggard, Kenneth Fearing, Michael Gold, and others. The New Masses has steadily advanced to the position of a radical political magazine. It is now a "Stalinist" weekly, and literary interests and activities are fairly well confined to the book review section. The first step in that direction came in 1928, when Michael Gold became the sole editor. In the thirties the New Masses enjoyed, with other magazines, the great interest taken by writers in radical politics; and, at the turn of the decade, when Communists were being divided into "Trotskyists" and "Stalinists," the magazine took the latter position and has since held to it. A study of the New Masses together with its predecessors, the old *Masses* and *The Liberator*, will give a clear picture of the leftwing literary development from 1911 to the present.

❖

POETRY FOLIO. Mar./Apr. 1926-May/June 1929. Irregular. Pittsburgh, Pa. Editors: Stanley Burnshaw (Mar./Apr. 1926-Mar./Apr. 1927, May/June 1929); Milton Kovner (Mar./Apr.-July/Aug. 1926, Sept./Oct. 1927, May/June 1929); E. Merrill Root (Jan./Feb. 1928); Haniel Long (Apr./May 1928). H NN
Haniel Long also appeared as contributing editor in the early issues.

A little magazine of verse and brief critical notes, its aim to publish "those poems and ideas on poetry which have the most enduring qualities." Contributions include poems by Haniel Long, Harold Vinal, Eda Lou Walton, Howard McKinley Corning, Witter Bynner, and E. Merrill Root.

❖

THE STRATFORD MAGAZINE; a periodical for creative readers. Feb. 1926-Apr. 1932. Monthly. Boston. bk. rev. NN Editor: Henry T. Schnittkind.

The purpose of *The Stratford Magazine* is to present a varied fare for what it calls "Creative Readers." To this end it features translations from the work of foreign authors, together with a liberal sampling of modern American and English writing. Examples of the latter are poems by Harry Kemp, Margaret Tod Ritter, Paul Eldridge, Helene Mullins, Raymond Kresensky, Royall Snow, Winfield T. Scott, Michael Fraenkel, and Merrill Moore.

❖

TWO WORLDS MONTHLY; devoted to the increase of the gaiety of nations. [1926]-Sept. 1927. New York. NN Editor: Samuel Roth.

With much the same kind of format and table of contents as *Two Worlds*, *Two Worlds Monthly*, like its predecessor, is "devoted to the increase of the gaiety of nations." It promises in the first issue that it "will be gay. It will be sophisticated. It will present fine fiction by noted writers. . . . And it will speak freely without ever overstepping the bounds of good taste." Among the contributions designed to fulfill the magazine's announced purpose are those by important and already well established contemporaries. To supplement these, Samuel Roth draws upon translations from poetry and prose of foreign writers (Heinrich Heine, Arthur Schnitzler, among them) and has much material from prominent British writers, such as D. H. Lawrence, A. E. Coppard, and Laurence Housman. Joyce's *Ulysses* appears in installments through most of the magazine's career. It is this unauthorized use of Joyce's work which provoked protests from Joyce and his many friends, and an injunction against Roth's piracy was finally issued in December 1928, over a year after the magazine had ceased publication. *Two Worlds Monthly*, like its predecessor, is the result of its editor's eclectic tastes and of his interest in foreign literatures.

❖

THE VOICE; a magazine for lovers of verse and for students of poetry. Mar. 1926-Spring 1927. Quarterly. North Manchester, Ind. NN Editor: Lulu Frances Warner.

A little poetry magazine which publishes the verse of N. Bryllion Fagin, Henry Harrison, and Raymond Kresensky.

❖

WILL-O'-THE-WISP; a magazine of verse. (Poetry Society of Suffolk.) May 1926-Winter 1935. Bimonthly. Suffolk, Va. NN Editor: E. E. Taylor.

A small poetry magazine, publishing, among others, the poems of Benjamin Musser, Ernest Hartsock, J. Corson Miller, and Josephine Johnson.

## 1927

THE AMERICAN CARAVAN; a yearbook of American literature. 1927-1936. New York. NN
(1929 as: *The New American Caravan*; 1936, *The New Caravan*.) Editors: Van Wyck Brooks (1927); Alfred Kreymborg, Lewis Mumford, and Paul Rosenfeld (1927-1936).

An annual volume of new American writing, *The American Caravan* is begun in 1927 "in the interests of a growing American literature." Its editors explain in the first volume that its establishment was an answer to the need for "a medium able to accommodate a progressively broader expression of American life. . . ." The annual provides examples of the work of twentieth century American writers in the fields of poetry, fiction, the drama, and criticism. The contributions to *The American Caravan* do not demonstrate the great interest in experimental writing which is immediately obvious in any one of James Laughlin IV's *New Directions* annuals. To *The American Caravan* annuals almost all of the writers of our American literary world contribute at one time or another. ❖

BOZART; the bi-monthly poetry review. Sept./Oct. 1927-Mar./Apr. 1935. Atlanta, Ga. bk. rev., illus. NN
(Jan./Feb. 1930 as: *Bozart and Contemporary Verse Combining Japm*; Mar./Apr. 1930-Mar./Apr. 1935, *Bozart and Contemporary Verse Combining Japm and The Oracle*.) (Absorbed *Japm*, and *Contemporary Verse*, Jan. 1930, *The Oracle*, Mar. 1930.) (Absorbed by *The Westminster Magazine* to form *Bozart-Westminster*, Spring 1935.)

Editors: Ernest Hartsock (Sept./Oct. 1927-Nov./Dec. 1930); Mary Brent Whiteside (Mar./Apr.-July/Aug. 1931); Thornwell Jacobs and James E. Routh (Sept./Oct. 1931-Jan./Feb. 1933); Robert Leseur Jones (May/June 1932-Jan./Feb. 1933); Wightman F. Melton (Mar./Apr. 1933-Mar./Apr. 1935), and others.

*Bozart* is Ernest Hartsock's reply to Henry L. Mencken's remark that the South is "the Sahara of the Bozart." By avoiding sectionalism in its editorial selection, the magazine hopes also to avoid the fate of many short-lived Southern magazines. "*Bozart* is to be dedicated to no exploitation of home talent nor to jingoism actuated by sentimental lovers of a too well-remembered past." With the issue of March/April, 1931, *Bozart* moves to Oglethorpe University, where it is ultimately absorbed by *The Westminster Magazine*. *Bozart* publishes some work by capable American poets: Mark Van Doren, Norman Macleod, Charles Henri Ford, and others. During 1930-1932 Benjamin Musser acts as associate editor. ❖

THE ENEMY; a review of art and literature. Jan. 1927-First quarter, 1929. Irregular. London. illus. NN
(Suspended, Oct. 1927-Dec. 1928.) Editor: Wyndham Lewis.

Wyndham Lewis' long and exciting career as painter, novelist, and one-man revolution receives its best literary expression in the few lengthy issues of this magazine. From the beginning, Lewis assumes responsibility for everything in *The Enemy*; in fact, he has chosen the name carefully, for "[it] secures for it this virtue: that it does not arrive under the misleading colours of friendship or of a universal benevolence." The magazine is, therefore, not impartial; Lewis is convinced that his age is in need of a "thorough cleansing." During the course of its career, *The Enemy* publishes Lewis' critical estimates of Bergson, Freud, Joyce, Gertrude Stein, D. H. Lawrence, and Sherwood Anderson, and engages in a spirited debate with Jolas' *transition* over the critical standards of that magazine. With the possible exception of *transition*, *The Enemy* received more notice in press and periodicals than any other little magazine—a recognition of, if not a tribute to, the intransigence of Lewis' mind and the brilliant effectiveness of his criticism. There are very few contributors, other than Lewis: T. S. Eliot writes an essay, and there are poems by Laura Riding and Roy Campbell.

❖

THE EXILE. Spring 1927-Autumn 1928. Semiannual. Dijon, France; Chicago. NN
Editor: Ezra Pound.

The four issues of Pound's *Exile* afford him an opportunity for full expression of his editorial temperament. Pound's career, since the early days of *The New Freewoman*, *The Egoist*, and *Poetry*, has always been marked by a wish to dogmatize, impress, or shock. He regards only a very small group of persons intelligent enough for conversation or friendship. There is always something of the poseur in Pound's attitudinizing, but his judgment, especially in matters aesthetic, is often surprisingly good, and always refreshing. Despite all this, *Exile* is a disappointment, probably because Pound operates most successfully as an "advisor" to editors. The title of the magazine is descriptive of its contents; herein are literary expressions of a few of the exiles from America: Ernest Hemingway's two-line poem, "Neo-thomist Poem," narrative by Robert McAlmon and John Rodker, poems by Carl Rakosi and others. No. 3 contains Yeats's "Sailing to Byzantium." Much space is taken by editorial announcements and opinions—scorn of the American mind, resentment at the U.S. Customs Office (*Exile* was withheld by customs officials), and proud recognition of the artist's position in a world otherwise overwhelmed by mediocrity.

❖

THE FIGURE IN THE CARPET; a magazine of prose. Oct. 1927-May 1929. Monthly. New York. NN
(Dec. 1928-May 1929 as: *Salient*.)
(No issues published June-Nov. 1928.)
Editors: Hansell Baugh (Oct. 1927-May 1928); John Riordan (Dec. 1928-May 1929).

For most of its career, *The Figure in the Carpet* is governed by a serious and unifying purpose—to investigate the aesthetic qualities and purposes of prose writing and to evaluate the twentieth century contributions to the history of prose. The magazine is eminently successful in achieving its purpose: William Troy writes important essays on the modern novel and tries his own skill in prose narrative; Hansell Baugh evaluates the ideas which have influenced twentieth century thought; Waldo Frank and Gorham B. Munson contribute critical and creative prose writings. With the issue of December 1928, the magazine changes its name to *Salient*, its editorial staff, and its point of view. Poetry appears for the first time, and the critical essays are less competently written.

❖

FREE VERSE; a contemporary gesture. 1927-Summer 1928? Quarterly. Brooklyn, N.Y. NN Y
Editor: Gremin Zorn.

Free verse, center of controversy in the second decade of our century, the subject of numerous articles, essays, and editorials, is the only object of attention in this magazine. Among the poets who "experiment" with free verse are Herman Spector, Kenneth Fearing, Eli Siegel, Charles Henri Ford, and Kathleen Tankersley Young.

THE HOUND AND HORN; a Harvard miscellany. Sept. 1927-July/Sept. 1934. Quarterly. Portland, Me. bk. rev., illus., index. NN
Consultative committee: Kenneth B. Murdock (Sept. 1927); Julian W. Mack (Dec. 1927-June 1928); Conrad Aiken, Martin Mower, William Allan Neilson, George Parker Winship (Sept. 1927-July/Sept. 1929). Editors: Bernard Bandler II (Jan. 1929-Sept. 1933); R. P. Blackmur (1929); Lincoln E. Kirstein (Jan. 1929-Sept. 1934); Varian Fry (Oct./Dec. 1929); A. Hyatt Mayor (Oct./Dec. 1931-Sept. 1933).

The *Hound and Horn* begins as a Harvard magazine: "Its pages will be open to creative work in any field and on any subject, provided that work is of a sufficiently non-technical nature to assure a general Harvard interest." This limitation does not prevent the magazine from publishing good material, but it does act as a check upon the scope of its inclusions. At the end of 1930 *The Hound and Horn* moves its editorial offices to New York City, under Bernard Bandler II and Lincoln Kirstein. In 1933 Kirstein becomes sole editor, with Allen Tate and Yvor Winters as regional associates. The difference between the earlier and later issues is specifically this: in the shadow of Harvard and the responsibilities of the magazine's subtitle, it pays close attention to Harvard men, printing original writings by them and critical essays on them; the shift in locale and editorial management is responsible for a more generous attention to modern arts and letters, irrespective of their origin. *Hound and Horn* throughout adheres to a policy of avoiding undue interference by political and social doctrine, though in later issues it does evaluate Marxism and assess its position in modern thought. The magazine is thus in a sense a "continuation of *The Dial*." Perhaps its great contribution to American letters is in the field of criticism: critical essays of considerable merit are contributed by T. S. Eliot, Kenneth Burke (who continues a series begun in *The Dial*), R. P. Blackmur, Allen Tate, and H. B. Parkes. Contributions include poetry of Theodore Spencer, R. P. Blackmur, Malcolm Cowley, Wallace Stevens, William Carlos Williams, E. E. Cummings, Horace Gregory, Selden Rodman, and J. V. Cunningham; the fiction of Katherine Anne Porter, John Dos Passos, Kay Boyle, Erskine Caldwell, Sean O'Faolain, and Yvor Winters. Cummings contributes his impressions of the Soviet Union; James Joyce, a letter "From a Banned Writer to a Banned Singer." The March and June, 1928, issues contain an article in two parts on T. S. Eliot by R. P. Blackmur and a bibliography of the writings of T. S. Eliot by Varian Fry. The entire issue of April/June, 1934, is devoted to Henry James.

❖

THE JONGLEUR; a quarterly sheaf of verses. Spring 1927-Summer 1940? Quarterly. Bradford, Eng. bk. rev., illus. B NN
Editor: Alberta Vickridge.

Alberta Vickridge's poetry magazine presents creditable performances by some minor English poets, including May Rita O'Rourke, Wilfred Childe, and the editor.

❖

THE JOURNAL OF AMERICAN POETRY; the magazine that discriminates. Spring 1927-Autumn/Winter 1928/1929. Irregular. Charlotte, N.C. bk. rev., illus. Editor: Wallace Stephen. NN

Wallace Stephen's *Journal* has no sympathy for experimentalism in verse. Poetry must be "exalted in mood"; it is the expression of "noble truths." Such critical judgments, which are frequent, are supplemented by a nostalgic view of the "great poets of 1914 who are now dead." The contributions reflect the tastes of the editor and the example of his favorites. They do not add substantially to the history of modern poetry, but prefer to be linked with more traditional poesy.

❖

LARUS; the celestial visitor, with which has been combined *Tempo.* Feb. 1927-June 1928. Irregular. Lynn, Mass. bk. rev.     NN
Editor: John Sherry Mangan (French ed., Virgil Thomson).

*larus* prints intelligent though opinionated criticism and much experimental poetry. The function of any magazine, says its American editor, and especially of this magazine, "properly lies at a variable point between the extremes best represented by a one-sided telephone conversation and a grand literary *garden-partouze.*" Mangan's editorials concern in the main the right of the artist to spiritual privacy, as against the literature produced to meet a popular taste. As a poet, Mangan wishes to have his motives respected and his work evaluated honestly. This position is not antidemocratic or antisocial; rather, it recognizes the difficulties of the creative artist and wishes to protect him from enervating popular attention. The magazine publishes the verse of R. P. Blackmur, Yvor Winters, Robert Hillyer, Robert McAlmon, Hart Crane, Conrad Aiken, and others; prose fiction by Gertrude Stein and Henry de Montherlant, and criticism by Blackmur.

❖

THE NEW COW OF GREENWICH VILLAGE; a monthly periodical sold on the seven arts as such. April 1927. (Only one issue.) New York.     NN
Editor: Tom Boggs.

Another Greenwich Village magazine, this time dedicated to the notion that "Literature is not life in deception: it is life in essence. Gayety is the goal of all, so it is to a gay essence of life, in Literature's life of essence, This Cow mediates." There are poems by Maxwell Bodenheim, Eli Siegel, Ralph Cheyney, and Tom Boggs.

❖

PARNASSUS; a wee magazine of poetry. Sept. 15, 1927-Apr. 1937? Irregular. New York.     NN
Editor: Lew Ney.

Lew Ney's five-cent poetry magazine is interesting as a Greenwich Village "idea"—the support of poetry by means of various publicity schemes. Verse appears here from the pens of Maxwell Bodenheim, Norman MacLeod, Charles Henri Ford, Parker Tyler, and Kathleen Tankersley Young.

❖

THE PRAIRIE SCHOONER. (University of Nebraska.) 1927+. Quarterly. Lincoln, Neb. bk. rev., index. Supplement.     NN
Editor: Lowry Charles Wimberly (with board of editors, 1927-Summer 1928).

In various editorial capacities appear Roscoe Schaupp, Jacob H. Gable, Jr., John G. Neihardt, Gilbert H. Doane, R. P. Crawford, Margaret Deming, Robert D. Scott, Weldon Kees, Lowell Thomas, and others.

Another of the Midwest's little magazines, *The Prairie Schooner* begins as ". . . an outlet for literary work in the University of Nebraska and a medium for the publication of the finest writing of the prairie country." Its emphasis is consistently regional. Included are short stories by Weldon Kees, Karlton Kelm, José Garcia Villa, William March, Albert Halper, and Raymond Kresensky; poetry by Norman Macleod, Jesse Stuart, Kerker Quinn, José Garcia Villa, and August Derleth.

❖

TRANSITION. Apr. 1927-Spring 1938. Monthly. Paris; The Hague. illus., index (Nos. 1-12, Apr. 1927-Mar. 1928),

cum index ("*transition bibliography,*" Nos. 1-22, in No. 22, Feb. 1933). (Suspended between Summer 1930 and Mar. 1932.) NN
Editors: Eugene Jolas and Elliot Paul.

Robert Sage is mentioned as associate editor and later as contributing editor. Beginning with Summer 1928, Matthew Josephson, Harry Crosby, and others appear as advisory or contributing editors.

Newsreporter, poet, and linguist, Eugene Jolas went to Paris in 1926, eventually to establish *transition*, one of the most interesting and challenging of all little magazines. From the time of his first meeting with James Joyce (see Jolas' article in the March-April, 1941, issue of *Partisan Review*), he was convinced of Joyce's significance for modern letters; Joyce's "Work in Progress" (*Finnegans Wake*) appeared in *transition*, and a series of "explanatory essays" ran concurrently. Aside from the purely literary value of many of its contributions—and there is scarcely an *avant gardist* who is omitted—*transition* is important for its revaluation of romanticism, its campaign for a "Revolution of the Word," and its attempt to build a new philosophy from subliminal and preconscious materials. The development of Jolas' philosophy begins with his repudiation of conventional rational structures; this, of course, is not new. Since language is the immediate channel of discourse, Jolas insists that conventional language patterns are also inadequate. "We are tired of the word that does not express the kinetic and subconscious." Hence he encourages experiments by Gertrude Stein (who contributed until 1935), James Joyce, A. Lincoln Gillespie, and others. But his philosophy must expand from this point. The ultimate expression of the artist lies in the union of the subconscious with the supernatural. Thus he has drawn upon the negativism of *dada*, the aesthetics of the unconscious as formulated by the surrealists (though he denies the validity of their political and moral inferences), and the researches of psychoanalysis, chiefly that of Carl G. Jung. From the purely technical point of view, Jolas' "vertigralism" derives much from the "kinetic" value of word and image and from the dream mechanism, as it is described for us by Freud and Jung. *transition* is a reflection of all these developments; its later issues present vertigralism as a complete philosophy and aesthetics; it is in the earlier issues that one finds Jolas' thought taking shape with all of its important consequences for modern letters. Much of the way Jolas traveled with some form of editorial aid: first that of Elliot Paul, as co-editor, then that of Robert Sage as associate; and his wife, Maria McDonald, a brilliant linguist also, helped him with the numerous translations from the French and German to be found in *transition*. The early issues present a much greater variety of contributors; in the last issues the contributions seem selected in the light of a theory. Only a partial list of contributors is possible: poems by Kenneth Fearing, Genevieve Taggard, Horace Gregory, Archibald MacLeish, Hart Crane, Malcolm Cowley, Allen Tate, Yvor Winters, and St.-J. Perse; prose by Kay Boyle, Matthew Josephson, André Breton, William Carlos Williams, Gertrude Stein, Ludwig Lewisohn, Robert Sage, Gilbert Stuart, Harry Crosby, and Franz Kafka.

✧

WESTWARD; a magazine of verse. Aug. 1927+. Quarterly. San Francisco. bk. rev., illus., index (in each vol.: 1-3, Aug. 1927-Nov. 1934). NN
(Absorbed *The Golden Fawn*, Jan. 1935.)
Editors: Florence R. Keene (Aug. 1927-Nov. 1933); Kent Goodnough Hyde (Feb. 1933-Nov. 1934); Hans A. Hoffmann (Jan. 1935+).

*Westward* is published with the aim of printing "forgotten poems by forgotten singers of California." There are occasional contributions from August Derleth, Robin Lampson, and Kathleen Sutton.

## 1928

THE ADOLESCENT; a literary quarterly by young people. Summer 1928-Feb./Apr. 1929. Baltimore. bk. rev.　NN
(Feb./Apr. 1929 as: *Youth*; a quarterly review of literature and art.)
Editors: Leonard Darvin, Alan Calmer, Hyman Rosen, Hilda Preissman, Arthur Musgrave, and Helen Alpert-Levin.

The *Adolescent* is edited and published entirely "by people under twenty-two years of age." The title and contents both betray an unfortunate self-consciousness which makes the magazine interesting but not important.

❖

EXPERIMENT. (Trinity College.) Nov. 1928-Oct. 1930. Irregular. Cambridge, Eng. illus.　NN
Editors: William Empson (Nov. 1928-May 1929); J. Bronowski and Hugh Sykes (Nov. 1929-Oct. 1930).

William Empson's work in poetics is already widely known. As editor of *Experiment*, he is able to give wide scope to his talents, and to publish the writing of other talented artists, most of them of the "Cambridge Group." In the sixth number the magazine, mainly under the influence of J. Bronowski, who had become an editor in November 1929, changed its policy, to give freer access to non-Cambridge writers. The magazine belongs definitely to the literature and aesthetics of the third decade of our century, and makes important experimental contributions to both. Included is the verse of William Empson, J. Bronowski, Richard Eberhart, and Conrad Aiken; and the criticism of Empson, Bronowski, and W. G. Archer.

JACKASS; a magazine of the Southwest. Jan. 1928-[1929]? Irregular. Albuquerque, N.M. bk. rev.　NN
(May 1928-[1929] as: *Palo Verde*.)
Editor: Norman W. Macleod (with D. Maitland Bushby, 1928-[1929]).

Contributing editors are: Benjamin Musser, Willard Johnson, Edith Tatum, and Herman Spector.

Norman Macleod founded *Jackass* "to fill a gaping need and a gaping hiatus in the existing periodicals, namely, the encouragement and articulation of Southwestern literature." It prints the poems of Paul Horgan, Norman Macleod, Kathleen Tankersley Young, Charles Henri Ford, and others.

❖

JAPM; the poetry weekly. July 1928-Dec. 1929. Atlantic City, N.J. index. (Absorbed by *Bozart*, Jan. 1930.)　NN
Editor: Ben Musser.

Like *Voices* and many other poetry magazines, *Japm* publishes a variety of writings by minor American poets. Some of these deserve mention: Charles Henri Ford, Norman Macleod, Parker Tyler, Robert Coffin, and Paul Engle.

❖

THE LONDON APHRODITE. Aug. 1928-July 1929. Bimonthly. London. illus.
Editors: Jack Lindsay and P. R. Stephensen.　NN

Lindsay and Stephensen publish six issues of their magazine, on the assumption that no literary magazine can last longer without getting dull. *The London Aphrodite* is exceptional for its consistent development of the editors' Nietzschean critique of modern society. From the point of view of the German philosopher (who is aided somewhat by references to Freud), the editors take most modern writers to task—Eliot and Joyce especially—for their preoccupation with the depressing minutiae of modern experience. They would oppose this pessimism with the plea that the modern writer once more face life without the sentimentalities or the illusions of the Victorians. Of all little reviews this magazine is the best application of the Nietzschean philosophy to modern culture and letters.

❖

OUTSIDERS. May 1928-May 1929. Semiannual. Mt. Vernon, N.Y. NN Editorial board: Ruth Heller, Rosalind Rosenwasser, Edna Rosenmond, Phyllis Barthman, Gerald D. Heller, and others.

*Outsiders* is "frankly an experiment. The Editors feel that there are innumerable talented young writers unable to obtain publication of their material in professional magazines.... We feel that by publishing the best and most promising material submitted to us and then circulating *Outsiders* to editors and publishers, that perhaps we may assist young writers to a more rapid recognition."

❖

SONNET SEQUENCES. June 1928+. Monthly. Landover, Md. illus. NN Editor: Murray L. Marshall (with Hazel S. Marshall, June 1936+).

This magazine is devoted almost entirely to experiments with the sonnet form. The early issues carry reprints of great English sonnet sequences. Included among the moderns who try their skill with the sonnet pattern are Stanton Coblentz, Benjamin Musser, Jesse Stuart, Harold Vinal, and Ralph Cheyney. The magazine frequently devotes all or almost all of a single issue to a modern sonnet sequence. Discussions of the history of the sonnet appear occasionally.

❖

TROUBADOUR; a magazine of verse. June 1928-Autumn 1932, (undated issue 1935?). Irregular. San Diego, Calif. bk. rev., illus., index (v. 1 and 2, June 1928-May 1930). NN Editorial board (June 1928-Dec. 1929). Editor: Whitley Gray (with Pauline Moyer, June-Autumn 1932).

*Troubadour* is an answer to an insistent demand of the San Diego Poetry Society and generally "of the fraternity of poets of the Pacific Coast, for an unbiased medium of expression." It is catholic in its tastes, holding no brief for "any given type of verse, new or old." The first issue prints Carl Sandburg's "38 Definitions of Poetry." Other contributions include poems by Norman Macleod, C. E. S. Wood, and Hildegarde Flanner. Single issues are often devoted to the work of poets from a certain state as, for example, the "Oregon Number," April 1929, and the "California Number," May 1929, edited by guest editors.

❖

THE VENTURE. (Cambridge University.) Nov. 1928-June 1930. Irregular. Cambridge, Eng. illus., index. NN Editors: Anthony Blunt (Nov. 1928-June 1929); H. Romilly Fedden and Michael Redgrave.

*The Venture*, a British magazine of the arts, prints poetry and fiction, and also contributes a number of critical essays on music and art. The magazine's contents are a cross section of British talent of the late twenties: there are poems by Louis MacNeice, Basil Wright, John Drinkwater, John Davenport, William Empson, John Lehmann, Humbert Wolfe, and others; short stories by Clemence Dane, John Davenport, and Michael Redgrave; and a variety of essays on music, painting, and poetry by such critics as Anthony Blunt, Martin Turnell, and George Oglethorpe. Some little attention is also paid the literature of England's past.

## 1929

BLUES; a magazine of new rhythms. Feb. 1929-Fall 1930. Monthly. Columbus, Miss. bk. rev., index (v. 1, Feb.-July 1929). NN
Editor: Charles Henri Ford.

The associate editors are Kathleen Tankersley Young and Parker Tyler. Among contributing editors are William Carlos Williams, Jacques Le Clercq, Joseph Vogel, and Eugene Jolas.

The experimentalism of *Blues* is self-conscious, enthusiastic, and daring. As William Carlos Williams puts it in an essay in the May 1929 issue: "Poetry lives where life is hardest, hottest, most subject to jailing, infringements and whatever it may be that groups of citizens oppose to danger." The poetry can therefore be expected to offer a variety of new departures and experiments in the use of imagery and language. These come from a varied assortment of writers: Charles Henri Ford, Horace Gregory, Eugene Jolas, Norman Macleod, Kay Boyle, Kathleen Tankersley Young among them.

⋄

THE CARILLON; a national quarterly of verse. Autumn 1929-1931. Irregular. Stanford University, Calif. illus. (Midsummer 1930-Twelfth Night number, 1931, as: *Roon*.) CU ICU
Editor: Ruth Mantz.

A California little magazine of creative writing, *The Carillon*, which changed its name to *Roon* after the first issue, publishes the verse of Yvor Winters, Janet Lewis, Henry Ramsey, David DeJong, and others; and a translation from the French of Paul Verlaine, by Yvor Winters.

⋄

THE CARILLON; a national quarterly of verse. Oct. 1929-Oct. 1933. Washington, D.C. NN
Editors: Caroline Giltinan, Anne Robinson, Catherine Cate Coblentz, and Courtland Baker.

Among contributing editors are Lew Sarett and Leonora Speyer.

*The Carillon*, on fairly frequent occasions, publishes poetry by such American poets as Lizette Reese, Witter Bynner, Winifred Welles, Eunice Tietjens, Countée Cullen, and Hildegarde Flanner.

⋄

CONTEMPORARY VISION. Winter 1929/30-Fall/Winter 1931. Quarterly. Chicago. NN
(Supersedes *Scepter*. Caption title: *The New Contemporary Vision and Scepter*.) (Absorbed by *Poetry World*, Feb. 1932.)
Editors: Lucia Trent, Ralph Cheyney (with William Sawyer, Winter 1929-Autumn 1930).

Among those who appear on the advisory board are: William Braithwaite, Glenn Ward Dresbach, Louis Ginsberg, Margaret Widdemer, Jack Conroy, Angela Morgan, Blanche Shoemaker Wagstaff.

*Contemporary Vision* expresses the firm conviction of its editors that poetry is a kind of divine key to knowledge, that the poet is also a prophet, and that the poem's contribution to thought is somehow "vital." The editors will "give no quarter to the sad young men"—that is, those contemporaries who would sing of the defeat of man. It is hard to translate such editorial aesthetics into an effective policy. Represented in its pages are such poets as Arthur Davison Ficke, Clement Wood, Norman Macleod, and Gale Wilhelm.

⋄

THE ECHO; a quarterly review of American and British college literature. (College Poetry Guild.) Mar. 1929-Autumn 1932. Hamilton, N.Y. bk. rev. (Superseded by *Connecticut Echo*.) NN

Editors: Arthur B. Berthold (Mar. 1929-Sept. 1930); George Scott Gleason (Autumn 1930-Autumn 1932).

The *Echo* is one of several magazines which attempt, by precept and model, to foster and publish the writings of college students. There are poems by Jesse Stuart and Norman Macleod.

❖

THE GYROSCOPE. May 1929-Feb. 1930. Quarterly. Palo Alto, Calif.   P Y
Editors: Yvor Winters, Janet Lewis, and Howard Baker.

A mimeographed quarterly which announces itself as opposed "to all forms of spiritual extroversion ... and emotional expansionism." Its editors suggest that recent theories and practices have tended to overemphasize "emotional escape" and have neglected important responsibilities in modern aesthetics. They prefer to regard style as an indication of "spiritual strength," and maintain "that spiritual precision and strength can be developed in a satisfactory degree only through the serious and protracted study of the masters of art and thought, as well as of self and of living human relations." *The Gyroscope* presents the poetry and prose of the California group, most of whom have belonged to the Yvor Winters "circle" at Stanford University. In his book, *The Anatomy of Nonsense*, published in 1943, Winters mentions some of these writers as "the most promising" in modern letters. Important contributions to modern short fiction are made by Janet Lewis, Caroline Gordon, and Katherine Anne Porter. Poetry is contributed by Howard Baker, Grant H. Code, Yvor Winters, Janet Lewis, and Henry Ramsey. Winters' comments on modern criticism are an interesting part of his development as a literary critic. For Winters, classicism in literary taste and judgment is based upon the discreet exercise of the reason: "The basis of Evil is in emotion; Good rests in the power of rational selection in action...." His criticism of many of his contemporaries is that they submit to one or another of emotional pressures and thus yield to the temptation to "escape" the responsibilities of the reason. Though the contributions do not always demonstrate overtly the principles of its critical leader—for it is an experimental collection of writings, of varied types and quality—the members of *The Gyroscope* group do represent a distinct and singular addition to serious writing in America. The Pacific Coast writers and Winters have continued to appear since the death of *The Gyroscope*, in their varied roles of poet, critic, and teacher.

❖

HARLEQUINADE. Oct. 15, 1929-June 1930. Frequency varies. Abilene, Tex. bk. rev., illus., index (v. 1, Oct. 15, 1929-Apr. 1, 1930).   NN
Editor: Franz A. Finberg.

*Harlequinade* is a mimeographed little magazine of limited scope and quality. The editor suggests, however, that a repetition of such efforts as his may eventually produce "one really first rank poet." Jay Sigmund and Benjamin Musser publish poems in the magazine.

❖

JANUS; a quarterly review of letters, thought, and the new theology. Nov. 1929-? Washington, D.C.   Y
Editor: Solon R. Barber.

A magazine of criticism and original writing, *Janus* "is sincerely and honestly devoted to the policy of having no policy. It symbolizes individualism gone loco and ideational freedom carried to a licentious excess." T. Swann Harding is listed as a "Dissenting Editor," whose function, the editorial announcement in the first issue explains, is to keep the principal editor from "going fundamentalist." The first issue carries critical essays or notes by V. F. Calverton, Henshaw Ward, and T. Swann Harding; poetry by E. Merrill Root, Charles Henri Ford, Norman Macleod, Parker Tyler, and others; prose fiction by Josephine Hemphill, Eleanor Trott, and others.

❖

THE KALEIDOSCOPE; a national magazine of poetry. May 1929+. Monthly. Dallas, Tex. bk. rev., illus., index. (May 1932+ as: *Kaleidograph*.) NN
Editors: Whitney Montgomery and Vaida Stewart Montgomery.

Another of a group of small poetry magazines which make payment in prizes for best poems and publish a great variety of materials. Contributions include poems by Benjamin Musser, David Cornel DeJong, Glenn Ward Dresbach, Paul Engle, Ralph Cheyney, Frances M. Frost, Stanton M. Coblentz, Kathleen Sutton, and Raymond Kresensky. Jessie B. Rittenhouse appears on the advisory board.

❖

THE MORADA. Autumn [1929-Dec. 1930?] Quarterly. Albuquerque, N.M. bk. rev. NN
Editorial board: Norman Macleod, William Flynn, C. V. Wicker, and Donal McKenzie.

Among contributing editors are: Charles Henri Ford, Benjamin Musser, Harry Crosby, Jack Conroy, Joseph Vogel, and Eugene Jolas. No. 5 [Dec. 1930] is a trilingual issue in English, French, and German, published in Italy.

One issue is devoted to the memory of Harry Crosby, with tributes by Pound, Macleod, and others, and examples of Crosby's writing. There is much discussion of and debate over the role of the artist in society.

POETRY WORLD. Aug. 1929-Apr./Aug. 1940. Monthly. New York. bk. rev. (Absorbed *Contemporary Vision*, Feb. 1932; *The Spinners*, Mar. 1936.) (Feb. 1932-May 1933 as: *Poetry World and Contemporary Vision*.) H NN
Editors: Parmenia Migel (Aug. 1929-Mar. 1931); Alice Rogers Hager (Aug. 1929-Mar. 1930); Jerry Clason (Aug. 1929-Mar. 1930); Gertrude White (Aug. 1929-June 1931), and others.

*Poetry World* publishes, among others, poems by Helen Hoyt, Carl John Bostelmann, Louis Ginsberg, Marie de L. Welch, Benjamin Musser, Glenn Ward Dresbach, Jay G. Sigmund, and others. Critical essays on the nature and meaning of poetry are also frequently printed.

❖

POET'S MAGAZINE. Nov. 1929-Jan./Feb. 1932. Bimonthly. New York. bk. rev. NN Y
Editor: George A. Sakele.

*Poet's Magazine* combines an interest in the history and biography of poets of the past with the publication of poems of the present. Among these latter are verses by Charles Henri Ford, Eli Siegel, Stanton A. Coblentz, Harry Roskolenkier, Parker Tyler, and Clifford Gessler.

❖

SCEPTER; the arbiter of rhyme. Mar.-Sept./Oct. 1929. Monthly. Franklin, Tenn. bk. rev. NN
(Absorbed by *Contemporary Vision*, Winter 1929/30.)
Editor: William Sawyer.

Contributing editors: D. Maitland Bushby, Lucia Trent, Ralph Cheyney, and Ernest Hartsock.

The "Arbiter of Rhyme" publishes a few of the poems of Benjamin Musser, Ralph Cheyney, Kathleen Tankersley Young, Norman Macleod, Charles Henri Ford, E. Merrill Root, and others.

STAR-DUST; a journal of poetry. Autumn 1929-Summer 1932. 3 issues a year. Washington, D.C. bk. rev.   NN
Editors: Edith Mirick (with John Lee Higgins, Autumn 1929-Spring/Summer 1930).

A little poetry magazine which publishes some of the poems of E. Merrill Root, Norman Macleod, Ralph Cheyney, Benjamin Musser, Clement Wood, L. A. G. Strong, Marie de L. Welch, Witter Bynner, Idella Purnell, Harold Vinal, and Raymond Kresensky. Each issue also prints translations of work by foreign poets. The issue of Winter 1932 is devoted entirely to poems done by American poets in Japanese forms.

✧

TAMBOUR. (Text in English and French.) [Feb. 1929]-June 1930. Irregular. Paris. bk. rev., illus.   NN
Editor: Harold J. Salemson.

Harold J. Salemson's lively Paris magazine has the advantage of a vigorous critical direction and an admirable selection of materials. What is significant in *Tambour* is its contribution to the question of the importance of the twentieth century writer—especially the writer of the twenties, whose exciting but at least superficially confusing career is drawing to a close during the publication of *Tambour*. These writers, says Salemson, have been too much preoccupied with *form*, with the development of a craft. It remains for the artist to "look at his day with the point-of-view of his day, as he understands it and without making us feel his presence in it." The writers of the thirties were to heed this advice in their own way. In an important sense, Salemson's editorial (No. 7, 1930) is a fitting concluding comment upon the writing of the twenties. Contributions to *Tambour* include the poetry of Charles Henri Ford, Maxwell Bodenheim, Norman Macleod, Parker Tyler, and others; prose fiction by James T. Farrell and Karlton Kelm, and criticism by Stuart Gilbert.

✧

TOM-TOM; a magazine of Southwestern poetry. Nov. 1929-Spring 1931? Quarterly. Scottsdale, Ariz. bk. rev.
Editor: D. Maitland Bushby.   H NN

From the editorial notice of the Autumn 1930 issue: "We want particularly poetry with a Southwestern atmosphere: the Indian, his mythology, his chants, his life past and present; historical, the old pioneer days when this section was Spanish territory and later; mountain and desert themes. *Tom-Tom* is conventional in poetic form and spirit. We rarely use free verse and have no time for radical or sex poetry." The magazine publishes, among others, the poems of Witter Bynner, Arthur Truman Merrill, Benjamin Musser, C. E. S. Wood, E. Merrill Root, and Helen Hoyt.

✧

VERSE. 1929-May/June 1930? Bimonthly. Melbourne, Australia.   ICU
Editor: Louis Lavater?
*Issues other than May/June 1930 not consulted.*

Verse, an Australian poetry magazine, publishes the poems of Ethel Davies, A. D. Hardy, Enid Derham, Louis Lavater, and others.

✧

WESTERN POETRY. Dec. 1929-Nov. 1931. Monthly. Holt, Minn.   NN (Nov. 1930-Nov. 1931 as: *The Northern Light*.)
Editor: B. C. Hagglund.

B. C. Hagglund's little magazine reflects the interest of writers of its time in social problems and their willingness to use verse as a medium of political and social expression. The editorial of the first issue complains that American poetry has been too discreet and cautious, insufficiently vigorous and "earthy." Poetry must, the editor insists "come into its own again, as the militant foe of injustice. . . ." Contributions which may be said to have accepted the editor's challenge include poems by Joseph Kalar, H. H. Lewis, David Cornel DeJong, William Pillin, Ralph Cheyney, Jack Conroy, and others.

## 1930

THE AGORA; a magazine of the New South. Sept. 1930-May 1931. Monthly. Chapel Hill, N.C.     Y
Editor: Richard A. Chace.

Paul Green, Addison Hibbard, and others appear on the advisory board.

A little magazine of the South, designed as a place for the publication of new writers of the South, "to offer these people a field for their earlier development." Among the contributions are poems by Joseph Upper, Lucia Trent, Benjamin Musser, Ed Winfield Parks, Ralph Cheyney, Norman Macleod, and Helene Mullins.

✧

ARGO; an individual review. Nov.-Dec. 1930. (Only two issues.) Princeton, N.J. bk. rev., illus.     NN
Editors: W. P. Vogel, Jr., and James Webb.

Argo begins with an editorial announcing the "decade of the '30's" and claiming that during the years ahead "a new generation" will awaken to "the consciousness of its strength." Among the contributions to the magazine Selden Rodman's poems are most deserving of note.

✧

CARMINA. Aug. 1930-1932. Irregular. London. bk. rev.     NN
Editor: Maurice Leahy.

Carmina reflects the Catholic influence upon poetry and criticism. Poetry is not "in the absolute sense, creative. The artist can hold the gleam, he cannot create it." Both in criticism and in the poetry published, the Catholic influence is avowed and strong.

✧

EARTH. Apr. 1930-July 1932. Monthly. Wheaton, Ill. bk. rev., illus.     NN
(Suspended, July 1931-Jan. 1932.)
Editors: J. Niver (Apr. 1930-July 1932); Konstantin Karloff (Apr.-June 1930, Mar. 1931); Ernest Schelander (Apr. 1930-Feb., June 1931); Upton Terrell (May 1930); Ralph Chaplin (Feb.-Mar. 1931); Fred Hardy (Feb.-Mar. 1931).

Earth begins at the source of much literature and criticism; it has its origin in lively discussions among young writers who subsequently yield to the wish to see their words in print. The issue of May 1930 changes its subtitle to "A Midwestern Expression." The later issues reflect an interest in radical politics and literature; an essay by James T. Farrell in the February 1931 issue clarifies the position of the young radical. Contributions include poems by E. Merrill Root, Winfield Scott, Sterling North, and Norman Macleod.

✧

FARRAGO. Feb. 1930-June 1931. Quarterly. Oxford, Eng. illus.     NN
Editor: Peter Burra.

This "farrago of incongruous rickshaws," made possible solely by the financial support of the Viscount Esher, runs its appointed six issues and then brings itself to an end already prepared for. Though the patronage of the Viscount removes from the magazine the honor which so many little magazines have had of suffering dire poverty and distress, the freedom of editorial supervision and the absence of any jaundiced control by the sponsor endow Farrago with a goodly abundance of the other qualities which go to make up the little review. Its contents are almost equally divided between the critical and the creative. John Sparrow and John Haldane Blackie enjoy a controversy over the criticism of I. A. Richards; there is a lengthy essay by P. J. S. Burra on "Baroque and Gothic Sentimentalism"; and an estimate by R. H. S. Crossman of D. H. Lawrence. Included among the other contributions are poems by Goronwy Rees, Randall Swingler, Evelyn Waugh, and Cecil Day Lewis; prose fiction by Gilbert Highet. The magazine is well illustrated; among the reproductions are two sketches by Max Beerbohm.

❖

THE FIVE ARTS. Apr. 1930-? Hanover, N. H. illus.    NN
*Editor not established.*

Like many of its American partners, *The Five Arts* attempts an understanding of a variety of expressions: poetry, fiction, drama, music, and painting.

❖

FRONT. (Text in English, French, and German.) Dec. 1930-June 1931. Bimonthly. The Hague. bk. rev., index. Editor: Sonja Prins. (Foreign editors: Spain, Xavier Abril; Japan, Masaki Ikeda; U.S.A., Norman Macleod; Russia, Secretariat F.O.S.P.)    NN

Beginning as a literary magazine with leftwing tendencies, but interested primarily in literature *per se*, *Front*, an excellent trilingual review, emphasizes more and more the urgent necessity for a socially informed literature and art. The last issue announces its complete agreement with radical politics: "Henceforth, we will only concern ourselves with literature as an art when it arms the workers against the bourgeoisie." The magazine attracts writers who are alive to experimental tendencies in modern letters and who eagerly anticipate the fullest use of literature as a social weapon. V. F. Calverton's essay in the issue of December 1930, with its emphasis upon the "demands of social organizations," establishes a platform for many of the writers of the thirties. Contributions include poetry by Norman Macleod, Charles Henri Ford, Louis Zukofsky, Richard Johns, William Carlos Williams, and others; fiction by Kay Boyle, Robert McAlmon, John Dos Passos, and many young writers who are later to be published frequently in proletarian literary magazines; criticism by V. F. Calverton, Ezra Pound (a "dissenting voice"), and Louis Zukofsky.

❖

THE GAREN MAGAZINE. Spring 1930-Spring 1940? Quarterly. Ridgewood, N.J. bk. rev., illus.    NN
(Summer 1931-Spring 1940 as: *Expression.*)
Editors: James Gabelle (with Patty Endicott, and Beatrix Reynolds, Spring 1930-Summer 1931).

The little poetry magazine often, from sheer multiplication of issues, publishes verse of some importance to modern letters. *The Garen Magazine* has its share of mediocre verse. Occasionally there are poems by minor but not undistinguished writers: Norman Macleod, Louis Ginsberg, Ralph Cheyney, and Benjamin Musser.

❖

THE HARKNESS HOOT; a Yale undergraduate review. (Yale University.) Oct. 1, 1930-Apr. 1934. Irregular. New Haven, Conn. illus.    NN
Editors: William Harlan Hale and Selden Rodman (Oct. 1, 1930-Apr./May 1931); Richard M. Bissell and Richard S. Childs (Oct. 7, 1931-June 7, 1932), and others.

One of Yale's undergraduate literary magazines, *The Harkness Hoot* is distinguished by a wide-awake editorial policy, an interest in modern letters, and a feeling ". . . that the undergraduate body of Yale needs a medium for progressive writing and liberal discussion." The first editors, William Harlan Hale and Selden Rodman, insist that the title of the magazine does not imply that it is just another freshman humor sheet; the title "merely emphasizes the fact of its freedom and lack of pretensions. No radical secret society, no literary I.W.W., shapes the editor's policy." Selden Rodman's contributions are frequent and include several of his poems and a study of Archibald MacLeish. Other modern writers who are the subject of *The Harkness Hoot* criticism are Stephen Vincent Benét, William Rose Benét, and Ezra Pound. James Laughlin IV (who is mentioned as one of the associate editors) adds an estimate of MacLeish. Towards the end of its career, the magazine is much taken up with political and economic issues, debating with some seriousness the effect of Communist ideology upon literature and upon life on an American campus. Other contributions include poetry by James Laughlin IV, Robert R. Fitzgerald, Wallace Stevens, Ezra Pound; prose fiction by James Laughlin IV and two critical essays by Ezra Pound. *The Harkness Hoot* is a lively member of a group of university magazines which may be said to have belonged to the little magazine family.

✧

HESPERIAN. Summer 1930-Spring 1931. Irregular. San Francisco. illus.   NN
Editors: James D. Hart (with Jan Maris, Summer 1930).

The aims of *hesperian* appear to be two: to emphasize the peculiar character and great necessity of the little magazine; and to dispel the illusion that "there is no culture in the West." Western writers are frequently published, but they do not dominate the magazine's interesting contents. Among the poems published are those of George Sterling, Norman Macleod, Yvor Winters, C. E. S. Wood, and Hildegarde Flanner. Contributions in prose include stories by Achilles Holt, Clarkson Crane, and critical essays by Carey McWilliams and Theodore Dreiser. There are translations from the poetry of Tristan Corbière, Charles Baudelaire, and Francis Viele-Griffin, by Yvor Winters. In the issue of Winter 1930, James D. Hart contributes an informative and provocative essay on "Little Magazines and Their Battle."

✧

THE MISCELLANY. Mar. 1930-Mar. 1931. Bimonthly. New York. bk. rev. (Prospectus number issued Dec. 1929.)
Editors: Frederick W. Dupee, Geoffrey T. Hellman, Dwight Macdonald, and George L. K. Morris.   NN Y

The great value of *The Miscellany* rests upon two advantages which it seems to have over many other magazines: its editorial control is not dictatorial; it attracts the writings of important men. Critical articles are of a high standard. The poetry of Yvor Winters, William Carlos Williams, Conrad Aiken, and David Cornel DeJong is published. There is criticism by Dwight Macdonald, Frederick W. Dupee, Hervey Allen, and George L. K. Morris. Contributions include short stories by L. A. G. Strong, Robert Cantwell, and H. L. Davis.   ✧

THE MODERN SCOT; the organ of the Scottish renaissance. Spring 1930-Jan. 1936. Quarterly. Dundee, Scotland. bk. rev., illus., index.   NN
Editor: J. H. Whyte.

*The Modern Scot* is a vigorous statement of aesthetic autonomy for Scottish writers and critics. "Nothing will be gained from the imitation of such cultural institutions as the English provinces now enjoy," the first editorial reads in part. There are a number of essays on the Scotch political scene, but for the most part the magazine is interested in Scottish literature and criticism, with an occasional translation from German or French writers, or an American contribution. The *Scot* is a little review with a national emphasis, but modern as well as "Scottish." The important Scottish writer, Edwin Muir, contributes criticism, fiction, and poetry. Willa Muir contributes short stories. C. M. Grieve writes political essays in his own name and poetry under the pseudonym of "Hugh M'Diarmid." Among other contributions are poems by Catherine Carswell, Norman Macleod, and Randall Swingler; fiction by Adam Kennedy; critical essays by Catherine Carswell, Séan O'Fáolain, A. T. Cunninghame, and Herbert Read; and translations of the prose of Franz Kafka and Thomas Mann and the poetry of Paul Eluard.

❖

NATIVITY; an American quarterly. Winter, 1930-Spring, 1931. Columbus, Ohio. bk. rev.   NN
Editor: Boris J. Israel.

Boris Israel's little magazine presents the American literary scene primarily for the purpose of commenting upon America's political and social decline. Short stories and poems frequently underline the sad state of American affairs during the first of the depression years. This emphasis is a direct attack upon the "most obnoxious" of all American cults, "the cult of respectability." To counteract the failure of respectable letters, *Nativity* publishes the verse of Charles Henri Ford, Louis Zukofsky, Gale Wilhelm, Lucia Trent, Ralph Cheyney, Norman Macleod, Harry Roskolenkier, and Kathleen Tankersley Young; the short stories of Erskine Caldwell, Albert Halper, and David Cornel DeJong.

❖

NEW WORLD MONTHLY. Jan.-Feb. 1930. New York. bk. rev.   NN
Editors: C. A. Tacke and H. Gilfond.

What gives the *New World Monthly* its importance is its editorial conviction that its age is one of critical evaluation rather than of creation: "Most of the work now done by poets and writers has little more than documentary significance. . . . The process of critical analysis must come first to eradicate the error of the past." This assumption is supported by serious and sometimes penetrating comment upon the major influences upon twentieth century thought: articles on Nietzsche, Bergson, John Dewey, and Whitehead. Other contributions include poems by Parker Tyler, Charles Henri Ford, and Norman Macleod; essays by H. A. Potamkin and Claude Bragdon.

❖

PAGANY; a native quarterly. (Some articles in French.) Winter 1930-Jan./Mar. 1933. Boston. illus.   NN
Editor: Richard Johns.

The value of Richard Johns's *Pagany* lies in the great consciousness of itself as a literary magazine, freed from all commercial pressures. One of its most valuable contributions is to modern American fiction: Erskine Caldwell's pieces throw an interesting new light upon his talents; William Carlos Williams' *White Mule* runs through most issues; a section of John Dos Passos' *U.S.A.* is published; and a host of young writers are represented by their short stories—James T. Farrell, William March, Edward Dahlberg, and Albert Halper among them. Critical articles by Sherry Mangan enliven many issues; other criticism is written by William Carlos Williams, Gorham Munson, Ezra Pound, and Pierre Loving. Poems include those by Kenneth Rexroth, Conrad Aiken, Millen Brand, Gertrude Stein, Louis Zukofsky, and Horace Gregory.

❖

THE POET AND THE CRITIC. May-Sept. 1930. (Only two issues.) New York.

bk. rev. illus.                  NN
Editor: Alan Frederick Pater.

Criticism (chiefly editorial) and verse combine in this magazine, which is very much aware of the necessity for publishing "material by known or unknown authors who have something important or interesting to say." There are poems by Clement Wood, Arthur Davison Ficke, Lola Ridge, and Babette Deutsch.

❖

POETRY QUARTERLY. Feb. 1930-Spring 1931. New York. bk. rev.    NN
Editors: Martha Fox Wolcott (Feb. 1930-Spring 1931); Alan Frederick Pater and Donald Colton (Feb. 1930); and Albert Philip Cohen (Summer 1930-Spring 1931).

Poetry Quarterly opens with a curious editorial announcement: since modern life is lived at high speed, it is possible that "a short lyric may focus, like the spectral glass, all of the colors of human emotion and artistic beauty." Thus the reader may adjust his wish for beauty to the other demands upon himself. The magazine publishes poems by Parker Tyler, David Cornel DeJong, Norman Macleod, Richard Johns, Langston Hughes, and others.

❖

THE POET'S FORUM. Jan. 1930-Mar. 1934. Monthly. Howe, Okla.    NN
Editors: Estil Alexander Townsend (Jan. 1930-Nov. 1932); Wilbur T. Townsend (Dec. 1932-Mar. 1934).

At various times Katharine Coe appears as associate and assistant editor.

A little poetry magazine, The Poet's Forum publishes some of the poems of Margaret Ball Dickson, Ralph Cheyney, and Faith Vilas.

❖

THE RACKET. 1930-May 1931? Irregular. Laguna Beach, Calif. illus.
Editor: Arthur Whipple.       NN

A California little magazine, The Racket is started with the aim of encouraging the talent in its part of the country. Among the contributions are poems by Dilwyn Parrish and Perry McCullough.

❖

THE SYMPOSIUM; a critical review. Jan. 1930-Oct. 1933. Quarterly. Concord, N.H. bk. rev., index.    NN
Editors: James Burnham and Philip E. Wheelwright.

In the pages of The Symposium criticism becomes a major art. The articles, many of them on modern poetics and on modern poets, are arranged loosely in a "symposial structure [which] will perhaps modify the chaotic impression so often given by contemporary magazines. . . ." Some of the most important criticism is here published for the first time: articles by Philip E. Wheelwright, I. A. Richards, Herbert Read, Louis Zukofsky, Harold Rosenberg, and Philip Blair Rice, among others. Toward the close of its brief career, The Symposium becomes troubled by two things which interfere with its heretofore unified purpose: the apparent necessity to yield to the pressure of the Marxists (See the "Thirteen Propositions," issue of April 1933), and the introduction of "creative" writing, the quality of which is a poor substitute for the excellence of the magazine's earlier issues.

❖

THE WHIRL; art-plus. Mar. 15, 1930-? Monthly. Santa Fe, N.M. bk. rev.
Editor: Richard Miller.      ICU

Among the contributions which The Whirl editorially announces as "expressive work from various sources," there are poems by Norman Macleod, Richard Johns, Dorothy Ellis, and others; and critical essays by Solon R. Barber, Haniel Long, Eaton Reeve, and others.

THE WINDOW; a quarterly magazine. Jan.-Oct. 1930. London. NN
Editors: Eric Partridge and Bertram Ratcliffe.

A magazine with book format, The Window publishes chiefly prose, including many short stories by English writers: H. E. Bates, George Barker, Dorothy Richardson, and T. F. Powys. There is poetry by Humbert Wolfe and John Drinkwater.

## 1931

CLAY; a literary notebook. (University of New Mexico.) Autumn 1931-Spring 1932?. Quarterly. Albuquerque, N.M. Editor: José Garcia Villa. NN

Clay began as a mimeographed magazine, sponsored and edited by José Garcia Villa. In its brief life, its chief claim to distinction is its publication of the "new American short story." It is a little magazine both in guiding spirit ("If the commercial magazines turn your stories down, give them away to Clay") and in the quality of its contents. Short stories are contributed by David Cornel DeJong, Erskine Caldwell, José Garcia Villa, Albert Halper, and William Carlos Williams; poems by Witter Bynner, Norman Macleod, and William Saroyan (one of a very few occasions on which Saroyan has attempted to write poetry).

❖

CONTEMPO; a review of ideas and personalities. May 1931-Feb. 1934. Irregular. Chapel Hill, N.C. bk. rev., index (v. 1, May 1931-Apr. 1932). NN
Editors: M. A. Abernethy (with S. R. Carter, May-July 1931, Phil Liskin, May-June 13, 1931, V. N. Garoffolo, May-Sept. 15, 1931, A. J. Buttitta, May 1931-Sept. 25, 1932), and others.

For a period Louis Adamic, Langston Hughes, Ezra Pound, Barrett Clark, Paul Green, Lewis Mumford, William Faulkner, Bob Brown, Kay Boyle, and Samuel Putnam were contributing editors.

Chapel Hill's "literary newspaper" is a lively organ of criticism which reviews almost all significant trends in modern letters—from the Fugitives to dada. Feb. 15, 1934, issue is devoted to Joyce. The magazine boasts of being free of all literary cliques, an "asylum for aggrieved authors." Contributions are valuable to a student of twentieth century literature; fiction by James T. Farrell, Erskine Caldwell, Kay Boyle; poetry by Wallace Stevens, Conrad Aiken, Evelyn Scott, William Faulkner, D. H. Lawrence, and others.

❖

FANTASY. Summer 1931-1943. Quarterly. Pittsburgh, Pa. bk. rev., illus. Editor: Stanley Dehler Mayer. NN

Stanley Mayer's magazine begins as a magazine primarily interested in free verse, but subsequent issues extend its scope and purpose. Almost every idea or tendency of interest to the intellectual is given prominence; the critical articles are generally of high quality, especially those by Charles I. Glicksberg. As the magazine develops, increasing interest in modern experimental literature is reflected both by the criticism and by the creative writing included. Contributions are many and varied: criticism by Eugene Jolas, Philip Rahv, Parker Tyler, Carl Burklund, and Harlan Hatcher; poetry by Kenneth Patchen, John Peale Bishop, Eve Merriam, Paul Eluard, Wallace Stevens, Garcia Lorca, Eugene Jolas, Charles Henri Ford, and others; fiction by Jesse Stuart, Meridel Le Sueur, James Laughlin IV, and others.

❖

FIFTH FLOOR WINDOW. Apr. 1931-May 1932? Irregular. New York. bk. rev., illus. B
Editors: Harvey N. Foster, Ulick Sullivan, Marianne Brown, and others.

*Fifth Floor Window* is a little magazine of creative and critical writing, interested in modern literary experiment and structural reform. The issue of February 1932 is a surrealist number, and includes, among other things, a critical essay on dadaism and superrealism, by H. B. Parkes, a note on E. E. Cummings by Helen Mears, an essay by H. R. Hays on "Lewis Carroll and the Moderns," and poetry and fiction by Harvey Foster. Other contributions include poems by Parker Tyler, Louis Zukofsky, Harry Roskolenkier, and David Cornel DeJong.

❖

IMPROMPTU. Jan.-Apr. 1931. Quarterly. New York. LC
Editor: J. L. Moreno.

A magazine "pledged . . . to interpret and elaborate a philosophy of the creator as an anti-mechanical corrective to our age," and, among other things, to present the "already known Impromptu techniques." The creational qualities which *Impromptu* tries to stimulate "are what they become through the spontaneous confluence of sub-conscious, conscious, emotional, intellectual and spiritual elements, as they are at the disposal of the nervous system in man." The magazine is an expression of the "modern Impromptu Movement" which is linked with the theater and finds its best expression there. In one sense, *Impromptu* is closely allied with psychoanalysis, although Helen Jennings claims that they are to each other "as water is to fire." Criticism of the psychoanalyst is that he dissipates and diffuses the creative urge by "curing" one of his "creative diseases."

❖

INTERNATIONAL LITERATURE. (International Union of Revolutionary Writers.) 1931+. Irregular. Moscow, U.S.-S.R. bk. rev., illus., index (in each year: 1933-1936). NN

(Continues *Literature of the World Revolution*.)
Editorial board with Bruno Jasienski (1931-1932); S. Dinamov (1933-1937), and others.
In the early volumes Henri Barbusse, Michael Gold, Maxim Gorky, John Dos Passos, Upton Sinclair, and others appear on the advisory board.

The creative life of the young man of the twenties is in many cases at least temporarily directed and channelized by extraliterary interests. *International Literature* furnishes an appraisal of that development in modern letters. It is by far the best document for the student of Marxist aesthetics; and since much attention is paid American writers, the magazine is a valuable guide to a Marxist evaluation of our own writing; articles appear on Ernest Hemingway, Robinson Jeffers, Sherwood Anderson, Theodore Dreiser, and others. Poetry is contributed by Norman Macleod, Langston Hughes, Michael Gold, and Bob Brown; fiction by Jack Conroy, Karlton Kelm, Joseph Kalar, F. C. Weiskopf, and Ramon Sender.

❖

THE ISLAND. June 15-Dec. 1931. Quarterly. London. illus. Y
Editor: Joseph Bard.

*The Island* is the voice of a group of artists and writers who "believe in the power and significance of imagination, and in the realisation of the artistic self through an imaginative and spiritual existence. . . . The collaboration of painters and sculptors with writers and poets has thus become possible through the conviction that all artistic activity rises from the same central core, differing only in accordance with the direction and medium chosen to express it." In the first issue there are poems by Ralph Chubb, Josef Bard, Grace Rogers, and others. Many of the contributions are accompanied by wood engravings done by the same contributor, who thus combines the roles of artist and poet.

✧

THE LEFT; a quarterly review of radical and experimental art. Spring 1931-? Davenport, Iowa. bk. rev.　　NN
Editors: George Redfield, Jay du Von, Marvin Klein, R. C. Lorenz, and W. K. Jordan.
Among the associate editors are V. F. Calverton, John Herrmann, Joseph Kalar, Herbert Klein, Norman Macleod, Donal McKenzie, Seymour Stern.

The two issues of The Left are important documents in the literary history of the thirties. The magazine's purpose is to give a vigorous welcome to the changing point of view of many writers, who through pressure of events and persuasions of spirit were turning more and more of their attention to the proletariat and the aesthetic application of Marxist principle. "The Left, a quarterly review of radical and experimental art, is born of this revolutionary movement and will provide a new medium for its expression in the arts . . . and attempt to win over to the movement those artists who have hitherto found their material and ideology in the bourgeois tradition. . . ." There are poems, vocal in the support of the revolution or openly sympathetic with those who have suffered for it; fiction which presents the travail of the exploited; and a department of the cinema, in which the technique of Soviet film directors is lauded, and a campaign for a workingman's cinema is launched. Among the contributions, one finds poetry by Norman Macleod, Sherry Mangan, Louis Zukofsky, Horace Gregory, Lola Ridge, and Ralph Cheyney; fiction by Albert Halper and Jack Conroy; and critical essays by V. F. Calverton, Bernard Smith, Donal Mackenzie, and Harold J. Salemson.

✧

LITERATURE OF THE WORLD REVOLUTION. (International Union of Revolutionary Writers.) June-Oct. 1931? Irregular. Moscow, U.S.S.R. bk. rev., illus.　　NN
(Superseded by International Literature.)
Editor: Bruno Jasienski.
On the advisory board are included Henri Barbusse, Michael Gold, Maxim Gorki, John Dos Passos, A. Serafimovich, Upton Sinclair, and others.

Like International Literature, its successor, Literature of the World Revolution is certain of its purpose and direction, both of which are controlled and circumscribed by the Marxist political and aesthetic doctrines. "Literature must become party literature. As a counterpart to the bourgeois customs, bourgeois commercial and commercialized press, a counterpart to bourgeois literary self-seeking and individualism, 'aristocratic anarchism' and money hunting—the socialist proletariat must put forward the principle of Party Literature, must develop this principle and carry it out in its fullest, completest form." The magazine demonstrates best the effect of an ideology upon the critical position and the literary tastes of the early thirties. It is a part of the Marxist, socialist, realist, declamatory thirties, and as such an extreme demonstration of the artist's abrogation of his aesthetic independence. Along with translations from numerous Soviet writers of poetry, fiction, and criticism, the magazine prints a translation by E. E. Cummings of Louis Aragon's "The Red Front," an editorial survey of the first four numbers of Front magazine, and evaluations of American writers by Sergei Dinamov.

✧

MANUSCRIPTS. (Author's Forum.) Jan. 1931-Mar. 1932. Monthly. Washington, D.C.　　NN
(Jan. 1931 as: Fifty Manuscripts; Mar. 1932 as: Author's Forum; cap-

tion and running title: *The Author's Forum*, throughout.)
*Editor not established.*

The purpose of *Manuscripts* is to bring author and publisher together, to present "The meritorious work of aspiring authors who, through our co-operation, seek to bring to the literary world, heretofore unpublished genius." A collection of writings, varied in form and quality, all by unknown writers.

✧

MANUSCRIPTS; a miscellany of art and letters . . . Nov. 1931-May 1935? Irregular. Geelong, Australia. bk. rev., illus. NN
Editor: H. Tatlock Miller.

*Manuscripts* is another of the Australian little magazines, one of whose purposes seems to be to encourage literary and artistic development "down under." Its editorial hope is that "it would become an acknowledged channel for the expression of our writers and our artists, especially our writers, who for so long have suffocated if not able to return to the Old World as prodigal sons and daughters." The interest is primarily Australian—the encouragement and development of native talent within home borders. "Why is it that in the new countries the life of so many journals of arts and letters should be so short?" the magazine asks. "Is it that our colonial feet are too heavy with the soil of the land to know 'the stillness where our spirits walk,' and our eyes so full of the yet unsettled dust of new-built cities, to notice 'the thin blown shape of a rhyme'?" *Manuscripts* publishes essays on Australian literature, reproductions of the work of Australian artists, and poetry and prose by comparatively little known Australian writers. Included among the contributions are poems by A. W. R. McNicoll, Ray M. Begg, Myra Morris, P. M. Kaberry, C. Gregory Kerr, W. A. Morrison, and Hector Bolitho. Reflections on and criticisms of contemporary European literature are numerous.

✧

THE NEW REVIEW; an international notebook for the arts . . . Jan. 1931-Apr. 1932. Quarterly. Paris. bk. rev., illus. NN
Editors: Samuel Putnam (with Peter Neagoe, Winter 1931/32-Apr. 1932).

The associate editors are Ezra Pound, Maxwell Bodenheim, and Richard Thoma.

Samuel Putnam's *New Review* has for its chief purpose "an international reportage for the arts, the higher journalism of ideas." The magazine seriously attempts to evaluate the new developments in science and to equate them with experiments in literature. The issue of Winter 1931-32 devotes much space to the effect of the machine upon aesthetics and creative expression. Criticism is contributed by Samuel Putnam, Ezra Pound, A. Lincoln Gillespie, Maxwell Bodenheim, and others.

✧

PROCESSION. Summer 1931-Feb. 1932. Quarterly. Ann Arbor, Mich. illus.
Editors: Derek Fox, Harold Courlander, and Peter Ruthven. NN

*Procession* reflects the best and most active of university interests in modern literature. It appeals to the universities to emphasize "more reasonably" the study of twentieth century literature. Critical articles by Peter Monro Jack, Gorham Munson, and William J. Gorman are supplemented by the poetry of Yvor Winters and others, and fiction by Achilles Holt and Barbara Gibbs.

✧

THE REBEL POET; official organ of rebel poets, the Internationale of song. Jan. 1931-Oct. 1932. Monthly. Holt, Minn. bk. rev., illus. NN
(Superseded by *The Anvil*, May 1933.)

Editors: B. C. Hagglund (Jan. 1931); Jack Conroy (Feb. 1931-Oct. 1932).

The early thirties found many young poets turning away from the "individualist manifestos" of the twenties, and aligning themselves definitely with some form of Marxist aesthetics. *The Rebel Poet* underlines this tendency, and is therefore essential to a study of Marxism in American literature. Contributions include poems by H. H. Lewis, Gale Wilhelm, Boris J. Israel, Joseph Freeman, Herman Spector, Fred Miller, and Kenneth Patchen.

❖

SMOKE. June 1931-May/Aug. 1937. Bimonthly. Providence, R.I. illus.　NN
Editors: Winfield Scott (June 1931-Oct. 1932); R. Wade Vliet (June-Oct. 1931); W. H. Gerry (June 1931-Oct. 1932); David Cornel DeJong (Dec. 1933-Winter 1934); S. Foster Damon (Dec. 1933-Winter 1934); Frank Merchant (Dec. 1933-Winter 1934); Susanna Valentine Mitchell (Dec. 1933-May/Aug. 1937).

David Cornel DeJong, S. Foster Damon, and Frank Merchant appear as assistant editors or advisory editors, except for two issues, when they appear as editors.

One of the best of American little poetry magazines, *Smoke* devotes no space to notices, reviews, or criticism. Its sole aim is to present the poetry of twentieth century American poets. Its contents reveal serious experiments by unknowns, together with contributions by important poets: Yvor Winters, Wallace Stevens, John Wheelwright, S. Foster Damon, Conrad Aiken, Robert Hillyer, R. P. Blackmur, William Carlos Williams, Muriel Rukeyser, Marya Zaturenska, Marianne Moore, Merrill Moore, Kenneth Patchen, and others.

❖

STORY; the only magazine devoted solely to the short story. Apr./May 1931+. Bimonthly. Vienna; Majorca, Spain; New York. index.　NN
Editors: Whit Burnett (with Martha Foley, Apr./May 1931-Sept./Oct. 1941).

Whit Burnett and Martha Foley, two American correspondents in Europe, established *Story* magazine in Vienna, because they felt that experiments in the story had received slight notice and almost no encouragement. The magazine since 1933 has been published in America. Among its outstanding contributions are stories by Erskine Caldwell, Kay Boyle, José Garcia Villa, Conrad Aiken, William Saroyan, H. E. Bates, and William Faulkner. Not the first story magazine in modern literary history, *Story* is most important for its consistent policy of sponsoring genuine talent and important innovation in the short story form. It may be said to have furnished a proving ground for many of its writers who subsequently turned to the serious business of illustrating the leftist revolution in literature, in such story magazines as *The Anvil* and Fred Miller's *Blast*. *Story* published the early writings of William Saroyan, and gave other writers of the modern short story their first opportunities for publication.

❖

STREAM. July 1931-? Monthly. Melbourne, Australia. bk. rev.　ICU
*Editor not established.*

*Stream* is an international magazine of the arts and of art criticism. It "is universal in outlook, and does not definitely ally itself with any particular art movement of the day: it seeks, in short, only what is vital and genuine in contemporary art, literature, and thought." Though *Stream* pays some attention to the work of Australian artists, writers, and critics, it is also very much interested in "the European scene." To this end, it publishes several essays on European art, music, and literature. Among the critics whose essays are published are Arthur Hanneger, Sacha Youssevitch, and G. Ribemont-Dessaignes. There are poems by Bertram Higgins, Ernest Harden, and others.

❖

VERSE CRAFT. (Emory University.) Mar./Apr. 1931+. Bimonthly (Sept.-June). Atlanta, Ga. bk. rev.   LC
(Absorbed *Horizons*, 1938?)
Editors: Wightman F. Melton (July/Aug. 1931-Jan./Feb. 1933); Lawrence W. Neff (Mar./Apr. 1933+).
*Issues earlier than July/Aug. 1931 not consulted.*

Many American poetry magazines editorialize self-consciously and sentimentally about "the beautiful" and "the divine creative impulse," and print verses in which the thought is buried in and the emotion stifled by clichés. This tendency in *Verse Craft* is only occasionally relieved by the verse of such poets as August Derleth, Ralph Cheyney, Stanton Coblentz, and Kathleen Sutton.

---

## 1932

THE AMERICAN SPECTATOR; a literary newspaper. Nov. 1932-Apr./May 1937. Monthly. New York. bk. rev., illus. (Suspended, Apr.-May 1935.)   NN
Editors: George Jean Nathan, Ernest Boyd, James Branch Cabell, Eugene O'Neill (Nov. 1932-Mar. 1935); Theodore Dreiser (Nov. 1932-Feb. 1934); Sherwood Anderson (Dec. 1933-Mar. 1935); anonymously edited (June-Sept. 1935); Charles Angoff (Oct. 1935-July/Aug. 1936); Max Lehman (Sept. 1936-Apr./May 1937).
Contributing editors: Art Young, Norman Macleod, Louis Ginsberg, E. M. Josephson, Witter Bynner, and others.

Like *Contempo* and *The Chicago Literary Times*, *The American Spectator* is a "literary newspaper," offering comment on a wide variety of subjects interesting to the student of modern letters. Unlike its Chicago brother, its point of view is serious, and its purpose to evaluate our age without "commercial or advertising" prejudice. Theodore Dreiser and Eugene O'Neill appear in the role of critics. The prose of Sherwood Anderson is also in evidence. The criticism of Joseph Wood Krutch, Ernest Boyd, and Robert Linn also appears. There are frequent satirical references to certain writers and movements—as, for example, Rita Wellman's "Up in Mabel's Room." Short stories are contributed by Jerome Weidman and Sherwood Anderson.

❖

BETTER VERSE. Sept. 1932-Sept. 1938. Bimonthly, St. Paul, Minn.   NN
(Absorbed *Nebulae*, Nov. 19, 1935.)
Editor: Irl Morse.

*Better Verse* prints, among others, the poems of Stanton Coblentz, Lucia Trent, and Glenn Ward Dresbach.

❖

CONTEMPORARY POETRY. Oct. 3-Dec. 5, 1932. Semimonthly. West Chicago, Ill.   H
Editor: George Henry Kay.

" 'Contemporary Poetry' has no quarrel with free verse, but whether rhymed or free, I maintain that verse should possess clarity and thought.... 'Free verse is good, but NEVER fresh verse,' shall be my motto." The magazine publishes, among others, the poems of Stanton Coblentz, Kathleen Sutton, J. Corson Miller, and Lucia Trent.

❖

DECIMAL; a modicum of verse. Mar. 1932-Dec. 1935. Quarterly. Newport, R.I. bk. rev.   NN
Editor: Ada Borden Stevens.

A small quarterly collection of verses, with some contributions by Harold Vinal, Margaret Widdemer, Benjamin Musser, Stanton Coblentz, and August Derleth.

❖

DOPE. 1932-? Frequency not given. London. illus.     ICU
Editor: Bernard Causton.

Dope is a literary newssheet, devoted to a rapid and satirical survey of the modern literary scene, but accessible also to young and unknown writers "who are recommended by their work and by their work alone." Somewhat in the manner of the early *American Mercury*, *Dope* prints excerpts from the British press which strike it as being especially amusing or foolish. Included in the first issue are poems by W. H. Auden and J. Bronowski, and critical notes by Oswell Blakeston and Bernard Causton.

❖

HERITAGE. May/June-Sept./Oct. 1932? Bimonthly. Amherst, Mass. bk. rev.
Editor: Cecil Herbert Hemley.   NN

*Heritage* is a kind of "counter-revolution" in the history of the little magazine. Its aim is not to present "a collection of youthful remedies to all sorts of conditions," but rather to assert traditional values, to relate the past with the present. The contents of the magazine consistently carry out its purpose.

❖

HOUSATONIC; a magazine for and about New England. July 15-Sept. 1, 1932. Fortnightly. Roxbury, Conn.   H
Editors: Eleanor Clark, Eunice Clark, and Muriel Rukeyser.

A New England magazine, *Housatonic* announces as its purpose ". . . to outline for a certain region the direction of this change [of the early thirties], in social standards, politics, economic organization, philosophy and art." To this end, the magazine contains several essays on New England culture and society. But it is not merely a magazine of regional debate. Its editors have been able to collect and publish a number of contributions in original writing, among them poems by Frances Frost, Selden Rodman, Eleanor Clark, Sherry Mangan, John Wheelwright, and James Rorty.

❖

LEFTWARD. (John Reed Club.) Nov. 1932-Aug. 1933? Monthly. Boston. bk. rev., illus.   Y
Editor: M. P. Hyde.

Like other John Reed Club magazines, *Leftward* is interested in the direct application of literature to the needs of radical politics. The magazine and the club are convinced "that the interests of all writers and artists should be identified with the interests of the working class." There are discussions of events in the Soviet and labor news from American sources. But the primary emphasis is upon literary demonstrations of leftwing ideas and principles. Among the contributions are poems by Paul Burns, Warner Wolcott, Eduard d'Orme; short stories by Paul Burns, Geraldine Whitney, and Peter Gillis.

❖

MASSES. (Progressive Arts Club.) Apr. 1932-Apr. 1934? Monthly. Toronto. bk. rev., illus.   Y
*Editor not established.*
*Issues other than Sept. 1933 not consulted.*

*Masses* is a leftwing magazine of literature and political comment. Its short stories are concerned mainly with underscoring the plight of the worker, or with describing conditions which strikes or other moves might help to alleviate. There are short stories by Robert Hall and Ruby Ronan, and poetry by Joseph Kalar and others.

MEASURE. (Gerard Manley Hopkins Poetry Society.) Christmas 1932-Christmas 1933. Semiannual. Washington, D.C. NN
Editors: James C. Hendrickson, Theodore Maynard, John Shields, and others.

By critical precept and poetic example, Measure pays tribute to the Catholic poet, Gerard Manley Hopkins. The poetry is for the most part imitative of Hopkins' manner and limited to religious themes.

❖

SCOPE; A Rocky Mountain review. Fall, 1932-? Quarterly. Denver, Colo. Editors: H. B. Noland and H. S. Pulse. Y

A Western little magazine, Scope has for its aim to act "as a nucleus for genuine talent" and to "provide a forum for adventurous thinkers." Contributions include poems by Witter Bynner and Margaret Pond, and fiction by H. S. Pulse and Fern Lane.

❖

SILHOUETTES. Oct. 1932-1938. Quarterly. Ontario, Calif. bk. rev., illus. (Absorbed *Five*, Winter 1935.) (Combined with *Poetry Caravan*, to form *Poetry Caravan and Silhouettes*, Winter 1939/40.) NN
Editor: James Neill Northe.

*Silhouettes* follows the familiar pattern of the little poetry magazine. "While we wish subscriptions," says the opening editorial, "a subscription will have no influence upon the publication of a poem." Poetry, for the editor, "is the quintessence of refinement, expressing the utmost in humanity in the most expressive way known to man, rhythm, meter and rhyme." Contributions include some of the poems of Benjamin Musser, Ralph Cheyney, Arthur Truman Merrill, Margaret Widdemer, Raymond Kresensky, Helen Hoyt, Robert P. Tristram Coffin, Witter Bynner, and other poets.

❖

TRAILS; a literary magazine of the outdoors. Winter 1932+. Quarterly. Esperance, N.Y. H NN
Editor: Fred Lape.

A little poetry magazine which publishes, among others, the poems of Helen Hoyt, Robert P. Tristram Coffin, Harold Vinal, Glenn Ward Dresbach, August Derleth, Clement Wood, and Stanton Coblentz.

❖

TREND; a quarterly of the seven arts. (Society of Teachers and Composers, Inc.) Mar./May 1932-Mar./Apr. 1935. Brooklyn, N.Y. bk. rev., illus., index. Supplement: "Prelude to Immortality," Eric Ely-Estorick, May/June 1934. NN
Editorial board: Harrison Kerr, Jeanne McHugh, Samuel Loveman, Edward G. Perry, and others.

Among the interesting developments in magazine publishing is the magazine of the "several arts." Many of the representatives of this type simply pay tribute to the arts of painting, sculpture, and music by publishing reproductions, photographs, and musical scores. Some few attempt a synthesis of the arts, or at least search for apparent or real relationships among them. The unity of *Trend's* treatment of the arts is only occasionally evident. By means of critical articles on American culture, the magazine seeks to give its separate treatments of the arts a larger reference to aesthetics as a whole. Literary contributions to *Trend* are numerous, and seem best adapted to its purpose. *Trend* publishes the poetry of Alfred Kreymborg, Countée Cullen, Langston Hughes, Norman Macleod, Kerker Quinn, Babette Deutsch, Millen Brand, Paul

Goodman, Muriel Rukeyser, Kenneth Patchen, and others; fiction by Millen Brand, August Derleth, Albert Halper, and Sanora Babb.

❖

THE VERSEMAKER; a quarterly magazine of popular verse. Spring 1932-Autumn 1936? Lawrenceville, Ill. Editors: R. Albright (with Jeanette Seletz, Summer 1935-Autumn 1936). H NN

A little poetry magazine which publishes, among others, the poems of Louis Ginsberg, Benjamin Musser, Joseph Upper, Lucia Trent, Glenn Ward Dresbach, and Ralph Cheyney.

## 1933

ADAMANT; a quarterly of beautiful verse. Winter 1933/34-Winter 1935. Waukegan, Ill. bk. rev. H
Editor: Lillian Candler.

A small poetry magazine whose five issues publish, among others, the poems of Lucia Trent, Benjamin Musser, Glenn Ward Dresbach, Stanton Coblentz, Ralph Cheyney, Clifford Gessler, and Kathleen Sutton.

❖

AMERICAN POETRY JOURNAL. July 1933-July/Aug. 1935. Monthly. Flushing, N.Y. bk. rev. NN
Editor: Frances Frost.

Among the aims of Frances Frost's magazine is that of publishing in each issue a poem of from three hundred to fifteen hundred lines or longer. Since most poetry magazines have neglected the longer forms, *American Poetry Journal* offers a valuable service to American verse. Among the longer poems published are those of Mark Van Doren, Evelyn Scott, Conrad Aiken, and Genevieve Taggard. Shorter poems are contributed by Theodore Roethke, John Wheelwright, Norman Macleod, Willard Maas, John Gould Fletcher, and others.

❖

THE ANVIL; stories for workers. May 1933-Oct./Nov. 1935. Bimonthly. Moberly, Mo. illus. NN
(Supersedes *The Rebel Poet*.) (Absorbed by *Partisan Review*, Feb. 1936.)
Editors: Jack Conroy (with Walter Snow, Mar./Apr.-Oct./Nov. 1935, Clinton Simpson, May/June-Oct./Nov. 1935, and Michael Gold, Oct./Nov. 1935).
B. C. Hagglund, Joseph Kalar, Erskine Caldwell, and Langston Hughes are among the associate or contributing editors.

Among those who turned to proletarian literature in the thirties one finds writers of two kinds: those who had already received some notice before the thirties, but whose convictions now led them to accept leftwing ideas as a guide to their writings (some of these submitted to a rather rigid doctrinal scrutiny of their work); those who gained their position as literary artists almost exclusively through their contributions to proletarian art. *The Anvil* prints contributions from members of both groups. Jack Conroy insists in the opening issue that contributors to *The Anvil* "need not be Communists." One of the most active and most successful of leftwing literary magazines, it publishes a great variety of short stories, of varying degrees of merit, most of them concerned with portraying the decadence of bourgeois life, the oppression of the workers, or heroic struggles against "the system." Contributions include short stories by Boris Israel, August Derleth, Erskine Caldwell, Paul Corey, Meridel Le Sueur, Louis Zara, and James T. Farrell; poems by Langston Hughes, Norman Macleod, and Orrick Johns.

ARTISTS' AND WRITERS' CHAP BOOK. Dec. 15, 1933-May 3, 1935. (Only two issues.) New York. illus. NN Editors: J. George Frederick (1933); David George Plotkin (1935).

In the midst of much proletarian activity, a few little magazines held fast to the pattern of the twenties—that is, either no editorial policy at all, or a policy based primarily upon individualist aesthetics. The *Artists' and Writers' Chap Book* (issued on the occasion of the Costume Ball by the Artists' and Writers' Dinner Club) is one of these few. It is still interested in Ezra Pound as a poet and critic, and publishes the work of a variety of writers, with very little regard for their political persuasions: poetry by Parker Tyler, Charles Henri Ford, William Carlos Williams, Harold Rosenberg, and Maxwell Bodenheim; critical prose by Tyler, Henry Miller, and Theodore Dreiser.

✧

BARD; a quarterly of verse. Oct. 1933-Summer 1941? Jackson, Mo. H NN Editors: Myrtle Vorst Sheppard (Oct. 1933-Apr. 1935?); Margaret Ferguson Henderson (Apr. 1935-Summer 1941; with Nina Harrington Cracraft, Spring 1940-Summer 1941?).

A little magazine of verse, which publishes, among others, poems by Byron Vazakas, August Derleth, Alan Swallow, and Oscar Williams.

✧

BLAST; a magazine of proletarian short stories. Sept. 1933-Nov. 1934. Bimonthly. New York. NN Editors: Fred R. Miller (with Sam Sorkin, Sept. 1933.)

Another of the proletarian magazines, *Blast* emphasizes the realistic detail of which most readers seemed intensely aware during the depression years. In the magazine appear many of the "depression-bred" writers, whose range of achievement is great, their subject matter generally limited by their social and political convictions: Benjamin Appel, Alfred Morang, Fred Miller, and others. Some of the best of William Carlos Williams' stories appear here.

✧

CAMBRIDGE LEFT. (Queens' College.) Summer 1933-Autumn 1934. 3 issues a year. Cambridge, Eng. bk. rev. *Editor not established.* NN

*Cambridge Left* reflects the strong swing of literary interest toward the left in the thirties in England. It is interested primarily in evaluating the role of the writer in terms of his social prerogatives and obligations, and in studying the effects of Marxist ideology upon poetry. "The motives for writing, of those who are writing for this paper, have changed, along with their motives for doing anything. It is not so much an intellectual choice, as the forcible intrusion of social issues." *Cambridge Left* exists as a means for writers of the left to work out an aesthetic consistent with the ideology of which they approve. Critical essays are contributed by J. D. Bernal, J. Cornford, Helen Davis, and H. V. Kemp; poetry, by W. H. Auden, Richard Goodman, Charles Madge, and Gavin Ewart.

✧

THE CONNECTICUT ECHO; a magazine of verse. Spring 1933-Summer 1935. Quarterly. Woodmont, Conn. illus. Editor: Marjorie Dugdale Asche. NN

A few minor poets contribute to the pages of this magazine: Kathleen Sutton, Olive Scott Stainsby, and Stanton Coblentz, among them.

✧

CONNECTICUT LORE. Jan./Mar. 1933-July 1934. Quarterly. Portland, Conn. bk. rev. NN Y Editor: Hollis M. French.

*Connecticut Lore* is interesting for its sponsorship of "a regional movement" in Connecticut letters. To this end are published sketches, essays, and poems. One sketch is contributed by Odell Shepard.

❖

CONTEMPORARIES AND MAKERS. Spring 1933-1934. Quarterly. Cambridge, Eng. (Summer 1933-1934 as: *Contemporaries.*) NN
Editor: John Kaestlin.

A college literary magazine, *Contemporaries and Makers* contributes to the literary scene several poems and stories by contemporary writers and a number of critical essays on modern literary figures and trends. Among these latter are essays on James Joyce, on the *Cantos* of Ezra Pound, and on contemporary drama and music. There are also poems by Ernest Reynolds, Robert Hamer, Charles Madge, and others; and stories by Wynyard Browne, Mark Appleby, and others.

❖

COUNTERPOINT; a poetic vanguard. July 1933-? Monthly. St. Louis, Mo.
Editor: Cardinal Le Gros. ICU

A little magazine of poetry, *Counterpoint* publishes, among others, contributions by Clark Mills and Harold Vinal.

❖

EUROPA; an all Europe review. May/July 1933-June/Aug. 1934. Quarterly. New York. illus. NN
Editor: William Kozlenko.

Samuel Putnam is indicated as the European editor.

The object of *Europa* is chiefly to survey the literature, the arts, and the politics of contemporary Europe. Its critical essays are of great value and importance to a study of what might well be called the "most self-conscious decade of our century." Among the critics represented are Clive Bell, William Kozlenko, and Lion Feuchtwanger.

❖

THE GREENWICH VILLAGER. May 15, 1933-Feb. 1934? Semimonthly. New York. bk. rev., illus. NN
Editor: Edison Smith.

A literary and critical magazine of the Village, *The Greenwich Villager* features such prose essays as V. F. Calverton's "Music and Morals" and C. Hartley Grattan's "On the Meaning in Novels." Editorially, the magazine speaks against other Village periodicals which have in the past been established to favor literary cliques, and hopes that "*The Greenwich Villager* will be accepted as a real asset to the Village and will be instrumental in the discovery of unknown and unpublished talent." The magazine also furnishes information about the Village and the Villagers. There are contributions in prose by Bob Brown, Genevieve Larsson, Joe Gould, Harold Loeb; poems by Harry Kemp, Mary Carolyn Davies, and others.

❖

KOSMOS; dynamic stories of today. Nov./Dec. 1933-July/Aug. 1935. Bimonthly. Philadelphia. bk. rev. NN
(Merged with *American Columnists* to form *Creative*, Nov./Dec. 1936.)
Editors: Jay Harrison (with S. Beryl Lush, Nov./Dec. 1933-May/June 1934, and Bernice Pittala, May/June-July/Aug. 1935).

José Garcia Villa appears in the early issues, as a contributing editor.

Like *Anvil* and *Blast*, *Kosmos* features proletarian fiction. The form of the short story is peculiarly suited to a proletarian literary movement, primarily because it is closest to the actual reporting of fact, yet less "objective" and more maneuverable by the writer than reportage. *Kosmos* attracts almost all of the "depression realists" and some of the best of the leftwing poets: stories by William Kozlenko, Benjamin Appel, James Laughlin IV, Karlton Kelm, James T. Farrell, Paul Corey, Langston Hughes, and Millen Brand; poems by Kenneth Fearing, Muriel Rukeyser, José Garcia Villa, and Norman Macleod. An essay by Thomas H. Uzzell in the issue of February/March 1935 discusses the influence of psychoanalysis upon radical literature.

❖

THE LATIN QUARTER-LY. Sept. 1933-Autumn 1934. New York. bk. rev., illus.　　　　　　　　　　　　　NN
Editors: Lew Ney and Ruth Widen.
　Contributing editors: Art Young, Sherwood Anderson, Norman Macleod, Louis Ginsberg, E. M. Josephson, Witter Bynner, and others.

Specifically, *The Latin Quarter-ly* is a magazine of gossip about Greenwich Village affairs; as such it is valuable. But, in its short career, it does little to justify its frequent editorial boasts and promises. The letters of Kathleen Tankersley Young to Lew Ney and Ruth Widen are published. There is poetry from the pens of John Gould Fletcher, Norman Macleod, and Benjamin Musser. There is much interesting comment about little magazines and the *avant garde*.

❖

LEFT FRONT. (John Reed Club of Chicago.) June 1933-June 1934? Bimonthly. Chicago, Ill. bk. rev., illus.　NN
Editor: Bill Jordan.

One of a group of John Reed Club publications, *Left Front* openly avows its dedication to the "proletarian culture front." Middle-class letters have fallen into senility and decay; sensible and intelligent middle-class intellectuals "are swinging left and learning the Marxian idea about art." The satire is less subtle and clever, the criticism more direct and self-confident, than that of *The Masses*; the change reflects the growing strength of the left wing since the years of the First World War. Proletarian fiction is contributed by J. S. Balch, Edith Margo, and others; poetry by Norman Macleod, Richard Wright, and William Pillin.

❖

THE LITERARY MONTHLY. Dec. 1933-May/June 1934. Portland, Ore. bk. rev., illus.　　　　　　　　　　BI UO
(Absorbed *Outlander*, Feb. 1934.)
(May/June 1934 as: *Literary Magazine*.)
Editors: Dec. 1933 editor not established; Philip Irwin, Padraic Merrick, Dan Northup, and Kenneth Tillson (Jan.-May/June 1934).

The aim of *The Literary Monthly* is to present the literature of its region, the Northwest. Among the contributions are stories by Dan Northup and Ken Tillson, and a poem by Philip Irwin.

❖

THE LITTLE MAGAZINE. Dec. 1933/Jan. 1934-Sept./Oct. 1934? Bimonthly. New York.　　　　　　　　　　NN
Editors: Harry Davis and Henrietta Tepper.

*The Little Magazine* steers a middle course between the two currents of letters of the thirties: the individualist and the Marxist. It announces as its chief purpose, ". . . to supply a medium for material which, by virtue of its being creative rather than manufactured according to formula, sets its own standards, thereby making it unacceptable to magazines with an 'editorial' policy." There are many shades of thinking and political belief represented; most writers, however, belong to "the left." Norman Macleod and Maxwell Bodenheim present two varying opinions of the revolutionary artist: Macleod is firmly convinced of the revolutionary role of the artist; Bodenheim, more moderate, warns against making art subserve propaganda. In the rather creditable list of contributions one finds poems by Samuel Putnam, José Garcia Villa, Harry Roskolenkier, James Laughlin IV, Kerker Quinn, and Philip Rahv; fiction by Millen Brand, David Cornel DeJong, and August Derleth. Ezra Pound submits two short pieces, of consequence only as they reflect the current of his interests in the thirties.

✧

LOVAT DICKSON'S MAGAZINE; new short stories. Nov. 1933-June 1935. Monthly. London. index (v. 3, July-Dec. 1934, only). NN
Editors: P. Gilchrist Thompson (Nov. 1933-Sept. 1934); Lovat Dickson (Oct. 1934-Mar. 1935); L. A. G. Strong (Apr.-June 1935).

Like *Story* and *New Stories*, *Lovat Dickson's Magazine* is dedicated to the furtherance of the short story as an "art form." The editorial policy calls for a magazine "free from political or other features, and attractive alike to those who want only an hour or two of interesting reading and to those who value the short story as a significant form of literature." The magazine wishes especially to honor with publication the great number of "writers struggling for recognition." But writers with "established reputation" are also published, because even they are not always able to place their work readily. In the issue of December 1933, Edward J. O'Brien sums up the history of the short story of the past twenty years. In this summary O'Brien gives some information about the short story little magazine of that time—most notably, about *Story*. *Lovat Dickson's Magazine* publishes, along with its careful selection of worth-while short stories, comments upon the short story by O'Brien, H. E. Bates, L. A. G. Strong, R. Ellis Roberts, and Edwin Muir; these comments, taken together, form an excellent critical treatment of the short story form. Among its many important contributions one finds the short stories of Louis Golding, Ernest Hemingway, H. E. Bates, Séan O'Fáolain, L. A. G. Strong, V. S. Pritchett, D. H. Lawrence, Hans Fallada, Kay Boyle, William Saroyan, Liam O'Flaherty, Erskine Caldwell, and Rhys Davies.

✧

THE MAGAZINE; a literary journal. Dec. 1933-June 1935. Monthly. Beverly Hills, Calif. index. NN
Editors: John McAllister, Richard Perry, Fred Kuhlman, and Arthur Rohman.

*The Magazine* is one of a few little magazines of the early thirties not committed, either directly or tacitly, to a political program or a social emphasis. It publishes much material from the "California group of writers," many of them influenced by the teaching and example of Stanford University's Yvor Winters. In all respects the magazine fulfills the requirements of *avant-garde* publications—with the single exception that its preoccupation with matters of style does not allow for startling innovation or experiment. There is poetry here by R. P. Blackmur, Don Stanford, J. V. Cunningham, Barbara Gibbs, Allen Tate, Kenneth Patchen, Yvor Winters, Howard Baker, Janet Lewis, José Garcia Villa, Norman Macleod, and Muriel Rukeyser; fiction by Robert Penn Warren, Meridel Le Sueur, Achilles Holt, Josephine Herbst, William Carlos Williams (parts of *White Mule*), Howard Baker, and others. "The Tunnel," from Muriel Rukeyser's *Theory of Flight*, is printed here for the first time.

✧

THE MOMENT. Feb. 1933-? Monthly. New York. NN
Editor: Martin Panzer.
*Issues later than Feb. 1933 not consulted.*

Chief interest of *The Moment* is the development of the form known as "short-short story"; much space is devoted to it, though poetry is also published, as are editorial comments.

❖

THE NEW ACT; a literary review. Jan. 1933-May 1934? Irregular. New York. bk. rev.     NN
Editors: H. R. Hays and Harold Rosenberg.
*Issues later than June 1933 not consulted.*

The New Act presents some of the best of all the little magazine's contributions to criticism, especially to poetics. Harold Rosenberg's essay-editorial in issue No. 1 states succinctly the problem of the *avant-garde* magazine. Important critical essays are contributed by Rosenberg, René Taupin, H. R. Hays, Ezra Pound, and others.

❖

THE NEW HOPE; art, literature, crafts, music. Oct. 1933-Oct. 1934. Monthly. New Hope, Pa. bk. rev., illus.    NN P
Editor: Peter Keenan.
Samuel Putnam, Thomas Benton, George Antheil appear, among others, on the editorial board (June-Oct. 1934).

Competent critics help to make The New Hope an interesting collection of revaluations. The editors are aware that "many of the still quite recent modernisms now seem as hopelessly demoded as the old rubber-tired phaeton . . ." and seek to measure the future possibilities of the arts and letters in America. Critical essays are contributed by Klaus Mann, Stanley Mayer, Samuel Putnam, and others.

❖

THE NEW OXFORD OUTLOOK. May 1933-Nov. 1935. Twice a year. Oxford, Eng. bk. rev.     NN
(Supersedes *The Oxford Outlook*.)
Editors: Richard Crossman and Gilbert Highet (with Derek Kahn, May 1933-Feb. 1934, Jack Winocour, May 1934-Jan. 1935, and Paul Engle, Nov. 1935).

Like its predecessor, The New Oxford Outlook is published in association with university affairs. Its interests, however, are considerably extended and varied, to include many aspects of modern aesthetics. Such modern poets as Stephen Spender, C. Day Lewis, Sherry Mangan, O. Blakeston, and Paul Engle appear in its pages. There are critical essays as well, some on politics, others on modern poetry and the arts.

❖

THE NEW TALENT; the new quarterly. June 1933-Jan./Mar. 1936. New York. bk. rev., illus.    NN
Editors: E. G. Arnold (with Weldon Giniger, June 1933-Apr./June 1935, and David Bernstein, Apr./June 1935-Jan./Mar. 1936).

The New Talent promises to publish the work of unknown writers who wish to see their names in print, but offers no other remuneration but "fame." The contents are an earnest of a sincere and fairly successful effort to remain true to the principles of the little magazine. There is much interesting comment on "the meaning of advance guard"—"It is of necessity a magazine for a minority, simply because only a minority of the people lives in an honest present, while the great mass reposes in a wish-dream."

❖

NEW VERSE. Jan. 1933-May 1939. Bimonthly. London. bk. rev., illus.    NN
Editors: Geoffrey Grigson, and others.

Because of its serious and intelligent interest in modern poetics, and also the excellence of its contributions, New Verse can justly be called the best of all recent poetry magazines. All of England's recent "poetry renaissance" is reflected and encouraged in its pages.

By means of editorials, essays, and enquiries on matters of poetics and aesthetics, New Verse exercises a constant self-criticism, thus furnishing the student of modern poetry both with the poetry and the technical means of appraising it. Special issues contain the answers to questionnaires on the nature of poetry and the self and poetry and society; herein are gathered serious statements by the poets themselves on Freudianism, Marxism, and related matters. The issue of April 1935 is devoted to a consideration of the poetry of Gerard Manley Hopkins; that of November 1937, to criticism of W. H. Auden's poetry. Criticism in New Verse is contributed by Horace Gregory, Herbert Read, I. A. Richards, Geoffrey Grigson, Stephen Spender, Charles Madge, and others. Only a partial list of the poets published in New Verse is possible: Frederic Prokosch, C. Day Lewis, Stephen Spender, Theodore Spencer, Allen Tate, W. H. Auden, Dylan Thomas, Kenneth Allott, George Barker, Herbert Read, William Empson, Archibald MacLeish, and John Crowe Ransom. An interesting experiment in "collective poetry" is reported upon in the issue of May 1937, "The Oxford Collective Poem."

❖

1 9 3 3; a year magazine. June/Dec. 1933-Dec. 1933/Apr. 1934. (Only two issues.) Philadelphia. bk. rev. (Dec. 1933/Apr. 1934 as: A Year Magazine.)    NN
Editors: J. Louis Stoll, J. B. Hoptner, and Ada Tier.

The aim of 1933 is ". . . to collect a vivid, vital, important cross section of the various schools of the advance guard." American realism in the short story of the thirties pictures the small town as a dreary, spiritually dead place —waiting dully to be reborn. An example of the detailed description of the small world of capitalism follows, from one of the stories: ". . . the room was small and its week-end yellowness squatted with a dull thud as she awoke heavily after a hot glowering night. The immovable silence and the quietly laughing bottle of wine. And ashes . . ." 1933 presents in its second number an important survey of opinion regarding the position of the advance guard magazine: participating in the symposium are Thomas Uzzell, Frederick Maxham, William Carlos Williams, Fred Miller, Norman Macleod, and others. Both conservative and radical opinions are expressed, but the latter are much more in evidence. Contributions to the magazine include short stories by James T. Farrell, Jack Conroy, Paul Corey, and others; poetry by Parker Tyler; and a "critical" essay by D. Lincoln Gillespie, Jr.

❖

THE NORTH CAROLINA POETRY REVIEW. (North Carolina Poetry Society.) July 1933-June 1936. Monthly. Gastonia, N.C. bk. rev.    NN
(Absorbed by Poetry World.)
Editor: Stewart Atkins.

At the beginning The North Carolina Poetry Review emphasizes "the writing of meritorious poetry in North Carolina"; gradually, however, it abandons its sectional policy and allows poetry from a wider selection of writers. The magazine publishes such minor poets as Archibald Rutledge, Benjamin Musser, Louis Ginsberg, and Ralph Cheyney.

❖

THE OBSERVER; a literary publication. Feb. 15, 1933-Jan./Feb. 1934. Monthly. Memphis, Tenn. bk. rev.    NN
Editor: Blaine Treadway and others.

Born of literary discussions by "the Socratic Club," The Observer presents a lively appearance, marked by enthusiasm for the avant garde. The issue of April 1933 is dedicated to Ezra Pound, "because he has done more than any other one man for the liberation of poetry." Contributions include verse by Norman Macleod and Gertrude Stein.

❖

THE OUTLANDER; a quarterly literary review. 1933. Portland, Ore. illus.
(Absorbed by The Literary Monthly, Feb. 1934.)
Editors: Albert Richard Wetjen and Roderick Lull.

The mimeographed little magazine of Richard Wetjen and Roderick Lull, The Outlander, publishes a number of stories, poems, and critical articles; contributors include August Derleth, Louis Adamic, Paul F. Corey, Ethel Romig Fuller, and Fred B. Maxham.

❖

THE OUTRIDER; a journal for literates. Nov. 1, 1933-May 1934? Bimonthly. Cincinnati, Ohio. illus.   NN
Editors: Norwood Chamberlin (with Howard Eustice, Nov. 1, 1933).

The Outrider devotes much critical attention to the modern American literary scene; among the subjects which come up for critical discussion are Greenwich Village, D. H. Lawrence and sex prudery, Gertrude Stein ("Chaos in Syntaxia"), and Ezra Pound. Satirical moods are frequent. There is a poem by Kerker Quinn, a short story by Alfred Morang.

❖

PANORAMA; a monthly survey of people and ideas. Oct. 1933-Jan. 1935. Boston.   NN
Editor: Isaac Goldberg.
Among the contributing editors are: Barrett H. Clark and Paul Eldridge.

A magazine chiefly of the leftist persuasion, Panorama combines the good critical talent of Charles I. Glicksberg (who surveys most of modern literature in a series of articles) with the writing of many of the best leftist advance-guardists. Contributions include the criticism of Isaac Goldberg, Albert Mordell, Benjamin De Casseres, and Anthony Netboy; the poetry of B. A. Botkin, Louis Ginsberg, Charles Glicksberg, Kerker Quinn, and Frederick Maxham; the short stories of William Kelm and Bryllion Fagin.

❖

THE PARTISAN; journal of art, literature and opinion. (John Reed Clubs of Hollywood, Carmel, San Francisco.) Dec. 1933-Sept./Oct. 1934? Monthly. Los Angeles, Calif. bk. rev., illus.   NN
Editors: Michael Quin, Douglas Hammer, Joseph Gower, and others.

Another of the John Reed Club magazines, The Partisan is interested chiefly in debate over social issues, and in prose and poetry which most closely approximate reportage. In the course of its campaign for a new world, it publishes such literary materials as the following: short stories by Ella Winter, John McGregor, and others; poems by Orrick Johns, Langston Hughes, Walker Winslow, and Marie de L. Welch.

❖

THE POETRY QUARTERLY; devoted to British and American poetry and drama. Winter 1933-Spring 1934. London. bk. rev.   NN
(Spring 1934 as: The Poetry Quarterly and Dramatic Review.)
Editors: William Kingston Fudge (Jan.-July 1933); George Whybrow (Autumn 1933-Spring 1934).

A British poetry magazine whose aim is to accept and publish poems from whatever source, known or unknown. "The magazine is not endowed, nor is it the official organ of any association or body. . . . We invite new and known poets to submit their verses for consideration. We are not impressed by 'best-selling' names; we want real poetry." The magazine conducts a lively editorial column discussing matters of interest to students of modern poetry. Contributions include poems by Sanora Babb, Stanton Coblentz, and Louis Ginsberg.

❖

POETRY STUDIES. Spring 1933-1938. Quarterly. London. bk. rev., illus. NN (Superseded by *Poetry Quarterly,* Spring 1939.)
Editors: Katherine Hunter Coe and E. M. Channing-Renton.

A British poetry magazine which publishes, among other things, the verse of Lucia Trent, Ralph Cheyney, Rev. T. Pittaway, Stanton Coblentz, and Clifford Gessler.

❖

THE RAVEN ANTHOLOGY. Dec. 1933-Oct. 1940. Monthly. New York.
Editor: Francis Lambert McCrudden.

A Greenwich Village little poetry magazine which publishes, among others, poems by Anca Urbooska, Vincent Beltrone, Jane O'Ryan, Joe Gould, and Eli Siegel.

❖

THE ROCKING HORSE; a literary magazine. (The Arden Club, University of Wisconsin.) Sept. 1933-Summer 1935? 4 issues a year. Madison, Wis. bk. rev. ICU P Y
Editor: John Moe.

The University of Wisconsin's literary magazine suddenly shifts its position (Spring 1935), to include contributions from most of the important writers of the time. The explanation for the change is that "local literary activity" will be stimulated by the presence of the literary great. *The Rocking Horse* demonstrates a noticeable self-criticism in its editorials, and casts an appraising eye over the avant-garde magazines in general; it is concerned over "the discredit which can be brought upon our endeavors generally by little magazines which have neither artistic merit nor political principle nor ethical passion to justify their existence." Contributions to the issue of Spring 1935 include the poetry of Wallace Stevens, William Ellery Leonard, Marya Zaturenska, Raymond E. F. Larsson, and Grant Code; an essay by William Carlos Williams on Ezra Pound and Gertrude Stein, and a brief note on economics by Pound.

❖

SEED. Jan.-July 1933. Quarterly. London. NN
Editors: Herbert Jones and Oswell Blakeston.

A short-lived but excellent little magazine, anxious for "new talent" but willing to publish authors already established. Contributions include poetry by H. D., Mary Butts, [Winifred] Bryher, Rhys Davies, John Pudney, Oswell Blakeston, Richard Thoma, and others; prose fiction by Sidney Hunt, Oswell Blakeston, Kay Boyle, and others.

❖

SHARDS. Feb. 1933-Nov. 1939. Quarterly. Augusta, Ga. bk. rev. NN
Editor: Constance Deming Lewis.

*Shards* would like to remedy a situation it deplores—a contemporary failure to appreciate good poetry. To that end it editorializes about the nature of the beautiful and its meaning for civilization: "A civilization that has the capacity for appreciation of the beautiful is a civilization that will need no military spur to prod it in the general direction of what has been conceived as the happy estate." As a means of putting civilization on the right train, *Shards* publishes the poems of Lucia Trent, Laura Benét, Kathleen Sutton, Stanton Coblentz, Ralph Cheyney, Norman Macleod, August Derleth, Benjamin Musser, and others, and many brief essays on poetry and allied subjects.

TONE; modern poetry. Sept. 1933-Jan. 1935. (Only four issues.) Irregular. Buffalo, N.Y. bk. rev.   NN
Editor: Joseph Rodman Manch.

Tone publishes poetry by a group of avant-garde writers, many of them editors of other little magazines. The quality of the verse varies. Contributions include the poetry of Frederick Maxham, José Garcia Villa, Norman Macleod, James Laughlin IV, Kerker Quinn, Evelyn Scott, and Parker Tyler.

◊

THE WANDERER. Dec. 1933-Nov. 1934. Monthly. London. index.   NN
Editor: John Middleton Murry.

The Wanderer is John Middleton Murry's little magazine, written entirely by him and distributed by him to his following, "in lieu of his next book." Subject matter varies but Murry's principal concern is "to make a new approach to politics." His writing is frankly a search for a "simple synthesis" of Christianity, art, and politics. Other subjects include marriage, crime, and D. H. Lawrence.

◊

THE WINDSOR QUARTERLY; modern American literature. Spring 1933-Fall 1935. Hartland Four Corners, Vt. bk. rev., cum. index (v. 1-3, Spring 1933-Fall 1935).   NN
Editors: Frederick B. Maxham and Irene Merrill.

The Windsor Quarterly moves South and left with the issue of Autumn 1934. It is at first hospitable to all tendencies, publishing essays by objective analysts, but eventually comes to the conclusion that the best materials are to be had from the leftwing groups. The career of The Windsor Quarterly, therefore, furnishes material for a valuable study of the dilemma of the artist of the thirties. The magazine is an excellent organ of advance guard expression. Contributions include poems by Evelyn Scott, José Garcia Villa, Norman Macleod, David Cornel DeJong, James Laughlin IV, and Harry Roskolenkier; stories by Alvah C. Bessie, Meridel Le Sueur, and others; and criticism by Samuel Putnam, Parker Tyler, and Louis Zukofsky.

◊

WINGS; a quarterly of verse. Spring 1933+. New York. bk. rev., index.
Editor: Stanton A. Coblentz.   NN

Stanton Coblentz's little poetry magazine is "dedicated to no cause but the furtherance of the highest poetic standards." It serves no school; the editor is "free in his decisions and unobstructed by any restraining authority." Wings publishes, among others, the poems of Witter Bynner, David Morton, Harold Vinal, Benjamin Musser, Bryllion Fagin, and Helene Mullins. Stanton Coblentz contributes a regular critical statement, in which he analyzes the poetry of his contemporaries and discusses allied subjects.

## 1934

ALCESTIS; a poetry quarterly. Oct. 1934-July 1935. New York.   NN
Editor: Ronald Lane Latimer.

The hold of revolutionary thinking and of the apparent necessity for social action upon the writers of the early thirties was so strong that it was difficult for any little magazine to exclude it from its pages. Alcestis begins by insisting that the ". . . poet's political opinions do not concern the editor, but his aesthetic theories and the manner in which he expresses them are of real importance." This editorial promise is fulfilled, with the exception of the issue of July 1935, the "Revolutionary number," in which all of the leftwing poets are lumped together—Ruth Lechlitner, Muriel Rukeyser, William Carlos Williams, Isidore Schneider, and others. Wallace Stevens is a frequent contributor to the other issues; other contributions include the poems of John Peale Bishop, Willard Maas, Herbert Read, E. E. Cummings, R. P. Blackmur, Parker Tyler, and Merrill Moore.

❖

AMERICAN SCENE. Feb./Mar. 1934-? Bimonthly. New York. bk. rev.   LC
Editor: Lawrence C. Woodman.

*American Scene* is an ambitious effort to convey to its readers the impression of America as a living and important cultural unit of many peoples and diverse expression. Among the contributions to its pages are poems by Robert Gates, Norman Macleod, Jacob Hauser, and David Cornel DeJong; and stories by James Burlie McCubbin, Dudley Carroll, Susie Karloff, Erling Larsen, Robert Traver, Alfred Morang, Kerker Quinn, and others.

❖

AVENUE. Jan. 8, 1934-Apr. 1935. Semimonthly. Syracuse, N.Y.   NN
Editors: Virginia Phillips, Weller Embler, Leonard Brown, and Arthur E. DuBois (Jan. 22, 1934-Apr. 1935).

*Avenue* is a distinctive and lively addition to the little magazines of America. Its critical attention to modern poetry, and the problems in poetics which seem always to accompany it, combines good taste with a wide range of interest. The issues improve in content as they proceed, the last issue being by far the most interesting composite of critical and "original" writing. *Avenue* publishes poems by Lynn Riggs, Theodore Spencer, Merrill Moore, Millen Brand, Yvor Winters, and Dudley Fitts; critical essays by Warren Taylor, Arthur E. DuBois, H. B. Parkes, and Geoffrey Stone.

❖

THE CALITHUMP. Mar.-Sept. 1934? Monthly. Austin, Tex. illus.   NN
Editors: Wailes Gray and Albert Gray.

The stories and poetry in *The Calithump* form an interesting but minor collection of modern American letters. Their authors experiment with words, structure, and rhythm. Among the more interesting results are the stories of Peter De Vries and Karlton Kelm, and the poems of Lawrence Harper and Harry Roskolenkier.

❖

CARAVEL; a national magazine of new poetry. Autumn-Winter 1934. Quarterly. Lowell, Mass.   LC
(Superseded by *Alentour*, Spring 1935.)
Editor: Michael W. Largay.

A little magazine of verse, *Caravel* publishes, among others, poems by Joseph Joel Keith, Philip J. Garrigan, Jr., and Florence Kauffman.

❖

CARAVEL; an American quarterly . . . Summer 1934-Mar. 1936? Majorca, Spain. bk. rev.   NN
Editors: Sydney Salt, Jean Rivers (with Charles Henri Ford, Mar. 1936).

One of the later "exile" magazines, *Caravel* demonstrates their best qualities. Many of the writers who published frequently in the exile magazines of the twenties are also represented here. The emphasis is entirely upon freedom of creation; what criticism we find is marked by its emphasis upon aesthetic matters. Among the contributions may be mentioned the poetry of Kathleen T. Young, Norman Macleod, Harry Roskolenkier, Charles Henri Ford, William Carlos Williams, Dylan Thomas, and Edith Sitwell; stories by Kay Boyle, Sydney Salt, and James Laughlin IV; criticism by Parker Tyler.

❖

THE CENTAUR. Feb.-Dec. 1934. Irregular. Washington, D.C. bk. rev. NN

Editors: Diana Kearny Powell, Henrietta Randolph Wirt, and John Dillon.

Benjamin Musser appears as one of the associate editors.

*The Centaur*, an invitation to spend some time "with Mr. Greatheart among the Delectable Mountains," publishes, among others, poems by Benjamin Musser and August Derleth.

❖

CHALLENGE; a literary quarterly. Mar. 1934-Fall 1937? Boston. bk. rev.   NN
(Fall 1937 as: *New Challenge*.)
Editors: Dorothy West (with Marian Minus, Fall 1937).

A magazine for Negro writers principally, *Challenge* wishes to advance the cultural and social position of the race and to point to "the great fertility of folk material as a source of creative material." The fiction is primarily social realism; poetry is contributed by Langston Hughes and Countée Cullen, aided by contributions by Norman Macleod, Charles Henri Ford, and Parker Tyler. Richard Wright writes critical prose in his dual role of associate editor and contributor.

❖

CHANTICLEER. Jan. 1934-? Frequency not given. New York.   Y
Editor: Jacob Hauser.

In its first issue, *Chanticleer* announces that it is opposed to the modern wastelanders who are guilty of "croaking their pessimistic and defeatist requiem upon watermarked paper." The editor of and contributors to this magazine support a more affirmative point of view: "Perhaps we are romanticists; but there is a great likelihood that all life is romance, when it is not a funeral." Among the essays on modern letters and on other cultural aspects of the thirties are those by Henry Gerber, B. C. Hagglund, and William H. Chiles. The first issue also publishes poetry by Jacob Hauser.

CHARACTERS. Jan./Feb. 1934-Mar./Apr. 1935. Bimonthly. Santa Cruz, Calif. illus., index (v. 1, 1934).   NN
Editor: Paul Pfeiffer.

*Characters* introduces to its readers, not the "big names" of its contributors, but the names of fictional characters—the assumption being that they are the substance of prose and poetic narrative. This mimeographed little magazine is interesting for its dominating idea, and publishes creditable performances by Karlton Kelm, August Derleth, Kathleen Sutton, and others.

❖

DIRECTION; a quarterly of new literature. Autumn 1934-Apr./June 1935. Peoria, Ill. bk. rev.   NN
Editors: Kerker Quinn, Rhody Fisher, Howard Nutt, and Nelson Bittner.

The literary-critical review of Kerker Quinn and his fellow-editors (see also *Accent*) is one of the more important little magazines of the thirties. The excellent essays by R. P. Blackmur are landmarks in modern criticism. Other critics represented are Richard Aldington and Herbert Read. Contributions include poetry by C. Day Lewis, Ruth Lechlitner, Wallace Stevens, Conrad Aiken, Horace Gregory, Stephen Spender, and Marianne Moore; and short stories by Erskine Caldwell, August Derleth, William Saroyan, Vardis Fisher, Kay Boyle, and Paul Horgan.

❖

THE DUBUQUE DIAL. June/Dec. 1934-Dec. 1935. Semiannual. Dubuque, Iowa.   NN
Editor: Karlton Kelm.

The purpose of Karlton Kelm's short-lived magazine is to encourage experiment with the form of the short story. Much of the material is typical of the social realism and implicit social criticism of the thirties; there are also experiments in the Saroyanesque manner. Contributors include Meridel Le Sueur, Josephine Herbst, David Cornel DeJong, William Saroyan, James T. Farrell, Kay Boyle, and Jean Toomer.

✧

DYNAMO; a journal of revolutionary poetry. Jan. 1934-Sept./Dec. 1936. Bimonthly. New York. bk. rev.   NN
(Suspended, Sept. 1934-Apr. 1935.) Editors: S. Funaroff, Herman Spector, Joseph Vogel, Nicholas Wirth (Jan.-Summer 1934), and Stephen Foster (May/June 1935).
*Issues later than May/June 1935 not consulted.*

Characteristic revolutionary poetry is rough in line, direct in statement, hard in finish, self-confident in tone. Figures are usually unadorned comparisons, the "ambiguities" held to a minimum. There is no reason, however, why such subject matter cannot be subtilized—the "message" stated more indirectly or implied—except that doctrinal considerations usually favor direct statement. Dynamo presents an interesting cross section of revolutionary poetry of the thirties—from the prosaic lines of Ben Maddow to the subtler poetic textures of W. H. Auden; contributors also include Horace Gregory, Joseph Freeman, Kenneth Fearing, C. Day Lewis, Muriel Rukeyser, Orrick Johns, and Isidore Schneider. Critical essays point to the inconsistencies sponsored by capitalism in much modern poetry.

✧

THE EUROPEAN QUARTERLY; a review of modern literature, art and life. May 1934-Feb. 1935. London. bk. rev., illus.   NN
Editors: Edwin Muir and Janko Lavrin.

The "cultural survey," like the college catalogue, too often fails to give more than a miscellany, with scarcely any unifying purpose. *The European Quarterly* is, in the main, a critical survey of the literatures of modern Europe. It is animated by a serious purpose, and directed by two intelligent editors. "There is no mechanical device that can overcome the obstacles, some palpable, like that of language, others subtle beyond definition, which lie between the ordinary citizen and the culture of a foreign people." The aim, therefore, is to inform English-speaking peoples of Continental cultures. Edwin Muir's essays interpret Bolshevism, Oswald Spengler, and Hölderlin. Translations of Russian, German, and Danish writings are published. There is some discussion of modern poetry and fiction, and a series of "Reminiscences" of D. H. Lawrence, by E. T., the Miriam of *Sons and Lovers*. Contributions also include poetry by George Barker, Garcia Lorca, and Sergei Essenin.

✧

FIVE; presenting five poems of the month. Feb. 1934-Jan. 1935. Monthly. Ontario, Calif.   H
(Absorbed by *Silhouettes*, Winter 1935.)
Editor: Margaret Scott Copeland.

It is the purpose of *Five* "to publish significant work of such quality that each poem will stand out in bold relief against a background of beauty, strength and poetic values, presenting a strong thought content, characterization or picture." Among the poems published in this little poetry magazine are those by Robert P. Tristram Coffin, Benjamin Musser, J. Corson Miller, Margaret Widdemer, Witter Bynner, Stanton Coblentz, C. E. S. Wood, and Howard McKinley Corning.

✧

THE FOURTH DECADE; a magazine of new writing. Jan./Feb.-Aug. 1934? Bimonthly. Washington, D.C.   P
Editors: Lee Alexander, James Whiting Saunders, Benjamin Klein Schwarz, Helen Swick, and others.

Confident that "The Jazz Age—the wasted Third Decade—is dead and needing to be buried . . ," the editors of *The Fourth Decade* view their time as alive with possibilities for serious work and heavy with responsibility. Editorial comment condemns the twenties as irresponsible, frivolous, almost quaint, and warns us to protect ourselves against a painful hangover. Short stories, poems, and essays, competently but not brilliantly written, make up the magazine's contents.

❖

HINTERLAND. (Midwest Literary League.) Nov./Dec. 1934-Jan. 1936; [n.s. Sept.] 1936-1939. Irregular. Cedar Rapids, Iowa. bk. rev., index ([n.s. v. 1, Sept.] 1936-1937). NN
Editor: Dale D. Kramer (Nov./Dec. 1934-Jan. 1936); editorial board: Raymond Kresensky, David McLaughlin, Mary Hudson, Jan Du Von, and others.

A magazine with a distinctly sectional tone and emphasis, *Hinterland* in its stories and essays underlines the problem of the Midwestern farmer and portrays the life on the farm or in small Midwestern towns. There is much comment on and justification for the little magazine as an organ for unknown and revolutionary writers. In its new series, beginning with the issue of September 1936, the magazine enlarges its range of contributors and confines itself in the main to purely literary contributions. Because of its sectional aim and emphasis, *Hinterland* is one of the most interesting of the little magazines of the middle thirties. Though it had less actual success than *The Midland*, it does carry on the sectional tradition of that magazine. Short stories, most of them characterized by the "agrarian realism" of Midwestern fiction, are contributed by Alfred Morang, Weldon Kees, Raymond Kresensky, Peter DeVries, Paul Corey, Jay G. Sigmund, William Saroyan, and Sanora Babb; poetry is published by Alan Swallow, Merrill Moore, Raymond Kresensky, and John Wheelwright.

❖

HUB; a quarterly magazine. Spring-Summer 1934. Cedar Rapids, Iowa. Editors: Harold Allison and William E. Henning. NN

Like *Hinterland*, *Hub* presents a detailed picture of Midwestern life, though its emphasis is more directly upon the need for social reform. For the most part, little magazines like *Hub* hoped to prove the desirability of a socialistic world by pointing to the undesirability of present conditions; they left to the more avowedly left-wing publications the responsibility of pointing to the future and of campaigning for it. Thomas Hart Benton contributes an assessment of modern American art. There are short stories by Benjamin Appel, Karlton Kelm, and others; poems by Norman Macleod are the most distinguished of the magazine's contributions.

❖

THE LANCE; a magazine of the new literature. 1934-Mar./Apr. 1935. Bimonthly. Dayton, Ohio. NN
Editors: J. G. Whitaker (Nov./Dec. 1934-Mar./Apr. 1935); Ralf Kircher (Nov./Dec. 1934-Jan./Feb. 1935); Ellington Curtis (Mar./Apr. 1935).
*Issues earlier than Nov./Dec. 1934 not consulted.*

Another Midwestern little magazine, *The Lance* publishes a number of *avant-gardists* and in general contributes to the aims and purposes of the little magazine movement. Among its contributions we note short stories by Alfred Morang and Walker Winslow, and poetry by Frank Ankenbrand and Lawrence A. Harper.

❖

LEFT REVIEW. (Philadelphia John Reed Club.) [1934]-? Monthly. Phila-

delphia. bk. rev., illus.  Y
Editor: Vincent Norman Hall.
*Issues other than v. 1, no. 3 [1934] not consulted.*

Like the other John Reed Club magazines, *Left Review* enlists the talents of writer and artist in the cause of the proletariat and in the fight against Fascism, "a menace to world culture." Ezra Pound lectures to his readers on economics in the third issue. Among other contributions there are poems by H. H. Lewis and Alan Sidney, stories by Jerry Sullivan and Robert Whitcomb.

✧

THE LEFT REVIEW. (Writers' International, British Section.) Oct. 1934-May 1938. Monthly. London. bk. rev., illus., index.  NN
(Absorbed *Viewpoint,* Oct. 1934.)
Editors: Montagu Slater, Amabel Williams-Ellis, T. H. Wintringham, and others (Oct. 1934-1935); Edgell Rickword (1936-June 1937); Randall Swingler (July 1937-May 1938).

Committed from the beginning to the principles and purposes underlying the leftwing literary movement of the thirties, *The Left Review* presents by far the most distinguished leftist poets and critics of our times. Its deliberate consistency of aim gives the contributions a clarity and assurance which is lacking in many other radical magazines. *The Left Review* is proof that acceptable and often great writing can be done within a circumscribed doctrinal framework. From their vantage point, such critics as C. Day Lewis and Ralph Fox survey tendencies of the past and present, condemn political developments and their immediate expression in the Spanish Civil War, and in general give the writer's social consciousness a voice. England's vigorous and in some respects notable "poetic renaissance," supported as it has been by interest in Communism, is well represented here by the poetry of W. H. Auden, C. Day Lewis, Hugh MacDiarmid, Stephen Spender, George Barker, and Sylvia Townsend Warner, supplemented by translations of the Russian poet, Vladimir Mayakowsky, and the Spaniard, Garcia Lorca. Contributions include fiction by Storm Jameson and Ralph Bates, reportage by Ralph Bates, and criticism by George Bernard Shaw, Stephen Spender, Alistair Browne, and others. The critical doctrine which *The Left Review* admirably fulfills is summed up in an editorial by Montagu Slater: "I imagine that it is generally accepted by readers of *The Left Review* that 'literature is propaganda.' But I am not sure that we emphasize often enough the converse that the most lasting and persuasive propaganda is literature."

✧

LITERARY AMERICA; devoted to the American scene. Apr. 1934-Winter 1936. Monthly. New York. bk. rev. Editors: Kenneth Houston (Apr. 1934-July 1936); S. Robert Morse (Fall-Winter 1936).  NN

In contrast with leftwing magazines, *Literary America* is impartial and tolerant in its editorial attitudes, generous and inclusive in its publication of materials. It is this inclusiveness which gives *Literary America* its value for a study of the literature of its time; it is quite literally a cross section of modern American letters. Original contributions are ably supplemented by critical evaluations of modern writers and by essays on aesthetics. In general *Literary America* regards preoccupation with nonaesthetic doctrine as damaging to the value of literature, but admits that writing must deal with social affairs and problems if it is to fulfill itself. Aldous Huxley, the only non-American contributor, publishes a series of essays, beginning with the issue of April 1935. The list of contributors is long: poetry by Langston Hughes, Millen Brand, Jesse Stuart, John Malcolm Brinnin, Marie de L. Welch, August Derleth, Kerker Quinn, William Carlos Williams, Charles Henri Ford, and others; short stories by Erskine Caldwell, Norman Macleod, David Cornel DeJong, Leane Zugsmith, Langston Hughes, Jerome Weidman, Morley Callaghan, and Meridel Le Sueur; criticism by Parker Tyler, Isidore Schneider, W. J. V. Hofmann, and William Kozlenko.

❖

THE LITERARY ARTS. Feb./Mar. 1934-? Frequency not given. New York. bk. rev.     Y
Editor: Lawrence C. Woodman.

Among the contributing and regional editors are: David Cornel DeJong, Norman Macleod, August Derleth, Karlton Kelm, Jay G. Sigmund, Alfred Morang, J. M. Sherby, Willard Maas, Kerker Quinn, and others.

A mimeographed little magazine, the literary arts attempts to present "the American Scene" in a variety of poems, sketches, brief playlets, short stories. There is some attempt to combine regional with national literature, in the hope of representing as varied a portrait of America as possible. There are poems by Paul Engle, David Cornel DeJong, Norman Macleod, Jay Sigmund, and others; short stories by Frederick Maxham, August Derleth, Erling Larsen, and others.

❖

THE LITERARY WORKSHOP; the national organ for student expression. (The Writers Laboratory Guild.) 1934-Jan. 1935. Irregular. New York. bk. rev.     NN
Editors: Edward A. Sand and Richard C. Sidon.

This interesting intercollegiate magazine presents original writing by college undergraduates and, in subsequent issues, reviews and criticisms of that writing by well known American poets, novelists, and critics: among those who offer encouragement and criticism to the young writers are Sherwood Anderson, William Carlos Williams, Erskine Caldwell, Jack Conroy, and Reinhold Niebuhr.

❖

THE LITERARY WORLD; a monthly survey of international letters. May 1934-June 1935. New York. bk. rev., illus. (Suspended, Jan.-May 1935).     NN
Editors: Angel Flores (May-Nov. 1934); Victor Robinson (Dec. 1934-June 1935).

Among others appearing in an editorial capacity are: Samuel Putnam, Pierre Loving, Clifton Fadiman, and Willy Haas.

Like *Contempo* and *The European Quarterly*, *The Literary World* is essentially a critical survey of modern Western literature and culture. The general method employed involves concentration upon a single figure in each issue, with contributions from him and a survey of his importance to modern letters. Among those whose work is thus evaluated are James Joyce, Franz Kafka, Louis Ferdinand Celine, and André Gide. The issue of July 1934 presents a symposium on the "Artist and the World Today"; contributors to it include W. Somerset Maugham, Thomas Burke, and Louis Golding. Original writing is contributed by Jaroslav Hasek, Franz Kafka, and Jules Romains.

❖

MANUSCRIPT. 1934-1936. Frequency varies. Athens, Ohio. bk. rev.     NN
Supplement: *Manuscript news*, no. 1-7, Sept. 1935-Apr. 1936.
Editors: John Rood and Mary Lawhead (with Flola Shepard, 1934).

The Ohio *Manuscript* begins with the valuable and genuine aim of encouraging young and comparatively unknown writers. It is essentially a magazine of the short story, and it is in examples of this form that the excellence of the magazine lies. Some poetry is published in the earlier issues, but it is in the main undistinguished, and the editors give up printing poetry with the issue of December 1935. *Manuscript* is an excellent proving ground for young writers of fiction in the thirties. In this magazine are published the first stories of Hilde Abel, George Dixon Snell, and Eudora Welty—the last named one of the most promising writers of fiction of the thirties. The style of *Manuscript's* fiction is influenced though not dominated by the sociological and political emphases of the time; there is some proletarian fiction. Reflected also in the fiction of such familiar writers as Benjamin Appel and Alfred Morang is the "hard-boiled, tough guy" manner ascribed to the "Hemingway" school. Other noteworthy contributors to the magazine's collection of fiction are Warren Bower, Meridel Le Sueur, August Derleth, Karlton Kelm, and Fred Miller.

❖

THE MEDALLION; an unbiased literary magazine. May/Aug. 1934-? Irregular New York. bk. rev., illus.   NN
Editors: Abbott S. Cohen and Louis S. Glassheim.
*Issues other than May/Aug.-Sept. 1934 not consulted.*

The Medallion is "an unbiased literary magazine"; that is, it pledges that it "will not cater to any one clique or society. We make our selection of material on the basis of the literary value it has—not on the basis of the author's eminence." At least one new writer is to be published each issue. Out of these editorial promises come the following results: poetry by August Derleth, David Cornel DeJong, Norman Macleod, and Samuel Putnam; short stories by Alfred Morang, William L. Kelm, Karlton Kelm, August Derleth, and Benjamin Appel.

THE MIDWEST; a . . . review of literature, news and opinion. Sept.-Nov. 1934. Monthly. Chicago. bk. rev., illus.   NN
Editor: George E. Hoffman.

This literary "newspaper" discusses and publishes literature of the Midwest, and is editorially convinced of the important position of the arts in society: "[It is] dedicated to the belief that the social, economic and spiritual structure of a nation cannot progress without complete recognition, appreciation and support of art, and that through art alone comes the only true expression of a people." It furnishes news notes about Midwestern writers. Included among the original writings are poems by Raymond Larsson, Arthur Nethercot, Kenneth Rexroth, and Norman Macleod; and fiction by Upton Terrell, Mackinlay Kantor, and Theodosia Paynter.

❖

THE MONTHLY REVIEW. June 1934-Mar. 1938? Plainfield, N.J. bk. rev., illus.   NN
Editor: Joseph Koven.
*Issues later than 1934 not consulted.*

The Monthly Review, like many of its contemporaries, commits itself to a program of leftwing criticism and editorial selection. James Joyce, Oswald Spengler, and others are subjected to the scalpel of radical criticism. Among the contributions one finds short stories by James T. Farrell, Karlton Kelm, and Fred Miller.

❖

MOSAIC. Nov./Dec. 1934-? Bimonthly. New York. bk. rev.   P
Editors: Sigmund and Vivienne Koch and Alvin Schwartz.

Delmore Schwartz appears as associate editor and Norman Macleod as advisory editor.

The purpose of *Mosaic* is ". . . to encourage and develop American writers who are sensitive to shifts and implications in the contemporary social landscape and who can transfer this awareness into the fields of short story, poetry and criticism." This purpose it fulfills with admirable intelligence and reasonableness; its contents are often marked by an intelligent awareness of milieu, but their literary value is not dulled by a too blatant partisanship. Contributions include poetry by Delmore Schwartz, R. P. Blackmur, and Norman Macleod; short stories by Alfred Morang and others; criticism by Samuel Putnam (an estimate of Ezra Pound) and William Carlos Williams.

❖

NEBULAE; verse of today. May 1934-Oct. 1935. Monthly. Imlay City, Mich. bk. rev. H Y
(Absorbed by *Better Verse*, Nov. 1935.)
Editor: Leon J. Gaylor.

A little poetry magazine, which publishes, among others, the poems of Stanton Coblentz, Ben Field, and August Derleth.

❖

THE NEW QUARTERLY. Spring-Summer 1934. Rock Island, Ill. NN
Editor: Jay du Von.

Like many of its fellows, *The New Quarterly* reflects the preoccupation of many of its writers with political subject matter; its effort to make the arts an important contribution to contemporary thought brings about the symposium of the Summer 1934 issue, in which more than twenty writers answer the question "For Whom Do You Write?" Among the answers are those of Joseph Freeman, Kenneth Burke, Norman Macleod, James T. Farrell, and Philip Rahv. Other contributions include poems by Norman Macleod, Bertold Brecht (translated by H. Orr and H. Back), Jay du Von, Ezra Pound, Virgil Geddes, and W. D. Trowbridge; fiction by James T. Farrell, Bob Brown, and Edward Dahlberg.

❖

NEW STORIES. Feb./Mar. 1934-Apr./May 1936. Bimonthly. Oxford, Eng. bk. rev., index (v. 1, Feb. 1934-Jan. 1935). NN
Editorial board: H. E. Bates, Edward J. O'Brien, Arthur Calder-Marshall, Hamish Miles, L. A. Pavey, and Geoffrey West.

Stimulated by the success of Whit Burnett's and Martha Foley's *Story*, *New Stories* proposes to offer an English counterpart. Its editors suggest a guiding principle of selection: "No particular school or type is favoured; accomplishment and originality are the qualities sought. . . . [The editors] are agreed upon a proper economy of effect and a sensibility to significant detail, as essential elements in the best contemporary short stories." Illustrating these qualities are the contributions of Stephen Spender, Janko Lavrin, John Lehmann, Dylan Thomas, Benjamin Appel, Alfred Morang, Gavin Ewart, August Derleth, Michael Sayers, and Randall Swingler.

❖

THE NEW TIDE; a magazine of contemporary literature. Oct./Nov. 1934-? Bimonthly. Hollywood, Calif. NN
Editor: Carl Bulosan.

Though *The New Tide* is "not limited by society forms, class, or sectionalism," its editorial selection indicates a preference for writers of leftist persuasion; its aim is to emphasize "the fight of sincere intellectuals against fascism and racial oppression in concrete national terms." Contributions include short stories by Fred Miller, Alfred Morang, and José Garcia Villa; poetry by William Carlos Williams and Carl Bulosan.

PARTISAN REVIEW; a bi-monthly of revolutionary literature. (John Reed Club of New York.) Feb./Mar. 1934+. New York. bk. rev., illus.   NN
(Absorbed *The Anvil*, Feb. 1936.) (Feb.-June 1936 as: *Partisan Review and Anvil*.) (Suspended, Nov. 1936-Nov. 1937.)
Editorial board: Nathan Adler, Edward Dahlberg, Joseph Freeman, Philip Rahv, and others (1934-1935). Editors: Jack Conroy, Dwight MacDonald, Delmore Schwartz, F. W. Dupee, and others.

During the period of February-June 1936, J. S. Balch, Erskine Caldwell, Kenneth Fearing, Joseph Kalar, Meridel Le Sueur, Samuel Putnam, Walter Snow, and others appear as associates.

Best of all leftwing literary magazines, *Partisan Review* demonstrates *pari passu* the contradictions real and imagined of the revolutionary writer of the thirties. Since the beginning of that decade the lines of controversy over the role of the artist in society had been tightened. Marxism, and more specifically Stalinist Communism, presented a challenge to the socially conscious writer. Many writers had abandoned their position of aesthetic individualism, to become champions of the proletariat. The Stalinist "purge" of Trotzky and his followers threw many artists into confusion and convinced some of them that Stalin had abandoned the Marx-Lenin program for a world revolution. More recently some groups of writers have sought to return to a solution more personal and subjective, and have busied themselves either with the strengthening of their command of the craft or with an estimate of their times from others than a Marxist point of view. *Partisan Review* reflects all of these tendencies; and, since its list of contributions is almost regularly representative of the best of modern writing, it is indispensable to a study of our age. The magazine begins as a publication of the John Reed Clubs. Its contents at this point are similar to those of other John Reed publications. Joseph Freeman is on the editorial board, and publishes his poetry and criticism. Sections from James T. Farrell's novels appear. We find short stories similar in subject to those in *Anvil* and *Blast*: Ben Field, Meridel Le Sueur, and John Dos Passos. The poetry of Genevieve Taggard, Kenneth Fearing, Muriel Rukeyser, and others gives the leftwing movement literary expression. With the issue of February 1936 *Partisan Review* absorbs *The Anvil*, and its contents are in the main an expression of social realism. The editorial in the issue of December 1937 announces that it has become a mature revolutionary magazine, and proclaims its independence of doctrinal control. The quarrel with *The New Masses* and the Stalinists begins. Under a new editorship, Dwight MacDonald, F. W. Dupee, and others, the magazine combines political discussion (following for the most part an anti-Stalinist "line") with original writing and criticism. A more recent policy substitutes Delmore Schwartz for MacDonald as editor, and calls for closer attention to matters essentially non-political. Such a history, brilliant in its outlines, but full of the divisions and controversies of the age, is responsible for important contributions to the literature of our times: poetry by Delmore Schwartz, Wallace Stevens, George Barker, Allen Tate, Louis MacNeice, John Berryman, Randall Jarrell, T. S. Eliot (first American publication of "East Coker" and "The Dry Salvages"), Karl Jay Shapiro, and others; fiction by Katherine Anne Porter, Franz Kafka, Nathan Asch, and others. Critical essays of great value include those of Philip Rahv, William Troy, Lionel Trilling, Edmund Wilson, F. O. Matthiessen, Morton D. Zabel, and R. P. Blackmur.

POEMS FOR A DIME. June 17, 1934-Nov. 7, 1937. Irregular. Boston.   H
Editor: John Wheelwright.

Like *Poems for 2 Bits*, this magazine attempts to give single poets a more extensive hearing than they usually get. The first issue is, however, a miscellany of contributions by Kenneth Patchen, Kenneth W. Porter, John Wheelwright, and others. No. 2 publishes "Footsteps: A Mass Recitation"; No. 3, Kenneth W. Porter's "A Christmas Carol"; No. 4, John Wheelwright's "Masque with Clowns"; No. 5, two poems by Leonard Spier; and No. 6, Arthur Saxe's "Teachers' Oath Hearing."

❖

POINT; an independent literary quarterly. Spring 1934. (Only one issue.) Madison, Wis. bk. rev.   Y
Editors: Bernard Hankin and Sol Sniderman.

The chief purpose of *Point*, as established in its one issue, is to link literary expression with the problems and status of the proletariat; to this end the magazine emphasizes the values of literary realism. Realism, say the magazine's editors, "need not be entirely a social luxury; it may on the contrary be a social necessity." Among the contributions are poems by Theodore Ward, Guy Savino, J. M. Sherby, and stories by Ken W. Purdy and Paul Marcus.

❖

POLLEN. Mar./Apr.-Dec. 1934. Irregular. Los Angeles, Calif. bk. rev.   NN
Editors: Walker Winslow, Lawrence A. Harper, and Irene Kilbourne.

The editors of *Pollen* hail the little magazine as the only medium of publication in which the writer "can be himself." The contents for the most part are taken up by writers of leftwing persuasion: poetry by David Cornel DeJong, John Wheelwright, and August Derleth; short stories by Paul Corey, Fred Maxham, Karlton Kelm, and Alfred Morang.

❖

PRELUDE; an expression of youth. 1934?-June 1935. Bimonthly. Detroit, Mich.   NN
(Superseded by *New Writers*, 1936.) Editors: John Malcolm Brinnin and Gordon Smith (Jan.-June 1935).
*Issues previous to 1935 not consulted.*

This magazine is a miscellany of poetry and prose, mainly by writers of the Detroit area. In it the first poems of John Malcolm Brinnin, who has since demonstrated his talent as a poet, appear. Other contributions include poems by Gordon Smith, Arthur Caswell, and short stories by John H. Thompson, John Malcolm Brinnin, and David R. Fielding.

❖

PROVINCETOWN. Apr.-Sept. 1934? Monthly. Provincetown, Mass. bk. rev., illus.   NN
Editors: Lloyd Frankenberg, Saul Yalkert, Bernard C. Schoenfeld, Paul Smith, Erik Huneker, and others.

*Provincetown* prints a variety of essays, some of them on the Provincetown community and the sea, some few on modern painting and painters. Essays by Lloyd Frankenberg appraise the value of D. H. Lawrence and comment satirically upon the "Freudian faddists" of our time. Original writing includes poetry by Winfield Townley Scott.

❖

RED PEN. (John Reed Club.) Jan. 1934-? Monthly. Philadelphia.   Y
Editor: Vincent Norman Hall.

One of several John Reed Club magazines, *Red Pen* of course emphasizes radical leftwing politics, and the writing in it is designed to illustrate or underscore the radical attitude toward political and economic issues. Among the contributions to the first number are short stories by Vincent Norman Hall and E. Clay.

SCOPE; a magazine of proletarian literature. Sept./Oct. 1934-? Bimonthly? Bayonne, N.J., illus.    Y
Editors: Harold Lambert and Nathan B. Levine.

Like *Blast*, *Scope* emphasizes the short realistic narrative; its contents for the most part reflect leftwing tendencies. There are short stories by Ben Hecht, Fred Miller, and Alfred Morang.

❖

THE SOUTHERN REVIEW. Winter 1934-? Quarterly. Jackson, Miss.    Y
Editor: Hubert Creekmore.

A little magazine of Southern writers, *The Southern Review* of Jackson, Miss., publishes poetry by George Marion O'Donnell, fiction by Benjamin Appel, Robert White, and others.

❖

SPACE. May 1934-Apr. 1935. Monthly. Norman, Okla. index.    NN
Editor: Benjamin Albert Botkin.

B. A. Botkin's magazine fits well the tradition of regionalism in American letters and encourages it by means of historical notes and remarks about folklore and tradition of the Southwest. The issue of September 1934 is dedicated to the memory of Mary Austin. John Gould Fletcher and the editor contribute summaries of the history of little magazine publication, and discussion of its problems. Other contributions include the poetry of Norman Macleod, John Gould Fletcher, Witter Bynner, and José Garcia Villa; the fiction of David Cornel DeJong and Frederick Maxham.

❖

THE SPINNERS; a bi-monthly of women's verse. Mar./Apr. 1934-Jan./Feb. 1936. New York. bk. rev.    NN
(Combined with *Poetry World*, Mar. 1936?)

Editors: Antoinette Scudder (with Eugenia T. Finn, Sept./Oct. 1934-May/June 1935, and Virginia Keating Orton, Sept./Oct. 1934-Jan./Feb. 1936).

Benjamin Musser's objection to "feminine poetry" inspired or provoked the establishment of a magazine devoted to poetry by women. Women, said Musser, when they write verse become "painfully self-conscious, stilted, trite, pedantic. . . ." Among those who attempt to prove Musser a mistaken critic are Lucia Trent, Blanche Shoemaker Wagstaff, and Antoinette Scudder.

❖

UNIVERSAL POETRY MAGAZINE. Jan.-May/June 1934? Monthly. Philadelphia.    NN
(Mar.-May/June 1934 as: *Universal Magazine*.)
Editors: Leo Konopka (with James Bolger, Jan.-Feb. 1934).

In its ambitious editorial announcement, *Universal Poetry Magazine* pledges itself to "attempt to present the best modern poetry and light, humorous satirical verse obtainable." Contributions are for the most part by unknown poets.

❖

THE UNIVERSITY REVIEW. (University of Kansas City.) Winter 1934+. Quarterly. Kansas City, Mo. illus., index., cum. index: v. 1-5 (1934-1939).    NN
(Supersedes *The University of Kansas Bulletin*.) (Summer 1944+ as: *The University of Kansas City Review*.)
Editor: Clarence Decker.

*The University Review* is associated definitely with the University of Kansas City and with the region in which it is published. Thus it is both a university review and a regional magazine. It has something of a Ph.D'ish cast, publishing a number of "studies"; but it is also interested in modern criticism and in original writing. This fact and the general excellence of its contents merit its being considered as a little review—or, rather, as the university's contribution to the idea of the little review. Much critical attention is paid modern literature, as evidenced by the following selection from its contents: an essay on Edgar Lee Masters, a discussion of art and social struggle by Diego Rivera and Thomas Hart Benton, Pearl Buck on "Fiction and Propaganda," James Laughlin's study of Ezra Pound, an essay on Robinson Jeffers, one on Thomas Mann, etc. Original writing includes poetry by Robinson Jeffers, Edgar Lee Masters, Humbert Wolfe, John Gould Fletcher, William Carlos Williams, Witter Bynner, and others; fiction by Hazel Cullen, Jesse Stuart, Charles Angoff, Brewster Ghiselin, Benedict Thielen, and others. The *University Review* is most active in the matter of evaluating contemporary writing—and, though its contents reveal a generous collection of that writing itself, its great merit is its appraisal of modern literature while it is being written. This is an important function of any university review and perhaps the greatest service magazines sponsored or tolerated by the academic environment can perform for modern letters. The issue for Autumn 1943 contains a selective bibliography of the criticism of poetry, 1920-1942, by Robert Stallman.

❖

VESPERS; a magazine of beautiful poetry. 1934+. Irregular. Paterson, N.J. bk. rev.                                        NN
Editor: Henry Picola.
*Issues previous to Sept. 1935 not consulted.*

One of a large number of small poetry magazines whose chief virtue seems to be their having afforded a haven of print to some few minor poets of our time. *Vespers* prints, among other contributions, a few of the poems of August Derleth, Harold Vinal, Stanton Coblentz, Kathleen Sutton, Benjamin Musser, and Ralph Cheyney.

❖

YANKEE POETRY CHAPBOOK. Summer 1934-Spring 1935. Quarterly. Flushing, N.Y.                                         NN
Editor: Leo Leonard Twynham.

A little poetry magazine whose chief interest is the literature of New England, though it does publish a number of poems from other parts of the country. "We make no attempt to praise New England. We try to show portraits and scenes accurately drawn from nature, revelatory of the true genius and contour of this land." Among the poems contributed are those by Frances Frost, Harold Vinal, Robert P. Tristram Coffin, August Derleth, Norman Macleod, and Thomas Caldecot Chubb.

## 1935

ADVANCE; Michigan's independent literary magazine. 1935-? Monthly. Ann Arbor, Mich. bk. rev.                      Y
Editor: J. C. Seidel.
*Issues other than Mar. 1935 not consulted.*

A mimeographed magazine of essays, short stories, and poetry. Included among the contributions is a short story by Alfred Morang.

❖

ALENTOUR; a national magazine of new poetry. Spring 1935-Winter 1942/43. Quarterly. Lowell, Mass. bk. rev. (Suspended publication between Summer 1937 and Fall 1940.) (Supersedes *Caravel*.)                                NN
Editors: Michael Largay (Spring 1935-Summer 1937); David Brook (Fall 1940-Winter 1942/43).

A small magazine of verse which publishes, among others, the poems of Joseph Joel Keith, Isabel Fiske Conant,

Arthur E. DuBois, Dorothy Quick, Jack Greenberg, and August Derleth.

❖

AMERICAN PREFACES; a journal of critical and imaginative writing. (University of Iowa.) Oct. 1935-Summer 1943. Monthly. Iowa City, Iowa. illus., cum. index: v. 1-5 (Oct. 1935-June 1940). Editors: Wilbur L. Schramm (Oct. 1935-Autumn 1941); Paul Engle (Autumn 1940-Summer 1943); Frederick Brantley (Winter 1941/42-Autumn 1942); Jean Garrigue (Autumn 1942-Summer 1943). NN

American Prefaces, one of many little magazines sponsored but only moderately controlled by American universities, is sufficiently aware of its regional position to emphasize the writings of many Midwestern artists. Its contents are not, however, limited to materials of any one section, and a fair representation of English writings also is to be found. T. S. Eliot contributes an essay on "Literature and the Modern World" to the issue of November 1935. Critical essays also include an article by John Gould Fletcher on literary regionalism, and articles on Robert Frost, Robert Penn Warren, Thomas Wolfe, and other modern writers. Ferner Nuhn contributes a section of his work on American literature, and Louis Adamic portions of My America. Other contributions include the poetry of Paul Engle, Stephen Vincent Benét, Muriel Rukeyser, William Ellery Leonard, Raymond Kresensky, Kenneth Patchen, Norman Macleod, Robert Frost, C. Day Lewis, Eugene Jolas, Eve Merriam, Theodore Roethke, and Richard Eberhart; short stories by William March, Jesse Stuart, Eudora Welty, and Wallace Stegner.

❖

ANATHEMA; an unorthodox quarterly. Apr./June 1935-Winter 1938. Frequency varies. Boston. bk. rev. NN (Apr./June-July/Sept. 1936 as: The Monarchist Quarterly; Spring 1937-Winter 1938 as: The Nationalist Quarterly.)
Editor: David Page.

Anathema begins with the conviction that literature should remain outside of orthodox, institutional influences. It hopes to publish "authors consciously indebted for their varying degrees of felicity to the mellow influences of the Pagan learning. . . ." Toward the end of its career, its name changed to The Monarchist Quarterly, its policy appears definitely to favor reactionary, Fascist politics, and the contents become almost wholly nonliterary. Listed among the contributions are poems by Sherry Mangan, John Wheelwright, R. P. Blackmur, Geoffrey Stone, and David Cornel DeJong; criticism by Stone and others.

❖

CORNELL COLLEGE CHAPBOOKS. (Cornell College. English Club.) 1935+. Irregular. Mount Vernon, Iowa. illus. Editor: Clyde Tull. H

Among the writers featured in single issues of the Chapbooks are Jay G. Sigmund, whose poems begin the series, Winifred Mayne Van Etten, whose short stories make up No. 7, Edward Weismuller, whose poetry is in No. 10, and Eugene Jolas, whose poems "Planets and Angels" make up No. 14 of the series. Jolas' poems are preceded by an essay on vertigralism. Other issues feature the poems and drawings of Iowa poets and artists.

❖

CYCLE. Mar. 1935-Mar. 1943. Quarterly. Homestead, Fla. NN
Editor: Lily Lawrence Bow.

A little poetry magazine from Florida, Cycle publishes a few poems from such American poets as Witter Bynner, Ralph Cheyney, Harold Vinal, August Derleth, Alan Swallow, and Kathleen Sutton.

THE DRAGON-FLY. Oct. 15, 1935-May 15, 1936? Annual. De Land, Fla.  NN
Editor: R. H. Barlow.

An amateur little magazine, in which R. H. Barlow delivers himself of his opinions on diverse subjects, and August Derleth and Elizabeth Toldridge contribute poems. Barlow's essays on poetry merit some attention.

❖

EPILOGUE; a critical summary. 1935-1938? Annual. Deya Majorca, Spain; London. illus.  NN
Editor: Laura Riding.

*Epilogue* presents much critical and original matter both by Laura Riding and by Robert Graves, associate editor; they are anxious to present the magazine as a mature, coherent expression of their thought and that of others. For that reason they prefer that *Epilogue* not be considered "a precipitation on the public of accidental pieces of writing; it is not a literary trying-out ground." It should therefore be considered as successive issues of a book. The last appearance is published as a book, edited by Laura Riding, *The World and Ourselves*. Contributions include critical remarks by Madeleine Vara, Thomas Mathews, Harry Kemp, and Alan Hodge; poetry by Harry Kemp, Kenneth Allott, Laura Riding, and Robert Graves. The whole may be considered a "continuous symposium," animated by a serious interest in poetics and philosophy.

❖

EXPERIENCES IN UNDERSTANDING; a new philosophical journal of youth. Spring 1935-Summer 1938. Quarterly. Cedar Rapids, Iowa. illus., index (nos. 1-8, Spring 1935-Spring 1937).  NN
(Summer 1937-Summer 1938 as: *Quest*.)
Editors: Maurice Taylor (with Marceil Taylor [1936]-Summer 1938).

*Experiences in Understanding* is published chiefly for the purpose of allowing expression to young writers who are either troubled or solaced by their readings in philosophy. Much of the prose is self-conscious and ponderously vague, the poetry declamatory. Among the more mature contributions is an essay by Charles W. Morris, a verse play by Hartley B. Alexander, and poems by Witter Bynner and Alan Swallow.

❖

GENESIS; a magazine of creative youth. Nov. 1935-Mar. 1937. Monthly. Detroit, Mich. bk. rev.  NN
(Nov. 1936-Mar. 1937 as: *Phenix*; a new literary magazine.)
Editors: Charles Samarjian (with Paul Nagel, Nov. 1935-Apr. 1936).

The prose and verse of *Genesis* are often adolescent, imitative, and immature; the magazine improves as it proceeds on its short-lived career. Among the contributions are stories by Alfred Morang, William Saroyan, August Derleth, and poetry by Derleth and Robert E. Hayden.

❖

HORIZONS; presenting poets of the West. (The Western Poetry League.) Summer 1935-Winter 1937/38. Quarterly. Los Angeles, Calif. illus.  NN
(Absorbed by *Verse Craft*, 1938.)
Editors: Lucia Trent, Ralph Cheyney, Wayland A. Dunham, Henry E. Swensen, Jane Rawlins Sheean, and Joseph C. Williams.

Lucia Trent's and Ralph Cheyney's little poetry magazine celebrates frequently the beauty of the West in appropriate verses, and in later issues is active in pledging its poets to take a pacifist stand with regard to international policy. Its issues celebrate in various ways the natural and scenic attractiveness of the West. A few poems can be singled out for mention—those by Ben Field, Helene Mullins, Lucia Trent, and Ralph Cheyney.

LETTERS; a quarterly of unpublished letters and other belles-lettres. Spring 1935-? New Hope, Pa. illus.  P
Editor: Allison Delarue.

Letters publishes correspondence by various notables of modern literature (the issue of Spring 1935 prints a letter from Gertrude Stein to "Cousins in Baltimore"), and a number of other contributions, including art reproductions, photographs, and musical scores.

❖

THE LONE WOLF; poems. 1935+. Quarterly. Jersey City, N.J.  NN
Editor: A. Zimmerman.

*The Lone Wolf* is exclusively the preoccupation of Mr. Zimmerman, who writes it, edits it, and prints it. The earlier issues are taken up entirely by his poetry; in later issues he adds a few brief prose comments. His poems are vigorous, strongly subjective statements about a variety of subjects, and vary widely in form. Much of his verse reveals a questing and questioning mind, and he is concerned with the task of apostrophizing his spiritual superiors, perhaps with an excessive and unpoetic awkwardness. Some of his poems, especially in the latter issues, deal with the War, coming and arrived. These topical pieces are often in vigorous free or blank verse.

❖

POEMS FOR 2 BITS. June 7, 1935-June 16, 1936. (Copyright dates.) Irregular. Boston.  H
(June 7, 1935, as: *Poems for a Dime*.)
Editor: John Wheelwright.

A small poetry chapbook designed to accommodate the works of one poet each issue. No. 2 contains Kenneth Porter's *Pilate Before Jesus*; No. 3, Kenneth Whelan's "Murder at Pottsville," and "Decade."

❖

PROGRAMME. 1935-Nov. 1937? Irregular. Oxford, Eng. bk. rev.  B
Editors: George Sayer, Veronica Ward, Alan Hodge, Kenneth Allott, and others.
*Issues earlier than May 1935 not consulted.*

The English little magazine, *Programme*, publishes the work of both British and American advance guard writers. Among these are poems by William Carlos Williams, Frank T. Prince, Oswell Blakeston, Dylan Thomas, Frederic Prokosch, Kenneth Allott, and Alan Hodge; and prose by H. E. Bates, Herbert Howarth, John Short, and others.

❖

RENEGADE. Spring 1935-? Frequency not given. Chicago.  ICU
Editor: Milton Wolford.

A little magazine of poetry, published in Chicago, *Renegade* publishes, among others, poems by Troy Garrison.

❖

VERNIER; a quarterly magazine of salient short stories. Fall 1935-Fall 1936. Dumont, N.J. illus.  NN
Editors: Charles A. Abels and H. Beatrice Abels.

A lively short-story magazine, *Vernier* supplements the contributions in that form by numerous editorial comments upon the short story in general and specific criticism of the stories submitted. The editors regret the lack of point in so much advance guard fiction; they are opposed also to aimless unintelligibility in certain developments of the short story. Fiction is contributed by August Derleth, Raymond Kresensky, Alfred Morang, Peter De Vries, and others.

---

# 1936

AVON; the international humorous verse magazine. Winter 1936?-Winter 1938? Quarterly. Detroit, Mich. bk. rev., illus.  Y

(Absorbed *Readers' World.*)
Editor: David Raymond Innes.
*Issues other than Autumn 1937 and Spring 1938 not consulted.*

A little magazine of comic verse, Avon publishes poems by Alan Swallow, Jack Greenberg, Benjamin Musser, and others.

❖

CANDOR; a magazine for modern youth. Oct. 1936+. Monthly. Puxico, Mo. illus.
(Dec. 1939-Sept. 1941 as: *Candor Magazine.*) H NN
Editor: Elvin Wagner.

A magazine for "modern youths. It will be devoted to their problems and to their very best interests. No age limits will be set in considering just who is or is not a 'youth.'" The magazine publishes essays on the problems of contemporary youth, and verses. The editor takes part frequently in the controversies of his time; his stand is for peace until the issue of September 1941, in which he advises sacrifice and trust in "those who have been chosen to direct the destiny of our Country."

❖

CHAMELEON; a national quarterly of poetry and prose. Sept. 1936-Summer 1937. Rochester, N.Y. bk. rev., illus.
Editor: Rae Beamish. NN

A mimeographed quarterly, *Chameleon* is a little magazine in its encouragement to writers of little or no reputation but with some promise. Among the contributions are short stories by Alfred Morang, L. L. Foreman, and Joan Cafaro; poems by Arthur E. DuBois, Kenneth L. Beaudoin, and Glen Stirling.

❖

CONTEMPORARY POETRY AND PROSE. May 1936-Autumn 1937. Monthly. London. index (v. 1, May-Dec. 1936).
Editor: Roger Roughton. NN

Though this British magazine is not a "little magazine" in the sense of encouraging unknown writers, it is an important *avant-gardist* publication, for it gives space to many of the important writers who began in one little magazine or another in the twenties and early thirties. The magazine's emphasis is frequently put upon the surrealists and latter-day extensions of their theories and practices. The issue of June 1936 is devoted solely to surrealists; and several selections from Lautréamont's *Maldoror* are presented in translation from time to time. Among the contributions are poems by David Gascoyne, E. E. Cummings, William Empson, Dylan Thomas, Wallace Stevens, Pablo Picasso, George Barker, Frederico Garcia Lorca, and Alfred Jarry; and prose fiction by Dylan Thomas, Kenneth Allott, David Gascoyne, and Alfred Morang.

❖

CREATIVE. Nov./Dec. 1936-? Frequency not given. Philadelphia. LC
(Formed by the merger of *Kosmos* and *American Columnists.*)
Editors: Michael Ligocki and James Rowenberg.

The magazine *Creative* "dedicates itself to publishing mainly stories and sketches in slightly lighter vein but of literary merit." "The editors have no quarrel with all experimental publications holding that literature and life are inextricably intertwined and that publishing theirs is a serious mission. Lighter work of import is not escape literature necessarily, as our pages will illustrate." There are contributions from the pens of Erling Larsen, Peter De Vries, K. C. Shelby, and others.

❖

GREEN-HORN; a herald of coming writers. Aug./Sept. 1936-? Bimonthly. Philadelphia. Y
Editors: Henry Schultz, John W. Dougherty, Richard Zink, Si Podolin.

Jack Conroy and Howard Rushmore are among the advisory editors.

Green-Horn is "The organ of America's new young writers." It "offers its pages to those sincere young writers who have something vital to say, and who reflect, in interesting story, poem and sketch forms, the warmth, vigor and progressiveness of present-day America." Among the contributions to the first issue are poems by H. H. Lewis, Harold Norse, and short stories by Alfred Morang and Howard Rushmore.

❖

HILL TRAILS; a bimonthly magazine dedicated to the renaissance of literature in Vermont. 1936+. Burlington, Vt. illus.　　　　　　　　NN Y
Editor: Blanche Finkle Gile.

As is indicated in the subtitle, Hill Trails is interested primarily in the literature of Vermont. To that end essays in criticism and appraisal point to the state's literary achievements, and Vermont writers of poetry and fiction are featured. There is, however, a fair quantity of verses from other parts of the country.

❖

HORIZON. Sept./Oct. 1936-March/April 1937. Bimonthly. Brooklyn, N.Y. Editors: Noah Landau, Matthew Kamm, and Sidney Young.　　NN

Horizon follows the pattern of many little magazines of our time: a group of young and enthusiastic writers establish a magazine so that they may be heard; a writer already established, and sympathetically interested in the careers of unknowns, contributes his bit to the table of contents, thus giving the magazine some chance of survival. In this case it is William Saroyan, whose interest in little magazines has been unceasing and healthful. He contributes a short story, "The Boy from Coalinga," to the first issue. Other contributions include poetry by Vladimir Babikoff and William Hudspeth; prose fiction by Lester G. Cohen, Merlin H. Hanson, and Agnes Albrecht Foote.

❖

MANHATTAN POETRY PARADE. June 15, 1936-? Fortnightly. New York. illus.　　　　　　　　　　　　　BI
Editor: Coleman Denton Squires.

A mimeographed little poetry magazine, Manhattan Poetry Parade has as its aims "to present the best of the new poetry available; to introduce new poets to a new public; to present the work of well known poets who will work along with us until such time when we shall be able to pay for contributions." Among the contributions to the first issue are poems by Elmo Russ and Frances M. Lipp.

❖

MIDWEST. (Midwest Federation of Arts and Professions.) Nov. 1936-Jan. 1937. Monthly. Minneapolis, Minn. bk. rev., illus.　　　　　　　　NN
Editors: Mcridcl Le Sueur and Dale Kramer.

Kerker Quinn, Raymond Kresensky, Jack Conroy, and Weldon Kees are among those mentioned as regional editors.

In a "Preview" issue of Midwest, Dale Kramer, one of its editors, explains that the magazine is the expression of a number of writers who wish to interpret the Midwest "as it was, is and is likely to be." Midwest is a protest against exclusiveness in aesthetic matters and argues for a vigorous championing of social and public reforms through the use of the artist's talents. It is concerned with the culture of the Midwest and with defining the limits and weighing the merits of regionalism in literature. To this problem B. A. Botkin devotes an essay in the issue of November 1936. Contributions also include poems by Norman Macleod,

Kerker Quinn, Kenneth Rexroth, and H. H. Lewis, and a short story by Alfred Morang. The issue of November 1936 includes a series of statements in memory of Harriet Monroe.

✧

NEW DIRECTIONS IN PROSE AND POETRY. 1936+. Annual. Norfolk, Conn. Editor: James Laughlin.　　　　NN

A collection of new writing, James Laughlin's *New Directions* has presented since 1936 the work of European and American *avant-gardists*. There is no narrowly defined policy which controls the selection of materials, except that the writing should be of some importance for the development of new ideas, forms, and methods. Surrealism has been well represented in its pages; the 1940 issue has a considerable exhibition of surrealist writing, together with explanations and critical appraisals. The first issue is prefaced by its editor's insistence that "it is the poet—the word-worker—who must lead." Unlike *Twice-a-Year, New Directions* confines itself almost entirely to creative and critical writing and does not divide its attention between political and aesthetic comment. The annual is above all motivated by its editor's conviction that experimental writing has value and needs to be encouraged. It is alive to the uses of and reforms in language, and is thus of even greater value than political writing, or such attempts to simplify the English language as Basic English, "in that it attacks more radically the visual and conceptual fronts of the congealed associations as well as the oral one." *New Directions* has grown and developed on the single policy of encouragement to experiment with word usage and literary structure. In the preface to the 1942 issue, Laughlin grants that both "tradition" and experiment are necessary to the continuing health of the arts:

"Working against each other, they produce a lively literature; neither one can be dispensed with." *New Directions* hopes to insure for experimental writing a suitable and safe place in modern letters. Among the contributions to its pages one can point to the poetry of Wallace Stevens, Ezra Pound, William Carlos Williams, Richard Eberhart, John Berryman, Kenneth Patchen, Kenneth Rexroth, Weldon Kees, William Everson, and many others; prose fiction by Henry Miller, Dylan Thomas, Paul Goodman, Robert Lowry, and others; and critical essays by Laughlin, Kenneth Burke, James T. Farrell, Henry Miller and others. Of increasing importance are the translations from foreign writers, appearing in the volumes from time to time: French, Spanish (particularly Latin-American) and Russian literatures have been well represented.

✧

NEW WRITERS. (Writers Guild.) Jan.-June 1936. Monthly. Detroit, Mich. (Supersedes *Prelude*.)　　　　NN
Editorial board: Maxine Finsterwald, Lewis Fall, John M. Brinnin, and others.

*New Writers* carries on and elaborates upon the tradition of John Malcolm Brinnin's *Prelude*, publishing a number of *avant-gardists*. Among the contributions are short stories by Kay Boyle, Alexander Godin, Michael Seide, and others; poems by August Derleth, H. H. Lewis, William Pillin, Josephine Miles, and others.

✧

NEW WRITING. Spring 1936+. Irregular. London. illus. (1940-1941 as: *Folios of New Writing*; 1942+ as: *New Writing and Daylight*.)　　　　NN
Editor: John Lehmann.

Under various titles, *New Writing* presents a competent selection of materials, chiefly by English writers. The editorial selection is excellent, its aim to "provide an outlet for those prose writers, among others, whose work is too unorthodox in length or style to be suitable for the established monthly and quarterly magazines." Critical essays of great merit come from the pens of Edwin Muir, Stephen Spender, Helen Gardiner, Virginia Woolf, and Rex Warner. Contributions include the poetry of Spender, David Gascoyne, C. Day Lewis, George Barker, and Louis MacNeice; short stories by V. S. Pritchett, Dylan Thomas, and Alan Lewis.

In 1940, *New Writing* enterprises entered into an agreement with Penguin Books, which has since published a number of small anthology volumes of new writing, called *Penguin New Writing*. The object of this agreement is to "appeal to a far wider public than that which a book costing 6s. or 7s. 6d. reaches." The anthology continues under this arrangement to publish the work of contemporary British writers, among which may be mentioned poetry by Louis MacNeice, William Plomer, W. H. Auden, C. Day Lewis, Stephen Spender, and others; fiction by James Hanley, Graham Greene, Dylan Thomas, and others; critical essays and a series of discussions by Stephen Spender on "Books and the War." This serial anthology is a book of new *writing* and not always of new *writers*, though the latter are certainly not excluded if the quality of their work is acceptable.

❖

THE POET. July/Aug. 1936+. Bimonthly. Balerno, Midlothian, Scotland. bk. rev. NN
Editors: ₍Harry Crouch₎ (July/Aug. 1936-July/Aug. 1938), G. L. Wilson (Sept./Oct. 1938+).

The editorial position of *The Poet* is conservative, its first editor (H₍arry₎ C₍rouch₎) believing that the true function of poetry is to repeat traditional truths. The magazine publishes "inspirational criticism" and the poems of Maurice Samuel, Alberta Vickridge, T. Pittaway, Harry Crouch, and others.

❖

POETRY CARAVAN. Winter 1936-Winter 1941/42. Quarterly. Lakeland, Fla. bk. rev., illus. NN
(Absorbed *Silhouettes*.) (Winter 1939/40-Winter 1941/42 as: *Poetry Caravan and Silhouettes*.)
Editor: Etta Josephean Murfey.

The following associate editors are mentioned: Robert L. Dark, Jr., Kathleen Sutton, Clement Wood, and others.

*Poetry Caravan* publishes a few fairly successful contributions by Harold Vinal, Benjamin Musser, Stanton Coblentz, and Kathleen Sutton.

❖

THE PORTFOLIO; annual of stories, poems, and plays. 1936-? [Sweetwater, Tex.] illus. NN
Editor: Jim Boothe.

A collection of original writings, including a short story by Alfred Morang.

❖

PSEUDOPODIA. 1936+. Quarterly. Clayton, Ga. bk. rev. (Spring 1937-Winter 1941 as: *The North Georgia Review*; Spring 1942+ as: *South Today*.) NN
Editors: Lillian E. Smith and Paula Snelling.

*Pseudopodia* adheres consistently to its original purpose: to review the work of Southern writers—Faulkner, Wolfe, Caldwell; to study the problems of Southern society (a portion of W. J. Cash's *The Mind of the South* is published in the issue of Fall 1936); and to publish the work of Southern writers. Among these last may be listed the poetry of Glenn Rainey, James Still, Ed. Winfield Parks, Laura Benét, and Evelyn Scott. Lillian Smith's work as editor and critic and her great interest in Southern problems are worth following, in view of the recent success of her novel, *Strange Fruit*.

SHUCKS. (Works Progress Administration. Federal Writers' Project.) Oct. 1936. Lincoln, Neb.    Y
"Shucks has had no editorial staff." Its single issue is published in mimeographed form.

A collection of writing of WPA writers, *Shucks* publishes poetry and prose done by "project workers," "solely as recreation and practice." Among the contributions is a humorous sketch by Weldon Kees and Norris Getty.

✧

SIGNATURES; work in progress. Spring 1936-Winter 1937/38. Quarterly. Detroit, Mich. index.    NN
Editors: John H. Thompson and John M. Brinnin.

A magazine of "work in progress," *Signatures* features the as yet unpublished writing of "representative American and foreign authors," most of which is being prepared for publication in book form. Much well known material is published here for the first time: fiction by Katherine Anne Porter, Séan O'Fáolain, Kay Boyle, James T. Farrell, Dorothy Richardson, Glenway Wescott, and others; poetry by Kenneth Patchen, Muriel Rukeyser, Ruth Lechlitner, Louis MacNeice, and others; and critical essays by Horace Gregory, Newton Arvin, and Granville Hicks.

✧

6 x 9 (SIX BY NINE). (Works Progress Administration. Federal Writers' Project.) Sept. 1936-? Morristown, N.J. illus.    Y
Editor: Albert Truman Boyd.

An "experiment in initiative, done in free time outside of regular project hours," *6 x 9* presents the writings of WPA writers—among them, poems by Carl John Bostelmann and fiction by Albert Truman Boyd.

TALARIA; a quarterly of poetry. 1936+. Cincinnati, Ohio. bk. rev.    NN
Editors: B. Y. Williams and Annette P. Cornell.
*Issues earlier than Spring 1943 not consulted.*

A little poetry magazine which publishes, among others, the poems of Glenn Ward Dresbach, Isabel Fiske Conant, Stanton A. Coblentz, August Derleth, Robert P. Tristram Coffin, Oscar Williams, Benjamin Musser, Ralph Cheyney, and Kathleen Sutton.

✧

VERS LIBRE; the magazine of free verse. 1936-Mar. 1938. Bimonthly. Waco, Tex. illus.    Y
Editor: J. C. Crews.
Bruce Kapustka appears as associate editor.

*Vers Libre*, a magazine of experiments in the medium of free verse, contains poems by Kenneth L. Beaudoin, Bruce Kapustka, Glen Sterling, W. Caldwell Webb, and others.

## 1937

THE AMERICAN YELLOW BOOK; a cooperative literary magazine. Winter-Summer 1937. Quarterly. Hartford, Conn. bk. rev.    NN
Editors: Joseph Baker (with Rachel Baker, Winter, Spring, 1937).

*The American Yellow Book* is a cooperative little magazine: "Each issue of this magazine is cooperatively owned and published by the writers whose work appears therein, the costs and earnings of each issue being shared by its contributors." The purpose of the magazine is to allow its writers the opportunity of avoiding the difficulties of commercial publication and "to keep the literary aim paramount to all commercial considerations." The problem of the young unknown is a matter of especial concern to the editors: the danger of his losing his original talent in order to subscribe to the rules for success in commercial publications. Of principal interest and concern, however, is the danger that commercial influences may help to corrupt public taste. The contributions to the magazine include poetry by Harry I. Zeidner; fiction by Joseph Baker, Luman Beckett, and others; and critical essays by Lucy L. Hatcher, George Anders Noring, and others.

❖

ANALYTIC. [1937]-? Frequency not given. New York. bk. rev.    LC
Editor: David Ignatew.

Analytic, a mimeographed little magazine, carries poetry by Jay G. Sigmund and August Derleth; and short stories by Harry Roskolenkier, Erling Larsen, Robert Traver, Newton J. Hustead, Alfred Morang, Raymond Kresensky, and others.

❖

THE BOOSTER; a monthly in French and English. Sept. 1937-Xmas 1938. Paris. illus.    NN
(Apr.-Xmas 1938 as: *Delta*.)
Editors: Alfred Perlès, Lawrence Durrell, Henry Miller, William Saroyan, and others.
*Issues earlier than Sept. 1937 not consulted.*
Associate editors: Anais Nin, Hilaire Hiler, Patrick Evans, and others.

*The Booster*, for a time a respectable magazine of "tourist aids," under the leadership of Henry Miller, Lawrence Durrell, Alfred Perlès, and others, becomes a riotous, reckless, provocative magazine of shock. One of the strangest ironies in little magazine history is the inclusion within one magazine of trade advertisements with the "advanced" writing of Henry Miller and friends. With the issue of April 1938, the advertisements cease, the name is changed to *Delta*, and the former back-ers of the magazine disclaim any responsibility for its contents. The striking personality of the magazine is, of course, Henry Miller, whose sportive exploration of the world of the subconscious fills many of its pages. Much of the material subsequently published by the New Directions Press appears here for the first time. Part of the correspondence between Miller and Michael Fraenkel on the subject of Hamlet is published in the magazine. Other contributions include poetry by Lawrence Durrell, Kay Boyle, and Dylan Thomas; fiction by William Saroyan, and others.

❖

THE CATAMOUNT. Sept. 1937-? Frequency not given. Montpelier, Vt.
Editorial board: Clifton Blake, Dana Doten, and Roaldus Richmond.

Though *The Catamount* is begun by a group of members of the Federal Writers' Project in the Vermont region, its contents are not confined to the work of that region or to writers working for the Project: "The editors desire the greatest possible range, both in personnel and in subject matter." Contributions include stories by Herman Buxbaum, Lee Hingston, Robert Whitehand, Mary Tomasi, and Roaldus Richmond, and an essay by Dana Doten on Henry Mencken.

❖

THE COAST; a magazine of Western writing. Spring 1937-? Quarterly. San Francisco.    LC Y
Editorial board: Lawrence Estavan, Miriam Allen De Ford, Ben Hamilton, Kenneth Rexroth, and others.
*Issues later than Spring 1937 not consulted.*

A little magazine whose purpose is to spare young writers the uncertainty and agony of striving for publication in commercial periodicals, *The Coast*, "an unofficial co-operative publication of writers on the San Francisco Writers' Project," is another of a growing list of important Western American publications. Among its contributions may be noted a prose piece by Hilaire Hiler, "Pieces of an Autobiography," a critical essay by Kenneth Rexroth, and poems by Kenneth Rexroth and Raymond E. F. Larsson.

❖

DIALECTICS. (Critics Group.) 1937-1939? Irregular. New York.　　H NN
Editor: Angel Flores.

*Dialectics* is a periodical devoted to the examination of literature, of the present and the recent past, from a Marxist point of view. This point of view, it is the purpose of this magazine to show, has a wholesome effect upon criticism and a not harmful one upon creation. "If it does not bestow genius upon a writer, it does untie the hands of genius." Many, but by no means all, of the essays are written by Soviet critics. Among the subjects treated in *Dialectics* are "The Dialectical Development of Thomas Mann," André Gide's quarrel with the Soviet, the realism of Emile Zola, and James Joyce's *Ulysses*. There are also several essays on Marxist aesthetics, and No. 5 has a bibliography of Soviet literature.

❖

DIRECTION. Dec. 1937+. Monthly. Darien, Conn. bk. rev., illus.　　NN
Editors: John Hyde Preston (Dec. 1937-Nov./Dec. 1938); Thomas Cochran (Dec. 1937-Summer 1940); Harriet Bissell (Dec. 1937-Apr. 1938); M. Tjader Harris (Dec. 1937+); H. L. River (May 1938-Summer 1940); William Gropper (Mar./Apr. 1939-Summer 1940).

In the recent issues Kenneth Burke, Thomas Cochran, and William Gropper appear, among others, as advisory or associate editors.

Using the "lively format" of a modern photographic magazine, *Direction* attempts a survey of modern man. *Direction* "is an independent liberal monthly, devoted to the arts, and seeking to present a true picture of the social scene through them." The social aim of the magazine is responsible for a number of essays and brief statements on the artist's responsibility to society; by dint of typographic arrangement and photographs, *Direction* seeks to give the arts a foundation of familiarity and a relationship to the ordinary world of the reader. No. 3 of 1938 is a special issue, featuring the writing of members of the Federal Writers' Project, and introduced by Harold Rosenberg, who discusses the problem of young writers and the little magazine "movement." The April/May, 1944, issue is devoted to Art Young. Contributions to *Direction's* varied career include criticism by Kenneth Burke, Harry Slochower (on Thomas Mann), Charles Glicksberg, and John Hyde Preston; poetry by Raymond E. F. Larsson, William Pillin, Harry Roskolenko, and Harry Kemp; fiction by Sherwood Anderson, Josephine Herbst, Albert Halper, John Dos Passos, and Erskine Caldwell.

❖

HUBVERSE. Aug. 1937-Fall/Winter 1939. Quarterly. Mattapan, Mass.
Editor: H. M. Tibbetts.　　NN

Published because of the urgent conviction of its editor that "Poetry is to become a National Necessity," this small magazine of verse prints the poems of Virginia Wainwright, Harriet W. Baxter, and others.

❖

INTERMOUNTAIN REVIEW OF ENGLISH AND SPEECH. Jan. 1, 1937+. Monthly. Murray, Utah. bk. rev., illus.　　NN
(Summer 1937-Winter 1938 as: *Intermountain Review*; Spring 1938-Summer 1946 as: *Rocky Mountain Review*; Autumn 1946+ as: *The Western Review*.)
Editors: Ray B. West, Jr. (with George

Snell and Grant H. Redford, Fall 1940+; and Jack Wallace, Winter 1944+).

In the capacity of associate or contributing editors appear Weldon Kees, Wallace Stegner, Alan Swallow, Wanda Burnett, and Thomas Hornsby Ferril. Brewster Ghiselin is the poetry editor.

The editors of the Intermountain Review justify their magazine on the grounds that the literature and culture of the "intermountain West" has been misrepresented by "pulp Westerners." The emphasis of the magazine is strongly sectional. Among the contributions are short stories by Meridel Le Sueur, Wallace Stegner, Vardis Fisher, Weldon Kees, William March, and Walter Van Tilburg Clark; poetry by Alan Swallow, Langston Hughes, Norman Macleod, William Carlos Williams, Bertold Brecht, Byron Vazakas, and Raymond Kresensky; criticism by Kenneth Burke, Wallace Stegner, Sherwood Anderson, Ray West, and Alan Swallow. Recent issues have carried an interesting series of articles on modern criticism.

✧

LEAVES. Summer 1937-? Frequency not given. Leavenworth, Kan.   LC
Editor: R. H. Barlow.

The mimeographed leaves offers, among other contributions, poems by E. Toldridge and Arthur H. Goodenough, and prose by Edith Miniter, A. Merritt, and August Derleth.

✧

MANUSCRIPT. Nov. 1937-? Monthly? Beverly Hills, Calif.   P
Editor: Lucien C. Mandelik.

The purpose of Manuscript is to alter the "film script situation" in Hollywood—to force upon the attention of Hollywood directors worthwhile scripts which would otherwise not be used.

POINT; an Australian quarterly of independent expression. (Point Writers' Group.) 1937-? Melbourne, Australia. illus.
Editor not established.
Issues other than Spring 1938 not consulted.

Point "stands for truth, freedom, security, and peace. . . . When these themes are expressed fearlessly they cease, it appears, to make the basis of an 'attractive commercial proposition,' but Point believes that there are many hundreds of intelligent Australians who, if they can be convinced of the possibility of our publication exerting an influence for the realisation of these aims, will assist in the further expression of them." Contributions include stories by L. P. Fox, Hal. Porter, and Alan Marshall; poetry by Mark Haynes, Jack Maugham, and Norman Macleod; and criticism by Harvey Flynn, A. F. Howells, and Alex Bell.

✧

RIVER; a magazine in the deep South. Mar.-June 1937. Monthly. Oxford, Miss.   P Y
Editor: Dale Mullen?

This interesting Southern little magazine publishes literature of importance to a study of the South as a source of modern letters, but it is not a regional magazine. Its contributors have been members of the avant garde for some years. The editorial policy is eclectic but discreet. Among the many contributions in the field of the short story are examples of the work of Eudora Welty, August Derleth, Hubert Creekmore, and others. Poems are contributed by Harry Brown, George Marion O'Donnell, W. R. Moses, James Laughlin IV, and others.

✧

SKYLINES. Apr. 1937-Sept. 1940. Bimonthly. Brooklyn, N.Y. bk. rev., illus.   NN

(Caption title: *Skylines Magazine*.)
Editor: Edgar H. Ryniker.

A little magazine of poetry, *Skylines* contains much editorial material, and a large collection of poems of varied quality. Among them are poems by Kenneth L. Beaudoin, Judson C. Crews, Bruce Kapustka, and others. The early issues publish some short stories.

❖

TALENT; a monthly magazine publishing the best previously rejected literary and pictorial works of America's unknowns. June-Sept. 1937. Cleveland, Ohio.   NN
Editor: Fred Borden.

The purpose of *Talent* is to afford unknown writers who seem to have had great difficulty breaking into print some opportunity to be heard. Its editor feels that rejection by an established publisher is frequently not a fair indication of the worth of a work —or of its lack of worth. Therefore, *Talent* will consider unknown writers and accept or reject only on the basis of merit. Its editorial policy includes acceptance of photographs and cartoons.

❖

TWENTIETH CENTURY VERSE. Jan. 1937-June/July 1939. 8 times a year. London. bk. rev., index (nos. 9-16, Mar. 1938-Feb. 1939).   NN
Editor: Julian Symons.

Published, its editor insists, "for a 'civilized' minority," *Twentieth Century Verse* avoids involvement in any modern issues which may give its poetry a peculiar character. Critical materials are generally stimulating and penetrating, though in some measure they are marked by certain editorial tastes and judgments. The issue of November/December, 1937, is devoted to a consideration of Wyndham Lewis as artist and critic. That of September/October, 1938, features the poetry of American writers and includes a symposium on the question, "Do you Believe in American Poetry?" Contributions to the magazine include poems by Wallace Stevens, Dylan Thomas, Allen Tate, Delmore Schwartz, Ruthven Todd, John Pudney, Gavin Ewart, and George Barker. Samuel French Morse serves as the American editor.

❖

WALES. Summer 1937-Winter 1939/40; [n.s.] July 1943+. Quarterly. Llangadock, Carmarthenshire, Wales. bk. rev.   NN
Editors: Keidrych Rhys (Summer 1937-Mar. 1939; July 1943+; with Dylan Thomas, Mar. 1939); Nigel Heseltine (Aug. 1939-Winter 1939/40).

One of a small group of Welsh and Scottish little magazines, *Wales* establishes itself as ". . . a sort of forum where the 'Anglo-Welsh' have their say as poets, story writers, and critics, chiefly." Among the Welsh contributions are the poems of Dylan Thomas, Vernon Watkins, Ll. Wyn Griffith, J. F. Hendry, and Gwyn Jones; short stories by Thomas, Ewart Evans, and Rhys Davies. Non-Welsh writing is represented by the poetry of George Barker, Norman Macleod, and Harry Roskolenko, and two narrative fragments by Franz Kafka.

## 1938

ACORN. Apr. 1938-? Quarterly. New York. bk. rev.
Editor: John Sidney, with editorial associates.

*Acorn*, "entirely written and edited by young writers," attempts in part to fill a need for a magazine in which "the rising young and talented writer" will have an opportunity to "exhibit and publish his work." The magazine prides itself in the youth of its editors and contributors. "The higher teens will be the predominating age which usually will not exceed the lower twenties." Among the contributions are poems by Harry Goldschlag, Rebecca Horn, Raphael Hayes, and Martha Millet; fiction by Kingsley Johnson and Seymour Gregory.

❖

BOLERO; a magazine of poetry. (Worcester College.) Summer 1938-? 3 issues a year. Oxford, Eng. bk. rev. Editor: John Waller.    ICU

A British poetry magazine, *Bolero* advances the suggestion that twentieth century poetry needs to be the product of what it calls "Mass-Observation": "The poet of today, if he is to be of any future significance, must come down to earth. Present day scenery is made up of factory chimneys, slums, cinema houses, advertisement hoardings, and dance halls. . . . 'Look in thy heart and write,' said Sidney when he desired to pen love sonnets to Stella. Nowadays it should be a case of 'Look around you and write.' The 20th century is an interesting age and those who can paint it vividly will be read at a future date." Among the contributions to *Bolero* are poems by Clifford Dyment, John Waller, Peter Viereck, and John Stead.

❖

BY—presenting the new writer. Spring 1938-? Quarterly. New York. bk. rev. Editor: Paul J. Frank.    NN

The purpose of *By*—is to provide a place for new writers. It publishes only new writers. It believes therefore that it "expresses the freshness and diversity which only new writers, sustained by an unfettered editorial policy, can create." Its material includes poetry, short stories, and essays.

❖

CREATIVE WRITING. Nov. 1938-Mar./Apr. 1941? Monthly. Chicago. illus. (July/Aug. 1940-Mar./Apr. 1941 as: *New Horizons*.)    NN
Editors: Robert and Margaret Williams.

*Creative Writing* begins as a mimeographed magazine for Chicago writers, later publishes the writing of Henry Miller, Gertrude Stein, and other well known writers, and finally decides to oppose the war. The magazine publishes short stories by William Carlos Williams and August Derleth; the poetry of Edouard Roditi, August Derleth, Robert Lowry, Lawrence Durrell, and Coleman Rosenberger.

❖

THE LITTLE MAN. 1938+. Irregular. Cincinnati, Ohio. illus.    NN
Editor: Robert James Lowry.

A letter from the University of Cincinnati states: "There was only one issue of *The Little Man* published on our campus and as far as we have been able to ascertain, that was the only number published until the new series of 1939 was started." This publishing venture of Robert Lowry, who, according to Albert Levin, moved it from the University of Cincinnati after a first trial in the spring of 1938, has several peculiarities which make it the despair of bibliographers but the delight of *avant-gardists*. The numbers have come out irregularly and each is a separate, distinct booklet, quite different from its fellows in format, price, and contents. The series was suspended temporarily during World War II; three issues, however, were published by Lowry in Italy during the war. The first regular issue, 1939, appeared as a small pamphlet containing some short stories by William Saroyan and selling for eight cents. Subsequent issues have been taken over by Robert Lowry, Albert Levin, and James Caldwell, the last named having written a report on "Defense in University City," based on his experience in Madrid during the

Spanish Civil War. There have also been at least two issues of varied contents, more like the regular issue of a magazine: "Pip Pap Po, a Book of Many Things," with stories by Weldon Kees, Robert Lowry, and others; and "The State of a Nation," an anthology of short stories by Albert Levin, Weldon Kees, and others, with running commentary by Lowry. The series is an interesting little magazine venture and has had results of some importance, most notably for the short story.

✧

MY WORD. Apr.-June? 1938. Monthly. Brooklyn, N.Y. NN
Editor: I. J. Alexander.

A "one-man magazine, written and published in this form only because nobody else cares to carry my work." I. J. Alexander publishes his poetry, criticism, and fiction in "The Personal Magazine of I. J. Alexander."

✧

THE PHOENIX; a quarterly. Spring 1938-Autumn 1940. Woodstock, N.Y. bk. rev. NN
Editor: James Peter Cooney.

More than any other group of writers since the death of D. H. Lawrence, the editors of and contributors to The Phoenix faithfully and vigorously advance the proposals and respect the opinions of "the master." He himself appears posthumously in numerous essays, stories, and letters. Lawrence's horror of industrialism, his love of physical activity, his proselytism and tendentiousness, his opposition to military conflict—are all given expression here, for the most part in editorials by James Cooney. Henry Miller writes about the significance of Lawrence, but his range of interest in him is more limited than Cooney's. From an unpublished book, The World of Lawrence, Miller contributes an essay contrasting the affirmative spirit of Lawrence with the negative attitudes of Proust and Joyce, who "emerged, took a glance about, and fell back again into the darkness whence they came." Toward the end of its career, The Phoenix takes a stand definitely opposed to World War II, supported by the publication of Lawrence's War Letters of 1914-1918. Other contributions include criticism by Derek Savage, Frieda Lawrence (via letters to the editor), and Michael Fraenkel; a novelette by Kay Boyle; and poems by Reuel Denney, Oscar Williams, and Geoffrey Johnson.

✧

PLANES. [1938-1939?] Irregular. Santa Fé, N.M.
Editor: William Lumpkins.

Planes, a "magazine devoted to the expression of the contemporary scene through the mediums of the short story, articles, and poetry," publishes, among other things, stories by Alfred Morang and George Snell, and poetry by William Pillin, Rowland O. Barber, and W. D. Trowbridge.

✧

POETRY AND THE PEOPLE. July 1938-1940. Monthly. London bk. rev., illus. (Absorbed by Our Time, 1941.) BY
Editor not established.

A British little poetry magazine, Poetry and the People wishes to reach as many people as possible—to give them some understanding of the value of poetry, and to eliminate the idea that the writing and reading of poetry are idle pastimes. The editorials comment upon political issues of the day, criticizing them from a liberal point of view. Among the contributions are poems by F. C. Ball, Miles Carpenter, Jack Lindsay, Randall Swingler, Albert Brown, David Moffat, Geoffrey Parsons, and Idris Davies. The poetry published is often simple, straightforward free verse or conversational, ballad style; the aim is to give to the reader a poetry of power but also of simplicity. All of this is designed to make poetry a popular means of communication. Essays by Jack Lindsay on "Neglected Aspects of Poetry" discuss the popular poems of the past—ballads and political broadsides. The magazine also attempts to make the reading and writing of poetry popular activities, and to this end sponsors the establishment of "Poetry Groups." The issue of May 1939 is a special May Day issue. *Poetry and the People* is both a little magazine and a leftwing development. In the interests of making an appeal to the working class, its editors declare that "it is high time the written and spoken propaganda in the progressive movement had a poetic quality, that is to say, became humanised, appealed to people on the basis of their own actual real life experience as it affects them in every way. . . ."

❖

POETRY PRESENTS; poems from the heart of man. June 1938-Winter 1940. Irregular. Burbank, Calif.   OU
Editor: C. Henry Hicks.

A Western poetry magazine, which publishes with some regularity the poems of August Derleth, Helene Mullins, Stanton A. Coblentz, and has one poem by Harry Roskolenko.

❖

SEVEN; the new magazine. Summer 1938-Spring 1940. Quarterly. Taunton, England. bk. rev.   H NN
Editors: John Goodland (Summer-Winter 1938); Nicholas Moore (Summer 1938-Spring 1940).

The seven issues of this magazine bring together an important group of writers, many of whom also wrote for *The Booster* in Paris. Perhaps an important contribution by such writers as Henry Miller and Lawrence Durrell is a form of prose-writing one may call "psychic fiction," deeply subjective in tone, autobiographical, yet written within a narrative framework. Several examples of this type of writing by Anaïs Nin, Lawrence Durrell, Henry Miller, and others appear in *Seven*. Added to the *Booster* group are a number of British writers, notably Nicholas Moore, Dylan Thomas, with brief appearances by Hugh MacDiarmid (C. M. Grieve). Contributions include poetry by Ruthven Todd, Frederic Prokosch, Lawrence Durrell, George Barker, Kay Boyle, Wallace Stevens, Parker Tyler, Dylan Thomas, Henry Treece, Merrill Moore, Richard Eberhart, David Gascoyne, Keidrych Rhys; prose fiction by Nigel Heseltine, Kay Boyle, William Saroyan, Emanuel Carnevali, and James Laughlin IV; and critical essays by Parker Tyler, Henry Treece, and Herbert Read.

❖

TOWNSMAN. Jan. 1938+. Quarterly. London. bk. rev., illus.   NN
(Some issues have title: *Scythe*.)
Editor: Ronald Duncan.

*Townsman's* principal consistency is that of the rebellious spirit which animates it. It changes size and format with almost every issue, and carries on in reduced form during World War II, advocating for the most part a serious reconsideration of the agrarian foundations of society. In a letter, its editor, Ronald Duncan, has said: "*Townsman* was first printed in January, 1938, and its contents were mostly of a literary or political nature. Gradually its contents changed more and more to those of an agricultural nature until such articles were almost all of its contents." Ezra Pound's frequent contributions, in the exaggerated prose (or typographic) style he seems latterly to have adopted, discourse principally upon the "fundamentals of economics." Among the contributions we find poems by E. E. Cummings, Ezra Pound, Norman Macleod, and Lawrence Olson; criticism by John Drummond, Katue Kitasano (translated by Pound); a verse play by Ronald Duncan; stories by William Saroyan and Jean Canayénne.

❖

TWICE A YEAR; a . . . journal of literature, the arts and civil liberties. Fall/Winter 1938+. Semiannual. New York. illus. NN
Supplement to nos. 5-6: A *Franz Kafka miscellany; pre-Fascist exile.* [c1940].
Editor: Dorothy Norman.

The function of *Twice a Year* gives it a deserved position among avant-garde publications. Like the *New Directions* anthologies, it accommodates in its pages the work of recent writers, both known and unknown; unlike *New Directions*, it attempts to support and defend the independence of these writers by devoting a large part of each issue to a report on Civil Liberties in the United States. The justification for this grouping of original literature and progressive reportage and comment is to be found in the publication's editorial announcements: "Because we believe that man must be given every possible opportunity whereby he may maintain his necessary dignity and integrity—so that he may fulfill himself as responsible individual and as responsible member of society—we are printing those expressions, in Literature, in the Arts, and in the fight to safeguard and to achieve Civil Liberties that seem most effectively directed towards such ends." Despite this interesting and promising statement, *Twice a Year* is eclectic rather than synthetic in its table of contents. The separation of the "Civil Liberties Section" from the other units of each issue (the issue of Fall/Winter, 1943, and Spring/Summer, 1943, does provide an interesting effort to synthesize the various "disciplines," to the neglect of original or creative writing) implies that political and social thinking is still distinct from aesthetic preoccupations. One of the important contributions to an understanding of literature as a reflection of society is the publication of some of Randolph Bourne's letters in the second issue. Of interest to the student of modern letters are the following contributions: poetry by Muriel Rukeyser, Kenneth Patchen, Harvey Breit, Harry Roskolenko, Kerker Quinn, and Garcia Lorca; fiction by Marcel Proust, Franz Kafka, and William Saroyan; criticism by James Laughlin IV, William Carlos Williams, Muriel Rukeyser, Paul Rosenfeld, and Henry Miller. In the Fall/Winter 1942 issue there is a special Stieglitz section. Many reproductions of his photographic studies appear throughout the volumes. *Twice a Year* may be considered as within the tradition established by *The Seven Arts*, in its attempt to achieve some synthesis of aesthetic, cultural, and social expression.

❖

UPWARD; a quarterly magazine of worth-while verse. Summer 1938-Apr. 1941? Prairie City, Ill. bk. rev. (Spring 1939-Apr. 1941? as: *Compass*.) H NN
Editor: James A. Decker.

Norman Macleod, Parker Tyler, and Tom Boggs appear, among others, as associate editors.

Originally published as a magazine, *Upward* became a quarterly anthology of verse in April 1941. It has published some work which has been printed elsewhere, but much that appears for the first time. Of interest to modern poetics is the department called "Credos" in the issue of April 1941, in which the poets themselves express their opinions about their art. Among the contributions are poems by Robert Clairmont, Kenneth Fearing, Marianne Moore, Malcolm Cowley, Lloyd Frankenberg, Langston Hughes, Oscar Williams, Tom Boggs, John Wheelwright, Witter Bynner, Harry Roskolenko, Norman Macleod, Edouard Roditi, William Carlos Williams, Wallace Stevens, Charles Henri Ford, D. S. Savage, Parker Tyler, Nicholas Moore, Kenneth Rexroth, August Derleth, and others.

## 1939

THE ABINGER CHRONICLE. Christmas 1939-Sept. 1944. Monthly. Dorking, Surrey, Eng. index.    NN
Editor: Sylvia Sprigge.

*The Abinger Chronicle's* unruffled contents include sketches by Max Beerbohm, E. M. Forster, and R. C. Trevelyan; poems by Nicholas Moore and Douglas Gibson. It is avowedly a magazine not in any way designed to "give you a bang for your sixpence."

❖

THE AMATEUR WRITER. Nov. 1939-July? 1942. Monthly. Yellow Springs, Ohio. index (in v. 1 and 2, Nov. 1939-Apr. 1942).    NN
(Jan. 1940-July? 1942 as: *The Writer's Forum.*) (Suspended, July-Dec. 1941.)
Editors: Freeman Champney (Nov. 1939-June 1941); Paul H. Rohmann (Jan.-July? 1942).

A magazine of "non-professional" writing, *The Amateur Writer* exists for the purpose of affording the unknown opportunity of being published and criticized at the same time. Comment is furnished usually at the end of each contribution. Contributions include prose writings by Charles Angoff, Mary Graham Lund, Len Zinberg, Frank Brookhouser, Hollis Alpert, and others.

❖

CROSSROAD; for art and thought in Cleveland and the Midwest. Apr. 1939-Spring 1940? Quarterly. Cleveland, Ohio. illus.    LC NN
Editorial Board: Winfield H. Rogers, Manuel G. Silberger, Rowena Woodham Jelliffe, Spencer D. Irwin, Dan Levin, Joseph A. Cully.

"*Crossroad* is a non-profit quarterly magazine. Its aim is to bring the best of art and thought to a greater public in Cleveland and the Middle West. *Crossroad's* only standard is artistic merit—efficient and distinguished expression of significant thought or feeling." A magazine of attractive format, *Crossroad* is well supplied with illustrations by modern young artists. Contributions include stories by John Edgar Webb and others, and poetry by Powell Jones, Robert Weaver Kollar, and Ted Robinson.

❖

DECADE OF SHORT STORIES. May 1939+. Bimonthly. Chicago.    NN
Editor: Lee Lukes.

*Decade of Short Stories* proposes editorially to present the stories of writers who have lived through "ten years of depression, turmoil, years of struggle, followed by a twisted turn to normalcy." Stories are contributed by Jesse Stuart, William Saroyan, Meridel Le Sueur, August Derleth, Louis Zara, Louis Paul, and Eve Merriam, among others.

❖

FOOTHILLS. Spring 1939-Fall 1940. Quarterly. Washington, D.C.    NN
Editors: John Zeigler (Spring-Winter 1939); Jack Deasy (Spring-Fall 1940).

This mimeographed little magazine is founded on the simple realization that "There are many young writers who want to write and be read. *Foothills* will try to give them the opportunity. It will allow the unknown writer to reveal his ability and to make himself heard. . . . *Foothills* confines itself to no one form, nor does it favor any school of technique or thought."

❖

FURIOSO; a magazine of verse. Summer 1939+. Irregular. New Haven, Conn.

bk. rev. NN
(None issued in 1942.)
Editors: James Angleton, E. Reed Whittemore, Jr. (with Carmen Mercedes Angleton, 1943).

Furioso, a magazine of modern poetry, begins with the "blessing" of Archibald MacLeish, whose letter to James Angleton is published in the first issue. MacLeish's primary objection to poetry magazines in general is that they are only a convenient place for mutual admiration societies of poets. He insists that poetry must find "greater audiences" and that criticism and the critics ought to be "put in their place"—that is, made to serve only a minor part in modern poetics. The first issue of Furioso leaves criticism out altogether; subsequent issues devote considerable attention to the reviewing of important collections of poems and to the problem of poetic language. Such an "intrusion" upon the domain of creation strengthens the magazine. If it is true that modern poets are a self-conscious and a self-critical lot, that fact has its advantages as well as its disadvantages. For the work of I. A. Richards, F. C. S. Northrup, Wm. M. Urban, and John Crowe Ransom, in the issue of Summer 1941, clarifies the problem of the modern metaphor and throws "linguistic light" upon the important question of poetic language. Furioso is primarily a meeting place for the major figures of the "poetic renaissance" of the forties. The editorial policy—never announced directly, but abundantly implied by the magazine's contents—is not dogmatic or superficial. In short, the poems published are the "prevailing expression of poets arriving and arrived," and the emphasis and subject matter shifts as these poets alter their points of view or develop new interests. Since Poetry can no longer serve as the sole "guardian" and sponsor of the "new and recent" in modern verse, such magazines as Furioso are an important supplement to Poetry's leadership and may (like Others of an earlier date) offer fuller opportunity for specific developments in poetics than Poetry can usefully accommodate. The contributions include the poetry of Horace Gregory, William Carlos Williams, Marya Zaturenska, E. E. Cummings, Richard Eberhart, John Peale Bishop, Theodore Spencer, Dylan Thomas, Genevieve Taggard, W. H. Auden, Marianne Moore, Wallace Stevens, Lawrence Durrell, John Malcolm Brinnin, Dunstan Thompson, and others.

◊

KINGDOM COME; the magazine of wartime Oxford. (Oxford University.) Nov. 1939+. Irregular. Oxford, Eng. bk. rev., illus. H
Editors: John Waller (Nov. 1939-?); Kenneth Harris (Nov. 1939-Summer 1940); Miles Vaughan Williams (Summer 1940-?) Mildred Clinkard (Summer 1940); Alan Rook, Stefan K. Schimanski, Henry Treece (Nov./Dec. 1941-?).
*Issues between Summer 1941 and Nov./Dec. 1941 and later than Nov./Dec. 1941 not consulted.*

Kingdom Come appears at the beginning of the war, as a magazine determined to continue the traditions of British poetry and prose through the years of World War II. The character of its contents, both original and critical writing, reflects a general preoccupation with matters associated with the War. Among the contributions are poems by Keith Douglas, Gervase Stewart, André Breton, Nicholas Moore, Alan Rook, Herbert Read, Hugh MacDiarmid, Paul Eluard, C. Day Lewis, Julian Symons, Oscar Williams, Ruthven Todd, Charles Madge, and others; stories by Kay Boyle, H. B. Mallalieu, Henry Treece, H. E. Bates; and many essays on literary and aesthetic subjects, or on social and political problems of World War II. Contemporary English poetry is the subject of a controversial brace of essays.

LITTLETOWN; written by the people of littletowns. Dec. 1939?-May 1940? Monthly. Lancaster, Wis. Y
Editor: Larry B. Clementson.
*Issues other than May 1940 not consulted.*

Littletown exists for the purpose of affording a place for members of small communities to publish their writings —and in the interests of presenting the small town, where is preserved "what is timeless and eternal, what is human and divine . . . where men still live close to the soil. . . ." Included among the contributions are poems by August Derleth.

◆

LYRICAL POETRY. Fall 1939-Spring 1941. Irregular. San Benito, Tex. bk. rev. NN
Editors: Ben and Isabel Hagglund.

The little poetry magazine of Ben and Isabel Hagglund publishes some interesting verses by Jack Greenberg, August Derleth, William Saroyan, and Alfred Morang.

◆

MATRIX; a magazine of creative writing. (Matrix Association.) 1939-Winter 1942/43; [n.s.] Fall 1943+. Bimonthly. Philadelphia. bk. rev. P Y
Editors: Hollis Alpert, Morton Fineman, and Jack Mashman (Dec. 1939/Jan. 1940-Sept./Oct. 1940); Bernard B. Gross and James Rochlis (Dec. 1939/Jan. 1940-May/June 1940); Joseph Moskovitz (Nov./Dec. 1940+).
*Issues earlier than Dec. 1939/Jan. 1940 not consulted.*

The files of *Matrix* present the writings of a number of young unknowns, as well as those of a few established writers. During the years of World War II, *Matrix* substitutes for its regular appearances an irregular series, a collection called "Little Books." This, the editors say, "will be published irregularly until regular publication of Matrix Magazine can be resumed." Contributions to both the magazine and the World War II substitute series include poems by James Franklin Lewis, Bernard Raymund, Nicholas Moore, Walter Lowenfels, Samuel Putnam, August Derleth, James Laughlin IV, Raymond Souster, Carlos Bulosan, and others; short stories by William Carlos Williams, George Snell, Martin Dreyer, Charles Angoff, Jack Shapiro, Anaïs Nin, and others.

◆

THE NEW ALLIANCE; a quarterly printing chiefly the work of Scottish and Irish writers and artists. Autumn 1939+. Frequency varies. Edinburgh. bk. rev., illus. NN
*Editor not established.*

This magazine expresses a "new alliance" among the writers of Scotland, Wales, and Ireland. Poems are contributed by Edwin Muir, Hugh MacDiarmid, F. R. Higgins, and stories by Seán O'Fáolain and George Scott-Muncrieff. During World War II, the magazine is considerably reduced in size, but succeeds in carrying on a vigorous verbal battle with Nazism.

◆

THE NEW ANVIL. Mar. 1939-July/Aug. 1940. Monthly. Chicago. illus.
Editor: Jack Conroy. Y

*The New Anvil* picks up the task dropped by *The Anvil* when the latter magazine merges with *The Partisan Review*. *The New Anvil* resembles its predecessor closely in contents and editorial purpose (both of them leftist). There are short stories by Robert Ramsey, Milton U. Wiser; poems by Alexander F. Bergman and Troy Garrison, among others.

◆

ON THE BOILER. 1939-? Dublin. C
Editor: W. B. Yeats.

Yeats's magazine of personal comment, On The Boiler, discusses its editor's past and his country's present. "In this new publication," he announces, "I shall write whatever interests me at the moment, trying, however, to keep some kind of unity, and only including poem or play that has something to do with my main theme."

❖

OPUS. 1939?-Spring 1943. Quarterly. Tring, Herts, Eng.     NN
Editor: Denys Val Baker.

Opus is a British magazine of new writing, poetry, fiction, and criticism, and its aims (as announced in an editorial statement) are "To emphasize the importance of the individual, to fight for freedom of thought and expression, to propagate the philosophies of love and brotherhood and universal understanding." The contributors are generally young and as yet of little established reputation in the world of letters. Among the contributions are poems by Jack Bayliss, Robin Atthill, Nicholas Moore, Henry Treece, Wrey Gardiner, and Maurice Lindsay; short stories and sketches by Denys Val Baker, Patricia Johnson, and Edwin Allan; critical essays by Roland Grant, Eric Nixon, and Derek Stanford.

❖

POETRY (London); a bi-monthly of modern verse and criticism. Feb. 1939+. London.     ICU NN
Editor: Tambimuttu.

Because of its interest in the work of recent poets, both known and unknown, and its intense interest in poetry as a significant literary form, Tambimuttu's Poetry has become within a very short time a major vehicle for modern poetry. In one of the regular "Letters" the editor expresses the conviction that "a magazine like this which is catholic in viewpoint helps to create a modern anonymous tradition from which the important work of the future may be derived. . . ." Though this point of view has been consistently adhered to, the magazine has shown itself willing to recognize the growing importance of a group of modern poets who have been called, for various reasons, "the Apocalyptic writers." The poems of such members of this group as Dylan Thomas, Henry Treece, J. F. Hendry, Nicholas Moore, G. S. Fraser, and Tom Scott, have appeared with fair regularity in Poetry. But this fact is not an indication that the magazine is or will become the mouthpiece of any organized group of poets; rather, it points to critical recognition of the present and prevailing vigor and importance of the Apocalyptic "school." The prose commentary has been provided in letters by the editor and in book reviews by Stephen Spender, Francis Scarfe, and others.

❖

POETRY QUARTERLY. Spring 1939+. London. bk. rev.     NN
(Supersedes Poetry Studies.)
Editors: Katherine Hunter Coe (with E. M. Channing-Renton, Spring 1939-Spring 1940); Wrey Gardiner, Spring 1940+.

London's Poetry Quarterly is interesting for more than the even excellence of its contents. Since it has survived the beginning and the early years of World War II, it acts as a fairly accurate—or, at any rate, a sensitive—mirror reflecting the changes in attitude and point of view which are the natural consequence of a long and serious war. The magazine begins with an editorial policy which calls for "the best MSS." and goes on to condemn "poems in which cacophonously stuttered commonplaces usurp the place of true poetry for the sake of giving a very questionable semblance of actuality." Under the editorship of Wrey Gardiner, who took over in 1940, Poetry Quarterly not only reflects the contemporary predilections of its writers but also underscores them by pointing vigorously to the great impact of events upon the arts. Gardiner comments, in the issue of Autumn 1942, upon the poetry of the forties in these terms; the men of the forties "stand in absolute and irreconcilable contrast to the dessicated despair, honest niggling and brazen, rather bawdy cynicism of the pre-war decade." Thus the issues of recent years point in a decisive manner to the future of poetry and poetics. The younger, newer poets are favored in these late issues; they are vigorously defended and applauded by the magazine's editor. Among the contributions may be listed poetry by Dylan Thomas, Henry Treece, James Kirkup, Nicholas Moore, Ruthven Todd, Theodore Roethke, and some translations from the work of Rainer Maria Rilke. Through the pages of the Poetry Quarterly one sees the young poet of the thirties shocked by events, changing with them, and in his verse triumphing over them.

✧

THE TRAMP; a magazine of poetry. Summer 1939-Winter 1941. Quarterly. Anacortes, Wash. LC
Editorial board: Fannie M. Grinnell, Evelyn Lundberg, Walter Moberg, George Witter Sherman, Martha Johnston Sherman, and others.

A little magazine published in the Northwest, The Tramp presents a number of poems from the pens of Ruth Lechlitner, Norman Macleod, William Saroyan, Witter Bynner, Harry Roskolenko, Carlos Bulosan, Alan Swallow, Thomas McGrath, Henry Treece, Nicholas Moore, Stanton Coblentz, Helene Mullins, and others.

✧

THE WELSH REVIEW; a monthly journal about Wales, its people and their activities. Feb. 1939+. Cardiff, Wales. bk. rev., illus. NN
(Suspended, Dec. 1939-Feb. 1944.) Editor: Gwyn Jones.

In the tradition of the little review, The Welsh Review searches for and publishes a fresh, creative work in verse and prose. Like The Modern Scot, Voorslag, and Manuscripts (Australia), it is "regionalistic" in its emphasis upon the talent and culture of its part of the British world. The editor, Gwyn Jones, is well enough supported by the talent of this region, for the young writers of Wales show great promise. "I believe firmly that they will soon be recognized as the most valuable leaven in English literature since the Irishmen opened insular eyes at the beginning of the century," Jones remarks in his first editorial. "The Welsh Review does not intend to over-emphasize the regional bias to the detriment of the magazine's quality," he adds. Contributions include poetry by W. H. Davies, Huw Menai, Meurig Walters, Oliver Davies, Keidrych Rhys, Gwyn Williams, Hugh MacDiarmid and others; stories by Gwyn Jones, Alun Lewis, T. A. Radcliffe, Geraint Goodwin, Sian Evans, and others.

✧

YELLOWJACKET. March 1939-? Frequency not given. Oxford, Eng. Editor: Constantine Fitzgibbon.
Margaret Aye Moung and John Orbach are mentioned as sub-editors.

Yellowjacket is primarily a review of European letters, guided by a group of young British intellectuals, who hope to avoid the pitfalls of dogmatic literary preference and thus to make excellence of performance a single criterion for inclusion. The editors, however, do show some concern over the present state of European culture; the review is therefore in part dedicated to the hope of keeping alive certain intellectual and cultural interests which are endangered by a hostile world: "Yellowjacket hopes by breaking down barriers of language and of creed, to make the task of barbarians more difficult, and to provide us, who are not barbarians, with that sense of unity which we lack." The contents are broad and inclusive, revealing a proud eclecticism and an honest eagerness to find some proof in modern arts of the worth and value of the aesthetic point of view. There are essays on painting and on modern music; there is a brief appraisal of the worth of Franz Kafka. The noncritical writing includes a translation of a poem by Jean Cocteau, poems by Gavin Ewart, John Betjeman, and Mario Francelli; and fiction by Dylan Thomas, Michael Wharton, and Henry de Montherlant.

## 1940

ACCENT; a quarterly of new literature. Autumn 1940+. Urbana, Ill. bk. rev., index.    NN
Editors: Kerker Quinn, Kenneth Andrews, Charles Shattuck, W. R. Moses, Thomas Bledsoe, Keith Huntress, W. McNeal Lowry, and others.

   *Accent* is an excellent example of the *eclectic* little magazine. Its principal aim from the beginning has been to serve as a "representative collection of the best creative and critical writing of our time, carefully balancing the work of established authors with that of comparative unknowns." Such an announcement, fulfilled as it is throughout the magazine's successful career, contains in germ a criticism of magazines with too dogmatic or strident an editorial voice. *Accent* thus attempts to avoid "a biased viewpoint" and rejects what it calls the "stereotyped and the trivial and the unintelligible" from its pages. The magazine is published on the campus of the University of Illinois, and the members of that university's English department have had some small part in determining the quality of its contents. But this is not merely a university magazine. It reflects a variety of literary and critical tastes —all of them serving recent movements and reflecting the latest interests in modern letters. Among its most distinguished contributions are the fiction of Katherine Anne Porter, Kay Boyle, and Thomas Mann; the criticism of Harry Slochower, Edwin Berry Burgum, and Kenneth Burke; and the poetry of Horace Gregory, Wallace Stevens, and E. E. Cummings. The issue of Summer 1941 includes a valuable bibliography of American poetry, 1930-1940, compiled by Horace Gregory. The appearance in Spring 1943 of a section of Thomas Mann's last volume of the Joseph story is typical of the magazine's policy of presenting "work in progress" by important writers of our time. The book reviews are serious, critical, and free from all commercial or other pressures. Contributions include poetry by John Berryman, John Malcolm Brinnin, Ruth Lechlitner, Conrad Aiken, Harry Roskolenko, Clark Mills, Brewster Ghiselin, R. P. Blackmur, Ivan Goll, Eve Merriam, and Byron Vazakas; fiction by Jerome Weidman, Walter Van Tilburg Clark, Hans Otto Storm, Richard Wright, Eudora Welty, Irwin Shaw, and Franz Kafka; and criticism by Richard Aldington, Paul Rosenfeld, John Crowe Ransom, Delmore Schwartz, David Daiches, Horace Gregory, and R. P. Blackmur.

✧

ADVENT. Fall 1940. (Only one issue.) Easton, Pa.    LC
Editors: Joseph Shober, Seymour Keidan, and Robert Connolly.

   *Advent* is a magazine devoted to the printing of young, unknown writers. "We are all young men who are just beginning to write and we are sure that there are many others like us throughout the country. . . . We want unknown writers, and we are sure that there are enough of these people who write good material to warrant further publication of *Advent.*" Its one issue publishes, among other contributions, poetry by Seymour Keidan, and prose by Razel Kapustin.

❖

THE AMERICAN EPOCH. Summer 1940-? Quarterly. Sybial, W.Va. Editors: Don Young and Gypsy Johnston. ICU

*The American Epoch* is a magazine of original and critical writing, established for the purpose of encouraging young and unknown writers. "It is not of circulation that we boast, or of advertising lineage. We feel, however, that we offer something which magazines of circulation and advertising do not have, even if it is only our freedom and independence." Contributions include fiction by Helen Addison Howard, poetry by Constance Carrier and Arthur Flagg, and critical essays by Don Young and George Turley.

❖

ANGRY PENGUINS. [1940]+. Irregular. Adelaide, Australia. illus. NN
Editors: Max Harris (with D. B. Kerr, [1940]); and John Reed (Sept. 1943+).

An Australian magazine of original and critical writing, *Angry Penguins* is interested in, and encourages, a rapidly developing Australian literature and art, but is also concerned over political matters: "The editors firmly believe that the issues involved are of vital importance to all artists and that to shirk them or to refuse to have them fought out in the pages of *Angry Penguins* would be to show a completely unrealistic approach to the complex situation which confronts the artist today." A critical essay by Ivor V. Francis, "Reintegration and the Apocalypse," in the issue of September 1943, discusses the Apocalyptic school of writers in England, and points out its relationship with surrealism. Among other contributions are poems by Elizabeth Lambert, Muir Holburn, H. M. Swan, Henry Treece, Geoffrey Dutton, Robert Penn Warren, Max Harris, James Gleeson, Ern Malley, Harry Roskolenko, and Vincent Ferrini; and stories by Frank Kellaway, Alister Kershaw, Peter Cowan, and others; and critical essays by Leonhard Adam, J. M. Keon, and others. The magazine is also of interest because of the "Ern Malley Hoax" which has occupied its editors since May 1944. The sixteen poems attributed to Ern Malley in that issue were discovered to be the work of two men whose purpose was to expose and censure the modern literary movement.

❖

BABEL; a multi-lingual critical review. Jan.-Summer 1940. (Only three issues.) Cambridge, Eng. bk. rev., illus. Editors: Peter G. Lucas, John Fleming, and G. Gordon Mosley. NN

*Babel* strives for a multiplication, but not a confusion of tongues. Together with essays explaining the literatures of Europe to each other, the magazine publishes translations of verse—such as the poetry of W. H. Auden, translated into French, and the verse of Baudelaire, done in English. Denis Saurat explains modern criticism in a French essay. Louis Gillet offers a French elucidation of Joyce's *Finnegans Wake.* David Gascoyne adapts Mallarmé to the English.

❖

CADENCE; a quarterly of verse and verse appreciation. Sept. 1940-Winter/Spring 1941. St. Louis, Mo. NN
Editor: M. C. Savore.

*Cadence*, a little poetry magazine, is begun because its editor feels that "a not inconsiderable quantity of acceptable and perhaps even superior verse may be lurking in obscure corners...."

Among the contributions are poems by William E. Graves, J. F. Stewart, and Katherine A. Paulsen.

❖

CALENDAR; an anthology of . . . poetry. (Poetry Center, Young Men's Hebrew Association.) 1940+. Annual. Prairie City, Ill.  NN
Editor: Norman Macleod.

The very active Poetry Center of the Young Men's Hebrew Association, New York City, has now published two anthologies of recent poetry, chiefly by American and British poets. The Center is supervised by Norman Macleod, who also acts as editor of the anthologies. The contributions are in some cases a product of the interest in modern poetic theory and practice sponsored by the Center; as such, they provide an important means of testing and evaluating the growth of twentieth century poets, from year to year. Poets who have contributed to the anthologies so far include Hugh MacDiarmid, Louis Zukofsky, Allen Tate, William Carlos Williams, Marya Zaturenska, Norman Macleod, Robert McAlmon, R. P. Blackmur, Alan Swallow, and Ruthven Todd.

❖

THE CLIPPER; a Western review. (Hollywood Chapter, League of American Writers.) Aug. 1940-Nov. 1941. Monthly. Los Angeles, Calif. illus. (Supersedes *Black and White*.)  NN
Editorial board: Sanora Babb, Cedric Belfrage, Wolfe Kaufman, Lester Koenig, Meyer Levin, John Sanford, and others.

The Los Angeles *Clipper* attacks the commercial magazine both cleverly and seriously, including in its pages a burlesque "writer's market." Its serious purpose is "to print the sort of honest writing which cannot be published in commercial magazines." In its interesting contents are included the poetry of J. Bronowski, John Sanford, and others; criticism and reportage by Cedric Belfrage, Meyer Levin, and Wolfe Kaufman; short stories by Guy Endore, A. I. Bezzerides, Sanora Babb, and others.

❖

A COMMENT. 1940+. Irregular. Melbourne. Australia. illus.  B NN
Editor: Cecily Crozier.

An Australian little magazine, A *Comment* features writings (short stories, poems) by local writers, and in some issues by American soldiers stationed in or near Australia. The poetry of Karl Jay Shapiro (most of it since published in book form in America) is found in several issues. There are also poems by Muir Holburn, James Gleeson, Elizabeth Galloway, and others; short stories by Mark Kronenberg, Elizabeth Halls, Cecily Crozier, and others. Brief critical notes and notices are also published.

❖

DESIGN; an Australian review of critical thought. 1940. (Only three issues.) Melbourne, Australia. bk. rev.  NN
Editor: P. I. O'Leary.

An Australian little review, *Design* "aims to be critical, inquiring, expository, and provocative, but not irruptively, destructively or behaviouristically. Inciting to thought by expressing thought, it seeks to awaken slumbering minds—and to make more active minds already awake." Much of *Design's* contents is in the form of critical prose: essays on modern culture, on the arts, and on literature are strongly in evidence. These, and the book reviews which support them, are accompanied by contributions in verse by Paul L. Grano, Mary Finnin, Ian Mudie, and others.

❖

DIOGENES. Oct./Nov. 1940-Jan. 1941? Bimonthly. Madison, Wis.  NN
Editors: Arthur Blair and Frank Jones.

The *Diogenes* of Madison, Wis., is less interested in finding an honest man than in keeping alive those honest men of letters whom he has already discovered. The editors are much concerned over the dangers affecting modern society and hope to help prevent their realization by publishing good writing. "We intend to print what we think good, regardless of the author's status among either the intelligentsia or those whose reading is restricted to best sellers." In this interesting and genuine little magazine are published the poems of William Carlos Williams, Charles Henri Ford, James Laughlin IV, Berthold Brecht (translated by Frank Jones), John Wheelwright, and John Malcolm Brinnin; criticism by John Wheelwright and Austin Warren.

✧

EXPERIMENTAL REVIEW. Spring 1940-Sept. 1941. Irregular. Woodstock, N.Y. bk. rev., illus.　　　　　　　　NN
(Spring 1940 as: *Ritual<Experimental Review No. 1>*) Supplement, Jan. 1941.
Editors: Robert Symmes (1940); Sanders Russell (1941).

A magazine devoted to literary experiment, *Experimental Review* explains that "The experiment is not to foster an eccentricity or a novelty of language, nor to create a new literature: it is to extend the understanding, to bring everything into consciousness, to develop the artist's awareness in the field of observation. . . ." The magazine not only tolerates and accepts experimental writing; it insists on it. Contributions include many poems by Kenneth Patchen, Sanders Russell, and Lawrence Durrell; prose sketches by Henry Miller and Anaïs Nin.

✧

FLORIDA MAGAZINE OF VERSE. 1940+. Bimonthly (Nov.-May). Winter Park, Fla. bk. rev.　　　　　　　　NN
Editor: Charles Hyde Pratt.

"Florida Magazine of Verse . . . will try to serve a balanced poetic ration of the traditional and the modern, in various styles and moods. . . ." Among its contributions are included poems by Jessie B. Rittenhouse, Isabel Fiske Conant, Stanton Coblentz, Witter Bynner, Ralph Cheyney, Gustav Davidson, and Louis Ginsberg.

✧

HORIZON; a review of literature and art. 1940+. Monthly. London. bk. rev., illus.　　　　　　　　NN
Editor: Cyril Connolly.

London's *Horizon* remains an important critical review of our immediate times. "Our standards are aesthetic and our politics are in abeyance." This, says the opening editorial, is for the best in a time when issues are confused. "At the moment civilization is on the operating table and we sit in the waiting room." Perhaps because of this "neutral" position (though *Horizon* has long since adopted a definite position with regard to World War II), the magazine has been able to publish excellent and relatively impartial surveys of contemporary culture and letters. Among these we find essays by Herbert Read, Clement Greenberg, William Empson, Henry Miller, Stephen Spender, T. S. Eliot, and D. S. Savage. Included in the list of poems are many by British writers: Dylan Thomas, George Barker, W. H. Auden, Louis MacNeice, William Empson, and C. Day Lewis.

✧

ICONOGRAPH. Fall 1940-[1942]. Quarterly. New Orleans, La. bk. rev., illus. (Absorbed *Motive*, Mar. 1941.) (Absorbed by *Crescendo*, 1943.)　　NN
Editor: Kenneth Lawrence Beaudoin.

*Iconograph*, a mimeographed little magazine, publishes short stories, poems, and criticism by comparatively unknown young writers of the early forties. Among the contributions are poems by Judson C. Crews, Alan Swallow, and Hubert Creekmore; short stories by Kenneth Lawrence Beaudoin, Jesse Stuart, and Walter Gaulke.

❖

THE KAPUSTKAN; an American journal of discovery. May 1940+. Monthly. Chicago. bk. rev. NN
Editors: Bruce Kapustka and Stan Lee Kapustka.

The mimeographed little magazine, The Kapustkan, is known principally for contributions by its editors. There are a great number of statements of principle and discussions of aesthetics and modern letters. The Kapustkas also contribute poetry, fiction, and book reviews to the magazine. There are contributions in poetry and fiction from others as well.

❖

M S; a literary workshop. 1940?+. Irregular. Los Angeles, Calif. bk. rev., illus. NN
Editor: Stephen Mathews?
Issues other than Sept./Oct. 1941 and no. 10 (n.d.) not consulted.

M S is "published in behalf of the new writers of Southern California." Contributions include poetry by Wendell Anderson, Scott Greer, James Franklin Lewis, Raymond Kresensky, J. C. Crews, and others; brief stories by Charles Angoff, Kenneth L. Beaudoin, and others; and a critical essay by Alan Swallow.

❖

MEANJIN PAPERS; contemporary Queensland prose and verse. Dec. 1940+. Bimonthly. Brisbane, Queensland, Australia. bk. rev., illus. NN
Editor: C. B. Christesen.
Issues earlier than Aug. 1941 not consulted.

The magazine of contemporary Australian verse and prose takes its position firmly with those who believe in the importance of creative art for society, and in the necessity for the artist to "take notice of the individual" in society and in his social and political needs. Among the contributions to this Australian little magazine are poems by C. B. Christesen, Brian Vrepont, Peter Miles, Karl Jay Shapiro, John Henderson, and others. Included in the critical prose are several essays in aesthetics and studies of Australian literature. Meanjin Papers has recently become associated with the University of Melbourne, Australia.

❖

MOTIVE. Apr./June-Aug./Oct. 1940. Irregular. Waco, Tex. bk. rev. Y
(Absorbed by Iconograph, Mar. 1941.)
Editor: J. C. Crews.

J. C. Crews's mimeographed little magazine publishes interesting materials from both unknown and well established writers. Quality, says its editor, is the requirement for acceptance: "We will use only the highest quality material available." Among the contributions are poems by J. F. Hendry, Nicholas Moore, Alan Swallow, Raynar Heppenstall, Kenneth L. Beaudoin, and D. S. Savage.

❖

Now. 1940-1941? [n.s.] 1943+. Irregular. London. bk. rev., illus. B NN
Editor: George Woodcock.

The magazine Now has had an interesting publishing history. It first appeared in 1940 as a "cyclo-styled sheet," at that time an effort to continue the tradition of some British literary magazines (New Verse and Twentieth Century Verse) which had been forced to suspend with the outbreak of World War II. In 1943 the name Now was attached to what its editor calls "a series of volumes of literary and social writings," an annual collection of criticism and original writing. "So far as their social content is concerned, the volumes of Now will be edited from an anarchistic point of view," says its editor, George Woodcock, in the first number of the annual series. "So far as their literary content is concerned, our criterion will be the quality of writing. Nor do we intend to exclude poets, essayists, story writers, because their political views do not coincide with our own." The first of this new series contains essays by Herbert Read, George Woodcock, D. S. Savage, and others; poetry by Julian Symons, Alan Rook, Theodore Spencer, and others; and a short story by Alagu Subramaniam.

✧

OASIS. 1940?+. Irregular. Croydon, Surrey, Eng. bk. rev.   NN
(Superseded by Leaven, Easter 1946.)
Editors: John Bate (with Conan Nicholas, Summer 1944+).
*Issues earlier than Spring 1944 not consulted.*

"Oasis is not a magazine, but an anthology, a collection." Some issues are without date or volume number.

The purpose of Oasis is not to sponsor a program. "Writing is a profession and an art, and it is for those who view it as such that we write." Among the contributions to this British collection of new writing, there are translations from Baudelaire by Edith Turner; critical essays by Derek Stanford and Victor Turner; and poetry by Victor and Edith Turner, John Bayliss, and John Bate.

✧

PYRAMID. Book 1, Oct. 1940-? San Benito, Tex. illus.   NN
Editors: Ben and Isabel Hagglund.
"This venture started as a magazine. We soon realized we would never be able to bring it out periodically, if at all. We decided simply to make a book of it, get out one issue, see what reaction there was, then go on from there."

Pyramid presents the work (poems, short stories, essays) of Ben and Isabel Hagglund.

✧

"RESURGAM" YOUNGER POETS. [1940?]+. Irregular. London.   NN
*Editor not established.*

This series of broadsheets by young British poets is one of England's many answers to the spiritual and cultural needs of World War II: "In the belief, in the knowledge, that a new era will arise, phoenix-like, from the ashes of our so-called civilisation, we know that culture must be preserved. This series, in however humble a way, seeks to play its part." The series includes poems by Peter Baker, Patricia Ledward, Bertram Warr, Douglas Gibson, Paul Scott, Emanuel Litvinoff, and Alex Comfort. The editorial note in No. 1 promises that "Other Resurgam works—essays, fiction, science, sociology, politics, philosophy—are being planned."

✧

THE SWALLOW PAMPHLETS. 1940+. Irregular. Baton Rouge, La.   NN
Editor: Alan Swallow.

These individual booklets, edited and published by Alan Swallow, present the work of young and comparatively unknown poets: Thomas McGrath, Clayton Stafford, Barbara Gibbs, Lincoln Fitzell, Robert Brown, and Clark Mills's translation of the *Chansons Malaises* of Ivan Goll.

✧

UNQUOTE. 1940-? Irregular. Yellow Springs, Ohio.   Y
Editorial staff: Paul Rohman, David Linhart, Gilbert Wilson, and others.
*Issues other than June 1940 not consulted.*

A mimeographed little magazine, Unquote publishes poems by Langston Hughes and Frances Power; fiction by Bruce Fessenden and Margaret Drury.

UPSTATE; a magazine for readers and writers of Buffalo and surrounding regions. Dec. 1940-Winter 1944. Monthly. Buffalo, N.Y. bk. rev., illus.  B
Executive board: George W. Poole, Emmanuel J. Fried, Ruth Lurie, John Myers, Charlotte Cherry, and others. *Issues earlier than July 1941 not consulted.*

A magazine of original and critical writing, whose purpose is "to develop new writers and a native and regional literature," Upstate publishes poetry by Howard Moss, Parker Tyler, Gordon Smith, and others; short stories by Reuel Denny, David Newton, and John Myers.

❖

VICE VERSA. Nov. 1940-Jan. 1942? Bimonthly. New York. bk. rev.  NN
Editors: Harry Brown and Dunstan Thompson.

Editorial invective is Vice Versa's chief weapon against "the smugness, the sterility, the death-in-life which disgrace the literary journals of America." Chief victims of the magazine's unallayed scorn are Edna St. Vincent Millay, Carl Sandburg, and others who in the editor's estimation have sold their heritage for a mess of patriotism. As recompense for their defection, Vice Versa offers the poetry of George Barker, W. H. Auden, John Malcolm Brinnin, Conrad Aiken, Horace Gregory, Oscar Williams, Ezra Pound, Richard Eberhart, Marya Zaturenska, and Edith Sitwell.

❖

VIEW; "through the eyes of poets." Sept. 1940+. 4 issues a year. New York. bk. rev., illus., index (ser. 2, Apr. 1942-Jan. 1943; ser. 3, Apr.-Dec. 1943). Editor: Charles Henri Ford.  NN
With Series 3 Parker Tyler becomes assistant editor, and later associate editor.

The surrealists draw much by way of suggestion from the researches of Freud. But they have gone far beyond Freud in the matter of attributing great significance to almost any state which either approximates or induces "the unconscious." They have added a political and social theory to the original explorations of the unconscious made by Freud. View evaluates the surrealist position chiefly with reference to its followers in poetry and painting. Single issues are devoted to the painters Max Ernst, Pavel Tchelitchew, and Yves Tanguy. The issue of October 1942 explains the great aesthetic value of "vertigo." Materials included are diverse, but the editorial pronouncements of Charles Henri Ford, aided by the remarks of Nicholas Calas and André Breton, give the magazine a direction. Poetry is contributed by Ford, Parker Tyler, William Carlos Williams, E. E. Cummings, Randall Jarrell, and Philip Lamantia; essays by Wallace Stevens, Kenneth Burke, Lionel Abel, and others.

❖

WHISPERS; a magazine of poetry. Nov. 1940-1942? 8 issues a year. Washington, D.C. bk. rev.  NN
Editor: Katherine W. Fulton.

A little magazine of poetry, which publishes, among others, the poems of Charles Angoff, August Derleth, and James Franklin Lewis.

## 1941

THE AMERICAN POET. Apr. 1941-Mar. 1944. Monthly. Brooklyn, N.Y.  NN
Editor: James Meagher.

James Meagher's little magazine of poetry succeeds in maintaining a fairly uniform degree of poetic achievement, though its editorials are perhaps a bit overly "instructorial" and much of its contents overstrain the limited possibilities of a theme. Verse is contributed by Ralph Gordon, Alfred Kreymborg, and Eve Merriam. There are many essays on poetic technique and on the aesthetics of poetry.

❖

CONTEMPORARY VERSE; a Canadian quarterly. Sept. 1941 +. Caulfield, B.C. Editor: Alan Crawley.   NN

A little magazine, chiefly of Canadian poetry; among the poets represented are A. M. Klein, Paul Halley, Donald Stewart, Ralph Gustafson, Harry Roskolenko, Kenneth Beaudoin, and Dorothy Livesay.

❖

CRESCENDO; a laboratory for young America. Sept. 1941-Autumn 1944. Quarterly. Waco, Tex. bk. rev., illus. (Absorbed *Iconograph*, 1943.)  B NN Editors: Scott Greer (Sept. 1941-Winter/Spring 1943); James Franklin Lewis (Autumn 1944).

*Crescendo's* pages demonstrate amply the sincerity of the purpose announced in its subtitle. It is essentially a magazine of writings by competent but as yet unknown young writers. Among the contributions are poems by James Franklin Lewis, Hubert Creekmore, Wendell Anderson, Kenneth L. Beaudoin, William Peterson, and others; fiction by Oscar Collier, Joseph Crowley, Paul Grossberg, and Judson C. Crews; and several critical essays, among them one by Alan Swallow.

❖

DAYLIGHT; European arts and letters yesterday, today, tomorrow. 1941. (One vol.) London. illus.   B (Combined with *Folios of New Writing* to form *New Writing and Daylight*, 1942.)
Editor: John Lehmann.

*Daylight* is established "by a group of English and Czech authors.... Two ideas were uppermost in their minds ... first, that though much had been done to bring British people and their European allies, whose representatives are in England at the moment, together in a political sense, a bridge still needed to be built between them on those things that touched their lives more deeply; in the things of the mind and the imagination, books, painting, music, the theatre and poetry.... They also felt that, at a time like the present, it was necessary to reaffirm a belief that the culture of Europe is fundamentally one, however important it may be to preserve the individuality of its manifestations in each people or entity within a people, and that it not only has common roots but also a common future." The purpose and aim are therefore centered upon the cultural unity of nations, somehow effected by an exchange of creative work and intellectual temperaments. More specifically, the editor of *Daylight* speaks of preserving "the unity of European arts and letters, the culture denied by the Nazis." In the brief space of its career, before it combines with *Folios of New Writing*, *Daylight* offers, among others, the following contributions: poetry by David Gascoyne, George Seferis (translated from the Greek), Vitezslav Nezval, and Frantisek Halas (translated from the Czech); and prose by Stephen Spender and John Lehmann.

❖

DECISION; a review of free culture. Jan. 1941-Jan./Feb. 1942. Monthly. New York. bk. rev., illus., index.   NN Editor: Klaus Mann.

On the board of editorial advisors are mentioned: Thomas Mann, Sherwood Anderson, W. H. Auden, Stephen Vincent Benét, Ernest Boyd, Julian Green, Horace Gregory, Somerset Maugham, Stefan Zweig, Bruno Frank, and others. With the issue of July 1941, Muriel Rukeyser becomes associate editor.

Klaus Mann's "Review of Free Culture" strives to strengthen the cause of anti-Nazism by calling upon the leading opponents to Nazism, many of them refugees, to reaffirm their faith in a free world. In view of this avowed "political" purpose and the magazine's frequent exhibitions and "anthologies" of writers from nations conquered by or fighting Nazism, Decision succeeds in presenting a defense of democratic culture and a plea for unity among those who believe in a democratic ideology. Perhaps the best parts of the magazine are the occasional European evaluations of American letters (though these are sometimes overly polite) and the cultural-political essays of Thomas Mann. Contributions include critical essays by Stephen Vincent Benét, Aldous Huxley, Horace Gregory, William Carlos Williams, Maurice Samuel, Ernest Boyd, and W. Somerset Maugham; poetry by Muriel Rukeyser, Eugene Jolas, Eve Merriam, C. Day Lewis, Stephen Spender, W. H. Auden, Stefan George, Bert Brecht, and George Barker; stories by Weldon Kees, William Carlos Williams, Sherwood Anderson, Hans Otto Storm, and Eudora Welty.

⋄

HERE AND NOW; a group production—poetry—prose—drawing. 1941+. Irregular. London. illus.   NN
Editor: Sylvia Read?

Here and Now is a periodical collection of the creative writing in prose and poetry of comparative unknowns. The first number suggests that "The auspices for saying something new could not be bettered, for the old sayings are worn out. Further, each of us is unknown; we therefore make no bow before prejudice." In the first issue there are poems by Francis King, Sylvia Read, Kenneth Ireland, and others; the second issue presents such fairly well known British poets as Nicholas Moore and Alex Comfort.

MINIATURE; tomorrow's literature in profile. July/Aug. 1941-? Irregular. Brush Valley, Pa.   LC
Editor not established.

The mimeographed sheet, Miniature, attempts to fulfill one of the functions of the little magazine by pledging to offer "its readers the chance to study the work of young and ambitious experimenters." Among the contributions are poems by Raymond Souster, Henry Schultz, and others; prose by Morton Fineman, Joseph Michaux, and others.

⋄

MODERN READING. 1941+. Irregular. London. illus.   Y
Editor: Reginald Moore.

Modern Reading is a collection of modern writing; its publishers "started their collection with the idea of stimulating interest in the short story which prior to the present war was hardly accepted in this country [England] at all. . . . Here then is the platform for all writers today. If their work is original and vital, if they are trying to express themselves significantly, if they are non-commercial, if they are in other words writers because they must write and for no other reason, they will find an echo in these collections and their work will always be sympathetically considered." Contributions include the work of Julian Symons, Graham Greene, William Saroyan, Ruthven Todd, Frederic Prokosch, Kay Boyle, Alun Lewis, Alex Comfort, Denys Val Baker, Henry Treece, and Storm Jameson.

⋄

MODERN VERSE. 1941. Quarterly. Albuquerque, N.M. bk. rev.   NN
(Absorbed by New Mexico Quarterly Review, 1942.)
Editor: Alan Swallow.

Alan Swallow's little poetry magazine features verse by poets of the Southwest and the Pacific Coast: Yvor

Winters, J. V. Cunningham, and Barbara Gibbs. Charles Henri Ford contributes a translation from Baudelaire.

❖

NEW REJECTIONS. Nov. 1941-May 1943. Irregular. Berkeley, Calif. illus.
Editors: Doris Woodhouse, George Leite and Warren d'Azevedo.

New Rejections, edited and written by students from the campus of the University of California at Berkeley, is designed for the purpose of supplementing "the present publications on the campus, certainly not to realize a quixotic ambition of driving them out of circulation." "New Rejections was introduced for the purpose of affording a medium for tiro writers with ambitions of a literary nature who wish to see their experimental and occasionally fortunate work in print." The contributors are mainly undergraduates; a few of them have since been active in publication of the West Coast little magazine, The Circle. Among the contributions there are poems by George Leite, George P. Elliott, Jeanne McGahey; short stories by George Leite, Warren d'Azevedo, and Jordan Brotman; and a critical essay by Jeanne McGahey. The third issue contains drawings by Giacomo Patri.

❖

Now. Aug. 1941. (Only one issue.) New York.
Editors: John Roberts and William Johnson.

The single issue of Now, both in its opening editorial and in an essay by William Carlos Williams ("Midas: A Proposal for a New Magazine") asserts the imminent and ever-present need for an aesthetic restatement of political and moral truths—since the very basis of communication is language, the principal equipment of the writer. It is only the intellectual and the poet who use language for other than selfish ends, the magazine maintains. Contributions include a narrative fragment by Norman Macleod, an essay by Stuart Davis, poems by Robert Lowry and Kenneth Patchen, and criticism by Henry Miller.

❖

THE POET OF THE MONTH; a series of poetry pamphlets. 1941+. Monthly. Norfolk, Conn.  NN
(1943+ as: The Poet of the Year.)
*Each number is edited by a different editor.*

James Laughlin's New Directions publishing venture has resulted in a number of unusual and important additions to modern letters. The Poet of the Month series is not the least of these (the title of the series was changed to The Poet of the Year, in 1943, in answer to objections from the Book of the Month Club). The series is partial to the work of poets prominent in contemporary literary history, but several of its issues have been devoted to the work of the past, if such work is important to a study of influences upon contemporary poets. Among the poets represented in The Poet of the Year issues are William Carlos Williams, F. T. Prince, Yvor Winters, Theodore Spencer, Harry Brown, Delmore Schwartz, Malcolm Cowley, and Dylan Thomas. Reprintings of the poems of John Donne, Robert Herrick, and the Earl of Rochester have also been included in the series, as have translations of the poems of Arthur Rimbaud, Rainer Maria Rilke, Charles Baudelaire, Friedrich Hoelderlin, and Bertold Brecht. An occasional special anthology varies the pattern; A Wreath of Christmas Poems and A Little Anthology of Canadian Poetry are examples. Because its contents are sufficiently complete to be representative of their individual contributors, and because intelligent editorship has made the selections judicious and properly representative, the series may be called the best single effort to keep the reader informed of developments in modern poetry.

POETRY FORUM. Apr. 1941+. Quarterly. Baltimore. bk. rev., index.   NN
(Autumn 1941+ as: *Contemporary Poetry.*)
Editor: Mary Owings Miller.

Baltimore's poetry magazine, with the aid of Oliver St. J. Gogarty, who is on the Advisory Board, publishes a fairly large number of poems conventional in idea and treatment. Included among British poets are Gogarty, Walter de la Mare, and Lord Dunsany; American poets represented are Alfred Kreymborg, Witter Bynner, Karl Jay Shapiro, Marya Zaturenska, and Robert P. Tristram Coffin.

❖

READ; the book world magazine. Mar.-May 1941. Monthly. New York. bk. rev., illus.   NN
Editor: Boris Todrin.

Read is "dedicated to the encouragement and publication of new writing by hitherto unpublicized authors, as well as work by established and recognized writers.... The single inflexible criterion is that *something must be said.* Mere verbal acrobatics will not suffice." Some of the materials here have already been published, but much of it makes its first appearance. A number of brief book reviews also appear. Among the contributions are poems by Boris Todrin, Millen Brand, and others; fiction by James Still and I. J. Alexander, a critical statement by Allen Tate, and a radio sketch by William Saroyan.

❖

THE SILVER BOUGH; a literary journal. Summer 1941. (Only one issue.) Los Angeles, Calif. illus.   NN
Editor: Dion O'Donnol.

A California literary magazine, *The Silver Bough* publishes contributions from its own state and a considerable minority from other parts of the country. The publication does not limit itself to unknown writers. Among the contributions are poems by Robinson Jeffers, Genevieve Taggard, and August Derleth; short stories by David Cornel DeJong and Florence Stewart.

❖

THE SPAN. Apr. 1941+. Bimonthly. St. Louis, Mo. bk. rev. (Suspended between June/July 1941 and Summer 1942.)   NN
Supplement: *Crossing the span.*
Editor: Joseph Hoffman.

*The Span* is a part of its editor's and contributors' battle "to give poets and writers the status of research workers essential to the free and sound development of society." The battle to establish writers as members of society "worthy of their hire" had been begun by the Federal Writers' Projects, the opening editorial of *The Span* acknowledges; but those ventures have since been enfeebled by "reaction and war hysteria." *The Span* is therefore a venture designed to help the young writer to help himself. The magazine's contents show the effect of a strong left-wing political preoccupation in the minds of its contributors. Among the writings published in *The Span* are poems by H. H. Lewis, Ralph Cheyney, August Derleth, Alfred Morang, Raymond Kresensky, Langston Hughes, and others; and short stories by Alfred Morang and Juliette Elkon.

❖

THE WIND AND THE RAIN. Jan. 1941+. Quarterly. London. bk. rev.   NN
Editors: Michael Allmand, Neville Braybrooke, and others.

An English magazine begun in the midst of our second World War, *The Wind and the Rain* shows an active patriotism in its editorials and a mildly traditionalist attitude in its other contributions. Contributions include poetry by Robin Atthill, Charles Williams, John Edward, Eleanor Farjeon,

Nicholas Moore, and Jon White; criticism by Arthur Machen, Maud Bodkin, and Christina Dawson.

❖

THE WINDMILL. 1941?+. London. illus.
Editors: Reginald Moore and Edward Lane.
Issues earlier than no. 5, 1946 not consulted.

In his editorial of the fifth issue of The Windmill, Reginald Moore discusses the problem of modern science's conflict with "the creative imagination." The Windmill, he says, is designed to encourage and stimulate interest in creative work. "We are becoming so accustomed to crouching in the shadow of scientific reckonings," he continues, "that merely to affirm our belief in art and philosophy seems an act of daring!" Contributions to the magazine include poetry by John Lehmann, Alex Comfort, W. S. Graham, Bernard Spencer, Anne Ridler, and Patric Dickinson; prose fiction by Jonathan Curling, Nigel Heseltine, and P. H. Newby; and critical prose by William Plomer, Paul Tabori, and Sybil de Souza.

❖

THE WINGED WORD. Autumn 1941+. Quarterly. Brunswick, Me. bk. rev.
Editor: Sheldon Christian. NN

The little poetry magazine of Maine, The Winged Word, publishes a number of comparatively unknown but promising poets, and a few who are already quite well known. Its contributors include Robert P. Tristram Coffin, Kathleen Sutton, Clifford Gessler, Charles G. Wilson, David Morton, and Stanton Coblentz. There is considerable comment, in editorials and essays, on poetics, and on the poet in a time of war.

## 1942

ARSON; an ardent review, part one of a surrealist manifestation. 1942. (Part I only.) London. bk. rev., illus. NN
Editor not established.

Arson is important for the information it gives concerning the development of surrealism since the inception of that doctrine. This information is given substantially in two essays, by André Breton and Nicholas Calas. According to Calas, surrealism, while not repudiating psychoanalysis, has become disillusioned by the tedious monotony of dream symbols, and has decided to draw a line between the "psychoanalytic unconscious" and the "aesthetic unconscious." "I think we have exaggerated the poetic value, not of the unconscious image, but of the free association method which is the modus operandi of psychoanalytic confession."

❖

THE CHIMERA; a rough beast. June 1942+. Quarterly. New York. bk. rev., illus. B NN
Editors: Benjamin Ford (June 1942); William Arrowsmith, Fearon Brown, Frederick Morgan, and others.

One of the most challenging and excellent of recent little magazines, The Chimera is eclectic in its table of contents, but marked by an editorial taste and discrimination which brings to the magazine poetry and criticism of important modern writers. Its principal editorial concern is with presenting the "aesthetic point of view": poetry which exploits our most recent interest in the organic and integrative metaphor, and criticism of two sorts: 1) a careful and intensive study of the structure and import of single works; and 2) speculation over larger issues, governed usually by an aesthetic appraisal of the intellectual environment. Kenneth Burke and R. P. Blackmur contribute critical essays of a quality consistent with that of their earlier contributions to The Dial and The Hound and Horn. Blackmur's study of Crime and Punishment in the issue of Winter 1943 combines his unusual critical intensity with a grasp of its subject that marks the essay as an important addition to modern appraisals of Dostoevski. But Chimera does not confine its attention to writers already well known. Its contents are duly aware of an important function of avant-garde magazines; young writers are fairly represented. Among these are several poets who will undoubtedly be heard from in the future: Milton Klonsky, Ruth Hershberger, June Cannan, Joseph Bennett, and Frederick Brantley. Contributions from established writers give the magazine stability and importance: poems by Mark Van Doren, Allen Tate, Eve Merriam, Clark Mills, John Berryman, Karl Jay Shapiro, Wallace Stevens, Richard Eberhart, R. P. Blackmur, and Byron Vazakas: criticism by Philip Wheelwright, R. P. Blackmur, and Kenneth Burke. The issue of Spring 1943 discusses the "Failure of Nerve" controversy which was begun by the Partisan Review of January-February, 1943. Briefly, the subject of the controversy is the alarm of certain critics over the loss of faith in the scientific method and the consequent substitution for it of religious and political "cures" for present ills. The controversy, engaging as it does the attention of many of our best critics, can be considered the current version of the critical evaluation of twentieth century thought, an evaluation which inevitably acquires the complexion of the times. The attention of The Chimera to this controversy is marked principally by its refusal to regard the "crisis" as seriously as do the critics of Partisan Review.

❖

DYN. (Text in English and French.) Apr./May 1942+. 6 times a year. Mexico, D. F. bk. rev., illus.   NN
Editor: Wolfgang Paalen.

Dyn exists primarily for the purpose of reappraising the surrealist and other extreme and modern developments in painting and poetry. It is opposed, as ever, to traditional rationalism, which only leads to "contradictory and diverse 'movements.'" Dyn advocates a search for "novelty," for such a search, if sincerely motivated, stimulates the function of imagination, the only truly creative faculty. Surrealism must itself be discarded, for it lacks essentially the power of "objective organization" which only the imagination can effect. The vital function of art in the future, says Wolfgang Paalen, will be to synthesize the "life of the interior" with "the objective light of the external world." No. 4/5 is devoted to the study of Amerindian art, with contributions by Miguel Covarrubias, Wolfgang Paalen, and others.

❖

FIRST STATEMENT; Canadian prose and poetry. Aug. 1942?-June/July, 1945. Monthly. Montreal. bk. rev.   NN
(Merged with Preview to form Northern Review, Dec., 1945/Jan., 1946.)
Editor: John Sutherland (with editorial board).
Issues earlier than Oct. 1943 not consulted.

First Statement, "a non-profit magazine, printed co-operatively," publishes poems by A. M. Klein, Paul Halley, Irving Layton, and others; a critical essay by Geoffrey Ashe, and prose fiction by William McConnell.

❖

POETRY; a quarterly of Australian and New Zealand verse. Dec. 1942+. Lucindale, South Australia.   NN
Editor: Flexmore Hudson.

Aware of the need for publicizing Australian and New Zealand verse and of giving it an adequate hearing, *Poetry* wishes to support the belief of its editor that "the best contemporary Australian and New Zealand verse, though little heard of, is equal, if not superior, to any contemporary English and American verse." Most of the poems appear here for the first time, though a few have seen the light of print before. The contributions include poems by Ambrose Pratt, Flexmore Hudson, J. R. Hervey, Myrle Desmond, and Arnold Wall.

❖

THE POETRY CHAP-BOOK. Oct./Nov. 1942+. Bimonthly. New York. NN
Editorial board: Sydney King Russell, Albert Ralph Korn, and Leslie Nelson Jennings.

Beginning almost with the entrance of the United States in World War II, *Poetry Chap-Book* has carried on bravely and with some success in its effort to encourage the product of good but not radical or experimentalist poets. The few issues which have thus far come out have printed the poems of Robert P. T. Coffin, August Derleth, Robert Hillyer, Witter Bynner, Byron Vazakas, Jesse Stuart, Byron Herbert Reese, and others.

❖

POETRY FOLIOS. 1942+. Irregular. Barnet, Herts, Eng. BY
Editors: Alex Comfort and Peter Wells.

A collection of modern poetry, which appears in separate volumes at irregular intervals, *Poetry Folios* has for its purpose "to present outstanding verse, selected as far as possible without literary prejudice, to a small interested public." Among the contributions are poems by Henry Treece, Nicholas Moore, Keidrych Rhys, Oscar Williams, Dudley Fitts, Stephen Spender, E. E. Cummings, Kenneth Patchen, and Ormond Thomas.

THE POETRY PALISADE. Spring 1942-Winter 1943. Quarterly. Indianola, Iowa. bk. rev., index. NN
(Winter 1942-Winter 1943 as: *Palisade*.)
Editor: Gordon H. Felton.

This little magazine of verse, like many of its kind, publishes a remarkably wide variety of poems—varied both in style and in quality—the best of which come from the pens of Raymond Kresensky, Jesse Stuart, August Derleth, William Carlos Williams, Norman Macleod, Alan Swallow, and William Van O'Connor.

❖

POETS NOW IN THE SERVICES. 1942+. Irregular. London. NN
Editor: A. E. Lowy.

A small collection of war verse by British soldiers, arranged by A. E. Lowy, *Poets Now in the Services* presents a series of poets' reactions to the realities of war. There is much attention paid in these poems to the bomb, the blitz, and to the confusion of sense and motive suffered by the modern soldier; but some of the poems are quiet and without reference at all to the facts of war. Among the contributions are poems by James R. Blyth, Derek Reade, Patrick Savage, and Alan White.

❖

PREVIEW. Mar. 1942-May 1945? Irregular. Montreal. NN Y
(Merged with *First Statement* to form *Northern Review*, Dec., 1945/Jan., 1946.)
Editors: F. R. Scott, P. K. Page, Bruce Ruddick, and others.

*Preview*, Canadian mimeographed little magazine, presents some of Canada's young and promising writers. Among contributions to its pages are poems by F. R. Scott, P. K. Page, Patrick Anderson, Kay Smith, and Bruce Ruddick; and short stories by

Patrick Anderson, P. K. Page, and Neufville Shaw.

❖

RETORT; a quarterly of social philosophy and the arts. Winter 1942+. Bearsville, N.Y. bk. rev. index. NN
Editor: Holley R. Cantine, Jr.

Dissatisfied with the "retreat" of radicals from their principles and programs, the editors of *Retort* retired to Bearsville, N.Y., for a reconsideration of the problems of the revolutionary. Since society is in an important sense "artistic"—that is, the materials of the artist are *social* and not private—the editors hope that the literary contributions will aid in their task of reorientation. The magazine publishes the poetry of Kenneth Patchen, Kenneth Rexroth, James Rorty, Kenneth Porter, Byron Vazakas, and others.

❖

TREND. (University of Chicago.) 1942+. Monthly. Chicago. bk. rev., illus. Y
Editor: John W. Barnes.

Allan Dreyfuss appears as assistant editor and David Daiches, George Dillon, and Norman Maclean as advisory editors.

A university magazine, *Trend* announces that "we wish to publish the writers who are doing new things in verse and prose." There are "no academic requirements for publication." Among the contributions to No. 1 is an essay by William Carlos Williams on "The Invisible University." Other contributions include fiction by David Daiches and Marian Castleman and an essay on the theater by William Saroyan.

❖

VVV; poetry, plastic arts, anthropology, sociology, psychology. June 1942+. Irregular. New York. bk. rev., illus.
Editor: David Hare. NN
Editorial advisers: André Breton, Max Ernst, Marcel Duchamp.

A genuinely and avowedly surrealist magazine, VVV supports ". . . Historical Materialism in the social field and Freudian analysis in psychology. Armed with these perspectives we are prepared to deal with all forms of transcendentalism." Mere experimentalism is too "naïvely skeptical" for effective results. The contents of the magazine for the most part reflect a desire to recognize the eccentricities and ambiguities of the dream mechanism and to reproduce them in the arts. Contributions include the poetry of Charles Henri Ford and William Carlos Williams, the prose of Harold Rosenberg, Benjamin Peret, and André Breton. Frederick Kiesler contributes "Some Testimonial Drawings of Dream Images," and the March 1943 issue contains a Surrealist Bibliography by Kurt Seligmann.

## 1943

AUSTRALIAN NEW WRITING; short stories, poetry, criticism. 1943+. Frequency not given. Sydney, Australia. Editors: Katharine Susannah Prichard, George Farwell, and Bernard Smith.
NN
"A non-profit-making publication," *Australian New Writing* begins in the interest of making Australian writers "face up to the present day." The opening editorial suggests that art may well, if it is not handicapped by a desire for profit, serve "as a means of coming to grips with reality, of understanding the processes of society and the human heart and mind." The magazine is interested in finding young Australian writers and in giving them the encouragement of early publication. Among the contributions are poems by John Quinn, Muir Holburn, and Kathleen Watson; short stories and sketches by Alfred Burke, Alan Marshall, and Margaret Trist; and critical essays by Noel Hutton and V. G. O'Connor.

DIRECTION. [Nov. 20, 1943]+. Irregular. Outremont, P. Q., Canada.
Editors: William Goldberg, Raymond Souster, and David Mullin. NN

Canada's *Direction*, a mimeographed little magazine, wishes to establish and prove the assertion that Canada has a number of young writers who have not as yet received their full measure of attention and praise. Speaking of the "gloomy future for our native productions," Raymond Souster suggests that it is by means of such magazines as *Direction* that Canadian literature might be revived, and rescued from its present regrettable position. Among the "few hopeful signs" which appear in the pages of *Direction* are poems by Souster, William Goldberg, Wesley Scott, David Mullen, and Saul Brott. The poetry treats of a variety of themes; among them, youth and the war, modern machinery, and city life. The magazine also prints broadly satirical cartoons about the sad state of Canadian culture. It is perhaps in an examination of the contributions to this magazine and to others, like *Circle*, published in Berkeley, Calif., that one may discern the emergence of a group of young writers who in the postwar world of the forties may assert themselves as the spokesmen of a new generation.

✧

HEMISPHERES; French American quarterly of poetry. Summer 1943+. Brooklyn, N.Y. illus. NN
Editor: Yvan Goll.

The first issue of *Hemispheres* suggests a strong union of aesthetic taste and principle among certain American, English, and French poets and critics, most of whom have long been familiar to the student of experimental writing. Much attention is paid the status of poetry in a time of international crisis, and it is suggested that the poet is vital to the maintenance of human liberties. Parker Tyler contributes an essay, principally on the influence of Rimbaud upon several American poets. Poetry in English is contributed by George Barker, Charles Henri Ford, William Carlos Williams, Kenneth Patchen, and Dunstan Thompson; in French, by Saint-John Perse, Yvan Goll, and Alain Bosquet. Roger Caillois discusses the art of Saint-John Perse.

✧

LIVING POETRY. Autumn 1943+. Quarterly. La Porte, Ind. bk. rev. NN
Editors: Margaret Dierkes and Henry Dierkes.

Taking its cue from Edwin Markham's "Come let us live the poetry we sing!" *Living Poetry* seeks to present a varied assortment of talents. The editors feel that poetry is a personal and subjective matter, but that its beauty can be shared. "Man's intellectual interests, as well as his emotions, are tempered by his background and the things that have happened to him." Among the contributions are poems by Glenn Ward Dresbach, Clement Wood, Gustav Davidson, Witter Bynner, Stanton Coblentz, Raymond Kresensky, Paul Engle, and Vincent Starrett.

✧

POETRY-SCOTLAND. [1943]+. Irregular. Glasgow. NN
Editor: Maurice Lindsay.

"One of the main purposes of *Poetry-Scotland* is to show Scotland herself, and the outside world, that she can produce poetry to-day, which is as strong and moving as the poetry of England, Ireland, Wales or America." *Poetry-Scotland* is a collection of newly written poetry presented by Scottish poets, who are in the majority but are supplemented by poets from Wales, England, and Ireland. The Scottish section "contains poems written in English, in Gaelic, and Lallans." Among those poets writing in English "there are perhaps two camps—the older poets, with Edwin Muir as their leader, and the Scottish writers of the New Apocalypse." Hugh MacDiarmid (C. M. Grieve) writes a critical essay on "Poetry in Scotland To-Day." Contributions from Scottish poets include those of Francis Scarfe, Edwin Muir, Hugh MacDiarmid, J. F. Hendry, and Ruthven Todd; English poets include Nicholas Moore, Kenneth Gee, and Alex Comfort; Welsh poets, Henry Treece and Kiedrych Rhys; and Irish, John Hewitt, Maurice James Craig, and Donagh Macdonagh.

❖

QUARTERLY REVIEW OF LITERATURE. Autumn 1943+. Chapel Hill, N.C. bk. rev. NN
Editors: Warren Carrier (with T. Weiss, Winter 1944+).

"We belong to no school, advocate no trend, preach no credo. We like ideas that are original and interesting, execution that is appropriate and fresh. We are not unaware of the war, but we hold to a modest disbelief in its preclusion of new expression in the somewhat lesser arts of literature and criticism" (Prepublication announcement). The issues of The Quarterly Review of Literature fulfill more than adequately the expectations aroused by its preliminary announcement. Among the contributions to the magazine we have poems by E. E. Cummings, T. Weiss, Mark Van Doren, Wallace Stevens, Genevieve Taggard, and John Malcolm Brinnin; fiction by Paul Green, Warren Beck, and Ramon J. Sender; and critical essays by Louis Gillet, Henry W. Wells, Edouard Roditi, and Edwin Berry Burgum.

❖

REVIEW-43; a quarterly review of literature, art and science. Spring 1943+. London. illus. NN
(Winter 1944/45+ as: Review-45.)
Editors: Walter Berger and Pavel Tigrid.

The principal aim of Review-43 is to furnish a medium of cultural exchange between the artists of England and Czechoslovakia. Janko Lavrin contributes an excellent appraisal of the work of Franz Kafka. There are several surveys of contemporary European poetry, one by Stephen Spender, "English Poetry in 1942," and a number of poems by Czech poets. Criticism is provided by Edwin Muir and Herbert Read, among others.

❖

THE SONNETEER; a magazine dedicated exclusively to the sonnet in all its forms. Winter 1943/44+. Quarterly? New York. bk. rev. NN
Editors: Nathaniel Thornton and Louis Valentine.

A magazine "controlled and financed by the editors themselves," and devoted to the publication of poems in the sonnet form. Among the poets represented in the first issue are David Morton, Alfred Kreymborg, Harold Vinal, and Dorothy Quick.

❖

TEMPEST. Oct. 1943+. Irregular. London. Y
Editors: John Leatham and Neville Braybrooke.

Tempest, an irregular series, "exists for the writers and readers of some sadly neglected trends in present literature: the fantasy, the allegory, the letter and the creative essay. The critical essay, the review article and the short-story are well and aptly served in other magazines." In the first series there are contributions in fiction by Denys Val Baker, Alan Storey, Eric Nixon, and others.

❖

TRANSFORMATION. 1943+. Annual. London. H
Editors: Stefan Schimanski and Henry Treece.

The title of Transformation gives some hint of its purpose and promise:

"We ... wish to present some aspects of the change which has taken place in the heart of man ... [since September 1939]." The position taken by the editors and called "Personalism," differs from that of the "Apocalyptics," as these latter contributors to Seven, Contemporary Poetry and Prose, and other magazines call themselves. ". . . Its survey of personality is wider-reaching, broader rather than deep-cutting. Instead of tunnelling into subterranean depths of each single individual, it stretches out its roots to embrace the widest sphere. . . ." Among the contributions to the first volume are poems by Fred Marnau, Henry Treece, Herbert Read, and others; and critical essays by Read, J. F. Hendry, Alexander Blok, and others.

❖

ULSTER VOICES. Spring 1943+. Quarterly. Belfast. NN
Editors: Roy McFadden and Robert Greacen.

A "series of Broadsheets, whose object is to provide a mouthpiece for the voice of contemporary Ulster poetry, and to give the general public an opportunity of observing existing trends in the poetic development of the Province." Among the young poets published in Ulster Voices are Roy McFadden, Robert Greacen, John Hewitt, Richard Rowley, and Alex Comfort.

## 1944

THE ALBATROSS; a quarterly magazine of verse for Bohemian poets and writers. Spring 1944+. Brooklyn, N.Y. bk. rev. NN
Editor: W. M. Evers.

A mimeographed poetry magazine, The Albatross advises in its first issue that "Imagist poems written in symbolic language that is difficult or impossible to understand; banal poems; poems of personal frustration; war poems, untrue, and pessimistic poems will not be accepted." Among the contributions are poems by Raymond Kresensky, Clement Wood, Anton Romatka, and Bernard Raymund.

❖

CIRCLE. 1944+. Irregular. Berkeley, Calif. illus. NN
Editor: George Leite.

A new little magazine of the Pacific Coast, Circle demonstrates in its first issue its adherence to the principles of little magazine publication; its principal concern is for freedom of literary expression as opposed to repressive censorship. The first issue of Circle reveals several influences upon its contributors: among these might be mentioned the surrealists and the writers of the "Apocalyptic School" who have achieved some prominence recently both in England and America. The effect of the novels of Franz Kafka upon the work of young modern writers may also be noted in at least one of the magazine's contributions, a short story by George P. Elliott, "The Red Battery." Among the other contributions are poems by Philip Lamantia, Jeanne McGahey, George Leite, Hubert Creekmore, Kenneth Patchen, Wendell Anderson, and Josephine Miles, and critical essays by George Leite and Lawrence Hart. A long letter from Henry Miller, giving advice to young writers and editors, heads the list of contributions.

❖

EXPERIMENT; a quarterly of new poetry. Apr. 1944+. Salt Lake City, Utah. NN
Editor: Meade Harwell.

The poetry magazine, Experiment, supports and explains its policy by pointing to the need for experimental poetry, as "an extension of the poetic norm toward new peripheries." Experimental poetry, says Meade Harwell in the first issue, can be defined as the poetry "which is innovative, or even a discovery, and whose effort is comparatively unknown to the reading public, and is not yet in the mainstream of the poetic tradition." The contributions include poems by Will Gibson, Alan Swallow, William Carlos Williams, Meade Harwell, Le Garde S. Doughty, and Byron Vazakas.

✧

HERE TO-DAY. June 1944+. Irregular. Reading, Berkshire, Eng. bk. rev.
Editors: Pierre Edmunds and Roland Mathias.

Four unnumbered issues published without dates during the war period.

Though *Here To-Day* is concerned often with local matters (each issue contains some notice of cultural affairs in and near Reading), its contents are selected with a view to surveying a considerably wider range of contemporary literature. Such modern writers as Robert Frost and André Gide are the subjects of interesting studies and appreciations; in addition, there are essays of a general nature as well, on the novel, the theatre, the short story and poetry; and included among the contributions are poems by Alan Jones, Ernest M. Frost, Roland Mathias, Ronald Tuckey, and Michael Gardner, and short stories by Pierre Edmunds, Sheila Bolton and Elizabeth Taylor. The policy of the magazine, as stated in its second issue, is to combine local or regional interests (the magazine "is to be regarded in the first place as a local or regional publication, having a real relation to the life of the town in which it makes its appearance") with work "of a more general nature."

✧

THE ILLITERATI. no. 3, Summer 1944+. Irregular. Waldport, Ore. illus. NN

Editors: Kermit Sheets and Kemper Nomland.

A mimeographed little magazine of new writing by members of a conscientious objectors' camp, *The Illiterati* explains itself editorially as "a magazine of directed pattern in creative expression. Its editors hold to the thesis that all organisms form an interconnected whole and that separation is possible only on the mental or verbal level." Its pages publish a variety of offerings: linoleum cuts, sketches, musical scores. Among the literary contributions are poems by Irwin Stark, Roy Finch, Harry Prochaska, William Everson, Kermit Sheets, and others; prose by Bill Stafford, Kermit Sheets, and Bill Read.

✧

INTERIM. Summer 1944+. Quarterly. Seattle, Wash. NN
Editors: Wil Stevens and Elizabeth Dewey Stevens.

*Interim* is a magazine publishing principally the literature of the Northwestern United States. "We have purposely refused to embrace any specific coterie of artists, because we believe policy in literature makes for isolation and possibly smugness in art." Among the contributions are poems by Wendell Anderson and Carol Ely Harper, a critical essay by Thomas Howells, and a selection from Henry Miller's "The Air-Conditioned Nightmare."

✧

MARSYAS. 1944+. Quarterly. New York. NN
Editor: Claire Nicolas.

A mimeographed little magazine, *Marsyas* is interesting because it contains work done by the "second generation" of the *avant garde*: there are contributions by the daughter of Kay Boyle ("S. Vail") and by the children of Eugene Jolas.

MARYLAND QUARTERLY. (University of Maryland; Briarcliff Junior College.) 1944+. College Park, Md. bk. rev., illus.   NN
(Dec. 1944+ as: *Briarcliff Quarterly*.)
Editors: Jane Woodring, Pauline Howland, Norman Macleod, and Arthur O'Keefe.

The three issues of *Maryland Quarterly* represent another in a long list of Norman Macleod's associations with little magazines. After a final issue of *The Old Line* (a campus magazine, forced to suspend during World War II), the Creative Writing Workshop, under Macleod's directorship, began the publication of a new magazine. The issues of that magazine, and of its continuation under the name of *Briarcliff Quarterly*, are a collection of important modern poetry and prose, collected from a variety of sources, and lending support and encouragement to a number of contributions from university and college students. Though the magazine devotes a large share of its pages to the publication of original writing, to this are added book reviews and critical essays; among the latter are Allen Tate's essay on the novel, and Vivienne Koch (Mrs. Macleod) on "An Approach to the Homeric Content of Joyce's *Ulysses*." Other contributions include poetry by Stephen Spender, Denis Devlin, Louis Aragon, Kenneth Patchen, Ruthven Todd, Norman Macleod, Wallace Stevens, Karl Jay Shapiro, Weldon Kees, Tennessee Williams, Merrill Moore, Nicholas Moore, E. E. Cummings, José Garcia Villa, and James Franklin Lewis; stories by Caroline Gordon, Denys Val Baker, Louise Lewis, and Erskine Caldwell. In their selection of materials and in their critical emphasis upon avant-gardist writing, the editors of *Maryland Quarterly* and *Briarcliff Quarterly* associate themselves closely with the very healthy tradition of university-inspired magazines, of which perhaps the best example is Illinois' *Accent*. Macleod's magazine is noteworthy also for its use as a student laboratory of creative writing and editorial activity.

❖

NEW POETRY. [1944?]+. Frequency not given. [London.]
Editor: Nicholas Moore.

*New Poetry*, published by the Fortune Press, gives no date or place of publication on its first issue. It publishes poems by Nicholas Moore, Lawrence Durrell, Paul Goodman, Ronald Bottrall, Kenneth Allott, Horace Gregory, Ruthven Todd, and others.

❖

THE NEW SAXON PAMPHLETS. March 1944+. Irregular. Prettyman Lane, Nr. Edenbridge, Kent, Eng. (no. 4 as: *The New Saxon Review*.)
Editor: John Atkins.

The general policy of *The New Saxon Review*, as its editor, John Atkins, has said, "has been to provide literature of a high quality which was, in my opinion, within the British tradition. I have accepted experimental writing but not where I felt it was pseudo-French or pseudo-American. On the other hand, I don't mind alien styles where the author belongs to an alien tradition himself." The attempt of the magazine to prove that the English can write as good poetry as the Celt explains the title; but this is no mere expression of English nationalism. The "new saxon," celebrating his rebirth, "enjoys the productive capacity of the celt as much as the celts themselves, but he boldly demands his place in the sun. . . ." The four issues of the magazine which have so far appeared (the magazine is to change its name to *Albion*, according to word from John Atkins) contain a variety of lively critical essays and controversial notes on present-day literary affairs in Britain; there is also fiction by Reginald Moore, Jack

Aistrop, Rachel Harvey, and others; and poetry by John Atkins, Brian Allwood, Earle Birney, John Singer, Ross Nichols, John Bate, and others.

❖

OUTPOSTS. [1944?]+. Frequency not given. London.　　　　　　B NN
Editor: Howard Sergeant.

"This poetry folio has been established to provide a convenient platform for the younger writers. We are concerned not only with the publication of outstanding poetry at a reasonable price, but also in assembling those poets, recognised and unrecognised, who, by reason of the particular outposts they occupy, are able to visualise the dangers and opportunities which confront the individual and the whole of humanity, now and after the war." Contributions include poems by Nicholas Moore, Henry Treece, Howard Sergeant, Pamela Davies, Maurice Lindsay, and others.

❖

PROSPECT. [1944?]+. Frequency not given. Birmingham, Eng.　　　B
Editor: Edward Toeman.

An English little poetry magazine, "Prospect has been launched to give voice and audience to the Younger Generation of Poets, whose poetry deserves recognition. . . . [It] stands for poetry for the people and by the people. We have neither prejudices nor political bias, nor is our policy dominated by any clique." Contributions include poems by John Anstey, Douglas Cole, Ernest Hopkins, Edward Toeman, and others.

## 1945

FOCUS. 1945+. Irregular. London. illus.
Editors: B. Rajan and Andrew Pearse.

Focus is defined by its editors as a "serial miscellany," to be published irregularly and to be devoted to extended criticism of contemporary literature. An important feature of its policy is the publication of a symposium of articles in each issue on contemporary literature and criticism. The first issue contains such a collection of articles on the writings of Franz Kafka and Rex Warner, with contributions by B. Rajan, D. S. Savage, John Atkins, Tom Harrisson, Julian Symons, George Woodcock, and others. The symposium method appeals to the editors of Focus as "the best available means of organization. We should like to use it in two ways, (a) by concentrating on a particular writer, or comparison, or literary theme, and (b) by applying the same method to widely different writers." Besides the critical work on Kafka and Warner, number one of Focus contains critical essays by Andrew Pearse (on John Dos Passos), Julian Symons (on the writing of the 1930's), two essays on modern music and one on modern painting. The poetry section contains work by George Barker, John Atkins, H. B. Mallalieu, Vernon Watkins, George Woodcock, and others. "We want to encourage the long poem and the detailed critical essay," says B. Rajan in a letter to the authors (August 10, 1946). "We prefer poems in which we can find definite reasons for every element being what and where it is. There aren't many such poems in England today; but this is because the generation writing them is indiscriminate, mentally teen-age and generally lacking in critical criteria. Good poetry will not be written until better criticism is read." What distinguishes Focus from other recent magazines is its effort to form a practical union of its criticism with its creative work—so that the one can stimulate, inspire, and complement the other.

❖

GANGREL; literature, poetry, music, philosophy. 1945+. Irregular. London.

Editor: J. B. Pick assisted by Charles Neill.

With the second issue Charles Neill becomes associate editor. The term "Gangrel pamphlet" appears in the second and third issues.

"My first aim was to publish criticism, philosophy and poetry of a high standard, and little more," writes J. B. Pick, editor of Gangrel, in a letter to the authors (December 12, 1946). "But it became obvious that a small review, if it is to justify its existence, must do a very *definite* and necessary job. There are too many aimless small reviews about. Gangrel now attempts, therefore, to fulfill a function other than that of a miscellany. Broadly, our view is that the world is suffering from the disease of self-consciousness, the lonely separation of the abstracting, analysing intellect from life, at its crisis in egoism. This results in the exaltation of the will in extreme theoretical idealism, replacing the value of persons for the concept of the welfare of society; in the search for a material and spiritual absolute; in failure of responsibility; in violence; eventually in nihilism; in intellectualism in poetry and the disintegration of the novel." Gangrel, the letter continues, attempts to provide what its editor calls "*moral criticism*, . . . mainly by means of an analysis of the ego and the will-to-power in politics and literature." The magazine contains a series of articles by writers, entitled "Why I Write," to which Rayner Heppenstall, George Orwell, Neil M. Gunn, and Alfred Perlès have contributed. Other criticism is provided by Fredrick Lohr, Henry Miller, Nicholas Moore, J. B. Pick, and others; there is poetry by Lawrence Durrell, George Woodcock, Ronald Bottrall, John Waller, Howard Sergeant, John Atkins, Kenneth Patchen, Richard Wright, James Kirkup, and others.

PACIFIC. (Mills College.) Nov. 1945+. Quarterly. Oakland, Calif. illus.   NN
Edited by students of Mills College.

*Pacific* publishes a number of pieces from established writers, as well as student material. Included among the contributions are poems by Witter Bynner, Wallace Stevens, E. E. Cummings, Josephine Miles, Edith Henrich, Robinson Jeffers, and George P. Elliott, prose fiction by Robert Lowry and Bernhard Blume, and critical essays by Dwight Kirsch, Manuel Olguin and George Hedley.

✧

PHAROS. Spring 1945+. Irregular. Murray, Utah.   NN
Editor: William Candlewood.

*Pharos* is a magazine, "published intermittently," for the purpose of accommodating work "too long for inclusion in the other literary magazines," and "the work of a single writer." The first issue (Nos. 1 and 2) contains Tennessee Williams' play, *Battle of Angels*, together with a note on the play by Margaret Webster and an account by Williams of the play's production in Boston.

✧

PHOENIX. 1945+. Quarterly. Lewes, Sussex, Eng. bk. rev.
Editors: Norman Swallow (Spring 1946); Nigel Storn (Autumn 1946+). *Issues other than Spring 1946 and Autumn 1946 not consulted.*

". . . before 1945 . . . edited for some years by Norman Hampson, Norman Swallow and Basil Widger, published from Manchester and went out of circulation about 1943."

The *Phoenix* under Norman Swallow and Nigel Storn exists for the simple purpose of securing and printing "only what we (a competent editorial board) consider significant and worth-while in short stories, poems and critical essays. We are limited by our prejudices but not by theories or politics. We publish ourselves and are free from pressure of advertisers." (Letter to the authors from Nigel Storn, November 12, 1946.) Among the contributions to the magazine are poems by A. L. Rowse, Henry Treece, Norman Hampson, Mervyn Peake, Elizabeth Bartlett, and others; stories by Diana Gardner, John Morrison, Nigel Storn, Denis Webbe, John Atkins, and others; and critical essays by Norman Swallow, W. H. Mason, Arturo Barea, C. P. Hennessy, and Kenneth Hudson.

❖

PORTFOLIO; an international quarterly. (The Black Sun Press.) Summer 1945+. Washington, D.C.; Paris; Rome. bk. rev., illus.      NN
Editor: Caresse Crosby.

Numbers one and two give Harry Thornton Moore as assistant editor; Henry Miller, Selden Rodman, and Sam Rosenberg as editorial advisors. In numbers three and four all four names appear as associate editors.

Portfolio, product of Caresse Crosby's interest in literature and the arts, is a publication of her Black Sun Press. Each piece printed in it is designed as "a movable unit, to carry away or to have bound or to frame upon the wall." The editorial note of number one gives some information about the Black Sun Press and lists some of the titles it has published. In addition to the writing published in Portfolio, there are drawings by Jean Helion, Henry Moore, Pablo Picasso, Henry Miller. Contributions include poems by Kay Boyle, Karl Shapiro, Ruth Herschberger, Paul Eluard, Robert Lowell, Weldon Kees, Garcia Lorca, Stephen Spender, William Abrahams, Hubert Creekmore; critical prose by Henry Miller, David Daiches, Alex Comfort, Jean-Paul Sartre, and Albert Camus; fiction by Réne Crevel (translated by Kay Boyle), Gwendolyn Brooks, Eleanor Clark, Jerome Weidman, Jean-Paul Sartre, and Kay Boyle.

❖

YALE POETRY REVIEW. (YPR) Summer 1945+. Quarterly. New Haven, Conn. bk. rev.      NN
Editorial board: Keith Botsford, Sydney Croog, Rolf Fjelde, Thomas McMahon, Harvey Shapiro and others. *Issues other than Autumn 1945 and Autumn 1946 not consulted.*

The Yale Poetry Review provides a place for the writing of the younger and unknown poets, who appear alongside more established poets. There are several critical evaluations of modern poetry, and reviews of new books of verse. The contributions include poetry by T. Weiss, Dorothy Hobson, John Maher Murphy, Babette Deutsch, Carlos Baker, Coleman Rosenberger, Hubert Creekmore, and Leonard Bacon; critical essays by Kenneth Bache, Keith Botsford, and Louis L. Martz.

## 1946

ANGRY PENGUINS BROADSHEET. [1946]+. Frequency not given. Melbourne, Australia. bk. rev., illus.
Editors: Max Harris and James McGuire.

The Angry Penguins Broadsheet announces in its first issue the following purpose: "It aims to improve taste and judgment in the realm of 'popular art' such as the cinema, jazz, or journalism. On the other hand it aims to increase the accessibility and immediacy of the significant art of the time, whether it is obscure or social-realist." Contributions to the first issue include critical essays by Henry Miller, Albert Tucker, and R. L. Rover, and poetry by Niall Brennan, W. S. Graham, and Eithne Wilkin.

THE CHICAGO REVIEW. Winter 1946+.
Quarterly. University of Chicago. Chicago. bk. rev., illus.   NN
Editors: Carolyn Dillard and J. Radcliffe Squires (Winter 1946); J. Radcliffe Squires (Winter 1946-Spring 1946); Ray N. Kilgore (Summer 1946+).
With no. 3 (Summer 1946), J. Radcliffe Squires becomes advisory editor.

The Chicago Review endeavors to meet what it calls "the problem of a cultural as well as an economic reconversion" in the literary scene following the conclusion of World War II. "The emphasis in American universities has rested too heavily on the history and analysis of literature—too lightly on its creation," the editorial of the first issue states. The Chicago Review exists, therefore, as a university magazine designed to encourage creative writing among student-writers "all over the country." Its early issues contain contributions from established writers; but, as its editor states in a letter (July 29, 1946) to the authors, "we feel that in the future the real test of the magazine will be our ability to foster and cultivate the talent of the unknown writer. By serving as a vehicle for those who will help us create an awareness of good writing among our readers, we will afford a norm against which our contributors can measure their own efforts." Contributions to the first three issues include fiction by James T. Farrell, Kenneth Patchen, Ray Kilgore, Ralph Marcus; poetry by Tennessee Williams, Byron Vazakas, Karl Shapiro, Radcliffe Squires, John F. Nims, Brewster Ghiselin, Gerald Hill, and Jeremy Ingalls; and criticism by James T. Farrell, Cecil M. Smith, Harold H. Watts, and Margaret Webster.

❖

CONTEMPORARY. Winter 1946+. Quarterly. Detroit, Mich. bk. rev. illus.   NN
Editor: Mel Jerome Ravitz.

Many of the critical essays in the first issue of Contemporary (those by Stephen Spender, Howard Fast, Eduard C. Lindeman, and Eric Russell Bentley) are reprinted from other magazines. These are supplemented by poetry from the pens of Leo Cierpial, Sarah Zweig, and Harriet Waratt; fiction by Jack Sessions and Leo Litwak, and critical prose by Mel Jerome Ravitz and Bernard Rosenberg. The editor suggests the hope that in the future, "gradually the emphasis will be thrown to the experimental, to the new, the untried."

❖

DEATH; a literary quarterly. Summer 1946+. New York. illus.   NN
Editor: Harry Herschkowitz.

Death is dedicated to the ideas and influences of Michael Fraenkel, "whose 'death theme' has inspired the founding and editorial views" of the magazine. The editor explains his choice of title by maintaining that "the first sense of life must come from the awareness of Death," and by asserting that we can have that awareness only if we courageously face the "stubborn fact" of the crisis in modern thinking and acting. In its attempt to offer "an expression of the crisis on all fronts," the magazine's first issue publishes excerpts from Fraenkel's Journal, essays by Neil Montgomery, Victor Serge (on existentialism), Henry Miller, Harry Herschkowitz, and others; and poetry by Scott Greer, Yvan Goll, J. C. Crews, Robert Duncan, Charles Angoff, and others.

❖

FOREGROUND; a creative and critical quarterly. Winter 1946+. Cambridge, Mass. bk. rev. illus.
Editors: André duBouchet, Lyle Glazier, Feb Grobman, Herbert Kramer, Henry Popkin, and John L. Sweeney.
Issues other than Spring-Summer 1946 not consulted.

A magazine edited by graduate students of Harvard University. Foreground has editorial representatives in thirteen other universities, throughout the country. Its purpose is to encourage and to publish the writings of "writers of merit who have not yet established literary reputations." The magazine's contents are fairly well divided between creative writing by young writers and critical essays on a variety of subjects of contemporary intellectual interest. Its contributions include poetry by Richard Eberhart, Robert Lowell, Byron Vazakas, Jean Garrigue, Coleman Rosenberger, and others; fiction by Allan Seager, David Cornel De Jong, and Elaine Gottlieb; and criticism by André duBouchet, Robert Garis, Reuben A. Brower, and others. The issue of Spring-Summer 1946 contains a translation and reprint of Jean-Paul Sartre's essay, "What is Existentialism?" originally written in answer to some of Sartre's French critics.

◆

GREEK HORIZONS. Summer 1946+. Quarterly. Athens, Greece. illus.
Editor: Derek Patmore.

Greek Horizons gives as its aim the attempt to "give friends and lovers of Greek life and culture a chance to read studies and impressions written by various English speaking writers and artists now resident in Greece. From time to time, it will also publish new works, and poems by outstanding or gifted new modern Greek authors, but its main purpose will be to present Anglo-Saxon impressions of contemporary Greek life." The first issue offers poems by John Waller and translations from the poetry of Kostas Kavafis, a portion of Rex Warner's new translation of Aeschylus' *Prometheus Bound*, and prose sketches of Greek life and impressions by Lawrence Durrell, Derek Patmore, Ronald Crichton, and others.

◆

JAZZ FORUM. 1946+. Quarterly. East Mill, Fordingbridge, Hants, Eng. bk. rev. illus.

Editor: Albert J. McCarthy (U.S. editor Frederic Ramsey, Jr.)

The British magazine of jazz offers an interpretation of jazz music and its relationship to modern thought and the arts: "One could say," says its editor in the first issue, "that this magazine was specifically designed to appeal to those readers who see jazz as part of the general art movement, and who are interested in art in general." The first two issues include such speculative discussions of jazz and modern "movements" as that by Eithne Wilkins, "Jazz, Surrealism, and the Doctor" and Nicholas Moore's "Notes on Jazz and Poetry." Other essays discuss the history of jazz, and offer notes on jazz performers and performances, past and present; there are discographies as well, and reviews of books on jazz, and reports on the status of jazz in several countries. Poetry is contributed by George Leite, David Boyce, Langston Hughes, Raymond Tong, W. S. Graham, and others.

◆

LEAVEN. Easter 1946. (Only one issue.) Croydon, Surrey, Eng. bk. rev. (Supersedes *Oasis*.)
Editor: John Bate.

Leaven was published after its editor's conversion to Catholicism and its editorial, "Words Are Not Enough," testifies to the serious religious purpose of its publication. "The skill of writing has not been lost by this generation," the editorial states, "but many other skills have, and we must recover them, or watch our civilization decay. . . . If thought does not move the soul, but only finds its way into words, then the soul grows sick." And it concludes on a still more somber note: "Man is without faith and confidence, the ingredients of patience. . . . Man to-day is restless, agitated, anxious, too proud even in his humility to be quiet and trust and wait." The issue of *Leaven*, published Easter 1946, contains an essay by D. S. Savage on "Socialism and the Problem of Evil," other essays by John Bate, Walter Princess, and Kathleen M. Hall.

❖

THE MEDUSA. Fall 1946+. Irregular. Amherst College, Amherst, Mass.
Editors: James Merrill and William Burford.

*The Medusa*, the product of a group of writers at Amherst College (though it is published "independently of the College"), prints work by members of that group and by "their guests during the past year." Included are poems by Kimon Friar, James Merrill, and Sprague Johnson, translations by George F. Whicher, prose fiction by Anais Nin and William Burford, and critical prose by Kimon Friar, Maya Deren, Janet Morgan, and John Oliver Cook.

❖

NORTHERN REVIEW; new writing in Canada. Dec., 1945/Jan., 1946+. Bimonthly. Montreal. bk. rev., illus. NN
Formed by the union of *Preview* and *First Statement*.
Editor: John Sutherland (with editorial board).

Though the majority of contributions to the *Northern Review* are by Canadian writers, it is interested in writing from England and the United States as well. "We shall try to fulfill the classic function of the 'little magazine'—to afford a means of expression for the serious writer who, without a reputation and without the advantages of commercial publicity, is nevertheless determined to make no concessions to the slick, the theatrical, and the popular." The editorial of the first issue points to the danger of falsification which might come from the commercial exploitation of Canadian writers. To this danger, the editors address themselves: "All work printed will be examined to the best of our ability, not in the light of a dubious nationalism or regionalism, not in obeisance to 'big Canadian names' or so-called national traditions, but in respect to that general cosmopolitan culture to which we all adhere." Contributions to the first issue include poetry by Ray Souster, Irving Layton, Patrick Anderson, Harry Roskolenko, A. M. Klein, A. J. M. Smith, and Dorothy Livesay; a story by William McConnell; and critical essays by Ralph Gustafson, Patrick Anderson, A. J. M. Smith, and F. R. Scott.

❖

RENASCENCE. (Usher Society and Vanguard Amateur Press Association.) Aug. 1945-Sept. 1946. Bimonthly. New York. NN
Supplement.
Editor: James Blish (with Robert Lowndes, Aug. 1945-Apr. 1946).

The first mimeographed issue of *Renascence* announces itself as "a vehicle for the expression of aesthetic values, as nearly free from commercial considerations as is possible in an economics-minded century." As the "official organ" of the Usher Society, an organization set up for the purpose of sponsoring "all serious artforms," *Renascence* publishes critical essays by Kenneth Patchen, Henry Sostman, and Mallory Kent, and a translation of Ezra Pound's essay, "James Joyce and Pecuchet." There are poems by Herbert Cahoon, Robert Lowndes, Laurence Josephs, William Hulse and others. In the issue of February, 1946, Kenneth Patchen contributes a statement about the question of Ezra Pound's guilt.

# SUPPLEMENTARY LIST

The following list contains magazines which, for one reason or another, do not answer strictly to the definition of the little magazine; however, their interests and histories are similar to those of the advance guard periodicals. They ought, therefore, to be considered as an important but supplementary part of little magazine history.

## 1892

THE SEWANEE REVIEW. (University of the South.) Nov. 1892+. Quarterly. Sewanee, Tenn. bk. rev., index, cum. index: v. 1-10 (Nov. 1892-Oct. 1902). Editors: Telfair Hodgson (Nov. 1892-Aug. 1893); William P. Trent (Nov. 1893-July 1900); Benjamin W. Wells (Jan. 1897-Apr. 1899); J. B. Henneman (Oct. 1900-Jan. 1909); John M. McBryde, Jr. (Jan. 1910-Oct./Dec. 1919); George Herbert Clarke (Jan. 1920-Oct./Dec. 1925); Seymour Long (1926); William S. Knickerbocker (Jan./Mar. 1926-Oct./Dec. 1942); Tudor S. Long (acting editor, Jan./Mar. 1943-July/Sept. 1944); Allen Tate (Oct./Dec. 1944+). NN

Beginning with January 1943 Gilbert E. Govan, Walter B. C. Watkins, John Donald Wade, and Cleanth Brooks appear as associate editors.

Started in 1892, *The Sewanee Review* is today the oldest critical and literary quarterly in the United States. In its first years, the magazine devoted much of its attention to biographical and historical essays, many of them concerned with Southern history and personalities. The academic interest in literary scholarship has always been strongly represented, but *The Sewanee Review* has in recent years manifested a growing interest in modern literature, and has had critical essays on almost all of the major contemporary writers and critics, whose work has been so important in little magazine history. In 1920, George Herbert Clarke, the editor, opened the magazine to poetry; and it has since published verses from the pens of such poets as John Crowe Ransom, Merrill Moore, John Wheelwright, Theodore Roethke, William Meredith, Laura Riding, Donald Davidson, and Wallace Stevens. Its principal service to modern literature, however, is its frequent publication of critical evaluations of modern literary figures, and essays on aesthetics. A series of essays by Charles I. Glicksberg on modern criticism is one evidence of the magazine's interests. Among the other critical essays are those by John Crowe Ransom, Louis Untermeyer, William Y. Tindall, Theodore Spencer, Edwin Berry Burgum, Harry Slochower, Gorham Munson, and Allen Tate. During the editorship of W. S. Knickerbocker, the magazine became an important university critical review; and the recent appointment of Allen Tate as its editor argues well for the continuance of its interest in modern literature.

## 1902

A BROADSHEET. 1902-1903. Monthly. London. illus. NN
*Editor not established.*

A sheet of ballads and songs, illustrated by Jack B. Yeats, Pamela Colman Smith, and others, and containing contributions by W. B. Yeats, A. E., Wilfrid Wilson Gibson, John Masefield, Ernest Rhys, and others, including translations by Lady Gregory.

## 1903

CAMERA WORK; a photographic quarterly. Jan. 1903-June 1917. New York. illus. NN
Supplements.
Editor: Alfred Stieglitz.
Joseph T. Keiley was associate editor until 1913.

Camera Work is Alfred Stieglitz's magazine of art photography and criticism. It is an important auxiliary to the little magazine for two reasons: its interest in photography as an art comparable with the other arts; the importance of Stieglitz himself, and his influence upon many modern writers and artists. This latter fact is attested to in No. 47 of the magazine (1914), in which a number of Stieglitz's contemporaries pay tribute to him and to "291"; among them are statements by Hutchins Hapgood, Alfred Kreymborg, Marsden Hartley, Man Ray, and Francis Picabia. There are many exhibits of modern photography in the successive issues of the magazine; and critical essays, often written by the artists themselves, accompany these displays. Among the critical essays we find Benjamin De Casseres, Sadakichi Hartmann, Roland Rood, and Alfred Stieglitz represented.

## 1906

MOTHER EARTH. Mar. 1906-Apr. 1918. Monthly. New York. NN
Editors: Emma Goldman (Mar. 1906-Oct. 1908?; Apr. 1915-Apr. 1918); Alexander Berkman (Nov. 1908-Mar. 1915).

Emma Goldman's radical and "anarchist" magazine, Mother Earth, is devoted chiefly to radical political comment. But it is a pioneer spokesman for radical thinking in the twentieth century and deserves attention here because of the regard in which both it and its publisher were held by the young radical intellectuals of the second decade. The first issue announces that "Mother Earth will endeavor to attract and appeal to all those who oppose encroachment on public and individual life. It will appeal to those who strive for something higher, weary of the commonplace. . . ." With Alexander Berkman and Hippolyte Havel, two of her most regular contributors, Miss Goldman reports on radical political affairs. Frequently there are reprints of Russian writing (Gorky, Dostoevski), in translation, and borrowings from such Americans as Emerson and Whitman. The issue of July 1915 reports on "The Trial and Imprisonment of Emma Goldman and Alexander Berkman." There is some attention paid, in book reviews and separate essays, to contemporary literature; and original poetry is contributed by Anna Louise Strong, Lola Ridge, C. E. S. Wood, Mabel Dodge, and Arturo Giovannitti.

## 1908

A BROADSIDE. June 1908-May 1915; n.s. 1935-1937. Monthly. Dublin. illus. (1936 not published.) NN
Editors: E. C. Yeats (June 1908-May 1915); W. B. Yeats and F. R. Higgins (1935); Dorothy Wellesley and W. B. Yeats (1937).

Presented by Dublin's Cuala Press (formerly Dun Emer Press), the Dublin Broadside prints ballads chiefly by Irish poets, set to music by several composers, and illustrated by such Irish artists as Jack Yeats. Among the poets who contribute ballads for the Broadside are W. B. Yeats, Dorothy Wellesley, John Masefield, Walter de la Mare, James Stephens, Oliver St. John Gogarty, James Guthrie, Gordon Bottomey, Padraic Colum, Seumas O'Sullivan, Ernest Rhys, and others. Translations from the Gaelic are supplied by Lady Gregory, Seumas O'Kelly, and other Irish writers.

## 1910

THE HARVARD MONTHLY. v. 51-63 (Oct. 1910-Apr. 1917). Cambridge, Mass. bk. rev., index (except in v. 57-63, Oct. 1913-Apr. 1917). NN
Editors: Kenneth MacGowan, Herbert J. Seligmann, Gilbert V. Seldes, J. R. Dos Passos, Robert G. Nathan, Robert Hillyer, Robert Littell, and others.

The Harvard Monthly, for the period under consideration (1910-1917), is interesting as a college companion of the little magazine and important chiefly for the light it throws upon the early careers of some of our important modern writers. Among other matters of interest are the early, prewar poems of E. E. Cummings, remarkably different from his postwar performances. The short stories and poems of John Dos Passos also offer interesting materials for a study of critical biography. Among other contributions which are important to modern literary history are poems by Robert G. Nathan, Robert Hillyer, S. Foster Damon, and Joseph Auslander; stories by Norman Foerster, Gilbert V. Seldes, and Walter Lippmann; and critical essays by Norman Foerster, Robert G. Nathan, and Robert Littell.

✧

THE VINEYARD. (Peasant Arts Guild.) Oct. 1910-Sept. 1920. Monthly. London. illus., index (in each vol.: v. 1-7, Oct. 1910-Mar. 1914). LC
(Suspended between Sept. 1914 and Christmas 1918.) (Superseded by The Country Heart, Jan./Mar. 1921.)
Editors: Oct. 1910-Mar. 1911 not established; Maud Egerton King (Apr. 1911-Sept. 1920).

"The aim of The Vineyard is to cultivate everything that has proved essential in the real progress of man.... It believes that literature is in this day necessary to the restoration of all other arts, and, like them, must, if it would be strong, live in aspiration." Contributions include poems by Katharine Tynan, Lascelles Abercrombie, John Galsworthy, Eleanor Farjeon, and others.

✧

THE YALE LITERARY MAGAZINE. (Yale University.) v. 75, No. 4, Jan. 1910+. Monthly. (Sept.-May.) New Haven, Conn. bk. rev., index (in each vol.: v. 75-81, 84, 86, Oct. 1909-June 1921). Editors: Arthur E. Baker, Richard D. Hillis, Robert D. French, Howard V. O'Brien, T. Lawrason Riggs, and others. NN

The Yale Literary Magazine, the "Oldest Monthly Magazine in America," is interesting for modern literary historians and students for several reasons. In the period we are considering (1910 to the present) the magazine publishes early work by Archibald MacLeish—poems, prose essays, short stories—and he appears occasionally in more recent issues as well. For a study of the early work of MacLeish, as well as of several other distinguished Yale alumni (Stephen Vincent Benét, Thornton N. Wilder, Leonard Bacon, F. O. Matthiessen, among them), The Yale Literary Magazine is indispensable. Another reason for regarding it as an interesting college cousin of the little magazine is the presence in its pages of a number of contributions from persons who subsequently became active as editors of or contributors to The Partisan Review: among them, Dwight MacDonald, Jr., Frederick W. Dupee, and George L. K. Morris. The magazine also publishes a number of critical essays on modern literature: F. O. Matthiessen on Greenwich Village writers, William H. Hale on modern experiments in language, and Eugene Rostov on T. S. Eliot, among them.

## 1911

THE DRAMA. Feb. 1911-June 1931. Quarterly. Chicago. bk. rev., index (in each vol.: v. 4-21, 1914-June 1931). (Oct. 1930-June 1931 as: *The Drama Magazine*.) NN
Editors: William Norman Guthrie (Feb.-Nov. 1911); Charles Hubbard Sergel (Feb. 1911-Nov. 1912); Theodore Ballou Hinckley (Feb. 1913-Jan. 1931); Albert E. Thompson (Oct. 1930-June 1931).
Advisory and contributing editors: Brander Matthews, Thomas H. Dickinson, Robert Herrick, George P. Baker, Richard Burton, Stark Young, Benedict Papot, S. H. Clark, Nathaniel W. Stephenson, and in late issues as associate editors: Walter Prichard Eaton, Barrett H. Clark, Harley Granville-Barker, J. Vendervoort Sloan, Paul Green, and others.

Established in 1911, *The Drama* serves for a few years as the center of comment and criticism of the new theater. An early editorial by William Norman Guthrie announces the main object of the magazine as "to serve as organ and free forum for all who are interested in realizing a great native drama." Especially in its earlier years, *The Drama* is active in bringing to the attention of American theatergoers the plays of continental Europe; translations are printed of plays by Arthur Schnitzler, Leonid Andreyev, Anton Chekhov, Gerhart Hauptmann, Hugo von Hofmannsthal, and others, and each appearance is accompanied by critical comment. From 1916 to 1919 the magazine has the character of a little magazine of the theater. Printed during those years are Ezra Pound's essay on "Mr. James Joyce and the Modern Stage" and a translation by Richard Aldington of a play by Remy de Gourmont. In October 1919 the magazine becomes a monthly and its purpose changes; one of its chief aims after this time is to act as an organ for amateur drama circles, "to meet the needs of women's clubs, schools, amateur and little theatre groups. . . ." Among the essays devoted to modern drama are those by Rabindranath Tagore, Thomas Seltzer, W. B. Yeats, Jacques Copeau, and Alexander Bakshy. Edwin Arlington Robinson's poem, "Ben Jonson Entertains a Man from Stratford," appears in the issue of November 1915.

✧

THE IRISH REVIEW; a monthly magazine of Irish literature, art and science. Mar. 1911-Nov. 1914. Dublin. bk. rev., illus., index (in each vol.: v. 1-3, Mar. 1911-Feb. 1914). NN
Editors: Mar. 1911-Feb. 1912 *not established*; Padraic Colum (Mar. 1912-July 1913); Joseph Plunkett (Aug. 1913-Nov. 1914).

*The Irish Review* is a magazine of comment, criticism, and original writing, "founded to give expression to the intellectual movement in Ireland. By the intellectual movement we do not understand an activity purely literary; we think of it as the application of Irish intelligence to the reconstruction of Irish life." The magazine discusses science, economics, and Irish political and economic life. Prominent Irish writers are well represented and are much talked about. The Irish theater is given adequate attention, and plays by Irish dramatists are published. Among the contributions are poems by W. B. Yeats, Seumas O'Sullivan, Padraic Colum, A. E., James Stephens, Joseph Plunkett, Katharine Tynan, and Thomas MacDonagh; stories by Lord Dunsany, Eleanor Farjeon, and James Stephens; and critical essays by Ernest A. Boyd, Joseph Plunkett, John Eglinton, and Forrest Reid.

## 1912

ART. Oct. 1912-May 1916. Monthly. Chicago. bk. rev., illus., index (v. 1 and 2, Oct. 1912-Sept./Oct. 1913; Nov. 1913-May 1914). NN (Mar. 1914-May 1916 as: *The Trimmed Lamp.*) (Absorbed by *The Dial,* June 1916.)
Editor: Howard Vincent O'Brien and others.

Beginning as a magazine commentary upon painting, its purpose "to keep the art world of Chicago and the West familiar with the contents of our [The O'Brien] galleries," *Art* changes its format and scope of interests. Toward the end of its career—when it is called *The Trimmed Lamp*—the magazine publishes original writing, including poetry by Vachel Lindsay, Mary Aldis, Helen Hoyt, Margaret Widdemer, and Amy Lowell, and some criticism by John Gould Fletcher.

❖

THE BLUE BOOK; conducted by Oxford undergraduates. May 1912-June 1913. Bimonthly. London. bk. rev., index. *Editor not established.* Y

The *Blue Book* is a review of contemporary letters, conducted by undergraduates of Oxford University. These students contribute poetry and fiction, and discuss the intellectual interests of the day in critical studies. Among these latter are studies of or notes on Gordon Craig, Henry James, and futurism.

❖

THE SMART SET; a magazine of cleverness. v. 36-72 (1912-Dec. 1923). Monthly. New York. bk. rev. NN
Editors: Willard Huntington Wright (1912-Nov. 1914?); George Jean Nathan and Henry Louis Mencken (Dec. 1914-Dec. 1923).

From 1912 to December 1923, *The Smart Set* is an important magazine of modern letters. In December 1914 Henry L. Mencken and George Jean Nathan appeared for the first time as editors—though even before that they wrote for the magazine, and it carried stories and poems by important writers. Mencken's monthly comment on books, his occasional discussion of the American desert of Philistia, and Nathan's reviews of drama are to be found in every issue during the years of their editorship. As for the contents, these are always predominantly fiction, though poetry and criticism receive more attention during the Mencken-Nathan leadership than before or after. Among those who contribute fiction during *The Smart Set's* long career are Edgar Saltus, James Branch Cabell, James Huneker, Ludwig Lewisohn, Theodore Dreiser, D. H. Lawrence, James Joyce, Sherwood Anderson, Ruth Suckow, Kenneth Burke, and Waldo Frank. Poems are contributed by Madison Cawein, Lizette Woodworth Reese, Louis Untermeyer, John G. Neihardt, Ezra Pound, D. H. Lawrence, Amy Lowell, Maxwell Anderson, Elinor Wylie, and others. In his last contribution to the magazine, in December 1923, Mencken comments upon the great change in attitude and point of view in American letters: Today, he says, "The American imaginative writer ... is quite as free as he deserves to be." With the departure of Mencken and Nathan, *The Smart Set* becomes a popular fiction magazine, with success stories along the pattern of *The American Magazine.* It loses its importance for American literary history altogether.

## 1913

THE PLAY-BOOK. (Wisconsin Dramatic Society.) Apr. 1913-May 1915. Monthly. Madison, Wis. illus., index (v. 1, Apr. 1913-Mar. 1914). NN
Editor: Thomas H. Dickinson.

Zona Gale and Laura Sherry are mentioned among others on the Board of editors.

Thomas H. Dickinson's magazine of the theater is interested in the variety of suggestions which the theater of its time has for the arts; it "is not primarily the voice of the theatre as an institution. The goings-on in things dramatic to-day have a much broader reference than merely to the stage. These refer to a society discovering itself." It is also interested in the theater as an art and in the conventions of dramatic art. The magazine has a number of articles on contemporary developments in dramatics; among these studies are essays by Dickinson, Mary Austin, Floyd Dell (who writes on dramatic criticism), Zona Gale, and H. M. Kallen. Original writing in the drama is also printed: plays by Mary Austin, Laura Sherry, and Hartley Alexander.

## 1915

EAST AND WEST; devoted to Jewish life, literature, art. Apr. 1915-Mar. 1916. Monthly. New York. illus. Editor: Harry Rogoff. NN

The purpose of *East and West* is to "reveal to those who are sufficiently interested in the fountain of spiritual life in the Jewish Ghettoes, here and abroad," to present important Yiddish writers to the American public. Among the writings translated from Yiddish into English are poems by Morris Rosenfeld, Joseph Jaffe, Abraham Reisen, and others; prose fiction by Sholom Aleichem, Sholom Asch, Leon Kobrin, Moissaye Olgin, and others.

❖

THE HARVARD ADVOCATE. v. 98, No. 8 (Jan. 1915-June 1943). Quarterly. Cambridge, Mass. bk. rev., illus. NN (Superseded by *The Harvard Wake*, Sept. 1944.)
Editors: R. M. Jopling, L. Osborne, T. J. Putnam, W. C. Sanger, K. B. Murdock, and others.

*The Harvard Advocate*, a university review, is important for modern literature primarily because of its distinguished list of contributors, who at one time or another spent some of their college years in Cambridge, Mass. One of its most important alumni is T. S. Eliot, and the magazine made note of that fact in December 1938, when it published an issue devoted to an appreciation of the work of Eliot, and published poems which Eliot had written while he was at Harvard. Among those included in the critical section of that number ("Homage to T. S. Eliot") are Conrad Aiken, Wallace Stevens, and Robert Penn Warren. Another Harvard alumnus, Wallace Stevens, received similar notice in the issue of December 1940. In the twenties and thirties *The Harvard Advocate* was alive to all of the advance guard developments, and published many poems and essays by *avant-gardists*. Among the prose essays contributed are those by James Laughlin IV, Delmore Schwartz, F. O. Matthiessen, Van Wyck Brooks, T. S. Eliot, and Wallace Stegner; poems published in the magazine include those by Wallace Stevens, Horace Gregory, Dunstan Thompson, Robert Fitzgerald, Harry Brown, and T. S. Eliot. *The Harvard Advocate* is important for advance guard literature for two reasons: some of the earliest work of important modern writers is published in it; and its interest in modern criticism and literature has encouraged it to favor them in its pages.

❖

THE NASSAU LITERARY MAGAZINE. (Princeton University.) v. 71, Apr. 1915+. Monthly. (Nov.-June). Princeton, N.J. illus. NN
Editorial board: Edmund Wilson, Jr., Hamilton Fish Armstrong, B. B. Atterbury, John Peale Bishop, and others.

*The Nassau Literary Magazine*, like *The Harvard Advocate* and *The Yale Literary Magazine*, is important for having helped to sponsor the early, undergraduate efforts of a number of American writers who have subsequently become important in American letters. Among these F. Scott Fitzgerald, John Peale Bishop, and Edmund Wilson are especially deserving of mention. Contributions by Princeton students include poems by Bishop, Fitzgerald, Wilson, Raymond Holden, Theodore Spencer, David Newton, and Donald A. Stauffer; fiction by Fitzgerald, Bishop, and James Burnham; and critical essays by Wilson, T. S. Matthews, and A. Hyatt Mayor.

❖

THE TEXAS REVIEW. (University of Texas; Southern Methodist University.) June 1915+. Quarterly. Austin, Tex. bk. rev., illus., index.   NN
(Oct. 1924+ as: *Southwest Review*.) (Absorbed *Reviewer*, Oct. 1926.)
Editors: Stark Young (June-Sept. 1915); (Jan. 1916-Jan. 1917, *editor not established*); Robert Adger Law (Apr. 1917-July 1924); Jay B. Hubbell (Oct. 1924-July 1925, Apr.-Summer? 1927); George Bond (Oct. 1925-Jan. 1927).

During the long career of this magazine there are many changes in its editorial setup. Occasionally editors, having relinquished that title and become associate editors, resume editorship for a period. In various editorial capacities appear, among others, Witter Bynner, Mary Austin, J. Frank Dobie, John Chapman, Howard Mumford Jones, B. A. Botkin, Cleanth Brooks, Jr., John Gould Fletcher, George Bond, Fred D. Gealy, Samuel Wood Geiser, John H. McGinnis, and Donald Day.

In view of its frequent sponsorship of "new literature," *The Texas Review* may accurately be listed with the advance guard magazines. Under Stark Young, *The Texas Review* fulfills his early promise "neither to upset nor convert the world, but only to speak with it in its finer and quieter moments." Writings by Howard Mumford Jones, Babette Deutsch, Mary Carolyn Davies, and others appear in its pages. Jay B. Hubbell, as first editor of the reconstituted *Southwest Review*, sponsors the writings of many moderns: John Gould Fletcher, Lizette Woodworth Reese, Mary Austin, Conrad Aiken, Paul Green, Norman Macleod, and Jesse Stuart among them. The magazine is for the most part regional in its emphasis, and in some issues ceases to be literary in its interests.

❖

291. Mar. 1915-Feb. 1916. Monthly. New York. illus. (Superseded by 391.) Editor: Alfred Stieglitz.   NN

Stieglitz's *Two-Ninety-One* strives, by typographical arrangement and photography, to effect a geometric synthesis of word and picture. The magazine's literary value lies in its attention to "experiment with the word," and its considering photography as an art allied with poetry and worthy of *avantgardiste* attention.

## 1916

THE INK POT. Aug. 1916-? Bimonthly. New York. illus.   P
Editor: Peter Newton.

*The Ink Pot* is of interest entirely as an apology for and a description of Greenwich Village life. Greenwich Village is not just a Bohemia, this magazine maintains: "Here live many hard-working young men and women (of from 17 to 70) who are creators or dispensers (or dreamers) of all those things which tend to gladden our pilgrimage through this Vale of Tears."

❖

THEATER ARTS MAGAZINE. (Society of Arts and Crafts.) Nov. 1916+. Quar-

terly. Detroit, Mich. bk. rev., illus., index. NN
Editors: Sheldon Cheney (1916-1921), Edith J. R. Isaacs (1919+), Kenneth Macgowan (1919-June 1924), Marion Tucker (1919-1921), Stark Young (1922-June 1924).

As associate or assistant editors appear Ashley Dukes (also as English editor), John Mason Brown, Carl Carmer, Rosamond Gilder, and Morton Eustis. Stark Young and Kenneth Macgowan after 1924 continue for a period as associate editors also. Among the contributing editors are: Winthrop Ames, Maurice Browne, Walter Prichard Eaton, Clayton Hamilton, Frank Cheney Hersey, Charles Rann Kennedy, Percy Mackaye, Ruth St. Denis, Arthur Hopkins.

*Theatre Arts Magazine* is established in 1916 to meet what its first editor calls "dramatic conditions existing in this country to-day." The magazine is designed "for the artist who approaches the theatre in the spirit of the arts and crafts movement, and for the theatregoer who is awake artistically and intellectually. . . ." Its chief interest is of course in commenting upon the events in the modern theater as they happen, evaluating current productions, and considering the art of the theater in its relation with the other arts. There is much lively discussion of the theater and of allied matters by such critics as Mary Austin, Huntly Carter, Barrett Clark, Gordon Craig, Norman Bel Geddes, W. B. Yeats, Stark Young, Ernest Boyd, Edith Hamilton, and Hallie Flanagan. The interest in stagecraft is demonstrated by photographs of designs by Norman Bel Geddes, Robert Edmond Jones, Claude Bragdon, Gordon Craig, Max Reinhardt, and others. Though the first issue of the magazine announces that it will not be "taken in" by the rising interest in the cinema, *Theatre Arts Magazine* publishes many critical discussions of the art of the film. Among the plays printed here either in full or in part are contributions by Stark Young, Susan Glaspell, Padraic Colum, Eugene O'Neill (*Emperor Jones* is published in the issue of January 1921), Alfred Kreymborg, Paul Green, and Maxwell Anderson. A few poems also appear, most notably the verse of William Rose Benét, Padraic Colum, E. A. Robinson, Eunice Tietjens, Carl Carmer, and Frances Frost.

✧

WHEELS; an anthology of verse. 1916-1921? Annual. Oxford, Eng. C
Editor: Edith Sitwell.

An anthology of important British verse, *Wheels* contains, in its successive issues, the verse of Osbert Sitwell, Nancy Cunard, Edith Sitwell, Sacheverell Sitwell, Helen Rootham, Aldous Huxley, Iris Tree, Sherard Vines, Arnold James, E. W. Tennant, Alan Porter, and others. Some of the verse has been printed elsewhere.

## 1917

THE GREENWICH VILLAGE SPECTATOR. Apr. 1917-June 1918. Monthly. New York. illus. NN
(May-Nov. 1917 as: *The Spectator*.)
Editor: Roderic C. Penfield.

Penfield's *Spectator* is little more than a Greenwich Village newssheet, but as such it is valuable for the student of Village local color.

✧

POETRY; a magazine of verse, comment and criticism. 1917-1931? Monthly. London. bk. rev. NN
(July 1925-1931 as: *Poetry and the Play*.)
Editors: C. J. Arnell (1917-?); (*1920-Aug. 1921, editor not established*); S. Fowler Wright (Oct. 1921-1931).
*Issues earlier than Oct. 1920 not consulted.*

A British magazine of poetry and criticism which among other things publishes a number of essays on poetics and on the history of English poetry. Surveys of poetry, such as that by Australian poets, are also printed. The poems published here are mainly by British poets, many of them serious and competent, but imitative efforts. Beginning with the issue of July 1925, the magazine adds to its critical matter treatments of the drama. In the issue of Autumn 1929, American verse magazines are analyzed and discussed. The contributions include poems by S. Fowler Wright, Edwin Faulkner, C. A. Renshaw, W. R. Childe, and W. H. Davies.

---

## 1919

THE AMERICAN POETRY MAGAZINE. (American Literary Association.) May 1919+. Monthly. Milwaukee, Wis. bk. rev., illus.               NN
Supplements.
Editor: Clara Catharine Prince (with M. H. Hedges and Kenneth Ellis, May-Oct. 1919).

The American Poetry Magazine is the organ of the American Literary Association, the purpose of which "was from the beginning (September 1918) to arouse a new interest in poetry, and drama, to encourage both the reading and writing of verse, to assist deserving talent, and to group together in reading circles people of similar literary tastes." It belongs, therefore, to a class of magazine whose source of financial and aesthetic security is the backing of a co-operative organization. So far as its task of encouraging the writing of unknowns is concerned, this type of magazine can legitimately be called a little magazine, but it often ceases to be one when the interests of its sponsors become more important than those of the writers. The American Poetry Magazine publishes a wide variety of poetic forms, and some interesting early poems by men who have since acquired fame and reputation in one field or another. Among its contributors are Jessica Nelson North, H. H. Bellamann, Hazel Hall, Oliver Jenkins, Harold Vinal, Mortimer J. Adler, Raymond Ellsworth Larsson, Rolfe Humphries, Margaret Widdemer, Robert Penn Warren, Howard McKinley Corning, and Raymond Kresensky.

◆

THEATRE-CRAFT; a book of the new spirit in the theatre. 1919-1921? Irregular. London. bk. rev., illus.   H
(Absorbed by The English Review, Oct. 1921.)
Editors: Norman Macdermott, Hermon Ould, and Horace Shipp.

Theatre-Craft is a little magazine of the theater. Its purpose is to evaluate and to protest against "the state of the English Theatre." Among other things, it wishes to advertise in England the soundness of the Little Theatre movement which has been so successful in America. The effort to free the theater from the pressure of commercial interests is allied with a variety of other problems with which Theatre-Craft deals. Gilbert Cannan writes an essay on "The Future of the Theatre" for the first issue, claiming that there is no use reforming the theater unless the people associated with it are also reformed. Through them the world might be re-educated and reformed. Ezra Pound pleads in the first number for "small and simplified theatres." Essays on varied subjects—the Russian Ballet, Architecture in the Theatre, Nietzsche in Modern Drama, Studies of the German and French Stage, etc. —are included.

---

## 1920

THE OXFORD AND CAMBRIDGE MISCELLANY. June 1920-? Frequency not given. Oxford, Eng. illus.     Y

Editors: Herbert Baxter and Alan Porter (Oxford); L. de G. Sieveking and Alec Macdonald (Cambridge).

A magazine designed to give "the creative work of our sister Universities" an adequate outlet, *The Oxford and Cambridge Miscellany* publishes the work mainly of persons connected with the two universities. "The Oxford editors are responsible only for Oxford contributions; the Cambridge editors for Cambridge contributions." Included among the contributions are poems by Edmund Blunden, Robert Graves, L. A. G. Strong, Edith Sitwell, Louis Golding, Edgell Rickword, and Royston Campbell. There are also prose sketches, short stories, and plays.

❖

THE SACKBUT. May 1920-Feb. 1934. Monthly. London. bk. rev., illus., index (v. 3-13, Aug. 1922-July 1933).   NN
(Absorbed *The Organist*, May 1920.)
Supplements: Dec. 1927-Mar. 1934.
Editors: Philip Heseltine (May 1920-June 1921); Ursula Greville (July 1921-Feb. 1934).

The importance of *The Sackbut* lies in its presentation of music as an art form allied in purpose and importance with the other arts. Though the earlier issues presented the problems of modern music with a certain heavy seriousness, since the magazine was at the time a journal for the teachers of music, its last few years found it more actively interested in music as one of the lively arts. During these later years the magazine also widened the scope of its interests, publishing poems and commentary upon films and the theater. Among the contributions included are poems by Osbert Sitwell, Ernest Rhys, Ezra Pound, Robert Frost, H. D., Richard Aldington, Roy Campbell, Isaac Rosenberg, and others; critical essays by Arthur Symons, Cecil Gray, T. W. Earp, Gordon Craig, Herbert Trench, and others.

## 1921

FANFARE; a musical causerie. Oct. 1, 1921-Jan. 1, 1922. Fortnightly. London. illus.   NN
(Absorbed by *Musical Mirror*, Dec. 1930.)
Editor: Leigh Henry.

The seven numbers of *Fanfare* contain much of interest to the student of advance guard literature and music. The magazine's chief purpose is to consider critically and to advocate new trends in musical composition. To this end numerous essays are published, among which Jean Cocteau's essay on Eric Satie may be given special mention. In recognition of poetry as another of the lively modern arts, *Fanfare* publishes poems by Richard Aldington, John Gould Fletcher, Jean Cocteau, John Rodker, Ivan Goll, and others.

❖

THE GREENWICH VILLAGER. July 9, 1921-May 6, 1922. Weekly. New York. illus.   H Y
*Editor not established.*

A newspaper of Village news and comment, like Bobby Edwards' *Quill* and Bruno's efforts, *The Greenwich Villager* is an important source for study of Village manners, customs, literary lights, and pranksters. "We have but one thought and that is that Greenwich Village is the best place on earth." Though it is officially known as a newspaper and so sold, it earns a place among the periodicals from which scholars may someday gain information about the capital of Bohemia. The issue of July 27, 1921, announces that "Greenwich Village Secedes . . . Van Loon To Be Emperor." Among those who contribute critical essays to the paper are Phillips Russell, Willard Huntington Wright, and Pierre Loving. Sketches by Hendrik Van Loon and William Gropper are occasionally to be found. Much attention is paid the current plays by Eugene O'Neill. Poems by Edna St. Vincent Millay are also published.

## 1922

THE CRITERION; a quarterly review. Oct. 1922-Jan. 1939. Frequency varies. London. bk. rev., index.　　　　NN (Jan. 1926-Jan. 1927 as: *The New Criterion;* May 1927-Mar. 1928 as: *The Monthly Criterion.*)
Editor: T. S. Eliot.

T. S. Eliot's *Criterion* opens with his "Wasteland"; it publishes the poetry and fiction of D. H. Lawrence, Hart Crane, and others, paying attention to European writers, neglecting many important Americans. The *Criterion* shall be judged primarily, however, on its merits as a critical review; and it is here that Eliot's genius for moderating disputes and his remarkably penetrating intellect best serve him. The vigorous but diffuse criticism of Ezra Pound is found in the company of John Middleton Murry's hesitant, speculative, hedging "meditations." Eliot's real value as a critic lies in his efforts to look to the literature of the past with an eye for its contemporary value. In all estimates of the review, reaction to Eliot himself as a person, and as an intellect, will inevitably play an important part.

## 1923

THE ADELPHI. June 1923+. Monthly. London. bk. rev., index (except v. 1-3, June 1923-May 1926).　　　　NN (Sept. 1927-Aug. 1930 as: *New Adelphi.*)
Editors: John Middleton Murry (June 1923-June/Aug. 1930; July 1931?-Sept. 1938; July 1941+); Max Plowman (Oct. 1930-June 1931; Oct. 1938-May 1941); Richard Rees (Oct. 1930-June 1931).

One of several postwar little reviews of commentary and controversy, *The Adelphi* is noted for its being the mouthpiece for the ideas (political and aesthetic) of John Middleton Murry, who guided it editorially for much of its career. The idea of the magazine had been developed in conversations and correspondence with D. H. Lawrence; but, though his contributions appear frequently and a memorial issue is devoted to him in June/August 1930, the plans for collaboration between Lawrence and Murry never quite materialized. Like Eliot's *Criterion*, *The Adelphi* may be said to have borne the imprint of its editor from the start, and, in a similar measure, as was characteristic of Eliot's magazine, the introductory essays in each issue and the running commentary by Murry give *The Adelphi* a definite stamp. The comment of the first issue shows the continuity of Murry's thought, for there are reminiscences in it of his earlier editorial expressions in other English reviews. "*The Adelphi* is nothing if it is not an act. It is not a business proposition, or a literary enterprise or a nice little book in a pretty yellow cover; it is primarily and essentially an assertion of a faith that may be held in a thousand different ways, of a faith that life is important, and that more life should be man's chief endeavour. . . ." During the course of his career as editor and commentator, Murry delivers himself of his opinions on a great variety of matters—ranging in extent and interest from a study of the life of Christ to a consideration of the Marxist doctrine. In its later years the magazine has become marked by a position which is a blend of socialism and pacifism. Among the literary and critical events of the magazine may be listed the publication of much biographical and autobiographical material concerning Katherine Mansfield, the first publication of much of D. H. Lawrence's critical prose, the printing of translations by S. S. Koteliansky and others, of representative samplings from Russian literature, and the appearance, in successive issues, of much important English and American verse. Among these latter are poems by Wilfrid Gibson, Katherine Mansfield, Robert Hillyer, Michael Roberts, W. H. Auden, Allen Tate, D. H. Lawrence, and C. Day Lewis. There are stories by Stella Benson, D. H. Lawrence, Liam O'Flaherty, A. E. Coppard, H. E. Bates, T. O. Beachcroft, and James Thurber; critical essays by Aldous Huxley, Edwin Muir, Waldo Frank, George Santayana, T. S. Eliot, Edmund Wilson, and Herbert Read; and a dramatic sketch by W. B. Yeats.

❖

THE BERMONDSEY BOOK; a quarterly review of life and letters. Dec. 1923-May 1930. London. bk. rev., illus. NN
Editor: Frederick Heath.

The Bermondsey Book is established as the literary organ of the Bermondsey Bookshop; "in point of fact, [it] was an extension of the work of the Bookshop with the same object in view; whereas the Bookshop was able to bring literature and the love of books within reach of those to whom such opportunities had hitherto been lacking, so The Bermondsey Book was a means by which the unknown author could express himself." The magazine is in its early issues primarily a critical review, but within a short time expands, to accommodate much original writing by British and American writers. Among the writers whom Mr. Sidney Gutman claims (in "Seven Years' Harvest") The Bermondsey Book first introduced to the world of letters are H. E. Bates, H. A. Manhood, Sheilla Fitzgerald, and Ashley Smith. Contributions include poems by R. H. Mottram, Thomas Hardy, Humbert Wolfe, Aldous Huxley, Siegfried Sassoon, and Edna St. Vincent Millay; and short stories by Kathleen Coyle, T. O. Beachcroft, A. E. Coppard, Liam O'Flaherty, Conrad Aiken, Albert Halper, Herbert Read, and R. H. Mottram.

❖

THE DUBLIN MAGAZINE. Aug. 1923-Aug. 1925; n.s. Jan. 1926+. Monthly. Dublin. bk. rev. illus., index (in each vol.: v. 1-3, Aug. 1923-Aug. 1925). (Suspended, Sept.-Dec. 1925.) NN
Editor: Seumas O'Sullivan.

A review of both original and critical writing, The Dublin Magazine is important for its interest in and preoccupation with Irish letters, and more particularly with the Irish theater, about which there is much historical and critical discussion. Its long life and its position as spokesman for Irish literature give it the status of an almost "official organ" for the thought and writing of its country, and its long critical essays and its many bibliographical summaries of Irish writing make it an important source for study of Irish literature. But there is also more than an adequate collection of original writings in its pages. Among these may be mentioned poems by F. R. Higgins, Padraic Colum, Oliver St. John Gogarty, Lord Dunsany, Alun Lewis, A. E., L. A. G. Strong, and others. Stories by Frank O'Connor, Vincent O'Sullivan, L. A. G. Strong, Liam O'Flaherty, and others. Critical essays include a series by A. J. Leventhal on modern literature and thought, and others on various subjects by Herbert E. Palmer, Louis Golding, W. B. Yeats, Séan O'Fáolain, and J. M. Hone.

❖

ORIENT; a magazine of art and culture. (The Orient Society.) Feb. 1923-Jan. 1927. Bimonthly. New York. bk. rev., illus., index (v. 1 and 2, Feb. 1923-Sept. 1925). NN
(May/June 1924-Jan. 1927 as: The New Orient.)
Editors: Hari G. Govil (Feb.-Oct./Nov. 1923); Syud Hossain (May/June 1924-Jan. 1927).

In *Orient* an attempt is made, with some little success, to bring together a variety of criticisms and appreciations of Oriental culture and the arts, and to publish translations of Oriental verse and prose. There are numerous reproductions of Oriental paintings and photographs of sculpture. Among the "Western" minds who write essays on the Orient are Romain Rolland, Claude Bragdon, Giovanni Papini, and Glenn Hughes. Oriental writers include Ananda K. Coomaraswamy and Rabindranath Tagore.

## 1924

THE ECHO. 1924-May 1928. Monthly. Denver. Colo. bk. rev., illus.   NN
Editor: David Raffelock.

The *Echo* from Denver is a magazine of local gossip and comment of the Denver and Western areas, but its contents include a large number of poems and stories by important twentieth century writers. Among these are poems by Horace Gregory, Haniel Long, Witter Bynner, Carl Rakosi, Kathleen T. Young, and Willard Johnson; short stories by Fiswoode Tarleton, N. Bryllion Fagin, and Meridel Le Sueur.

## 1925

THE CALENDAR OF MODERN LETTERS. Mar. 1925-July 1927. Monthly. London. bk. rev., index (v. 1-2, Mar. 1925-Mar. 1926).   NN
(Apr. 1926-July 1927 as: *The Calendar*.)
Editors: Edgell Rickword, Douglas Garman, and Bertram Higgins.

The *Calendar of Modern Letters* is an ambitious and successful review, notable, among other things, for its publication of some of D. H. Lawrence's best tales, and a few of his essays in modern criticism. The magazine divides its space well between critical and creative work. Contributions include poems by Hart Crane, Allen Tate, and John Crowe Ransom, fiction by A. E. Coppard and Liam O'Flaherty, and critical essays by Edwin Muir, John Crowe Ransom, Wyndham Lewis (critical comments on Shakespeare), and Desmond MacCarthy. Translations of the work of Dostoevski are furnished by S. S. Koteliansky.

## 1926

VOORSLAG; a magazine of South African life and art. June 1926-July 1927. Monthly. Durban, South Africa. bk. rev., illus.   NN
*Editor not established.*

A South African review, *Voorslag*, like many of its British fellows of Wales, Scotland, and Australia, attempts to present the arts and letters of its place and time, along with essays on the culture and politics of its region. The magazine is well supplied with original writing, from which the following may be singled out for mention: poetry by Hector Bolitho, Leon Picardy, and Philip Page, and fiction by Ethelreda Lewis.

## 1927

CLOSE-UP. July 1927-Dec. 1933. Monthly. Territet, Switzerland; London. bk. rev., illus., index (in each vol.: v. 6-10, 1930-1933).   NN
Editor: Kenneth Macpherson.

It is inevitable that the intellectuals of the century should have become interested in the two new art forms: photography and the film. For the second, *Close-up* is the voice of serious and advanced thinkers on the subject. Dorothy Richardson's almost regular column, "Continuous Performance," speaks wisely of the aesthetics of the cinema. Besides many articles on cinema technique, and essays on the probable or actual influence of the cinema upon literary style, there are such other contributions as poetry by H. D., Marie de L. Welch, Marianne Moore, and prose by Gertrude Stein.

❖

THE PANTON MAGAZINE; literature, art, music, drama. (Panton Arts Club.) 1927. Quarterly. London. bk. rev., illus. *Editor not established.* NN

A British version of the noncommercial magazine of the arts, which is sponsored by a union or co-operative group of writers. "The objects both of the Panton Arts Club and of the magazine being strictly professional and noncommercial, the Editorial Committee is in a position to consider work submitted to it upon its intrinsic merits alone and to remain indifferent to the fictitious value lent by reputation." Attention is paid to the art of painting by means of reproduction and critical discussion.

---

## 1928

---

THE CANADIAN MERCURY. Dec., 1928—? Monthly. Montreal. bk. rev. NN
Editorial board: Jean Burton, F. R. Scott, Leo Kennedy, Felix Walter.
*Issues later than Apr./May, 1929 not consulted.*

The Canadian Mercury, "a Journal of Literature and Opinion conducted along the necessarily liberal lines of an open forum," is designed—so its editors say in the first issue—to assist in "the emancipation of Canadian literature from the state of amiable mediocrity and insipidity in which it now languishes." The magazine carries a number of essays on Canadian politics and economics. It publishes, as well, the work of young Canadian writers, including the early poetry of A. J. M. Smith and A. M. Klein. Other contributions include poems by Mona Weiss, F. R. Scott, Erica Selfridge, and N. W. Hainsworth; short stories by Jean Burton, Dorothy Livesay, Russell Maccallum, and Douglas McPhee; and criticism by George Humphrey, S. Ichiyé Hayakawa, Leo Kennedy, Leonard Bullen, Harcourt Brown, and A. J. M. Smith.

❖

THE CAROLINA PLAY-BOOK. (Carolina Playmakers; The Carolina Dramatic Association.) Mar. 1928+. Quarterly. Chapel Hill, N.C. illus. NN
Supplement: *The Carolina Stage*, Mar. 1936+.
Editor: Frederick Koch.

Like many another little magazine of the theater, *The Carolina Play-Book*, published at the University of North Carolina, is an active commentary on immediate events in the theater, an elaborate and suggestive "play bill." Plays written and produced by local writers and actors are published and commented upon, and the position of the drama in contemporary letters is given much comment and discussion. Among the most frequent contributors is Paul Green, important spokesman for Southern drama. His essays appear almost regularly. In addition, there are essays by Archibald Henderson, a member of the Board of the Carolina Playmakers, and one essay by Howard Mumford Jones. The issue of March/June 1943 is published "To the Memory of Thomas Wolfe" and contains much material by him and essays on him by Henderson and Koch.

❖

LIFE AND LETTERS. June 1928+. Monthly. London. bk. rev., index (except in v. 12-20, no. 18, Apr. 1935-Feb. 1939). NN
(Sept. 1935+ as: *Life and Letters Today.*) (Absorbed *The London Mercury*, May 1939.)
Editors: Desmond MacCarthy (June 1928-Dec. 1933/Feb. 1934); Hamish

Miles (Mar.-Aug. 1934); R. Ellis Roberts (Oct. 1934-Apr. 1935); Petrie Townshend (Sept. 1935-Spring 1937); Robert Herring (Sept. 1934+).

The literary history of the twentieth century includes a number of reviews which, though they cannot be said to answer the requirements of the "little magazine," nevertheless played an important accompaniment to the "major performers." *Life and Letters* is such a magazine. If it may be said that modern literature is furnishing its own mature evaluation and thus anticipating by several decades at least the conclusions and decisions of future historical scholarship, such magazines as *The Kenyon Review, The Southern Review, The University Review,* and *Life and Letters* have been greatly instrumental in satisfying inquiries about literature as it is being written. Critical evaluations are supplied, in *Life and Letters,* of the work of T. S. Eliot, Baudelaire, Rainer Maria Rilke, Edith Sitwell, James Joyce, Franz Kafka, and Gerard M. Hopkins, among others. Critical essays of a general aesthetic interest are provided by Paul Valéry, André Gide, Thomas Mann, Edgell Rickword, Stefan Schimanski, and others. Among the contributions are poems by Roy Campbell, D. H. Lawrence, Herbert Read, Charles Madge, George Barker, Marianne Moore, Horace Gregory, William Carlos Williams, Merrill Moore, John Malcolm Brinnin, Alun Lewis, Edith Sitwell, Henry Treece, and others; fiction by David Garnett, V. Sackville-West, Evelyn Waugh, Stephen Spender, Dylan Thomas, Thomas Mann, Franz Kafka, H. E. Bates, and others.

---

## 1929

ALHAMBRA; a literary monthly. Hispano and American Alliance, Inc.) (Text in English and Spanish.) June 1929-Jan. 1930. New York. bk. rev., illus. NN
Editor: Angel Flores.

*Alhambra,* a magazine "devoted primarily to Spanish and American letters," is an attempt to bring to Spanish and English writing some understanding and appreciation. "We form part of no radical movement, of no literary clique. But we will project any significant gesture which may imply a 'decent' expansion of tradition." In the first issue, the American contributions are presented in Spanish, the Spanish in English; all other issues are entirely in English. Included among the contributions are fiction by A. Hernandez-Cata and Miguel de Unamuno; poems by Garcia Lorca, Ramon de Basterra, Kathleen Tankersley Young, and Conrad Aiken; and critical essays by Houston Peterson and V. J. McGill.

✧

FOLK-SAY; a regional miscellany. (Oklahoma Folklore Society.) 1929-1932. Annual. Norman, Okla. NN
Editor: B. A. Botkin.

The advisory editors include Percy MacKaye, J. Frank Dobie, Mary Austin, Witter Bynner, Barrett H. Clark, Charles J. Finger, Alain Locke, John G. Neihardt, Carl Sandburg, Frank Shay, and Edna Lou Walton.

This annual collection of folk literature and of essays on folk culture is an important appendix to the literature of regionalism in Midwestern and Southwestern America. B. A. Botkin's lengthy essay on "The Folk in Literature: An Introduction to the New Regionalism," fairly well establishes the critical purpose, direction, and defense of the annual's contents. The identity of folk lore with literature, he says, is borne out by the fact that "in every age literature moves on two levels—that of folk and that of culture; and that whenever the latter is in need of being strengthened and revitalized, it returns to the lower of the folk. . . ." The annual publishes fables and stories stemming from Oklahoma folk culture, and selections showing folk motifs in literature. Among the critics who discuss regionalism and folklore are Mary Austin, Louise Pound, and Sterling A. Brown. Contributions include poems by John Gould Fletcher, Norman Macleod, Mary Austin, Haniel Long, Pat Morrissette, and Alice Corbin. The volume for 1930 includes bibliographical material and a summary of the current research in folk materials.

❖

MAIN STREET; a magazine of American opinion, arts and letters. Mar.-July 1929. Bimonthly. New York. illus.   Y
Editors: Harold Hersey (with Elinor Hersey, May-July 1929).

A magazine of and for young American writers: "We are trying to give birth and rebirth to American letters: birth for the new, rebirth for the old. We hope to make this magazine a 'Main Street' of opinion and art: not a medium for personally destructive criticism." Opposed to Henry L. Mencken's habits of criticism, *Main Street* asserts that it "will struggle to publish what is worthy and gallant in American arts and letters." This positive point of view is the occasion for the publication of the following contributions: poems by Bert Cooksley, Herbert Bruncken, and others; short stories by Edward Vernon Burkholder, Robert W. Sneddon, and others. The issue of May 1929 publishes a series of Art Young cartoons, and a note on his art.

❖

OPINION. Oct. 1929-May 1930? Monthly. Los Angeles, Calif. illus. Editor: José Rodriguez.   NN

Though *Opinion* does not confine itself to literary matters—being concerned often with the state of Southern California ethics and politics—its major emphasis is upon criticism and evaluation of current literary interests on the Pacific Coast. Some new letters of Ambrose Bierce are published in the issue of May 1930. Included among contributions are poems by Hildegarde Flanner, Herman Salinger, and Jake Zeitlin.

❖

PURPOSE. 1929-1940? Quarterly. London. bk. rev., indcx.   ICU NN
Editors: John Marlow (1929); W. T. Symons (1930-1940) (with Philippe Mairet, 1930-1935; A. Desmond Hawkins, 1936-1940).

Though *Purpose* publishes little creative writing, its contribution to modern criticism is important. An entire issue (Jan.-March, 1938) is devoted to essays on modern poetry. Ezra Pound, T. S. Eliot, George Barker, Robert Penn Warren contribute articles of importance to modern critical thought. There are poems by Dylan Thomas, Lawrence Durrell, Frederic Prokosch, and Michael Roberts.

## 1930

EXPERIMENTAL CINEMA; a monthly projecting important international film manifestations. Feb. 1930-June 1934? Irregular. Philadelphia. illus.   NN
Editors: David Platt, Lewis Jacobs, Seymour Stern, Alexander Brailovsky, and Barnet G. Braver-Mann.

An awareness of the great importance of the film for modern art informs the contents of this magazine. The cinema "is great enough in possibilities to not only *contain* but to give *direction* and *purpose* to poetry, music, painting, sculpture. . . ." To a very lively interest in the technique of the film, the magazine adds, in the later issues, an interest in radical social issues. It announces itself as opposed to the "reactionary political, psychological, and conventional formalistic tendencies of the capitalistic film industry." Contributions include critical essays by S. M. Eisenstein and H. A. Potamkin.

---

## 1931

---

COLLEGE VERSE. (College Poetry Society of America.) Nov. 1931-May 1941? Monthly (Nov.-May). Grinnell, Iowa.                      LC H
Editors: Eda Lou Walton (Nov. 1931-May 1933); Arthur H. Nethercot (Nov. 1933-May 1935); and others.

"Board of Sponsors" includes Edna St. Vincent Millay, Harriet Monroe, Jessie B. Rittenhouse, Sara Teasdale, Lucia Trent, Joseph Auslander, Witter Bynner, Arthur Davison Ficke, Robert Frost, William Ellery Leonard, John Neihardt, Carl Sandburg, Lew Sarett, and John V. A. Weaver.

The "simple program" of *College Verse*, according to Robert Hillyer, president of the College Poetry Society of America, is not to "organize" undergraduate poets, but "simply to put in touch with each other people who are interested in the same subject." Among the contributions are found the verses of Audrey Wurdemann, William Kimball Flaccus, Lionel Wiggam, Philip Horton, Kerker Quinn, Alan Swallow, Ted Olson, and others. Each issue publishes a number of critiques and brief notes about modern poetry.

✧

THE FORTNIGHTLY. Sept. 11, 1931-May 6, 1932. Campbell, Calif. bk. rev., illus., index.            NN
Editor: Carlton S. Hyman.

In this Pacific Coast magazine much attempt is made to "chronicle" activities in the various arts. Its contents, however, include several contributions of some importance; and critical attention is paid to most of the important persons and events of modern letters. There is poetry here by Willard Maas, John Cowper Powys, C. E. S. Wood, and others.

✧

THE NEW MEXICO QUARTERLY. (University of New Mexico.) Feb. 1931+. Albuquerque, N.M. bk. rev., illus., index.                                    NN
(1941+ as: *The New Mexico Quarterly Review*.) (Absorbed *The New Mexico Business Review*, 1941; *Modern Verse*, 1942.)
Editorial board: J. F. Zimmerman, John D. Clark, J. W. Diefendorf, and others; editors: T. M. Pearce (Nov. 1932-Nov. 1939); Dudley Wynn (Feb. 1940+).

From February 1940 to date T. M. Pearce continues as associate editor. Alan Swallow appears as poetry editor.

Like the *Texas Review* and *Prairie Schooner*, *The New Mexico Quarterly* begins as a means of publishing materials written by faculty and students. The emphasis is frequently upon Southwestern folklore tradition and its possibilities for art. But its principal function is to serve as an "outlet" for Southwestern writers and as a means of critical commentary upon them. The magazine's interest in literary regionalism is highlighted by essays on the subject by B. A. Botkin, J. C. Ransom, and Mary Austin. The interest in D. H. Lawrence as a one-time resident of New Mexico is the occasion for essays on his work and on his significance for twentieth century thought. Beginning with the issue of February 1941, the magazine publishes several articles on Southwestern politics and economics, but it continues its very liberal emphasis upon modern letters, and its contributions include many representative modern poems, selected by Alan Swallow. The great virtue of *The New Mexico Quarterly* is its intelligent compromise between regionalism and universalism in its attitudes and contents. Among the contributions are poems by Witter Bynner, Norman Macleod,

José Garcia Villa, Haniel Long, John Gould Fletcher, Spud Johnson, Oscar Williams, Alan Swallow, Federico Garcia Lorca, Yvor Winters, and J. V. Cunningham; prose narratives by Paul Horgan, Alfred Morang, Jesse Stuart, and William March; and critical essays by Mary Austin, John C. Ransom, Alan Swallow, and Eric Russell Bentley.

✧

WORKERS THEATRE. (League of Workers Theatres.) Apr. 1931-1933. Monthly. New York. illus.   NN
*Editor not established.*
*Issues other than May-Aug. 1932 not consulted.*

A magazine of proletarian drama, *Workers Theatre* discusses the problem of the worker's drama and publishes sections of new proletarian plays.

---

## 1932

CINEMA QUARTERLY. Autumn 1932-Summer 1935. Edinburgh, Scotland. bk. rev., illus., index.   NN
(Superseded by *World Film News and Television Progress*, Apr. 1935.)
Editor: Norman Wilson.

The British magazine of film comment and criticism deserves a place among the little reviews because of its intelligent evaluation of the cinema as a companion art to those of writing, painting, and music. "For our guidance we depend on a deep-rooted faith in the ultimate value of the film, not as an art form with an end in itself, but as a medium for the communication of ideas and the exposition of ideals." *Cinema Quarterly* is against the commercialized movie. "Technical swagger too often misleads the critics and the public into accepting as works of first-rate importance films entirely devoid of purpose or any idea of value." Among the interesting critical appraisals of the cinema are Herbert Read's "Towards a Film Aesthetic," which appears in the first issue; Alexander Werth on the "Average French Talkie," Read's "The Poet and the Film"; Eric Knight on American films; Hugh MacDiarmid's "Poetry and Film"; and Rudolf Arnheim's "The Film Critic of To-day and To-morrow." The quarter's output of films is reviewed in each issue.   ✧

DAVID; an international review of politics and literature. Mar.-May 1932. Monthly. London. bk. rev.   NN
Editors: A. J. Henderson, Allan N. Taylor, and Erik Warman.

The essays in *David* are fairly evenly divided in subject matter between politics and literature. In the former, subjects important to the British mind are taken up. The latter attempts to act as a check upon the sad state of commercialized reviewing in our day. Among the critical essays are those by Lionel Britton, A. J. Henderson, C. K. Ogden, and Alaric Jacob.

✧

THE INTERNATIONAL THEATRE. Bulletin. (International Union of the Revolutionary Theatre.) 1932-Oct., 1934? Irregular. Moscow, U.S.S.R. illus.   NN
Editor: S. S. Podolsky.

*The International Theatre* is a news magazine of theatrical events within the Soviet Union. Included also is a brief report of events in other countries among organizations committed to the advancement of "the revolutionary theatre." The magazine merits a mention here because, like *International Literature*, it furnishes information about the effect of radical political movements upon literature in the thirties. For this reason, its influence was not inconsiderable upon writers of the time who were interested in the doctrinal direction of the arts in general.

✧

THE LION AND CROWN. Fall 1932-[Jan. 1933?] 4 issues a year. New York. bk. rev.   NN

(Supersedes *The New Broom and Morningside.*)
Editor: James G. Leippert.

College literary magazines often confine themselves to undergraduate writing. Occasionally, however, they expand to include a variety of writers, and thus become important sources for study of the *avant garde*. *The Lion and Crown*, one of several Columbia University literary magazines, publishes the work of many well known modern writers: poetry by Conrad Aiken, Carl Rakosi, Norman Macleod, Gertrude Stein, and José Garcia Villa, among others; fiction by Charles Reznikoff, Erskine Caldwell, and Villa.

❖

MOTLEY. Mar. 1932-May 1934. Monthly. Dublin. illus.
Editor: Mary Manning.

*Motley* is the expression of Irish critical comment on matters concerning the theater. As such it publishes a series of lively essays on the modern theater; its more restricted interest is indicated by discussions of Irish literature. Poems, though not given "first billing" in the magazine, are frequently published; among the poets are Michael Sayers, Padraic Colum, John Betjeman, and John Lane. Séan O'Fáolain writes an essay on "Provincialism and Literature" in the August 1932 issue.

❖

THE NEW BROOM AND MORNINGSIDE. (Philolexian Society, Columbia College.) Jan.-Apr. 1932. 5 issues a year. New York. illus.   NN
(Formed by the union of *The New Broom* and *The Morningside*.) (Superseded by *The Lion and Crown*, Fall 1932.)
Editor: James G. Leippert.

One of Columbia University's literary magazines, *The New Broom and Morningside* strives to remain aloof from current aesthetic quarrels; "we do not wish it to be the mouthpiece of any particular artistic clique." Contributions are mainly by undergraduate writers; two poems by Ben Maddow, alumnus, are included in the March 1932 issue.

❖

SCRUTINY. May 1932+. Quarterly. Cambridge, Eng. bk. rev.   NN
Editors: L. C. Knights (with Donal Culver, May 1932-June 1933); F. R. Leavis (Dec. 1932+); Denys Thompson (Dec. 1932-June 1939); D. W. Harding (Sept. 1933+); W. H. Mellers (Jan. 1942+).

*Scrutiny*, like T. S. Eliot's *Criterion*, attempts to evaluate modern literature and thought, and also reviews much of the literature of the past. F. R. Leavis' valuable critical articles are published here. *Scrutiny* also publishes a small number of "original compositions": "Since, however, more people are able to write good criticism than good verse or short stories, we commit ourselves to no large or constant proportion of creative work." Included among the relatively few good poems are those by Richard Eberhart, Selden Rodman, and Ronald Bottrall. Among the modern writers and critics who are given critical attention in *Scrutiny* are T. S. Eliot, Ezra Pound, William Empson, D. H. Lawrence, and I. A. Richards. Bergson and Whitehead are also the subjects of critical essays.

## 1933

CADENCES; a magazine of criticism. Apr. 1933-Jan. 1936? Quarterly. New York. illus.   NN
Editor: Marion Blodgett.

Another Greenwich Village magazine, *Cadences* is of little value except as a reflection of the Village "color." There is much poetry, of negligible value, on the Village and Villagers.

FILM ART; international review of advance-guard cinema. 1933-Spring 1937. Quarterly. London. bk. rev., illus.
Editors: B. Vivian Braun (Spring-Winter 1934); Irene Nicholson and John C. Moore (Autumn 1935-Spring 1937, with Robert Fairthorne, Second quarter 1936-Spring 1937). NN
*Issues earlier than Spring 1934 not consulted.*

film art is dedicated to the task of giving the art of the cinema an enlightened and informed audience. "The new cinema film ... must be collected, informal and guided in order that the genuinely good film may be supported." To this end the magazine publishes essays on the film by S. M. Eisenstein, Oswell Blakeston, Terence White, and others, as well as a running commentary upon "The Film Today."

✧

OXFORD CRITERION. June 1933-Spring 1935. Quarterly. Oxford, Ohio. bk. rev., illus. Y
Editors: Arthur M. Coon (June 1933); James H. Beardsley (Fall 1933-Mid-Winter 1934?) and others.

A review associated with the academic community of Miami University in Ohio, the *Oxford Criterion* publishes essays on a variety of subjects, politics, economics, literature, and the arts. Among the contributions there are poems by Ridgely Torrence and fiction by Walter Havighurst and John Rood.

---

## 1934

---

ART FRONT. (Artists' Union; also sponsored by the Artists' Committee of Action, Nov. 1934-Jan. 1935.) Nov. 1934-Dec. 1937. Monthly. New York. bk. rev., illus. NN
Editorial board: Hugo Gellert, Stuart Davis, Ethel Olenikov, Max Spivak, Clarence Weinstock, H. Glintenkamp, and others.

A leftwing magazine of the arts, *Art Front* calls for a vigorous alignment of the arts with leftwing political thought and action. "Art Front is the crystallization of all the forces in art surging forward to combat the destructive and chauvinistic tendencies which are becoming more distinct daily." Thus the art of our time is evaluated in terms of its political or economic associations, real or imagined. There are essays on surrealism, on painting and propaganda, short articles by Thomas Hart Benton and John Steuart Curry, and studies of the painting of Diego Rivera and William Gropper.

✧

THE COLOSSEUM. Mar. 1934-July/Sept. 1939. Quarterly. London. bk. rev., index (v. 1-3, Mar. 1934-Dec. 1936).
Editor: Bernard Wall. NN

A critical magazine, *The Colosseum* presents an interpretation of contemporary affairs, cultural and literary, from the Catholic point of view. "Its function is to investigate the chief problems—particularly the spiritual problems—of our time in the light of Catholicism." It is interested in a very active application of principle to the immediate present, what it calls the "actualization of principle." "Our work then is to develop an outlook, or better a mode of consciousness ... which will be capable of sympathy with forms of experience, offered by the contemporary world." Critical and philosophical essays are offered by Nicholas Berdyaev, Jacques Maritain, Eric Gill, Georges Cattani, Bernard Wall, Bernard Fay, Wallace Fowlie, and Pierre Balascheff.

✧

THE CRITIC. Oct. 1934-Feb. 1935. Monthly. Glenbrook, Conn. bk. rev., illus. NN
Editors: Sabin Leake, C. D. Smith, Revington Arthur, and Charles Baldwin.

The purpose of The Critic "is to present to its readers an analysis of contemporary problems which affect the average person in his daily activity.... [The] foundation for individual thinking ... will be laid by means of articles, essays, and critical columns, satire, poems, and stories." There are many art reproductions, book and film reviews, critical essays.

❖

THE INLAND REVIEW. (University of Michigan.) Apr.-June 1934? Quarterly. Ann Arbor, Mich.  Y
Editor: Arthur M. Coon.

A University of Michigan quarterly, The Inland Review publishes verse, fiction, and criticism written by students, with contributions also from outsiders. Ezra Pound contributes "Epitaph" to the first issue, a satirical comment upon conservatism in American literary tastes.

❖

THE LION AND THE UNICORN; an American review of the arts. Oct./Nov. 1934. (Only one issue.) New York. bk. rev., illus.  NN
Editors: Russell Cloud, G. Jerome Francis, and Kenneth Seeman Giniger.

The single issue of this little magazine announces a program typical of much little magazine editorial history. "Since we have adopted no particular political or literary editorial viewpoint, work will be selected on the basis of intrinsic merit and artistic value rather than because of the name, politics, morals, or subject matter of the author.... We are particularly interested in those new writers of merit who cannot find a place for their work in the commercial publications." This magazine attempts in a sense to be a replacement of The Hound and Horn or at any rate proposes to "remedy the situation" caused by the death of that and other little reviews. The contents of the single issue include poems by Norman Macleod, José Garcia Villa, Yvor Winters, and others; and short stories by Alfred Morang, Eugene Armfield, and August Derleth.

❖

THE NEW FRONTIER. Jan. 1934-Oct. 1935. Bimonthly. Exeter, N.H. bk. rev., illus.  H
Editors: Brooks Otis and Reuben Brower.

The New Frontier is marked by its definiteness of editorial policy which advocates a solution of the problems of modern society—a form of "Techno-democracy" which includes a suggestion for leadership by an "intellectual aristocracy." This position dominates a major proportion of the magazine's contents.

❖

NEW THEATRE; drama, film, dance. (League of Workers Theatres of the USA.) Jan. 1934-Apr. 1937. Monthly. New York. bk. rev., illus.  NN
(Suspended, Dec. 1936-Feb. 1937.) (Supersedes Workers' Theatre.) (Absorbed Filmfront, Apr. 1935.) (Mar.-Apr. 1937 as: New Theatre and Film.)
Editors: Ben Blake (Jan.-June 1934); Herbert Kline (June 1934-Nov. 1936); editorial board: George Redfield, Robert Stebbins, Edna Ocko, Eleanor Flexner, and Mark Marvin (Mar.-Apr. 1937).

In the early issues Joseph Freeman, Virgil Geddes, Michael Gold, Alfred Kreymborg, John Howard Lawson, Romain Rolland, Langston Hughes, and Sidney Howard are listed among the contributing editors.

New Theatre is one of drama's contributions to the leftwing movement in modern letters. Its radical interests include attention to the technique of stagecraft and the film and expression of the drama as a form of proletarian literature. Most prominent among the leftist dramatic critics is John Howard

Lawson. Much attention is paid the Russian dramatists and film directors. Among those whose scripts and plays are published, in part or as a whole, are Clifford Odets ("Waiting for Lefty") and Archibald MacLeish ("Panic"). Critical essays include a survey of Eugene O'Neill by Charmion von Weigand, an estimate of the work of Elmer Rice by Joseph Freeman, and an article on poetry in the theater by Archibald MacLeish.

❖

SPIRIT; a magazine of verse. (Catholic Poetry Society of America.) Mar. 1934+. Bimonthly. New York. bk. rev., index. NN
Editor: John Gilland Brunini.

This, the organ of the Catholic Poetry Society of America, represents a direction similar in kind, but not in purpose, to the ideologically controlled literary magazines of the thirties. In this case, the hitching of the poetic wagon to a spiritual instead of an economic star, the effect is altogether different. "Poetry springs not from the material but from the spiritual," says the opening editorial; "and *Spirit*, our magazine, leaps into a new dawn from those qualities of our members which are concerned with the true sources of poetry." *Spirit* is "a universal poets' magazine—not that of the poets of one-school but of all schools which are unconcerned with a strident campaign against the very essentials of poetry...." Among the poems contributed are those of Theodore Maynard, Glenn Ward Dresbach, J. Corson Miller, John Frederick Nims, Louise Townsend Nichols, and Oscar Williams.

❖

VIEWPOINT; a critical review. Apr./June 1934-? Quarterly. Croydon, Eng. (Absorbed by *The Left Review*, Oct. 1934.) Y
Editor: D. A. Willis?

A critical review, *Viewpoint* "attempts to interpret the arts in the only justifiable way, as integral parts of life in its fullest and most absolute sense. It regards literature, drama, cinema, music, painting and sculpture as essential to the full life of every man in the new state which must supersede capitalism." There are essays on radio, the cinema, the theater, and on various problems in the arts today. *Viewpoint* is Communist in its political stand, but believes in "individualism and metaphysics in the arts. It declares that the work of art is an organic individual creation and that it can only exist in its integrity in a classless society...."

## 1935

AXIS; a quarterly review of contemporary "abstract" painting and sculpture. 1935-Early Winter 1937. London. bk. rev., illus. NN
Editor: Myfanwy Evans.

*Axis* is a review of modern "abstract" painting and sculpture, sponsoring one form of *avant-gardism* in the arts. "Abstract," says the editor, "is used as a general term for the painting and sculpture of to-day that is not naturalistic, nor surrealist, nor purely decorative." There are many reproductions and photographs of "abstract" art; there are also essays by Herbert Read, Geoffrey Grigson, James Johnson Sweeney, and others.

❖

THE BURLINGTON CHAPBOOKS. 1935-? (Imprint date.) Irregular. Philadelphia. NN
Editor: Frank Ankenbrand, Jr.

The Burlington Chapbooks are little collections of verse, usually devoted to the work of single authors. One of them, called *Firebrands*, has five contributors, among them Norman MacLeod.

THE SCOTTISH BOOKMAN. Sept. 1935-Feb. 1936. Monthly. Edinburgh. bk. rev., illus.　　　　　　　　　NN
Editor: David Cleghorn Thomson.

Though *The Scottish Bookman* prints a number of items scarcely to be called "original writing," and though it relies heavily upon advertising in its pages, the magazine deserves its place in a study of little reviews for its accommodation of a number of young Scottish writers in its pages. It is more than a book review; the proportion of original writing is high, and its quality equally so. Contributions include short stories by John Gough, Halliday Sutherland, Hector MacIver, Alison Fleming, and others; poetry by Randall Swingler, Jan Struther, Desmond Hawkins; and a number of critical essays, including one by Séan O'Fáolain.

❖

THE SOUTHERN REVIEW. (Louisiana State University.) July 1935-Apr. 1942. Quarterly. Baton Rouge, La. bk. rev., index.　　　　　　　　　NN
Editors: Charles W. Pipkin (July 1935-Spring 1941); Cleanth Brooks, Jr. (Winter 1941-Spring 1942); Robert Penn Warren (Winter 1941-Spring 1942).

*The Southern Review* was established in July 1935, at the Louisiana State University, and continued until spring of 1942 as one of the most important university critical reviews in the United States. There have always been essays on historical, political, and cultural subjects, but the majority of essays are critical in nature; and many of these are devoted to an analysis of individual poets as well as to the general problem of modern poetics. *The Southern Review* has favored the kind of close structural and textural analysis of poetry which has come to be regarded as one of the distinctive contributions of modern literature to the history of criticism. Among the critics who have made contributions of this nature to the review's pages are John Crowe Ransom, Cleanth Brooks, R. P. Blackmur, F. O. Matthiessen, Allen Tate, and Leonard Unger. The issue of Winter 1942 is devoted entirely to an examination and analysis of the poetry and career of W. B. Yeats, and is perhaps the best single collection of critical essays on one man ever furnished by a critical review. *The Southern Review* has fulfilled well the purpose of the critical quarterly which Allen Tate summarized in an essay in the issue of Winter 1936: "The ideal task of the critical quarterly is not to give the public what it wants, or what it thinks it wants, but what—through the medium of its most intelligent members—it ought to have." Among the contributions to the magazine are many poems and short stories by men and women recognized as artists in modern literature: poetry by Yvor Winters, R. P. Blackmur, Wallace Stevens, W. H. Auden, Randall Jarrell, Donald Davidson, and Mark Van Doren; fiction by Katherine Anne Porter, Robert Penn Warren, Eudora Welty, and Caroline Gordon.

## 1936

THE AMERICAN ARTS MONTHLY; the champion and cultural voice of the four arts. 1936-? Monthly. New York. illus.　　　　　　　　　　　P
(v. 1-2, no. 2 as: SFZ.)
Editor: Marcel Honoré.
*Issues other than Sept. 1936 not consulted.*

Marcel Honoré justifies the publication of *the american arts monthly* with the announcement that "... a great and far-flung plan for the future of our American arts is in process of being unfolded, and of this plan *the american arts monthly* shall be the untiring exponent and protagonist." Originally SFZ, a magazine of music commentary, its expanded form includes articles on music, the dance, the theater, and painting, in addition to "original" writing.

❖

CANADIAN POETRY MAGAZINE. (Canadian Authors' Association.) Jan. 1936+. Quarterly. Toronto. bk. rev.   NN
Editor: E. J. Pratt.

The magazine admits the purpose of its beginning—to furnish Canadian poets with a voice similar to Harriet Monroe's *Poetry* and other American poetry magazines. Some brief critical essays and reviews supplement the poetry contributed by a variety of Canadian writers.

---

## 1937

---

NEW LETTERS IN AMERICA. [1937]. (One issue only.) New York.   NN
Editor: Horace Gregory.

A "periodical in book form," *New Letters in America* publishes the new writing of many modern writers, most of whom are already well established in little magazine history. In explaining his publication, Horace Gregory says "there are never enough new places for younger writers to gain a hearing. . . ." Among the contributions are poems by Richard Eberhart, T. C. Wilson, Muriel Rukeyser, Robert Fitzgerald, and David Schubert; fiction and prose sketches by Elizabeth Bishop, James Agee, and W. H. Auden.

❖

ONE ACT PLAY MAGAZINE. May 1937-May/June 1942. Monthly. New York. index.   NN
(Suspended between Mar. 1939 and Jan. 1940.) 1940 as: *One Act Play Magazine and Theatre Review*; 1941-May/June 1942 as: *One Act Play Magazine and Radio-Drama Review*.) (Absorbed by *Plays*, Oct. 1942.)

Editors: William Kozlenko (May 1937-Jan./Feb. 1941); J. Emerson Golden (Mar./Apr. 1941-May/June 1942).

This magazine is a successful attempt to further the cause of dramatics. It is interested in publishing "the dramatic efforts of known and unknown playwrights, both of Europe and America. The only consideration for being published will be the aim and merit of play submitted . . . no restrictions regarding choice of theme, subject, treatment, or form. . . ." Several "departments" of comment supplement the magazine's main purpose by discussing play production and allied matters. In the course of its career, the magazine has added to its contents and broadened its policy, to accommodate experiments in radio and film script. Among the essays on the theater and the allied arts are those by Paul Rosenfeld, William Saroyan, Maxim Gorky, and John W. Gassner. Plays are contributed by William Kozlenko, Langston Hughes, Alfred Kreymborg, Irwin Shaw, and others.

❖

PLASTIQUE. (Text in English, French and German.) Spring 1937-1939? Irregular. Paris; New York. illus.
*Editor not established.*

A magazine "devoted to the study and appreciation of Concrete Art; its editors are themselves painters and sculptors identified with the modern movement in Europe and America." There are essays, in English, French, and German, on modern painting and sculpture. Eugene Jolas contributes an essay on *transition* to the third issue.

❖

VERVE; an artistic and literary quarterly. (Text in English and French.) Dec. 1937-Sept./Nov. 1940. Paris. illus.   NN
Editor: E. Tériade.

An elaborate magazine of the arts, Verve "proposes to present art as intimately mingled with the life of each period and to furnish testimony of the participation by artists in the essential events of their time." The essays on painting, literature, art history, and aesthetics are abundantly and expensively illustrated. Among the critical essays included are those by André Gide, André Malraux ("Psychology of Art," translated by Stuart Gilbert), Paul Valéry, and Alfred Jarry. Literature is represented by prose sketches by John Dos Passos, André Gide, and Paul Valéry, a poem by Garcia Lorca, and translations of Chinese poems.

## 1938

THE CANDLE. Jan. 1938-June 1940? Irregular. London.    NN
Editor: Oliver W. F. Lodge.

A magazine of English poetry, *The Candle* appears with the poems of William Foster and Oliver W. F. Lodge. No. 4 was printed for Lodge by the College of William and Mary, Virginia. Its contents are made up exclusively of Lodge's poems.

✧

LONDON BULLETIN; published by the Surrealist Group in England. (Text in English and French.) Apr. 1938-June 1940? Monthly. London. illus.    C H
Editor: E. L. T. Mesens.

The *London Bulletin* is a magazine of the arts; more specifically it presents, explains, and defends the surrealist artists, publishing as well essays and poems by surrealists in English and French. One of the most active in behalf of surrealist painting and writing is the British poet and critic, Herbert Read, whose essays appear in the *London Bulletin*. In addition to a generous attention to and reproduction of surrealist paintings, the magazine publishes the poetry of Paul Eluard, Humphrey Jennings, Djuna Barnes, Charles Madge, Benjamin Peret, Charles Henri Ford, Herbert Read, Ruthven Todd, Pablo Picasso, and others; surrealistic statements in prose by André Breton, Herbert Read, and others.

## 1939

THE KENYON REVIEW. (Kenyon College.) Winter 1939+. Quarterly. Gambier, Ohio. bk. rev., illus., index.    NN
Editor: John Crowe Ransom.

The advisory editors include R. P. Blackmur, Allen Tate, Mark Van Doren, Eliseo Vivas, and Robert Penn Warren.

One of several excellent "college reviews" of modern literature, *The Kenyon Review* has since its inception occupied an enviable position with respect to modern criticism. In one sense it may be said to be "John Crowe Ransom's magazine"; but, though the critical taste of its principal editor is discernible in the quality and nature of its contents, and identifiable in Ransom's own editorial remarks, the review does not suffer from any oppressive or narrow control over the thought and creation of contributors. Since 1939 the magazine has served as a meeting place for such modern critics as Allen Tate, Yvor Winters, Robert Penn Warren, and Philip Wheelwright. Several of its issues have had surveys of important trends in modern thought. The magazine has also published materials of interest to the student of music, painting, and of importance to general aesthetics. After the suspension of *The Southern Review*, in 1942, John Crowe Ransom's magazine took over its subscription list and *The Kenyon Review* was enlarged to include a number of examples of modern fiction. It has always managed to publish a representative collection of recent poems, together with a variety of explanations of and debates over modern poetics. Among the contributions are included poems by John Berryman, Muriel Rukeyser, Allen Tate, R. P. Blackmur, Robert Penn Warren, Marianne Moore, Delmore Schwartz, Louis MacNeice, and others; fiction by Jean Garrigue, Walter Elder, David Cornel DeJong, and others; critical essays by Robert Penn Warren, Kenneth Burke, Charles W. Morris, Philip Wheelwright, Herbert J. Muller, Klaus Mann, John Peale Bishop, Delmore Schwartz, Yvor Winters, Eliseo Vivas, R. P. Blackmur, F. O. Matthiessen, Herbert Read, and others. The issue of Autumn 1943 is devoted entirely to essays on the work and art of Henry James.

tions of the poems of five young, unknown, but promising American poets. Some of these poems are reprinted from little magazines in which they had their original appearance, but a considerable proportion of them appear here for the first time. Among the important events in the history of this annual volume, the first substantial selection of Karl Jay Shapiro's poems appeared in the 1941 issue. Other young poets who take their bow in full costume before the reading public by means of this series include Mary Barnard, John Berryman, Randall Jarrell, W. R. Moses, Paul Goodman, Eve Merriam, John Frederick Nims, and Tennessee Williams.

❖

## 1940

THE BELL; a survey of Irish life. Oct. 1940+. Monthly. Dublin. bk. rev., illus.     NN Y
Editor: Séan O'Fáolain.

Séan O'Fáolain's "Survey of Irish Life," besides discussing the culture and society of Ireland, is interested in publishing original work by its writers. As for the first part of its purpose, there are O'Fáolain's editorials on "That Typical Irishman" and on other Hibernian matters; there is a monthly department of the theater; and there are essays on political and social questions. Among the other contributions are poems by John Hewitt, Thomas Irwin, Nick Nickolls, and others; prose fiction by Jim Edwards, Patrick Campbell, Mary Field, Lochlinn MacGlynn, James Plunkett, and others.

❖

THE FIVE YOUNG AMERICAN POETS. 1940+. Annual. Norfolk, Conn.    NN
Editor: James Laughlin IV.

Another of James Laughlin IV's New Directions enterprises, this annual volume publishes substantial selec-

INDIAN WRITING. Spring 1940-Summer 1942? Quarterly. London. bk. rev.    LC
Editors: Iqbal Singh, Ahmed Ali, K. S. Shelvankar, and A. Subramaniam.

Indian Writing is a magazine of stories, sketches, articles, and reviews, for the most part written by Indian writers who are living in the British Isles. The contributions, while they exhibit a strong nationalistic point of view, are valuable for two other reasons: 1) they are a sign of a growing and promising Indian literature; 2) they underscore the strong editorial point of view and are in a sense the spokesmen for it. Of this latter the editors of the magazine speak in an opening announcement: "It does not seem altogether fantastic to suggest that we are witnessing today a significant shift of the bases of culture, that initiative in cultural matters is passing to those vast masses of humanity who have so far served only as pawns for the profit of Western Imperialism."

## 1941

ENGLISH STORY. 1941+. Irregular. London.    NN

Editors: Woodrow Wyatt (with Susan Wyatt, 1941).

Among others on the advisory committee are Edward O'Brien, H. E. Bates, L. A. Pavey, Geoffrey West.

The book-form series of *English Story* is so arranged because it was the only way its editors could manage the publication of new stories at the time. Since it tries to present a considered best from among the candidates for publication and since it also makes a definite statement about the short story's qualifications, *English Story* can be said to have substantially continued the tradition of the British magazine, *New Stories*. "There are no celebrity rates and no story is accepted because of the author's distinction." Among the stories contributed are those by Sylvia Townsend Warner, Alun Lewis, Nicholas Moore, Dorothy Richardson, Henry Treece, Osbert Sitwell, and Elizabeth Bowen. *English Story* "is run on non-commercial lines. That is to say, the first to benefit from the profits are the contributors."

❖

OUR TIME, incorporating Poetry and the People. 1941+. Monthly. London. bk. rev., illus.　　　　　　B NN
Editors: Beatrix Lehmann, John Banting, Birkin Howard, Ben Frankel, Randall Swingler, and others.

A review of contemporary affairs, political, social, and cultural, *Our Time* is a magazine of leftwing persuasion which judges its contemporaries from that critical point of view. Its interests are many and include modern education, music, painting, and literature. Original writing is represented by the short stories of W. R. Cottingham, Arnold Rattenbury, William MacGregor, and others; poetry by Jack Lindsay, Randall Swingler, James Constant, Leslie Daiken, and others.

POEMS FROM THE FORCES; a collection of verses by serving members of the Navy, Army, and Air Force. [1941]. Frequency not given. London.　　NN
Editor: Keidrych Rhys.

A collection of poems by members of the British services in World War II, *Poems from the Forces* is introduced by Keidrych Rhys and contains poems by John Cromer, Gavin Ewart, G. S. Fraser, Roy Fuller, J. F. Hendry, Rayner Heppenstall, Alun Lewis, Mervyn Peake, Keidrych Rhys, Alan Rook, Tom Scott, John Waller, and others.

## 1943

BUGLE BLAST; an anthology from the services. [1943]+. Annually. London.　　　　　　　　　　　　　　　　NN
Editors: Jack Aistrop and Reginald Moore.

A collection of writings from British forces during World War II, *Bugle Blast* presents a variety of contributions from both known and unknown writers. Included are poems by Henry Treece, Alan Rook, John Pudney, and Keidrych Rhys; fiction by Jack Aistrop, John Atkins, and Alun Lewis.

❖

ETC; a review of general semantics. (Society of General Semantics.) Aug. 1943+. 4 issues a year. Chicago. bk. rev. illus.　　　　　　　　NN
Editor: S. I. Hayakawa.

etc is "devoted to the encouragement of scientific research and theoretical inquiry into non-Aristotelian system and General Semantics." It performs a valuable service to critics, scholars, and poets, by making available information about the current interest in semantics and its application to various fields of learning. Though it is not a literary magazine, it is important for the timeliness and appropriateness of its subject. The first issue includes, among other things, an essay on "General Semantics and Modern Art," and Charles I. Glicksberg's "General Semantics and Psychoanalysis: Korzybski and Freud."

❖

NEW ROAD; new directions in European art and letters. 1943+. Annual. Billericay, Essex, Eng. NN
Editors: Alex Comfort and John Bayliss.

New Road, an annual collection of writings published in England, attempts by means of critical and editorial essays and in its other contributions to point to recent and new developments in literature. The emphasis of both seems to indicate an interest in recent experiments with the surrealist idiom and methodology. The surrealists are given a respectable but separate place; and the "Apocalyptic Movement" in modern poetry, an extension of surrealist doctrines, is recognized and encouraged. Both of these facts seem to underline the wish of the editors "to humanize Socialism, to establish a society with a less impersonal shape, and to reassert the importance of individual effort and the individual as final criterion of society." Some of the contributions, but by no means all, are by writers long familiar to the reader of modern literature. The bulk of them can be identified as the product of persons still interested in surrealism but exploring all possibilities for extending its range and scope, and strengthening its importance. Contributions include poetry by John Bayliss, Alex Comfort, Lawrence Durrell, Wrey Gardiner, Nicholas Moore, Herbert Read, Ruthven Todd, Henry Treece, and others; fiction by Julien Gracq, Kay Boyle, Henry Miller, and others; and critical essays by Derek Stanford, Alex Comfort, Jean Giono, Denis Preston, Ruthven Todd, and L. J. Cole.

VOICES; an anthology of individualist writings. 1943+. Irregular. Wigginton, Herts, Eng. NN
Editor: Denys Val Baker.

Voices is a collection of new writings, designed to put into convenient anthology form a representative cross section of British poetry and prose. Its first issue contains critical articles by John Hargrave, Kenneth Bourke, Eric Nixon, and W. Roy Nash; prose fiction by Fred Urquhart, Anna Kavan, Mulk Raj Anand, and Roland Gant; and poetry by Douglas Gibson, John Atkins, Nicholas Moore, and others.

## 1944

AIR FORCE POETRY. [1944]. Frequency not given. London. NN
Editors: John Pudney and Henry Treece.

The collection of poems done by members of RAF and FAA is offered in the hope that "it will demonstrate, as clearly as an anthology twice its size, that a man may fight and yet keep his soul, that a poet is a poet whatever he is called on to face." Contributions include poems by H. E. Bates, John Bayliss, T. R. Hodgson, John Pudney, H. G. Porteus, Henry Treece, and Vernon Watkins.

❖

CONVOY; stories, articles, poems, drawings from the factories, services, fields and mines. 1944?+. Irregular. London. illus.
Editor: Robert Maugham.

Convoy's series of literary and political anthologies is concerned chiefly with the problem of keeping the civilian and military populations of England in touch with each other. The magazine carries a number of articles on England's domestic problems, both during the war and after its conclusion; these and its efforts to support itself through advertising suggests the classification of commercial magazine. But in the course of its career, it has published poems and short stories from the pens of comparatively unknown English writers, many of them in the armed services: poems by Alun Lewis, John Jarmain, E. H. R. Altounyan, Maurice Lindsay, John Atkins, Robin Atthill, A. S. J. Tessimond, and others; fiction by G. B. Stern, Alec Smith, Elizabeth Myers, A. G. Morris, and others.

❖

HARVARD WAKE. Sept. 1944+. Quarterly. Cambridge, Mass. illus.   NN
(Supersedes The Harvard Advocate.)
Editors: Austryn Wainhouse (Sept. 1944); Seabury Quinn (Dec. 1944 and Mar. 1945); Seymour Lawrence, Robert Leed and Hugh Whitehouse (June 1945); Seymour Lawrence (Mar. 1946+).

The Harvard Wake began as "an outlet for the student talent which was blocked with the temporary failure of the [Harvard] Advocate," which suspended in June 1943. The magazine is a student publication, and most of the writing is done by student writers, supplemented occasionally by work from such Harvard graduates or faculty members as E. E. Cummings, Conrad Aiken, and Theodore Spencer. Number three announces a change in policy, to allow for contributions from persons not of the undergraduate student body. In it I. A. Richards appears, as well as Theodore Spencer. Issue number four continues and extends the changed policy, and here we find poems by Kenneth Patchen, E. E. Cummings, Harry Levin, Conrad Aiken, José Garcia Villa, and a translation from Stéphane Mallarmé. Issue five is a Cummings number, devoted to a number of critical estimates of his work, and publishing for the first time his "Santa Claus: A Morality." Criticism of Cummings in issue five is contributed by Horace Gregory, Paul Rosenfeld, Alfred Kreymborg, Lloyd Frankenberg, Theodore Spencer, and others.

❖

MILLION; new left writing. [1944?]+.
Irregular. Glasgow. illus.   NN
Editor: John Singer.

A collection of work by leftwing writers, million announces editorially that it will search for "a new synthesis in society." This synthesis, it believes, "is a Left synthesis." But the effective means of reaching its goal, the magazine maintains, is the work of artists and writers: "The 'Field of Action' is cultural, the work of art." Among the contributions to the first issue of million are poems by Langston Hughes, Hugh MacDiarmid, Bertold Brecht (translated by Honor Arundel), and John Singer; short stories by Sean O'Casey and Reginald Moore; and critical essays by John Singer and Anthony Hern.

❖

SCOTTISH ART AND LETTERS. 1944+.
Frequency not given. Glasgow, Scotland. bk. rev., illus.   NN
Editor: R. Crombie Saunders.

Scottish Art and Letters is designed to encourage native talent and to free it from the necessity of looking toward London for guidance and direction: "It is only when the writers and artists find an interest and encouragement among their own people that they are likely to use their best material," states the editorial of the first issue. It also encourages the new, younger poets, who are writing in the Scots language. Contributions to the magazine include essays on Scottish cultural affairs by various hands; fiction by Morley Jamieson, Marius Blum, and Fred Urquhart; poetry by Maurice Lindsay, J. F. Hendry, Norman McCaig, W. S. Graham, G. S. Fraser, and others.

## 1945

THE ARIZONA QUARTERLY; a journal of literature, history, folklore. (University of Arizona.) Spring 1945+. Tucson, Ariz. bk. rev.     NN
Editors: Frederick Cromwell and Harry Behn.

Like its neighboring New Mexico Quarterly, The Arizona Quarterly, started in the Spring of 1945, combines scholarly and critical essays with imaginative writing. There is some attention paid Southwestern folk-lore, and considerable attention to contemporary letters, by way of critical appraisal and by example. Poetry in the first issue is contributed by Wallace Stevens, Randall Jarrell, Arthur Blair, Maynard Dixon, and Genevieve Taggard; there are critical essays by Yvor Winters, M. R. Schenck, Desmond Powell, and others.

◆

ORION; a miscellany. 1945+. Frequency not given. London.
Editors: Rosamond Lehmann, Edwin Muir, Denys Kilham Roberts, and C. Day Lewis.

A British collection of writing, Orion "aims to publish good writing, creative and critical, in prose and verse. It is attached to no group or movement. If it has a bias, it is towards the 'written' and away from the impoverished, towards the imaginative and away from reportage. Orion will publish experimental work, if the particular experiment seems to the editors a successful one: it is equally open to traditional work provided the work has character." The first publication prints poetry by Walter de la Mare, Edith Sitwell, Stephen Spender, Edwin Muir, Andrew Young, John Lehmann, and others; critical essays and prose sketches by Rose Macaulay, John Piper, Frank O'Connor, Mary Macrae, and others.

PINNACLE. (The League for Sanity in Poetry.) [1945?]+. Irregular. Corpus Christi, Tex.     NN
[Editorial] Committee: Stanton A. Coblentz, Albert Ralph Korn, Lilith Lorraine, Etta Josephean Murfey, Lawrence W. Neff.

This bulletin is designed as a means of expressing the aims and purposes of "The League for Sanity in Poetry," an organization opposed to obscurity and typographical eccentricity in modern poetry. Of its position and its mission in modern letters the League is absolutely certain, and it is even more sure of the great need for its fight for "sanity" in modern poetry: "One can hardly turn to a sophisticated magazine without finding prosy, obscure, unrhythmical and often meaningless gabble occupying the poetic seat of honor. In the colleges no less than in the smoky dens of the bohemians, this old-man-of-the-sea that goes by the name of modernism and surrealism has fastened itself parasitically upon the shoulders of poetry...." The prominence of this kind of poetry, its overwhelming popularity with anthologists, Pinnacle says, has succeeded in pushing into the very remote background those poets who uphold "the eternal poetic values." Pinnacle is interesting, therefore, as a natural and perhaps inevitable reaction against the Cummings-Marianne Moore-Pound form of *avantgardism* of the twentieth century.

◆

POLEMIC. Sept. 1945+. Irregular. London. bk. rev. illus.
Editor: Humphrey Slater.
*Issues earlier than Jan. 1946 and later than Sept./Oct. 1946 not consulted.*

Polemic, a magazine of political and critical prose, "was projected a few months before the end of the war by a small group of people who were dissatisfied with the fact that in England we had no serious theoretical magazine apart from the very highly technical ones like Mind and Philosophy—there is nothing for people equally interested and informed about philosophy, psychology, aesthetics and sociology." (Letter from Humphrey Slater to the authors, August 28, 1946.) Editorially, Polemic takes a stand against current expressions of irrationalism, and wishes "to encourage the growth of an integrated and rational world outlook which includes and synthesizes certain revolutionary trends in contemporary thought which are evolving, at the moment, independently of one another." It is opposed to what it calls "the ubiquitous romantic reaction now showing itself in almost every sphere of intellectual and aesthetic life," and points especially to such evidence of it as Existentialism, "the richly romantic ideas of Jung," the writings of Henry Miller, and the paintings of the surrealists. Articles and essays in defense and explanation of rationalism are contributed by George Orwell, Bertrand Russell, Adrian Stokes, Geoffrey Grigson, C. H. Waddington, Philip Toynbee, Humphrey Slater, John Wisdom, Arthur Waley, and others.

## 1946

THE NEW QUARTERLY OF POETRY. (The League to Support Poetry.) Fall 1946+. New York. bk. rev.
Editor: Gerard Previn Meyer.

Marcia Nichols Holden appears as poetry editor and J. Donald Adams, Thomas Ollive Mabbott and Jean Starr Untermeyer compose the advisory committee.

The "League to Support Poetry" bases its choice of poems and its support of poetry upon the conviction that, as Henry W. Wells puts it in the first issue, the poet's need "requires a few relatively simple beliefs, taught him even more from experience than from books." The magazine looks unfavorably upon the work of many modern poets, who, Wells asserts, have suffered from "a prolixity and often a sterile intricacy where aesthetic criticism is concerned." The advance guard of the twenties and thirties, Wells concludes, "must be the rear guard of the forties and fifties." Contributions to issue one include prize-winning poems (sponsored by the League) by Kenneth Slade Alling, Ted Olson, Gerard Previn Meyer, and others.

# LIST OF REFERENCES

ALLEN, CHARLES, "The Advance Guard," *Sewanee Review*, v. 51, no. 3, July/Sept. 1943, p. 410-29.
———, "American Little Magazines: I. Poetry; a magazine of verse," *American Prefaces*, v. 3, no. 2, Nov. 1937, p. 28-32.
———, "American Little Magazines: II. The Little Review," *American Prefaces*, v. 3, no. 4, Jan. 1938, p. 54-59.
———, "American Little Magazines: III. Seven Arts," *American Prefaces*, v. 3, no. 6, Mar. 1938, p. 94-96.
———, "American Little Magazines: IV. The Midland," *American Prefaces*, v. 3, no. 9, June 1938, p. 136-40.
———, "American Little Magazines: transition," *American Prefaces*, v. 4, no. 8, May 1939, p. 115-18, 125-28.
———, "American Little Magazines: 1912-1944," *The Indiana Quarterly for Bookman*, v. 1, no. 2, Apr. 1945, p. 43-54.
———, "The Dial," *The University Review*, v. 10, no. 2, Winter 1943, p. 101-8.
———, "Director Munson's Secession," *The University Review*, v. 5, no. 2, Winter 1938, p. 95-102.
———, "The Fugitive," *The South Atlantic Quarterly*, v. 43, no. 3, Oct. 1944, p. 382-89.
———, "Glebe and Others," *College English*, v. 5, no. 8, May, 1944, p. 418-23.
ANDERSON, MARGARET C. *My Thirty Years' War*. New York, Covici, Friede, 1930. 274 p.
ANDERSON, SHERWOOD, "New Orleans, The Double Dealer and the Modern Movement in America," *The Double Dealer*, v. 3, no. 15, Mar. 1922, p. 119-26.
BAKER, DENYS VAL. *Little Reviews, 1914-1943*. London, George Allen and Unwin, Ltd., [1943]. 53 p.
BARRY, IRIS, "The Ezra Pound Period," *The Bookman*, v. 74, no. 2, Oct. 1931, p. 159-71.
BERNSTEIN, DAVID, "The Little Magazines," *Scholastic*, v. 25, no. 4, Oct. 13, 1934, p. 10, 13.
BLODGETT, MARION, "A Little More about Little Magazines," *The Literary Record*, v. 2, no. 1, July 1937, p. 16-24.
BOTKIN, B. A., "Folk-Say and Space: Their Genesis and Exodus," *Southwest Review*, v. 20, no. 4, July 1935, p. 321-35.
———, "The Paradox of the Little Magazine: A Postscript," *Space*, v. 1, no. 12, Apr. 1935, p. 113-15.
BRONOWSKI, J., "Experiment," *transition*, no. 19/20, June 1930, p. 707-12.
BROWN, BOB, "Them Asses," *The American Mercury*, v. 30, no. 120, Dec. 1933, p. 403-11.
CALVERTON, V. F., "The Decade of Convictions," *The Bookman*, v. 71, no. 5, Aug. 1930, p. 486-90.
CANTWELL, ROBERT, "Little Magazines," *The New Republic*, v. 79, no. 1025, July 25, 1934, p. 295-97.
CLARK, EMILY. *Innocence Abroad*. New York, Alfred A. Knopf, 1931. 270 p.
CLEATON, IRENE and ALLEN. *Books and Battles: American Literature, 1920-1930*. Boston, Houghton Mifflin Co., 1937. 282 p.
C[OONEY] J. P., "Among the Magazines," *The Phoenix*, v. 1, no. 2, June/Aug. 1938, p. 134-50.

Cowley, Malcolm. *After the Genteel Tradition: American Writers Since 1910.* New York, W. W. Norton & Co., Inc., [c1937]. 270 p.

———, *Exile's Return: A Narrative of Ideas.* New York, W. W. Norton & Co., Inc., [1934]. 308 p.

Cunningham, J. V., "Envoi," *Hound and Horn,* v. 6, no. 1, Oct./Dec. 1932, p. 124-30.

———, "The Gyroscope Group," *The Bookman,* v. 75, no. 7, Nov. 1932, p. 703-8.

Damon, S. Foster. *Amy Lowell: A Chronicle . . .* Boston, Houghton Mifflin Co., 1935. 773 p.

Dell, Floyd. *Homecoming.* New York, Farrar & Rinehart, Inc., 1933. 368 p.

Derleth, August W., "The Cult of Incoherence," *The Modern Thinker and Author's Review,* v. 11, no. 9, Dec. 1932, p. 612-18.

———, "The Plight of The Midland," *Commonweal,* v. 15, no. 16, Feb. 17, 1932, p. 439-40.

Dupee, F. W., "British Periodicals," *Partisan Review,* v. 5, no. 1, June 1938, p. 45-48.

Eastman, Max, "Bunk about Bohemia," *Modern Monthly,* v. 8, no. 4, May 1934, p. 200-8.

———, "John Reed and the Old Masses," *Modern Monthly,* v. 10, no. 1, Oct. 1936, p. 19-22, 31.

———, "New Masses for Old," *Modern Monthly,* v. 8, no. 5, June 1934, p. 292-300.

Eliot, T. S., "The Idea of a Literary Review," *Criterion,* v. 4, no. 1, Jan. 1926, p. 1-6.

Elistratova, A., "New Masses," *International Literature,* no. 1, 1932, p. 107-14.

Ely-Estorick, Eric, and Oscar H. Fidell, "The Masses Tradition in Contemporary Literature," *Contempo,* v. 3, no. 8, Apr. 5, 1933, p. 1-3, 8.

Emmart, A. D. [Richel North], "The Limitations of American Magazines," *The Modern Quarterly,* v. 1, no. 3, Dec. 1923, p. 17-26.

Evans, Oliver, "The Fugitives," *Commonweal,* v. 40, no. 11, June 30, 1944, p. 250-54.

Falkowski, Ed, "Guido Bruno—Romantic Ghost," *The Bookman,* v. 69, no. 2, Apr. 1929, p. 167-69.

Fletcher, John Gould. *Life Is My Song.* New York, Farrar & Rinehart, Inc., [c1937]. 406 p.

———, "The Little Reviews: Yesterday and To-day," *Space,* v. 1, no. 8, Dec. 1934, p. 84-86.

Ford, Charles Henri, and Parker Tyler, "Blues," *Sewanee Review,* v. 39, no. 1, Jan./Mar. 1931, p. 62-67.

Ford, Ford Madox. *Return To Yesterday.* New York, Horace Liveright, 1932. 417 p.

Freeman, Joseph. *An American Testament.* New York, Farrar & Rinehart, Inc., 1936. 678 p.

F[riend], J[ulius] W[ise], "Innocents Abroad," *The Double Dealer,* v. 4, no. 22, Oct. 1922, p. 201-4.

Grattan, C. Hartley, "The Present Situation in American Literary Criticism," *Sewanee Review,* v. 40, no. 1, Jan./Mar. 1932, p. 11-23.

Gregory, Horace, "The Unheard of Adventure—Harriet Monroe and Poetry," *The American Scholar,* v. 6, no. 2, Spring 1937, p. 195-200.

GUTMAN, SIDNEY. *Seven Years' Harvest: An Anthology of The Bermondsey Book, 1923-1930.* London, William Heinemann, Ltd., 1934. 454 p.
HANIGHEN, FRANK C., "Vance Thompson and 'M'lle New York,'" *The Bookman,* v. 75, no. 5, Sept. 1932, p. 472-81.
HANSEN, HARRY. *Midwest Portraits: A Book of Memories and Friendships.* New York, Harcourt, Brace and Co., [c1923]. 357 p.
HAPGOOD, HUTCHINS. *A Victorian in the Modern World.* New York, Harcourt, Brace and Co., 1939. 604 p.
HART, JAMES D., "Little Magazines and Their Battle," *Hesperian,* Spring 1931.
HAYAKAWA, S. ICHIYÉ, "Harriet Monroe as Critic," *The Rocking Horse,* v. 1, no. 2, Dec. 1933, p. 20-24.
H[AYAKAWA, S. I.], "Straight from the Horse's Mouth," *The Rocking Horse,* v. 2, no. 3, Spring 1935, p. 35-38.
HEYL, LAWRENCE, "Little Magazines," *The Princeton University Library Chronicle,* v. 2, no. 1, Nov. 1940, p. 21-26.
HICKS, GRANVILLE. *John Reed: The Making of a Revolutionary.* New York, The Macmillan Co., 1937. 445 p.
HOFFMAN, FREDERICK J., "The Little Magazines: Portrait of an Age," *Saturday Review of Literature,* v. 26, no. 52, Dec. 25, 1943, p. 3-5.
HORTON, PHILIP. *Hart Crane: The Life of an American Poet.* New York, W. W. Norton & Co., [c1937]. 352 p.
HUBBELL, JAY B., "Southern Magazines," *Culture in the South,* edited by W. T. Couch, Chapel Hill, 1934, p. 159-82.
HUGHES, GLENN. *Imagism and the Imagists: A Study in Modern Poetry.* Stanford University, Calif., Stanford University Press, 1931. 283 p.
JOLAS, EUGENE, "Surrealism: Ave Atque Vale," *Fantasy,* v. 7, no. 1, 1941, p. 23-30.
———, "Ten Years Transition," *Plastique,* no. 3, 1938, p. 23-26.
———, "Transition: An Epilogue," *The American Mercury,* v. 23, no. 90, June 1931, p. 185-92.
KAZIN, ALFRED. *On Native Grounds.* New York, Reynal & Hitchcock, 1942. 541 p.
KIRSTEIN, LINCOLN, "The Hound and Horn, 1927-1934" (With a letter from Varian Fry as a note). *The Harvard Advocate,* v. 121, no. 2, Christmas 1934, p. 6-10, 92-94.
KRAMER, DALE, "The Revolt Against the 'Little' Magazines," *Midwest,* Aug. 1936, p. 1, 8 (Preview number).
KREYMBORG, ALFRED. *Troubadour: An Autobiography.* New York, Boni and Liveright, 1925. 415 p.
LAUGHLIN, JAMES, IV, "The Little Mags: 1934," *Harkness Hoot,* v. 4, no. 4, Apr. 1934, p. 41-48.
LEWIS, WYNDHAM, "Art and 'Radical' Doctrines," *The Enemy,* no. 2, Sept. 1927, p. xxiii-xxviii (Editorial notes).
———, "The Diabolical Principle," *The Enemy,* no. 3, First quarter, 1929, p. 11-84.
"Little Magazines What Now?" *The New Republic,* v. 104, no. 13, Mar. 31, 1941, p. 424.
MCALMON, ROBERT. *Being Geniuses Together: An Autobiography.* London, Secker and Warburg, 1938. 373 p.
MAYER, STANLEY DEHLER, "The Poetry Magazines," *Scholastic,* v. 26, no. 8, Mar. 23, 1935, p. 6.

MEACHAM, ALICE. *Little Magazines in Twentieth Century America, 1912-1920.* New York, Columbia University, M. A. thesis, June 1941. 162 p.

MONROE, HARRIET, "Editorial Amenities," *Poetry*, v. 14, no. 5, Aug. 1919, p. 262-66.

———, "The Enemies We Have Made," *Poetry*, v. 4, no. 2, May 1914, p. 61-64.

———, Letter to *Hound and Horn*, v. 6, no. 2, Jan./Mar. 1933, p. 320-22.

———, "Looking Backward," *Poetry*, v. 33, no. 1, Oct. 1928, p. 32-38.

———, *A Poet's Life.* New York, The Macmillan Co., 1938. 488 p.

———, "These Five Years," *Poetry*, v. 11, no. 1, Oct. 1917, p. 33-41.

———, "Twenty-One," *Poetry*, v. 43, no. 1, Oct. 1933, p. 32-37.

MOSS, DAVID, "A Bibliography of the Little Magazines Published in America Since 1900," *Contact*, v. 1, nos. 1-3, Feb.-Oct. 1932, p. 91-109, 111-24, 134-39.

MUNSON, GORHAM B., "The Fledgling Years, 1916-1924," *Sewanee Review*, v. 40, no. 1, Jan./Mar. 1932, p. 24-54.

———, "How to Run a Little Magazine," *The Saturday Review of Literature*, v. 15, no. 22, Mar. 27, 1937, p. 3-4, 14, 16.

———, "The Mechanics for a Literary 'Secession,'" *S 4 N*, Year 4, no. 22, Nov. 1922.

———, "The Others Parade," *The Guardian*, v. 1, no. 6, Apr. 1925, p. 228-34.

———, "The Skyscraper Primitives," *The Guardian*, v. 1, no. 5, Mar. 1925, p. 164-78.

NORTH, RICHEL (pseud. of A. D. Emmart), "The Limitations of American Magazines," *The Modern Quarterly*, v. 1, no. 1, Mar. 1923, p. 2-12; v. 1, no. 2, July 1923, p. 18-30; v. 1, no. 3, Dec. 1923, p. 17-26.

O'BRIEN, EDWARD J., "The Little Magazines," *Vanity Fair*, v. 41, no. 2, Oct. 1933, p. 20-21, 58.

OPPENHEIM, JAMES, "The Story of The Seven Arts," *The American Mercury*, v. 20, no. 78, June 1930, p. 156-64.

"Our Little Magazines," *Pulse of the Nation*, v. 1, no. 11, Dec. 1935, p. 13-15.

PARKER, CLARA M., "The New Poetry and the Conservative American Magazine," *The Texas Review*, v. 6, no. 1, Oct. 1920, p. 44-66.

PARRY, ALBERT. *Garrets and Pretenders: A History of Bohemianism in America.* New York, Covici, Friede, 1933. 383 p.

PATTEE, FRED LEWIS. *The New American Literature, 1890-1930.* New York, The Century Co., [1930]. 507 p.

"Poetry and Miss Monroe," *The Saturday Review of Literature*, v. 9, no. 2, July 30, 1932, p. 13, 17.

POUND, EZRA, "A Few Don'ts by an Imagiste," *Poetry*, v. 1, no. 6, Mar. 1913, p. 200-6.

———, "Small Magazines," *The English Journal*, v. 19, no. 9, Nov. 1930, p. 689-704.

RORTY, JAMES, "Life's Delicate Children," *Nation*, v. 128, no. 3328, Apr. 17, 1929, p. 470-71.

R[OSENBERG], H[AROLD], "Literature Without Money," *Direction* (Darien, Conn.), v. 1, no. 3 [1938], p. 6-10.

SCHWARTZ, DELMORE, "The Criterion, 1922-1939," *Purpose*, v. 11, no. 4, Oct./Dec. 1939, p. 225-37.

SIEGEL, ELI, "The Scientific Criticism: The Complete Criticism," *The Modern Quarterly*, v. 1, no. 1, Mar. 1923, p. 37-50.

SINGER, HERMAN, "The Modern Quarterly, 1923-1940," *The Modern Quarterly*, v. 11, no. 7, Fall 1940, p. 13-19.

STEVENS, JAMES, "The Northwest Takes to Poesy," *American Mercury*, v. 16, no. 61, Jan. 1929, p. 64-70.

TATE, ALLEN, "The American Caravan," *Bookman*, v. 68, no. 3, Nov. 1928, p. 353-55.

———, "The Fugitive, 1922-1925." *The Princeton University Library Chronicle*, v. 3, no. 3, April 1942, p. 75-84.

TELL, WALDO, [Review of Radical Little Magazines], *Partisan Review*, v. 1, no. 1, Feb./Mar. 1934, p. 60-63.

TIETJENS, EUNICE. *The World at My Shoulder*. New York, The Macmillan Co., 1938. 341 p.

TODD, RUTHVEN, "The Little Review," *Twentieth Century Verse*, no. 15/16, Feb. 1939, p. 159-62.

———, "Pat-a-Cake, Pat-a-Cake, Baker Man" (Review of *Little Reviews, 1914-1943*, by Denys Val Baker), *Wales*, no. 3, Jan. 1944, p. 101-3.

TROY, WILLIAM, "The Story of the Little Magazines," *The Bookman*, v. 70, nos. 5, 6, Jan.-Feb. 1930, p. 476-81, 657-63.

UNTERMEYER, LOUIS. *From Another World*. New York, Harcourt, Brace and Co., 1939. 394 p.

UZZELL, THOMAS H., and others, "A Symposium: The Status of Radical Writing," *A Year Magazine*, section 2, Dec. 1933/Apr. 1934, p. 122-43.

VAN DOREN, CARL CLINTON. *Three Worlds*. New York, Harper & Brothers, 1936. 317 p.

VORSE, MARY HEATON. *A Footnote to Folly* . . . New York, Farrar & Rinehart [1935]. 407 p.

WALSH, ERNEST J., "What is Literature?" *This Quarter*, v. 1, no. 3, Spring 1927, p. 59-87.

WARREN, AUSTIN, "Some Periodicals of the American Intelligentsia," *The New English Weekly*, v. 1, no. 25, Oct. 6, 1932, p. 595-97.

WAYNE, JOHN LAKMORD, "Some Little Magazines of the Past," *Hobbies*, v. 45, no. 3, May 1940, p. 106-7.

[WHEELER, EDWARD J.] "An Illinois Art Revivalist," *Current Literature*, v. 50, no. 3, Mar. 1911, p. 320-23.

WHITELEY, MARY N. S., "Shall We Let It Die?" *The Saturday Review of Literature*, v. 9, no. 2, July 30, 1932, p. 19.

WILSON, T. C., "The Literary Avant-Garde," *The Inland Review*, v. 1, no. 1, Apr. 1934, p. 10-14.

WINKLER, JEAN, "William Marion Reedy," *Saint Louis Review*, v. 2, no. 7, Jan. 28, 1933, p. 5-7; v. 2, no. 8, Feb. 11, 1933, p. 7-10.

WOOD, CLEMENT, "The Story of Greenwich Village," *Haldeman-Julius Quarterly*, v. 1, no. 1, Oct. 1926, p. 169-85.

"Wyndham Lewis's 'Enemy,'" *Experiment*, no. 3, May 1929, p. 2-5 (signed: Five).

YOUNG, ARTHUR. *Art Young, His Life and Times*. New York, Sheridan House, 1939. 467 p.

———, *On My Way*. New York, Horace Liveright, 1928. 203 p.

ZABEL, MORTON DAUWEN. "Appendix III: American Magazines Publishing Criticism," *Literary Opinion in America*. New York, Harper & Brothers, 1937. p. 621-26.

———, "The Way of Periodicals," *Poetry*, v. 34, no. 6, Sept. 1929, p. 330-34.

# INDEX

NOTE: Page numbers set in italics refer to a magazine's own entry in the Bibliography.

Abel, Hilde, 323
Abel, Lionel, 356
Abels, Charles A., 331
Abels, H. Beatrice, 331
Abercrombie, Lascelles, 245, 258, 378
Aberle, Will, 271
Abernethy, M. A., 299
The Abinger Chronicle, *345*
Abrahams, William, 372
Abril, Xavier, 295
Accent, 9, *350*, 369
Acorn, *340*
Adam, Leonhard, 351
Adamant, *307*
Adamic, Louis, 280, 314, 329
Adams, Franklin P., 239
Adams, J. Donald, 406
The Adelphi, *386*
The Adelphi Magazine, *265*
Adler, Mortimer J., 250, 384
The Adolescent, *288*
Advance, *328*
advance guard, 3, 4, 6, 155, 189, 195, 218, 223-24
Advent, *350*
A.E., 237, 376, 379, 387
Aengus, 255
Aesthete, 227-28, 275
Agee, James, 399
The Agora, *294*
Aiken, Conrad, 70, 112, 126, 242, 248, 250, 255, 256, 259, 261, 263, 267, 271, 276, 286, 288, 296, 297, 299, 303, 307, 318, 350, 356, 381, 382, 387, 390, 394, 404
Air Force Poetry, *403*
Aistrop, Jack, 370, 402
The Ajax, *248*
Akins, Zoë, 235
The Albatross, *367*
Albright, R., 307
Alcestis, *316*
Aldington, Richard, 18, 19, 22, 25, 37, 39, 54, 242, 243, 244, 245, 246, 248, 249, 250, 251, 256, 258, 262, 279, 318, 350, 379, 385

Aldis, Mary, 380
Aleichem, Sholom, 381
Alentour, *328*
Alexander, Hall, 260
Alexander, Hartley, 330, 381
Alexander, I. J., 342, 360
Alexander, Lee, 319
Alhambra, *390*
Ali, Ahmed, 401
Allan, Edwin, 348
Allen, Hervey, 263, 277, 296
Alling, Kenneth Slade, 406
Allison, Harold, 320
Allmand, Michael, 360
Allott, Kenneth, 313, 330, 331, 332, 369
All's Well, or The Mirror Repolished, *258*
Allwood, Brian, 370
L'Alouette, 126, *261*
Alpert, Hollis, 345, 347
Alpert-Levin, Helen, 288
Altenberg, Peter, 256
Altounyan, E. H. R., 404
The Amateur Writer, *345*
the american arts monthly, *398*
The American Bard, see The Country Bard
The American Caravan, *283*
The American Epoch, *351*
The American Intercollegiate Magazine, *261*
The American Mercury, 226, 275
The American Parade, *280*
The American Poet, *356*
American Poetry Journal, *307*
The American Poetry Magazine, *384*
American Prefaces, 9, *329*
The American Quarterly, 45
American Scene, *317*
The American Spectator, *304*
American Yellow Book, *336*
Analytic, *337*
Anand, Mulk Raj, 403
anarchism, 245
Anathema, *329*

# INDEX

Anderson, Margaret C., 20-21, 41, 52-66, 68, 245
Anderson, Maxwell, 125, 192, 247, 256, 263, 380, 383
Anderson, Patrick, 363, 364, 375
Anderson, Paul Y., 248
Anderson, Sherwood, 1, 37, 60, 65, 91, 245, 250, 257, 261, 262, 266, 271, 274, 278, 279, 284, 300, 304, 322, 338, 339, 358, 380
Anderson, Wendell, 354, 357, 367, 368
Andrews, Kenneth, 350
Andreyev, Leonid, 243, 379
Angarola, Anthony, 270
Angleton, Carmen Mercedes, 346
Angleton, James, 346
Angoff, Charles, 304, 328, 345, 347, 354, 356, 373
Angry Penguins, 351
Angry Penguins Broadsheet, 372
Ankenbrand, Frank, 320, 397
Ansley, C. F., 141
Anstey, John, 370
The Antidote, 241
The Anvil, 159, 167, 303, 307
Apollinaire, Guillaume, 63, 245
Appel, Benjamin, 146, 274, 308, 310, 320, 323, 324, 327
Appleby, Mark, 309
The Apple (of beauty and discord), 258
Aragon, Louis, 62, 301, 369
Archer, W. G., 288
Arens, Egmont, 74, 257, 281
Arensberg, Walter Conrad, 46, 47, 49
Argo, 294
The Arizona Quarterly, 405
Armfield, Eugene, 396
Arnell, Charles John, 272, 383
Arnheim, Rudolf, 393
Arnold, E. G., 312
The Arrow, 238
Arrowsmith, William, 361
Arson, 181, 361
Art, 380
Art and Letters, 251
Art Front, 395
Arthur, Revington, 395
Artists' and Writers' Chap Book, 308
Art Young Quarterly, 265
Arundel, Honor, 404
Arvin, Newton, 336

Asch, Nathan, 259, 325
Asch, Sholom, 381
Asche, Marjorie Dugdale, 308
Ashe, Geoffrey, 362
Atkins, John, 369, 370, 371, 372, 402, 403, 404
Atkins, Stewart, 313
The Atlantic Monthly, 34, 35, 38
Atthill, Robin, 348, 360, 404
Auden, W. H., 241, 305, 308, 313, 319, 321, 335, 346, 351, 353, 356, 358, 387, 398, 399
Auer, H. C., Jr., 264
Auslander, Joseph, 249, 268, 272, 378, 392
Austin, Mary, 262, 266, 277, 327, 381, 382, 383, 390, 391, 392, 393
Australian New Writing, 364
Author's Forum, see Manuscripts (Washington, D.C.)
automobilism, see futurism
avant garde, see advance guard
Avenue, 317
Avon, 331
Axis, 397

Babb, Sanora, 307, 315, 320, 352
Babel, 351
Babikoff, Vladimir, 333
Bache, Kenneth, 372
Bacon, Leonard, 249, 378
Bacon, Peggy, 256
Baker, Arthur E., 378
Baker, Carlos, 372
Baker, Courtland, 290
Baker, Denys Val, 348, 358, 366, 369, 403
Baker, George P., 379
Baker, Howard, 291, 311
Baker, Joseph, 336, 337
Baker, Peter, 355
Baker, Rachel, 336
Bakshy, Alexander, 379
Balascheff, Pierre, 395
Balch, J. S., 310
Baldwin, Charles, 395
Ball, F. C., 342
Bandler, Bernard, II, 285
Banting, John, 402
Barber, Rowland O., 342
Barber, Solon R., 291, 298
Bard, 308

## INDEX

Barea, Arturo, 372
Barker, George, 299, 313, 319, 321, 325, 332, 335, 340, 343, 353, 356, 358, 365, 370, 390, 391
Barlett, Elizabeth, 372
Barlow, Jane, 237
Barlow, R. H., 330, 339
Barnard, Mary, 401
Barnes, Djuna, 260, 400
Barnes, John W., 364
Barr, Ronald Walker, 275
Basterra, Ramon de, 390
Bate, John, 355, 370, 374, 375
Bates, H. E., 277, 299, 303, 311, 331, 346, 387, 390, 402, 403
Bates, Katharine Lee, 268, 274, 280
Bates, Ralph, 321
Baudelaire, Charles Pierre, 247, 264, 296, 351, 355, 359, 390
Baugh, Hansell, 284
Bax, Clifford, 266
Baxter, Harriet W., 338
Baxter, Herbert, 385
Bayliss, John, 348, 355, 403
Beachcroft, T. O., 387
Beals, Carleton, 248
Beamish, Rae, 332
Beardsley, James H., 395
Beardsley, W. A., 276
Beaudoin, Kenneth L., 332, 336, 340, 353, 354, 357
Beck, Warren, 366
Beckett, Luman, 337
Beechman, N. A., 257
Beerbohm, Max, 238, 295, 345
Begg, Ray M., 302
Béguin, Albert, 178-79
Behn, Harry, 405
Behrman, S. N., 250, 254
Belfrage, Cedric, 352
Belgion, Montgomery, 258
*The Bell, 401*
Bell, Alex, 339
Bell, Clive, 250, 309
Bellamann, Henry, 264, 265, 274, 384
Bellemin, Frank J., 270
Belloc, Hilaire, 247
*Beltaine, 236*
Beltrone, Vincent, 315
Benét, Laura, 249, 315, 335
Benét, Stephen Vincent, 15, 67, 249, 250, 260, 296, 329, 358, 378

Benét, William Rose, 38, 235, 240, 242, 248-49, 252, 273, 296, 383
*Ben Hecht's Chicago Literary Times,* see *The Chicago Literary Times*
Bennett, Arnold, 237
Bennett, Gwendolyn, 280
Bennett, Joseph, 362
Benson, Stella, 387
Bentley, Eric Russell, 373, 393
Benton, Thomas Hart, 320, 328, 395
Berdyaev, Nicholas, 395
Berenberg, David P., 269
Beresford, J. D., 91, 246, 261
Berger, Walter, 366
Bergman, Alexander F., 347
Bergson, Henri, 22, 57-58, 63, 245, 284, 297, 394
Berkman, Alexander, 377
*The Bermondsey Book, 387*
Bernal, J. D., 308
Bernstein, David, 312
Berry, Matilda, see Katherine Mansfield
Berryman, John, 325, 334, 350, 362, 400, 401
Berthold, Arthur B., 291
Bessie, Alvah C., 316
Betjeman, John, 350, 394
*Better Verse, 304*
Bezzerides, A. I., 352
Bierce, Ambrose, 391
Birney, Earle, 370
Bishop, Elizabeth, 399
Bishop, John Peale, 257, 299, 317, 346, 381, 382, 401
Bissell, Harriet, 338
Bissell, Richard M., 295
Bittner, Nelson, 318
Black, MacKnight, 281
Blackie, John Haldane, 295
Blackmur, R. P., 9, 207, 208, 209, 285, 286, 303, 311, 317, 318, 324, 325, 329, 350, 352, 361, 362, 398, 400, 401
Blair, Arthur, 352, 405
Blake, Ben, 396
Blake, Clifton, 337
Blakeston, Oswell, 305, 312, 315, 331, 395
*Blast (London), 23, 244*
*Blast (New York), 303, 308*
*Blast (San Francisco), 148*

Bledsoe, Thomas, 350
The Blind Man, *251*
Blish, James, 375
Bloch, Ernest, 88
Blodgett, Marion, 394
Blok, Alexander, 269, 367
The Blue Book, *380*
The Blue Review, 27, *243*
Blues, 14, *290*
Blum, Marius, 404
Blum, W. C., see Dr. J. S. Watson, Jr.
Blume, Bernhard, 371
Blunden, Edmund, 385
Blunt, Anthony, 289
Blyth, James R., 363
Bodenheim, Maxwell, 37, 49, 155, 235, 245, 251, 252, 267, 268, 272, 273, 278, 280, 286, 293, 302, 308, 310
Bodkin, Maud, 361
Bogan, Louise, 263, 264
Boggs, Tom, 274, 286, 344
The Bohemian (Chicago), *275*
The Bohemian (Toledo, Ohio), *275*
Bolero, *341*
Bolger, James, 327
Bolitho, Hector, 302, 388
Bolton, Shelia, 368
Bond, George, 382
Boni, Albert, 46, *243*
Boni, Charles, 46, *243*
Bonier, Chester W., 273
Bonner, Sue Grundy, 278
Bonnet, Theodore F., 247
The Booster, 186, *337*
Booth, Frederick, 91
Boothe, Jim, 335
Borden, Fred, 340
Bosquet, Alain, 365
Bostelmann, Carl John, 292, 336
Botkin, B. A., 327, 334, 382, 390, 392
Botsford, Keith, 372
Bottomley, Gordon, 238, 242, 377
Bottrall, Ronald, 369, 371, 394
Bourke, Kenneth, 403
Bourne, Randolph, 92, 198, 240, 250, 344
Bow, Lily Lawrence, 329
Bowen, Elizabeth, 402
Bower, Warren, 323
Bowra, C. M., 257
Boyce, David, 374

Boyce, Neith, 235
Boyd, Albert Truman, 336
Boyd, Ernest, 226-27, 274, 275, 304, 358, 379, 383
Boyle, Kay, 259, 279, 285, 287, 290, 295, 299, 303, 311, 315, 317, 318, 319, 334, 336, 337, 342, 343, 346, 350, 358, 368, 372, 403
Bozart, *283*
Bozart and Contemporary Verse Combining Japm, see Bozart
Bozart and Contemporary Verse Combining Japm and The Oracle, see Bozart
Bozart-Westminster, see The Westminster Magazine
Bracque, George, 262
Bradford, Gamaliel, 247, 268, 280
Bragdon, Claude, 297, 383, 388
Brailovski, Alexander, 391
Braithwaite, William Stanley, 242, 250, 251, 280, 291
Brancusi, Constantin, 60
Brand, Millen, 297, 306, 307, 310, 311, 317, 322, 360
Brantley, Frederick, 329, 362
Braun, B. Vivian, 395
Braver-Mann, Barnet G., 391
Bray, Will, see Matthew Josephson
Braybrooke, Neville, 360, 366
Brecht, Bertold, 324, 339, 353, 358, 359, 404
Breit, Harvey, 344
Brennan, Niall, 372
Breton, André, 63, 182, 287, 346, 356, 361, 364, 400
Briarcliff Quarterly, see *Maryland Quarterly*
Brinnin, John Malcolm, 2, 322, 326, 334, 336, 346, 350, 353, 356, 366, 390
Britton, Lionel, 393
A Broadsheet, *376*
A Broadside, *377*
Broder, William Albert, 278
Brodsky, Horace, 261, 269
Brody, Alter, 249, 265
Broinowski, R. A., 275
Bronowski, J., 279, 288, 305, 352
Brook, David, 328
Brooke, Rupert, 37, 240, 242, 244, 245

## INDEX

Brookhouser, Frank, 345
Brooks, Cleanth, 122, 257, 376, 382, 398
Brooks, Gwendolyn, 372
Brooks, Van Wyck, 86, 88, 89, 250, 283, 381
Broom, 9, 79, 96, 99, 100, 101-107, 261
Brotman, Jordan, 359
Brott, Saul, 365
Brower, Reuben, 374, 396
Brown, Albert, 342
Brown, Bob, 300, 309, 324
Brown, Edmund R., 242
Brown, Fearon, 361
Brown, Harcourt, 389
Brown, Harry, 334, 339, 356, 359, 381
Brown, Leonard, 317
Brown, Marianne, 299
Brown, Robert, 355
Brown, Slater, 106, 261, 275
Brown, Sterling A., 391
Browne, Alistair, 321
Browne, Maurice, 273, 383
Browne, Wynyard, 309
Bruncken, Herbert, 247, 391
Brunini, John Gilland, 397
Bruno, Guido, 27, 225, 243, 246, 251, 253, 255, 258
*Bruno Chap Books*, 27, 246
*Bruno's*, 27, 251
*Bruno's Bohemia*, 14, 253
*Bruno's Review of Life, Love and Letters*, 27, 255
*Bruno's Review of Two Worlds*, 27, 258
*Bruno's Weekly*, 27, 246
Bryher, Winifred, 279, 315
B.S.C., 274
*The Buccaneer*, 272
Buck, Pearl, 328
*Bugle Blast*, 402
Bullen, Leonard, 389
Bulosan, Carl, 324, 347, 349
Burford, William, 375
Burgum, Edwin Berry, 350, 366, 376
Burke, Alfred, 364
Burke, Kenneth, 49, 96-97, 98, 100, 101, 106, 107-108, 205, 227, 228, 243, 245, 253, 257, 259, 261, 267, 268, 273, 275, 285, 324, 334, 338, 339, 350, 356, 361, 362, 380, 401
Burke, Thomas, 255, 322
Burkholder, Edward Vernon, 391
Burklund, Carl, 299
*The Burlington Chapbooks*, 397
Burnett, Whit, 160, 281, 303
Burnham, James, 298, 382
Burns, Paul, 305
Burnshaw, Stanley, 274, 277, 282
Burra, Peter, 294, 295
Burton, Jean, 389
Burton, Richard, 379
Bushby, Don Maitland, 288, 293
Buttitta, A. J., 299
Butts, Mary, 315
Buxbaum, Herman, 337
*By—*, 341
Bynner, Witter, 235, 242, 248, 250, 253, 254, 260, 262, 266, 268, 271, 274, 281, 282, 290, 293, 299, 306, 316, 319, 327, 328, 329, 330, 344, 349, 353, 360, 363, 365, 371, 382, 388, 390, 392

Cabell, James Branch, 263, 304, 380
*Cadence*, 351
*Cadences*, 394
Cafaro, Joan, 332
Cahoon, Herbert, 375
Caillois, Roger, 365
Calas, Nicholas, 181, 356, 361
Caldwell, Erskine, 1, 14, 259, 279, 285, 297, 299, 303, 307, 311, 318, 322, 335, 338, 369, 394
Caldwell, James, 341
*The Calendar* (London), see *The Calendar of Modern Letters*
*Calendar* (Prairie City, Ill.), 352
*The Calendar of Modern Letters*, 388
*The Calithump*, 317
Callaghan, Morley, 279, 322
Calmer, Alan, 288
Calverton, V. F., 153, 156, 157, 270, 292, 295, 301, 309
*Cambridge Left*, 308
*Camera Work*, 377
Campbell, Patrick, 401
Campbell, Royston, (Roy), 284, 385, 390
Camus, Albert, 372

The Canadian Mercury, *389*
Canadian Poetry Magazine, *399*
Canayénne, Jean, *344*
Canby, Henry Seidel, *132*
The Candle, *400*
Candler, Lillian, *307*
Candlewood, William, (pseud.), *371*
Candor, *332*
Candor Magazine, see Candor
Cannan, June, *362*
Cannan, Gilbert, *239*, *384*
Cantine, Holley R., Jr., *364*
Cantwell, Robert, *296*
Capek, Karel, *277*
Caprice, *265*
Caravel (Lowell, Mass.), *317*
Caravel (Majorca, Spain), *317*
The Carillon (Stanford University, Calif.), *290*
The Carillon (Washington, D.C.), *290*
Carman, Bliss, *235*
Carmer, Carl, *267*, *276*, *383*
Carmina, *294*
Carnevali, Emanuel, *265*, *334*, *343*
The Carolina Play-Book, *389*
The Carolina Stage, see The Carolina Play-Book
Carpenter, Miles, *342*
Carrier, Constance, *351*
Carrier, Warren, *366*
Carroll, Dudley, *317*
Carswell, Catherine, *297*
Carter, Huntly, *245*, *383*
Carter, S. R., *299*
Casements, *268*
Cash, W. J., *335*
Cassidy, G. L., *268*
Cassidy, Jane M., *261*
Castelli, N. L., *269*
Castleman, Marian, *364*
Caswell, Arthur, *326*
The Catamount, *337*
Cattani, Georges, *395*
Causton, Bernard, *305*
Cawein, Madison, *235*, *380*
Celine, Louis Ferdinand, *322*
The Centaur, *317*
Chace, Richard A., *294*
Challenge, *163*, *318*
Chameleon, *332*

Chamberlin, Norwood, *314*
Champney, Freeman, *345*
Chandler, Robert W., *278*
Channing, William Ellery, *7*
Channing-Renton, E. M., *315*, *348*
Chanslor, Roy E., *266*
Chanticleer, *318*
The Chap-Book, *7*, *235*
The Chapbook, see The Monthly Chapbook
Chaplin, Ralph, *294*, *330*
Chapman, Edith, *265*
Characters, *318*
Chase, Stuart, *254*
Chatfield-Taylor, Hobart C., *18*, *34*, *35*, *36*
Chekhov, Anton, *240*, *379*
Cheney, Sheldon, *383*
Cheyney, Ralph, *249*, *256*, *267*, *272*, *274*, *278*, *280*, *286*, *289*, *290*, *292*, *293*, *294*, *295*, *297*, *298*, *301*, *304*, *306*, *307*, *313*, *315*, *328*, *329*, *330*, *336*, *353*, *360*
The Chicago Literary Times, *268*
The Chicago Review, *373*
Childe, Wilfred R., *272*, *285*, *384*
Childs, Richard S., *295*
Chiles, William H., *318*
The Chimaera, *248*
The Chimera, *10*, *362*
Christesen, C. B., *354*
Christian, Sheldon, *361*
Chubb, Ralph, *300*
Chubb, Thomas Caldecot, *328*
Cierpial, Leo, *373*
Cinema Quarterly, *393*
The Circle (Baltimore), *272*
Circle (Berkeley, Calif.), *365*, *367*
Clairmont, Robert, *274*, *344*
Clapp, Henry, *7*
Clark, Barrett, H., *379*, *383*, *390*
Clark, Donald B., *255*
Clark, Eleanor, *305*, *372*
Clark, Emily, *263*
Clark, Eunice, *305*
Clark, John D., *392*
Clark, S. H., *379*
Clark, Walter Van Tilburg, *339*, *350*
Clark, William Russell, *272*
Clarke, George Herbert, *376*
Clason, Jerry, *292*

## INDEX

Clay (Albuquerque, N.M.), *299*
Clay (Brooklyn, N.Y.), *265*
Clay, E., 326
Clelland, Lucy S., 269
Clementson, Larry B., 347
Clinkard, Mildred, 346
*The Clipper, 352*
*Close-up, 388*
Cloud, Russell, 396
Coady, Robert, 31-32, 251, 280
*The Coast, 337*
Coates, Grace Stone, 37, 260
Coates, Nettie Allen, 280
Coates, Robert, 262
Coates, Walter John, 280
Coblentz, Catherine Cate, 290
Coblentz, Stanton, 281, 289, 292, 304, 305, 306, 307, 308, 315, 316, 319, 324, 328, 335, 336, 343, 353, 361, 365, 405
Cochran, Thomas, 338
Cocteau, Jean, 245, 350, 385
Code, Grant H., 267, 291, 315
Coe, Katherine Hunter, 315, 348
Coffin, Robert P. Tristram, 288, 306, 319, 328, 336, 360, 361, 363
Cohen, Abbott S., 323
Cohen, Albert Philip, 298
Cohen, Lester G., 333
Cole, Douglas, 370
Cole, L. J., 403
Coleman, Carroll D., 276
*College Verse, 392*
Collier, Oscar, 357
*The Colosseum, 395*
Colton, Donald, 298
Colum, Padraic, 37, 237, 238, 268, 276, 377, 379, 383, 387, 394
Comfort, Alex, 355, 358, 361, 363, 366, 367, 372, 403
*A Comment, 352*
Communism, 149, 165, 254
*Compass*, see *Upward*
Conant, Isabel Fiske, 328, 336, 353
Conkling, Grace Hazard, 36
*The Connecticut Echo, 308*
*Connecticut Lore, 308*
Connolly, Cyril, 221, 353
Connolly, Robert, 350
Conroy, Jack, 290, 294, 300, 301, 303, 307, 313, 322, 325, 347

Constant, James, 402
*Contact*, 49, 69, *258*
*Contempo, 299*
Contemporaries, see *Contemporaries and Makers*
*Contemporaries and Makers, 309*
*Contemporary, 373*
Contemporary Poetry (Baltimore, Md.), see *Poetry Forum*
*Contemporary Poetry* (Dublin), *276*
*Contemporary Poetry* (West Chicago), *304*
*Contemporary Poetry and Prose, 332*
Contemporary Poetry and Song, see *Contemporary Poetry* (Dublin)
*Contemporary Verse* (Caufield, B.C.), *357*
*Contemporary Verse* (Philadelphia), 8, *249*
*Contemporary Vision, 290*
*Convoy, 403*
Cook, John Oliver, 375
Cooksley, Bert, 391
Cooley, Mary Elizabeth, 278
Coomaraswamy, Ananda K., 388
Coon, Arthur M., 395, 396
Cooney, James Peter, 185, 342
Copeau, Jacques, 379
Copeland, Margaret Scott, 319
Coppard, Alfred E., 258, 262, 282, 283, 387, 388
Corbière, Tristan, 296
Corbin, Alice, 391
Corey, Paul F., 307, 310, 313, 314, 320, 326
Cornell, Annette Patton, 336
*Cornell College Chapbooks, 329*
Cornford, J., 308
Corning, Howard McKinley, 260, 261, 271, 274, 277, 282, 319, 384
*Coterie*, 33, *255*
Cottingham, W. R., 402
*Counterpoint, 309*
*The Country Bard, 253*
Courlander, Harold, 302
Covarrubias, Miguel, 362
Cowan, Peter, 351
Cowley, Malcolm, 37, 76, 94, 95, 98, 99, 100, 102, 105, 106, 226, 228, 249, 253, 255, 259, 261, 262, 268, 281, 285, 344, 359

Coyle, Kathleen, 387
Cracraft, Nina Harrington, 308
Craig, Gordon, 238, 254, 255, 380, 383, 385
Craig, Maurice James, 366
Crampton, Savington, 270
Crane, Clarkson, 296
Crane, Harold, see Hart Crane
Crane, Hart, 14, 42, 98-99, 100, 101, 102, 104-5, 119, 227, 245, 249, 250, 253, 256, 257, 259, 262, 263, 266, 268, 274, 275, 286, 287, 386, 388
Crane, Stephen, 235
Crawley, Alan, 357
*Creative, 332*
*Creative Writing, 341*
Creekmore, Hubert, 211, 279, 327, 339, 354, 357, 367, 372
*Crescendo, 357*
Crevel, Réne, 372
Crews, Judson, C., 336, 340, 354, 357, 373
Crichton, Ronald, 374
*The Criterion, 9, 82, 386*
*The Critic, 395*
Cromer, John, 402
Cromwell, Frederick, 405
Cronyn, George, 46
Croog, Sydney, 372
Crosby, Caresse, 372
Crosby, Harry, 71, 287, 292
Crosland, T. W. H., 241
Cross, Enrique, 251
*Crossing the Span, see The Span*
Crossman, Richard H. S., 295, 312
*Crossroad, 345*
Crouch, Harry, 335
Crowley, Joseph, 357
Crozier, Cecily, 352
cubism, 58-59, 245
Cullen, Countee, 269, 271, 280, 290, 306, 318
Cullen, Hazel, 328
Culver, Donal, 394
Cummings, E. E., 108, 153, 212, 241, 256, 257, 259, 261, 274, 275, 279, 281, 285, 300, 301, 317, 332, 334, 343, 346, 350, 356, 363, 366, 371, 378, 404

Cunard, Nancy, 259, 383
Cunningham, J. V., 285, 311, 359, 393
Cunninghame, A. T., 297
Cunningham-Graham, R. B., 237
Curling, Jonathan, 361
Curry, John Steuart, 395
Curry, Walter Clyde, 118
Curtiss, Ellington, 320
*Cycle, 329*

dadaism, 3, 9, 62-63, 180, 245, 287, 299, 300
*Dadaist Disgust, 62*
Daehler, Albert Hartman, 277
Dagnal, Deverell, 265
Dahlberg, Edward, 297, 324
Daiches, David, 350, 364, 372
Daiken, Leslie, 402
*The Damn, 255*
Damon, S. Foster, 38, 303, 378
*Dana, 237*
Dane, Clemence, 289
Danielson, Henry, 265
Darmuzey, Jack, 265
Darvin, Leonard, 288
Davenport, John, 289
Davenport, Russell W., 277
*David, 393*
Davidson, Donald, 12, 118, 119, 121, 123, 262, 263, 264, 265, 269, 271, 376, 398
Davidson, Gustav, 252, 271, 353, 365
Davidson, John, 235
Davies, Ethel, 293
Davies, Idris, 342
Davies, Mary Carolyn, 309, 382
Davies, Oliver, 349
Davies, Pamela, 370
Davies, Rhys, 311, 315, 340
Davies, W. H., 240, 242, 247, 249, 258, 265, 349, 384
Davis, Harry, 310
Davis, Helen, 308
Davis, H. L., 296
Davis, Stuart, 359, 395
Dawson, Christina, 361
*Daylight, 357*
d'Azevedo, Warren, 359
Dean, Joseph, 280

## INDEX

Deasy, Jack, 345
Death, *373*
The Decachord, 126, *272*
Decade of Short Stories, 161, *345*
De Casseres, Benjamin, 252, 278, 314, 377
Decimal, *304*
Decision, 222-23, *357*
Decker, Clarence, 327
Decker, James A., 344
DeJong, David Cornel, 274, 290, 292, 294, 296, 297, 298, 299, 300, 311, 316, 319, 322, 323, 326, 327, 329, 360, 374, 401
De la Mare, Walter John, 239, 246, 249, 360, 377, 405
Dell, Floyd, 7, 8, 29, 37, 53, 69, 71, 150, 240, 252, 253, 254, 260, 271, 381
Delta, see The Booster
Dennen, Grace Atherton, 262
Denney, Reuel, 342, 356
Deren, Maya, 375
Derham, Enid, 293
Derleth, August, 247, 279, 280, 286, 288, 304, 306, 307, 308, 311, 314, 315, 318, 322, 323, 324, 326, 328, 329, 330, 331, 334, 336, 337, 339, 341, 343, 345, 347, 356, 360, 363, 396
Derwood, Gene, 271
Design, *352*
Desmond, Myrle, 363
Destinations, 95
Deutsch, Babette, 24, 151, 235, 252, 254, 262, 263, 281, 298, 306, 372, 382
Devlin, Denis, 369
De Voto, Bernard, 273
De Vries, Peter, 43, 241, 317, 320, 331, 332
Dewey, Frank, 278
Dewey, John, 90, 266, 297
The Dial (1840-44), 7
The Dial (1920-29), 9, 11, 13, 41, 51, 68, 82, 196-206, 215, *259*
Dialectics, *338*
Dickinson, Patric, 361
Dickinson, Thomas H., 379, 380, 381, 382
Dickson, Lovat, 311

Dickson, Margarette Ball, 254, 267, 280, 298
Diefendorf, J. W., 392
Dierkes, Henry, 365
Dierkes, Margaret, 365
Dillard, Carolyn, 373
Dillon, George H., 39, 43, 241, 266, 273, 277, 364
Dillon, John, 276, 318
The Dill Pickler, *272*
Dinamov, Sergei, 301
Diogenes, 10, *352*
Direction (Darien, Conn.), 223, *338*
Direction (Outremont, P.Q.), 365
Direction (Peoria, Ill.), *318*
Dixon, Maynard, 405
Dodds, E. R., 255
Dodge, Mabel, see Mabel Dodge Luhan
Donne, John, 359
Donohue, Jay H., 239
Doolittle, Hilda, see H.D.
Dope, *305*
Dos Passos, John R., 90, 275, 285, 295, 297, 325, 338, 370, 378, 400
Dostoevsky, Feodor M., 362, 377, 388
Doten, Dana, 337
The Double-Dealer, 9, 10-14, 15, 68, 192, *262*
Dougherty, John W., 332
Doughty, Le Garde S., 368
Douglas, Alfred Bruce, Lord, 241
Douglas, Cole, 370
Douglas, Keith, 346
The Dragon-Fly, *330*
The Drama, *379*
The Drama Magazine, see The Drama
Dreiser, Theodore, 90, 150, 239, 250, 256, 296, 300, 304, 308, 380
Dresbach, Glenn Ward, 258, 276, 278, 280, 292, 304, 306, 307, 336, 365, 397
Dreyer, Martin, 347
Dreyfuss, Allen, 364
The Drift-Wind, *280*
The Drift-Wind from the North Hills, see The Drift-Wind
Drimbonigher, see Alec Brock Stevenson
Drinkwater, John, 239, 245, 289, 299
Drummond, John, 241, 343

Drury, John, 270
Drury, Margaret, 355
*The Dublin Magazine, 387*
Du Bois, Arthur E., 317, 329, 332
duBouchet, André, 373, 374
*The Dubuque Dial*, 161, *318*
Duchamp, Marcel, 364
Dulac, Edmond, 238
*The Dumbook, 276*
Duncan, Robert, 373
Duncan, Ronald, 343, 344
Dunham, Wayland A., 330
Dunsany, Edward, Lord, 238, 239, 243, 255, 260, 360, 379, 387
Dupee, Frederick W., 296, 325, 378
Durboraw, Charles L., 106
Durrell, Lawrence, 337, 341, 343, 346, 353, 369, 371, 374, 391, 403
Dutton, Geoffrey, 351
Du Von, Jay, 301, 320, 324
Dyment, Clifford, 341
*Dyn*, 183-84, *362*
*Dynamo, 319*

Earp, T. W., 250, 385
*Earth*, 163, *294*
*East and West, 381*
Eastman, Chrystal, 254
Eastman, Max, 7, 8, 29, 152, 240, 254, 270
Eaton, Walter Pritchard, 379, 383
Eberhart, Richard, 241, 288, 329, 334, 343, 346, 356, 362, 374, 394, 399
*The Echo* (Denver, Colo.), *388*
*The Echo* (Hamilton, N.Y.), *290*
Edmonds, J. G., 274
Edmunds, Pierre, 368
Edward, John, 360
Edwards, Jim, 401
Edwards, Robert, 69, 252
Eglinton, John, 237, 238, 379
*The Egoist*, 22, 23, 82, *244*
Eisenstein, S. M., 392, 395
Elder, Walter, 401
Eldridge, Paul, 256, 277, 282
Eliot, T. S., 1, 9, 33, 37, 41, 77, 112-13, 115, 242, 244, 245, 248, 251, 255, 256, 259, 264, 284, 285, 288, 325, 329, 353, 379, 381, 386, 387, 390, 391, 394
Elkon, Juliette, 360

Elliott, George P., 359, 367, 371
Ellis, Dorothy, 298
Ellis, Kenneth, 384
Elliston, George, 276
Eluard, Paul, 279, 297, 299, 346, 372, 400
Embler, Weller, 317
Emerson, Ralph Waldo, 7, 377
Emery, Byron, 248
Em Jo, 255
Empson, William, 288, 289, 313, 332, 353, 394
Endicott, Patty, 295
Endore, Guy, 352
*The Enemy*, 82-83, *283*
England, E. M., 275
England, Robert, 241
Engle, Paul, 247, 262, 273, 277, 279, 288, 292, 312, 322, 329, 365
*English Story, 401*
*Epilogue, 330*
Erling, Larsen, 337
Ernst, Max, 356, 364
Essenin, Sergei, 319
E. T., 319
etc, *402*
*Europa*, 216, *309*
*The European Quarterly*, 216, *319*
Eustice, Howard, 314
Evans, Ewart, 340
Evans, Myfanwy, 397
Evans, Sian, 349
Evers, W. M., 367
Everson, William, 368
Ewart, Gavin, 308, 324, 340, 350, 402
*The Exile*, 79, 83, *284*
existentialism, 373, 374, 406
expatriates, 22, 75-80
*Experiences in Understanding, 330*
*Experiment* (Cambridge, Eng.), *288*
*Experiment* (Salt Lake City, Utah), *367*
*Experimental Cinema, 391*
experimentalism, 9, 42, 57, 66, 84, 115, 127, 212, 364
*Experimental Review, 353*
Expression, see *The Garen Magazine*
expressionism, 3, 58-59

Fagin, N. Bryllion, 282, 314, 316, 388
Fairthone, Robert, 395

## INDEX

Fall, Lewis, 334
Fallada, Hans, 311
*Fanfare, 385*
Fanning, M. A., 235
*Fantasia, 276*
*Fantasy,* 169, 299
Farjeon, Eleanor, 242, 360, 378, 379
*Farrago, 294*
Farrell, James T., 14, 167, 215, 279, 293, 294, 297, 299, 307, 310, 313, 319, 323, 324, 325, 336, 373
Farwell, George, 364
Fast, Howard, 373
Faulkner, Edwin, 272, 384
Faulkner, William, 1, 12, 13, 262, 299, 303, 335
Faust, Henri, 271
Fawcett, James Waldo, 256
Fay, Bernard, 395
Fearing, Kenneth, 13, 241, 247, 264, 277, 279, 281, 284, 287, 310, 319, 325, 344
Fedden, H. Romilly, 289
Felton, Gordon H., 363
feminism, 22, 244, 245
Ferrini, Vincent, 351
Fessenden, Bruce, 355
Feuchtwanger, Lion, 309
Ficke, Arthur Davison, 36, 38, 54, 226, 242, 245, 266, 290, 298, 392
Field, Ben, 271, 324, 325, 330
Field, Mary, 401
Fielding, David R., 326
*Fifth Floor Window, 299*
*Fifty Manuscripts,* see *Manuscripts* (Washington, D.C.)
*The Figure in the Carpet, 284*
*film art, 395*
Finberg, Franz A., 291
Finch, Roy, 368
Fineman, Morton, 347, 358
Finger, Charles J., 235, 258, 390
Finn, Eugenia T., 327
*Finnegans Wake,* 175-76, 189, 275, 287
Finnin, Mary, 352
Finsterwald, Maxine, 334
*Fire!!, 280*
*First Statement, 362*
Fisher, Dorothy Canfield, 139-40
Fisher, Mahlon Leonard, 253, 273

Fisher, Rhody, 318
Fisher, Vardis, 318, 339
Fitts, Dudley, 317, 363
Fitts, Norman, 257, 269, 281
Fitzell, Lincoln, 355
Fitzgerald, F. Scott, 382
Fitzgerald, Robert R., 271, 296, 381, 399
Fitzgerald, Sheilla, 387
Fitzgibbon, Constantine, 349
*Five, 319*
*The Five Arts, 295*
*The Five Young American Poets, 401*
Fjelde, Rolf, 372
Flaccus, William Kimball, 392
Flagg, Arthur, 351
Flanagan, Hallie, 279, 383
Flanner, Hildegarde, 260, 264, 271, 289, 290, 296, 391
Fleming, Alison, 398
Fleming, John, 351
Fleming, Thomas, 236
Fletcher, John Gould, 22, 25, 37, 74, 154-55, 242, 244, 245, 248, 250, 252, 255, 256, 258, 262, 266, 267, 271, 272, 273, 277, 307, 310, 327, 328, 329, 380, 382, 391, 392
Flint, F. S., 37, 111, 242, 256, 266
Flores, Angel, 322, 338, 390
*Florida Magazine of Verse, 353*
Flynn, Harvey, 339
Flynn, William, 292
*Focus, 370*
Foerster, Norman, 378
Foley, Martha, 160, 303
*folio, 268*
*Folios of New Writing,* see *New Writing;* see also *Daylight*
*Folk-Say, 390*
Foote, Agnes Albrecht, 333
*Foothills, 345*
Ford, Benjamin, 361
Ford, Charles Henri, 182, 283, 284, 286, 288, 290, 292, 293, 295, 297, 299, 308, 317, 318, 322, 345, 353, 356, 359, 364, 365, 400
Ford, Ford Madox, 60, 244-45, 246, 275
Ford, Webster, see Edgar Lee Masters
*Foreground, 373*
Foreman, L. L., 332

The Forge, 272
Form, 249
Forster, E. M., 239, 345
The Fortnightly, 392
Foster, George Burman, 72
Foster, Harvey N., 299, 300
Foster, Stephen, 319
Foster, William, 400
Four, 269
The Fourth Decade, 319
Fowler, Alfred, 250, 273
Fowlie, Wallace, 395
Fox, Derek, 302
Fox, L. P., 339
Fox, Ralph, 321
Fraenkel, Michael, 271, 276, 277, 278, 282, 337, 342, 373
France, Anatole, 80
Francelli, Mario, 350
Francis, G. Jerome, 396
Francis, Ivor V., 351
Frank, Paul J., 341
Frank, Waldo, 86, 88, 90, 91, 92, 108, 249, 250, 257, 258, 264, 267, 271, 273, 284, 380, 387
Frankel, Ben, 402
Frankenberg, Lloyd, 326, 344, 404
Fraser, G. S., 348, 402, 404
Frederick, J. George, 308
Frederick, John T., 8, 129, 131, 132, 133, 140-47, 247
The Free Spirit, 256
free verse, 41, 112-13, 248, 249
free verse, 284
Freeman, John, 242
Freeman, Joseph, 33, 69, 150, 154, 167, 254, 281, 303, 319, 324, 325, 396, 397
Freeman, Margaret, 263
Freeman, Rose Florence, 256, 277
The Freewoman, 22
French, Hollis M., 308
French, Robert D., 378
Freud, Sigmund, 57, 58, 63, 69-72, 75, 153-54, 170-72, 176, 180-81, 184, 188, 258, 278, 284, 287, 288, 313, 356, 403
Friar, Kimon, 375
Friend, Julius Weis, 10, 11, 262
Front, 156, 295

The Frontier, 8, 130, 131, 139, 259
The Frontier and Midland, see The Frontier
Frost, Ernest M., 368
Frost, Frances, 276, 280, 292, 305, 307, 328, 383
Frost, Robert, 37, 38, 242, 244, 250, 256, 263, 280, 329, 368, 385, 392
Fry, Varian, 285
Fudge, William Kingston, 314
Fuessle, Milton, 243
The Fugitive, 8, 12, 42, 116-25, 265
Fuller, Ethel Romig, 314
Fuller, Margaret, 7
Fuller, Roy, 402
Fulton, Katherine W., 356
Funaroff, S., 319
Furioso, 10, 345
Furst, Herbert, 258
futurism, 24-25, 58, 269, 380
Futurist Aristocracy, 269

Gabelle, James, 295
Gaer, Yossef, 269
Gale, Zona, 380, 381
The Galleon, 273
Galloway, Elizabeth, 352
Galsworthy, John, 378
The Gammadion, 276
Gangrel, 370, 371
Gangrel Pamphlet, see Gangrel
Gant, Roland, 403
Gard, Wayne, 278
Gardiner, Helen, 335
Gardiner, Wrey, 348, 403
Gardner, Diana, 372
Gardner, Michael, 368
The Garen Magazine, 295
Gargoyle, 80, 262
Garis, Robert, 374
Garland, Hamlin, 235
Garman, Douglas, 388
Garnett, David, 390
Garoffolo, V. N., 299
Garrigan, Philip J., Jr., 317.
Garrigue, Jean, 329, 374, 401
Garrison, Troy, 331, 347
Gascoyne, David, 332, 335, 343, 351, 357
Gassner, John W., 399
Gates, Robert, 317

## INDEX

Gaulke, Walter, 354
Gaw, Allison, 263
Gaw, Etheleen Tyson, 263
Gaylor, Leon J., 324
Geddes, Norman Bel, 246, 383
Geddes, Virgil, 249, 250, 267, 324, 396
Gee, Kenneth, 366
Gellert, Hugo, 281, 395
*Genesis, 330*
gently, brother, *273*
George, Stefan, 358
Gerber, Henry, 318
*Germinal, 269*
Gerry, W. H., 303
Gessler, Clifford, 292, 307, 315, 361
Getty, Norris, 336
Ghiselin, Brewster, 328, 350, 373
Gibbs, Barbara, 302, 311, 355, 359
Gibson, Douglas, 345, 355, 403
Gibson, Wilfrid Wilson, 245, 249, 376, 387
Gibson, Will, 368
Gide, André, 322, 338, 368, 390, 400
Gilbert, Stuart, 293, 400
Gile, Blanche Finkle, 333
Gilfond, H., 297
Gill, Eric, 395
Gill, Ottie, 276
Gillespie, A. Lincoln, 287, 302, 313
Gillet, Louis, 351, 366
Gilliam, Florence, 262
Gillis, Peter, 305
Gilman, H., 251
Giltinan, Caroline, 290
Giniger, Kenneth Seeman, 396
Giniger, Weldon, 312
Ginner, Charles, 251
Ginsberg, Louis, 274, 278, 292, 295, 307, 313, 315, 353
Giono, Jean, 403
Giovannitti, Arturo, 29, 149-50, 240, 254, 377
*Gipsy*, see *The Gypsy* (Cincinnati, Ohio)
Glaspell, Susan, 383
Glassheim, Louis S., 323
Glazier, Lyle, 373
Gleason, George Scott, 291
*Glebe,* 8, 19, 41, 45-46, *243*
Gleeson, James, 351, 352

Glicksberg, Charles I., 299, 314, 338, 376, 403
Godin, Alexander, 334
Gogarty, Oliver St. John, 237, 238, 360, 377, 387
Gold, Michael, 273, 281, 300, 307, 396
Goldberg, Isaac, 251, 314
Goldberg, William, 365
Golden, J. Emerson, 399
*The Golden Galleon*, see *The Galleon*
*The Golden Hind, 266*
*Golden Quill, 276*
Golding, Louis, 258, 277, 311, 322, 385, 387
Goldman, Emma, 52, 148, 377
Goldschlag, Harry, 341
Goldstein, Albert, 10, 12, 265
Goll, Yvan, 350, 355, 365, 373, 385
Goodenough, Arthur H., 339
Goodland, John, 343
Goodman, Edward, 239
Goodman, Henry, 265
Goodman, Paul, 307, 369, 401
Goodman, Richard, 257, 308
*Good Morning, 256*
Goodwin, Geraint, 349
Gordon, Caroline, 291, 369, 398
Gordon, David, 281
Gordon, Ralph, 356
Gorky, Maxim, 237, 269, 377, 399
Gorman, Herbert S., 274
Gorman, William J., 302
Gottlieb, Elaine, 374
Gough, John, 398
Gould, Joe, 106, 309, 315
Gourmont, Remy de, 379
Govil, Hari G., 387
Gower, Joseph, 314
Gracq, Julien, 403
Graham, Howard S., Jr., 249
Graham, W. S., 361, 372, 374, 404
Grakowsky, David N., 265
Grano, Paul L., 352
Grant, Roland, 348
Granville-Barker, Harley, 379
Grattan, C. Hartley, 309
Graves, Robert, 113, 249, 257, 258, 266, 272, 330, 385
Graves, William E., 352
Gray, Albert, 317

Gray, Cecil, 385
Gray, Wailes, 317
Gray, Whitley, 274, 289
Greacen, Robert, 367
*Greek Horizons*, 374
Green, Paul, 263, 366, 379, 382, 383, 389
Green, Russell, 255
Greenberg, Clement, 353
Greenberg, Jack, 329, 332, 347
Greene, Graham, 335, 358
Greene, Ralph E., 261
Greenhood, Clarence David, 260
*Green-Horn*, 332
Green-Leach, Leacy Naylor, 272
*The Green Sheaf*, 237
Greenwich Village, 28, 246, 252, 286, 309, 310, 314, 378, 382, 383, 385
Greenwich Village, 27, 246
*The Greenwich Village Quill*, see *The Quill*
*The Greenwich Villager* (July 9, 1921-May 6, 1922), 385
*The Greenwich Villager* (May 15, 1933-Feb. 1934?), 309
*The Greenwich Village Spectator*, 383
Greer, Scott, 354, 357, 373
Gregory, Horace, 247, 269, 281, 285, 287, 290, 297, 301, 313, 318, 319, 336, 346, 350, 356, 358, 369, 381, 388, 390, 399, 404
Gregory, Isabella, Lady, 236, 376, 378
Gregory, Seymour, 341
Greville, Ursula, 385
Grieve, C. M., see Hugh MacDiarmid
Griffith, Llewellyn Wyn, 340
Griffiths, Alexander, 265
Grigson, Geoffrey, 312, 313, 397, 406
Gris, Juan, 62
Grobman, Feb, 373
Grokowsky, David N., 269
Gropper, William, 256, 281, 338, 385, 395
Gross, Bernard B., 347
Grossberg, Paul, 357
Grudin, Louis, 114, 265
Grunewald, Isaac, 262
*The Guardian*, 273
*The Guild Pioneer*, 269
Guiterman, Arthur, 239
Gunn, Neil M., 371

Gustafson, Ralph, 357, 375
Guthrie, James, 242, 377
Guthrie, Ramon, 257, 261
Guthrie, William Norman, 379
Gwynn, Stephen, 237
*The Gypsy* (Cincinnati, Ohio), 276
*The Gypsy* (London), 246
*The Gyroscope*, 164, 291

Hager, Alice Rogers, 292
Hagglund, Ben C., 293, 303, 318, 347, 355
Hagglund, Isabel, 347, 355
Hainsworth, N. W., 389
Halas, Frantisek, 357
Hale, William Harlan, 269, 295, 296, 378
Hall, Hazel, 256, 384
Hall, Kathleen M., 375
Hall, Robert, 305
Hall, Vincent Norman, 321, 326
Halley, Paul, 357, 362
Halls, Elizabeth, 352
Halper, Albert, 13, 286, 297, 299, 301, 307, 338, 387
Hamer, Robert, 309
Hamilton, Edith, 383
Hammer, Douglas, 314
Hampson, Norman, 371
Hanes, Leigh, 262
Hankel, Walter S., 275
Hankin, Bernard, 326
Hanley, James, 335
Hanneger, Arthur, 304
Hansen, Harry, 55
Hanson, Merlin H., 333
Hapgood, Hutchins, 377
Harden, Ernest, 304
Harding, D. W., 394
Harding, T. Swann, 291, 292
Hardy, A. D., 293
Hardy, Fred, 294
Hardy, Thomas, 235, 387
Hare, David, 364
Hargrave, John, 403
*The Harkness Hoot*, 295
*Harlequinade*, 291
*The Harp*, 277
Harper, Carol Ely, 368
Harper, Don, 276
Harper, Lawrence A., 317, 320, 326

*Harper's*, 34, 35, 38
Harris, Frank, 246, 255
Harris, Kenneth, 346
Harris, Max, 351, 372
Harris, M. Tjader, 338
Harrison, Henry, 252, 274, 276, 282
Harrison, Jay, 309
Harrisson, Tom, 370
Hart, James D., 296
Hart, Lawrence, 367
Hartley, Marsden, 88, 259, 377
Hartmann, Sadakichi, 276, 377
Hartsock, Ernest, 272, 274, 275, 276, 283
*The Harvard Advocate, 381*
*The Harvard Monthly, 378*
*Harvard Wake, 404*
Harvey, Rachel, 370
Harwell, Meade, 367, 368
Hasek, Jaroslav, 322
Haskins, H. D., 268
Hatcher, Harlan, 299
Hatcher, Lucy L., 337
Hauptmann, Gerhardt, 379
Hauser, Jacob, 317, 318
Havel, Hippolyte, 246, 277, 377
Havighurst, Walter, 395
Haviland, Walter, 280
Hawkins, A. Desmond, 391, 398
Hawthorne, Julian, 235
Hayakawa, S. I., 389, 402
Hayden, Robert E., 330
Hayes, Raphael, 341
Haynes, Mark, 339
Hays, H. R., 300, 312
H. D., 18, 19, 37, 242, 244, 245, 248, 259, 262, 279, 315, 385, 389
Heap, Jane, 55, 65, 245
Hearst, James, 138
Heath, Frederick, 387
Hecht, Ben, 65, 265, 268, 327
Hedges, M. H., 384
Heine, Heinrich, 247, 264, 282
Helion, Jean, 372
Hellman, Geoffrey T., 296
Hemingway, Ernest, 1, 12, 13, 14, 76, 262, 275, 279, 284, 300, 311
*Hemispheres, 365*
Hemley, Cecil Herbert, 305
Hemphill, Josephine, 292
Hempson, Norman, 371, 372

Henderson, A. J., 393
Henderson, Alice Corbin, 241
Henderson, Archibald, 389
Henderson, John, 354
Henderson, Margaret Ferguson, 308
Hendrickson, James, 306
Hendry, J. F., 340, 348, 354, 366, 367, 402, 404
Henley, William Ernest, 237
Henneman, J. B., 376
Hennessy, C. P., 372
Henning, William E., 320
Henrich, Edith, 371
Henry, Leigh, 385
Heppenstall, Raynar, 354, 371, 402
Herbst, Josephine, 161, 311, 319, 338
Herdman, Edward F., 248
*Here and Now, 358*
*Here To-Day, 368*
Hergesheimer, Joseph, 263, 266
*Heritage, 305*
Hern, Anthony, 404
Hernandez-Cata, A., 390
Herrick, Robert, 359, 379
Herring, Robert, 390
Hersey, Elinor, 391
Hersey, Harold, 247, 252, 391
Herschkowitz, Harry, 373
Hershberger, Ruth, 362, 372
Herts, B. Russell, 239
Hervey, J. R., 363
Heseltine, Nigel, 340, 343, 361
Heseltine, Philip, 250, 385
*hesperian, 296*
Hewitt, John, 366, 367, 401
Hicks, C. Henry, 343
Hicks, Granville, 336
Higgins, Bertram, 304, 388
Higgins, F. R., 238, 255, 347, 377, 387
Higgins, John Lee, 293
Highet, Gilbert, 295, 312
Hiler, Hilaire, 338
Hill, Frank E., 263
Hill, Gerald, 373
Hillis, Richard D., 378
*Hill Trails, 333*
Hillyer, Robert, 262, 286, 303, 363, 378, 387, 392
Hinckley, Theodore Ballou, 379
Hingston, Lee, 337
Hinrichsen, Steen, 270

## INDEX

Hinterland, *320*
Hirsch, Sidney Mttron, 117, 120
Hobson, Dorothy, 372
Hodel, George Hill, 276
Hodge, Alan, 330, 331
Hodgson, Telfair, 376
Hodgson, T. R., 403
Hofer, E., 270
Hoffman, George E., 323
Hoffman, Joseph, 360
Hoffmann, Hans A., 287
Hofmann, W. J. V., 322
Hofmannsthal, Hugo von, 379
Holburn, Muir, 351, 352, 364
Holden, Marcia Nichols, 406
Holden, Raymond, 382
Hölderlin, Johann Christian Friedrich, 319, 359
Hole, Philippa, 272
Holmes, C. J., 239
Holt, Achilles, 296, 302, 311
Hone, J. M., 387
Honoré, Marcel, 398
Hopkins, Ernest, 370
Hopkins, Gerard Manley, 306, 313, 390
Hoptner, J. B., 313
Horan, Robert, 182
Horgan, Paul, 288, 318, 393
*Horizon* (Brooklyn, N.Y.), *333*
*Horizon* (London), 221, *353*
*Horizons*, *330*
Horn, Rebecca, 341
Horton, Philip, 392
Hossain, Syud, 387
*The Hound and Horn*, 9, 206-10, 215, *285*
*Housatonic*, *305*
Housman, A. E., 247
Housman, Laurence, 247, 249, 266, 282
Houston, Kenneth, 321
Hovey, Richard, 237
Howard, Birkin, 402
Howard, Helen Addison, 351
Howarth, Herbert, 331
Howden, Molly, 275
Howells, A. F., 339
Howells, Thomas, 368
Howland, Pauline, 369

Hoyt, Helen, 244, 248, 253, 260, 271, 274, 292, 293, 306, 380
*Hub*, *320*
Hubbard, Press, 243
Hubbell, Jay B., 11, 131, 382
*Hubverse*, *338*
Hudson, Flexmore, 362, 363
Hudson, Kenneth, 372
Hudson, Mary, 320
Hudspeth, William, 333
*The Hue and Cry*, *269*
Hueffer, Ford Madox, see Ford Madox Ford
Hughes, Glenn, 388
Hughes, Langston, 272, 280, 298, 300, 306, 307, 310, 314, 318, 322, 339, 344, 355, 360, 374, 396, 399, 404
Hulme, Thomas Ernest, 111
Hulse, William, 375
Humphrey, George, 389
Humphries, Rolfe, 263, 271, 272, 384
Huneker, Erik, 326
Huneker, James Gibbons, 73-74, 235, 236, 380
Hunt, Richard M., 242
Hunt, Sidney, 315
Huntress, Keith, 350
Hurst, Fannie, 235
Hurston, Zora Neale, 280
Hustead, Newton J., 337
Hutton, Noel, 364
Huxley, Aldous, 26, 33, 249, 250, 251, 255, 266, 277, 279, 321, 358, 383, 387
Hyde, Kent Goodnough, 287
Hyde, M. P., 305
Hydeman, Albert L., 261
Hyman, Carlton S., 392

Ibanez, Vincent Blasco, 255
*Iconograph*, *353*
Ignatew, David, 337
Ikeda, Masaki, 295
*The Illiterati*, *368*
imagism, 9, 18, 19, 22, 39-40, 49, 54, 111, 113, 241-42, 243, 246
*Imagist Anthology*, 40
*Impromptu*, *300*
*Indian Writing*, *401*
Ingalls, Jeremy, 373
*The Ink Pot*, *382*

## INDEX 429

*The Inland Review, 396*
Innes, David Raymond, 332
*Interim, 368*
*Interludes, 273*
*Intermountain Review,* see *Intermountain Review of English and Speech*
*Intermountain Review of English and Speech, 338*
*The International,* see *Moods*
*International Arts, 277*
*International Literature,* 157, 300
*The International Theatre, 393*
*Inwhich, 246*
Ireland, Kenneth, 358
*The Irish Review, 379*
Irwin, Thomas, 310, 401
Isaacs, Edith J. R., 383
Ishill, Joseph, 256, 277
*The Island, 300*
Israel, Boris J., 297, 303, 307

Jack, Peter Monro, 302
*jackass, 288*
Jackson, Holbrook, 273
Jackson, Schuyler B., 261
Jacob, Alaric, 393
Jacobs, Lewis, 391
Jacobs, Thornwell, 241, 283
Jaffe, Joseph, 381
James, Arnold, 383
James, Henry, 235, 285, 380, 401
Jameson, Storm, 321, 358
Jamieson, Morley, 404
*Janus, 291*
*Japm, 288*
Jarmain, John, 404
Jarrell, Randall, 325, 356, 398, 401, 405
Jarry, Alfred, 332, 400
Jasienski, Bruno, 301
*Jazz Forum, 374*
Jeffers, Robinson, 281, 300, 328, 360, 371
Jenkins, Oliver, 260, 264, 265, 271, 277, 278, 384
Jennings, Helen, 300
Jennings, Humphrey, 400
Jennings, Leslie Nelson, 363
Joffe, Eugene, 259
Johns, Orrick, 31, 49, 235, 280, 307, 314, 319

Johns, Richard, 295, 297, 298
Johnson, Frank C., 271
Johnson, Geoffrey, 342
Johnson, Helene, 280
Johnson, Josephine, 261, 283
Johnson, Kingsley, 341
Johnson, Lionel, 236
Johnson, Martyn, 196
Johnson, Patricia, 348
Johnson, Sprague, 375
Johnson, Spud, see Willard Johnson
Johnson, Stanley, 118
Johnson, Willard, 266, 271, 276, 278, 388, 393
Johnson, William, 359
Johnston, Gypsy, 351
Jolas, Eugene, 3, 80, 115, 172-80, 181, 249, 270, 271, 274, 279, 281, 287, 290, 299, 329, 358, 368, 399
Jones, Alan, 368
Jones, Carter Brooke, 273
Jones, Ellis O., 256
Jones, Frank, 352
Jones, Gwyn, 340, 349
Jones, Herbert, 315
Jones, Howard Mumford, 143, 247, 258, 382, 389
Jones, Jack, 272
Jones, Llewellyn, 268, 272
Jones, Powell, 345
Jones, Robert Edmond, 383
Jones, Robert Leseur, 283
*The Jongleur, 285*
Jopling, R. M., 381
Jordan, Bill, 310
Jordan, W. K., 301
Josephs, Devereux C., 249
Josephs, Laurence, 375
Josephson, Matthew, 94, 95, 96, 97, 98, 99, 100, 102, 105, 106, 228, 261, 267, 275, 287
Joslin, H. A., 275, 276, 277
Joslin, Olin, 275
*The Journal of American Poetry,* 125, 126, *285*
Joyce, James, 21, 23, 37, 59, 174-76, 189, 243, 244, 245, 257, 258, 275, 279, 282, 284, 285, 287, 288, 299, 309, 322, 323, 338, 342, 351, 369, 375, 379, 380, 390
Jung, Carl G., 177, 287, 406

## INDEX

Kaberry, P. M., 302
Kaestlin, John, 309
Kafka, Franz, 215, 216-17, 287, 297, 322, 325, 334, 340, 344, 350, 366, 367, 370, 390
Kahn, Derek, 312
Kalar, Joseph, 162, 276, 294, 300, 305
Kaleidograph, see The Kaleidoscope
The Kaleidoscope, 292
Kallen, Horace M., 269, 381
Kamer, Herbert, 373
Kamm, Matthew, 333
Kantor, Mackinlay, 261, 323
Kapustin, Razel, 351
Kapustka, Bruce, 336, 340, 354
Kapustka, Stan Lee, 354
The Kapustkan, 354
Karloff, Konstantin, 294
Karloff, Susie, 317
Kauffman, Florence, 317
Kauffman, Roma, 278
Kaufman, Wolfe, 352
Kavafis, Kostas, 374
Kavan, Anna, 403
Kay, George Henry, 304
Kazin, Alfred, 107
Keenan, Peter, 312
Keene, Florence R., 287
Kees, Weldon, 286, 320, 336, 339, 342, 358, 369, 372
Keidan, Seymour, 350, 351
Keith, Joseph Joel, 317, 328
Kellaway, Frank, 351
Kelleher, D. L., 255
Kelm, Karlton, 279, 286, 293, 300, 310, 314, 317, 318, 320, 323, 326
Kemp, Harry, 240, 282, 309, 330, 338
Kemp, H. V., 308
Kennedy, Adam, 297
Kennedy, Leo, 389
Kennedy, Thomas, 268
Kent, Mallory, 375
The Kenyon Review, 2, 9, 210, 400
Keon, J. M., 351
Keown, Anna G., 255
Kerr, C. Gregory, 302
Kerr, D. B., 351
Kershaw, Alister, 351
Kiesler, Frederick, 364
Kilbourne, Irene, 326
Kilgore, Ray N., 373

King, Francis, 358
King, Maud Egerton, 378
Kingdom Come, 346
Kirch, Curtis J., 243
Kirchner, Ralf, 320
Kirkup, James, 349, 371
Kirsch, Dwight, 371
Kirstein, Lincoln E., 207, 208, 285
Kitasano, Katue, 344
Klein, A. M., 357, 362, 375, 389
Klein, Marvin, 301
Kline, Herbert, 396
Kling, Joseph, 69, 249, 264, 267, 277
Klonsky, Milton, 362
Knickerbocker, William S., 376
Knight, Eric, 393
Knights, L. C., 394
Knopf, Alfred A., 266
Kobrin, Leon, 381
Koch, Frederick, 389
Koch, Sigmund, 323
Koch, Vivienne, 323, 369
Kollar, Robert Weaver, 345
Komroff, Manuel, 261
Konopka, Leo, 327
Korn, Albert Ralph, 363
Korzybski, Alfred, 403
Kosmos, 309
Koteliansky, S. S., 386, 388
Koven, Joseph, 323
Kovner, Milton, 282
Kozlenko, William, 309, 310, 322, 399
Kramer, Dale D., 320, 333
Krause, Herbert, 135
Kresensky, Raymond, 260, 273, 274, 276, 278, 279, 282, 286, 292, 293, 306, 320, 329, 331, 337, 339, 354, 360, 363, 365, 367, 384
Kreymborg, Alfred, 19, 44-50, 102, 103, 105, 242, 243, 246, 247, 248, 250, 256, 260, 261, 269, 274, 276, 277, 283, 306, 356, 360, 366, 377, 383, 396, 399, 404
Kronenberg, Mark, 352
Krutch, Joseph Wood, 279, 304
Kuhlman, Fred, 311
Kyle, Galloway, 242

The Labor Herald, 30, 151
Lall, Chaman, 255
Lamantia, Philip, 356, 367

# INDEX

Lambert, Elizabeth, 351
Lambert, Harold, 327
Lampson, Robin, 288
*The Lance, 320*
Landau, Noah, 333
Lane, Edward, 361
Lane, Fern, 306
Lane, John, 394
*The Lantern* (Chicago), *243*
*The Lantern* (New York), *280*
*The Lantern* (San Francisco), *247*
Lape, Fred, 306
Lapolla, Garibaldi M., 239
Lardner, Ring, 268
Largay, Michael W., 317, 328
*The Lariat, 270*
Lark, 7
Larsen, Erling, 317, 322, 332, 337
Larsson, Genevieve, 309
Larsson, Raymond E. F., 315, 323, 338, 384
*larus, 286*
Latimer, Ronald Lane, 316
*The Latin Quarter-ly, 310*
*Laughing Horse,* 225-26, *266*
Laughlin, James, IV, 9, 210-15, 223, 241, 283, 296, 299, 310, 311, 316, 317, 328, 334, 339, 343, 344, 347, 353, 359, 381, 401
Laurvik, John, 276
Lautréamont, Isidore Ducasse, 332
Lavater, Louis, 293
Lavrin, Janko, 319, 324, 366
Law, Robert Adger, 382
Lawhead, Mary, 322
Lawlor, Adrian, 275
Lawrence, D. H., 25-26, 37, 90, 91, 184-85, 240, 242, 243, 244, 247, 248, 250, 252, 257, 258, 259, 266, 277, 279, 281, 282, 284, 295, 299, 311, 314, 316, 319, 326, 342, 380, 386, 387, 388, 390, 392, 394
Lawrence, Frieda, 342
Lawrence, Seymour, 404
Lawson, John Howard, 396, 397
Layton, Irving, 362, 375
Leach, Marcia Lewis, 272
Leahy, Maurice, 294
Leake, Sabin, 395
Leatham, John, 366
*Leaven, 374*
*Leaves, 339*

Leavis, F. R., 394
Lechlitner, Ruth, 271, 273, 316, 318, 336, 349, 350
Le Clercq, Jacques, 280
Ledoux, Louis V., 242
Ledward, Patricia, 355
Leed, Robert, 404
*The Left,* 157-58, *301*
*Left Front,* 155, *310*
*The Left Review* (London), 165, *321*
*Left Review* (Philadelphia), *320*
*Leftward, 305*
leftwing writers, see proletarian literature
Le Gallienne, Richard, 237, 239, 246, 270, 280
Le Gros, Cardinal, 309
Lehman, Max, 304
Lehmann, Beatrix, 402
Lehmann, John, 289, 324, 334, 357, 358, 361, 405
Lehmann, Rosamond, 405
Leippert, James G., 394
Leite, George, 359, 367, 374
Lemley, Margaret, 278
Lench, W. H., 269, 271
Leonard, William Ellery, 40, 247, 315, 329, 392
Le Sueur, Meridel, 299, 307, 311, 316, 318, 322, 323, 325, 333, 339, 345, 388
*Letters, 331*
Leventhal, A. J., 387
Levin, Albert, 341
Levin, Harry, 404
Levin, Meyer, 352
Levin, Morton, 270
Levine, Nathan B., 327
Lewis, Alun, 335, 349, 358, 387, 390, 402, 404
Lewis, C. Day, 262, 272, 295, 312, 318, 319, 321, 329, 335, 346, 353, 358, 387, 405
Lewis, Constance Deming, 315
Lewis, Ethelreda, 388
Lewis, H. H., 156-57, 294, 303, 321, 333, 334, 360
Lewis, James Franklin, 347, 354, 356, 357, 369
Lewis, Janet, 270, 290, 291, 311
Lewis, Louise, 369

Lewis, Wyndham, 23, 24, 60, 82-83, 193, 244, 245, 264, 283, 340, 388
Lewisohn, Ludwig, 239, 253, 277, 279, 287, 380
The Liberator, 8, 28, 30, 80, 150-51, 152-53, *254*
*Life and Letters, 389*
*Life and Letters Today,* see *Life and Letters*
Light, James, 252
Ligocki, Michael, 332
Lindeman, Eduard C., 373
Lindin, Carl Eric, 243
Lindsay, Jack, 5, 74-75, 271, 288, 342, 343, *402*
Lindsay, Maurice, 348, 365, 370, 404
Lindsay, Vachel, 37, 54, 235, 239-40, 242, 245, 257, 263, 278, 380
*The Lion and Crown, 393*
*The Lion and the Unicorn, 396*
Lipp, Frances M., 333
Lippmann, Walter, 240, 378
Liskin, Phil, 299
*Literary America, 321*
*The Literary Arts, 322*
*Literary Magazine,* see *The Literary Monthly*
*The Literary Monthly, 310*
*The Literary Workshop, 322*
*The Literary World,* 216, 217, *322*
*Literature of the World Revolution, 301*
Littell, Robert, 378
*The Little Magazine, 310*
*The Little Man,* 6, *341*
*The Little Review,* 9, 20-21, 41, 52-66, 82, 96, 148, *245*
*Littletown, 347*
Litvinoff, Emanuel, 355
Litwak, Leo, 373
Livesay, Dorothy, 357, 375, 389
*Living Poetry, 365*
L.L.C., 274
Lobo, G. Edmund, 276
Lodge, Oliver W. F., 400
Loeb, Harold A., 46, 102, 103, 105, 261, 309
Loftus, John, 277
Lohr, Frederick, 371
*The London Aphrodite,* 5, 74-75, *288*
*London Bulletin, 400*
*The Lone Wolf, 331*

Long, Haniel, 253, 264, 268, 274, 282, 298, 388, 391, 392
Long, Seymour, 376
Long, Tudor S., 376
Lorca, Garcia, 299, 319, 321, 332, 344, 372, 390, 393, 400
Lorenz, R. C., 301
*Lovat Dickson's Magazine, 311*
Loveman, Samuel, 264
"The Love Song of J. Alfred Prufrock," 37
Loving, Pierre, 68, 253, 265, 297, 385
Lowden, Eleanor, 278
Lowell, Amy, 35, 37, 38, 242, 244, 248, 249, 250, 252, 255, 380
Lowell, Robert, 372, 374
Lowenfels, Walter, 347
Lowes, John Livingston, 112
Lowndes, Robert, 375
Lowry, Robert James, 211, 341, 359, 371
Lowry, W. McNeil, 350
Lowy, A. E., 363
Loy, Mina, 20, 248, 251, 259
Lucas, Peter G., 351
Luck, H. R., 260
Luhan, Mabel Dodge, 81, 266, 271, 377
Lukes, Lee, 345
Lull, Roderick, 279, 314
Lumpkins, William, 342
Lund, Mary Graham, 345
Lush, S. Beryl, 309
*The Lyric* (New York), *252*
*The Lyric* (Norfolk, Va.), *262*
*Lyrical Poetry, 347*
*The Lyric West, 262*

Maas, Willard, 273, 307, 317, 392
Mabbott, Thomas Ollive, 406
McAllister, C. B., 280
McAllister, John, 311
McAlmon, Robert, 77-78, 83, 228, 259, 264, 275, 277, 279, 284, 286, 295, 352
McAlmon, Mrs. Robert, see Winifred Bryher
Macaulay, Rose, 405
McBryde, John M., Jr., 376
McCaig, Norman, 404
Maccallum, Russell, 389
McCarthy, Albert J., 374

## INDEX

MacCarthy, Desmond, 388, 389
McClure, John, 10, 12, 262
McConnell, William, 362, 375
McCormick, Virginia Taylor, 262
McCoy, Samuel, 249
McCrae, Hugh, 271
McCrudden, Francis Lambert, 315
McCubbin, James Burlie, 317
McCullough, Perry, 298
Macdermott, Norman, 384
MacDiarmid, Hugh (Pseud. for C. M. Grieve), 241, 272, 296, 321, 343, 346, 347, 349, 352, 366, 393, 404
Macdonagh, Donagh, 366
MacDonagh, Thomas, 379
Macdonald, Alec, 385
Macdonald, Dwight, 296, 325, 378
McDonald, Maria, 287
McFadden, Roy, 367
McGahey, Jeanne, 359, 367
McGill, V. J., 390
MacGlynn, Lochlinn, 401
MacGowan, Kenneth, 378, 383
McGrath, Thomas, 349, 355
McGregor, John, 314
MacGregor, William, 402
McGuire, H., 278
McGuire, James, 372
Machen, Arthur, 246, 268, 361
MacIver, Hector, 398
Mackellar, Dorothea, 275
McKenzie, Donal, 157, 292, 301
McLaughlin, David, 320
Maclean, Norman, 364
MacLeish, Archibald, 38, 260, 287, 296, 313, 346, 378, 397
Macleod, Norman, 3, 162-63, 260, 274, 276, 280, 283, 286, 288, 289, 290, 291, 292, 293, 294, 295, 296, 297, 298, 299, 300, 301, 306, 307, 310, 311, 313, 314, 315, 316, 317, 318, 320, 322, 323, 324, 327, 328, 329, 333, 339, 340, 343, 344, 349, 352, 359, 363, 369, 382, 391, 392, 394, 396, 397
McMahon, Thomas, 372
MacNeice, Louis, 279, 289, 325, 335, 336, 353, 401
McNicoll, A. W. R., 302
McPhee, Douglas, 389
Macpherson, Kenneth, 388

Macrae, Mary, 405
McWilliams, Carey, 276, 297
Maddow, Ben, 319, 394
Madge, Charles, 308, 309, 346, 390, 400
*The Madrigal*, 252
*The Magazine*, *311*
*Main Street*, *391*
Mairet, Philippe, 391
"The Makers of Modern Literature Series," 214
Mallalieu, H. B., 346, 370
Mallarmé, Stéphane, 351, 404
Malley, Ern, (hoax), 351
Malraux, André, 400
Manch, Joseph Rodman, 316
Mandelik, Lucien C., 339
Mangan, John Sherry, 286, 297, 301, 305, 312, 329
Mangione, Jerre, 159-60
*Manhattan Poetry Parade*, *333*
Manhood, H. A., 387
*Le Manifeste du Surréalisme*, 64
*Manikin*, *270*
Mann, Klaus, 222, 312, 357, 358, 401
Mann, Thomas, 223, 259, 297, 328, 338, 350, 358, 390
Manning, Mary, 394
Mansfield, Katherine, 26, 240, 243, 248, 251, 386, 387
Mantz, Ruth, 290
*Manuscript* (Athens, Ohio), *322*
*Manuscript* (Beverly Hills, Calif.), *339*
*Manuscripts* (Geelong, Australia), *302*
*Manuscripts* (New York), *267*
*Manuscripts* (Washington, D.C.), *301*
March, William, 145, 279, 286, 297, 329, 339, 393
Marcus, Paul, 326
Marcus, Ralph, 373
Margo, Edith, 310
Marin, John, 269
Marinetti, Filippo Tommaso, 23, 24-25, 58, 243, 269
Maring, Helen, 274
*The Marionnette*, *254*
*The Marionnette To-night at 12-30*, see *The Marionnette*
Maris, Jan, 296
Maritain, Jacques, 395
Markham, Edwin, 252
Marlow, John, 391

Marnau, Fred, 367
Marquis, Neeta, 263
Marsden, Dora, 22, 244, 245
Marsden, Francis, 249
Marshall, Alan, 339, 364
Marshall, Hazel S., 289
Marshall, Murray L., 289
*Marsyas, 368*
Marten, G. I., 276
Martz, Louis L., 372
Marxism, 28, 69, 80, 149, 153, 154, 157, 159, 165-66, 188, 270, 300, 301, 303, 308, 313, 324, 338
*Maryland Quarterly, 369*
Masefield, John, 237, 238, 257, 376, 377
Mashman, Jack, 347
*The Mask, 238*
Mason, W. H., 372
The Masses (New York), 7, 8, 28-30, 149-50, 151, 152, 240, 254
Masses (Toronto), *305*
Masters, Edgar Lee, 7, 31, 37, 112, 235, 328
Mathers, E. Powys, 265
Mathews, Stephen, 354
Mathews, Thomas, 330
Mathias, Roland, 368
*Matrix, 347*
Matthews, Brander, 379
Matthews, T. S., 261, 382
Matthiessen, F. O., 325, 378, 381, 398, 401
Maugham, Jack, 339
Maugham, Robert, 403
Maugham, W. Somerset, 322, 358
Maxham, Frederick, 259, 313, 314, 316, 322, 326, 327
May, Beulah, 276
Mayakowsky, Vladimir, 321
Mayer, Stanley Dehler, 299, 312
Maynard, Theodore, 306, 397
Mayne, Ethel, 266
Mayor, A. Hyatt, 285, 382
Meagher, James, 356
*Meanjin Papers, 354*
Mears, Helen, 300
The Measure (New York), 8, 125, 192, *263*
Measure (Washington, D.C.), *306*
The Medallion, *323*

The Mediator, *270*
The Medusa, *375*
Meeter, George F., 163-64, 279
Mellers, W. H., 394
Melton, Wightman F., 283, 304
Menai, Huw, 349
Mencken, Henry L., 72, 90, 283, 337, 380, 391
Merchant, Frank, 303
Meredith, William, 376
Merriam, Eve, 299, 329, 345, 350, 358, 362, 401
Merriam, Harold G., 130, 131, 132, 134, 260
Merrick, Padraic, 310
Merrill, Arthur Truman, 293, 306
Merrill, Irene, 316
Merrill, James, 375
Merritt, A., 339
Merten, Jack, 255
The Mesa, *277*
Mesens, E. L. T., 400
Meyer, Gerard Previn, 406
Meynell, Alice, 38
Michaux, Joseph, 358
The Midland, 8, 129, 131, 132, 133, 136, 140-47, *247*
The Midwest (Chicago), *323*
Midwest (Minneapolis, Minn.), *333*
Migel, Parmenia, 292
Miles, Hamish, 390
Miles, Josephine, 334, 367, 371
Miles, Peter, 354
Millay, Edna St. Vincent, 37, 235, 356, 386, 387, 392
Miller, Fred, 162, 303, 308, 313, 323, 324, 327
Miller, Henry, 185-87, 308, 334, 337, 341, 342, 343, 353, 359, 367, 368, 371, 372, 373, 403, 406
Miller, H. Tatlock, 302
Miller, J. Corson, 283, 304, 319, 397
Miller, Mary Owings, 360
Miller, Richard, 298
Millet, Martha, 341
million, *404*
Mills, Clark, 309, 350, 355, 362
The Milwaukee Arts Monthly, *267*
The Minaret, 191-92, *247*
Miniature, *358*
Miniter, Edith, 339
Minor, Robert, 254

## INDEX            435

Minus, Marian, 318
Mirick, Edith, 293
The Mirror, 6, 30-31, *235*
The Miscellany, *296*
Mitchell, Susanna Valentine, 303
M'lle New York, 7, 73, *236*
Modernist, *256*
The Modern Monthly, see The Modern Quarterly
The Modern Quarterly, 152-53, *270*
"The Modern Readers Series," 214
Modern Reading, *358*
Modern Review, *267*
The Modern Scot, *296*
Modern S 4 N Review, *281*
Modern Verse, *358*
Moe, John, 315
Moffat, David, 342
The Moment, *311*
Monahan, Michael, 237, 245-46
The Monarchist Quarterly, see Anathema
Monro, Harold, 24, 240, 242, 244, 249, 256
Monroe, Harriet, 7, 18, 20, 34-44, 60, 191, 241-42, 334, *392*
The Montanan, see The Frontier
Montgomery, Neil, 373
Montgomery, Vaida Stewart, 292
Montgomery, Whitney, 292
Montherlant, Henry de, 286, 350
The Monthly Chapbook, *256*
The Monthly Criterion, see The Criterion
The Monthly Review, *323*
Moods, *239*
Moody, William Vaughn, 36, 235
Moore, George, 236, 237
Moore, Harry Thornton, 372
Moore, Henry, 372
Moore, John C., 395
Moore, Marianne, 37, 48, 199, 200-1, 241, 244, 246, 248, 249, 256, 258, 259, 268, 270, 303, 318, 344, 346, 389, 390, 401
Moore, Merrill, 119, 123, 262, 265, 271, 282, 303, 317, 320, 343, 369, 376, 390
Moore, Nicholas, 343, 345, 346, 347, 348, 349, 354, 358, 361, 363, 366, 369, 370, 371, 374, 402, 403

Moore, Reginald, 358, 361, 369, 402, 404
Moore, T. Sturge, 258
Moorhead, Ethel, 279
The Morada, *292*
Morang, Alfred, 308, 314, 317, 320, 323, 324, 326, 327, 328, 330, 331, 332, 333, 334, 335, 337, 342, 347, 360, 393, 396
Mordell, Albert, 314
Moreland, John R., 262, 267
Moreno, J. L., 300
Morgan, Angela, 290
Morgan, Frederick, 361
Morgan, Janet, 375
Morris, A. G., 404
Morris, Charles W., 330, 401
Morris, George L. K., 296, 378
Morris, Myra, 275, 302
Morrison, Arthur, 235
Morrison, John, 372
Morrison, W. A., 302
Morrissette, Pat, 391
Morse, Irl, 304
Morse, Samuel French, 340
Morse, S. Robert, 321
Morton, David, 266, 316, 361, 366
Mosaic, *323*
Moses, J., 263
Moses, W. R., 339, 350, 401
Moskovitz, Joseph, 347
Mosley, G. Gordon, 351
Moss, Arthur H., 80, 252, 262
Moss, David, 259
Moss, Howard, 356
Moss, Millia Davenport, 252
Mother Earth, 148, *377*
Motive, *354*
Motley, *394*
Mott, Frank Luther, 143, 144, 146, 247
Mottram, R. H., 387
Moult, Thomas, 258
Moyer, Pauline, 289
M S, *354*
Muddiman, Bernard, 265
Mudie, Ian, 352
Muilenburg, Walter J., 143
Muir, Edwin, 263, 297, 311, 319, 335, 347, 365, 366, 387, 388, 405
Muir, Willa, 297

Mullen, Dale, 339
Muller, Herbert J., 334, 401
Mullin, David, 365
Mullins, Helene, 262, 263, 267, 271, 277, 280, 282, 294, 316, 330, 343
Mumford, Lewis, 137, 283
Munson, Gorham B., 5, 93, 94, 95, 96, 97, 98, 99, 100, 101, 148, 243, 249, 256, 257-58, 261, 267, 268, 273, 274, 281, 284, 297, 302, 334, 376
Murdock, Kenneth B., 381
Murfey, Etta Josephean, 335, 405
Murphy, John Maher, 372
Murry, John Middleton, 26-27, 240, 243, 248, 257, 258, 316, 386
Muse and Mirror, 274
Musgrave, Arthur, 288
Musser, Benjamin, 249, 277, 278, 281, 283, 288, 289, 291, 292, 293, 294, 295, 305, 307, 310, 313, 316, 318, 319, 327, 328, 332, 335, 336
Myers, Elizabeth, 404
Myers, John, 356
My Word, 342

Nagel, Paul, 330
Narodny, Ivan, 278
Nasby, Petroleum V., see David R. Locke
Nash, W. Roy, 403
The Nassau Literary Magazine, 381
Nathan, George Jean, 304, 380
Nathan, Robert G., 378
The Nationalist Quarterly, see Anathema
Nativity, 297
Neagoe, Peter, 302
Nearing, Scott, 253
Nebulae, 324
Neff, Lawrence W., 304, 405
Neihardt, John G., 380, 390, 392
Neill, Charles, 371
Nelson, Jack, 276
Netboy, Anthony, 314
Nethercot, Arthur H., 274, 323, 392
The New Act, 312
New Adelphi, see The Adelphi
The New Alliance, 221, 347
The New American Caravan, see The American Caravan

The New Anvil, 347
new apocalypse, 366, 367, 403
The New Broom and Morningside, 394
Newby, P. H., 361
The New Caravan, see The American Caravan
New Challenge, see Challenge
"The New Classics Series," 214
The New Contemporary Vision and Scepter, see Contemporary Vision
The New Coterie, 277
The New Cow of Greenwich Village, 286
The New Criterion, see The Criterion
New Directions, 210-15, 283, 334
New Directions Press, 9, 211-15
The New Freewoman, 22, 244
The New Frontier, 396
The New Hope, 312
New Horizons, see Creative Writing
New Letters in America, 399
Newman, Israel, 277
Newman, Stanley, 272
New Masses, 151-52, 168, 281
The New Mexico Quarterly, 8, 129, 138, 139, 392
The New Mexico Quarterly Review, see The New Mexico Quarterly
New Numbers (Ryton, Gloucester, Eng.), 245
new numbers (Saint Paul, Minn.), 260
The New Orient, see Orient
The New Oxford Outlook, 312
The New Pen, 263
New Poetry, 369
The New Quarterly, 324
The New Quarterly of Poetry, 406
New Rejections, 359
The New Review, 83, 302
New Road, 403
The New Saxon Pamphlets, 369
Newsom, Francis Ward, 261
New Stories, 161, 324
The New Talent, 6, 312
New Theatre, 396
New Theatre and Film, see New Theatre
The New Tide, 324
Newton, David, 261, 356, 382
Newton, Peter, 382

## INDEX 437

New Verse, *312*
New World Monthly, *297*
New Writers, *334*
New Writing, *334*
New Writing and Daylight, see New Writing
The New Yorker, 152
Ney, Lew, 286, 310
Nezval, Vitezslav, 357
Nicholas, Conan, 355
Nicholas, Elmer, 271
Nicholl, Louise, 280
Nichols, Beverley, 257
Nichols, Louise Townsend, 397
Nichols, Ross, 370
Nicholson, Irene, 395
Nickolls, Nick, 401
Nicolas, Claire, 368
Niebuhr, Reinhold, 322
Nietzsche, Friedrich W., 23, 72-75, 236, 245, 288-89, 297, 384
Nims, John Frederick, 373, 397, 401
Nin, Anaïs, 343, 347, 353, 375
Nineteen-Ten Magazine, *239*
*1933*, 162, *313*
*1924*, *274*
Ninety-Eight-Six, *274*
Niver, J., 294
Nixon, Eric, 348, 366, 403
Noguchi, Yone, 237, 238
Noland, H. B., 306
The Nomad, *267*
Nomland, Kemper, 368
Noring, George Anders, 337
Norman, Dorothy, 9, 344
Norse, Harold, 333
North, Jessica Nelson, 241, 273, 384
North, Richel, 270
North, Sterling, 272, 294
The North Carolina Poetry Review, *313*
Northe, James Neill, 306
The Northern Light, see Western Poetry
Northern Review, *375*
The North Georgia Review, see Pseudopodia
Northrup, Dan, 310
Northrup, F. C. S., 346
Norton, Allan, 248
Now (London), 222, *354*
Now (New York), 220, *359*

Nuhn, Ferner, 329
Nutt, Howard, 279, 318

Oasis, *355*
objectivist poetry, 42
O'Brien, Edward J., 145-46, 160, 161, 241, 242, 311, 402
O'Brien, Howard Vincent, 378, 380
The Observer, *313*
O'Casey, Sean, 404
The Occident, *260*
O'Connor, Frank, 387, 405
O'Connor, V. G., 364
O'Connor, William Van, 363
O'Day, Edward F., 247
Odets, Clifford, 397
O'Donnell, George Marion, 327, 339
O'Donnell, T. C., 276
O'Donnol, Dion, 360
O'Faolain, Sean, 285, 297, 311, 336, 347, 387, 394, 398, 401
O'Flaherty, Liam, 275, 277, 311, 387, 388
Ogden, C. K., 393
Oglethorpe, George, 289
O'Keefe, Arthur, 369
O'Kelly, Seumas, 378
O'Leary, C., 255
O'Leary, P. I., 352
Olgin, Moissaye, 381
Olguin, Manuel, 371
Olson, Lawrence, 343
Olson, Ted, 263, 272, 277, 392, 406
One Act Play Magazine, *399*
One Act Play Magazine and Radio-Drama Review, see One Act Play Magazine
One Act Play Magazine and Theatre Review, see One Act Play Magazine
O'Neill, Dennis, 278
O'Neill, Eugene, 91-92, 250, 304, 383, 386, 397
On the Boiler, *347*
Open Vistas, *277*
The Open Window, *239*
Opinion, *391*
Oppenheim, James, 86, 88, 90, 92, 239, 250
Opus, *348*
The Oracle, *278*
Orient, *387*
Orion, *405*

d'Orme, Eduard, 305
Ornstein, Leo, 88
O'Rourke, May Rita, 285
Orpheus, 274
Orton, Virginia Keating, 327
Orwell, George, 371, 406
O'Ryan, Jane, 315
Osborne, L., 381
Osgoode, Addington, 265
O'Sullivan, Seumas, 237, 238, 377, 379, 387
O'Sullivan, Vincent, 387
Others, 8, 19-20, 45, 46-51, 247
Otis, Brooks, 396
Ould, Hermon, 384
Our Time, 402
The Outlander (Ann Arbor, Mich.), 278
The Outlander (Portland, Ore.), 314
Outposts, 370
The Outrider, 314
Outsiders, 289
Overtures, see The Quill
The Owl, 257
The Oxford and Cambridge Miscellany, 384
Oxford Criterion, 395
The Oxford Outlook, 257

Paalen, Wolfgang, 183-84, 362
Pacific, 371
The Pagan, 69, 249
Pagany, 297
Page, David, 329
Page, Philip, 388
Page, P. K., 363, 369
Painted Veils, 73-74
The Palatine Review, 33, 250
Palisade, see The Poetry Palisade
Palmer, Herbert E., 387
Palms, 8, 271
Palo Verde, see jackass
Panorama, 314
Pan, Poetry and Youth, 278
The Panton Magazine, 389
Panzer, Martin, 311
Papini, Giovanni, 388
Papot, Benedict, 379
The Papyrus, 237
Parabalou, 260
Parker, Charles A. A., 261
Parker, Theodore, 7

Parkes, H. B., 285, 300, 317
Parks, Ed Winfield, 294, 335
Parnassus (1924+), 274
Parnassus (1927-1937?), 286
Parrish, Dilwyn, 298
Parry, Albert, 77
Parsons, Geoffrey, 342
The Partisan, 314
Partisan Review, 8, 166-68, 325, 362, 378
Partisan Review and Anvil, see Partisan Review
Partridge, Eric, 299
Patchen, Kenneth, 211, 241, 264, 299, 303, 307, 311, 326, 329, 334, 336, 344, 353, 359, 364, 365, 367, 369, 371, 373, 375, 404
Pater, Alan Frederick, 298
Patmore, Derek, 374
Patri, Giacomo, 359
Patterson, Vernon, 260
Paul, Elliot, 173, 174, 177, 287
Paul, Louis, 345
Pauli, George, 243
Paulsen, Katherine A., 352
Paynter, Theodosia, 323
Peake, Mervyn, 372, 402
Pearce, T. M., 392
Pearse, Andrew, 370
Pegasus, 271
Peguy, Charles, 250
Penfield, Roderic C., 383
Penguin New Writing, see New Writing
Perelman, S. J., 259
Peret, Benjamin, 364, 400
Perlès, Alfred, 337, 371
Perlman, Jess, 253
Perry, Richard, 311
Perse, St. John, 287, 365
personalism, 367
Pessin, Samuel, 267
Peterkin, Julia, 263
Peterson, Houston, 390
Peterson, William, 357
Pfeiffer, Paul, 318
Phaër, Daniel, 242
Phantasmus, 274
Pharos, 371
Phenix, see Genesis
Phillips, Charles, 278
Phillips, Stephen, 242

# INDEX

Phillips, Virginia, 317
The Phoenix (South Norwalk, Conn.), 245
Phoenix (Sussex, Eng.), *371*
The Phoenix (Woodstock, N.Y.), 184-86, *342*
Picabia, Francis, 252, 377
Picardy, Leon, 388
Picasso, Pablo, 58, 105, 332, 372, 400
Pick, J. B., 371
Picola, Henry, 328
The Pilgrims Almanach, 193, 278
Pillin, William, 294, 310, 334, 338, *342*
Pinnacle, *405*
Piper, Edwin Ford, 141, 247
Piper, John, 405
Piper, Thaddeus, 281
Pipkin, Charles W., 398
Pirandello, Luigi, 105
Pittala, Bernice, 309
Pittaway, Rev. T., 315, 335
Planes, *342*
Plastique, *399*
Platt, David, 391
The Play-Book, *380*
The Playboy, 68, *257*
Plomer, William, 335, 361
Plotkin, David George, 308
Plowman, Max, 386
The Plowshare, see The Wild Hawk
Plunkett, James, 401
Plunkett, Joseph, 379
Podolin, Si, 332
Podolsky, S. S., 393
Poems for a Dime, 326
Poems for 2 Bits, *331*
Poems from the Forces, 402
Poesy, 248
The Poet, 335
The Poet and the Critic, *297*
The Poet of the Month, 214, *359*
The Poet of the Year, see The Poet of the Month
Poetry (Chicago), 5, 7, 8, 18, 19, 20, 34-44, *241*
Poetry (London) (1917-1931?), *383*
Poetry (London) (1939-), *348*
Poetry (Lucindale, South Australia), *362*
Poetry and Drama, 24, *244*

Poetry and the Play, see Poetry (London) (1917-31?)
Poetry and the People, *342*
Poetry Caravan, *335*
Poetry Caravan and Silhouettes, see Poetry Caravan
The Poetry Chap-Book, *363*
Poetry Folio, *282*
Poetry Folios, *363*
Poetry Forum, *360*
The Poetry Journal, 7, 8, 112, 126, *242*
Poetry of To-Day, see The Poetry Review
The Poetry Palisade, *363*
Poetry Presents, *343*
The Poetry Quarterly (London) (1933-1934), *314*
Poetry Quarterly (London, 1939+), *348*
Poetry Quarterly (New York), *298*
The Poetry Quarterly and Dramatic Review, see The Poetry Quarterly (London, 1933)
The Poetry Review, *242*
The Poetry Review of America, *250*
Poetry-Scotland, *365*
Poetry Studies, *315*
Poetry World, *292*
Poetry World and Contemporary Vision, see Poetry World
The Poet's Forum, *298*
Poet's Magazine, *292*
Poets Now in the Services, *363*
The Poets' Scroll, *267*
Point (Madison, Wis.), *326*
Point (Melbourne, Australia), *339*
Point Counterpoint, 26
Polemic, *405*
Pollen, *326*
Pond, Margaret, 306
Popkin, Henry, 373
Porter, Alan, 258, 383, 385
Porter, Hal, 339
Porter, Katherine Anne, 135, 208, 285, 291, 325, 336, 350, 398
Porter, Kenneth W., 326, 331, 364
Porteus, H. G., 403
The Portfolio (Sweetwater, Tex.), *335*
Portfolio (Washington, Paris, Rome), *372*

## 440 INDEX

A Portrait of the Artist as a Young Man, 23, 245
Potamkin, H. A., 297, 392
Pound, Ezra, 3, 18, 21-23, 24, 36, 42, 45, 59, 68, 77, 79, 82, 83, 109, 111, 112, 115, 156, 157, 191, 193, 211, 214, 241, 242, 243, 244, 245, 248, 250, 258, 259, 274, 275, 279, 284, 292, 295, 296, 297, 302, 308, 309, 311, 312, 313, 314, 315, 321, 324, 328, 334, 343, 344, 356, 375, 379, 380, 384, 385, 386, 391, 394, 396
Pound, Louise, 391
Powell, Dawson, 272
Powell, Desmond, 405
Powell, Diana Kearny, 318
Power, Frances, 355
Powers, T., 236
Powys, John Cowper, 392
Powys, T. F., 299
Prairie, see The Milwaukee Arts Monthly
The Prairie Schooner, 8, 130, 286
Pratt, Ambrose, 362
Pratt, Charles Hyde, 353
Pratt, E. J., 399
Pratt, Harry Noyes, 277
Preissman, Hilda, 288
Prelude, 2, 326
Prescott, Frederick Clarke, 70
Preston, Denis, 403
Preston, John Hyde, 338
Preview, 363
Prezzolini, Giuseppe, 103
Price, William James, 273, 274
Prichard, Katherine Susannah, 364
Prince, Clara Catharine, 384
Prince, Frank T., 331, 359
Princess, Walter, 375
Prins, Sonja, 295
Pritchett, V. S., 311, 335
Procession, 302
Prochaska, Harry, 368
Programme, 331
Prokosch, Frederick, 241, 331, 343, 358, 391
proletarian literature and art, 42, 158, 162, 165-66, 303, 305, 307, 308, 309-10, 314, 319, 321, 325, 343, 393, 395, 397, 404
Prospect, 370
Proust, Marcel, 342, 344

Provincetown, 326
Pseudopodia, 335
psychoanalysis, 70-72, 170-88, 245, 252, 270, 300, 310, 361, 364, 403
Puberty, see Youth (Chicago)
Pudney, John, 315, 340, 402, 403
Pulse, H. S., 306
Pulsifer, G. Bishop, 276
Purdy, Ken W., 326
Purnell, Idella, 260, 271, 293
Purpose, 391
Putnam, Samuel, 83, 264, 265, 267, 268, 272, 274, 302, 311, 312, 316, 323, 324, 347
Putnam, T. J., 381
Pyramid, 355

The Quarterly Notebook, 250
Quarterly Review of Literature, 366
Quest, see Experiences in Understanding
Quick, Dorothy, 329, 366
The Quill, 252
Quin, Michael, 314
Quinn, John, 364
Quinn, Kerker, 286, 306, 311, 314, 316, 317, 318, 322, 334, 344, 350, 392
Quinn, Seabury, 404

Raab, Helen, 260
Raab's Review, 260
The Racket, 298
Radcliffe, T. A., 349
Raffelock, David, 388
Rahv, Philip, 241, 299, 311, 324, 325
Rainbow, 260
Rainey, Glenn, 335
Rajan, B., 370
Rakosi, Carl, 259, 271, 279, 281, 284, 388, 394
Ralston, Harriet B., 261
Ramsey, Frederick Jr., 374
Ramsey, Henry, 290, 291
Ramsey, Robert, 347
Ransom, John Crowe, 9, 12, 38, 116, 119, 120, 123, 257, 262, 265, 271, 273, 313, 346, 350, 376, 388, 392, 393, 398, 400
Ratcliffe, Bertram, 299
Rattenbury, Arnold, 402
Ravitz, Mel Jerome, 373

*The Raven Anthology, 315*
Ray, Man, 45, 94, 377
Raymund, Bernard, 260, 347, 367
Read, *360*
Read, Bill, 368
Read, Herbert, 251, 255, 264, 271, 297, 298, 313, 317, 318, 343, 346, 353, 355, 366, 367, 387, 390, 393, 397, 400, 401, 403
Read, Sylvia, 358
Reade, Derek, 363
*The Rebel Poet, 302*
Redfield, George, 301, 396
Redford, Grant H., 339
Redgrave, Michael, 289
*Red Pen, 326*
Reed, John, (of Australia), 351
Reed, John, (of New York and Moscow), 29, 37, 80, 92, 150, 152, 240, 254
Reedy, Marion, 30-31, 235
*Reedy's Mirror, see The Mirror*
Rees, Goronwy, 295
Rees, Richard, 386
Reese, Byron Herbert, 363
Reese, Lizette Woodworth, 247, 262, 290, 380, 382
Reeve, Eaton, 298
regionalism, 128-47
Reid, Forrest, 379
Reinhardt, Max, 383
Reisen, Abraham, 381
*Renascence, 375*
*Renegade, 331*
Renshaw, C. A., 384
"Resurgam" Younger Poets, 355
*Retort*, 220, *364*
*The Reviewer*, 9, 10, 12, *263*
*Review-43*, 224, *366*
*Review-45, see Review-43*
Rexroth, Kenneth, 297, 323, 334, 338, 345, 364
Reynolds, Beatrix, 295
Reynolds, Ernest, 309
Reznikoff, Charles, 394
Rhys, Ernest, 376, 378, 385
Rhys, Keidrych, 340, 343, 349, 363, 366, 402
*Rhythm*, 27, *240*
*Rhythmus, 271*
Ribemont-Dessaignes, G., 304
Rice, Elmer, 254, 397

Rice, Philip Blair, 298
Rich, H. Thompson, 269
Richards, I. A., 295, 298, 313, 346, 394, 404
Richardson, Dorothy, 60, 251, 275, 299, 336, 388, 402
Richardson, James E., 249
Richardson, Nina Maud, 263
Richmond, Roaldus, 337
Rickword, Edgell, 321, 385, 388, 390
Ridge, Lola, 105, 261, 281, 298, 301, 377
Riding, Laura, 113, 119, 122, 123, 284, 330, 376
Ridler, Anne, 361
Riggs, Lynn, 263, 271, 317
Riggs, Thomas Lawrason, 378
Rilke, Rainer Maria, 349, 359, 390
Rimbaud, Jean Arthur, 359, 365
Riordan, John, 284
Rittenhouse, Jessie B., 292, 353, 392
Ritter, Margaret Tod, 277, 282
*Ritual, see Experimental Review*
*River, 339*
River, H. L., 338
Rivera, Diego, 328, 395
Rivers, Jean, 317
Roberts, Denys Kilham, 405
Roberts, Elizabeth Madox, 37
Roberts, John, 359
Roberts, Michael, 387, 391
Roberts, R. Ellis, 239, 311, 390
Roberts, Walter Adolphe, 265, 280
Robinson, Anne, 290
Robinson, Boardman, 239, 254, 256, 281
Robinson, Edwin Arlington, 7, 38, 110, 252, 255, 256, 379, 383
Robinson, Ellen, 269
Robinson, Henry Morton, 249
Robinson, Lennox, 238, 275
Robinson, Ted, 345
Robinson, Victor, 322
Roché, Henri Pierre, 251
Rochester, Earl of, 359
Rochlis, James, 347
*The Rocking Horse, 315*
*Rocky Mountain Review, see Intermountain Review of English and Speech*
Roditi, Edouard, 341, 344, 366

Rodker, John, 245, 258, 259, 264, 284, 385
Rodman, Selden, 279, 285, 294, 295, 296, 305, 372, 394
Rodriguez, José, 391
Roethke, Theodore, 307, 329, 349, 376
Rogers, Grace, 300
Rogoff, Harry, 381
*Rogue*, 46, *248*
Rohman, Arthur, 311
Rohmann, Paul H., 345
Rolland, Romain, 388, 396
Rollins, Leighton, 268
Romains, Jules, 322
Romatka, Anton, 267, 367
Ronan, Ruby, 305
*Rongwrong, 252*
Rood, John, 322, 395
Rood, Roland, 377
Rook, Alan, 346, 355, 402
Roon, see *The Carillon* (Stanford, Calif.)
Root, E. Merrill, 260, 282, 292, 293, 294
*Root and Branch, 242*
Rootham, Helen, 383
Rorty, James, 270, 273, 281, 305, 364
Rosen, Hyman, 288
Rosenberg, Bernard, 373
Rosenberg, Harold, 298, 308, 312, 338, 364
Rosenberg, Isaac, 385
Rosenberg, Sam, 372
Rosenberger, Coleman, 341, 372, 374
Rosenfeld, Morris, 381
Rosenfeld, Paul, 249, 283, 344, 350, 399, 404
Rosenthal, Albert A., 267
Roskolenkier, Harry, see Harry Roskolenko
Roskolenko, Harry (Pseud. for Harry Roskolenkier), 292, 297, 300, 311, 316, 317, 337, 338, 340, 343, 344, 349, 350, 351, 356, 375
Rostov, Eugene, 379
Roth, Samuel, 252, 279, 282
Rothenstein, William, 238
Roughton, Roger, 332
Routh, James, 241, 283
Rover, R. L., 372
Rowenberg, James, 332

Rowley, Richard, 255, 367
Rowse, A. L., 372
Royce, Josiah, 133
*Rubczac, 269*
Ruddick, Bruce, 363
Rukeyser, Muriel, 241, 303, 305, 307, 310, 311, 316, 319, 325, 329, 336, 344, 358, 399, 401
Rushmore, Howard, 333
Russ, Elmo, 333
Russell, Bertrand, 90, 259, 406
Russell, Phillips, 385
Russell, Sanders, 353
Russell, Sydney King, 363
Ruthven, Peter, 302
Rutledge, Archibald, 313
Rutter, Frank, 251
Ryder, Arthur, 276
Ryder, David Warren, 276
Ryniker, Edgar H., 340

*The Sackbut, 385*
Sackville-West, V., 390
Sadler, Michael T. H., 240
Sage, Robert, 177, 287
St. John, Christopher, 237
Sakele, George A., 292
Salemson, Harold J., 80, 84, 156, 293, 301
*Salient* (New York), see *The Figure in the Carpet*
Salinger, Herman, 391
Salt, Sydney, 317
Saltus, Edgar, 380
Samarjian, Charles, 330
*Samhain, 236*
Samsel, Helen M., 274
Samuel, Maurice, 335, 358
Sand, Edward A., 322
Sandburg, Carl, 19, 37, 235, 240, 250, 254, 259, 267, 279, 289, 390, 392
Sandoz, Paul, 274
Sanford, John, 352
*The San Francisco Review*, see *The Dumbook*
Sanger, W. C., 381
*The Sansculotte, 252*
Santayana, George, 259, 387
Saphier, William, 247
Sarett, Lew, 260, 261, 263, 265, 279, 392

## INDEX 443

Saroyan, William, 1, 299, 303, 311, 318, 319, 330, 333, 337, 341, 343, 344, 345, 347, 349, 358, 360, 364, 399
Sartre, Jean-Paul, 372, 374
Sassoon, Siegfried, 241, 247, 249, 251, 257, 272, 387
Satie, Eric, 379
Saturday Night Lantern, see The Lantern (Chicago)
Saturday Press, 7
The Saturnian, *264*
Saunders, James Whiting, 319
Saunders, R. Crombie, 404
Saurat, Denis, 217, 351
Savage, Derek, 185, 342
Savage, D. S., 245, 353, 354, 355, 370, 375
Savage, Patrick, 363
Savino, Guy, 326
Savore, M. C., 351
Sawyer, William, 290, 292
Saxe, Arthur, 326
Sayer, George, 331
Sayers, Michael, 324, 394
Scarfe, Francis, 348, 366
*Scepter*, *292*
Schachner, E. A., 164
Schauffler, Robert H., 247
Schelander, Ernest, 294
Schenck, M. R., 405
Schimanski, Stefan K., 346, 366, 390
Schlick, Robert, 276
Schmalhausen, Samuel D., 270
Schneider, Isidore, 279, 317, 319, 322
Schnittkind, Henry T., 251, 282
Schnitzler, Arthur, 282, 379
Schoenfeld, Bernard C., 326
Schoonmaker, Frank, 269
Schramm, Wilbur L., 329
Schubert, David, 399
Schultz, Henry, 332, 358
Schwartz, Alvin, 323
Schwartz, Delmore, 211, 324, 325, 340, 350, 359, 381, 401
Schwarz, Benjamin Klein, 319
Scollard, Clinton, 235
*Scope* (Bayonne, N.J.), *327*
*Scope* (Denver), *306*
Scott, Evelyn, 114, 299, 307, 316, 335
Scott, F. R., 363, 375, 389
Scott, Paul, 355

Scott, Tom, 348, 402
Scott, Wesley, 365
Scott, Winfield, 282, 294, 303, 326
*Scottish Art and Letters*, *404*
*The Scottish Bookman*, *398*
Scott-Muncrieff, George, 347
*Scribner's*, 34, 38
*Scrutiny*, *394*
Scudder, Antoinette, 327
*Scythe*, see *Townsman*
Seager, Allan, 374
Seaver, Edwin, 193, 269, 274
Seccombe, Anne Mary, 276
*Secession*, 5, 9, 79, 93-101, 102, 107, 108, 267, 281
*Seed*, *315*
Seferis, George, 357
Seide, Michael, 334
Seidel, J. C., 328
Seiffert, Marjorie Allen, 271
Seldes, Gilbert V., 378
"Selected Writings Series," 214
Seletz, Jeanette, 307
Selfridge, Erica, 389
Seligmann, Herbert J., 267, 378
Seligmann, Kurt, 364
Selincourt, Hugh de, 239
Seltzer, Thomas, 240, 379
Sender, Ramon J., 300, 366
Sergeant, Howard, 370, 371
Serge, Victor, 373
Sergel, Charles Hubbard, 379
Sessions, Jack, 373
*Seven*, *343*
*The Seven Arts*, 9, 86-92, 250
*The Sewanee Review*, 2, 210, *376*
*S 4 N*, 86, 107-8, 257
*S 4 N Society*, see *S 4 N*
*SFZ*, see *the american arts monthly*
*The Shanachie*, *238*
Shannon, Charles, 238
Shapiro, Harvey, 372
Shapiro, Jack, 347
Shapiro, Karl Jay, 43, 325, 352, 354, 360, 362, 369, 372, 373, 401
*Shards*, *315*
Sharp, Clarence A., 254
Shattuck, Charles, 350
Shaw, George Bernard, 321
Shaw, Irwin, 350, 399
Shaw, Neufville, 364
Sheean, Jane Rawlins, 330

## 444 INDEX

Sheeler, Charles, 269
Sheets, Kermit, 368
Shelby, K. C., 332
Shelvankar, K. S., 401
Shepard, Flola, 322
Shepard, Odell, 252, 309
Sheppard, Myrtle Vorst, 308
Sherby, J. M., 326
Sherry, Laura, 380, 381
Shields, John, 306
Shipp, Horace, 384
Shober, Joseph, 350
Short, John, 331
the short story, 160
*Shucks, 336*
Sidney, Alan, 321
Sidney, John, 340
Sidon, Richard C., 322
Siegel, Eli, 284, 286, 292, 315
Sieveking, L. de G., 385
Sigmund, Jay G., 254, 263, 265, 267, 276, 279, 291, 292, 320, 322, 329, 337
Signature, 26, *248*
Signatures, *336*
Silhouettes, *306*
*The Silver Bough, 360*
Simpson, Clinton, 307
Sinclair, Upton, 266
Singer, John, 370, 404
Singh, Iqbal, 401
Sitwell, Edith, 249, 251, 257, 317, 356, 383, 385, 390, 405
Sitwell, Osbert, 249, 251, 258, 383, 385, 402
Sitwell, Sacheverell, 251, 383
*6 x 9 (Six By Nine), 336*
*Skylines, 339*
Skylines Magazine, see *Skylines*
*Slate, 253*
Slater, Humphrey, 405, 406
Slater, Montagu, 321
Slessor, Kenneth, 271
Sloan, John, 281
Sloan, J. Vandervoort, 379
Slochower, Harry, 338, 350, 376
*The Smart Set, 9, 380*
Smith, Alec, 404
Smith, A. J. M., 375, 389
Smith, Ashley, 387
Smith, Bernard, 301, 364
Smith, C. D., 395

Smith, Cecil M., 373
Smith, Edison, 309
Smith, Gordon, 326, 356
Smith, Kay, 363
Smith, Lillian E., 335
Smith, Logan Pearsall, 249
Smith, Pamela Colman, 237, 376
Smith, Paul, 326
*Smoke, 8, 303*
Sneddon, Robert W., 391
Snell, George, 323, 338, 342, 347
Snelling, Paula, 335
Sniderman, Sol, 326
Snow, Royall, 249, 253, 255, 282
Snow, Walter, 158-59, 307
*The Soil, 31-32, 251*
Sokoloff, Ivan, 270
*The Soldier,* see *Art Young Quarterly*
Solow, Herbert, 168
*The Sonnet, 253*
*The Sonneteer, 366*
Sonnet Sequences, *289*
Sorkin, Sam, 308
Sostman, Henry, 375
Souster, Raymond, 347, 358, 365, 375
Southerland, John, 362
*The Southern Review* (Baton Rouge, La.), 2, 9, 210, *398*
*The Southern Review* (Jackson, Miss.), *327*
South Today, see *Pseudopodia*
Southwest Review, see *The Texas Review*
Souza, Sybil de, 361
*Soviet Russia Pictorial,* 30, 151
*Space,* 154-55, *327*
*The Span, 360*
Spare, Austin O., 249, 266
Sparrow, John, 295
*The Spectator,* see *The Greenwich Village Spectator*
Spector, Herman, 284, 303, 319
Spencer, Bernard, 361
Spencer, Theodore, 285, 313, 317, 346, 355, 359, 376, 382, 404
Spender, Stephen, 221-22, 257, 312, 313, 318, 321, 324, 335, 348, 353, 357, 358, 363, 366, 369, 372, 373, 390, 405
Spengler, Oswald, 259, 319, 323
Speyer, Leonora, 249, 262
Spier, Leonard, 326

# INDEX 445

The Spinner, *275*
The Spinners, *327*
*Spirit, 397*
*Spoon River Anthology*, 31, 112, 235
Sprigge, Sylvia, 345
Squires, Colman Denton, 333
Squires, J. Radcliffe, 373
Stafford, Bill, 368
Stafford, Clayton, 355
Stagg, Hunter, 263
Stahl, C. Victor, 248
Stainsby, Olive Scott, 308
Stait, Virginia, 241
Stallman, Robert, 328
Stanford, Derek, 348, 355, 403
Stanford, Don, 311
*Star-Dust, 293*
Stark, Irwin, 368
Starrett, Vincent, 192-93, 235, 246, 247, 258, 268, 273, 365
Stauffer, Donald A., 382
Stead, John, 341
Stearns, Harold, 94
Steffens, Lincoln, 29, 266
Stegner, Wallace, 329, 339, 381
Stein, Gertrude, 82, 174, 248, 275, 284, 286, 287, 297, 314, 315, 331, 341, 389, 394
Stephen, Wallace, 285
Stephens, James, 239, 261, 377, 379
Stephensen, P. R., 5, 288
Stephenson, Nathaniel W., 379
Sterling, George, 37, 237, 258, 272, 277, 280, 281, 296
Sterling, Glen, 336
Stern, G. B., 404
Stern, Seimour, 391
Stevens, Ada Borden, 304
Stevens, Elizabeth Dewey, 368
Stevens, James, 239, 260, 276
Stevens, Wallace, 37, 48, 242, 248, 251, 256, 259, 263, 268, 285, 296, 299, 303, 315, 317, 318, 325, 332, 334, 340, 343, 345, 346, 350, 356, 361, 362, 366, 369, 371, 376, 381, 398, 405
Stevens, Wil, 368
Stevenson, Alec Brock, 118
Stewart, Donald, 357
Stewart, Ellsworth, 260
Stewart, Florence, 360
Stewart, Gervase, 346
Stewart, J. F., 352
Stieglitz, Alfred, 252, 267, 344, 377, 382
Still, James, 335, 360
Stirling, Glen, 332
Stokes, Adrian, 406
Stoll, J. Louis, 313
Stone, Geoffrey, 317, 329
Stone, Herbert Stuart, 235
Storey, Alan, 366
Storey, Walter, 240
Stork, Charles Wharton, 249
Storm, Hans Otto, 350, 358
Storn, Nigel, 371, 372
*Story*, 9, 160-61, *303*
*The Stratford Journal, 251*
*The Stratford Magazine, 282*
*The Stratford Monthly*, see *The Stratford Journal*
*Stream, 303*
Street, Mary D., 263
Strindberg, August, 243
Strobel, Marion, 241
Strong, Anna Louise, 377
Strong, L. A. G., 266, 293, 296, 311, 385, 387
Struther, Jan, 398
Stuart, Gilbert, 287
Stuart, H., 255
Stuart, Jesse, 136, 267, 274, 286, 289, 291, 299, 322, 328, 329, 345, 354, 363, 382, 393
Subramaniam, Alagu, 355, 401
Suckow, Ruth, 143-44, 380
Sullivan, Jerry, 321
Sullivan, Ulick, 299
Sulman, D. L., 239
*Sunday Mirror*, see *The Mirror*
surrealism, 3, 9, 40, 63-64, 180-84, 287, 300, 332, 334, 356, 361, 362, 364, 374, 395, 400, 403, 406
Sutherland, Halliday, 398
Sutherland, John, 362, 375
Sutton, Kathleen, 288, 292, 304, 307, 308, 315, 318, 328, 329, 335, 336, 361
Swallow, Alan, 279, 308, 320, 330, 332, 339, 349, 352, 354, 355, 357, 358, 363, 368, 392, 393
Swallow, Norman, 371, 372
*The Swallow Pamphlets, 355*
Swan, H. M., 351

Sweeney, James Johnson, 397
Sweeney, John L., 373
Sweet, Ione M., 269
Swenson, Henry E., 330
Swick, Helen, 319
Swingler, Randall, 295, 297, 321, 324, 342, 398, 402
Sykes, Hugh, 288
symbolism, 57, 236
Symmes, Robert, 353
Symons, Arthur, 237, 246, 355, 385
Symons, Julian, 279, 340, 346, 358, 370
Symons, W. T., 391
*The Symposium*, 9, 164-65, 209, 210, 215, *298*
Synge, J. M., 236, 238

Tabori, Paul, 361
Tacke, C. A., 297
Taggard, Genevieve, 254, 263, 264, 271, 273, 274, 277, 281, 287, 307, 325, 346, 360, 366, 405
Tagore, Rabindranath, 37, 379, 388
*Talaria*, *336*
*Talent*, *340*
Tambimuttu, 348
*Tambour*, 80, 84, *293*
*The Tanager*, *278*
Tanaquil, Paul, 260, 275
Tanguy, Yves, 356
Tanko, Boris de, 261
Tannenbaum, Frank, 150, 252
Tarleton, Fiswoode, 249-50, 267, 281, 388
*Tarr*, *23*
Tate, Allen, 12, 42, 117, 118, 119, 123, 124, 207, 227, 228, 257, 262, 264, 265, 267, 268, 273, 275, 285, 287, 311, 313, 325, 340, 352, 360, 361, 362, 369, 376, 387, 388, 398, 400, 401
Taupin, René, 312
Taylor, Allan N., 393
Taylor, E. E., 282
Taylor, Elizabeth, 368
Taylor, Marceil, 330
Taylor, Maurice, 330
Taylor, Warren, 317
Tchelitchew, Pavel, 356
Teasdale, Sara, 7, 235, 392
*Tempest*, *366*

*Tempo*, *264*
the *tendenz* magazine, 85-86
Tennant, E. W., 383
Tepper, Henrietta, 310
Tériade, E., 399
Terrell, Upton, 294, 323
Tessimond, A. S. V., 404
*The Texas Review*, 8, 129, 131, 138, 139, *382*
Thayer, Scofield, 68, 196, 199, 200, 259
*Theatre Arts Magazine*, *382*
*Theatre-Craft*, *384*
Thielen, Benedict, 328
*This Quarter*, 7, 80, 82, 279
Thoma, Richard, 315
Thomas, Dylan, 219, 313, 317, 331, 332, 334, 335, 337, 340, 343, 346, 348, 349, 350, 353, 359, 390, 391
Thomas, Edward, 239, 242
Thomas, Ormond, 363
Thompson, Albert E., 379
Thompson, Basil, 10, 12, 262, 265
Thompson, Denys, 394
Thompson, Dunstan, 346, 356, 365, 381
Thompson, John H., 326, 336
Thompson, Lloyd S., 273
Thompson, P. Gilchrist, 311
Thompson, Roy Towner, 262
Thompson, Vance, 236
Thomson, David Cleghorn, 397
Thoreau, Henry David, 7
Thornton, Nathaniel, 366
Thurber, James, 387
Thurman, Wallace, 280
Tibbetts, H. M., 338
Tier, Ada, 313
Tietjens, Eunice, 37, 54, 245, 250, 265, 277, 290, 383
Tillson, Kenneth, 310
Tindall, William Y., 376
Tirgrid, Pavel, 366
Titus, Edward W., 279
Tod, 280
Todd, Ruthven, 20, 241, 340, 343, 346, 349, 352, 358, 366, 400, 403
Todrin, Boris, 360
Toeman, Edward, 370
"To Faustus and Helen," 98-99
Toldridge, Elizabeth, 330, 339
Tomasi, Mary, 337

## INDEX 447

To-morrow, *275*
Tom-Tom, *293*
Tone, *316*
Tong, Raymond, 374
Toomer, Jean, 12, 261, 262, 267
Torrence, Ridgely, 395
Torrup, Ingeborg, 276
Townsend, Estil Alexander, 267, 298
Townsend, Wilbur T., 267, 298
Townshend, Petrie, 390
Townsman, *343*
Toynbee, Philip, 406
Trails, *306*
The Tramp, *349*
transatlantic review, 76, 79, 275
Transformation, *366*
transition, 9, 71, 80, 172-80, 286
Traver, Robert, 317, 337
Treadway, Blaine, 313
Tree, Iris, 383
Treece, Henry, 343, 346, 348, 349, 351, 358, 363, 366, 367, 370, 372, 390, 402, 403
Trench, Herbert, 385
Trend (Brooklyn, N.Y.), *306*
Trend (Chicago), *364*
Trent, Lucia, 249, 276, 290, 294, 297, 304, 307, 315, 327, 330, 392
Trent, William P., 376
Trevelyan, R. C., 345
Trilling, Lionel, 325
The Trimmed Lamp, see Art
The Tripod, *242*
Trist, Margaret, 364
Trott, Eleanor, 292
Troubadour, *289*
Trowbridge, W. D., 324, 342
Troy, William, 284, 325
Tucker, Albert, 372
Tucker, Marion, 383
Tuckey, Ronald, 368
Tull, Clyde, 329
Turley, George, 351
Turnell, Martin, 289
Turner, Edith, 355
Turner, Ethel, 271
Turner, Victor, 355
Turner, W. J., 238, 249
Twentieth Century Verse, *340*
Twice a Year, 9, *344*
*291, 382*
Two Worlds, *279*

Two Worlds Monthly, *282*
Twynham, Leo Leonard, 328
Tyler, Dorothy, 278
Tyler, Parker, 249, 259, 286, 288, 292, 293, 297, 298, 299, 300, 308, 313, 316, 317, 318, 322, 343, 345, 356, 365
Tynan, Katharine, 242, 246, 378, 379
The Tyro, *264*
Tyson, Anne Arrington, 280
Tzara, Tristan, 62, 245

Udell, Geraldine, 39
Ulster Voices, *367*
Ulysses, 21, 23, 59-60, 68, 245, 369
Unamuno, Miguel de, 390
Universal Magazine, see Universal Poetry Magazine
Universal Poetry Magazine, *327*
The University of Kansas City Review, see The University Review
The University Review, 10, *327*
Unger, Leonard, 398
Unquote, *355*
Untermeyer, Jean Starr, 249, 406
Untermeyer, Louis, 38, 150, 239, 240, 242, 249, 253, 262, 266, 267, 376, 380
Updegraff, Allan, 243
Upper, Joseph, 294, 307
Upstate, *356*
Upward, *344*
Urban, William M., 346
Urbooska, Anca, 315
Urquhart, Fred, 403, 404
Uzzell, Thomas H., 162, 310, 313

Vail, S., 368
Valentine, Louis, 366
Valéry, Paul, 279, 390, 400
Van Doren, Mark, 247, 249, 264, 283, 307, 362, 366, 398, 400
Van Etten, Winifred Mayne, 329
Van Loon, Hendrik, 256, 385
Van Rensselaer, James T., Jr., 266, 273
Van Vechten, Carl, 90, 252, 262, 268
Vara, Madeleine, 330
Vazakas, Byron, 308, 339, 350, 362, 363, 364, 368, 373, 374

# INDEX

The Venture, *289*
Verlaine, Paul, 264, 290
Vernier, *331*
Verse (Melbourne, Australia), *293*
Verse (Philadelphia), *280*
Verse Craft, *304*
Vers Libre, *336*
vers libre, see free verse
The Versemaker, *307*
verticalism, see vertigralism
vertigo, 183
vertigralism, 177-79, 287, 329
Verve, *399*
Vespers, *328*
Vice Versa, 6, *356*
Vickridge, Alberta, 285, 335
Viele-Griffin, Francis, 296
Viereck, George Sylvester, 239
Viereck, Peter, 341
View, 182, 183, *356*
Viewpoint, *397*
Vilas, Faith, 298
Villa, José Garcia, 286, 299, 303, 310, 311, 316, 324, 327, 369, 393, 394, 396, 404
The Village Magazine, *239*
Vinal, Harold, 257, 258, 264, 265, 266, 267, 268, 271, 272, 274, 277, 280, 282, 289, 293, 304, 306, 309, 316, 328, 329, 335, 366, 384
Vincent, J. Nolan, 274
Vines, Sherard, 383
The Vineyard, *378*
The Virginia Quarterly Review, 2
Vision (New York), *240*
Vision (Sydney, Australia), *271*
Vivas, Eliseo, 72, 400, 401
Vlag, Piet, 29, 240
Vliet, R. Wade, 303
Vogel, Joseph, 319
Vogel, W. P., Jr., 294
The Voice, *282*
Voices (Boston), 8, *264*
Voices (London), *258*
Voices (Wigginton, Herts, Eng.), *403*
Voorslag, *388*
Vorse, Mary Heaton, 152
vorticism, 3, 23, 24, 244
Vrepont, Brian, 354
VVV, 183, 364

Waddington, C. H., 406

Wagner, Elvin, 332
Wagstaff, Blanche Shoemaker, 239, 242, 290, 327
Wainhouse, Austryn, 404
Wainwright, Virginia, 338
Wales, 221, 340
Waley, Arthur, 249, 406
Wall, Arnold, 363
Wall, Bernard, 395
Wallace, Eunice, 277
Wallace, Jack, 339
Waller, John, 341, 346, 371, 374, 402
Walsh, Ernest J., 3, 80, 82, 192, 279
Walter, Felix, 389
Walters, Earl, 276
Walters, Meurig, 349
Walton, Eda Lou, 275, 282, 390, 392
The Wanderer (London), *316*
The Wanderer (San Francisco), *271*
Wanning, Andrews, 218-19
Ward, Henshaw, 292
Ward, May Williams, 277
Ward, Theodore, 326
Ward, Veronica, 331
Warman, Erik, 393
Warner, Lulu Frances, 282
Warner, Rex, 335, 370, 374
Warner, Sylvia Townsend, 321, 402
Warr, Bertram, 355
Warratt, Harriet, 373
Warren, Austin, 353
Warren, Robert Penn, 12, 118, 122, 123, 262, 264, 266, 279, 311, 329, 351, 381, 384, 391, 398, 400, 401
"The Wasteland," 259, 386
Watkins, Vernon, 340, 370, 403
Watson, Dr. J. S., Jr., 68, 196, 198, 199-200
Watson, Kathleen, 364
Watts, Harold H., 373
Waugh, Alec, 266
Waugh, Evelyn, 295, 390
The Wave, *268*
Weaver, Harriet Shaw, 244, 245
Webb, James, 294
Webb, John Edgar, 345
Webb, W. Caldwell, 336
Webbe, Denis, 372
Webster, Margaret, 371, 373
Wedekind, Frank, 243
Weidman, Jerome, 304, 322, 350, 372
Weigand, Charmion von, 397

# INDEX

Weiskopf, F. C., 300
Weismuller, Edward, 329
Weiss, Mona, 389
Weiss, T., 366, 372
Welles, Winifred, 249, 262, 290
Wellesley, Dorothy, 377
Wellman, Rita, 304
Wells, Benjamin W., 376
Wells, Henry W., 366, 406
Wells, Peter, 363
Welsh, Marie de L., 276, 292, 293, 314, 322, 389
*The Welsh Review, 349*
Welty, Eudora, 279, 323, 329, 339, 350, 358, 398
Werth, Alexander, 393
Wescott, Glenway, 37, 259, 270, 336
West, Dorothy, 318
West, Nathaniel, 259
West, Ray B., Jr., 338, 339
West, Rebecca, 244
*Western Poetry, 293*
*The Westminster Magazine, 240*
*Westward, 287*
Wetjen, Albert Richard, 162, 314
Whartoe, Christian, 270
Wharton, Michael, 350
Wheeler, C. E., 239
Wheeler, Monroe, 270
Wheelock, John Hall, 35, 38, 258
*Wheels, 383*
Wheelwright, John Brooks, 98, 241, 275, 303, 305, 307, 320, 326, 329, 331, 353, 376
Wheelwright, Philip E., 298, 362, 400, 401
Whelan, Kenneth, 331
Whicher, George F., 375
Whipple, Arthur, 298
*The Whirl, 298*
*Whispers, 356*
Whitaker, J. G., 320
Whitcomb, Robert, 321
White, Alan, 363
White, Gertrude, 292
White, Hervey, 243
White, H. O., 255
White, Jon, 361
White, Kenneth, 243
White, Robert, 327
White, Terence, 395
Whitehand, Robert, 337

Whitehead, Alfred N., 297, 394
Whitehouse, Hugh, 404
Whiteside, Clara, 265
Whiteside, Mary Brent, 283
Whitman, Walt, 377
Whitney, Geraldine, 305
Whittemore, E. Reed, Jr., 346
Whybrow, George, 314
Whyte, J. H., 296
Wicker, C. V., 292
Widdemer, Margaret, 247, 272, 273, 280, 305, 306, 319, 380, 384
Widen, Ruth, 310
Widger, Basil, 371
Wiggam, Lionel, 392
Wilde, Oscar, 246, 256, 279
Wilder, Thornton, 12, 257, 262, 378
*The Wild Hawk, 243*
Wilhelm, Gale, 290, 297, 303
Wilkins, Eithne, 372, 374
Williams, Alberta, 243
Williams, B. Y., 336
Williams, Charles, 360
Williams, Gwyn, 349
Williams, Joseph C., 330
Williams, Margaret, 341
Williams, Miles Vaughan, 346
Williams, Oscar, 247, 250, 262, 265, 268, 271, 281, 308, 336, 342, 344, 346, 356, 363, 393, 397
Williams, Robert, 341
Williams, Tennessee, 368, 369, 371, 373, 401
Williams, William Carlos, 3, 46, 48-49, 69, 192, 220, 241, 242, 243, 244, 259, 261, 267, 268, 270, 274, 275, 279, 285, 287, 290, 295, 296, 297, 299, 303, 308, 311, 313, 315, 316, 317, 322, 324, 328, 331, 334, 339, 341, 344, 345, 346, 347, 352, 353, 356, 358, 359, 363, 364, 365, 368, 390
Williams-Ellis, Amabel, 321
Willis, D. A., 397
*Will-o'-the-Wisp, 282*
Wills, Ridley, 265
Wilson, Charles G., 361
Wilson, Edmund, 270, 325, 381, 382, 387
Wilson, G. L., 335
Wilson, Norman, 393
Wilson, T. C., 241, 399
Wimberly, Lowry Charles, 286

*The Wind and the Rain*, *360*
*The Windmill*, *361*
*The Window*, *299*
*The Windsor Quarterly*, 163-64, *316*
*The Winged Word*, *361*
*Wings*, *316*
Winocour, Jack, 312
Winslow, Horatio, 240
Winslow, Walker, 314, 320, 326
Winter, Ella, 314
*The Winter Owl*, see *The Owl*
Winters, Yvor, 100, 101, 207, 209, 259, 267, 268, 274, 279, 285, 286, 287, 290, 291, 296, 302, 303, 311, 317, 358, 359, 393, 396, 398, 400, 401, 405
Wintringham, T. H., 321
Wirt, Henrietta Randolph, 318
Wirt, Nicholas, 319
Wisdom, John, 406
Wiser, Milton U., 347
Wolcott, Martha Fox, 298
Wolcott, Warner, 305
Wolfe, Humbert, 272, 289, 299, 328, 387
Wolfe, Thomas, 329, 335, 389
Wolford, Milton, 331
Wood, C. E. S., 258, 289, 293, 296, 319, 377, 392
Wood, Clement, 267, 269, 272, 274, 276, 277, 290, 293, 298, 306, 365, 367
Woodberry, George Edward, 235, 268, 273
Woodbridge, William, 276
Woodcock, George, 354, 355, 370, 371
Woodhouse, Doris, 359
Woodman, Lawrence C., 317, 322
Woodring, Jane, 369
Woolf, Virginia, 335
*The Worker's Monthly*, 30, 151
*Workers Theatre*, *393*
Wright, Basil, 289
Wright, Richard, 155-56, 310, 318, 350, 371
Wright, S. Fowler, 383, 384
Wright, Willard Huntington, 72, 90, 380, 385
*The Writer's Forum*, see *The Amateur Writer*
*Wrong-Wrong*, see *Rongwrong*
Wurdemann, Audrey, 274, 392

Wyatt, Susan, 402
Wyatt, Woodrow, 402
Wylie, Elinor, 37, 263, 380
Wynn, Dudley, 392

*The Yale Literary Magazine*, *378*, 381
*Yale Poetry Review*, *372*
*The Yale Review*, 2
Yalkert, Saul, 326
*Yankee Poetry Chapbook*, *328*
*A Year Magazine*, see *1933*
Yeats, E. C., 377
Yeats, Jack B., 238, 376, 377
Yeats, W. B., 60, 235, 236, 237, 238, 245, 249, 259, 275, 284, 347, 348, 376, 377, 379, 383, 387, 398
*Yellowjacket*, *349*
Young, Andrew, 405
Young, Art, 29, 254, 255, 256, 265, 281, 391
Young, Don, 351
Young, Kathleen Tankersley, 260, 278, 284, 286, 288, 290, 292, 297, 310, 317, 388, 390
Young, Sidney, 333
Young, Stark, 379, 382, 383
Youssevitch, Sacha, 304
*Youth* (Baltimore), see *The Adolescent*
*Youth* (Cambridge, Mass.), *255*
*Youth* (Chicago), *264*

Zabel, Morton Dauwen, 5, 39, 43, 241, 325
Zara, Louis, 307, 345
Zaturenska, Marya, 247, 303, 315, 346, 352, 356, 360
Zeidner, Harry I., 337
Zeigler, John, 345
Zeitlin, Jake, 391
Zimmerman, A., 331
Zimmerman, J. F., 392
Zimmern, Alfred E., 239
Zinberg, Len, 345
Zink, Richard, 332
Zola, Emile, 338
Zorn, Gremin, 284
Zugsmith, Leane, 322
Zukofsky, Louis, 13, 241, 259, 271, 279, 295, 297, 298, 300, 301, 316, 352
Zweig, Sarah, 373
Zweig, Stefan, 279